Lecture Notes in Computer Science 8225

Commenced Publication in 1973
Founding and Former Series Editors:
Gerhard Goos, Juris Hartmanis, and Jan van Leeuwen

T0183219

Martin Erwig   Richard F. Paige
Eric Van Wyk (Eds.)

Software Language Engineering

6th International Conference, SLE 2013
Indianapolis, IN, USA, October 26-28, 2013
Proceedings

 Springer

Volume Editors

Martin Erwig
Oregon State University
School of Electrical Engineering and Computer Science
Corvallis, OR 97331-5501, USA
E-mail: erwig@eecs.oregonstate.edu

Richard F. Paige
University of York
Department of Computer Science
Deramore Lane, York YO10 5GH, UK
E-mail: richard.paige@york.ac.uk

Eric Van Wyk
University of Minnesota
Department of Computer Science and Engineering
200 SE Union Street, Minneapolis, MN 55455, USA
E-mail: evw@cs.umn.edu

ISSN 0302-9743   e-ISSN 1611-3349
ISBN 978-3-319-02653-4   e-ISBN 978-3-319-02654-1
DOI 10.1007/978-3-319-02654-1
Springer Cham Heidelberg New York Dordrecht London

Library of Congress Control Number: 2013949676

CR Subject Classification (1998):
D.3.2-4, D.2.1-2, D.2.11-13, F.4.2, I.2.4, I.6.5, K.6.3

LNCS Sublibrary: SL 2 – Programming and Software Engineering

Typesetting: Camera-ready by author, data conversion by Scientific Publishing Services, Chennai, India

Printed on acid-free paper

Springer is part of Springer Science+Business Media (www.springer.com)

Preface

We are pleased to present the proceedings of the 6th International Conference of Software Language Engineering (SLE 2013). The conference was held in Indianapolis, USA, during October 26–28, 2013. It was co-located with the 12th International Conference on Generative Programming and Component Engineering (GPCE 2013), the 4th Conference on Systems, Programming, Languages and Applications: Software for Humanity (SPLASH 2013, which includes OOPSLA), the Dynamic Languages Symposium, the 5th International Workshop on Feature-Oriented Software Development, and three SLE workshops: the Industry Track of Software Language Engineering, the Systems Biology and Language Engineering, and the Parsing@SLE Workshop.

The SLE conference series is devoted to a wide range of topics related to artificial languages in software engineering. SLE is an international research forum that brings together researchers and practitioners from both industry and academia to expand the frontiers of software language engineering. SLE's foremost mission is to encourage, synthesize, and organize communication between communities that have traditionally looked at software languages from different and yet complementary perspectives. Supporting these communities in learning from each other, and transferring knowledge, is the guiding principle behind the organization of SLE.

The conference program included a keynote presentation, 17 technical paper presentations, 2 tool papers, and a number of poster presentations (which are not included in these proceedings, but in a complementary volume). The invited keynote speaker was Don Batory (University of Texas at Austin, USA), who spoke provocatively about "Dark Knowledge and Graph Grammars in Automated Software Design".

We received 56 full submissions from 63 abstract submissions. From these submissions, the Program Committee (PC) selected 19 papers: 17 full papers and 2 tool demonstration papers, resulting in an acceptance rate of 34%. Each submitted paper was reviewed by at least three PC members and discussed in detail during the electronic PC meeting.

SLE 2013 would not have been possible without the significant contributions of many individuals and organizations. We are grateful to the SPLASH 2013 general chairs and local organizing chairs, particularly Antony Hosking and Patrick Eugster, for taking care of logistical matters and hosting the conference in Indianapolis. The SLE Steering Committee provided invaluable assistance and guidance. We are also grateful to the PC members and the additional reviewers for their dedication in reviewing the submissions. We thank the authors for their efforts in writing and then revising their papers and addressing the recommendations of the referees in a constructive manner. Our final thanks go to the sponsoring and cooperating institutions for their generous support.

August 2013   Martin Erwig
                                                                                 Richard F. Paige

Organization

General Chair

Eric Van Wyk   University of Minnesota, USA

Program Co-chairs

Martin Erwig   Oregon State University, USA
Richard F. Paige   University of York, UK

Steering Committee

Mark van den Brand   Eindhoven University of Technology,
                                    The Netherlands
James Cordy   Queen's University, Canada
Jean-Marie Favre   University of Grenoble, France
Dragan Gašević   Athabasca University, Canada
Görel Hedin   Lund University, Sweden
Eric Van Wyk   University of Minnesota, USA
Jurgen Vinju   CWI, The Netherlands
Kim Mens   Catholic University of Louvain, Belgium

Program Committee

Emilie Balland   Inria, France
Olaf Chitil   University of Kent, UK
James R. Cordy   School of Computing, Queen's University,
                                    Canada
Davide Di Ruscio   Università degli Studi dell'Aquila, Italy
Iavor Diatchki   Galois Inc., USA
Anne Etien   LIFL - University of Lille 1, France
Jean-Marie Favre   University of Grenoble, France
Dragan Gašević   Athabasca University, Canada
Jeremy Gibbons   University of Oxford, UK
Andy Gill   University of Kansas, USA
Jeff Gray   University of Alabama, USA

Giancarlo Guizzardi	Federal University of Espirito Santo, Brazil
Görel Hedin	Lund University, Sweden
Markus Herrmannsdörfer	Technische Universität München, Germany
Zhenjiang Hu	NII, Japan
Oleg Kiselyov	USA
Paul Klint	CWI, The Netherlands
Thomas Kühne	Victoria University of Wellington, New Zealand
Kim Mens	Université Catholoque Louvain, Belgium
Pierre-Etienne Moreau	Ecole des Mines de Nancy, France
Klaus Ostermann	University of Marburg, Germany
Arnd Poetzsch-Heffter	University of Kaiserslautern, Germany
Fiona Polack	University of York, UK
Lukas Renggli	University of Bern, Switzerland
Bernhard Rumpe	RWTH Aachen, Germany
João Saraiva	Universidade do Minho, Portugal
Friedrich Steimann	FernUniversität in Hagen, Germany
Gabriele Täntzer	Philipps-Universität Marburg, Germany
Mark Van Den Brand	TU Eindhoven, The Netherlands
Jurgen Vinju	CWI, The Netherlands

Additional Reviewers

Alalfi, Manar
Arendt, Thorsten
Asadi, Mohsen
Bach, Jean-Christophe
Bieniusa, Annette
Boskovic, Marko
Bosnacki, Dragan
Brunnlieb, Malte
Chen, Sheng
Cho, Hyun
Corley, Jonathan
Cunha, Jácome
Dean, Thomas
Feller, Christoph
Fontaine, Pascal
Fort, Karën
Greifenberg, Timo
Groener, Gerd
Hermerschmidt, Lars
Horst, Andreas

Jacob, Ferosh
Kelter, Udo
Kolassa, Carsten
Kurnia, Ilham
Kurpick, Thomas
Martins, Pedro
Michel, Patrick
Pollet, Damien
Ressia, Jorge
Ringert, Jan Oliver
Serebrenik, Alexander
Smeltzer, Karl
Stephan, Matthew
Stevenson, Andrew
Sun, Yu
van Amstel, Marcel
van der Meer, Arjan
Verhoeff, Tom
Weber, Mathias

Table of Contents

Tools

Language Analysis

Meta- and Megamodelling

Dark Knowledge and Graph Grammars
in Automated Software Design*

Don Batory[1], Rui Gonçalves[2], Bryan Marker[1], and Janet Siegmund[3]

[1] University of Texas at Austin, Austin, TX 78712 USA
{batory,marker}@cs.utexas.edu
[2] Universidade do Minho, Braga, Portugal
rgoncalves@di.uminho.pt
[3] University of Passau, Germany
feigensp@ovgu.de

Abstract. Mechanizing the development of hard-to-write and costly-to-maintain software is the core problem of automated software design. Encoding expert knowledge (a.k.a. *dark knowledge*) about a software domain is central to its solution. We assert that a solution can be cast in terms of the ideas of language design and engineering. Graph grammars can be a foundation for modern automated software development. The sentences of a grammar are designs of complex dataflow systems. We explain how graph grammars provide a framework to encode expert knowledge, produce correct-by-construction derivations of dataflow applications, enable the generation of high-performance code, and improve how software design of dataflow applications can be taught to undergraduates.

1 Introduction

Like many of you, I read popular science articles. I especially enjoy discussions on current problems in theoretical physics. My favorite problem is that roughly 80% of the mass of our universe is made of material that scientists cannot directly observe. It is called *dark matter*. Dark matter emits no light or energy, but is not entirely invisible. Scientists know it exists because with it they can explain the otherwise unusual rotations of galaxies, the unexpected bending of light in empty space, and the surprising fact that the expansion of our universe is accelerating. The issue of dark matter has been known for at least 25 years [2], yet today it remains poorly understood.

Dark matter reminds me of a corresponding problem in software design. Software design is a series of decisions whose effects are seen in programs, but are not directly observable. In analogy to dark matter, I call it *dark knowledge*. Dark knowledge is fleeting. Programmers may know it one day and forget it the next. It is not present in source code. Yet we know dark knowledge exists, because with it we can explain program designs. If an engineer makes a certain decision, (s)he would expect to see algorithm α in a program; with an alternative choice, (s)he would see β. The presence of dark knowledge in programs has been known for at least 30 years [6,9,22], and today it too remains poorly understood.

---

* As this paper transcribes a keynote presentation, "I" refers to Batory's personal experience and "We" refers to the experience of all authors.

M. Erwig, R.F. Paige, and E. Van Wyk (Eds.): SLE 2013, LNCS 8225, pp. 1–18, 2013.
© Springer International Publishing Switzerland 2013

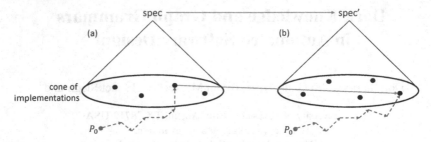

Fig. 1. Cone of Implementations for a Specification

Dark knowledge is important. Software design starts with a formal or informal specification. We know that there are huge numbers of possible programs that could implement a spec (indicated by the "cone of implementations" in Fig. 1a, [3]). With domain and software-engineering knowledge, an engineer makes a series of decisions to create a program to implement the spec. The dashed lines in Fig. 1a indicate "dark knowledge": the engineer starts with an existing program (possibly the empty program) P_0 that typically does not satisfy the spec, makes a series of modifications (one per decision) to ultimately arrive at a program that does satisfy the spec. This chain of decisions is fleeting—over time it is forgotten, thereby losing vital knowledge about the program's design. When the spec is updated (Fig. 1b), engineers who maintain the program effectively have to recreate the series of decisions that lead to the original program, erase a previous decision, and replace it with those that are consistent with the new spec. In time, these decisions are forgotten as before, bringing us back to square one where design knowledge is dark.[1]

The connection to language design is immediate in a shallow way: language design and language implementation are instances of these ideas. They too involve a series of decisions whose effects can be seen, but not explicitly encoded. Consequently, the same problems arise: vital design knowledge for maintenance and evolution is lost.

The importance of dark knowledge is well-known. Making dark knowledge white (explicit) was expressed in 1992 by Baxter in his paper on "Design Maintenance Systems" [6]. More recently, another version of this idea arises in self-adaptive and self-managing software [48] . Here, the goal is to encode design decisions explicitly in software to make dark knowledge white, so these decisions can be revisited and redecided automatically (possibly with a human in the loop). Illuminating dark knowledge embodies a new approach to software development [40].

The approach presented in this paper to make dark knowledge white is called *Design by Transformation (DxT)* [17,21,37,38,46,50].

2   How Dark Knowledge Can Be Encoded

The challenge is how to encode dark knowledge thereby making it white. Transformations can do this. Fig. 2 shows the basic idea. Starting with program P_0, a series of transformations $\tau_4 \cdot \tau_3 \cdot \tau_2 \cdot \tau_1$ is applied to produce the desired program P_4. Of course, today each of these transformations is accomplished manually: P_0 is hacked into P_1, P_1 is hacked into P_2, P_2 into P_3, and P_3 into P_4. With enough experience, an engineer can skip

---

[1] Dark knowledge can be encoded in code comments, but this is woefully inadequate.

Fig. 2. Program Derivation

intermediate steps. But if each transformation were programmed so that it could be applied by a tool, P_4 would be automatically derived from P_0. It is this automation mindset that drives DxT.

Program derivation in DxT is related to grammars and parse trees. A grammar G for a language is a set of rules called *productions* that describe how to form sentences (in the language's alphabet) that are valid according to the language's syntax. The set of derivable sentences is the language $L(G)$. Fig. 3a shows grammar G and its cone of sentences $L(G)$. What I have called dark knowledge is a sequence of decisions that derives a particular sentence S (the dashed arrows in Fig. 3a). Starting from a representation S_0 that likely does not belong to $L(G)$, a series of decisions (production invocations) derives S. This derivation, of course, is the parse tree of S: it is a proof that $S \in L(G)$ (Fig. 3b). It also represents the not-so-dark knowledge of S. Characteristic of dark knowledge is that there is no direct evidence of

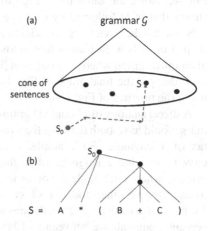

Fig. 3. The Language of a Grammar and a Parse Tree of Sentence S

these productions in S itself; all that appears are their after-effects. Such knowledge is important; given the *abstract syntax tree (AST)* of a program, one can automate program manipulations, such as refactorings. Without such knowledge, refactorings would be difficult, if not impossible, to perform correctly.

In over 25 years of studying program design, I have come to see typical programming languages and their grammars as one-dimensional; their sentences (*eg* Java programs) are simply 1D strings. This is not enough: to see the possibilities that arise in program development, one has to think in terms of $n \geq 2$ dimensional graphs, not 1D lines.

I focus on dataflow programs in this paper. They are not representative of all programs, but they do occupy a significant group of programs that are developed today. A dataflow program can be visualized as a graph of computations, where nodes are primitive computations and edges indicate the flow of data. Fig. 4a is an example: α, β, γ are computations; data enters on the left and exits on the right. Although it is always possible to map dataflow graphs to 1D programs, there is an important distinction between 1D and nD grammars, which I'll discuss later in Section 5.1.

Informally, *graph grammars* are generalizations of Chomsky string grammars. They extend the concatenation of strings to a gluing of graphs [10,15]. Productions are of the form $Graph_{left} \rightarrow Graph_{right}$; *ie* replace $Graph_{left}$ with $Graph_{right}$.[2] Derivations are

---

[2] There are different formalisms for graph grammars [47]. DxT grammars follow the algebraic (double-pushout) approach to (hyper-)graph grammars.

of the form $\text{Graph}_{\text{initial}} \Rightarrow^* \text{Graph}_{\text{final}}$; *ie* apply a sequence of rewrites to $\text{Graph}_{\text{initial}}$ to produce $\text{Graph}_{\text{final}}$. Graph grammars have been used for many purposes, such as design of visual languages [19,44,59], model synchronization [20,28], model validation [25,52], program compilation [49], and dynamic adaptation/evolution of architectures [11,14,33,55,56].

Fig. 4 shows three rewrites. Fig. 4b replaces a β computation with a graph of computations (*eg* a map-reduce of β). Fig. 4c shows the same for γ. Fig. 4d shows that of α followed by α^{-1} cancels each other, yielding an identity map. Fig. 5 is a derivation that starts at an initial graph where computation β precedes γ to the final graph of Fig. 4a using the rewrites of Fig. 4b-d.

A direct analogy of 1D and nD grammars would have both defining the syntax of a language. For example, it is easy to imagine a language of cyclic graphs, where each node is connected to exactly two other nodes. DxT goes further in that each production defines a semantic equivalence between its LHS and RHS graphs.

There is a subtle distinction between a graph grammar and a graph-rewriting system: the former enumerates all graphs from some starting graph and the latter transforms a given state (host graph) into a new state [57]. In this sense, DxT is closer to a graph grammar.

All of this is rather abstract, so let's pause here to see a concrete example.

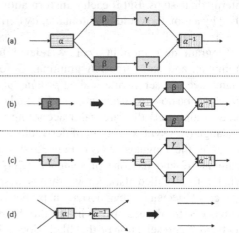

Fig. 4. A Dataflow Graph and 3 Rewrites

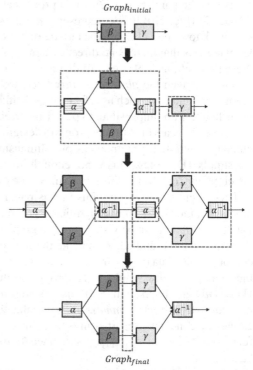

Graph$_{initial}$

Graph$_{final}$

Fig. 5. $\text{Graph}_{\text{initial}} \Rightarrow^* \text{Graph}_{\text{final}}$

3   Upright: A Synchronous Crash Fault Tolerant Server

Upright was the state-of-the-art Byzantine crash fault tolerant server in 2009 [8]. We were interested in its dataflow design. Talking to the Upright authors, we soon discovered that ~15 people on earth really understood it (and we certainly were not among them). It posed a challenging reverse engineering task [46]. In this section, we review Upright's *Synchronous Crash Fault Tolerant (SCFT)* design in terms of DxT. Doing so turns its dark knowledge white.

Upright's starting dataflow graph is Fig. 7a. (My apology for the size of this figure; it can be digitally enlarged). Such a graph in *Model Driven Engineering (MDE)* is called a *Platform Independent Model (PIM)*. Clients (the C boxes) asynchronously send requests to a stateful server (box VS); the network effectively serializes these requests (box Serialize). The server reads each request, updates its state, and then sends out a response. The network routes the response back to the originating client (box Demultiplex). In effect, messages exiting on the right of Fig. 7a re-enter the figure on the left, as if the graph were embedded on the surface of a cylinder (Fig. 6).

Fig. 6. Cylinder

The derivation of Upright's implemented dataflow graph, called a *Platform Specific Model (PSM)*, begins with the transition from Fig. 7a to Fig. 7b that exposes a network queue (L) in front of the server (S). Next, the transition from Fig. 7b to Fig. 7c effectively performs a map-reduce of both L and S [29]. Fig. 7d is a copy of Fig. 7c that shows the subgraphs to be replaced (to eliminate single points of failure). The SCFT dataflow design of Fig. 7e is a PSM for Fig. 7a [46]. We used this derivation to reimplement Upright's SCFT design [46].

The semantics of these rewrites are well-understood by experts of SCFT design; for this presentation, we view them as sterile graph transformations.

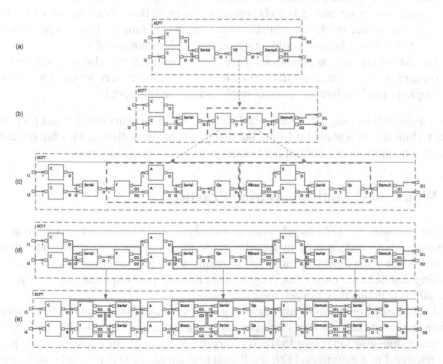

Fig. 7. Upright's SCFT PIM $\Rightarrow^*$ PSM Mapping

3.1 DxT and the Essence of Graph Grammars

A graph grammar $\mathcal{GG}$ is an ordered pair $(g, \mathcal{P})$; g is the starting graph and $\mathcal{P}$ is a set of graph productions. The language of $\mathcal{GG}$, $L(\mathcal{GG})$, is the set of graphs that can be derived by applying the rules in $\mathcal{P}$ to g [10,15,47].

DxT builds on this foundation: (1) the primitive computations (operations) of a domain are the alphabet of $\mathcal{GG}$, (2) the fundamental computational equivalences of the domain are its graph transformations (which encode the fundamental patterns of computation that were previously dark knowledge), and (3) the initial graph g is the PIM of an application and $L(\mathcal{GG})$ is the set of its PSMs—the cone of implementations for g. DxT goes further, in that the initial graph can be a member of a domain of PIMs, $g \in \mathcal{G}_{\text{pim}}$.

There are indeed distinctions between 1D and nD grammars. Here are a few:

- In general, the parse of a sentence in a 1D grammar should be unique; the grammar is either unambiguous or it is ambiguous with context making a parse unambiguous. Not so for nD grammars: multiple parses of a dataflow program simply means there are multiple equivalent ways of deriving that program—a perfectly acceptable situation.
- 1D productions do not need proofs of correctness—they simply define a textual pattern where there is nothing to prove. In contrast, each DxT rewrite defines a fundamental computational equivalence in a domain; there should be some evidence (ideally a proof) that each rewrite is correct.
- A parse tree for sentence S in a 1D grammar $\mathcal{G}$ is proof that S is a sentence of $L(\mathcal{G})$. A derivation tree for dataflow application S in an nD grammar $\mathcal{GG}$ is a proof that $S \in L(\mathcal{GG})$, *ie* S is a correct-by-construction implementation of g.
- 1D technology aims at parsing sentences. Although DxT can also be used for reverse engineering (parse the design of a legacy application), here we use it to derive programs (and explore the space of implementations of a spec).

It is not difficult to imagine the utility of Upright's DxT explanation. I could go into more technical details about DxT now, but that would be overkill. Instead, a big picture is needed to motivate this general field of research, which I consider next.

4   Who Cares? Motivations from Practice

Software Engineering (SE) largely aims at techniques and tools to aid masses of programmers whose code is used by hoards—these programmers need all the help they can get. At the same time, there are many domains where programming tasks are so demanding that there are only a few programmers that can perform them—these experts need all the help that they can get, too.

As said earlier, the focus of my research group is on dataflow domains which represent an important class of today's applications (*eg* virtual instrumentation [53] and applications of streaming languages [54]). The specific domains of our interest include parallel relational join algorithms [12], crash fault tolerant file servers [8], and distributed-memory, sequential, and shared-memory *Dense Linear Algebra (DLA)* kernels [37,38].

In practice, domain experts magically produce a *big bang* design: the dataflow graph of the complete application. Typically, it is a spaghetti diagram. *How it was created* and *why it works* are mysteries to all but its authors. For academic and practical reasons, it seems intuitively better to derive the graph from domain knowledge; doing so would answer both questions.[3] A digitally enlargeable Fig. 8 shows a DxT derivation of the parallelization of hash joins in the Gamma database machine [12]. Ask yourself: would you want only $Gamma_{final}$ or its derivation $Gamma_{initial} \Rightarrow^* Gamma_{final}$? I return to this point in Section 6.

Our current project focuses on the generation of DLA kernels/libraries. Kernel portability is a serious problem. First, porting may fail: kernels for distributed memory (where communication between cores is explicitly handled via a high-speed network [38]) may not work on sequential machines and vice versa. Second, if it does work, it may not perform well. The choice of algorithms to use on one hardware architecture may be different from those to use on another. One cannot simply "undo" optimizations and apply others—hopefully the reason for this is clear: such changes require dark knowledge. Third, in the worst case (which does frequently happen), kernels are coded from scratch.

Why is this so? The primary reason is *performance*. Applications that make DLA kernel calls

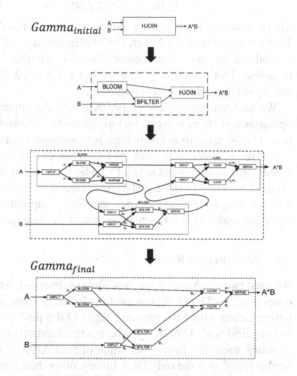

Fig. 8. Derivation of the Gamma Join Algorithm

are common to scientific computing, *eg* simulation of airflow, climate change, and weather forecasting. These applications are run on extraordinarily expensive machines. Time on these machines costs money; higher performance means quicker/cheaper runs or more accurate results. Bottom line: Application developers want the best performance to justify their costs [35].

Consider distributed-memory DLA kernels. They deal with *Single Program, Multiple Data (SPMD)* hardware architectures: the same program is run on each processor, but with different inputs and processors communicate with one another. The operations that a DLA kernel is expected to support is fixed—they have been well-known and

---

[3] This is no surprise to scientists. Physics students, for example, typically rederive equations to understand a paper. Similar activities occur in Computer Science.

well-defined for 40 years. Fig. 9 lists some of the *Level 3 Basic Linear Algebra Subprograms (BLAS3)*, which are matrix-matrix operations [13]. (Level 2 deals with vector-matrix operations and Level 1 vector-vector operations.) There is Gemm, general matrix-matrix multiply, Hermitian Hemm, symmetric Symm, and triangular Trmm matrix-matrix multiplies. Trsm solves non-singular triangular system of equations.

What is unusual from an SE perspective is that each operation has many variants. Consider Gemm. With constants α, β, the general form of this operation is:

$$C := \alpha \cdot A \cdot B + \beta \cdot C$$

where matrices A and B are either "normal" or transposed. That's 4 possibilities. Further, the implementation of Gemm is specialized for distributed memory based on whether A, B, or C is largest. That's another 3 for a total of $4 \times 3 = 12$. A similar variety is required for other operations.

BLAS3	# of Variants
Gemm	12
Hemm	8
Her2k	4
Herk	4
Symm	8
Syr2k	4
Trmm	16
Trsm	16

Fig. 9. The BLAS3

We also must consider "LAPACK-level" algorithms, which call DLA and BLAS3 operations, such as solvers, factorizations (*eg* Cholesky), and eigenvalue decompositions [1]. We have to generate high-performance algorithms for these operations, too.

Let me be clear: *our work on DLA kernels did not start from scratch.* We mechanized portions of van de Geijn's FLAME project [26] and the distributed-memory DLA library Elemental [42]. FLAME and Elemental leverage 15 years of polishing elegantly layered designs of DLA libraries and their computations. FLAME and Elemental provided the foundation for us to convert dark knowledge of DLA into white knowledge.

4.1 Performance Results

We used two machines in our benchmarks: Intrepid, Argonne's BlueGene/P with 8,192 cores and 27+ TFLOPS peak performance and Lonestar of the Texas Advanced Computing Center with 240 cores and 3.2 TFLOPS peak performance. We compared our results against ScaLAPACK [7], which is the standard linear algebra library for distributed memory machines. Each installation of ScaLAPACK is auto-tuned or manually-tuned. ScaLAPACK was the only DLA library, other than Elemental, for these machines.

DxTer is our tool that generates Elemental code [34,37]. It takes a PIM g of a *sequential* DLA program as input. It exhaustively applies all of the productions $\mathcal{P}$ in its library to produce the space of all of g's implementations $L((g, \mathcal{P}))$ *in distributed memory*. Using cost functions to estimate the performance of each derived graph, the most efficient graph is chosen.[4]

We used DxTer to automatically generate and optimize Elemental code for BLAS3 and Cholesky FLAME algorithms. Fig. 10 shows the performance for BLAS3. Overall, DxTer-generated code executes significantly faster than its hand-written ScaLAPACK counterparts. Fig. 11 shows the performance of Cholesky factorization. Again, DxTer generated-code is noticeably faster, which is the same or better than hand-coded Elemental implementations. These graphs are typical of DxTer results [36,37,38].

---

[4] This process of mapping an abstract specification to an efficient implementation is historically called *automatic programming*.

Today, *Elemental is shipped with DxTer-generated algorithms* [16].

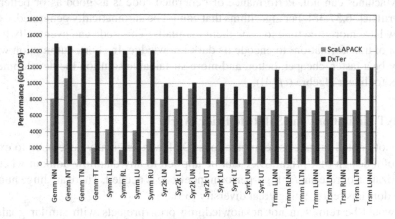

Fig. 10. BLAS3 Performance on Intrepid

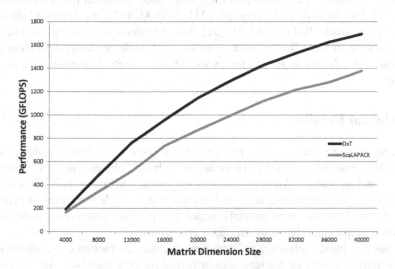

Fig. 11. Cholesky Performance on Lonestar

4.2   State-of-the-Art vs. Our Group's Vision

Today's linear algebra libraries exist as code. They are rewritten manually as the architecture du jour changes, and it changes rapidly. Consequently, library development lags far behind architecture development, by as much as a decade. Attaining sub-optimal performance on the latest and greatest machines carries a big price for end users.

This is not sustainable. We argue that linear algebra libraries written in a specific language for a specific architecture should never be developed entirely *manually*. Instead, tools, techniques, and theories are needed to encode algorithms, expert knowledge, and information about target architectures. The majority of code libraries can then be generated *automatically*. Experts can overlook optimizations and make mistakes. Machines can not. Performance of generated code is as good as or better than hand-written [36,37,38]. For algorithms that cannot be automatically generated, experts will now have more free time to code them manually. This code can eventually be cast in terms of transformations to encode its dark knowledge. In short, automation will ultimately be a faster, cheaper, better, and more sustainable solution the development of libraries for linear algebra (*cf* [4]).

4.3 DxT Limitations and Salute to Prior Work

DxT is not limited to stateless computations; DxT was originally developed to explain the stateful design of Upright. DxT can be applied to any dataflow domain where the mechanization of rote and/or high-performance code is needed. There are huge numbers of such domains representing great diversity [53].

We would be remiss in not acknowledging prior projects with similar goals and ideas. Among them are the pioneering works on correct-by-construction and deductive program synthesis [24], Amphion [32], rule-based relational query optimization (from which DxT is a direct descendant) [31], SPIRAL [43], the Tensor Contraction Engine [5], and Build-To-Order BLAS [51]. These projects were successful, because their authors put in the effort to make them succeed. Unfortunately, *the successes of these projects are known to far too few in the SE community*. I return to this point in Section 6.

5 Technical Details

With the big picture made clear, let's now drill down to see some details—what in MDE is called the metamodel—of DxT. There are three basic "objects" in DxT: interfaces, primitives, and algorithms. An *interface* is exactly what it suggests: It is a box that defines only the input/output ports and—at least informally—box semantics. A *primitive* is a box that implements a fundamental computation (operation) in code. An *algorithm* is a dataflow graph that references interfaces and primitives.

DxT has two basic "relationships": refinements and abstractions. A *refinement* replaces an interface with an implementation (primitive or algorithm). An *abstraction* rewrites in the opposite direction: from primitive or algorithm to an interface.[5]

Interfaces have preconditions (no surprise). But primitives and algorithms may have preconditions of their own that are *stronger* than the interfaces they implement (this is different). Fig. 12 is a classical example. The sort interface takes a stream of records as input and produces a sorted stream as output. (The sort key parameter is not shown). The first two refinements show quick-sort and merge-sort as primitives. The third shows a map-reduce implementation, where hash and omerge are primitive and any implementation of sort can be substituted for sort interfaces. The last refinement is the focus of this discussion: it says if the input stream is already in sort-key order, nothing needs to be done. This donothing algorithm has a precondition that is *stronger* than its sort interface.

---

[5] There is more to DxT, but this is sufficient for this paper. See [21,46] for more details.

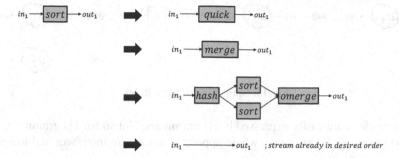

Fig. 12. The `sort` Interface and its Implementations

The *Liskov Substitution Principle (LSP)* is a hallmark of object-orientation [30]. It says if S is a subtype of T, then objects of type S can be substituted for objects of type T without altering program correctness. Substituting an interface with an implementing object (component) is standard fare today and is a way to realize refinement in LSP [39,58]. The key constraints of LSP are that preconditions for using S can *not* be stronger than preconditions for T, and postconditions for S are *not* weaker than that for T.

The `donothing` refinement is incompatible with LSP. In fact, LSP is too restrictive for graph rewriting; another principle is at work. In 1987, Perry [41] said a box A (read: algorithm or primitive) is upward compatible with box I (read: interface) iff:

$$\texttt{pre}(\texttt{A}) \Rightarrow \texttt{pre}(\texttt{I}) \quad \textit{; preconditions can be stronger}$$
$$\texttt{post}(\texttt{A}) \Rightarrow \texttt{post}(\texttt{I}) \quad \textit{; postconditions can't be weaker}$$

This is exactly what we need, which we call the *Perry Substitution Principle (PSP)* [41]. It is a practical alternative to LSP that dominates the DxT world. PSP takes into account the local conditions surrounding an interface to qualify legal refinements. *We could not re-engineer legacy designs without it.*

Abstraction—which replaces an implementation with an interface—has stronger constraints than refinement. It implies that a graph A must implement I. For this to hold, the pre- and postconditions of A and I must be equivalent [21]:

$$\texttt{pre}(\texttt{I}) \Leftrightarrow \texttt{pre}(\texttt{A})$$
$$\texttt{post}(\texttt{I}) \Leftrightarrow \texttt{post}(\texttt{A})$$

5.1 Optimizations

Earlier we used rewrites that replace a graph α_1 (more than a single node) with another graph α_2 (Fig. 13a), where Fig. 4d is an example. We call these rewrites *optimizations*. Optimizations effectively break "modular" boundaries of adjacent algorithms to expose inefficient graphs which are replaced with more efficient graphs. Optimization is equivalent to an abstraction (replacing graph α_1 with interface ι) followed by a refinement (replacing ι with graph α_2) (Fig. 13b). This allows DxT rewrites to assume the canonical form of interfaces on the left and implementations on the right (Fig. 13b).

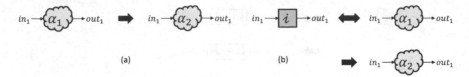

Fig. 13. Optimizing Rewrite Rules

Optimizations are easily expressed in nD grammars. Not so for 1D grammars. Consider the following 1D grammar, where uppercase names are interfaces and lowercase names are primitives:

$$A : a B c \mid \ldots ;$$
$$B : b \mid \ldots ;$$

A sentence of this grammar is abc. Suppose composition bc implements interface Z:

$$Z : bc \mid q ;$$

Further, domain experts know that bc is inefficient and can be replaced by box q, which is faster. This is accomplished by abstracting sentence abc to aZ and then refining to a faster program by replacing Z with q to yield aq. Although this makes perfect sense, abstraction is foreign to 1D grammars and parsing technology [45]; it is a natural part of nD grammars. I mentioned earlier (Section 2) that there is an important distinction between 1D and nD grammars; this is the point that I wanted to make.

Much of this should look familiar: it is similar to optimization techniques in compilers (esp. for functional languages) [27]. Optimizations break encapsulation boundaries to produce more efficient code. The novelties of DxT are (1) DxT uses graphs not trees, (2) DxT grammars derive software designs, which are *not* parse-trees or ASTs of programs and are *not* states of program executions, and (3) DxT rewrites should be clearly visible to domain experts and program designers, not hidden compiler internals.

5.2 Abstract Interpretation

Another fundamental idea (stolen from compiler playbooks) is *abstract interpretation*. A DxT graph g may have many interpretations. The default—what we have used up to now—is to interpret each box of g as the computation it represents. sort means "sort the input stream". We call this the *standard interpretation* S. The S interpretation of box b is denoted $S(b)$ or simply b, *eg* $S(\text{sort})$ is "sort the input stream". The standard interpretation of graph g is $S(g)$ or simply g.

There are other interpretations. $COST$ interprets each box b as a computation that *estimates the execution time* of $S(b)$ given statistics about $S(b)$'s inputs. So $COST(\text{sort})$ is "return an estimate of the execution time to produce sort's output stream". Each box $b \in G$ has exactly the same ports as $COST(b) \in COST(G)$, but the meaning of each box and its ports are different.

- We mentioned in Section 4.1 that DxTer forward-engineers (derives) all possible PSMs from an input PIM. The estimated run-time of a PSM p is determined by executing $\mathcal{COST}(\mathrm{p})$. The most efficient PSM that implements the PIM is the one with the lowest estimated cost [38].

- $\mathcal{M2T}(\mathrm{p})$ is a model-to-text interpretation that maps p to executable code.
- Pre- and postconditions help guarantee the correctness of DxT graphs. The $\mathcal{POST}$ interpretation computes properties that are output by a box given properties about box inputs. The $\mathcal{PRE}$ interpretation reads properties about box inputs (computed by $\mathcal{POST}$) and checks if the preconditions of that box are satisfied. A composition of these interpretations ($\mathcal{PRE} \cdot \mathcal{POST}(\mathrm{P})$) computes postconditions and validates preconditions of P [21].

6   The Reaction to DxT

Fellisen once remarked "It is not a problem to keep ourselves as researchers busy; we need to keep undergraduates busy" [18]. I saved the most important message about DxT for last. DxT is simple enough to teach to undergraduates.

Our thought has always been: once you have a proof or derivation of a design, you've hit the jackpot: you have turned dark knowledge into white knowledge. Having said this, we have been surprised at the reaction to DxT. Some of the reviews we received had breathtaking statements of technical acuity. In Letterman Show countdown order, our top 3 statements are:

3. "Refinement is not a transformation."
2. "Why will you succeed where others have not?"[6,7]
1. "The work lacks motivation."

We were comforted by the fact that conferences were being created solely for rejecting our papers. Overall, none of the reactions made sense to us.

This lead us to conduct user studies involving third-year CS undergraduates and first-year graduates. We split each set of students into two groups. To the first, we presented the big-bang design for Gamma (Fig. 8); to the second, we presented Gamma's derivation. We gave a written quiz that we graded. The result: *no difference!* There was no difference in the number of correct answers, no obvious benefit to DxT derivations over a big-bang. Both undergraduates and graduates were consistent on this point. This was counter-intuitive to us; it didn't make sense.

Perhaps, we thought, Gamma was too simple. So we re-ran the experiment using Upright. The result: again no difference! We were mystified.

Then it occurred to us: maybe these students and referees had *no* experience developing software in this manner. It could not be the case that DxT was difficult to grasp—the ideas are simple. And perhaps also the students and referees had no domain knowledge of parallel relational query processing or crash fault tolerant servers. They could not appreciate what we were telling them. If so, they could not recognize the value on our part to distill software-architecture knowledge as elementary graph rewrites. Nor could they see the practical implication of our results.

---

[6] They conveniently ignored our performance results.

[7] Others *have* been successful (Section 4.3). It helps to know the literature.

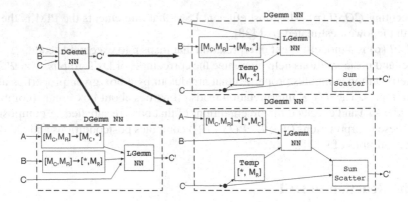

Fig. 14. Distributed Gemm Refinements

We had anecdotal evidence for this last conjecture. We asked ourselves "what are the refinements of DGemm (Distributed Gemm)?" Of course, we knew the answer (see Fig. 14), but how many others would? People who were familiar with distributed DLA algorithms should know. But very few would know a majority of the rules that we used in DxTer to derive DLA algorithms and how these rules could be applied. In short, the answer was: *very, very few*.

This again brings us back to the differences between 1D and nD grammars. It is relatively easy to understand 1D productions—there is little to know. Graph grammars as we use them are different. One needs deep knowledge of a domain to appreciate most rewrites. Very few have such knowledge. Cordell Green once told me "It takes effort" [23]. Few people have been in his (our) position to appreciate this point.

Our next user study in Fall 2012 explored these conjectures. We gave a programming assignment to an undergraduate class of 28 students. We had them build Gamma given its derivation. Once they completed the task, we gave them a questionnaire asking for them to compare their experiences with a big-bang approach (where derivation details were absent). As students had been exposed to big-bang implementations in other classes (and in previous assignments), they could compare DxT with a big-bang. We briefly review some of our questions and results [17,50]:

- **Comprehension.** Do you think the structured way DxT imposes gives you a deeper understanding of Gamma's design than you would get by not using it and doing it your own way?
- **Modification.** Do you think it would be easier or more difficult to modify Gamma with DxT compared to a big-bang approach?
- **Recommendation.** Would you recommend to your fellow students implementing Gamma using DxT or in a big-bang manner?

Analyzing the responses showed that 55% said DxT provided a deeper comprehension of Gamma's design; over 80% said DxT improved comprehension. 47% said it would be considerably easier to modify Gamma given its derivation; over 90% said it would make modification easier. None said it would make it harder. And 88% said they would recommend DxT over a big-bang.

More gratifying were the written comments, a few from different individuals are listed below:

- I have learned the most from this project than any other CS project I have ever done.
- I even made my OS group do a DxT implementation on the last 2 projects due to my experience implementing Gamma.
- Honestly, I don't believe that software engineers ever have a source (to provide a DxT explanation) in real life. If there was such a thing we would lose our jobs, because there is an explanation which even a monkey can implement.
- It's so much easier to implement (using DxT). The big-bang makes it easy to make so many errors, because you can't test each section separately. DxT might take a bit longer, but saves you so much time debugging, and is a more natural way to build things. You won't get lost in your design trying to do too many things at once.

In retrospect, these comments were familiar. In October 2003, NSF held a Science of Design Workshop in Airlie, Virginia. Fred Brooks (1999 Turing Award) summarized the conclusions of his working group to explore the role of science in design: "We don't know what we're doing and we don't know what we've done!". To paraphrase Edsger Dijkstra (1972 Turing Award): "Have you noticed that there are child prodigies in mathematics, music, and gymnastics, but none in human surgery?". The point being that there are bodies of knowledge that take years to comprehend and there are no short-cuts to achieve such understanding. We owe our success with DxTer to 15 years of research by van de Geijn and others to understand the domain of DLA. Not all domains are this hard to understand, but again, *it takes effort*. Our take-away conclusion is this:

Knowledge, experience, and understanding how to codify knowledge of efficient programs in a reproducible way is everything to automated design. Lacking any of these is a significant barrier to progress.

7 Conclusions

Programmers are geniuses at making the simplest things look complicated; finding the underlying simplicity is the challenge. Programmers are also geniuses at making critical white knowledge dark; reversing the color of knowledge is yet another challenge. It takes effort to understand a legacy application or domain to mine out its fundamental identities or rewrite rules that are key to (a) automated design, (b) correct-by-construction, and (c) transforming undergraduate education on software design from hacking to a more scientific foundation.

Software Language and Engineering (SLE) has great potential for the future of Software Engineering. Formal languages will be the foundation for automated software development. Knowledge of dataflow application designs will be encoded as graph grammars, not Chomsky string grammars, whose sentences define complex programs. Such grammars will enable the design of programs to be optimized automatically; they will remove the burden of rote, tedious, difficult, and error-prone activities of program development; they will scale domain expertise from a few people to the masses; and most importantly, they ultimately will help modernize undergraduate curriculums in software design.

Acknowledgements. We thank R. van de Geijn (Texas), T. Riche (NI), M. Erwig (Oregon), R. Paige (York), and C. Kästner (CMU) for their helpful comments on drafts of this paper. We gratefully acknowledge support for this work by NSF grants CCF-0724979, CCF-0917167, and ACI-1148125. Gonçalves was funded by the ERDF project FCOMP-01-0124-FEDER-010152 and FCT grant SFRH/BD/47800/2008. Marker held fellowships from Sandia National Laboratories and NSF (grant DGE-1110007). Siegmund was funded by BMBF project 01IM10002B. This research used resources of the Argonne Leadership Computing Facility at Argonne National Lab, which is supported by the Office of Science of the U.S. Department of Energy under contract DE-AC02-06CH11357. We are greatly indebted to Jack Poulson for his help to understand his Elemental library.

References

1. Anderson, E., et al.: LAPACK Users' Guide. SIAM, Philadelphia (1992)
2. Bahcall, J., Piran, T., Weinberg, S.: Dark matter in the universe. In: 4TH Jerusalem Winter School For Theoretical Physics (1987)
3. Batory, D., Azanza, M., Saraiva, J.: The Objects and Arrows of Computational Design. In: Czarnecki, K., Ober, I., Bruel, J.-M., Uhl, A., Völter, M. (eds.) MODELS 2008. LNCS, vol. 5301, pp. 1–20. Springer, Heidelberg (2008)
4. Batory, D., Singhal, V., Sirkin, M., Thomas, J.A.: Scalable software libraries. In: SIGSOFT (1993)
5. Baumgartner, G., et al.: Synthesis of high-performance parallel programs for a class of ab initio quantum chemistry models. Proceedings of the IEEE (2005)
6. Baxter, I.D.: Design Maintenance Systems. CACM (April 1992)
7. Blackford, L.S., et al.: ScaLAPACK: a portable linear algebra library for distributed memory computers - design issues and performance. In: SC (1996)
8. Clement, A., Kapritsos, M., Lee, S., Wang, Y., Alvisi, L., Dahlin, M., Riche, T.: Upright cluster services. In: SOSP (2009)
9. Curtis, B., Krasner, H., Iscoe, N.: A field study of the software design process for large systems. Comm. ACM (November 1988)
10. D'Antonio, F.: (October 2003), http://www.docstoc.com/docs/123006845/Introduction-to-Graph-Grammars-DAntonio
11. Derk, M., DeBrunner, L.: Reconfiguration graph grammar for massively parallel, fault tolerant computers. In: Cuny, J., Engels, G., Ehrig, H., Rozenberg, G. (eds.) Graph Grammars 1994. LNCS, vol. 1073, pp. 185–195. Springer, Heidelberg (1996)
12. Dewitt, D.J., Ghandeharizadeh, S., Schneider, D., Hsiao, A.B.H., Rasmussen, R.: The Gamma Database Machine Project. IEEE ToKaDE 2(1) (1990)
13. Dongarra, J.J., Du Croz, J., Hammarling, S., Duff, I.: A set of level 3 basic linear algebra subprograms. ACM Trans. Math. Software 16(1) (March 1990)
14. Dowling, J., Cahill, V.: Dynamic software evolution and the k-component model. In: Workshop on Software Evolution at OOPSLA (2001)
15. Ehrig, H., Pfender, M., Schneider, H.J.: Graph-grammars: An algebraic approach. In: SWAT (1973)
16. Elemental Team, http://libelemental.org/about/team.html
17. Feigenspan, J., Batory, D., Riché, T.L.: Is the derivation of a model easier to understand than the model itself? In: ICPC (2012)
18. Felleisen, M.: Private Correspondence (January 2007)

19. Ferrucci, F., Tortora, G., Tucci, M., Vitiello, G.: A predictive parser for visual languages specified by relation grammars. In: VL (1994)
20. Giese, H., Wagner, R.: Incremental model synchronization with triple graph grammars. In: Wang, J., Whittle, J., Harel, D., Reggio, G. (eds.) MoDELS 2006. LNCS, vol. 4199, pp. 543–557. Springer, Heidelberg (2006)
21. Gonçalves, R.C., Batory, D., Sobral, J.: ReFlO: An interactive tool for pipe-and-filter domain specification and program generation (submitted 2013)
22. Green, C., Luckham, D., Balzer, R., Cheatham, T., Rich, C.: Report on a knowledge-based software assistant. Tech. rep., Kestrel Institute (1983)
23. Green, C.: Private Correspondence (January 2009)
24. Green, C., Luckham, D., Balzer, R., Cheatham, T., Rich, C.: Report on a knowledge-based software assistant. Kestrel Institute Technical Report KES.U.83.2 (1983)
25. Grunske, L., Geiger, L., Zündorf, A., Van Eetvelde, N., Van Gorp, P., Varro, D.: Using graph transformation for practical model driven software engineering. In: Model-Driven Software Development. Springer, Heidelberg (2005)
26. Gunnels, J.A., Gustavson, F.G., Henry, G.M., van de Geijn, R.A.: FLAME: Formal Linear Algebra Methods Environment. ACM Trans. on Math. Softw. (December 2001)
27. Jones, S.L.P., Santos, A.L.M.: A transformation-based optimiser for haskell. Science of Computer Programming 32(1-3) (1998)
28. Königs, A., Schürr, A.: Tool integration with triple graph grammars - a survey. Electronic Notes in Theoretical Computer Science 148(1) (2006)
29. Lamport, L.: The part-time parliament. ACM Trans. Comput. Syst. 16(2) (1998)
30. Liskov, B.H., Wing, J.M.: A behavioral notion of subtyping. ACM Trans. Program. Lang. Syst. 16(6) (1994)
31. Lohman, G.M.: Grammar-like functional rules for representing query optimization alternatives. In: ACM SIGMOD (1988)
32. Lowry, M., Philpot, A., Pressburger, T., Underwood, I.: Amphion: Automatic programming for scientific subroutine libraries. In: Raś, Z.W., Zemankova, M. (eds.) ISMIS 1994. LNCS, vol. 869, pp. 326–335. Springer, Heidelberg (1994)
33. Maggiolo-Schettini, A., Peron, A.: A graph rewriting framework for statecharts semantics. In: Cuny, J., Engels, G., Ehrig, H., Rozenberg, G. (eds.) Graph Grammars 1994. LNCS, vol. 1073, pp. 107–121. Springer, Heidelberg (1996)
34. Marker, B., Batory, D., Shepherd, C.: Dxter: A dense linear algebra program synthesizer. Computer Science report TR-12-17, Univ. of Texas at Austin (2012)
35. Marker, B., Batory, D., van de Geijn, R.: DSLs, DLA, DxT, and MDE in CSE. In: SECSE (May 2013)
36. Marker, B., Batory, D., van de Geijn, R.: A case study in mechanically deriving dense linear algebra code. International Journal of High Performance Computing Applications (to appear)
37. Marker, B., Batory, D.S., van de Geijn, R.A.: Code generation and optimization of distributed-memory dense linear algebra kernels. In: ICCS (2013)
38. Marker, B., Poulson, J., Batory, D., van de Geijn, R.: Designing linear algebra algorithms by transformation: Mechanizing the expert developer. In: Daydé, M., Marques, O., Nakajima, K. (eds.) VECPAR. LNCS, vol. 7851, pp. 362–378. Springer, Heidelberg (2013)
39. Medvidovic, N., Rosenblum, D.S., Taylor, R.N.: A language and environment for architecture-based software development and evolution. In: ICSE (1999)
40. Müller, H.: Private Correspondence (May 2013)
41. Perry, D.E.: Version control in the inscape environment. In: ICSE (1987)
42. Poulson, J., Marker, B., van de Geijn, R.A., Hammond, J.R., Romero, N.A.: Elemental: A new framework for distributed memory dense matrix computations. ACM Trans. on Math. Softw. 39(2) (February 2013)

43. Püschel, M., et al.: SPIRAL: Code generation for DSP transforms. In: Proceedings of the IEEE, special issue on "Program Generation, Optimization, and Adaptation" (2005)
44. Rekers, J., Schürr, A.: Defining and parsing visual languages with layered graph grammars. Journal of Visual Languages & Computing 8(1) (1997)
45. Rich, E.A.: Automata, Computability and Complexity: Theory and Applications. Pearson-Prentice Hall (2008)
46. Riché, T., Goncalves, R., Marker, B., Batory, D.: Pushouts in Software Architecture Design. In: GPCE (2012)
47. Rozenberg, G.: Handbook of Graph Grammars and Computing by Graph Transformation. Foundations, vol. I. World Scientific (1997)
48. Salehie, M., Tahvildari, L.: Self-adaptive software: Landscape and research challenges. ACM Trans. Auton. Adapt. Syst. (2009)
49. Schürr, A.: Introduction to progress, an attribute graph grammar based specification language. In: Nagl, M. (ed.) WG 1989. LNCS, vol. 411, pp. 151–165. Springer, Heidelberg (1990)
50. Siegmund, J.: Framework for Measuring Program Comprehension. Ph.D. thesis, University of Magdeburg, School of Computer Science (2012)
51. Siek, J.G., Karlin, I., Jessup, E.R.: Build to order linear algebra kernels. Parallel and Distributed Processing (2008)
52. Taentzer, G.: AGG: A graph transformation environment for modeling and validation of software. In: Pfaltz, J.L., Nagl, M., Böhlen, B. (eds.) AGTIVE 2003. LNCS, vol. 3062, pp. 446–453. Springer, Heidelberg (2004)
53. The LabVIEW Environment, http://www.ni.com/labview/
54. Thies, W., Karczmarek, M., Amarasinghe, S.P.: StreamIt: A language for streaming applications. In: Conference on Compiler Construction (2002)
55. Tichy, M., Henkler, S., Holtmann, J., Oberthür, S.: Component story diagrams: A transformation language for component structures in mechatronic systems. In: Workshop on Object-oriented Modeling of Embedded Real-Time Systems, Paderborn, Germany (2008)
56. Wermelinger, M., Fiadeiro, J.L.: A graph transformation approach to software architecture reconfiguration. Sci. Comput. Program. (2002)
57. Wikipedia: Graph rewriting, http://en.wikipedia.org/wiki/Graph_rewriting
58. Wikipedia: Component-based software engineering (2013), http://en.wikipedia.org/wiki/Component-based_software_engineering
59. Wittenburg, K.: Earley-style parsing for relational grammars. In: Visual Languages (1992)

Developing a Domain-Specific Language for Scheduling in the European Energy Sector

Stefan Sobernig[1], Mark Strembeck[1], and Andreas Beck[2]

[1] Institute of Information Systems, New Media Lab
Vienna University of Economics and Business (WU Vienna), Austria
firstname.lastname@wu.ac.at
[2] VERBUND Trading AG, Austria
andreas.beck@verbund.com

Abstract. European electricity companies trade electric power across country and market boundaries. So called *schedules* are data sets that define the terms and conditions of such power trades. Different proprietary or standardized formats for schedules exist. However, due to a wide variety of different trading partners and power markets, a number of problems arise which complicate the standardized exchange of schedules. In this paper, we discuss a project that we conducted to develop a domain-specific language (DSL) for scheduling in a large Austrian electricity company running more than 140 power plants. The DSL is written in Ruby and provides a standardized programming model for specifying schedules, reduces code redundancy, and enables domain experts ("schedulers") to set up and to change market definitions autonomously.

Keywords: Domain-specific Language, DSL, Power Market, Power Trading, Scheduling, Industry Project, Europe.

1 Introduction

The VERBUND AG[1] is an Austrian electricity company and one of the largest producers of electricity from hydropower in Europe. VERBUND AG has about 3.300 employees and is running more than 140 power plants in Austria and other European countries (125 of which are hydropower plants) to serve about one million private households and corporate customers. The VERBUND Trading AG (VTR)[2] is a subsidiary company of VERBUND AG. VTR is the operating unit for the optimization of the power plants, for international power trading, and for the scheduling process of the VERBUND group and its subsidiaries. VTR trades about 500 GWh of electrical power on a daily basis (500 GWh correspond to an annual electricity consumption of some 120 000 households). In the VTR context, *schedules* are structured data sets which contain the technical details about the terms, the conditions, and the volumes of the power deals made within or across 21 European power markets in 18 countries.

---

[1] http://www.verbund.com/cc/en/
[2] http://www.verbund.com/cc/en/about-us/our-business-divisions/trading

M. Erwig, R.F. Paige, and E. Van Wyk (Eds.): SLE 2013, LNCS 8225, pp. 19–35, 2013.

A transmission system operator (TSO) is a company that runs an infrastructure (the power grid) for transporting (electrical) energy. The scheduling process ensures the transfer of schedules to the TSO concerning the amount of power traded in each of the TSO's markets. The liberalization of the energy market (which occurred in 2001 in Austria) requires that the exchange of the schedules between the TSO and its trading partners be carried out in a standardized way so as to guarantee the quick and automated processing of schedules and to ensure the maintenance of a stable power grid.

However, due to the large number of different energy markets and trading partners, VTR faces a number of problems with respect to a standardized exchange of schedules. The first problem is the heterogeneous set of applications and scripts that VTR currently uses to carry out its scheduling process. The legacy system that VTR employs to support the scheduling process has been in use since 2007. The system is based on a number of different Microsoft Excel workbooks and embedded spreadsheet applications (Visual Basic for Applications, VBA, macros). The bulk of the source code used for data retrieval, calculations, and format-building logic is the same in every workbook (code clones). There are, however, differences between the workbooks arising from the implementation of the local *market rules* (rules that are specific for a given power market) in each workbook. Therefore, the maintenance of the code requires substantial effort because, in order to maintain a consistent code basis, every change in one workbook must be incorporated into every other workbook. VTR reports on having spent an average of 30 person-days per year since 2007 on maintaining and further-developing the existing scheduling-support system. The second problem is to develop the technical knowledge needed to make changes to the workbooks throughout the organization and to render the scheduling system adaptable by non-technical domain experts ("schedulers"). At the same time, any scheduler wishing to make changes must comply with company requirements and work within the existing system landscape.

In this context, we developed a scheduling system based on a domain-specific language (DSL) to address the above problems. The project started in January 2011 and has evolved over 2.5 years. For this project, we applied an extraction-based DSL development style [15] to systematically define a DSL for scheduling in the energy sector based on the existing scheduling system. In the remainder, we report on this development project and its exploratory evaluation by first providing some background on the scheduling domain (see Section 2). We then document the DSL design and implementation in Section 3. Based on an early case-study evaluation reported on in Section 4, we review the achieved benefits of the DSL-based system refactoring (see Section 5) and the lessons learned from applying an extraction-based DSL development style (see Section 6).

2   Background: Scheduling Power Deals

During the scheduling process, VTR must handle different representation formats of schedules which detail the amounts of power VERBUND AG produces, the amounts of power it imports, the amounts it exports (deliveries that cross market boundaries), and the amounts of power it trades in internal areas (deliveries within a market). Furthermore, VTR must deliver those schedules to various market-specific recipients, including TSOs. Each market has its own schedule. Runtime occurrences of schedules are referred to as *schedule messages* (messages, hereafter), with each message having its particular format, covering a particular scope, and relating to a particular mode of transmission. The most common message formats are ESS (ETSO Scheduling System [5,6,7]) and KISS (Keep It Small and Simple [4]). ESS is a special-purpose XML-based data format, while KISS is based on Microsoft Excel. Moreover, for some markets VTR must provide proprietary (mostly Excel based) formats. The scope of a particular schedule can cover market-internal power deliveries, market-external power deliveries, or both. A schedule can be transmitted either via e-mail, FTP, Web applications, Web services, or any combination of these. Figure 1 illustrates this configuration space of schedules.

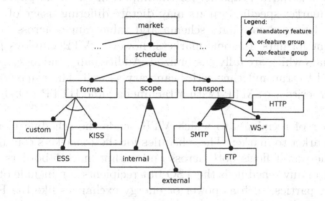

Fig. 1. Excerpt from the Scheduling Domain Model, depicted as Feature Diagram [2]

There are some principles that every schedule follows. Every delivery or receipt relationship is called a *time series*. Every time series is identified by a set of elements. Every schedule has the following elements (although the name for a particular element may differ, depending upon the format used for the particular schedule): In Area, Out Area, In Party, Out Party, and the Capacity Agreement ID. There are other elements that may elaborate upon the time series but those elements are not part of the distinct identification of a schedule. Each time series also contains the delivery quantities of the traded power. A particular time series covers either the amount of electrical power delivered to one particular customer or the amount of power received from a supplier in one control area.

The In and Out Area define the direction of the energy flow. The Out Area is the market area the energy comes from and the In Area is the market area to which the energy goes. For the identification of the areas, standardized codes are used. Time series covering deliveries within a market area (i.e., an internal delivery) have the same In and Out Area code, while time series covering deliveries across two market areas (i.e., external or cross border delivery) bear the respective area code for each market. The concept of the trading border is similar to geographical borders, except that a trading border only exists where there are power lines in place that link two markets. There are, for example, four different market areas within Germany but only three have a border with and power lines that link to Austria. As a result, there are trading borders between three of the German markets and the Austrian market. Another example is the border between Austria and Slovakia. There is a geographical border, but, because there are no power lines connecting the two countries, there is no trading border between them.

The In and Out Party elements define separately the party which delivers and the party which receives the energy. The Capacity Agreement ID is only applied to cross border deals and identifies capacity rights. The term "capacity right" refers to the right to export or import power across a specified trading border. On limited borders, i.e., borders with limited power transmission capacity, one of the parties must have a capacity for the import or export of power. Although the required market-specific formats may dictate differing usage of certain elements, VTR defines a core data schema and value ranges across markets and across different formats. In some markets, however, VTR employs proprietary message formats which are fully customized. Additionally, the message exchange protocols used to transmit time series can vary as well. The usual ways used to transmit such series are SMTP (with attachments) and HTTP POST (via a web application).

The number of recipients to which VTR sends the schedule messages also varies from market to market. The schedules for these markets contain information about the power flows both across and within market borders. A mandatory recipient of any schedule is the TSO but recipients can include other official power market parties, such as power or energy exchanges like the EPEX (European Power Exchange) in Germany and France or market makers in general like Borzen in Slovenia, or OTE in the Czech Republic. In Austria, there are two recipients. One is the TSO (the Austrian Power Grid AG) which receives only data concerning power flows across the country's borders and the other is the APCS (Austrian Power Clearing and Settlement AG), to which all the transaction data inside the Austrian market are sent.

The daily transactions result in a high number of schedules. On an average day, the number of schedules may go as high as about 200. The types of schedules that VTR generates include long-term, day-ahead, intra-day, and post-scheduling schedules. Long-term schedules cover the time frame before D-1, where D stands for the delivery day. That is, if the delivery day is June 14, every schedule sent before June 13 is considered to be long term. The valid time frame for a specific market can be found in the local market rules. The time frame for day-ahead usually begins the day before delivery and ends after the final schedules for the delivery day are sent, which usually is on D-1 at about 14:30. In our example that would be June 13, 14:30. Again, the valid time frame for a specific market can be found in the local market rules. Intra-day schedules cover the time frame between the start of intra-day (which is usually shortly after the end of day-ahead) and the end of the delivery day. Post-scheduling schedules cover the defined time frame after delivery.

At VTR, long-term and day-ahead schedules are handled by a group of 4 schedulers. Intra-day scheduling is handled by an intra-day trading team, which handles both intra-day scheduling and controls the power plants. Post scheduling is again handled by the schedulers group. For verifying data quality, the standing data (e.g., market definitions) and the transaction data (as retrieved by executing data queries in the trading system) entering a schedule message are subjected to review processes. The standing data must undergo a double-check by a second scheduler to ensure their correctness. The transaction data at VTR are double-checked upon processing by the power trader and the back-office staff.

Table 1. Key Figures for the Legacy Scheduling System

Number of implemented power markets	18
Number of Excel workbooks	14
Avg. SLOC[3] per workbook	1 500
Avg. market-specific SLOC[3] per workbook	50

3   A DSL for Scheduling

In addition to implementing the domain of scheduling as analyzed in Section 2, the DSL-based scheduling system sets out to address a number of objectives. The following four goals resulted from the actual difficulties with the existing scheduling system as experienced by administrator and schedulers at VTR.

Minimize Code Clones. In the existing scheduling system, 14 Excel workbooks generate different schedule types for 18 of the 21 markets (see Table 1). For the remaining three markets, third-party schedule generators are used which are not maintained by VTR. On average, there are about 1 500 source lines of code (SLOC[3]; mainly VBA code) in each workbook, for a total of approximately 21 000 SLOC in the 14 workbooks. The average number of market-specific SLOC per market is approximately 50, summing up to 700 lines in 14 workbooks. Therefore, when comparing the code bases of the workbooks, the workbooks share approximately 97% of their code bases. Only the remaining 3% are code fragments specific to single markets. Specialization involves local market rules relating to message generation, such as those used in the mapping of codes (e.g., market-area codes). Such rules usually follow a certain default rule that makes it easy for human beings to read and to understand them. In some cases, however, certain values must differ from default rules, such as crossing in and

---

[3] The source lines of code (SLOC) were measured using `cloc` [3].

Table 2. Schedule Configuration Specific to the RWE Market

Configuration point	Configuration value(s)
Format	ESS V2R3
Borders	EON, ENBW, LU, AT, FR, CH
SenderIdentification	13XVERBUND1234-P
SenderRole	A01
ReceiverIdentification	10XDE-RWENET—W
ReceiverRole	A04

crossing out of a control area for cross-border energy deliveries. Table 2 exemplifies configuration data specific to the power market of the German company "Rheinisch-Westfälische Elektrizitätswerks Aktiengesellschaft" (RWE).

The numerous code clones make the workbooks hard to maintain over time. Propagating the latest version of the code to every workbook is tedious and time-consuming. For example, one basic step within the scheduling process is the use of Business Objects reports provided by the SAP business intelligence software [12] as part of the power-trading system. SAP Business Objects offers a COM-based API for generating such reports. Whenever there are SAP vendor upgrades, there are API changes affecting any client application such as the workbooks. As a result, one must examine every workbook to reflect these API changes. In the majority of shared workbook code, a second source of redundancy are recurring configuration data, common to all or subsets of markets. For example, the various input and output identifiers (e.g., file names, output directory names for messages and temporary files) follow one naming convention.

Establish Participatory Maintainability. There are two main participant roles in the existing scheduling process. On the one hand, there is the scheduler as the non-technical domain expert, and, on the other hand, there is the administrator responsible for setting up new markets. The scheduler, as the domain expert, has a deep knowledge of the scheduling process, of the message formats used, of the local market rules, and of the delivery modes for messages. The administrator, as the primary workbook developer, knows the programming logic and the design of the workbook code. In the legacy system, almost everything from the GUI logic that governs the configuration to the business logic has been included in the monolithic workbook code. This means, of course, that the administrator is the only one who can make even the smallest changes or amendments to the code. The objective, therefore, is to develop a system that will allow the schedulers to participate in implementing new markets, with new rules, only requiring action by an administrator for non-routine tasks (e.g., code changes due to new interface versions of SAP Business Objects).

Cover Standard and Custom Message Formats. For 18 of the 21 power markets mentioned above, VTR uses standardized message formats, such as the

Excel-based KISS or the XML-based ESS formats. However, VTR must be able
to derive custom, market-local message formats from standard formats to ac-
commodate market rules deviating from the standards. The concrete format for
a market is usually a deviation from a standard format and may be defined by
the market operator or energy controlling authority. Occasionally, even the rules
set by a TSO may differ from the standard or officially advertised rules.

Integrate Refactored System into the Existing System Landscape. To
keep changes to the existing technical landscape at VTR to a minimum, the
DSL development should avoid the introduction of new software components.
Software components already in use in the existing scheduling process are Excel,
Business Objects, as well as VBA and VB.NET as frontend languages to .NET
as runtime platform.

Provide Uniform, but Variable Graphical User Interfaces (GUI). Each
workbook provides a unique UI form to the scheduler for entering configuration
data, such as the delivery date, delivery message, or the message format to use.
These scheduler forms tend to be narrowly focused and tailored to meet the
exact needs of each particular market. This is, however, not a flaw in the design
of the forms. Rather, the narrowness is simply a result of the extreme tailor-
ing towards scheduling needs in a particular market. Nevertheless, the deviating
form designs affect a scheduler's ease to move between the workbooks negatively,
because they require the user to interpret and to understand every different user
form. The goal, therefore, was to develop a uniform user interface that would
contain cross-market functionality to run schedules, but which would allow the
scheduler either to activate or to deactivate GUI parts deemed necessary or unnecessary for a given market.

Given these requirements and restrictions, it was decided to develop an embedded DSL using Ruby as its host-language infrastructure. An embedded DSL
meant a minimal and non-invasive addition to the existing system landscape
without the need for adding software components, for example, for parsing and
integrating an external DSL. Besides, an embedded DSL provides for seamless
integration with the existing runtime infrastructure such as the SAP business
intelligence software (see, e.g., [15,19]). The dominant interface for domain users
(schedulers) was to remain a revised, form-based GUI with the embedded DSL
serving as an alternative backend syntax for maintenance tasks, rather than as a
complete replacement. Ruby was adopted because of its suitability for developing embedded DSLs (see, e.g., [8]) and its availability as IronRuby for .NET [9],
including IDE support by Microsoft, which is the required development platform
at VERBUND Trading AG.

3.1   Language Model and Concrete Syntax

The language model and the concrete-syntax style were extracted from reviewing the documentation, the code base, and auxiliary documents of the existing

software system [15]. The reviews were performed by the DSL design team consisting of the three authors. The main domain abstractions, which constitute the core language model, were identified by studying, first, the Excel workbooks because they host the existing VBA source code and the existing market definitions. Second, Business Objects reports were investigated for the trading data they provide and for the business logic represented by data queries. Third, there are the standards documents defining the schedule-message formats, including markup-schema definitions such as the ETSO Scheduling System formats [5,6,7].

Abstract Syntax. Figure 2a shows the conceptual language model of the DSL. The key abstraction is the `Message` which represents a schedule in a specific message format. A `Market` models a power market and records important market-specific data such as the market symbol, border codes, and the allowed message formats. `Market` can refer to one direct `default Market` whose configuration data is inherited if not redefined. A `MessageBuilder` implements a generator for a specific message format which specifies a `Message` in terms of construction rules for a `ScheduleHeader` and a `ScheduleColumn`. The attributes of `ScheduleHeader` enter the message headers as required by the message format. A `ScheduleColumn` represents the different time series which form the body of a schedule message. The construction rules typically take the form of mappings and, if needed, transformations between message elements (e.g., as specified by the KISS and ESS message formats) and the elements of a given `Market` definition. Depending on the message representation (e.g., XML), the construction rules may also specify the representation creation. For writing XML markup, our DSL integrates with the Builder library available for Ruby [18].

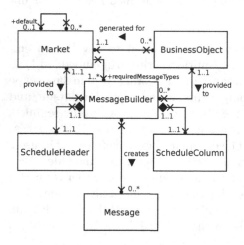

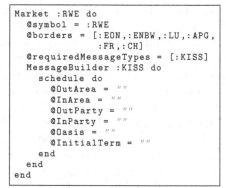

(a) Core Language Model   (b) Concrete Syntax Example

Fig. 2. Scheduling DSL

Concrete Syntax. In the existing, workbook-based scheduling system, the configuration data for markets and schedule messages are maintained in a rows-and-columns spreadsheet format with assigning certain rows, columns, or individual cells the role of meta-data stores identifying the meta-data type using a text label. Both roles, administrators and schedulers, performed their tasks using this tabulated syntax. To meet the requirements of a uniform GUI for domain users (i.e., schedulers) and to separate the user interfaces between administrators and schedulers (see requirements above), a textual concrete-syntax for administrators as primary users of the scheduling DSL was devised. Listing 2b shows the `Market` definition for the control area RWE and an exemplary `MessageBuilder` definition of the KISS message format, showing the assignment of a market-name symbol, the six transmission network borders relevant for this market, and the message format to use for this market: KISS. Note that for KISS only, the variables are initialized using empty strings.

As an embedded DSL, the textual-concrete syntax leverages and integrates with the concrete syntax of the Ruby host language. To reflect the use of the DSL for configuration programming of markets and message builders, especially mapping and construction rules, a single assignment form is promoted. Assignments establish correspondences between elements of market definitions and message formats, on the one hand, as well as between market attributes and configuration values, on the other hand. This syntax style is realized using the principles of object scoping and nested closures [8].

Constraints. There are constraints applying to a `Market` and a `Message-Builder`. The `Market` must have a unique name accompanied by a unique symbol or abbreviation (e.g., "RWE"). This pair represents the market or control area for which this definition stands. Furthermore, the possible borders for power import and export have to be stated and the message types applicable to this market. Each message format has then to be represented by a `MessageBuilder` referenced by a `Market`. In addition, there are specific constraints on the data representations of trading data. For example, value constraints on time stamps are set by the ESS family of standards (see, e.g., [5]).

Structural Semantics. The inheritance semantics between a `Market` and its default `Market` are those of concatenation-based prototypical inheritance [16]. This allows for factoring out common configuration data into single and reusable `Market` definitions. This way, creating incremental variants of single market definitions upon changed market requirements eases maintenance. Implementing this refinement scheme is facilitated by the use of nested closures (see below).

3.2 Implementation

The realized architecture is built from three interacting components: a GUI component (`VTRGUI`), a managed assembly (`VTRCore`), and the `IronRubyEngine` (see Figure 3). The GUI and the managed assembly are implemented using .NET 4.0 and VB.NET as frontend language. The retrieval process for transaction

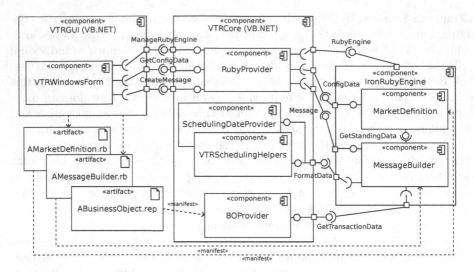

Fig. 3. An Architectural Overview of the DSL-Based Scheduling System

data uses Microsoft Excel 2010 and SAP Business Objects. The Ruby engine is provided by IronRuby 1.1.3, a Ruby implementation targeting the Microsoft Common and Dynamic Language Runtimes (CLR, DLR) and widely complying with MRI-Ruby 1.9.2.

The overall workflow of creating a `Message` is controlled by the GUI component in terms of a wizard. Once the scheduler has selected a market definition (`AMarketDefinition.rb`) and a message-builder definition (`AMessageBuilder.rb`), the GUI sets up a Ruby evaluation context using the `RubyProvider` component. Based on the standing data for the selected market, the `VTRCore` retrieves the transaction data in terms of a Business Objects report using the `BOProvider` and provides market-specific configuration data to update the message-creation wizard (e.g., available control areas). The scheduler then completes the message-configuration step and has the selected `MessageBuilder` create the final `Message`. The `MessageBuilder` formats the transaction data using helpers such as the `SchedulingDateProvider` provided by the `VTRCore`.

The language model is implemented by a Ruby class collaboration by mapping the entities in Figure 2a to Ruby classes. Ruby provides built-in language mechanisms to realize nested closures, object scoping, and instance evaluation [8]; the techniques used to implement the structural semantics and the concrete-syntax style outlined before. A Ruby block (also called a Ruby Proc or a closure) is a group of executable statements defined in the environment of the caller and is passed unevaluated to the called method as an implicit argument. The called method may then execute the block zero or more times, supplying the needed arguments for each block evaluation. For example, a context variable storing a reference to a `Market` can be provided to the `MessageBuilder` when processing the block which stores the message production rules. To populate a `Market` or

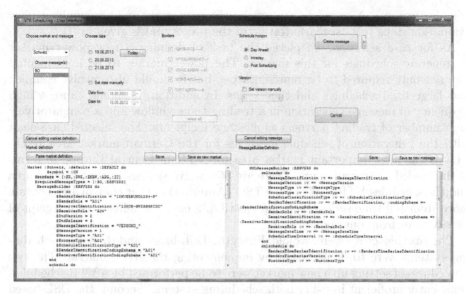

Fig. 4. The Controlling GUI of the DSL-Based Scheduling System

to construct a `Message` from a `MessageBuilder`, the market-definition scripts and the message-builder scripts, which are implemented as blocks, are evaluated in the scope of instance objects of `Market` and `MarketBuilder`. This principle is referred to as object scoping [8]. In addition, this allows for implementing the concrete syntax of `Market` and `MessageBuilder` as an expression builder [8]: For this reason, each `Market` and `MessageBuilder` keyword (see, e.g., `schedule` in Listing 2b) is implemented as a Ruby method. By limiting evaluation to defined accessors, methods, and classes, there is scaffolding of schedulers to only use this pre-defined vocabulary. Populating a `Market` and creating a `Message` are controlled by the `VTRCore` component, by instrumenting Ruby entities in their .NET representation using cross-language method invocations [14].

The Ruby-based DSL implementation is written in 500 SLOC[3], the VB.NET-managed `VTRCore` component has a code base of 1 100 SLOC, and the GUI amounts to 800 SLOC in VB.NET. Figure 4 shows the GUI wizard having loaded a definition of the Swiss market and the ESS 2.3 message builder. The wizard provides views for both the administrator and the scheduler roles, with the administrator being able to manipulate the market definitions and message-builder definitions directly.

4   DSL Evaluation

To assess whether the DSL-based scheduling system meets the previously defined requirements (see Section 3), we designed a case study [11]. In the following, we summarize the case study objectives, the real-world setting to be studied (the case), important details of data collection (collection techniques, actors), and key observations. A complete account on the case study and on supplementary evaluation steps (e.g., scenario testing of the prototype) is given in [1].

As for *case selection*, we picked the task of defining a new power market to generate schedules for this market. The power market to be implemented was not only required to be representative, but it should also involve complex and large-sized schedules and time series. In addition, it should cause a high frequency of message generation in a trading time window and a comparatively high number of trading partners as message recipients. The selected case dealt with the generation of schedule messages for the German market area RWE. This is the most important market area for VTR in Central Europe in terms of the traded energy amounts. There are 350 active traders in that control area and the schedules VTR sends to the TSO (Amprion) of that control area contain more than 100 time series, each one identifying either a delivery or a receipt of energy to or from one counterparty.

The *case objectives* were twofold: First, the DSL-based and the legacy scheduling systems were to be exercised by implementing the RWE market. The two procedures of setting up a new market were to be performed by a VTR scheduler, sufficiently proficient in using both scheduling systems. Second, the DSL-based prototype was to be evaluated against the critical timing requirements on generating schedules for the RWE market. Schedule generation and delivery are time-critical in the range of 1 or 2 minutes in certain markets including RWE. This is because energy trading happens in fixed time boxes (e.g., 15 minutes after the hour) and price increases tend to grow towards the end of trading windows. Trading, however, is stopped effectively before the end of a time box to create and to deliver the schedule messages reliably for completing the transaction. To optimize an intra-day trading portfolio, the energy seller seeks to minimize schedule-handling times to extend the effective trading time.

The *case work* was performed by the third author who, as a VTR energy manager, can take both the roles of the administrator and the scheduler for the legacy and the DSL-based scheduling system. Performing the case study involved preparatory steps identical for each system. These steps included gathering the market rules for the RWE market area and interfacing with the power-trading system to obtain the trading data in terms of Business Objects reports. The main task was then to implement the RWE market rules, once using the scheduling DSL and once using an Excel workbook. For this last step, we recorded the working time needed, collected the resulting code artifacts (VBA macros, DSL-based market definition), and monitored for runtime data to learn about the time and space efficiency of the DSL-based scheduling system, especially when generating schedules.

The key observation was that the effective market-definition time using the DSL amounted to approximately 10 minutes, while the definition process in the legacy system required an entire, 8-hours working day (i.e., one person-day). This substantial effort escalation in the legacy system was due to the tedious and time-consuming task of screening existing Excel workbooks for code fragments to be reused directly or, mostly, in a modified form.

Table 3. A Scheduler's Work Station Configuration at VTR

Processor	Intel U9600 @ 1.6 GHz
Memory (RAM)	3.00 GB
Hard Drive	60 GB SSD
Operating System	MS Windows 7 Enterprise x64
Office suite	MS Office 2010

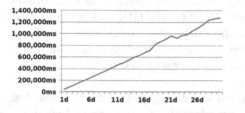
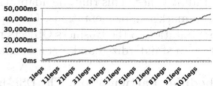

(a) 110 Time Series per Schedule/Day, 1-   (b) 1-110 Time Series per Schedule/Day,
30 Days   1 Day

Fig. 5. Schedule Generation Times of the DSL-Based Scheduling System

In light of the strict timing requirements, we ran time-efficiency measurements. Time efficiency was assessed by measuring the elapsed execution time between the start and the end of the schedule-creation process in milliseconds on a scheduler's typical work station (see Table 3). We devised different data sets as representative workloads for distinct scenarios: a fixed-size schedule containing 110 time series ("legs") of one market for 30 trading days and a schedule growing by one time series per iteration for one trading day. Overall, we found linear growth patterns for these workloads (see Figure 5a and Figure 5b). For large-sized schedules (110 time series per schedule), average processing times of 43 seconds were measured. This compares with approximately 1.5 minutes for similarly sized schedules in the legacy system. For smaller sized, growing schedules (one up to 110 times series per schedule), the average processing time was approximately 345 milliseconds.

5   Achieved Benefits

Reduction of Code Redundancy. Where the old system required separate Excel workbooks for each market implementation, the DSL only uses the market-specific configuration artifacts called *market definitions* expressed in a Ruby-based embedded DSL. In addition, general configuration settings, valid for several markets, can be placed once into reusable market definitions used together with specializations to generate a market-specific schedule. Different message formats (KISS, ESS) are defined in a second set of DSL scripts referred to as message builders. Again, message-format details only need to be maintained in one central location rather than in separate workbooks. This also applies to defining new, custom message formats.

Standardized Interface. The GUI implementation has been centralized and unified as well. Initially, the GUI component reads the available markets from the market definition, identifies the market-required message formats, and automatically updates that information in the GUI (e.g., by providing market-specific drop-down lists and check boxes). In a next step, the GUI provides market-specific configuration steps to the scheduler, such as the different trading borders or trading times. This runtime adaptation allows for the GUI code to be reused across market implementations. On top, the GUI is used to provide a uniform representation to the Business Objects reports, as basis for handling transaction data in a standardized and a consistent manner across markets.

Scheduler Participation. The DSL-based scheduling system renders selected internals of the scheduling accessible to and adaptable by the non-technical domain experts, the schedulers. That is, the scheduler can be trained with little effort to perform small and anticipated changes to market definitions and message builders on duty, based on a syntax reflecting her domain terminology and without requiring deep knowledge on the underlying software execution platform (.NET, Ruby). The revised GUI providing a consistent view on markets and transaction data facilitates collaborative tasks and context switching, such as in peer reviews of transaction data between schedulers (see Section 2).

Whereas the systematic design process was primarily driven by artifact reviews (see Section 3.1), a late prototype of the DSL-based scheduling system was used to set two schedulers, the target audience of the DSL, in the future situation of working with the prototype. In separate ad hoc sessions, each scheduler was guided through the schedule-generation process by the third author, a former scheduler at VTR himself. Immediate feedback was collected orally, in particular, feedback on the GUI, on the DSL-based procedure for defining a new market, and on whether the generation times were acceptable. Defining markets using the DSL was judged intuitive by the two schedulers. Having the GUI adapted immediately in response to changes in market definitions was deemed useful. This positive feedback did not require any modifications to the actual language design, that is, the abstract syntax, the concrete syntax, the constraints, and the structural semantics (see Section 3.1).

Improved Concern Separation. The DSL-based scheduling system cleanly separates between the concerns of defining/maintaining a market and defining/-maintaining a message format. For example, a scheduler can implement a new market and the pre-defined message formats (e.g., ESS 2.3 and KISS) can be applied to schedules for this market directly. Conversely, when implementing a new message format (e.g., another ESS revision), this format becomes available to the base of market definitions. In the legacy system, such additions or changes required modifications in all affected market implementations (workbooks).

6 Discussion

The development of this scheduling DSL did not occur in a vacuum. Rather, it was an enhancement of an existing system. The existing scheduling system presented us with a number of benefits and liabilities during the DSL development process. One benefit from working with the existing system was that we could derive the domain abstractions (e.g., market, schedule, message) from that system [15,19]. A second benefit of investigating the existing system was that this system clearly defined the scope of the DSL, as well as functional and non-functional requirements on the DSL [19]. For example, in the evaluation phase, we established a baseline of execution timings and working times using the legacy system. An existing system, however, poses the potential liability that relying upon the existing domain abstractions could hinder the critical review and adoption of revised domain concepts [19]. As a result, the extracted DSL could be limited in its expressiveness. We addressed this risk by conducting a domain analysis beyond the narrow boundaries of the existing scheduling system, by including standards documents available for the scheduling domain.

As for the concrete-syntax style of the embedded scheduling DSL, a textual concrete syntax and a graphical frontend syntax were adopted [15]. Under this approach, the basic configuration data are stored as text, and the representation of such data for the user is done by means of a GUI. The textual syntax representations of market and message-builder definitions are interpreted and rendered, especially for the scheduler role. The choice of using a textual concrete syntax for DSL development has a number of benefits. With this syntax, market and message-builder configurations can be specified in a compact manner and existing editors for Ruby can be reused [19]. Furthermore, a textual concrete syntax in support of a graphical frontend helps separate different working tasks for individual domain users. For the repetitive and routine task of generating schedule messages, the visual frontend allows for acquiring a quick overview of standing and transaction data. The non-routine task of modifying or creating market and message-builder definitions can be achieved in a compact textual form. A drawback of a mixed textual and graphical syntax is the need for scheduler awareness of subtle interdependencies between the two syntactic representations of domain concepts.

7 Conclusion

Documented and systematically collected empirical evidence on the alleged benefits of DSLs such as an improved maintainability [17] in an industry setting is rare (see, e.g., [13]). In this paper, we report on a successful development and deployment project of an embedded DSL for the VERBUND Trading AG (VTR), the subsidiary company responsible for power trading of the large-scale Austrian electricity company VERBUND AG. The project was carried out in a period of 2.5 years and included phases of domain analysis, DSL design and implementation, and an empirical evaluation based on a case study design and auxiliary software measurement. The DSL-based scheduling system is being actively used as a training tool for schedulers and as a backup scheduling system. VTR is planning to adopt the DSL-based system as a full replacement of the legacy system.

This project report shows that a DSL-based system refactoring can provide benefits in terms of reduced code redundancy for an improved maintainability of a code base. By enabling non-technical domain experts (schedulers) to participate in maintaining DSL-based system artifacts (e.g., market definitions, message builders), maintenance times can be reduced substantially. Finally, the project demonstrates that developing a DSL by extracting the DSL elements (e.g., its language model) from an existing system [15] represents a viable software-refactoring strategy [10] in otherwise rigid enterprise system landscapes. In follow-up work, we will perform more comprehensive and confirmatory empirical evaluations (e.g., domain-expert interviews, controlled experiments with domain-expert subjects) to reflect on the daily working routine based on the new DSL-based scheduling system at VERBUND Trading AG.

References

1. Beck, A.: Development of a domain specific language for scheduling in the energy sector. Master thesis, Institute of Information Systems and New Media, Vienna University of Economics and Business (August 2013)
2. Czarnecki, K., Eisenecker, U.W.: Generative Programming — Methods, Tools, and Applications. 6th edn. Addison-Wesley Longman Publishing Co., Inc. (2000)
3. Danial, A.: Count lines of code (2013), http://cloc.sourceforge.net/ (last accessed: May 02, 2013)
4. Electric System Operator: Schedule management (KISS). URL (April 2012), http://www.tso.bg/default.aspx/schedule-management/en (last accessed: May 02, 2013)
5. European Network of Transmission System Operators for Electricity (ENTSO-E): Scheduling system implementation guide 2.3. (April 2003), https://www.entsoe.eu/fileadmin/user_upload/edi/library/schedulev2r3/documentation/ess-guide-v2r3.pdf (last accessed: May 02, 2013)
6. European Network of Transmission System Operators for Electricity (ENTSO-E): Scheduling system implementation guide 3.1. (June 2007), https://www.entsoe.eu/fileadmin/user_upload/edi/library/schedulev3r1/documentation/ess-guide-v3r1.pdf (last accessed: May 02, 2013)
7. European Network of Transmission System Operators for Electricity (ENTSO-E): Scheduling system implementation guide 3.3. (April 2009), https://www.entsoe.eu/fileadmin/user_upload/edi/library/schedulev3r3/documentation/ess-guide-v3r3.pdf (last accessed: May 02, 2013)
8. Fowler, M., Parsons, R.: Domain-Specific Languages. Addison-Wesley (2010)
9. IronRuby: IronRuby – the Ruby programming language for the .NET framework (2012), http://www.ironruby.net/ (last accessed: May 02, 2013)
10. Mens, T., Tourwe, T.: A survey of software refactoring. IEEE Trans. Softw. Eng 30(2), 126–139 (2004)
11. Runeson, P., Höst, M.: Guidelines for conducting and reporting case study research in software engineering. Empirical Softw. Eng. 14(2), 131–164 (2009)

12. SAP AG: SAP Business Objects (2012), `http://www.sap.com/germany/solutions/sapbusinessobjects/large/business-intelligence/data-exploration/index.epx` (last accessed: May 02, 2013)
13. Sobernig, S., Gaubatz, P., Strembeck, M., Zdun, U.: Comparing complexity of API designs: An exploratory experiment on DSL-based framework integration. In: Proc. 10th Int. Conf. Generative Programming and Component Eng. (GPCE 2011), pp. 157–166. ACM (2011)
14. Sobernig, S., Zdun, U.: Evaluating Java runtime reflection for implementing cross-language method invocations. In: Proc. 8th Int. Conf. Principles and Practice of Programming in Java (PPPJ 2010), pp. 139–147. ACM (2010)
15. Strembeck, M., Zdun, U.: An approach for the systematic development of domain-specific languages. SP&E 39(15) (October 2009)
16. Taivalsaari, A.: On the notion of inheritance. ACM Comput. Surv. 28(3), 438–479 (1996)
17. Van Deursen, A., Klint, P.: Little languages: little maintenance? J. Softw. Maint. Evol.: Res. Pract. 10(2), 75–92 (1998)
18. Weirich, J.: Builder (2013), `http://builder.rubyforge.org/` (last accessed: June 15, 2013)
19. Zdun, U., Strembeck, M.: Reusable architectural decisions for DSL design: Foundational decisions in DSL projects. In: Proc. 14th Annual European Conf. Pattern Languages of Programming (EuroPLoP 2009). CEUR Workshop Proceedings, vol. 566 (2009)

Micro-Machinations
A DSL for Game Economies

Paul Klint[1] and Riemer van Rozen[2]

[1] Centrum Wiskunde & Informatica[**]
[2] Amsterdam University of Applied Sciences[**]

Abstract. In the multi-billion dollar game industry, time to market limits the time developers have for improving games. Game designers and software engineers usually live on opposite sides of the fence, and both lose time when adjustments best understood by designers are implemented by engineers. Designers lack a common vocabulary for expressing gameplay, which hampers specification, communication and agreement. We aim to speed up the game development process by improving designer productivity and design quality. The language Machinations has introduced a graphical notation for expressing the rules of game economies that is close to a designer's vocabulary. We present the language *Micro-Machinations* (MM) that details and formalizes the meaning of a significant subset of Machination's language features and adds several new features most notably modularization. Next we describe *MM Analysis in* RASCAL (MM AiR), a framework for analysis and simulation of MM models using the Rascal meta-programming language and the SPIN model checker. Our approach shows that it is feasible to rapidly simulate game economies in early development stages and to separate concerns. Today's meta-programming technology is a crucial enabler to achieve this.

1 Introduction

There is anecdotal evidence that versions of games like Diablo III[1] and Dungeon Hunter 4[2] contained bugs in their game economy that allowed players to illicitly obtain game resources that could be purchased for real money. Such errors seriously threaten the business model of game manufacturers. In the multi-billion dollar game industry, time to market limits the time designers and developers have for creating, implementing and improving games. In game development speed is everything. This applies not only to designers who have to quickly assess player experience and to developers that are under enormous pressure to deliver software on time, but also to the performance of the software itself. Common software engineering wisdom does not always apply when pushing technology to the limits regarding performance and scalability. Domain-Specific Languages (DSLs) have been successfully applied in domains ranging from planning and

---

[**] This work is part of the EQuA project. http://www.equaproject.nl/
[1] http://us.battle.net/d3/en/forum/topic/8796520380
[2] http://www.data-apk.com/2013/04/dungeon-hunter-4-v1-0-1.html

M. Erwig, R.F. Paige, and E. Van Wyk (Eds.): SLE 2013, LNCS 8225, pp. 36–55, 2013.
© Springer International Publishing Switzerland 2013

financial engineering to digital forensics resulting in substantial improvements in quality and productivity, but their benefits for the game domain are not yet well-understood.

There are various explanations for this. The game domain is diffuse, encompassing disparate genres, varying objectives and concerns, that often require specific solutions and approaches. Because the supporting technologies are constantly changing, domain analysis tracks a moving target, and opportunities for domain modeling and software reuse are limited [1]. Existing academic language-oriented approaches, although usually well-scoped, are often poorly adaptable, one-off, top-down projects that lack practical engineering relevance. Systematic bottom-up development and reuse have yielded libraries called game engines but such (commercial) engines are no silver bullet either, since they only provide general purpose solutions to technical problems and need significant extension and customization to obtain the functionality for a completely new game. Engines represent a substantial investment, and also create a long-term dependency on the vendor for APIs and support.

Our objective is to demonstrate that game development can benefit from DSLs despite the challenges posed by the game domain and the perceived shortcomings of existing DSL attempts. We envision light-weight, reusable, inter-operable, extensible DSLs and libraries for well-scoped game concerns such as story-lines, character behavior, in-game entities, and locations. We focus in this paper on the challenge of speeding up the game development process by improving designer productivity and design quality. Our main contributions:

- Micro-Machinations (MM), a DSL for expressing game economies.
- Micro-Machinations Analysis in RASCAL (MM AiR), an interactive simulation, visualization and validation workbench for MM.
- The insight that combining state-of-the-art tools for meta-programming (RASCAL[3] [2]) and model checking (PROMELA/SPIN[4] [3]) enable rapid prototyping of and experimentation in the game domain with frameworks like MM AiR.

2   Micro-Machinations

2.1   Background

Our main source of inspiration is the language Machinations [4] that has been based on an extensive analysis of game design practices in industry and provides a graphical notation for designers to express the rules of game economies. A *game economy* is an abstract game system governed by rules (e.g., how many coins do I need to buy a crystal) that offers players a playful interactive means to spend and exchange atomic game resources (e.g., crystals, energy). Resources are characterized by *amount* and *unit kind*.

---

[3] http://www.rascal-mpl.org/
[4] http://spinroot.com/spin/whatispin.html

Its focus is on the simulation of game designs. Various game design patterns have been identified in this context [4,5] as well. Machinations takes an approach that closely resembles Petri Nets that have been used in the game domain by others. For instance, Brom and Abonyi [6] use Petri nets for narratives, and Araújo [7] proposes general game design using Petri Nets. Other approaches to formalisms for game development related to design include hierarchical state machines [8], behavior trees [9], and rule-based systems [10].

Machinations is a visual game design language intended to create, document, simulate and test the internal economy of a game. The core *game mechanics* are the rules that are at the heart of a game. Machinations diagrams allow designers to write, store and communicate game mechanics in a uniform way. Perhaps the hardest part of game design is adjusting the game balance and make a game challenging and fun.

Figure 1a shows the Machinations framework as presented in [4]. Machinations can be seen as a design aid, that augments paper prototyping, which is used by designers to understand game rules and their effect on play. The Machinations tool[5] can be used to generate automatic random runs, that represent possible game developments, as feedback on the design process. Machinations is already in use by several game designers in the field.

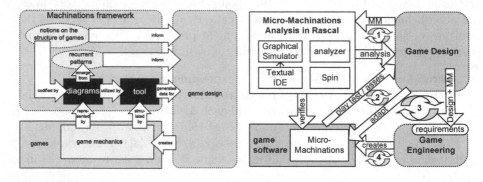

(a) Machinations Conceptual Framework   (b) Micro-Machinations Architecture

Fig. 1. Side-by-side comparison of Machinations (a) and Micro-Machinations (b)

Micro-Machinations (MM) is an evolutionary continuation of Machinations aiming at software prototyping and validation. MM is a formalized extended subset of Machinations, that brings a level of precision (and reduction of non-determinism) to the elements of the design notation that enables not only simulation but also formal analysis of game designs. MM also adds new features, most notably modularization. MM is intended as embedded scripting language for game engines that enables interaction between the economic rules and the so-called *in-game entities* that are characterized by one or more atomic resources.

---

[5] http://www.jorisdormans.nl/machinations/

An advantage of early paper prototyping is that loosely defined rules can be changed quickly and analyzed informally. Later, during software prototyping the rules have to be described precisely and making non-trivial changes usually takes longer. To start software prototyping as early as possible, a quick change in a model should immediately change the software that implements it. Therefore we study the precise meaning of the language elements and how they affect the game state. By leveraging meta-programming, language work-benches and model checking we can provide additional forms of analysis and prototyping. This enables us to answer questions about models designers might have, that affect both the design and the software that implements it. Figure 1b shows schematically how MM relates to game development.

Our objectives are to introduce short and separate design iterations (1 and 2) to free time for separate software engineering iterations (4) and alleviate relying on the usually longer interdependent development iterations (3).

2.2   Micro-Machinations Condensed

MM models are graphs that consist of two kinds of elements, *nodes* and *edges*. Both may be annotated with extra textual or visual information. These elements describe the rules of internal game economies, and define how resources are step-by-step propagated and redistributed through the graph. Here is a cheat sheet for the most important language elements[6].

◯ p pool p **Empty pool**	① p pool p at 1 **Pool & resource**	A *pool* is a named node, that abstracts from an in-game entity, and can contain *resources*, such as coins, crystals, health, etc. Visually, a pool is a circle with an integer in it representing the current amount of resources, and the initial
① max 2 p pool p at 1 max 2 **Limited capacity**	② max 2 p pool p at 2 max 2 **Full pool**	amount at which a pool starts when first modeled. Pools may specify a maximum capacity for resources, which can never be exceeded, that is visually a prefix max followed by an integer.
⟶ -> **Resource connection** flow rate of one	all ⟶ -all-> **Resource connection** unlimited rate	A *resource connection* is an edge with an associated expression that defines the rate at which resources can flow between source and target nodes. During each transition or *step*, nodes can *act* once by redistributing resources
/2 ⟶ -/2-> **Resource connection** half flow rate	4*p+1 ⟶ -4*p+1-> **Resource connection** flow expression	along the resource connections of the model. The *inputs* of a node are resource connections whose arrowhead points to that node, and its *outputs* are those pointing away.

---

[6] For conciseness we only give an informal description here, closely adhering to [4].

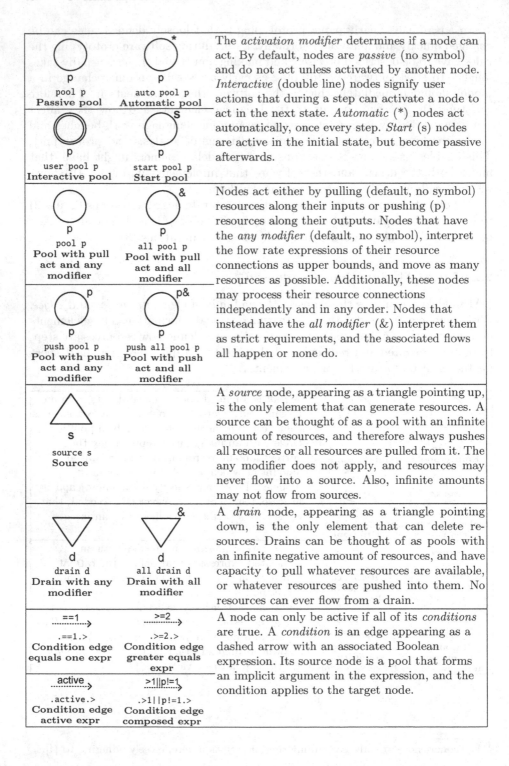

p / pool p / Passive pool	**p** * / auto pool p / Automatic pool	The *activation modifier* determines if a node can act. By default, nodes are *passive* (no symbol) and do not act unless activated by another node. *Interactive* (double line) nodes signify user actions that during a step can activate a node to act in the next state. *Automatic* (*) nodes act automatically, once every step. *Start* (s) nodes are active in the initial state, but become passive afterwards.
p / user pool p / Interactive pool	**p** s / start pool p / Start pool	
p / pool p / Pool with pull act and any modifier	**p** & / all pool p / Pool with pull act and all modifier	Nodes act either by pulling (default, no symbol) resources along their inputs or pushing (p) resources along their outputs. Nodes that have the *any modifier* (default, no symbol), interpret the flow rate expressions of their resource connections as upper bounds, and move as many resources as possible. Additionally, these nodes may process their resource connections independently and in any order. Nodes that instead have the *all modifier* (&) interpret them as strict requirements, and the associated flows all happen or none do.
p **p** / push pool p / Pool with push act and any modifier	p& **p** / push all pool p / Pool with push act and all modifier	
s / source s / Source		A *source* node, appearing as a triangle pointing up, is the only element that can generate resources. A source can be thought of as a pool with an infinite amount of resources, and therefore always pushes all resources or all resources are pulled from it. The any modifier does not apply, and resources may never flow into a source. Also, infinite amounts may not flow from sources.
d / drain d / Drain with any modifier	& / d / all drain d / Drain with all modifier	A *drain* node, appearing as a triangle pointing down, is the only element that can delete resources. Drains can be thought of as pools with an infinite negative amount of resources, and have capacity to pull whatever resources are available, or whatever resources are pushed into them. No resources can ever flow from a drain.
==1 / .==1.> / Condition edge equals one expr	>=2 / .>=2.> / Condition edge greater equals expr	A node can only be active if all of its *conditions* are true. A *condition* is an edge appearing as a dashed arrow with an associated Boolean expression. Its source node is a pool that forms an implicit argument in the expression, and the condition applies to the target node.
active / .active.> / Condition edge active expr	>1||p!=1 / .>1||p!=1.> / Condition edge composed expr	

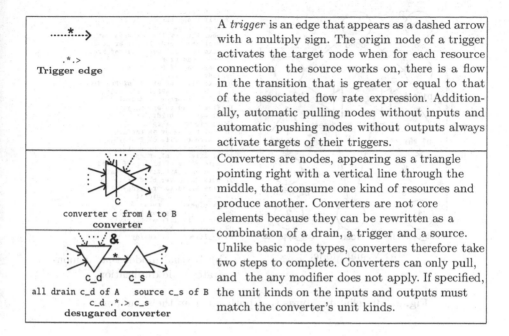

 ┄┄⋆┄┄⟩ .*.> **Trigger edge**	A *trigger* is an edge that appears as a dashed arrow with a multiply sign. The origin node of a trigger activates the target node when for each resource connection the source works on, there is a flow in the transition that is greater or equal to that of the associated flow rate expression. Additionally, automatic pulling nodes without inputs and automatic pushing nodes without outputs always activate targets of their triggers.
 c **converter c from A to B** **converter** c_d c_s **all drain c_d of A source c_s of B** **c_d .*.> c_s** **desugared converter**	Converters are nodes, appearing as a triangle pointing right with a vertical line through the middle, that consume one kind of resources and produce another. Converters are not core elements because they can be rewritten as a combination of a drain, a trigger and a source. Unlike basic node types, converters therefore take two steps to complete. Converters can only pull, and the any modifier does not apply. If specified, the unit kinds on the inputs and outputs must match the converter's unit kinds.

2.3   Introductory Example

Figure 2a shows an example how a designer might model a lady feeding birds in the original Machinations language. Figure 2b shows the textual equivalent as introduced in MM. The lady automatically throws bread crumbs in a pond (*p) one at a time, and two birds with different appetites compete for them. The first has a small appetite and the latter a big a appetite. Both birds automatically try to eat the whole amount (*&) their appetite compels them to. The edges from *small_ appetite* and *big_ appetite* are not triggers but *edge modifiers*, and we have replaced them by flow rate expressions in MM (lines 11 & 21). Birds digest food automatically which gives them energy and produces *droppings* on the road.

2.4   Game Designer's Questions

Given a model such as the example from Section 2.3, a designer might have the following questions.

- **Inspect:** Given a game state, what are the values of the pools, which nodes are active and what do they do?
- **Select:** Given a game state, what are the possible transitions? Are there alternatives? What are these alternatives and what are their successor states?
- **Reach:** Given this model, does a node ever act? Does a flow ever happen? Does a trigger ever happen? Where in the model can resources be scarce? Is an undesired state reachable, e.g., can the player ever have items from the

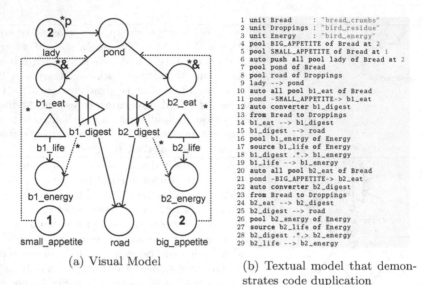

(a) Visual Model

```
 1 unit Bread      : "bread_crumbs"
 2 unit Droppings : "bird_residue"
 3 unit Energy     : "bird_energy"
 4 pool BIG_APPETITE of Bread at 2
 5 pool SMALL_APPETITE of Bread at 1
 6 auto push all pool lady of Bread at 2
 7 pool pond of Bread
 8 pool road of Droppings
 9 lady --> pond
10 auto all pool b1_eat of Bread
11 pond -SMALL_APPETITE-> b1_eat
12 auto converter b1_digest
13 from Bread to Droppings
14 b1_eat --> b1_digest
15 b1_digest --> road
16 pool b1_energy of Energy
17 source b1_life of Energy
18 b1_digest .*.> b1_energy
19 b1_life --> b1_energy
20 auto all pool b2_eat of Bread
21 pond -BIG_APPETITE-> b2_eat
22 auto converter b2_digest
23 from Bread to Droppings
24 b2_eat --> b2_digest
25 b2_digest --> road
26 pool b2_energy of Energy
27 source b2_life of Energy
28 b2_digest .*.> b2_energy
29 b2_life --> b2_energy
```

(b) Textual model that demonstrates code duplication

Fig. 2. Modeling two birds that both eat from the same pond

store without paying crystals? Is a desired state always reachable, e.g., can
the game be won or can the level be finished?
- **Balance:** Are the rules well balanced?

2.5   Technical Challenges

Before answering these questions (in Section 2.6), we discuss engineering challenges and how to tackle them leveraging meta-programming, language workbenches and model checking.

- **Parse:** To analyze any of these questions we need a representation that can
  easily be parsed. Therefore, MM introduces a textual representation of the
  game model, that serves as an intermediate format, that is compact and easy
  to read, parse, serialize and store.
- **Reuse:** Having a closer look at the example in Figure 2a, we see mirroring in
  the game graph that corresponds to code duplication in Figure 2b. We need
  modular constructs for reuse, encapsulation, scaling views, partial analysis
  and testing, and embedding MM in games (by way of connecting nodes and
  edges with in-game entities).
- **Inspect:** We need an environment that enables users to inspect states by
  visualizing serialized models.
- **Select:**   Detailed insight in the game behavior can be obtained by interactively choosing successors and seeing transition alternatives. This is similar
  to debugging when stepping through code, and requires the calculation of
  alternatives. This can, for instance, reveal a lack of resources or capacity.

– **Analyze Context Constraints:** Some structural elements of models, related to contextual constraints can introduce errors that we want to catch statically. Examples are: (i) Sources cannot have inputs; (ii) Drains cannot have outputs; (iii) Edges are dead code if no active node can use them by pushing or pulling; and (iv) Edges are doubly used when both origin and target are pushing and pulling, which can lead to confusing results. Modeling errors can also be detected. Optionally, resource types of nodes can be defined making resource connections easily checkable. Additionally, missing references can be reported.

– **Analyze Reachability:** Analyzing reachability is hard because it requires calculation of all possible paths through the game graph. Normally, we cannot calculate all possible executions of programs due to the sheer number of possibilities, and use abstractions to allow forms of analysis. Because a MM model is itself an abstraction of the actual game, and types and instances —MM's modularization mechanism is described in more detail in Section 2.7— enable partial analysis, we can exhaustively verify models in an experimental context using model checking techniques. The challenge is to translate MM diagrams to models that a model checker can analyze, and making that analysis *scalable*. Non-deterministic choices lead to a combinatorial explosion of execution path and this results in a state explosion in the model checker. When searching for undesired situations, an exhaustive search may not be necessary, since the moment an invalid state is found, the execution stack trace represents a result.

– **Balance:** Providing useful analysis to support balancing games is very hard, since this requires analyzing multiple types of play, each dynamic with different *unpredictable* player choices and non-deterministic events. Experimental set-ups in which instance interfaces are subjected to modeled input may provide designers with useful feedback, but building such set-ups is hard and is the expertise of game designers.

– **Prototype and Adjust:** Prototyping game software and making adjustments requires code. In addition to the MM format we require a light-weight embeddable interpreter that enables using script for prototyping and adjusting game software. A simple API for integrating MM in existing architectures should at least provide a means for calculating successor states (step), observing pools value changes, activating interactive nodes and reading and storing information. We require that this API relates the run-time state of models to the state and the behavior of game elements that affect how the game behaves when played. This is not further explored in the current paper.

2.6 Answers to Game Designer's Questions

We will now answer the questions raised in Section 2.4 and illustrate them using the bird feeding example.

Figure 3 shows a rewrite of the example using new language elements to be detailed in Section 2.7. Figure 3a shows the definition of *Bird*, which references

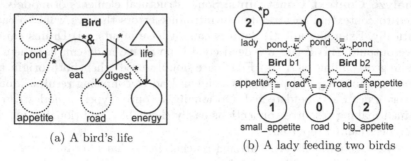

(a) A bird's life

(b) A lady feeding two birds

Fig. 3. Graphically modeling birds that eat, digest and live

```
1  Bird(ref appetite,ref pond,ref road)    1  unit Bread     : "bread_crumbs"         1  lady-1->pond
2  {                                        2  unit Droppings : "bird_residue"         2  step
3     //birds eat exactly all they want     3  unit Energy    : "bird_energy"          3  pond-1->b1_eat
4     auto all pool eat of Bread            4  pool BIG_APPETITE of Bread at 2         4  lady-1->pond
5     pond -appetite-> eat                  5  pool SMALL_APPETITE of Bread at 1       5  step
6     auto converter digest                 6  //a lady throws crumbs in the pond      6  pond-1->b1_eat
7        from Bread to Droppings            7  auto push all pool lady of Bread at 2   7  b1_eat-1->b1_digest_drain
8     eat --> digest //digest Bread         8  pool pond of Bread                      8  step
9     digest --> road //produce Dropping    9  pool road of Droppings                  9  b1_eat-1->b1_digest_drain
10    pool energy of Energy                 10 lady --> pond                           10 b1_life-1->b1_energy
11    source life of Energy                 11 Bird b1 //b1 has a big appetite         11 b1_digest_source-1->road
12    digest .*.> energy                    12 BIG_APPETITE .=.> b1.appetite           12 step
13    life --> energy                       13 pond .=.> b1.pond    road .=.> b1.road  13 b1_life-1->b1_energy
14    assert fed: energy > 0 || road < 2    14 Bird b2 //b2 has a small appetite       14 b1_digest_source-1->road
15       "birds_always_get_fed"             15 SMALL_APPETITE .=.> b2.appetite         15 step
16 }                                        16 pond .=.> b2.pond    road .=.> b2.road  16 violate b2_fed
```

(a) A bird's life   (b) A lady feeding two birds   (c) Bird b2 starves

Fig. 4. Textual model and analysis that shows birds with a big appetite starve

external nodes *pond*, *road* and *appetite*. These external nodes act as formal parameters of the Bird specification and are bound twice in Figure 3b. Figure 4a and Figure 4b show the textual equivalent of this model.

Next, we introduce assertions and pose that birds shall never starve by adding an assertion at line 14 of Figure 4a.

Then, we run the analysis to check for reachability and find that (i) bird *b2* starves because *b1_eat* always happens before *big_appetite* is available, and (ii) the acts of bird *b2_eat* and *b2_energy* are unreachable for all execution paths.

Finally, we can explore the model and understand it better by inspecting states, observing lack of alternative transitions, and automatically simulating the trace that lead to the assertion violation visually, shown textually in Figure 4c.

2.7 Language Extensions

We have designed MM and have introduced new language features as necessary to attain our goals. MM has modular constructs for reuse, encapsulation, scaling views, partial analysis and testing, and relating MM to in-game entities. MM has reduced non-determinism and increased control over competition for resources and capacity by introducing priorities. Time is modeled and understood, in a way that is embeddable in games. Finally, invariants are introduced for defining simple properties for analysis.

Types definitions and instances. The following table introduces[7] our modularization features *type definitions* and *instances*.

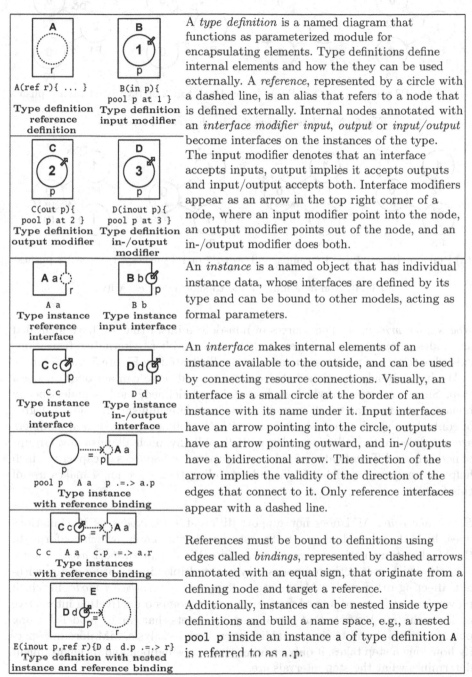

A *type definition* is a named diagram that functions as parameterized module for encapsulating elements. Type definitions define internal elements and how the they can be used externally. A *reference*, represented by a circle with a dashed line, is an alias that refers to a node that is defined externally. Internal nodes annotated with an *interface modifier input*, *output* or *input/output* become interfaces on the instances of the type. The input modifier denotes that an interface accepts inputs, output implies it accepts outputs and input/output accepts both. Interface modifiers appear as an arrow in the top right corner of a node, where an input modifier point into the node, an output modifier points out of the node, and an in-/output modifier does both.

An *instance* is a named object that has individual instance data, whose interfaces are defined by its type and can be bound to other models, acting as formal parameters.

An *interface* makes internal elements of an instance available to the outside, and can be used by connecting resource connections. Visually, an interface is a small circle at the border of an instance with its name under it. Input interfaces have an arrow pointing into the circle, outputs have an arrow pointing outward, and in-/outputs have a bidirectional arrow. The direction of the arrow implies the validity of the direction of the edges that connect to it. Only reference interfaces appear with a dashed line.

References must be bound to definitions using edges called *bindings*, represented by dashed arrows annotated with an equal sign, that originate from a defining node and target a reference. Additionally, instances can be nested inside type definitions and build a name space, e.g., a nested pool p inside an instance a of type definition A is referred to as a.p.

---

[7] Once again, for conciseness, only informally.

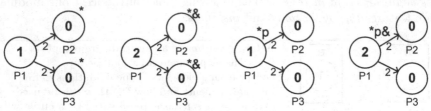

(a) P2 or P3 pulls   (b) P2 or P3 pulls (c) Push to P2 or P3 (d) P1 cannot push

Fig. 5. Non-determinism due to shortage of resources

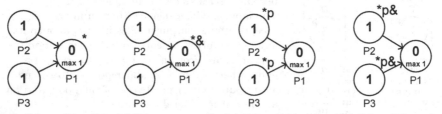

(a) Pull from P2 or P3 (b) P1 cannot pull   (c) P2 or P3 pushes (d) P2 or P3 pushes

Fig. 6. Non-determinism due to shortage of capacity

Nodes have priorities. The sources of non-determinism that we have identified are nodes *competing* for resources and the *any* modifier. Alternative transitions exist due to lack of resources or capacity, as illustrated by Figure 5 and Figure 6.

We have already mentioned that each activated node can act once during a step. Since the order in which nodes act is not defined, models under-specify behavior and this can result in undesirable non-determinism. To allow a degree of control, we specify that active nodes with the following actions and modifiers are scheduled in the following order: pull all, pull any, push all, push any. Groups of nodes from different categories do not compete for resources or capacity, which helps in analyzing models and in understanding them. Section 4 makes use of this feature.

Steps take time. MM does not support different *time modes* as Machinations does. In MM each node may act at most once during a step, which conforms to the Machinations notion of *synchronous time*. We do not support *asynchronous time*, in which user activated nodes may act multiple times during a step without affecting other nodes. Machinations supports a *turn-based mode*, in which players can each spend a fixed number of action points on activating interactive nodes each step. We note that *turns* are game assets that can be modeled, using pools, conditions and triggers, enabling turn-based analysis. MM does not specify how long a step takes, it only assumes that steps happen and its environment determines what the step intervals are.

Invariants. Defining property specifications to verify a model against can be hard, requiring knowledge of linear temporal logic. Defining invariants, Boolean expressions that must be true for each state, is easier to understand. MM adds *assertions* which consist of a name, a boolean expression that must invariantly be true, and a message to explain what happened when the assertion is violated, i.e. becomes false for some state. Figure 4a contains an example of an assertion (lines 14–15).

3   MM AiR Framework

Figure 7a shows the main functions of the MM Analysis in RASCAL (MM AiR) framework and Figure 7b relates them to the challenges they address. The framework is implemented as a RASCAL meta-program of approximately 4.5 KLOC. We will now describe the main functions of the framework.

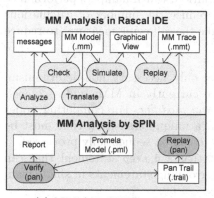

(a) MM AiR IDE functions

§	functionality	challenges
3.1	*check* contextual constraints (parse, desugar, perform static analysis)	define syntax, semantics, reuse, constraints
3.2	*simulate* MM model (interpret and evaluate successor states, interactive graphical visualizations)	make models debuggable, improve scalability and performance
3.3	*translate* MM to PROMELA	relate formalisms, ensure interoperability, improve scalability
3.4	*verify* MM in SPIN	ensure interoperability, improve scalability
3.5	*analyze* reachability	ensure interoperability
3.6	*replay* behaviors and verification results	source level debugging, ensure interoperability, readability

(b) Sections, functions and challenges

Fig. 7. MM AiR Overview

3.1   Check Contextual Constraints

Starting with a grammar for MM's textual syntax, using RASCAL we generate a basic MM Eclipse IDE that supports editing and parsing textual MM models with syntax highlighting. This IDE is extended with functionality to give feedback when models are incorrect or do not pass contextual analysis. This is implemented in a series of model transformations, leveraging RASCAL's support for pattern matching, tree visiting and comprehensions. This includes labeling the model elements, for storing information in states and for resource redistributions in transitions. We check models against the contextual constraints described in Section 2.5.

3.2 Simulate Models

Simulate provides a graphical view of a MM model and enables users to inspect states, choose transitions and successors, and navigate through the model by stepping forward and backward. We generate figures and interactive controls for simulating flattened states and transitions. This is easily done by applying RASCAL's extensive visualization library, which renders figures and provides callbacks we use to call an interpreter. The *interpreter* calculates successor states by evaluating expressions, checking conditions and generating transitions.

3.3 Translate to PROMELA

The biggest challenge in analyzing MM is providing a scalable reachability analysis. We achieve this by translating MM to PROMELA, the input language of the SPIN model checker. A naive approach is to model each node as a process, enabling every possible scheduling permutation to happen. However, not every scheduling results in a unique resource distribution, which hampers performance and scalability. Therefore we take steps to reduce the number of calculations without excluding possible behaviors. We take the following measures to reduce the state space explosion.

- **Reduce non-determinism.** We model only necessary non-determinism. We have identified two sources that are currently in MM: nodes *competing* for resources or capacity and the *any modifier*. For competing nodes every permutation potentially results in a unique transition that must be computed, but nodes that do not compete can be sequentially processed.
- **Avoid intermediate states.** PROMELA has a d_step statement that can be used to avoid intermediate states, by grouping statements in single transitions.
- **Store efficiently and analyze partially.** Pools can specify a maximum that we use to specify which type to use in PROMELA (bit, byte or int), minimizing the state vector. For partial analysis we can limit pool capacities.

Translating an MM model to PROMELA works as follows. We bind references to definitions and transform the model to core MM. We generate one proctype per model, schematically shown in Figure 8, and a monitor proctype that tests assertions for each state. Figure 8a depicts their general structure. At the beginning of a step the state is printed, and step guards are enabled if a node is active. This is followed by *sections* for each priority level as determined by node type. In each section, groups of nodes may be competing for resources or capacity.

For each group of competitors c_i consisting of nodes $n_1, ..., n_n$, we introduce a non-deterministic choice using guards that are disabled after a competing node acts as shown in Figure 8b. The remaining independent nodes $r_1, ..., r_n$ are just sequentially processed, since they never affect each other during a step. Figure 8c shows that each path in the monitor process remains blocked until an invariant becomes false, and a violation is found.

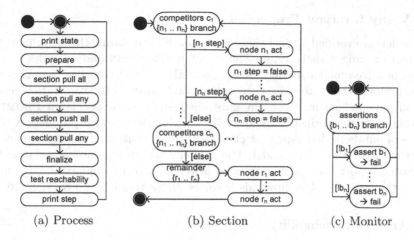

Fig. 8. Skeleton for generated PROMELA code: process, section and monitor

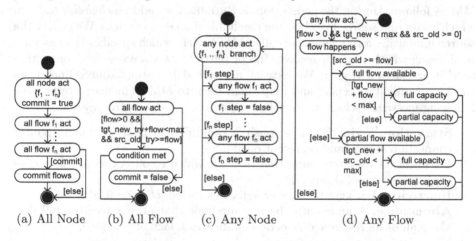

Fig. 9. Skeleton of generated PROMELA code for nodes

The behavior of nodes with the *all modifier* is deterministic, as shown in Figure 9a and Figure 9b. All flows $f_1, ..., f_n$ are executed sequentially and per flow conditions are checked. The effect of all flows is only committed if the conditions for all flows have been satisfied.

The behavior of nodes with the *any modifier* is shown in Figure 9c and Figure 9d models the non-determinism by introducing a non-deterministic choice between the flows $f_1, ..., f_n$.

Individual nodes act by checking shortages of resources on the old state from which subtractions are made and check shortage of capacity on the new state, to which additions are also made. Finally, when each node has acted the state is finalized by copying the new state to the current state. Temporary values and guards are reset, and active nodes are calculated by applying activation modifiers, triggers and conditions. Next reachability is tested, the step is printed and we start at the beginning to determine the next step.

3.4   Verify Invariant Properties

MM models are verified against their assertions by translating them to PROMELA and then running a shell script. The script invokes SPIN and compiles it to a highly optimized model-specific PROMELA analyzer (PAN). It then runs this verifier to perform the state space exploration, and captures the verification report PAN outputs, which may contain unreached states and associated PROMELA source lines. If the verifier finds an assertion violation, it also produces a *trail*, a series of numbers that represent choices in the execution of the state machine representing the PROMELA model. The challenge is interoperability, relating the verification report and the trail back to MM and showing understandable feedback to the user. We show how this is solved in Section 3.5 and Section 3.6.

3.5   Analyze Reachability

We tackle the interoperability challenge of relating a SPIN reachability analysis to MM as follows. During the generation of PROMELA we add *reachability tests*, in which states and source lines become reachable if an element acts. We collect the source lines using a tiny language called MM Reach, which specifies the test case by defining whether a node receives full or partial flow via a resource connection or if it activates a trigger. We extract unreached PROMELA source lines from the PAN verification report and map them back to MM elements to report the following messages, which are relative to a partial or exhaustive search.

- **Starvation.** Nodes that never push or pull full or partial flow via a resource connection starve, and represent dead code.
- **Drought.** A resource connection through which resources do not flow runs dry, and is unused dead code.
- **Inactivity.** A trigger that never activates its target node is idle.
- **Abundance.** A node with the any modifier that always receives full flow along all of its resource connections indicates a lack of shortage.

3.6   Replay Behaviors

We tackle the interoperability challenge of relating PAN trails for PROMELA models we obtained in Section 3.4 to MM model resource redistributions by introducing an intermediate language called MM Trace (MMT). A sequence of MMT statements forms a program that contains the transitions that an MM model performs, which MM AiR graphically replays in a guided simulation.

Replaying a trail on PAN simulates the steps of a PROMELA model while calling `printf` statements that generate an MMT program, ending in an assertion violation. The program is obtained by embedding the following MMT statements prefixed with `MM:` for filtering in the PROMELA model.

- **Flow.** Node causes flow to occur: `source-amount->target`
- **Trigger.** Trigger activates a target node in the next state: `trigger node`
- **Violation.** A state violates an assertion: `violate name`
- **Step.** Terminate a transition: `step`

4 Case Study: SimWar

SimWar is a simple hypothetical Real-Time Strategy (RTS) game introduced by Wright [11] that illustrates the game design challenge of *balancing* a game. This entails ensuring different player choices and strategies represent engaging and challenging experiences. Common strategies for RTS games are *turtling*, a low-risk, long-term strategy that favors defense, and *rushing*, a high-risk short-term strategy that favors attack. Adams and Dormans [4] study the game using the Machinations tool. By simulating many random runs, they show the game is indeed poorly balanced and that turtling is the dominant strategy.

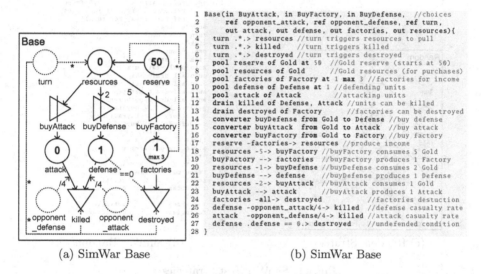

(a) SimWar Base

```
1  Base(in BuyAttack, in BuyFactory, in BuyDefense,  //choices
2      ref opponent_attack, ref opponent_defense, ref turn,
3      out attack, out defense, out factories, out resources){
4      turn .*.> resources //turn triggers resources to pull
5      turn .*.> killed    //turn triggers killed
6      turn .*.> destroyed //turn triggers destroyed
7      pool reserve of Gold at 50  //Gold reserve (starts at 50)
8      pool resources of Gold      //Gold resources (for purchases)
9      pool factories of Factory at 1 max 3 //factories for income
10     pool defense of Defense at 1 //defending units
11     pool attack of Attack        //attacking units
12     drain killed of Defense, Attack //units can be killed
13     drain destroyed of Factory      //factories can be destroyed
14     converter buyDefense from Gold to Defense //buy defense
15     converter buyAttack  from Gold to Attack  //buy attack
16     converter buyFactory from Gold to Factory //buy factory
17     reserve -factories-> resources //produce income
18     resources -5-> buyFactory //buyFactory consumes 5 Gold
19     buyFactory --> factories  //buyFactory produces 1 Factory
20     resources -1-> buyDefense //buyDefense consumes 2 Gold
21     buyDefense --> defense    //buyDefense produces 1 Defense
22     resources -2-> buyAttack  //buyAttack consumes 1 Gold
23     buyAttack --> attack      //buyAttack produces 1 Attack
24     factories -all-> destroyed        //factories destuction
25     defense -opponent_attack/4-> killed //defense casualty rate
26     attack  -opponent_defense/4-> killed //attack casualty rate
27     defense .defense == 0.> destroyed  //undefended condition
28 }
```

(b) SimWar Base

Fig. 10. The rules of SimWar

Our MM adaptation of SimWar, shown in Figure 10, is based on [4], but it models the rules for players in a definition called *Base*, avoiding duplication. It also replaces probabilities on resource connections with amounts. Two players compete by spending *resources*, choosing to buy *defense* (cost 1), *attack* (cost 2) or *factories* (cost 5). This is modeled by three converters in line 15–17 of Figure 10b that pull their respective costs from *resources* when activated.

Factories produce income every turn, and represent an investment enabling more purchases. We model this by *turn* triggering *resources* (line 5), which pulls from *reserve* (line 9) the current amount of factories (line 18). A player must destroy their opponent's factories to win. Two references, *opponent_defense* and *opponent_attack* determine the (rounded down) casualty rate of one in four (line 26, 27) for *attack* and *defense* respectively. Opponents fight until one player has no defense, and her factories are destroyed (line 28).

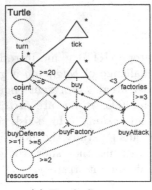

(a) Turtle Strategy

```
1  Turtle(ref buyAttack, ref buyDefense,
2          ref buyFactory, ref factories,
3          ref resources, ref turn){
4    source tick
5    turn .*.> count
6    tick --> count
7    pool count
8    auto source buy
9    buy .*.> buyAttack
10   buy .*.> buyFactory
11   buy .*.> buyDefense
12   count     .>=20.> buyAttack
13   factories .>=3.>  buyAttack
14   resources .>=2.>  buyAttack
15   count     .<8 .>  buyDefense
16   resources .>=1.>  buyDefense
17   count     .>=8.>  buyFactory
18   factories .<3.>   buyFactory
19   resources .>=5.>  buyFactory
20 }
```

(b) SimWar Turtle

```
1  Random(ref buyAttack, ref buyDefense,
2          ref buyFactory, ref factories,
3          ref resources, ref turn){
4    source tick
5    turn .*.> count
6    tick --> count
7    pool count
8    tick --> state
9    auto pool state max 1
10   auto all drain skip
11   auto all drain getFactory
12   auto all drain getAttack
13   auto all drain getDefense
14   getAttack  .*.> buyAttack
15   getFactory .*.> buyFactory
16   getDefense .*.> buyDefense
17   state --> skip
18   state --> getAttack
19   state --> getDefense
20   state --> getFactory
21   count     .>15.>   skip
22   resources .>= 2.>  getAttack
23   count     .>= 20.> getAttack
24   resources .>= 1.>  getDefense
25   count     .<10.>   getDefense
26   resources . >= 5.> getFactory
27   factories . <3.>   getFactory
28 }
```

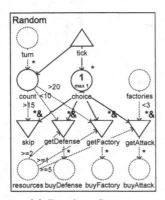

(c) Random Strategy

(d) SimWar Random

Fig. 11. SimWar Test Strategies

4.1 Experimental Setup

In an experiment with SimWar and two strategies shown in Figure 11 we apply the MM AiR framework, analyzing (i) the reachability of modeling elements, and (ii) the existence of a strategy that beats a turtling strategy.

The *Turtle* strategy, defined in Figure 11a and Figure 11b, simply counts turns, and based on this triggers references for buying. The *Random* strategy defined in Figure 11c and Figure 11d also counts, but adds a non-deterministic element which uses priorities. Drains *skip*, *getDefence*, *getFactory*, *getAttack* compete for the resource in *choice* before it pulls a resource from *tick*, enabling the next choice. In our test set-up shown in Figure 12, we bind instances of Random and Turtle to a Base instance in lines 16–20 & 25-29 of Figure 12b. We bind base instances as opponents in lines 13–14, 22–23 and bind *turn* to *doit*, our means for activity. Finally, we assert in lines 30–31 that the factories of Turtle are never destroyed. A violation of this assertion represents a behavior of Random that beats Turtle.

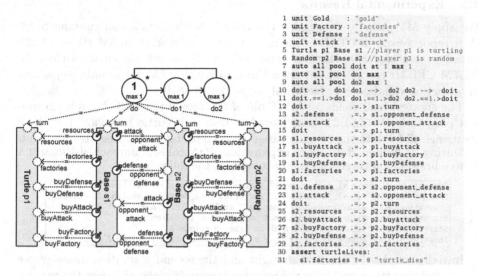

```
 1  unit Gold    : "gold"
 2  unit Factory : "factories"
 3  unit Defense : "defense"
 4  unit Attack  : "attack"
 5  Turtle p1 Base s1 //player p1 is turtling
 6  Random p2 Base s2 //player p2 is random
 7  auto all pool doit at 1 max 1
 8  auto all pool do1 max 1
 9  auto all pool do2 max 1
10  doit --> do1 do1 --> do2 do2 --> doit
11  doit.==1.>do1 do1.==1.>do2 do2.==1.>doit
12  doit         .=.> s1.turn
13  s2.defense   .=.> s1.opponent_defense
14  s2.attack    .=.> s1.opponent_attack
15  doit         .=.> p1.turn
16  s1.resources .=.> p1.resources
17  s1.buyAttack .=.> p1.buyAttack
18  s1.buyFactory .=.> p1.buyFactory
19  s1.buyDefense .=.> p1.buyDefense
20  s1.factories .=.> p1.factories
21  doit         .=.> s2.turn
22  s1.defense   .=.> s2.opponent_defense
23  s1.attack    .=.> s2.opponent_attack
24  doit         .=.> p2.turn
25  s2.resources .=.> p2.resources
26  s2.buyAttack .=.> p2.buyAttack
27  s2.buyFactory .=.> p2.buyFactory
28  s2.buyDefense .=.> p2.buyDefense
29  s2.factories .=.> p2.factories
30  assert turtleLives:
31    s1.factories != 0 "turtle_dies"
```

(a) A Turtle instance battling a Random instance   (b) SimWar Battle

Fig. 12. SimWar experimental test setup

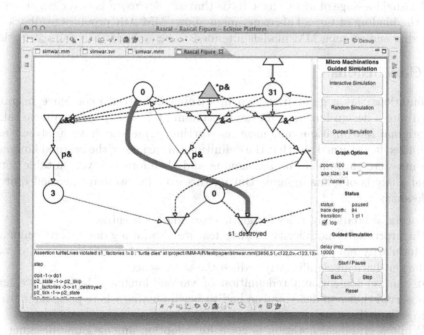

Fig. 13. MM AiR playing back a counter-example showing *Turtle* defeated

4.2   Experimental Results

We apply MM AiR by translating the models to PROMELA and running SPIN. PAN reports using 2500MB of memory, mostly for storing 10.5M states of 220 bytes, generating 188K states/second, taking 56 seconds on an Intel Core i5-2557M CPU. It reports 11.9M transitions, of which 9.5M are atomic steps, and an assertion violation (s1_factories!=0) at depth 8810.

The shortest trail yields an MMT file of 95 steps. Figure 13 shows its graphical play-back. We find 22 strategies that beat our Turtle behavior, but these strategies all fall into the turtling category, confirming the strategy is dominant.

During its limited state space exploration, PAN collects unreached PROMELA source lines. Using these, our analysis reports the following:

```
Drought: No flow via s1_factories -s1_factories-> s1_destroyed at line 25 column 2
Drought: No flow via s2_factories -s2_factories-> s2_destroyed at line 25 column 2
Starvation: Node s2_destroyed does not pull at line 14 column 2
Starvation: Node s1_destroyed does not pull at line 14 column 2
Starvation: Node p1_buy does not push at line 39 column 2
Inactivity: Node doit does not trigger s2_destroyed at line 7 column 2
```

Initially puzzled by the first drought and the second starvation message, we concluded that the assertion in the monitor process is violated before the reachability check happens. Indeed node *p1_ buy* never pushes, since it has no resource connections, it serves only to trigger choices.

The final message of inactivity tells us that *s2_ destroyed* is never triggered by *doit*, the binding of *turn*. This experiment shows MM AiR provides feedback for analyzing and refining MM models intended to be embedded in game software.

5   Conclusions

Machinations was a great first step in turning industrial experience in game design into a design language for game economies. In this paper we have taken the original Machinations language as starting point and have analyzed and scrutinized it. It turned out that the definitions of various of the original language elements were incomplete or ambiguous and therefore not yet suitable for a formal analysis of game designs. During this exercise, we have learned quite a few lessons:

- Formal validation of rules for game economies is feasible.
- Unsurprisingly, modularity is a key feature also for a game design language. Modularity not only promotes design reuse, but also enables modular validation that can significantly reduce the state space.
- In our refinement and redefinition of various language features, we have observed that non-determinism had to be eliminated where possible in order to reduce the state space.
- While a graphical notation is good for adoption among game designers, a textual notation is better for tool builders.
- PROMELA is a flexible language that offers many features to represent the model to be validated. Different representation choices lead to vastly different performance of the model checker and it is non-trivial to choose the right representation for the problem at hand.

– The RASCAL language workbench turned out to be very suitable for the design and implementation of MM AiR. In addition to compiler-like operations like parsing and type checking MM AiR also offers editing, interactive error reporting and visualization. It also supports generation of PROMELA code that is shipped to the SPIN model checker and the resulting execution traces produced by SPIN can be imported and replayed in MM AiR.

MM Air in its current form is an academic prototype, but it is also a first step towards creating embeddable libraries of reusable, validated, elements of game designs. Next steps include the use of probabilistic model checkers, mining of recurring patterns in game designs and finally designing and implementing embeddable APIs for MM. These will form the starting point for further empirical validation. We see as the major contributions of the current paper both the specific design and implementation of MM and MM AiR and the insight that the combination of state-of-the-art technologies for meta-programming and model checking provide the right tools to bring game design to the next level of productivity and quality.

Acknowledgements. We thank Joris Dormans for answering our many questions about Machinations, Tijs van der Storm for providing advice and feedback, and the anonymous reviewers for giving valuable suggestions.

References

1. Blow, J.: Game Development: Harder Than You Think. ACM Queue 1, 28–37 (2004)
2. Klint, P., van der Storm, T., Vinju, J.: EASY Meta-programming with Rascal. In: Fernandes, J.M., Lämmel, R., Visser, J., Saraiva, J. (eds.) GTTSE 2009. LNCS, vol. 6491, pp. 222–289. Springer, Heidelberg (2011)
3. Holzmann, G.: SPIN Model Checker, the: Primer and Reference Manual, 1st edn. Addison-Wesley Professional (2003)
4. Adams, E., Dormans, J.: Game Mechanics: Advanced Game Design, 1st edn. New Riders Publishing, Thousand Oaks (2012)
5. Dormans, J.: Level Design as Model Transformation: A Strategy for Automated Content Generation. In: Proceedings of the 2nd International Workshop on Procedural Content Generation in Games, PCGames 2011, ACM, New York (2011)
6. Brom, C., Abonyi, A.: Petri Nets for Game Plot. In: Proceedings of Artificial Intelligence and the Simulation of Behaviour (AISB) (2006)
7. Araújo, M., Roque, L.: Modeling Games with Petri Nets. In: Proceedings of the 3rd Annual DiGRA Conference Breaking New Ground: Innovation in Games, Play, Practice and Theory (2009)
8. Fu, D., Houlette, R., Jensen, R.: A Visual Environment for Rapid Behavior Definition. In: Proc. Conf. on Behavior Representation in Modeling and Simulation (2003)
9. Champandard, A.J.: Behavior Trees for Next-Gen Game AI (December 2007), http://aigamedev.com
10. McNaughton, M., Cutumisu, M., Szafron, D., Schaeffer, J., Redford, J., Parker, D.: ScriptEase: Generative Design Patterns for Computer Role-Playing Games. In: Proceedings of the 19th IEEE International Conference on Automated Software Engineering, pp. 88–99. IEEE Computer Society, Washington, DC (2004)
11. Wright, W.: Dynamics for Designers. Lecture delivered at the Game Developers Conference (2003)

xMOF: Executable DSMLs Based on fUML

Tanja Mayerhofer, Philip Langer, Manuel Wimmer, and Gerti Kappel

Business Informatics Group, Vienna University of Technology, Austria
{mayerhofer,langer,wimmer,gerti}@big.tuwien.ac.at

Abstract. The basic ingredients of a domain-specific modeling language (DSML) are its syntax and semantics. For defining the abstract syntax in terms of metamodels, MOF constitutes a standardized language. For specifying the behavioral semantics, however, no standardized language exists, which hampers the emergence of model execution facilities, such as debugging and simulation support. The contribution of this paper is an integrated approach for specifying the abstract syntax and behavioral semantics of DSMLs based exclusively on standardized modeling languages. In particular, we integrate fUML, a standardized executable subset of UML, with MOF leading to a new metamodeling language xMOF. Moreover, we propose a methodology for developing executable DSMLs fostering the separation of abstract syntax and behavioral semantics. To evaluate our approach, we provide an EMF-based implementation and report on lessons learned from performing three case studies in which we implemented executable DSMLs using xMOF.

1 Introduction

The success of model-driven engineering (MDE) depends significantly on the availability of adequate means for developing domain-specific modeling languages (DSMLs). The two key components that constitute a DSML are its *syntax* and its *semantics*. For defining the *abstract syntax*, the OMG standard MOF [19] provides a well-established and commonly accepted language for defining metamodels. Moreover, MOF fostered the emergence of (i) a variety of techniques for (semi-)automatically deriving *specific facilities* from a metamodel, such as modeling editors, and (ii) a multitude of *generic facilities*, e.g., for model persistence, validation, comparison, and transformation.

For developing the *behavioral semantics* of a DSML, no standard language has been established yet [1]. In practice, models are usually made executable by using code generators or by implementing model interpreters with general purpose programming languages (GPLs). However, code generators or model interpreters constitute only an *implementation* of the behavioral semantics rather than an explicit *specification*. The semantics is only implicitly, redundantly, and maybe only partially given (cf. Figure 1a). Thus, it is difficult to analyze, extend, and reuse the implemented semantics, as well as to verify whether the implementations are actually consistent with each other regarding the intended semantics, making it costly to create and maintain such implementations.

As a first important step towards addressing these drawbacks, we stress the need for a *standardized* way of specifying *explicitly* the behavioral semantics of a DSML (cf. Figure 1b). Moreover, we think that a *model-based* specification of the behavioral semantics would be beneficial because it enables to stay in the technical space of MDE

M. Erwig, R.F. Paige, and E. Van Wyk (Eds.): SLE 2013, LNCS 8225, pp. 56–75, 2013.

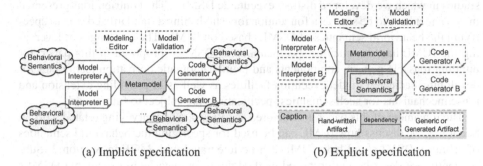

(a) Implicit specification   (b) Explicit specification

Fig. 1. Specification of the behavioral semantics

and hence to immediately apply MDE techniques for processing such specifications. An explicit specification of the behavioral semantics of DSMLs enables the *simulation and validation* of the behavior of DSMLs already in early phases of the language development process. Additionally, it may also provide similar benefits as MOF granted for implementing modeling facilities based on a DSML's abstract syntax: it may enable the emergence of *reusable generic components* and *(semi-)automatic derivation techniques* for developing dedicated model execution facilities, such as code generators, model interpreters, model debuggers, and model analysis components.

Therefore, we propose to use fUML [20] for explicitly specifying the behavioral semantics of DSMLs. fUML is standardized by the OMG and defines the semantics of a key subset of UML in terms of a virtual machine. This subset contains the UML modeling concepts for defining UML classes and for defining the behavior of these classes using UML activities. As UML classes and MOF metaclasses differ only in their intended usage (modeling of a software system vs. metamodeling), we argue that fUML might be well suited not only for specifying the behavior of UML classes but also for specifying the behavior of MOF metaclasses. Although OMG intended fUML to be sufficient for specifying the semantics of the remainder of UML [20], it is, however, an open question how fUML can be employed for this purpose and, even more, how fUML can be integrated with state-of-the-art metamodeling languages, techniques, methodologies, and tools for specifying the semantics of arbitrary DSMLs.

Based on first ideas which we have outlined in previous work [15], the contribution of this paper is threefold. First, we show how fUML can be integrated with MOF leading to a new metamodeling language called xMOF (eXecutable MOF) that allows specifying both the abstract syntax and the behavioral semantics of DSMLs. Second, we extend existing methodologies for developing DSMLs [25,26,27] with additional steps concerning the behavioral semantics specification, fostering a clear separation of abstract syntax and behavioral semantics ensuring compatibility with existing modeling frameworks. Third, we present an approach for deriving a model interpreter for DSMLs based on their semantics specified with xMOF which enables to execute models conforming to the DSML using the fUML virtual machine. To evaluate the applicability of our approach, we implemented a prototype that is integrated with the Eclipse Modeling Framework (EMF) [26] and report on lessons learned from performing three case studies in which we developed distinct executable DSMLs. The contributions presented in this paper have to be seen as a foundation for establishing a standardized way of specifying the behavioral semantics of DSMLs based on fUML. The challenges of leveraging the fUML-based semantics specifications of DSMLs, proposed in this paper, for building reusable generic components and (semi-)automatic derivation techniques for developing dedicated model execution facilities as well as of providing extension and reuse mechanisms for such semantics specifications are subject to future work.

The remainder of this paper is structured as follows. After surveying related work in Section 2, we discuss how fUML can be used for specifying the behavioral semantics of arbitrary DSMLs and how fUML can be integrated with MOF in Section 3. Subsequently, we describe the proposed methodology for specifying executable DSMLs using xMOF in Section 4. In Section 5, we present case studies evaluating the applicability of xMOF for specifying the behavioral semantics of DSMLs and discuss lessons learned, before we conclude this paper in Section 6.

2   Related Work

In this section we give an overview about existing approaches for specifying the behavioral semantics of DSMLs and briefly describe efforts in using UML action languages on the metamodel level.

2.1   Semantics Specification Approaches

For explicitly specifying the behavioral semantics of DSMLs, various approaches have been proposed in the past, which can be divided into two categories: *translational* approaches and *operational* approaches.

Translational semantics specification approaches map constructs of a DSML to constructs of another language whose semantics is already formally and explicitly defined. This has the advantage that existing tools for the target language, such as execution and analysis tools, can also be used for the source language. The drawback, however, is that the semantics of a DSML is defined by the mapping to the target language leading to an additional level of indirection. Thus, the semantics of the source language is hard to comprehend and to analyze. Furthermore, if tools of the target language are used, for instance, to execute or analyze models of the source language, obtained results also have to be mapped back to the source language. Examples for translational semantics specification approaches are the work of Chen *et al.* [2] who use the Abstract State Machine formalism, Rivera *et al.* [22] who use Maude, Kühne *et al.* [10] who use Petri nets, and Rumpe *et al.* [6] who use their System Model as target language for specifying the behavioral semantics of DSMLs. In addition, a common approach to define the behavioral semantics of domain-specific languages in a translational way is to utilize code generation. This has a long tradition in several technical spaces [11], such as in grammarware [7,16,30] and in modelware [26].

Compared to translational approaches, the *operational semantics* specification approach is more explicit in the sense that behavior is directly specified for the DSML without moving to a different language. One way for defining operational semantics is to define graph transformation rules operating on models as proposed by Engels *et al.* [5]. Another possibility is to follow an object-oriented approach by specifying the behavior of the operations defined for the metaclasses of a DSML's metamodel using a dedicated action language. A plethora of action languages has been proposed for this purpose including existing GPLs: Kermeta [17], Smalltalk [4], Eiffel [21], xCore [3], Epsilon Object Language [8], and the action languages proposed in the Model Execution Framework (MXF) [24] and by Scheidgen and Fischer [23] to name just a few.

Although several approaches for specifying the behavioral semantics of DSMLs have been proposed, these approaches do not seem to be commonly accepted in the MDE community [1], especially in comparison to the acceptance of MOF. As specifying the behavioral semantics of DSMLs is a core challenge in MDE, we believe that a standardized action language for metamodeling is required. Both MOF and fUML are standardized by OMG, which is an important standardization body in the MDE domain; thus, fUML may be considered as a promising candidate for serving as a well-established and standardized action language for metamodeling. However, it is an open question how fUML can be integrated with MOF and with currently applied metamodeling techniques, methodologies, and tools, as well as how appropriate fUML is for specifying the behavioral semantics of DSMLs and how an fUML-based semantics specification can be utilized to directly execute models conforming to the DSMLs. In this paper, we aim to address those research questions.

2.2 Using UML Action Languages on the Metamodel Level

The Action Semantics (AS) integrated with UML 1.5, the predecessor of fUML, was employed by Sunye *et al.* [28,29] for defining programs on the metamodel level. In particular, the authors proposed to implement refactorings, design patterns, as well as aspect-orientation for UML by using AS to realize transformations of the abstract syntax of UML models. In this paper, we go one step further and use fUML to define also the behavioral semantics of DSMLs in general.

Recently, Lai and Carpenter [12] also proposed the usage of fUML for specifying the behavioral semantics of DSMLs in an operational way. However, they focus on the static verification of fUML models to identify structural flaws, such as unused or empty model parts. The authors neither discuss possible strategies for using fUML as an action language on the metamodel level, nor do they consider the execution of models based on fUML. In contrast, the aim of our work is to enable the explicit specification of executable DSMLs and the execution of conforming models by providing a framework that seamlessly integrates with existing metamodeling environments.

3 Specifying Semantics with fUML

To use fUML for specifying the behavioral semantics of a DSML and for executing models conforming to this DSML, we may apply two distinct approaches: the *translational approach* and the *operational approach*.

With the *translational approach*, the behavioral semantics of a DSML is specified through a mapping of DSML concepts to fUML concepts. The mapping between the languages can be implemented using model transformation languages and the obtained fUML models may be executed using the fUML virtual machine. However, when developing DSMLs having a semantics diverging from fUML's semantics, this approach has the disadvantage of potentially complex mappings, which are difficult to specify due to the fact that three languages are involved: the DSML, the transformation language, and fUML. An additional challenge arises with this approach when the results of executing the fUML models have to be traced back to the original models.

Because of these drawbacks we advocate the *operational approach* where the behavioral semantics is introduced into the DSML's metamodel by adding operations to the metaclasses and implementing them using fUML activities that specify how models shall be executed, i.e., fUML is used as action language. Having the operational semantics of a DSML specified in terms of fUML activities, the fUML virtual machine can be used to directly execute models conforming to the DSML. In the following, we discuss how the operational approach for using fUML as semantics specification language can be realized for MOF.

3.1   The Gap between fUML and MOF

Before fUML can be used in MOF-based metamodels, the gap between both modeling standards has to be bridged. Therefore, let us consider how fUML is composed and how it relates to MOF. For modeling structural aspects of a system, fUML contains a subset of the *Classes::Kernel* package of UML. For modeling behavior, a subset of the UML packages *CommonBehaviors*, *Activities*, and *Actions* is included in fUML. As fUML uses the UML package *Classes::Kernel* and the same package is also merged into MOF, the structural part of the fUML metamodel overlaps with MOF. Although the same elements are used for structural modeling on a conceptual level, on a technical level, they are two distinct languages. Furthermore, there is a conceptual mismatch between an fUML class diagram and a MOF-based metamodel: considering the metamodeling stack [9] (cf. left-hand side of Figure 2), fUML models (*afUML Model*) are situated on the meta-level M1, whereas the metamodel of a DSML (*aDSML MM*) is located on the meta-level M2. However, an operational semantics specification of a DSML has to reside on the same meta-level as the metamodel of the DSML itself.

3.2   Bridging the Gap between fUML and MOF

To overcome the gap between MOF and fUML for enabling the usage of fUML as an action language for MOF two strategies can be applied.

By Transformation: The first strategy is to *transform* the MOF-based metamodel of the DSML into an fUML class diagram and extend the fUML classes with the operational semantics in terms of fUML activities as proposed by Lai and Carpenter [12]. For executing a model conforming to the DSML, it has to be transformed into an fUML-compliant object diagram consisting of objects representing ontological instances [9] of the fUML classes that correspond to the DSML's metaclasses. One advantage of this approach is that model transformations for the metamodel and models are all that is needed to obtain an executable model. However, one major drawback is that both metamodeling environments and UML environments have to be used in parallel. The

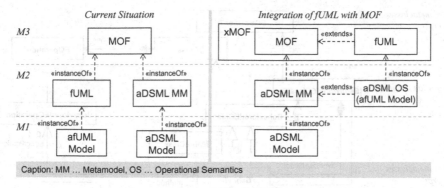

Fig. 2. Gap between fUML and MOF and how it is bridged

UML environment has to be used for defining the operational semantics, as well as for executing, analyzing, and debugging models and the metamodeling environment has to be employed for defining the syntax of the DSML, as well as conforming models. Consequently, users have to switch between different environments and constantly apply transformations on metamodels and models to obtain equivalent fUML class diagrams and fUML object diagrams, respectively.

By Integration: Because of the aforementioned drawbacks, we advocate a second strategy based on an *integration approach* as depicted on the right-hand side of Figure 2. In this strategy fUML is *integrated* with MOF by extending MOF with the behavioral part of fUML to obtain a language on M3 that we call eXecutable MOF (xMOF). By extending MOF with certain parts of fUML, these parts are pulled up from the meta-level M2 to the meta-level M3 enabling the specification of the abstract syntax as well as the operational semantics of a DSML with one metamodeling language that is composed of two standardized languages (MOF and fUML). As a result, the abstract syntax can be specified in terms of a metamodel (*aDSML MM*) using the modeling concepts provided by MOF and the operational semantics (*aDSML OS*) can be specified using fUML activities. Models (*aDSML Model*) can be executed by employing the fUML virtual machine.

3.3 Extending Ecore with fUML

As Ecore [26] constitutes the most prominent implementation of MOF (or to be more precise essential MOF (EMOF)), we show in this section how we extended Ecore with the behavioral parts of fUML leading to the novel metamodeling language *xMOF*. Please note that a corresponding extension can be applied also to MOF itself, instead of Ecore.

As depicted in Figure 3, xMOF extends Ecore in a way that enables to specify fUML activities for the operations of the metaclasses defined in the metamodel of a DSML. The fUML activity specified for an operation defines the implementation, i.e., the behavior, of this operation. Therefore, we introduced the metaclasses Behaviored-EClassifier, BehavioredEClass, MainEClass, and BehavioredEOperation serving as

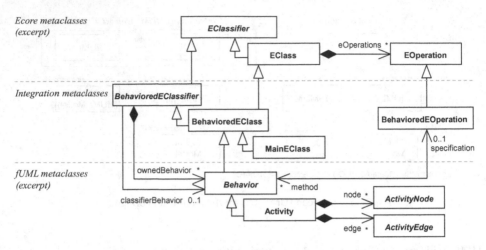

Fig. 3. Metamodel of xMOF (excerpt)

connection points between Ecore and fUML. A BehavioredEClassifier is an EClassifier that can own Behaviors in terms of Activities. One Behavior can serve as classifier behavior of the BehavioredEClassifier. As specified in UML, the classifier behavior is invoked when the owning BehavioredEClassifier is instantiated. BehavioredEClass is a concrete subtype of BehavioredEClassifier and EClass. Thus, a BehavioredEClass is an ordinary EClass but may own Activities in addition. The class MainEClass is introduced to distinguish one BehavioredEClass in a semantics specification as the main class controlling the execution of a model conforming to the DSML. An Activity serves as specification of a BehavioredEOperation which is a subtype of Ecore's EOperation.

Using xMOF it is now possible to use fUML activities (Activity) to specify the behavior of operations (BehavioredEOperation) of metaclasses (BehavioredEClass) in the metamodel of a DSML and therewith it is possible to specify the behavioral semantics of a DSML.

4   Methodology for Specifying Semantics with xMOF

With xMOF, as introduced in the previous section, it is possible to specify the abstract syntax as well as the behavioral semantics of DSMLs. In this section we will present the xMOF-based semantics specification of an example DSML. Furthermore, to foster a systematic and efficient development of behavioral semantics specifications using xMOF, as well as to maximize the reuse and the compatibility with existing EMF-based technologies, we propose a dedicated *methodology*, which is orthogonal to existing metamodeling methodologies [25,26,27]. Before we present this methodology by means of the example DSML, we first discuss the goals we aim to address with this methodology.

4.1   Goals of the Methodology

With the proposed methodology, we aim at supporting users in applying xMOF for specifying executable DSMLs. In particular, we aim at addressing the following six sub-goals. The proposed methodology shall *(i) integrate seamlessly* with existing method-ologies for developing DSMLs, including their techniques and tools, and only *extend* them concerning the specification of the behavioral semantics of DSMLs. Thus, the use of existing metamodeling techniques and tools, as well as any other techniques and tools for deriving modeling facilities or for processing models, shall not be affected. Further, the proposed methodology shall *(ii)* enable a *clear separation* of the abstract syntax specification from the specification of the behavioral semantics and *(iii)* allow users to develop *multiple behavioral semantics* for the same abstract syntax without interference. Moreover, the methodology should *(iv)* enable a clear distinction between *modeling concepts* of the DSML and *runtime concepts* that are only needed for execut-ing models (such as the specification of runtime variables and additional input param-eters). Finally, the methodology shall also provide the means for *(v) executing models* conforming to the DSML and *(vi)* for *representing the results* of the model execution on the level of the executed model (i.e., on the DSML level and not on the fUML level).

4.2   xMOF Methodology

The proposed methodology consists of the metamodeling language xMOF and a set of processes, techniques, and supporting tools for specifying the behavioral semantics of DSMLs, as well as for executing models conforming to the DSML. The processes of the methodology including the produced and consumed artifacts are depicted in Fig-ure 4, which also annotates the steps of the processes that are carried out automatically and the steps that have to be carried out manually. The relationships among the in-volved artifacts are shown in more detail in Figure 5. The methodology consists of five phases, which are discussed in the following by means of a running example; that is, the specification of a DSML for modeling Petri nets.

Language Design.   First of all the language designer has to specify the *abstract syntax* of the DSML with an *Ecore-based metamodel*. For specifying the behavioral seman-tics, an initial *xMOF-based configuration* is generated automatically from this meta-model. In particular, for each concrete metaclass in the metamodel, one Behaviored-EClass is generated, whereas one of them can be selected as MainEClass. Each of these generated classes (*configuration classes*) is defined as subclass of the respective metaclass it has been generated for and can now be extended to specify the behav-ioral semantics of this metaclass. Therefore, the language designer may add operations (BehavioredEOperations) providing an implementation of the designated behavior of the metaclass in terms of fUML Activities. In addition to the configuration classes, one class called Initialization, as well as a containment reference from the MainEClass to it, is generated. This *initialization class* can be used to define supplementary data that is needed as additional input for the execution of models based on the specified se-mantics. Therefore, attributes, references, and additional contained initialization classes (EClasses or BehavioredEClasses) can be added to this generated initialization class.

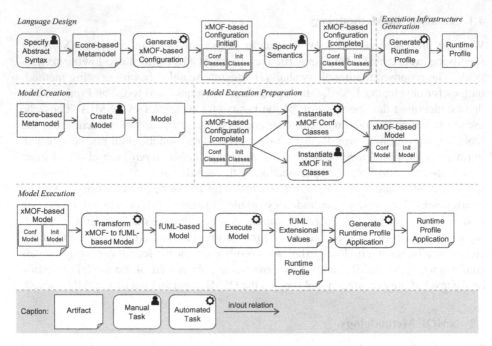

Fig. 4. Methodology for specifying the semantics of DSMLs with xMOF

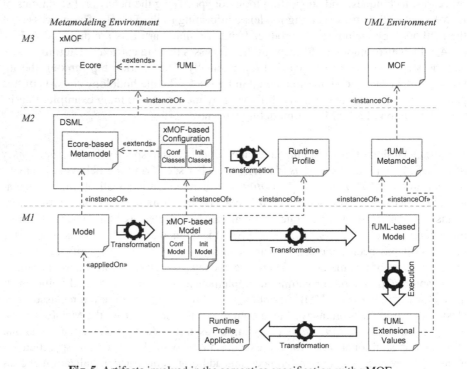

Fig. 5. Artifacts involved in the semantics specification with xMOF

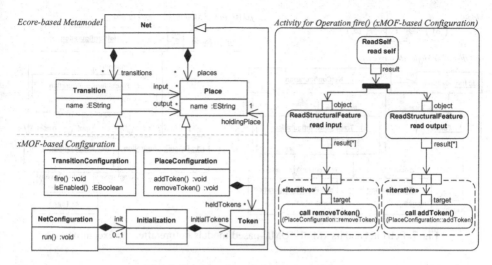

Fig. 6. Specification of the Petri net DSML

The xMOF-based configuration, consisting of configuration classes and optionally initialization classes together with their respective behavior specifications, completely define the behavioral semantics of a DSML.

Example. The metamodel of the Petri net DSML is depicted at the top left-hand side of Figure 6. A Net consists of Places and Transitions whereas Transitions reference their input and output Places. In the xMOF-based configuration of the Petri net DSML depicted at the bottom left-hand side of Figure 6, the configuration classes NetConfiguration, TransitionConfiguration, and PlaceConfiguration were generated for the metaclasses Net, Transition, and Place, respectively; NetConfiguration was selected to be the MainEClass. Next, we extend these classes with the behavioral semantics specification in terms of the operations addToken and removeToken for the configuration class PlaceConfiguration, fire and isEnabled for TransitionConfiguration, and run for NetConfiguration. As an example, the fUML activity specifying the behavior of the operation fire is depicted at the right-hand side of Figure 6. It calls the operation removeToken for each input Place and addToken for each output Place of a Transition. Besides the aforementioned operations, we added the class Token as a containment of the generated initialization class for representing the initial token distribution, which is the necessary input for executing a Petri net.

Model Creation. Using existing modeling facilities, a user may create *models* conforming to the DSML by instantiating the DSML's Ecore-based metamodel. Thus, the creation of models is not affected by our xMOF-based methodology at all and any modeling editor developed with, for instance, GMF[1] or Xtext[2], can be used to conveniently create models in the concrete syntax.

---

[1] http://www.eclipse.org/modeling/gmp
[2] http://www.eclipse.org/Xtext

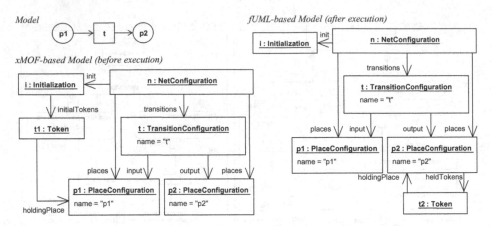

Fig. 7. Petri net and its xMOF/fUML-based models before/after the execution

Example. At the top left-hand side of Figure 7, an example of a Petri net is depicted in concrete syntax consisting of two places and one transition between them.

Model Execution Preparation. As the behavioral semantics of a DSML is specified in xMOF using fUML activities, models can be executed by leveraging the standardized fUML virtual machine. Therefore, the model to be executed has to be represented in terms of an instance of the xMOF-based configuration resulting in an *xMOF-based model*. Thus, for each element in the model, the configuration class defined for the element's metaclass is instantiated and initialized automatically, including its attribute values and references, to obtain a *configuration model*. In addition, the initialization classes have to be instantiated by the modeler in an *initialization model* to provide the additional information required for executing the model. Together with this initialization model, the configuration model is ready to be executed using the fUML virtual machine.

Example. At the bottom left-hand side of Figure 7 the xMOF-based model instantiated for the Petri net model created before is depicted. For the Petri net, the transition, and the places, the respective configuration classes NetConfiguration, TransitionConfiguration, and PlaceConfiguration were instantiated and initialized accordingly. As an input to the model execution, we manually instantiated the initialization classes for defining the initial token distribution consisting of one token residing in place p1.

Execution Infrastructure Generation. To provide the result of a performed model execution as feedback to the modeler in a comprehensible way, we annotate the execution result directly on the executed model. For this we again make use of a technique standardized by the OMG, namely the UML Profiles mechanism. However, as we deal with EMF-based models and not with UML models, we use EMF Profiles [13], which is an adaptation of the UML Profile concept to DSMLs in the realm of EMF. Thus, EMF

Profiles is a mechanism for adding and visually annotating additional information on EMF-based models without having to extend the respective metamodel. To annotate the executed model with the result of the model execution, we automatically generate a *runtime profile* from the xMOF-based configuration. More precisely, for each configuration class, a dedicated stereotype is generated with dedicated tagged values and references to represent the attributes and references of the respective configuration class.

Please note that the runtime profile itself is neither involved in the specification of the behavioral semantics of a DSML nor in the execution of a conforming model. Its sole purpose is to annotate the results of the model execution directly on the executed model itself in order to provide a visualization of the execution result to the modeler. Note that this visualization mechanism could be exchanged with another mechanism.

Example. The runtime profile generated for the xMOF-based configuration of the Petri net DSML is depicted at the top of Figure 8. This profile consists of the stereotypes NetConfigurationStereotype, TransitionConfigurationStereotype, as well as the Place-ConfigurationStereotype, which are applicable to model elements of the metaclasses Net, Transition, and Place, respectively. The attributes and references defined for the configuration classes were also accordingly introduced in the stereotypes.

Model Execution. Having obtained an xMOF-based representation of the model to be executed, as well as the means for representing the result of the model execution, we may perform the execution by leveraging the fUML virtual machine. Therefore, the xMOF-based model has to be converted into the in-memory representation (i.e., instantiated Java classes) of an fUML-compliant model dictated by the fUML virtual machine. For that reason, we provide an xMOF-to-fUML converter for accomplishing this translation automatically. The configuration classes are translated into fUML classes and the activities specifying their behavioral semantics are translated into fUML activities. This translation is a straightforward one-to-one transformation, as the language concepts for specifying behavior in xMOF (activities, actions, etc.) are basically identical to the concepts in fUML, due to the direct integration of fUML in xMOF. The language concepts in xMOF for defining the structure (classes, references, etc.) are taken from Ecore directly and hence can be translated easily into fUML. The elements of the xMOF-based model to be executed and their attribute values, as well as their references, are translated into fUML objects and fUML links (both called *extensional values* in fUML). During the execution of the obtained *fUML-based model* the fUML virtual machine interprets the activities specifying the behavioral semantics of the DSML and manipulates the objects and links representing the model to be executed accordingly. The result of the execution consists of the manipulated objects and links representing the runtime state of the executed model after the execution finished. This runtime information is then automatically transformed into an application of the generated runtime profile. This generated *runtime profile application* can now be loaded into the modeling editor to annotate the executed model with the result of the model execution.

Example. The fUML-based model resulting from the performed execution is depicted at the right-hand side of Figure 7. Basically, the token contained in the initial token

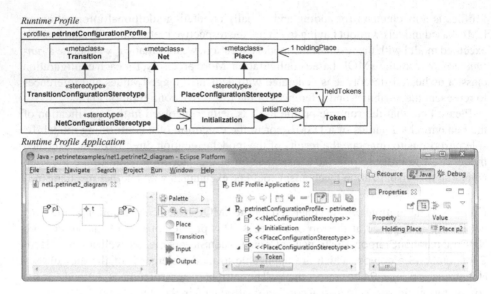

Fig. 8. Runtime profile and runtime profile application for Petri net DSML

distribution which was residing in the place p1 was removed and a new token was created for place p2, which means that the transition t fired in the model execution. To illustrate how the results of the execution is annotated, the generated runtime profile application for the executed model is depicted at the bottom of Figure 8. We can see in the *EMF Profile Applications* view that the stereotype NetConfigurationStereotype was applied on the net and contains the initial token distribution. Further the stereotype PlaceConfigurationStereotype was applied on both places, whereas the place p2 holds one token.

Tool Support. We provide an EMF-based implementation supporting the presented methodology. For further information on the tool support, such as demos, examples, and source code, we kindly refer the interested reader to our project website[3].

5   Case Studies and Lessons Learned

We used our xMOF prototype for carrying out several case studies in order to evaluate the applicability of our approach and to answer the following research questions: Is it possible to specify distinct languages' semantics by using fUML as action language? How appropriate and convenient is the usage of fUML and the proposed methodology for specifying the behavioral semantics of DSMLs?

---

[3] http://www.modelexecution.org

5.1 Case Studies Setup

We applied the presented methodology for developing three distinct DSMLs that follow different semantic paradigms: *(i)* token flow semantics, *(ii)* the semantics of imperative statements, and *(iii)* event-driven semantics.

As a first DSML, we chose the *Petri net DSML (PN)*, which we already presented as a running example in Section 4. In particular, we considered two implementation variants of the Petri net DSML: the first variant *PN1* incorporates the initial token distribution with an attribute in the metaclass **Place**, whereas the second variant *PN2* introduces the initial token distribution as initialization class (as presented in Section 4). The second DSML is an *imperative modeling language (IML)*, which allows to specify statements for defining variables, calculations of values, assignments to variables, and goto statements. The statements are executed top to bottom considering goto jumps. The distinct characteristic of this language is the need for a statement counter which holds the index of the statement to be executed in the next execution step. As a third DSML, we implemented the semantics of *finite state automata (FSA)* for processing a sequence of input symbols and verifying whether it conforms to a given alphabet. The distinct feature of this DSML is the event-driven nature of its behavioral semantics in terms of reacting to a sequence of input symbols. Table 1 shows some figures about the size of the Ecore-based metamodels and xMOF-based configurations specified for the considered DSMLs. All artifacts of the case studies can be found at our project website.

Table 1. Metrics about the size of the case study DSML specifications

Ecore-based Metamodel	PN1	PN2	IML	FSA	xMOF-based Configuration	PN1	PN2	IML	FSA
EClass	3	3	8	3	Activity	6	6	4	6
EReference	4	4	13	7	Action (all)	33	37	53	53
EAttribute	1	2	5	3	Read Action	15	16	29	22
xMOF-based Configuration	PN1	PN2	IML	FSA	Write Action	3	7	5	7
Conf Class	3	3	7	3	Call Action	9	9	12	11
Init Class	0	2	0	2	Other Action	6	5	7	13
EReference	0	4	0	3	Control Node	19	12	25	20
EAttribute	1	0	2	4	Object Flow	49	51	89	81
EOperation	5	5	3	5	Control Flow	18	10	24	15

5.2 Lessons Learned

In summary, the performed case studies confirmed that the proposed metamodeling language xMOF, as well as the presented methodology, are applicable for defining different kinds of executable DSMLs. In the following, we critically reflect on the lessons learned from performing the case studies by first outlining some strengths and, subsequently, challenges that might need to be addressed in future.

Strengths

Separation of Concerns. With the proposed methodology, the specification of the abstract syntax and the specification of the behavioral semantics of a DSML are *clearly separated* from each other in distinct artifacts. Thus, the Ecore-based metamodel does not incorporate any semantics-specific aspects and can be left as is. This separation also allows to define *multiple behavioral semantics* for the same metamodel by defining multiple xMOF-based configurations.

Explicit Runtime Representation. The xMOF-based configuration acts also as a representation for the *runtime information* of executed models (i.e., runtime variables, such as the pointer to the current state in *FSA*). Moreover, the xMOF-based configuration allows to define separately *additional and maybe complex input parameters* that are needed for executing models (e.g., the input sequence of symbols in *FSA*).

Non-invasive Methodology. The proposed methodology may be used *orthogonally to existing methodologies* for developing DSMLs. The usual steps for developing the abstract and concrete syntax, as well as for creating models, are not affected. Further, EMF was extended with appropriate *tool support* for this methodology enabling the integration of the semantics specification and model execution in any project that makes use of Ecore-based metamodels.

Support for Model Execution. By leveraging the fUML virtual machine, *models can be directly executed.* Only the behavioral semantics, the model to be executed, and the input parameter values have to be provided. The *execution result* is provided as feedback to the user on DSML level using the EMF Profiles mechanism, whereas the profile and its application are generated automatically.

Suitability of fUML. As fUML is designed to specify the behavior of UML classes and UML classes constitute the basis for MOF, fUML is a suitable candidate for an action language for MOF. The case studies showed that fUML is adequate for defining the behavioral semantics of executable DSMLs.

The first three listed strengths (separation of concerns, explicit runtime representation, and non-invasive methodology) concern the semantics specification methodology proposed in this paper and are not specific to the usage of fUML as semantics specification language. Indeed, the methodology might be compatible with other semantics specification languages as well. The latter two strengths (support for model execution and suitability of fUML) are specific to fUML whereas direct model execution support might be available for other action languages too.

Future Challenges

Semantics Specification Specialization. The behavioral semantics of a DSML may contain *semantic variation points*. For instance for *FSA*, a design decision was that if multiple transitions can process the next input symbol, the input is instantly declared as invalid; alternatively, one could prefer that one of those transitions is selected randomly. Although our methodology allows to define multiple xMOF-based configurations for the same metamodel, each alternative configuration has to be developed independently from scratch. Thus, it would be more efficient to have dedicated mechanisms for specializing existing behavioral semantics specifications by providing alternative behaviors for explicitly defined semantic variation points. A possible approach to achieve this in xMOF is the utilization of inheritance relationships among configuration classes. In this approach the behavioral semantics of a DSML could be specialized by overriding dedicated operations of the configuration classes which implement a semantic variation point.

Semantics Specification Reuse. Many DSMLs share a reoccurring set of semantic paradigms. For instance, the behavioral semantics of UML activity diagrams and diverse kinds of workflow languages, such as BPMN, incorporate the semantic paradigm of token flow as specified for the Petri net DSML. For instance, in our Petri net case study, the variant *PN1* differs from the variant *PN2* only in the representation and handling of tokens, apart from that the specified semantics are equivalent, e.g., the implementations of the operations run and fire are exactly the same for *PN1* and *PN2*. Nevertheless, no reuse was possible since this is currently not supported. Thus, dedicated means for reusing behavioral semantics specifications might increase the efficiency of the semantics specification tremendously. Therefore, we envision the definition of so-called *kernel semantics* that express reoccurring patterns in behavioral semantics specifications, such as control flow, data flow, events, statement counter, calculations etc. Having xMOF-based specifications of such kernel semantics at hand, we could use them to specify the behavioral semantics of comparable DSMLs very efficiently by reusing and combining the required kernel semantics.

Comprehensive Library Support. With xMOF, the behavioral semantics of a DSML is specified by means of the fUML action language which provides, besides basic actions for creating, updating, and destroying objects and links, also a set of functions for primitive data types in a so-called *fUML foundational model library* (e.g., the functions add and subtract for Integer values). However, when specifying the behavioral semantics in the case studies, we missed essential functions, such as indexOf for fUML lists, which we needed to implement the selection of the next statement to be executed in *IML*, or random, which would have enabled us to implement nondeterministic *FSA*. Furthermore, we noticed that functions for navigating and querying models more concisely are needed in fUML. Currently, even simple navigations over multiple references require one action for each navigated reference, which leads to long chains of reading actions. As indicated in Table 1, 42%-55% of all actions in the developed semantics specifications are reading actions. For collecting objects that fulfill certain conditions, even more complex combinations of reading and writing actions, decision and merge nodes are required. Thus, the size and complexity of the fUML activities developed in our case studies could be reduced significantly, if a support for OCL queries (such as collect and select) would be provided. fUML enables the extension of the fUML foundational model library by providing and registering Java implementations of the respective functions at the fUML virtual machine. However, functions for navigating and querying models more concisely are hard to integrate with this extension mechanism because the conditions for selecting certain objects would have to be passed from fUML to Java in terms of plain Strings, which can hardly be validated on model level.

Besides such general purpose functions, also external APIs might be required for the specification of the semantics of a DSML. Consider for instance a DSML for controlling robots. If the robot should actually be operated by executing models, operations of a dedicated robot API have to be invoked during the model execution. In such cases, a mechanism for integrating domain-specific model libraries in addition to the fUML foundational model library would be useful. As sketched in previous work [15], another solution would be to integrate the interfaces of the required external libraries into the xMOF-based configuration by reverse-engineering the library and to employ a dedicated integration layer which delegates calls to the external library.

fUML Notation. For specifying the activities in xMOF, we implemented a graphical editor that uses the well-known and standardized UML activity diagram notation. However, when specifying the behavioral semantics of a DSML with activities in a graphical way, they easily become very large because it is required to model on a very detailed level. In average, the activities of our case studies consist of 11 nodes, whereas large activities contain up to 33 nodes. Although this is not a huge number, the diagrams are already hard to read due to the large number of edges among them (on average 15 edges, maximum 44 edges per activity). While it might be useful to have a graphical view of activities that are not very detailed, i.e., which mainly call other activities, a textual representation would be more appropriate for more detailed activities. A potential solution for this issue is the integration of the standardized textual syntax for fUML called Alf [18] in xMOF.

Detailed Runtime Information. Our approach of specifying the behavioral semantics of a DSML with xMOF enables the execution of models by leveraging the fUML virtual machine. As runtime information about the performed model execution, the runtime state of the model after the execution finished is provided. While this runtime information allows to reason about the *result* of executing a model, no information is provided *during the runtime*, which, however, might be helpful to analyze the behavior of a model more thoroughly. In previous work [14], we extended the reference implementation of the fUML virtual machine by introducing a command API and an event mechanism allowing to control and observe the execution of fUML models at runtime. Further, a trace of the performed execution can be obtained. These extensions may be helpful for the language designer when analyzing and debugging the xMOF-based semantics specification. However, to also provide this detailed runtime information to the modeler, the runtime events, commands, and the trace should be tailored to the respective DSML, instead of being provided on the level of the executed fUML actions, because the modeler is only concerned with the concepts of the DSML and not with its behavioral semantics specification. Thus, it would be useful to derive a DSML-specific event model, command API, and trace model from the behavioral semantics specification of the DSML to enable the derivation of DSML-specific debuggers, as well as testing, analysis, and verification tools.

It has to be noted that these challenges are not specific to our semantics specification language xMOF, but are challenges generally faced when developing and maturing new software languages. Although we can build on existing notable solutions and approaches from general software language engineering research to address these challenges, it has to be investigated which of these solutions are most adequate and how they have to be adapted for the realm of metamodeling and under the consideration of the existing capabilities and peculiarities of fUML.

6   Conclusion

In this paper, we investigated the applicability of fUML for specifying the behavioral semantics of DSMLs. Therefore, we composed a novel metamodeling language called xMOF that integrates Ecore with the behavioral part of fUML. Moreover, we proposed a non-invasive methodology, including dedicated tool support, for developing executable DSMLs with xMOF that fosters a clear separation of concerns and enables the execution of models using the standardized fUML virtual machine. Based on the case studies presented in this paper, we may conclude that fUML seems to be very promising for being established as a standardized language for the specification of the behavioral semantics of DSMLs. However, a large-scale case study applying our proposed semantics specification approach based on fUML on more complex languages comprising more complex modeling concepts (e.g., inheritance), which is for now left for future work, is necessary to evaluate its scalability. In these large-scale case studies, we further plan to investigate how adequate our approach is for supporting DSMLs that are only partially executable; or that are only executable based on additional models. Furthermore, a comprehensive comparison of fUML with other action languages existing in the MDE domain might provide interesting insights into the strengths and weaknesses of fUML as semantics specification language. Based on our experiences gained by carrying out the case studies, we also revealed and discussed several challenges that need to be addressed in future for unleashing the full potential of using our fUML-based semantics specification approach. Another interesting line of future research concerns the development of techniques that exploit the explicit semantics specification to derive, for instance, code generators or model analysis support (semi-)automatically.

References

1. Bryant, B.R., Gray, J., Mernik, M., Clarke, P.J., France, R.B., Karsai, G.: Challenges and directions in formalizing the semantics of modeling languages. Computer Science and Information Systems 8(2), 225–253 (2011)
2. Chen, K., Sztipanovits, J., Abdelwalhed, S., Jackson, E.: Semantic anchoring with model transformations. In: Hartman, A., Kreische, D. (eds.) ECMDA-FA 2005. LNCS, vol. 3748, pp. 115–129. Springer, Heidelberg (2005)
3. Clark, T., Evans, A., Sammut, P., Willans, J.: Applied Metamodelling: A Foundation for Language Driven Development. Ceteva, Sheffield (2004)
4. Ducasse, S., Gîrba, T.: Using Smalltalk as a Reflective Executable Meta-language. In: Wang, J., Whittle, J., Harel, D., Reggio, G. (eds.) MoDELS 2006. LNCS, vol. 4199, pp. 604–618. Springer, Heidelberg (2006)

5. Engels, G., Hausmann, J.H., Heckel, R., Sauer, S.: Dynamic Meta Modeling: A Graphical Approach to the Operational Semantics of Behavioral Diagrams in UML. In: Evans, A., Caskurlu, B., Selic, B. (eds.) UML 2000. LNCS, vol. 1939, pp. 323–337. Springer, Heidelberg (2000)

6. Grönniger, H., Ringert, J.O., Rumpe, B.: System Model-Based Definition of Modeling Language Semantics. In: Lee, D., Lopes, A., Poetzsch-Heffter, A. (eds.) FMOODS 2009. LNCS, vol. 5522, pp. 152–166. Springer, Heidelberg (2009)

7. Kats, L.C.L., Visser, E.: The Spoofax language workbench. In: Companion to the 25th Annual ACM SIGPLAN Conference on Object-Oriented Programming, Systems, Languages, and Applications (OOPSLA), pp. 237–238. ACM (2010)

8. Kolovos, D.S., Paige, R.F., Polack, F.A.C.: The Epsilon Object Language (EOL). In: Rensink, A., Warmer, J. (eds.) ECMDA-FA 2006. LNCS, vol. 4066, pp. 128–142. Springer, Heidelberg (2006)

9. Kühne, T.: Matters of (Meta-)Modeling. Software and System Modeling 5(4), 369–385 (2006)

10. Kühne, T., Mezei, G., Syriani, E., Vangheluwe, H., Wimmer, M.: Explicit Transformation Modeling. In: Ghosh, S. (ed.) MODELS 2009. LNCS, vol. 6002, pp. 240–255. Springer, Heidelberg (2010)

11. Kurtev, I., Bézivin, J., Aksit, M.: Technological Spaces: An Initial Appraisal. In: Proceedings of the International Symposium on Distributed Objects and Applications, DOA (2002)

12. Lai, Q., Carpenter, A.: Defining and verifying behaviour of domain specific language with fUML. In: Proceedings of the 4th Workshop on Behaviour Modeling - Foundations and Applications (BM-FA) @ ECMFA 2012, pp. 1–7. ACM (2012)

13. Langer, P., Wieland, K., Wimmer, M., Cabot, J.: EMF Profiles: A Lightweight Extension Approach for EMF Models. Journal of Object Technology 11(1), 1–29 (2012)

14. Mayerhofer, T., Langer, P., Kappel, G.: A runtime model for fUML. In: Proceedings of the 7th Workshop on Models@run.time (MRT) @ MoDELS 2012, pp. 53–58. ACM (2012)

15. Mayerhofer, T., Langer, P., Wimmer, M.: Towards xMOF: Executable DSMLs based on fUML. In: Proceedings of the 12th Workshop on Domain-Specific Modeling (DSM) @ SPLASH 2012, pp. 1–6. ACM (2012)

16. Mernik, M., Heering, J., Sloane, A.M.: When and how to develop domain-specific languages. ACM Computing Surveys 37(4), 316–344 (2005)

17. Muller, P.-A., Fleurey, F., Jézéquel, J.-M.: Weaving Executability into Object-Oriented Metalanguages. In: Briand, L.C., Williams, C. (eds.) MoDELS 2005. LNCS, vol. 3713, pp. 264–278. Springer, Heidelberg (2005)

18. Object Management Group. Action Language for Foundational UML (Alf), Version Beta 1 (October 2010), http://www.omg.org/spec/ALF/1.0/Beta1

19. Object Management Group. OMG Meta Object Facility (MOF) Core Specification, Version 2.4.1 (August 2011), http://www.omg.org/spec/MOF/2.4.1

20. Object Management Group. Semantics of a Foundational Subset for Executable UML Models (fUML), Version 1.0 (February 2011), http://www.omg.org/spec/FUML/1.0

21. Paige, R., Brooke, P., Ostroff, J.: Specification-driven development of an executable metamodel in Eiffel. In: Proceedings of the 3rd Workshop in Software Model Engineering (WiSME) @ UML 2004 (2004)

22. Rivera, J.E., Durán, F., Vallecillo, A.: On the Behavioral Semantics of Real-Time Domain Specific Visual Languages. In: Ölveczky, P.C. (ed.) WRLA 2010. LNCS, vol. 6381, pp. 174–190. Springer, Heidelberg (2010)

23. Scheidgen, M., Fischer, J.: Human Comprehensible and Machine Processable Specifications of Operational Semantics. In: Akehurst, D.H., Vogel, R., Paige, R.F. (eds.) ECMDA-FA. LNCS, vol. 4530, pp. 157–171. Springer, Heidelberg (2007)

24. Soden, M., Eichler, H.: Towards a model execution framework for Eclipse. In: Proceedings of the 1st Workshop on Behaviour Modeling - Foundations and Applications (BM-FA) @ ECMFA 2009, pp. 1–7. ACM (2009)
25. Sprinkle, J., Rumpe, B., Vangheluwe, H., Karsai, G.: Metamodelling - State of the Art and Research Challenges. In: Giese, H., Karsai, G., Lee, E., Rumpe, B., Schätz, B. (eds.) Model-Based Engineering of Embedded Real-Time Systems. LNCS, vol. 6100, pp. 57–76. Springer, Heidelberg (2010)
26. Steinberg, D., Budinsky, F., Paternostro, M., Merks, E.: EMF: Eclipse Modeling Framework, 2nd edn. Addison-Wesley Professional (2008)
27. Strembeck, M., Zdun, U.: An approach for the systematic development of domain-specific languages. Software: Practice and Experience 39(15), 1253–1292 (2009)
28. Sunyé, G., Guennec, A.L., Jézéquel, J.-M.: Using UML Action Semantics for model execution and transformation. Information Systems 27(6), 445–457 (2002)
29. Sunyé, G., Pennaneac'h, F., Ho, W.-M., Le Guennec, A., Jézéquel, J.-M.: Using UML Action Semantics for Executable Modeling and Beyond. In: Dittrich, K.R., Geppert, A., Norrie, M. (eds.) CAiSE 2001. LNCS, vol. 2068, pp. 433–447. Springer, Heidelberg (2001)
30. van den Bos, J., Hills, M., Klint, P., van der Storm, T., Vinju, J.J.: Rascal: From Algebraic Specification to Meta-Programming. In: Proceedings of the 2nd International Workshop on Algebraic Methods in Model-based Software Engineering (AMMSE). EPTCS, vol. 56, pp. 15–32 (2011)

Variability Support
in Domain-Specific Language Development

Edoardo Vacchi[1], Walter Cazzola[1], Suresh Pillay[2], and Benoît Combemale[2]

[1] Computer Science Department, Università degli Studi di Milano, Italy
[2] TRISKELL (INRIA - IRISA), Université de Rennes 1, France

Abstract. Domain Specific Languages (DSLs) are widely adopted to capitalize on business domain experiences. Consequently, DSL development is becoming a recurring activity. Unfortunately, even though it has its benefits, language development is a complex and time-consuming task. Languages are commonly realized from scratch, even when they share some concepts and even though they could share bits of tool support. This cost can be reduced by employing modern modular programming techniques that foster code reuse. However, selecting and composing these modules is often only within the reach of a skilled DSL developer. In this paper we propose to combine modular language development and variability management, with the objective of capitalizing on existing assets. This approach explicitly models the dependencies between language components, thereby allowing a domain expert to configure a desired DSL, and automatically derive its implementation. The approach is tool supported, using Neverlang to implement language components, and the Common Variability Language (CVL) for managing the variability and automating the configuration. We will further illustrate our approach with the help of a case study, where we will implement a family of DSLs to describe state machines.

Keywords: Domain-Specific Languages, Language Design and Implementation, Variability Management, CVL and Neverlang.

1 Introduction

In computer science, we call *domain-specific language* (DSL) a language that is targeted towards a *specific problem area*. DSLs use concepts and constructs that pertain to a particular domain, so that domain experts can express their intentions using a language that is closely aligned with their understanding. For instance, mathematicians often prefer MATLAB or Mathematica, while in the modeling world we often talk about domain-specific *modeling* languages (DSMLs). In the last few years, industry has shown a growing interest in DSL development [15], because complex problems are more easily expressed using problem-tailored languages. However these complex problems tend to have variations, thus requiring different language implementations.

Traditional language development is a top-down, *monolithic process*, that provides very little support in terms of reuse and management of reusable parts.

M. Erwig, R.F. Paige, and E. Van Wyk (Eds.): SLE 2013, LNCS 8225, pp. 76–95, 2013.

Many modern programming languages include DSL-development oriented features (e.g., Scala's parser combinators, Groovy, and so on). However, language development is still far from being within everyone's reach. Language development tools are generally not built for direct interaction with the end user of the language; but rather the language developer. Thus, although componentized development is today the norm, even in the case of language development, complete language workbenches such as Xtext [9] or MPS [25] are usually top-down, end-to-end development tools that are meant for programmers, and therefore less suited for programming-illiterate users. Componentized language frameworks such as LISA [19], JastAdd [10], or Neverlang [2,3] support *reuse* of language components, but each component may have implicit dependencies on other parts, and often these dependencies are not managed automatically by the system, but are delegated to the developer.

We believe that combining variability and modular language frameworks would bridge the gap between developers and end users, thereby further promoting re-use. In *software product lines* [6], variability models represent the family of products. Some works [22, 28] have shown that variability modeling improves code reuse in DSL development, in that it makes *explicit* the way components in a collection may cooperate, how to avoid conflicts and how to ensure that dependencies are included. Even though it has been recognized as good practice, variability modeling in language development is still an overlooked aspect, and most language frameworks usually do not natively take into account its importance. The contribution of this work is an approach to apply variability modeling to component-based language development, that focuses on reuse of existing assets. In particular, we describe

1. a method to extract structured information from the set of existing assets in the form of a graph of dependencies,

2. a strategy to construct a variability model using the extracted information,

3. an implementation of a derivation operator to generate the language implementation from the VM automatically,

thereby facilitating the collaboration between the language developer and the domain expert, to the extent that the domain expert becomes autonomous in extracting a desired language. The implementation of this approach will be demonstrated using a real working toolset applied to a family of state machine languages.

The rest of this paper is structured as follows: in Sect. 2 we provide some background in terms of a modular language implementation and variability modeling; in Sect. 3 we give an overview of the approach. In Sect 4 we describe the approach in detail starting with a set of components and in Sect. 5 we apply variability techniques. In Sect. 6 a case study of a family of statemachines is provided. Finally, in Sect. 7 we discuss the related work and in Sect. 8 we draw our conclusions.

```
module com.example.AddExpr {
  reference syntax {
    AddExpr ←  Term
    AddExpr ←  AddExpr "+" Term;
  }
  role(evaluation) {
    0.{ $0.value = $1.value; }
    2.{ $2.value = (Integer) $3.value + (Integer) $4.value; }.
  }
}
slice com.example.AddExprSlice {
  concrete syntax from com.example.AddExpr
  module com.example.AddExpr with role evaluation
}
```

Listing 1. A simple Neverlang slice defining the syntax and semantics for the sum. Numbers refer to nonterminals.

```
module com.example.Numbers {
  reference syntax { Integer ←  /[0-9]+/; }
  role(evaluation) { ... }
}
slice com.example.NumbersSlice {
  concrete syntax from com.example.Numbers
  module com.example.Numbers with role evaluation
}
```

Listing 2. The slice that defines Term for sum

2 Background

In this section we present the tools that we are going to use in the description of our approach. As we already mentioned, we will employ Neverlang for the componentization of the language implementation, while we will use CVL for variability modeling and realization.

2.1 Neverlang

The *Neverlang* [2,3] framework for DSL development promotes code reuse and sharing by making language units first-class concepts. In Neverlang, language components are developed as separate units that can be compiled and tested independently, enabling developers to share and reuse the same units across different language implementations.

In Neverlang the base unit is the **module** (Listing 1). A module may contain a **syntax** definition or a semantic **role**. A role defines actions that should be executed when some syntax is recognized, as prescribed by the *syntax-directed translation* technique (for reference, see [1]). Syntax definitions are portions of BNF grammars, represented as sets of *grammar rules* or *productions*. Semantic actions are defined as code snippets that refer nonterminals in the grammar.

Syntax definitions and semantic roles are tied together using **slices**. For instance, moduleneverlang.commons.AddExpr declares a reference syntax for sum, and actions are attached to the nonterminals on the right of the two productions. Rules are attached to nonterminals by referring to their position in the

```
language com.example.CalcLang {
  slices com.example.AddExprSlice com.example.MulExprSlice
         com.example.ParenExprSlice com.example.ExprAssocSlice
         com.example.NumbersSlice
  roles syntax < evaluation < ... // other roles
}
```

Listing 3. Neverlang's language construct

grammar: numbering starts with 0 from the top left to the bottom right, so the first AddExpr is referred to as 0, Term as 1, the AddExpr on the second line would be 2 and so on. The slice neverlang.commons.AddExprSlice declares that we will be using *this* syntax (which is the **concrete syntax**) in our language, with that particular semantics.

Finally, the **language** descriptor (Listing 3) indicates which slices are required to be composed together to generate the interpreter or the compiler[1] for the language. Composition in Neverlang is therefore twofold:

1. between modules, which yields slices
2. between slices, which yields a language implementation

The result of the composition does not depend on the order in which slices are specified. The grammars are merged together to generate the complete parser for the language. Semantic actions are performed with respect to the parse tree of the input program; roles are executed in the order specified in the **roles** clause of the **language** descriptor. For lack of space, we cannot not give an in-depth description of Neverlang's syntax; for a more detailed description, see [3].

The set of generated components can be precompiled into JVM bytecode, and can be instantiated and queried for their properties using a specific API. For instance it is possible to retrieve the part of the syntax they define, the actions they include, etc. This API can be exploited to collect information from a given pool of slices.

In Neverlang the composition process is *syntax driven* and *implicit*. It is *syntax driven*, in that relations between slices are inferred from the grammar definitions that they contain. It is *implicit* in that these dependencies are implied by these definitions, and they are not stated in an explicit way. We will describe this with more detail in Sect. 4.

2.2 Variability Management and CVL

Variability modeling (VM) is a modeling approach in order to manage and express commonalities and differences in a family of products. These commonalities and differences are represented as features (particular characteristic or properties) of the family of products. Currently two approaches are possible,

---

[1] Although in the following we will take the liberty to always use the term *interpreter*, let it be known that Neverlang is perfectly capable of generating compilers.

the first being that the underlying asset provides mechanisms to support extensions which are used to introduce variations; and the second approach is when the variability is expressed orthogonally to the asset. In the second approach a binding is required between the features and the asset. A feature model is a common approach to specifying the relationship between features defined as a set of constraints between features.

The *common variability language* (CVL)[2] [11] is a domain-independent language for specifying and resolving variability over any instance of any MOF-compliant metamodel. Inspired by feature models, CVL contains several layers. The Variability Abstraction Model (*VAM*) is in charge of expressing the variability in terms of a tree-based structure. The core concepts of the VAM are the variability specifications (*VSpecs*). The *VSpecs* are nodes of the VAM and can be divided into three kinds: Choices, Variables and Classifiers. The Choices are *VSpecs* that can be resolved to yes or no (through *ChoiceResolution*), *Variables* are *VSpecs* that requires a value for being resolved (VariableValue) and *Classifiers* are *VSpecs* that imply the creation of instances and then providing per-instance resolutions (*VInstances*). In this paper, we mainly use the *Choices VSpecs*, which can be intuitively compared to features, which can or cannot be selected during the product derivation (yes/no decision). Besides the VAM, CVL also contains a Variability Realization Model (VRM). This model provides a binding between the base model which contains the assets and the VAM. It makes possible to specify the changes in the base model implied by the *VSpec* resolutions. These changes are expressed as Variation Points in the VRM. The variation points capture the derivation semantics, i.e. the actions to perform during the Derivation. The CVL specification defines four types of variation points, namely *Existence, Substitution, Value Assignment* and *Opaque Variation Point*. An *object existence variation point* is used to determine when an object found in the base model should be included or not. Finally, CVL contains resolution models (RM) to fix the variability captured in the VAM. The RM replicates the structure of the VAM, in the case of the *Choice* it would become a *ChoiceResolution* which allows the choice to be either selected or not. Similarly *VariableValueAssignments* are used to assign values to variables. Thereby providing a mechanism to configure the features required in the desired product.

3 Approach Overview

As noted in the introduction, each component that we add to a language usually has some dependencies, such as a semantic concept, a syntactic requirement, or both of them. For instance, if we want some looping construct to terminate, be it **for**, **while**, or whichever we may pick, we might as well include some concept of *truth value* and the idea of a *condition* to test. Likewise, we would need some syntax to express this concept. Similarly, there might be concepts that, together, in the same language may *conflict*. For instance, we cannot have a three-valued

---

[2] CVL is currently a proposal submitted to OMG. Cf.
http://variabilitymodeling.org.

logic and the simple boolean logic to just *coexist* in the same places: what if the condition of a loop evaluates to **null**? Should the loop exit or not?

Component-based language development is close to providing people with an easy way to implement a language by just selecting components, but implicit dependencies and conflicts between them creates a barrier to opening such development to a wider audience. The challenge lies in the fact that an in-depth knowledge of how the components are designed is required prior to using such an approach. Applying variability modeling to a modular language framework allows the explicit modeling of the relations between components in a manner understandable to the domain expert or end-user.

In our approach, component-based development is necessary for users to be able to selectively pick components; the feature model is necessary to represent how components may interact and to relieve users from the burden of satisfying complicated dependencies by hand. The variability model explicitly represents the constraints and the resolution model complies with these constraints, so that the result of the derivation is guaranteed to behave as expected. Typically a variability model is used to represent a family of products; in our case we will use it to represent a *language family*, that is a set of languages that share a common set of features. In a perfect world, language components would be developed from scratch, with the target variability model in mind, and therefore they would be guaranteed to compose well together. However, implementing a language from the ground requires a substantial investment. To minimize cost during component-based language development, one approach would be to maximize reuse of a set of already available language components.

We will focus on the case of Neverlang and CVL, but the approach that we present can be applied to any kind of feature modeling approach and any componentized language development tool that will fit our framework. In particular, the main requirement for the language framework is to support a way to define the language constructs in separate components. Although Neverlang includes some peculiar features [3], we believe that this approach can be applied by other modular language development frameworks (see Section 7 for other Neverlang-related work), provided that it is possible to extract from the language components the set of their relations (the *dependency graph*, see Section 4). The global approach is a two-level process: first, the reusable language components are capitalized and their possible combinations are captured in a variability model. Second, the variability model is used to select an expected set of features (or *configuration*) from which a woven model is produced by composition of the suitable reusable language components.

From a methodological perspective, we also distinguish two roles for users of our approach:

- **Language Developer**. A person experienced in the field of DSL implementation, and who knows how to break down a language into components.
- **Domain Expert**. A person that knows the concepts and the lexicon of the target domain. People in this category would also be end-users of the language.

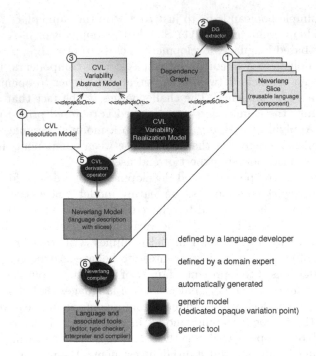

Fig. 1. CVL in Language Development

In practice, as illustrated in Fig. 1, the approach is divided into the following six steps:

① the *language developer* collects all of the available language components: these could be pre-existing components or newly created components.
② the relations between components are extracted automatically and represented as a *dependency graph*
③ the *language developer* and the *domain expert* collaborate to define a variability model using the dependency graph as a guide, in such a way as to define a language family most relevant for the given domain.
④ the *domain expert* becomes autonomous: it is now possible to extract a desired language by resolving the variability (selecting a set of features).
⑤ using a derivation operator, a list of composition directives is derived from the resolution of the variability model
⑥ the language development tool generates a complete interpreter/compiler for the desired language.

In our case, if Neverlang is the language framework, and CVL is the variability language, then we will implement the reusable language components (**slices**) using Neverlang (step ①) and extract the dependency graph from Neverlang (step ②); the specification of the variability (called *variability abstract model*) will use the choice diagram proposed by CVL (step ③); variability resolution will be CVL's *resolution model* (step ④); the composition directives (the **language** descriptor) will be derived (step ⑤) using a dedicated derivation operator, implemented using the CVL opaque variation point (and included in the *variability realization model*); finally Neverlang (step ⑥) will compose the slices contained in the language descriptor. Please notice that Neverlang provides an additional degree of composition: composition between slices (possibly) yields a language, but, as described in Sect. 2, composition between modules yields slices. This additional degree of freedom will not be discussed here as it would go beyond the scope of this paper: code reuse at the module level would raise the problem of multi-dimensional variability, that we reserve to explore in future work.

4   From Slices to Variability Modeling

The *domain expert* and the *language developer* interact to implement the variability model and map it onto a pool of slices. In this section we show that a variability model can be reverse-engineered from language components. We will show a simple DSL to express arithmetical expressions (similar to the ARI language found in [12]) that, however, has the right level of complexity to explain our approach. The language of arithmetical expressions is known to be more complicated than it looks. For instance, the grammar is known to be non-trivial to factorize, and the semantics is hard to modularize (cf. *"the expression problem"* in [26]). In this known setting, we imagine that a *language developer* and the *domain expert* collaborate to implement a variability model on top of a set of slices that implement a family of ARI-like languages. For the sake of brevity, we will consider expressions that include only addition and multiplication over the domain of positive naturals; e.g.: $12 + 5 \times (4 + 2)$.

In our example, the language has already been developed using Neverlang, and *a pool of slices* is already available. In this context the variability model would be a representation of all the possible language variants that can be obtained from different subsets of this pool, and a *language family* (Sect. 3) would be seen as the set of languages that share a common set of slices. In particular, given this pool of slices, then the first step (Sect. 3) to design their variability model (Fig. 3) is to derive a *dependency graph* (Fig. 2).

From Slices to Dependency Graph.   In Sect. 2 we briefly introduced the slices that implement the addition (Listing 1) and the definition of numbers (Listing 2), and we said that the composition process in Neverlang is *syntax-driven* and *implicit*. Slices are composed together automatically, because the

```
module neverlang.commons.ExprAssoc {
  reference syntax {
    Expr    ← AddExpr;
    Expr    ← ParenExpr;
    Term    ← MulExpr;
    Factor ← Integer;
  }
}
```

Listing 4. Traditional Associativity Rules

nonterminals that their grammars contain already *implicitly* declare something about what they *require* and *provide*. For instance, consider the production for `com.example.Numbers`:

$$\text{Term} \leftarrow /[0\text{-}9]\text{+}/$$

In this case, the right-hand side is a regex pattern, i.e., a *terminal symbol*: this is just a way to tell Neverlang's parser generator that the text of a program should contain a number, and has no implication on the way this slice composes with others. On the other hand, the *head* of the production (its left-hand nonterminal) represents something that the slice *makes available* to other slices. In other words, since this slice has Term in the head of its production, another production, possibly in another slice, may refer to it in its right-hand side. In this case, we might say that the slice `com.example.NumbersSlice` *provides* the nonterminal Term, which is bound to the high-level concept of *number* and *operand of a sum*. Similarly, a nonterminal occurring in the right-hand side of a production is predicating about what the slice *requires* to be available. For instance, in `com.example.AddExprSlice` we had:

$$\text{AddExpr} \leftarrow \text{Term}$$

In this case, the *head* says that the slice *provides* AddExpr, but, at the same time, this slice *requires* Term. This constraint would be satisfied if `com.example.AddExpr` and `com.example.Numbers` were part of the same language.

These *implicit dependencies* are not enforced. Satisfying these constraints is left to the knowledge of the language developer. In Neverlang we have fostered support to variability modeling by adding a high-level API to simplify extraction of this data from a given slice. The result is that now slices can be queried for what we call their *provide set* —i.e., the collection of all the nonterminals that the slice defines— and for their *require set* —i.e., the collection of all the nonterminals that should be made available by other slices— in order for this slice to make sense in the language. For instance, the slice for the addition that we presented does not make sense alone, but rather another slice in the same language should define what a Term is; that is, Term should be found in the *provide set* of another slice. It is then quite natural, that, given a pool of slices, it is possible to derive a *dependency graph* depicting the relations.

The concept of dependency graph for a set of slices is quite intuitive, but more formally, we may say that, given a set (a pool) of slices $S = \{s_0, s_1, \ldots, s_n\}$, we define for each $s \in S$ two sets $R_s \subset N$, the *require set* and $P_s \subset N$, the *provide set*, with N being the alphabet of all the nonterminals in the grammars of all the slices in S. A *dependency* is a pair (s, X), where $s \in S$ and $X \in R_s$. We can say that the dependency (s, X) is *satisfied* if there is at least one slice $s' \in S$ such that $X \in P_{s'}$, and then that s' satisfies s. A *dependency graph* for a pool of slices can be then defined as a tuple $G = \langle S, D \rangle$, with S being the set of slices and $D = \{(s, s') \mid s' \text{ satisfies } s\}$, with a function $\ell(d) = X$ for each $d = (s, s') \in D$, such that (s, X) is a dependency satisfied by s'. For instance, given the pool of slices that constitutes the language in Listing 3, the dependency graph is shown

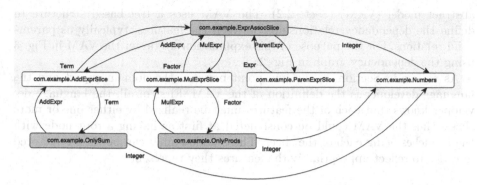

Fig. 2. A Slice Pool, including the ARI language

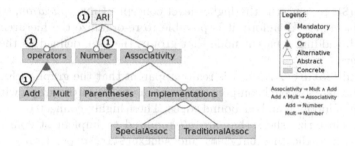

Fig. 3. VAM for the Expression Language

in Fig. 2, in the grey box. The arrows point in the direction of a dependency, and they are labeled by the nonterminal that represents that dependency. For instance, `com.example.ExprAssocSlice` (Listing 4) requires some slice to define the `MulExpr`, `AddExpr` and `ParenExpr` nonterminals. These dependencies are satisfied by the slices for multiplication, addition and parenthesized expressions, respectively; e.g., if s = `com.example.ExprAssocSlice` and X = `MulExpr`, then the dependency (s, X) is satisfied by `com.example.MulExprSlice`.

From Dependency Graph to VAM. The CVL variation model (VAM) presents a simple-to-use, feature-oriented view of a pool of Neverlang slices to the user. It encodes the set of choices and the constraints between choices. Constructing a VAM requires the collaboration between the language developer and the domain expert. The language developer has experience in using a language development tool (in our case, Neverlang) and can count on a code base of language components that he or his colleagues have developed over the years. Any arbitrary combination of slices from the pool of slices does not necessarily constitute a language. As each slice may have specific dependencies and conflicts may arise when combining certain slices. In order to establish such dependencies a *dependency graph* is provided. The DG Extractor is a tool that uses Neverlang to query a pool of slices and generate the corresponding dependency graph.

The language developer and the domain expert can exploit this graph as a basis to design the variability they intend to obtain implemented as a variability abstract model (VAM) (Sect. 2.2). The VAM uses a tree-based structure to define the dependency relationships between the features, typically as parent-child relations. For the purpose of this explanation we target the VAM in Fig. 3 using the dependency graph in Fig. 2.

As we see in Section. 3, the join point between the domain expert and the language developer is the definition of the VAM. First of all, the language developer knows that each of the features must be realized by either one or more slices, thus the VAM could be constructed at first as having a root node with the branches being each of the slices. These node names can be then refactored in order to reflect appropriately the features they represent.

Identifying simple features. First of all, the domain expert is able to recognize that `AddExprSlice` concerns the higher-level concept of *addition* and that `MulExprSlice` concerns the higher-level concept of *multiplication*, which are both *operators*. Therefore, it is possible to re-organize the hierarchy in the VAM, by adding a parent node that groups the two, defined as the feature *operators*.

Compound features. Now, it is really apparent that the graph in Fig. 2 contains highly-connected components; there are nodes in the graph with a high number of inbound and outbound edges. These highly-connected components usually clusterize slices that are *all* required to implement some feature. For instance, the slice `OnlySums` and `AddExprSlice` depend on each other, and `OnlySums` depends on `Numbers`. A similar reasoning applies to `OnlyProds`, `MulExprSlice` and `Numbers`. Both of these highly-connected components show no dependency on `ParenExprSlice`. The *domain expert* has the knowledge to abstract away from the language components that are shown in the graph, and suggest that a language variant having only sums can be represented in Fig. 3 as the feature `Add_NoParenthesis` being one of the alternative of the feature `Add`. Similarly, the same thought process can be applied to the multiplication operation. In addition, the fact that the dependency graph shows that exists a dependency from feature `Add` and feature `Mult` to the feature `Numbers`, implies that we have a cross-cutting constraint that when any operator is selected the feature `Number` *must* be included.

Extra features. More information can be added. For instance, the domain expert might require that there exist another type of associativity, such as feature `SpecialAssoc`. In this case it is also evident that in the current set of slices this is not possible: this reflects the notion that building such a model with the domain expert can also highlight missing features in the language. It is also shown in Fig. 3 additional constraints —predicate logic statements— which would need to be captured by the domain expert and language developer.

For the ARI example, we obtain the VAM as depicted in Fig. 3. This VAM contains a root choice ARI with three optional features. The *operators* feature allows you to choose either addition (Add Feature) or multiplication (Mult Feature) or both can be included in a language. Since these features are also dependent on

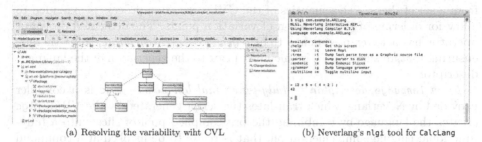

(a) Resolving the variability wiht CVL   (b) Neverlang's nlgi tool for CalcLang

Fig. 4. Example usage of the toolchain provided by CVL and Neverlang

numbers, additional constraints are shown below the legend as predicate logic statements. Including associativity in the language requires that parenthesis is also included shown as a mandatory child of feature *Associativity*. Finally *implementations feature* represents alternatives in terms of the associativity implementations. The rationale for building a VAM from a dependency graph, provides a mechanism to ensure that dependencies are included and conflicts are avoided. Also when the pool of slices needs to be maintained the variability model provides an indication of what the impact could potentially be. The current implementation merely provides the dependency graph, and it is left as a manual process to completely define the VAM. In future work we intend to provide additional facilities to cope with such a task.

5 From Variability Modeling to Language Implementation

The *domain expert* would select a set of features in order to derive a desired language variant. In this section we provide details on how the process is automated in order to obtain a fully-functional language by selecting a set of features.

From VAM to Resolution Model. The Resolution model (RM) contains a set of choices defined as *Choice Resolutions* which corresponds to the features found in the VAM. In addition the RM respects the constraints defined by the VAM. In the implementation, we automatically generate a resolution model according to the VAM and its constraints (`cardinalities`, `isImpliedByParent`, `DefaultResolution`, ...). The domain expert can select or reject a feature by changing the choice resolution decisions and in the implementation a graphical tool is provided depicted in Fig. 4(a).

From a resolution model to a language description. The mapping between the features in the VAM and the Neverlang slices is defined in the CVL variability realization model (VRM). The VRM takes as input a RM which effectively contains the selected set of features. An *object existence variation point* (Sect. 2.2) is used to include or reject a slice. An *opaque variation point* (OVP) is a black box variation point whose behaviour is defined with an action language. In our CVL implementation, we currently support OVPs defined in Groovy3, in Javascript or in Kermeta [16]. Using the OVP we define a dedicated derivation operator. This operator implements the semantics to generate a Neverlang language descriptor from a set of slices. The semantics of the CVL derivation process is extended to allow for ordering of the execution of variation points. The dedicated derivator operator has a lower precedence than *object existence variation point* thereby ensuring that all slices would be included prior to the generation of the language descriptor.

From **language** *descriptor to fully-functional language.* nlgc is a compiler provided by Neverlang, which translates the script generated by the VRM. nlgc creates the language by combining the pre-compiled pool of slices into a fully-functional language implementation, that is ready to be invoked at a command prompt with an input source file. The nlg tool can be invoked with the language name to start a minimal non-interactive interpreter that executes a program from a file input. Likewise, the nlgi tool starts an interactive interpreter that executes user-input programs shown in Fig. 4(b). An additional process or step is required in order to implement the variability model. However the benefit is that we have an explicit model of the relations between features of the set of languages. These features are also explicitly mapped to the slices in the VRM. These models can be exploited when the pool of slices need to be modified or new slices need to be introduced. In addition the resolution model provides a usable interface for the domain expert, who can immediately benefit by selecting a set of features and generating a desired fully-functional language. Which he/she can immediately test and use interactively or in batch mode, thereby allowing the domain expert to become completely *autonomous*.

6   Case Study: Family of Statemachines

Statemachines represented by statechart diagrams are typically used to model behavior. Over the years different implementations of statecharts have emerged, ranging from UML statechart diagrams, Harel's statechart and their object-oriented versions (implemented in Rhapsody). These implementations exhibit syntactic and semantic variations. In Crane *et al.* [7] a categorization is provided, highlighting the effects of such variations and the challenges in transforming from one implementation to another. Consider for example the pseudostate *fork* which would split an incoming transition into two or more transitions. In the case of classic statecharts simultaneous triggers/events can be handled; thus, in the *fork* implementation in the classic statechart the incoming and outgoing transitions support a trigger, shown in Listing 5(a) as evt1, evt2 and evt3. In UML or Rhapsody, when an event arrives, the machine must complete the processing of such an event prior to accepting a new event known as *run-to-completion* (RTC) events. Using the statechart fork implementation in UML or Rhapsody statecharts would result in an ill-formed statechart, as they do not handle simultaneous events. In Listing 5(b) the UML implementation is shown: in this case we have removed the triggers on the outgoing transitions, which makes it compliant with UML as outgoing fork transitions may contain labels or actions. However this implementation would still remain ill-formed for Rhapsody, as the fork is simply a split which is shown in Listing 5(c). In the next section a pool of slices in Neverlang is defined to support the fork implementations in the different statechart

```
statechart Classic {
  State: S1; State: S2; State: S3;
  State<Fork> : F1;
  Transition: T1 <S1,F> Trigger[evt1];
  ForkTransition: T2 <F,S2> Trigger[evt2] Effect[act1];
  ForkTransition: T3 <F,S3> Trigger[evt3] Effect[act2];
}
```

(a) Harel statechart

```
statechart UML {
  State: S1; State: S2; State: S3;
  State<Fork> : F1;
  Transition: T1 <S1,F> Trigger[e];
  ForkTransition: T2 <F,S2> Effect[act1];
  ForkTransition: T3 <F,S3> Effect[act2];
}
```

```
statechart Rhapsody {
  State: S1; State: S2; State: S3;
  State<Fork> : F1;
  Transition: T1 <S1,F> Trigger[e];
  ForkTransition: T2 <F,S2>;
  ForkTransition: T3 <F,S3>;
}
```

(b) UML statechart   (c) Rhapsody statechart

Listing 5. Textual DSL notation for the three kinds of Statecharts

Table 1. Statechart implementations in relation to the slices

Implementation	Neverlang Slices						
	Statechart	State	Transition	ForkState	ForkTriggerEffect	ForkEffect	ForkNoActions
Classic statechart	✓	✓	✓	✓	✓		
UML statechart	✓	✓	✓	✓		✓	
Rhapsody statechart	✓	✓	✓	✓			✓

variants. The CVL derivation engine and the Neverlang implementation can be downloaded from their websites[3].

Step ① Implementation of the language components. In Neverlang, such a set of statecharts in Neverlang is defined as a set of slices. In the implementation, the statemachine supports simple states, transitions and the pseudostate fork. For the sake of brevity we merely show the syntax of the slices which would support the variations in the different fork implementation. The slice ForkState represents the fork pseudostate, which is supported by the module ForkState. The slice includes the syntax for State<Fork>, and includes the keyword ForkTransitions, that introduces the outgoing transition in a fork. Finally the nonterminal ForkActions represents the possible actions that can be used in the fork transitions. Depending on the implementation the syntax for the ForkActions would vary, as shown in Listing 6. Similarly, states and transitions are implemented as slices. Using these slices we can implement each variation.

Classic State Chart. In this case we need to combine a set of slices that supports a simple statechart with a fork state, supporting simultaneous triggers. In this case we would combine the slices for the simple statemachines together with the slices ForkState and SimultaneousTriggers.

---

[3] people.irisa.fr/Suresh.Pillay/vm-neverlang and neverlang.di.unimi.it respectively.

```
module ForkState {
    reference syntax {
        StateDef ← Fork;
        Fork ← "State<Fork>" ":" Identifier;
        TransitionDef ← "ForkTransition" "<" Identifier "," Identifier ">" "(" ForkActions ")";
}}
slice ForkState {
    concrete syntax from ForkState
    module ForkState with role evaluation
}

module ForkTriggerEffect {
    reference syntax { ForkActions ← Trigger "," Effect; }
}
slice ClassicForkActions {
    concrete syntax from SimultaneousTriggers
    module ForkTriggerEffect with role evaluation
}

module ForkEffect {
    reference syntax { ForkActions ← Effect; }
}
slice UMLForkActions {
    concrete syntax from RTCEffects
    module ForkEffect with role evaluation
}

module ForkNoActions {
    reference syntax { ForkActions ← ""; }
}
slice RhapsodyForkActions {
    concrete syntax from RTCEffects
    module ForkNoActions with role evaluation
}
```

Listing 6. Slices and modules to support variations in Fork implementations

UML. In the case of UML we would use `ForkState` and `RTCEffects` as this kind of graph supports RTC with labels or effects.

Rhapsody. Finally, in the case of Rhapsody we can simply use the simple statemachine together with `ForkState` as there is no need for fork triggers or effects.

A summary of the possible choices is represented in Table 1. Using such a set of slices we can support the different language variants, and the right combination of slices is automatically generated according to the domain expert choices.

Step ② Dependency Graph. Figure 5 shows the dependency graph extracted from our pool of slices. Included in the pool is the states, transitions and the pseudostate fork slices that would support the different implementations (classic, UML and Rhapsody). The language developer and the domain expert can clearly see that they have slices for representing states and transitions. The transition supports three options `Trigger`, `Guard` and `Effect`. Using this set of slices, it is also possible to represent a feature to support the pseudostate fork. In addition, the different fork implementations reflect that the variability model should cater for the variations to support classic and UML statechart.

Partitioning the slices in features correctly requires domain knowledge. The major difference between the three implementations, with respect to the fork pseudostate, is a result of how events are handled, either simultaneously or RTC.

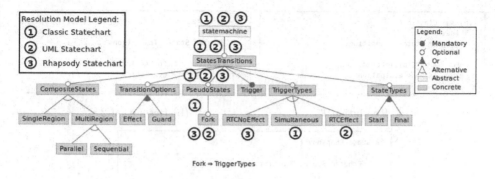

Fig. 6. Variability Model for a Family of Statemachines

From the dependency graph, it is only possible to infer that each implementation supports the different ForkActions. However only leveraging on the knowledge of the domain expert, it is possible to decide to model this against the type of event system adopted by the given implementation. The dependency graph provides some guidance towards reaching a VM, however it still requires human intervention.

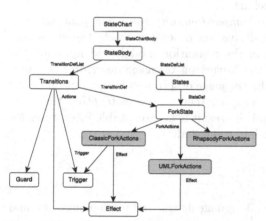

Fig. 5. Dependency graph for a family of statemachines

Step ③ *Variability Model.* Figure 6 shows the VAM for a family of statemachines, and shown in the legend it can be seen that different relations (e.g., *or, alternative*) can be modeled in such a structure. The focus is on the pseudostate fork part of the variability model. It is possible to choose the feature *fork*, which has a dependency on feature *TriggerTypes*. Feature *TriggerTypes* imposes an alternative between the *ForkActions* being either simultaneous triggers or RTC triggers with or without effects. Knowing how triggers/events are handled provides sufficient information to implement the fork correctly. The VRM allows us to map the features to the slices. These variation points are defined as *Object Existence* variation points in the VRM, which links the *feature* to the slice or slices which would implement the requirements of such a *feature* in the language. In Table 2 the mapping between the features and the slices supporting the fork variations is listed.

Step ④ *Resolution of the variability by selecting a set of features.* CVL provides a resolution model which is used to select or reject a feature. In Fig. 6 we show three sets of possible feature selections. The numbers 1, 2 or 3 represent the

```
language Classic {
  slices
    Program States Transitions
        ...
    ForkState ClassicForkActions
  roles syntax < evaluation
}
```

```
language UMLSC {
  slices
    Program States Transitions
        ...
    ForkState UMLForkActions
  roles syntax < evaluation
}
```

(a) Resolution 1   (b) Resolution 2

```
language Rhapsody {
  slices
    Program States Transitions
        ...
    ForkState RhapsodyForkActions
  roles syntax < evaluation
}
```

(c) Resolution 3

Listing 7. Neverlang **language** descriptor for (a) classic, (b) UML, (c) Rhapsody statechart

configurations for the different implementations. Using such a set of selections a desired statechart can be defined, 1 represents a classic statechart, 2 a UML statechart and 3 the Rhapsody statechart.

Step ⑤ and ⑥ Derivation of the composition directives and generation of the language implementation. The derivation process extracts the slices corresponding to the features selected in the resolution model, and applying the *opaque variation point* (see Sect. 5) the Neverlang **language** descriptor is generated. In Listing 7(a), 7(b) and 7(c) the **language** descriptors for resolution model 1, 2 and 3 is shown. The Neverlang compiler then composes together the slices that the **language** descriptor lists, and the result is an executable interpreter for the language variation that the user had requested.

7   Related Work

This section discusses related work on language design and implementation, and variability modelling approaches.

As we noticed in Section 3, the approach that we presented is general and can be applied even to other frameworks that support modular language

Table 2. Mapping Features to Neverlang Slices

Feature	Slice	Feature	Slice
Statemachine	Program	Fork	ForkState
StatesTransitions	States,Transition	Simultaneous	ClassicForkActions
Guard	Guard	RTCEffect	UMLForkActions
Effect	Effect	RTCNoEffect	RhapsodyForkActions

implementation. Several authors explored the problem of modular language design (e.g., [10,13,23,24]). For example, LISA [13] and Silver [23] integrate specific formal grammar-based language specifications supporting the automatic generation of various language-based tools (e.g., compiler or analysis tools). One practical obstacle to their adoption is a perceived difficulty to adopt specific grammar-based language specifications, and the relative gap with the development environments used daily by software engineers. JastAdd [10] combines traditional use of higher order attribute grammars with object-orientation and simple aspect-orientation (static introduction) to get better modularity mechanism. To develop our work, we chose Neverlang [2,3], a language development framework that focuses on modularity, and reuse of pre-compiled language modules for the JVM. In Neverlang, language components are compiled into regular JVM classes that can be instantiated and inspected using a public API, to retrieve rich, structured information. This is a departure from the classic source-based analysis found in other tools, and makes Neverlang's core easier to plug into a higher-level workflow, such as the one we described.

Many formalisms were proposed in the past decade for variability modeling. For an exhaustive overview, we refer the readers to the literature reviews that gathered variability modeling approaches [5,14,20,21]. All formalisms for variability modeling could be used following the approach we introduce in this paper. In our case, we use the choice diagram proposed by CVL, very similar to an attributed feature diagram with cardinalities.

Several works [8,12,22,28] have highlighted the benefits of coupling language development and variability approaches. Czarnecki [8] has shown that DSL implementation can be improved by employing feature description languages. Van Deursen *et al.* has proved the usefulness of their text-based Feature Description Language (FDL) using DSL design as a case study. In the work by Haugen *et al.* [12], the authors show how the features of DSLs such as the ARI language (an expression language similar to the one described in Sect. 4), the Train Control Language (TCL) and even UML can be modeled to design possible variations using CVL. White *et al.* [28] have demonstrated how feature modeling can be used to improve reusability of features among distinct, but related languages.

More recently, some work has applied variability management to language implementation. MontiCore [17] modularizes a language by extension. Extension is achieved by inheritance and language embedding. In [4] a variability model is used to manage language variants. In our case we focus on the reuse of existing components, not only varying a base language. Langems [27] uses role-based metamodeling in order to support modularization of languages. The roles play the role of interfaces and bind to concrete classes for the implementation. The concrete syntax is bound to the abstract syntax. A more restrictive version of EMFText is used to try to avoid ambiguities when the grammar is composed following the abstract syntax. However it is left to the language developer to avoid such conflicts. In [18] a family of languages is decomposed in terms of their features. The grammar is constructed using SDF and the semantics is implemented using re-writing rules in Stratego. However, in this work the focus is on the language developer, who implements the language components without any assistance from a domain expert. Their approach is bottom up, but they do not start from a set of pre-defined component, but rather they componentize an already existing language and develop the variability model to support it. Therefore, the relations between language components are imposed by the developers as they implement them, while in our approach we rely on the existing dependencies of the language components to direct the implementation of the VM using an intermediate artifact (the *dependency graph*, Sect. 4).

8   Conclusions and Future Work

Applying variability modeling techniques to language development bridges the gap between the language developer and the domain expert. The variability model not only represents the features of the domain and their relations, but also the relation between the features and the language components. In our approach, the dependency graph provides a useful artifact to direct the construction of the variability model. This graph helps the domain expert to recognize possible language variants, and assists the language developer in finding possible shortcomings in the implementation of language components. A dedicated derivation operator is provided to allow the domain expert to automatically generate a language implementation, supported by an interactive interpreter, without further assistance from the language developer. In future work we intend to provide a set of operators to fully-automate the implementation of a variability model from a pool of existing language components.

References

1. Aho, A.V., Sethi, R., Ullman, J.D.: Compilers: Principles, Techniques, and Tools. Addison Wesley, Reading (1986)
2. Cazzola, W.: Domain-Specific Languages in Few Steps: The Neverlang Approach. In: Gschwind, T., De Paoli, F., Gruhn, V., Book, M. (eds.) SC 2012. LNCS, vol. 7306, pp. 162–177. Springer, Heidelberg (2012)
3. Cazzola, W., Vacchi, E.: Neverlang 2: Componentised Language Development for the JVM. In: Binder, W., Bodden, E., Löwe, W. (eds.) SC 2013. LNCS, vol. 8088, pp. 17–32. Springer, Heidelberg (2013)
4. Cengarle, M.V., Grönniger, H., Rumpe, B.: Variability within Modeling Language Definitions. In: Schürr, A., Selic, B. (eds.) MODELS 2009. LNCS, vol. 5795, pp. 670–684. Springer, Heidelberg (2009)
5. Chen, L., Ali Babar, M.: A Systematic Review of Evaluation of Variability Management Approaches in Software Product Lines. Journal of Information and Software Technology 53(4), 344–362 (2011)
6. Clements, P., Northrop, L.: Software Product Lines: Practices and Patterns. Addison-Wesley (August 2001)
7. Crane, M.L., Dingel, J.: UML Vs. Classical Vs. RHAPSODY Statecharts: Not All Models Are Created Equal. In: Briand, L.C., Williams, C. (eds.) MoDELS 2005. LNCS, vol. 3713, pp. 97–112. Springer, Heidelberg (2005)

8. Czarnecki, K.: Overview of Generative Software Development. In: Banâtre, J.-P., Fradet, P., Giavitto, J.-L., Michel, O. (eds.) UPP 2004. LNCS, vol. 3566, pp. 326–341. Springer, Heidelberg (2005)
9. Efftinge, S., Völter, M.: Oaw xText: A Framework for Textual DSLs. In: Proc. of the EclipseCon Summit Europe 2006 (ESE 2006), Esslingen, Germany (November 2006)
10. Ekman, T., Hedin, G.: The JastAdd System — Modular Extensible Compiler Construction. Science of Computer Programming 69(1-3), 14–26 (2007)
11. Fleurey, F., Haugen, Ø., Møller-Pedersen, B., Svendsen, A., Zhang, X.: Standardizing Variability – Challenges and Solutions. In: Ober, I., Ober, I. (eds.) SDL 2011. LNCS, vol. 7083, pp. 233–246. Springer, Heidelberg (2011)
12. Haugen, Ø., Møller-Pedersen, B., Oldevik, J., Olsen, G.K., Svendsen, A.: Adding Standardized Variability to Domain Specific Languages. In: Proc. of SPLC 2008, Limerick, Ireland, pp. 139–148. IEEE (September 2008)
13. Henriques, P.R., Varanda Pereira, M.J., Mernik, M., Lenič, M., Gray, J., Wu, H.: Automatic Generation of Language-Based Tools Using the LISA System. IEE Proc.— Software 152(2), 54–69 (2005)
14. Hubaux, A., Classen, A., Mendonça, M., Heymans, P.: A Preliminary Review on the Application of Feature Diagrams in Practice. In: Proc. of VaMoS 2010, Linz, Austria, pp. 53–59. Universität Duisburg-Essen (January 2010)
15. Hutchinson, J., Whittle, J., Rouncefield, M., Kristoffersen, S.: Empirical assessment of MDE in industry. In: Proc. of ICSE 2011, Hawaii, pp. 471–480 (May 2011)
16. Jézéquel, J.-M., Barais, O., Fleurey, F.: Model Driven Language Engineering with Kermeta. In: Fernandes, J.M., Lämmel, R., Visser, J., Saraiva, J. (eds.) GTTSE 2009. LNCS, vol. 6491, pp. 201–221. Springer, Heidelberg (2011)
17. Krahn, H., Rumpe, B., Völkel, S.: MontiCore: A Framework for Compositional Development of Domain Specific Languages. International Journal on Software Tools for Technology Transfer 12(5), 353–372 (2010)
18. Liebig, J., Daniel, R., Apel, S.: Feature-Oriented Language Families: A Case Study. In: Proc. of VaMoS 2013, Pisa, Italy. ACM (January 2013)
19. Mernik, M., Žumer, V.: Incremental Programming Language Development. Computer Languages, Systems and Structures 31(1), 1–16 (2005)
20. Pohl, K., Metzger, A.: Variability Management in Software Product Line Engineering. In: Proc. of ICSE 2006, Shanghai, China, pp. 1049–1050. ACM (May 2006)
21. Rabiser, R., Grünbacher, P., Dhungana, D.: Requirements for Product Derivation Support: Results from a Systematic Literature Review and an Expert Survey. Journal of Information and Software Technology 52(3), 324–346 (2010)
22. van Deursen, A., Klint, P.: Domain-Specific Language Design Requires Feature Descriptions. Journal of Computing and Information Technolog 10(1), 1–17 (2002)
23. Van Wyk, E., Bodin, D., Gao, J., Krishnan, L.: Silver: An Extensible Attribute Grammar System. Science of Computer Programming 75(1-2), 39–54 (2010)
24. Van Wyk, E., de Moor, O., Backhouse, K., Kwiatkowski, P.: Forwarding in Attribute Grammars for Modular Language Design. In: Nigel Horspool, R. (ed.) CC 2002. LNCS, vol. 2304, pp. 128–142. Springer, Heidelberg (2002)
25. Völter, M., Pech, V.: Language Modularity with the MPS Language Workbench. In: Proc. of ICSE 2012, Zürich, Switzerland, pp. 1449–1450. IEEE (June 2012)
26. P.: Wadler. The expression problem. Java-Genericity Mailing List (1998)
27. Wende, C., Thieme, N., Zschaler, S.: A Role-Based Approach towards Modular Language Engineering. In: van den Brand, M., Gašević, D., Gray, J. (eds.) SLE 2009. LNCS, vol. 5969, pp. 254–273. Springer, Heidelberg (2010)
28. White, J., Hill, J.H., Gray, J., Tambe, S., Gokhale, A.S., Schmidt, D.C.: Improving Domain-Specific Language Reuse with Software Product Line Techniques. IEEE Software 26(4), 47–53 (2009)

Software Evolution
to Domain-Specific Languages

Stefan Fehrenbach[1], Sebastian Erdweg[2], and Klaus Ostermann[1]

[1] University of Marburg, Germany
[2] TU Darmstadt, Germany

Abstract. Domain-specific languages (DSLs) can improve software
maintainability due to less verbose syntax, avoidance of boilerplate code,
more accurate static analysis, and domain-specific tool support. However,
most existing applications cannot capitalise on these benefits because
they were not designed to use DSLs, and rewriting large existing applications from scratch is infeasible. We propose a process for evolving existing
software to use embedded DSLs based on modular definitions and applications of syntactic sugar as provided by the extensible programming
language SugarJ. Our process is incremental along two dimensions: A
developer can add support for another DSL as library, and a developer
can refactor more code to use the syntax, static analysis, and tooling of a
DSL. Importantly, the application remains executable at all times and no
complete rewrite is necessary. We evaluate our process by incrementally
evolving the Java Pet Store and a deliberately small part of the Eclipse
IDE to use language support for field-accessors, JPQL, XML, and XML
Schema. To help maintainers to locate Java code that would benefit from
using DSLs, we developed a tool that analyses the definition of a DSL to
derive patterns of Java code that could be represented with a high-level
abstraction of the DSL instead.

1 Introduction

Language-oriented programming [6,14,29] is the idea of decomposing large software systems into *domain-specific languages* (DSLs), which narrow the gap between the requirements of a software system and the implementation of these
requirements. Examples of DSLs are state machines for behavioural modelling,
XML for data serialisation, SQL for data querying, or BNF for parsing. According to language-oriented programming, a software system should be written in
a combination of many existing DSLs and, possibly, newly designed languages
specific to the application.

The ultimate goal of language-oriented programming is increased productivity and reduced maintenance effort [17]. DSLs address software maintenance
from four directions. First, domain-specific *syntax* reduces the representational
boilerplate associated with encoding domain concerns using regular programming constructs and allows developers to focus on the domain-relevant aspects
of a program. Thus, DSLs improve understandability and modifiability of source
code.

M. Erwig, R.F. Paige, and E. Van Wyk (Eds.): SLE 2013, LNCS 8225, pp. 96–116, 2013.
© Springer International Publishing Switzerland 2013

Second, domain-specific *static analysis* enables the encoding of domain invariants and compile-time detection of any violation. In contrast, if encoding domain concerns with regular programming constructs, errors are often only detectable through testing. For example, when dynamically generating an XML document through concatenating strings or calling an API such as JDOM, the validity of generated XML documents cannot be statically guaranteed. An explicit representation of the XML DSL enables a static analysis to guarantee that an XML document adheres to its schema in all possible runs of a program. In case of a violation, an analysis issues domain-specific error messages, which help programmers understand the problem. Consequently, DSLs improve the static safety and understandability of source code.

Third, domain-specific *semantics* abstract over recurring patterns found in the encoding of domain concerns, such as the application of string concatenation or calling conventions. For example, a domain-specific language can ensure proper escaping of injected code to prevent injection attacks, not relying on manually called escape commands. Since a DSL specifies the semantics of domain concerns once and for all, changes to the behaviour of domain concerns are local to the DSL definition and separate from DSL programs. This separation of concerns improves modularity and modifiability of source code, and allows programmers to focus on domain-relevant aspects instead of their encoding.

Fourth, domain-specific *editor support* communicates domain knowledge from the language implementation to developers: from domain-specific syntax highlighting to domain-specific content completion, editor support improves understandability and modifiability of source code. In summary, DSLs improve the quality and thereby the maintainability of source code.

Today, the vast majority of software systems are not designed in a language-oriented fashion. Instead, the long-standing success of C, C++ and Java has led to large procedural and object-oriented systems. The closest many of these applications come to making the best use of DSLs, is containing strings of SQL for database queries. As a consequence, those applications do not benefit from the maintenance advantages that DSLs provide.

Unfortunately, existing literature on language-oriented programming does not address existing code bases, but promotes methodologies useful only when employing them in the original design of an application [29,6,2]. Therefore, to introduce DSLs and their benefits into an existing application, we would have to rewrite the application from scratch. However, rewriting large parts of realistic applications all at once is infeasible [20].

Evolving existing Java applications to use DSLs requires a process that allows for adding new language extensions and incrementally adapting existing code to use them. In regular Java programming, libraries fulfil this role. On the one hand, they extend the standard library with new classes. On the other hand, they need to be imported explicitly in every file they are used, allowing existing code to coexist unmodified with new libraries and adapted code.

Embedded DSLs [17] allow for incremental introduction of DSLs using libraries. However, their flexibility and power is limited by the general flexibility of the host language. The rigid syntax, type system and missing metaprogramming facilities of Java limit the applicability of embedded DSLs [21]. In particular, the maintenance benefits of concrete syntax with domain-specific editor support and advanced static analyses like XML Schema validation cannot be achieved with embedded DSLs.

We propose a solution for evolving existing code bases to DSLs based on library-based embedding of DSLs in extensible host languages. A sufficiently extensible host language avoids the disadvantages of regular embedding (rigid syntax, no domain-specific editors or static analyses) by extending the corresponding facilities of the host language. Specifically, we use our previous work on the Java-based extensible programming language SugarJ [8,10,11], which permits DSLs as libraries of Java that can define domain-specific syntax, semantics, analyses and editor support. In our prior work on SugarJ, we focused on the expressiveness that SugarJ provides in building new applications, much like other works on language-oriented programming. For this paper, we extended the SugarJ compiler to handle code bases that consist of standard Java source files and *jar* files, and SugarJ source files that employ language extensions. Thus, the SugarJ compiler supports a mix of unchanged legacy code and adapted code that uses DSLs.

To assist maintainers in identifying code locations in an existing software systems where a DSL is applicable, we developed a tool that analyses a DSL definition to extract a pattern that represents the code generated from the DSL. We match this pattern against existing source code to find potential application sites for the DSL and to guide maintainers.

In summary, this work makes the following contributions:

- We explain why incremental introduction of DSLs is a necessary requirement for the evolution of software systems to DSLs. We show that SugarJ is a framework that supports incremental introduction of DSLs. In particular, SugarJ organises DSLs as syntactic sugar in libraries and thereby supports adding DSLs and adapting applications incrementally.
- To demonstrate the applicability of incremental introduction of DSLs in extensible languages, we reengineered Sun Microsystem's Java Pet Store, which "is the reference application for building Ajax web applications on Java Enterprise Edition 5 platform" [22]. We incrementally introduced four DSLs into the Java Pet Store, in particular, for field-accessor generation, data serialisation (XML), static XML Schema validation (which reveals what appears to be a bug in the Java Pet Store), and data querying (JPQL). The Java Pet Store remains executable throughout our maintenance activity.[1]
- We demonstrate the scalability of incremental introduction of DSLs to large applications with a partially reengineered Eclipse code base.
- We extended SugarJ to support a mix of SugarJ and original Java files to facilitate its use in a large code base. Previously, one would have had to change every Java file to a SugarJ file before using SugarJ.

---

[1] The source code of the reengineered Java Pet Store including all DSL definitions is available at http://sugarj.org.

- We explore SugarJ's self-adaptable DSL mechanism to support the reuse of existing language definitions that occur, for example, in documentation.
- We developed an analysis that finds source-code locations in a software system at which a given DSL is applicable.

2   Problem Statement and Proposed Solution

Domain-specific languages have several advantages over general-purpose languages that influence the maintainability of programs [2,23,14,17,29]: They reduce syntactic boilerplate, enforce domain invariants, abstract over recurring patterns, and provide domain-specific tool support. Unfortunately, the majority of applications is not written in a language-oriented fashion, despite these well-known benefits for software maintenance. Their size makes rewriting them from scratch infeasible [20]. Nevertheless, these applications are still evolving and important to their users.

Since software evolution is inherently incremental, any process for introducing DSLs into existing applications must support incremental application along two dimensions: (i) adding support for more DSLs and (ii) converting more code to use the supported DSLs.

2.1   First Dimension: Support More DSLs

Most applications need to deal with multiple domains, and over their lifetime the number of different domains is only going to increase. For applications developed in a language-oriented fashion, specific domains that would benefit from DSLs are identified in an initial design phase. For existing applications, potential domains for improvement through DSLs are usually only identified while performing a maintenance task. For example, imagine a programmer needs to understand and modify the code shown in Figure 1(a) because the serialisation format requires change. This code is a literate excerpt from the Java Pet Store [22] and serialises an item to its XML representation. It uses string literals to represent the static parts of the resulting XML document, that is, element names such as "<item>" or "<price>". Dynamic values like the item's ID are concatenated in between the static element names and the document tree as a whole is assembled through calls to a StringBuffer's append method.

This representation of XML documents as strings is common but has several weaknesses. First, it is hard to read due to string concatenation, character escaping, and the interspersion with calls to append. All of this is boilerplate code that has nothing to do with XML. Second, the structure of the code does not reflect the structure of the XML document. For example, to add an element currency as child of price, we have to disassemble the string describing price to inject the currency at the right place. Third, the encoding is unsafe because domain invariants are not enforced. For example, XML documents must be well-formed, that is, start and end tags must match. In the string encoding, this invariant is not explicitly stated, let alone statically enforced. An ill-formed document will

```
private String handleItem(String targetId) {
   Item i = cf.getItem(targetId);
   StringBuffer sb = new StringBuffer();
   sb.append("<item>\n");
   sb.append("  <id>" + i.getItemID()
             + "</id>\n");
   sb.append("  <price>" +
     NumberFormat.getCurrencyInstance(Locale.US)
                 .format(i.getPrice())
             + "</price>\n");
   [...]
   sb.append("</item>\n");
   return sb.toString();
}
```

```
import sugar.Xml;

private String handleItem(String targetId) {
   Item i = cf.getItem(targetId);
   return <item>
             <id>${i.getItemID()}</id>
             <price>${NumberFormat
                .getCurrencyInstance(Locale.US)
                .format(i.getPrice())}
             </price>
             [...]
          </item>;
}
```

(a) String-encoded XML document from the Java Pet Store.

(b) Semantically equivalent to (a) but uses XML language support.

Fig. 1. Embedded XML using string embedding and language support

lead to a runtime error. Fourth, string concatenation is semantically unsafe because it allows for injection attacks that can only be prevented by passing each concatenation argument to an escaping function, which is a global refactoring. Fifth, the string encoding inhibits domain-specific tool support such as syntax colouring; all strings appear the same. For all these reasons, data serialisation with string-encoded XML is a problem domain in the Java Pet Store. There are many others, we address some of them in Section 4.

A DSL-based solution to the problems with XML could look like the code in Figure 1 (b). In general, a DSL should avoid string embedding and instead provide a higher level of abstraction. A more abstract representation that actually represents the inherent structure of the domain also allows for static analysis and dynamic checking. In XML we want to reject documents that do not adhere to a given schema. In XML and SQL we want to prevent the injection of unsafe Java runtime values into documents or queries.

Note that it is not sufficient to merely identify all domains for a single application and use a language that supports them all. For example, Scala has built-in support for XML which addresses some of the problems mentioned, but consider a new browser-based front-end that requires JSON serialisation. Continuous software evolution requires adding language support for new domains.

2.2   Second Dimension: Convert More Code

Having language support for domain-specific problems is nice. Unfortunately, existing code does not immediately benefit from such support. It has to be converted from the original domain-unspecific encoding (such as string concatenation) to the DSL (using the domain-specific syntax). However, it is undesirable to require maintainers to locate all possible application sites of a DSL at once.

Likely, the maintainer of a code base would want to convert code to an existing DSL at an opportune moment. For example, there might be a bug report claiming a missing element in an XML document that so far went unnoticed. To address this issue, a maintainer might first refactor the relevant code to use an XML DSL with static validation against XML Schema, and then fix the resulting XML Schema compile-time error.

We need some modularity guarantees to achieve both dimensions of incrementality. Adding language support for a domain should not affect any existing code immediately. Reengineered code should activate language extensions explicitly. Also, reengineered code needs to coexist, or even better cooperate and coevolve, with unchanged code.

2.3 Proposed Solution

We propose the following process for the evolution of an application to use DSLs. First, choose a problem domain. Existing DSLs with weak embeddings, such string embeddings of XML or SQL, are an obvious target but there are likely other domains that can be improved with language support. Second, design and implement a DSL as *syntactic sugar*, enriched with domain-specific static analysis and tool support, in SugarJ [11]. Third, use SugarJ to *modularly activate* the new DSL in some source files and incrementally rewrite code to use the DSL.

To scale our process to the evolution of large existing applications, we designed it around syntactic sugar that is modularly activated. Syntactic sugar is semantically transparent. Therefore, we achieve cooperation and coevolution of old and new or reengineered code, because both remain semantically compatible and thus interoperable at all times. This allows for incremental rewriting of large code bases.

Modular activation of DSLs means that DSLs must be activated explicitly per source file. Conversely, a DSL definition can only affect those source files that activate the DSL. This is important for software evolution of large code bases, because it gives maintainers the guarantee that DSLs have no effect for files left unchanged by the maintainer. This way a single project can use multiple conflicting DSLs in different parts of the code, which would be impossible in tools that require global activation of DSLs. Moreover, in contrast to global build-script based DSL activation, modular activation of DSLs retains the incremental compilation character of Java, so that only affected source files require recompilation.

We propose to use SugarJ [11] for the implementation of DSLs as syntactic sugar that is modularly activated. SugarJ organises DSL definitions in regular Java libraries so that regular Java import statements activate DSLs in a source file. It is easy to add new DSLs as libraries, and it is even possible to use multiple DSLs in a single file by importing all corresponding libraries.

3 Background: DSL Development with SugarJ

SugarJ is an extensible programming language based on Java that supports library-based language extension [8,11]. SugarJ and its IDE [10] make all aspects of Java extensible: syntax, semantics, static analysis and tool support. In

```
package sugar;

import sugar.XmlSyntax;
import org.sugarj.languages.Java;
import concretesyntax.Java;

public extension Xml {
  context-free syntax
    Document -> JavaExpr {cons("XMLExpr")}
    "$" "{" JavaExpr "}" -> Element {cons("JavaEscape")}

  desugarings
    desugar-xml
  rules
    desugar-xml :
      XMLExpr(doc) ->
      |[ String.format(~xml-string, ~java-escapes) ]|
      where <xml-to-string> doc => xml-string;
            <xml-java-escapes> doc => java-escapes
    xml-to-string : ...
    xml-java-escapes : ...

    constraint-error :
      Element(lname, attrs, content, rname) ->
      [(lname, "element start and end tag need to coincide"),
       (rname, "element start and end tag need to coincide")]
      where <not(equal)> (lname, rname)

  colorer
    ElemName : blue (recursive)
    AttrName : darkorange (recursive)
    AttValue : darkred (recursive)
    CharData : black (recursive)
  folding
    Element
}
```

Fig. 2. Definition of the XML DSL in SugarJ

particular, SugarJ's extensibility is useful for embedding DSLs into Java [11]. In this section, we exemplify the development of a DSL with SugarJ using the XML DSL presented in the previous section.

SugarJ organises language extensions as regular Java libraries that, instead of a Java class or interface, define an extension with custom syntax, static analyses and tool support for a DSL. Figure 2 displays the SugarJ language extension that defines the XML DSL. Figure 1 (b) already showed how to use this extension, namely by importing the corresponding library sugar.Xml. SugarJ supports extension compositions [9], which is triggered by importing multiple extensions into a single scope. We explain the implementation of the different language aspects in turn.

Syntax. To define extended syntax, we employ the grammar formalism SDF [25] and write productions in a **context-free syntax** block. For example, the first production in Figure 2 declares that any valid syntax for the Document nonterminal is also valid syntax for the JavaExpr nonterminal. The second production enables writing a Java expression wrapped in $\{...\} in place of an XML element. Additionally, a production specifies the name of the corresponding node in the abstract syntax tree with a cons annotation.

We use the JavaExpr, Document and Element nonterminals to integrate XML syntax into Java syntax and Java expressions into XML. These nonterminals stem from the Java and XML base grammars defined in org.sugarj.languages.Java and sugar.XmlSyntax. We use import statements to bring the Java and XML syntax definitions into scope of the sugar.Xml library.

Semantics. The semantics of a DSL is given as a transformation from the extended syntax into SugarJ base syntax. In line with the notion of syntactic sugar, we call such a transformation a desugaring and use the Stratego transformation system [28] to implement it. A DSL defines transformations in a **rules** block. Each transformation has a name (before the colon), pattern-matches an abstract syntax tree (left-hand side of arrow) and produces another abstract syntax tree (right-hand side of arrow). Since the generation of abstract syntax trees is tedious for complex languages such as Java, we use concrete Java syntax within I[...]I for code generation [26]. To this end, we import the concretesyntax.Java library, which extends Stratego with support for concrete syntax [11].

The desugaring for XML matches on an XMLExpr node and transforms it into Java code that calls the String.format method of the standard Java library. Within concrete syntax, the ~ symbol allows us to escape back to Stratego code. In particular, we compute the arguments of String.format by applying the xml-to-string and xml-java-escapes transformations (definitions elided for brevity) to the embedded XML document. The former transformation pretty-prints the XML document and inserts a placeholder %s for each escape to Java. The latter transformation extracts the Java code from the XML document. Importantly, the string that results from the generated String.format invocation is semantically equivalent to the original string encoding; the DSL only provides syntactic sugar.

Static analysis. SugarJ represents static analyses as program transformations that transform the program under analysis into a list of errors. To this end, a programmer can define a special-purpose transformation named constraint-error. For XML, we have defined a static analysis that matches on XML elements and produces errors in case the start and end tag of the element differ. Accordingly, this static analysis verifies the domain invariant that embedded XML documents are well-formed. In case of an ill-formed document, our IDE uses the syntax tree that amends an error message (lname and rname in our example) to determine the position for displaying the domain-specific error message to the user.

Editor services. Finally, our SugarJ IDE enables domain-specific editor services such as syntax colouring, code folding, code completion, or reference resolution [10]. We provide an Eclipse plugin based on the Spoofax language workbench [18]. In Figure 2, we have defined XML-specific syntax colouring and code folding.

In summary, we defined the XML DSL from the previous section in SugarJ as a language extension: We provide a syntactic extension to integrate the domain syntax and semantics, use program transformations to encode domain invariants as static analyses and leverage the extensibility of our IDE plugin to support domain-specific editor services.

4   Evolution to DSLs in Practice

We conducted two case studies to gather experience with applicability of DSLs in existing software systems and to confirm the applicability of SugarJ for incrementally evolving an existing software system to use DSLs.

Our first case study is based on the Java Pet Store [22], an interactive web application developed by Sun Microsystems as a reference application for Java Enterprise Edition. Following the process proposed in Section 2.3, we incrementally identified four problem domains and designed and implemented corresponding DSLs in SugarJ. We used these DSLs to incrementally reengineer part of the Java Pet Store to improve subsequent maintainability; the code remained executable at all times. This case study shows that SugarJ enables evolution of an existing software system to use DSLs.

As a second case study, we reengineered a deliberately small part of the implementation of the Eclipse IDE to use DSLs. For the Eclipse IDE, it is essential to retain modular reasoning, which allows developers to assume local effects for local changes. In particular, a local improvement through a DSL should not affect other code. In SugarJ this is witnessed through Java-style separate compilation: Source files that are compiled separately cannot influence each others meanings. This case study shows that SugarJ enables local and small-scale evolution in large software systems.

4.1   Java Pet Store

First Iteration: XML As an interactive web application, the Java Pet Store makes use of Ajax technologies for data exchange between server and browser. In particular, it uses string-embedded XML for data serialisation. In Section 2.3, we already discussed the drawbacks of the string embedding of XML and designed a DSL, which integrates XML documents into Java more directly as syntactic sugar. The implementation of the XML DSL as a SugarJ library was illustrated in the previous section.

Within the Java Pet Store, use of XML is cross-cutting multiple classes and methods. In total, we reengineered 59 lines of legacy XML code to use the XML DSL. Our syntactic integration of XML and static analysis for well-formedness did not reveal any bugs in the original code, but increase confidence in its correctness.

Second Iteration: Field-Accessor Declarations

The second problem domain we identified are the getter and setter methods that clutter the code of the Java Pet Store, following the *JavaBeans* standard. The resulting amount of accessor methods is considerable and all of it is dispensable boilerplate. For example, consider the class definition shown in Figure 3 (a), which is a literate but shortened excerpt from the Java Pet Store. This class models a product with five properties: a product ID, an associated category ID, a name, a description and a URL to some image. These properties are private fields behind public getters and setters, and initialised by a constructor. The only nontrivial aspect of this class is the @Id annotation on the productID getter,

```
public class Product {
  private String productID, categoryID, [...];
  public Product(String productID,
                 String categoryID, [...])
  { this.productID = productID;
    this.categoryID = categoryID; }
  public String getCategoryID(){return categoryID;}
  public void setCategoryID(String categoryID)
  { this.categoryID = categoryID; }
  @Id
  public String getProductID(){return productID;}
  public void setProductID(String productID)
  { this.productID = productID; }
  [...]
}
```

```
import sugar.Accessors;

public class Product {
  private String productID {set; con};
  private String categoryID, description,
                 name, imageURL {get; set; con};

  @Id
  public String getProductID() {
    return productID;
  }
}
```

(a) Java class definition from the Java
Pet Store.

(b) Reengineered class definition using
the field-accessor DSL.

Fig. 3. The original Product class has 5 properties with corresponding accessors

which marks it as a primary key for the object-relational mapping employed by
the Java Pet Store.

The main problem with this class definition is the large amount of boilerplate code. Modern Java IDEs try to address this by automatically generating
getters and setters. However, this is insufficient because it does not solve the
maintainability issue. For a maintainer who reads such code, it is not immediately clear what fields are truly private, publicly readable, or publicly readable
and writable. Furthermore, actual application-specific code that deviates from
the standard template for accessors is masked by the large amount of boilerplate
code. For instance, the actually interesting @Id annotation of the productID getter is easily overlooked in a file consisting mostly of getter, setter, and constructor
boilerplate code.

Based on these observations, we designed a DSL that abstracts over the boilerplate associated with field accessors. In our DSL, programmers declare the
desired accessors instead of implementing them. The unshortened reengineered
class definition from Figure 3 (a) is shown in Figure 3 (b). The syntax is inspired
by C#'s syntax for properties. The annotations **get** and **set** declare getters and
setters respectively, **con** makes a field part of the initialising constructor. To
achieve compatibility with existing code, the new annotations desugar to usual
field-accessor method implementations. Therefore, we were able to apply the
field-accessor DSL locally in some files without affecting others.

Third Iteration: JPQL The third problem domain we identified in the Java Pet
Store is its string-based embedding of the Java Persistence Query Language
(JPQL) used to query databases. Figure 4 shows a JPQL query from the Java Pet
Store. The string encoding of JPQL shares many of the problems we previously
saw in the XML example, but its handling of dynamic data is much better:
Within a query, a programmer can use a parameter (identifier prefixed by a colon)
in place of a regular JPQL expression. After processing the query string into a
Query object, the programmer calls the query's setParameter method to provide
dynamic data for the parameters in the query. Thus, when used appropriately,

```
public List<Item> getItemsByCategoryByRadiusVLH(...) {
    Query query = em.createQuery(
        "SELECT i " +
        "FROM Item i, Product p " +
        "WHERE i.productID=p.productID " +
        "AND p.categoryID = :categoryID " +
        "AND((i.address.latitude BETWEEN :fromLatitude AND :toLatitude) " +
        "AND (i.address.longitude BETWEEN :fromLongitude AND :toLongitude )) " +
        "AND i.disabled = 0 " +
        "ORDER BY i.name");
    query.setParameter("categoryID",catID);
    query.setParameter("fromLatitude",fromLat);
    query.setParameter("toLatitude",toLat);
    query.setParameter("fromLongitude",fromLong);
    query.setParameter("toLongitude",toLong);
    return query.getResultList();
}
```

Fig. 4. JPQL query from the Java Pet Store

```
import sugar.JPQL;

public List<Item> getItemsByCategoryByRadiusVLH(...) {
    Query query =
      em.SELECT i
          FROM Item i, Product p
          WHERE i.productID = p.productID
            AND p.categoryID = :catID
            AND i.address.latitude BETWEEN :fromLat AND :toLat
            AND i.address.longitude BETWEEN :fromLong AND :toLong
            AND i.disabled = 0
          ORDER BY i.name;
      return query.getResultList();
}
```

Fig. 5. JPQL query from Figure 4 using the JPQL DSL

JPQL prevents injection attacks. However, there is not guarantee because string concatenation in queries is still possible.

Even though the JPQL string embedding avoids some of the problems the XML string embedding has, it is still problematic: Queries are not parsed and thus may contain syntax errors; query parameters are dynamically resolved, can be misspelled or forgotten; a query may illegally refer to a tuple variable not bound within the **FROM** clause; there is no editor support for queries; string concatenation is necessary to break long lines.

To address these problems, we implemented language support for JPQL as a DSL in SugarJ. A reengineered version of the previous query is shown in Figure 5. The reengineered query is statically syntax checked and does not require string concatenation to break lines. Instead of indirectly injecting dynamic data into a query, parameters (colon-prefixed identifiers) in our DSL refer to Java variables directly. Hence, a programmer needs to manage fewer namespaces and cannot forget calling setParameter. Our DSL desugars the reengineered query into the original one and generates all setParameter calls to relate the query namespace to the Java namespace.

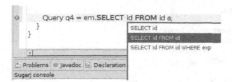

Fig. 6. Content completion for JPQL in Eclipse

To guarantee that queries do not refer to unbound tuple variables, we implemented a domain-specific static analysis. It traverses a query and checks that every variable in the query is bound within the query's **FROM** clause. Since SugarJ executes the analysis before desugaring at compile time, we statically ensure that no unbound variables can occur at runtime for reengineered queries and we provide domain-specific error messages in case of the developer made a mistake. Furthermore, the JPQL DSL includes editor support in the form of syntax highlighting, code folding and JPQL-specific code completion, as illustrated in Figure 6.

The BNF Meta-DSL. JPQL has many features and therefore its definition is rather involved. For example, a grammar provided by Oracle as part of the documentation of the JavaEE consists of 217 lines.[2] Unfortunately, Oracle employed a different grammar formalism than the one used in SugarJ. Therefore, we cannot directly reuse their grammar. However, DSLs in SugarJ are self-applicable, that is, a programmer can implement a DSL for writing other DSLs. We call this kind of DSL a *meta-DSL*. In particular, the dialect of BNF used by Oracle can be implemented as a meta-DSL in SugarJ, which enables us to reuse Orcale's grammar for the JPQL DSL.

Technically, the BNF meta-DSL is implemented as syntactic sugar on top of SugarJ's standard grammar formalism SDF. Accordingly, a BNF grammar desugars into an SDF grammar. It is even possible to mix BNF productions and SDF productions within a single library, which we have done to integrate JPQL into Java and Java variables as parameters into JPQL. The BNF meta-DSL can be reused with only minor changes in other contexts where BNF and its extensions are used for describing languages. For example, using a similar meta-DSL it would be possible to reuse the host of available ANTLR grammars.

We believe that self-applicability is particularly useful in the context of maintaining legacy applications, where it is more likely that a language description already exists in some form, for example, as documentation. Our embedding of BNF into SugarJ to reuse Oracle's JPQL grammar gives some evidence that a self-applicable DSL mechanism is not only theoretically desirable but indeed useful in practice.

Fourth Iteration: XML Schema After implementing and using the DSLs described above, we returned to the XML DSL described in Section 3 and added

---

[2] http://docs.oracle.com/javaee/5/tutorial/doc/bnbuf.html

```
import xml.schema.XmlSchema;

public xmlschema FileUploadResponseSchema {
  <xsd:schema targetNamespace="jpsfur">
  <xsd:element name="response" type="FileUploadResponse"/>
  <xsd:complexType name="FileUploadResponse">
    <xsd:sequence>
      <xsd:element name="message" type="string" />
[...]
```

Fig. 7. Excerpt of the XML Schema definition for file upload responses

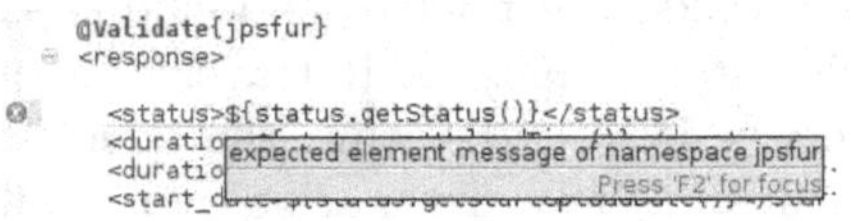

Fig. 8. Element <response> is missing its first child <message>

support for XML Schema validation. XML Schema allows programmers to specify the structure required from XML documents. We have built language support for XML Schema in SugarJ that performs XML Schema validation at compile time as a domain-specific analysis.

For example, Figure 7 shows an XML schema for file upload responses as they occur in the Java Pet Store. A programmer activates XML Schema validation for an XML document by annotating the document with **@Validate**{namespace}, where an XML schema for namespace must have been locally imported. In addition to the standard XML well-formedness checks, XML schema validation guarantees the presence or absence of tags and attributes and thus protects against incomplete data and misspelling, as seen in Figure 8. Static validation of schemas is particularly valuable if the serialisation format is to be changed. After changing the schema accordingly, compile-time error messages will point the maintainer to code that still needs to be adapted to the new format.

We defined three schemas by reverse engineering the XML documents that are actually used in the Java Pet Store. Thanks to these schemas we discovered several inconsistencies regarding XML documents in the Java Pet Store. First, the handling of composed words in tags is inconsistent: The XML response to a file upload contains both camelCase and under_score element names. Second, the XML encoding for categories contains redundant information, as seen below.

```
@Validate{jpsc}
<category>
  <id>${c.getCategoryID()}</id>
  <cat-id>${c.getCategoryID()}</cat-id>
  [...]
```

The elements id and cat-id always contain the same value. Third, there is an inconsistency between two instances of the XML representation of items, either using an element prod-id or product-id. The Java Pet Store front-end does not seem to use the generated XML documents and instead uses a JSON representation of essentially the same data. We believe these inconsistencies are previously undiscovered bugs in the Java Pet Store.

4.2 Eclipse

With the Eclipse case study, our goal is not to show new and interesting DSLs for IDE development. Rather, we aim to answer the question whether our approach of incremental introduction of DSLs and incremental adaption of code scales to very large code bases. We chose Eclipse because of the availability of its source code, its stability in terms of the plugin API combined with active development, and most importantly its size. According to a comparison of Eclipse's and Netbeans' code sizes in 2011 [15], Eclipse comprises 10 million lines of source code and is organised into just under 500 top-level folders which roughly equate to subprojects.

For this case study we checked out an arbitrary selection of 194 top-level folders from Eclipse's CVS. Out of these 194, we chose two top-level folders, namely org.eclipse.core.variables and org.eclipse.jdt.core.tests.model, for reengineering using the Accessors and XML language extensions, respectively. Together, these two folders contain 523342 lines of code in Java files.

Specifically for this case study, we extended the SugarJ compiler to support using a mix of Java and SugarJ source files. Previously, it would only accept SugarJ files. This was not a problem in the Java Pet Store, since every Java file is also a valid SugarJ file, except for the file extension. Nevertheless, renaming all source files of a project is contrary to our goal of incremental introduction.

We reused the existing DSL implementation code almost unchanged. The XML library was missing syntax rules for XML comments in its grammar, which required two new lines of SDF code. In Eclipse, field names are by convention prefixed with an f. We adapted the Accessors library's desugaring transformation to respect this convention.

4.3 Results

We reflect on the goals and expectations described at the beginning of this section. In summary, we expected easy identification of problem domains, need for language composition, and reuse of language libraries.

We successfully used SugarJ's syntactic-sugar based DSLs to improve the code quality of the Java Pet Store considerably. In Figure 9, we show an overview of the extent of code affected by our reengineering efforts. The main purpose of the Accessors DSL was eliminating boilerplate code and its application exceeded our expectations. It saves almost 10% of the Java back-end code of the Java Pet Store. The XML and JPQL DSLs improve static safety with domain-specific analyses, readability with domain-specific syntax and editing experience with domain-specific editor support. Their application sometimes increases and sometimes reduces code size. We attribute increases to easier line breaks for more natural code formatting in the respective DSL and reductions to more concise integration of dynamic data into static DSL code. In the table we report lines

DSL	Usage in Java Pet Store	New DSL imple-mentation code	Reused code
Accessors	avoid 506 lines of boilerplate in 13 classes	65 LoC	0 LoC
XML	check 59 lines in 7 XML documents	35 LoC	160 LoC
XML Schema	validate 51 lines in 5 XML documents using 3 schemas	20 LoC	713 LoC
JPQL	check 29 lines in 14 JPQL queries	101 LoC	140 LoC
BNF	reuse parts of the JPQL grammar	131 LoC	0 LoC

DSL	Usage in Eclipse	New DSL imple-mentation code	Reused code
Accessors	avoid 86 lines of boilerplate in 3 classes	3 LoC	62 LoC
XML	check 449 lines in 56 XML documents	2 LoC	192 LoC

Fig. 9. Reengineering results and DSL implementation effort

of reengineered code. By manual inspection of the Java Pet Store's source code, we found ample opportunity for improvement with DSLs. Besides the DSLs we implemented, there are further areas that would benefit from language support.

During this case study we often switched between implementing DSLs and adapting code to use them. We also did not always adapt all code at once. This shows that incrementality works as desired in both dimensions: making new DSLs available and adapting parts of the code base to use them. In the reengineered Java Pet Store, there is one file that uses two DSLs at once: the JPQL and Accessors DSLs. These DSLs compose without conflict. This confirms our expectation that language composability is needed in practice and that different DSLs rarely interact unintentionally.

The implementation effort for new DSLs was reduced by reusing existing code. Figure 9 lists the lines of new language-library-implementation code that were written as part of this case study and the amount of code that was reused from previous work. SDF's declarative nature makes new syntax definition easy. For example, there is no need to know details about parsing algorithms to avoid left-recursive productions. We believe that the focus on syntactic sugar especially helps reducing the complexity of implementing DSLs. All new desugaring transformations employed in this case study are straightforward. Nonetheless, reusability is essential in reducing the costs of DSL implementation. The XML DSL reuses the previously existing XML syntax. The XML Schema DSL is almost entirely reused from previous work [11] since it only operates on the abstract XML syntax. The XML schemas themselves are implemented in 42 lines of code on average. All DSLs implemented in this case study are immediately reusable for future reengineering efforts.

With 10 million lines of source code, Eclipse is a huge project. Any process for improving its maintainability has to be incremental, because programmers cannot be expected to change all of Eclipse's code at once. For this case study, we introduced two language extensions in two different parts of the code base. At this point, only a small part of Eclipse has been reengineered to use these DSLs. There are more opportunities to use both the XML and Accessors DSLs, and

```
String.format(                   Alt(                             public void id:{set ? ?*} (? id:?) {
   Alt( "< ? ? > ? </ ? >",        ?,                                this.id:? = id:?;
      " \"?\" ",                    ?.createQuery("?"),            }
      "%s",                         ?.createQuery("?")             public Alt(Boolean,?)
      ""),                            .setParameter("?", id:?)     Alt(id:{is ? ?*}, id:{get ? ?*}) () {
   new Object[] { ?* }           )                                   return id:?;
)                                                                 }
```

| (a) Pattern for XML. | (b) Pattern for JPQL. | (c) Pattern for field-accessors. |

Fig. 10. Automatically extracted patterns for code that can be refactored to use a DSL

others. Nevertheless, the whole project is fully functional, because the nature of syntactic sugar makes changes necessary only local to its point of use. Thus, the Eclipse case study shows that our process is incrementally applicable and therefore scales to large code bases.

5   Automatically Locating Code for DSL Usage

Finding existing code that can be refactored to use a DSL is not always easy, especially when working with a large code base. To assist maintainers, we developed a tool called *sweet tooth*[3] that takes the definition of a SugarJ DSL and a Java source file as input, and computes a ranked list of source locations at which the DSL could be used.

Sweet tooth first analyses the DSL definition to derive a syntax-tree pattern for the generated code, and then matches this pattern against a Java source file. We illustrate the patterns derived for the DSLs of our case study in Figure 10 (manually transcribed to use concrete Java syntax instead of abstract syntax trees). The question mark ? denotes an unknown subtree, the symbol ?* denotes an unknown list of subtrees. The form Alt(x,...,x) denotes alternatives in the pattern. The annotation id: denotes that the following tree is an identifier.

For example, for the XML DSL (see definition in Figure 2), sweet tooth analysed the recursive-descent XML pretty printer xml-to-string to derive a list of alternative strings that can be produced. The generated code of JPQL calls the createQuery method of a pre-existing entity-manager object on which the method setParameter is called if there is at least one parameter in the JPQL query. Compare this pattern to actual JPQL code from the Java Pet Store in Figure 4. For field-accessors, the desugaring generates setter and getter functions. The name of the setter function id:{set ? ?*} is composed of the string set followed by at least one character ? (for which the desugaring ensures it is upper case), followed by any number of characters ?*. The generated getter function is similar, but, depending on the type of the field, the method gets a different name using either the prefix is or get.

Technically, sweet tooth derives these patterns by extracting the transformation from a SugarJ library, normalising the transformation to a core transformation language [27] for easier analysis, and performing *abstract interpretation*

---
[3] Source code available online: http://github.com/seba--/sweet-tooth

of the core transformation. In our abstract interpreter, we directly represent abstract values as patterns, which thus are the result of abstract interpretation. The abstract interpreter of sweet tooth supports transformations that use conditional constructs (which lead to alternative patterns) and recursion (which is truncated after few steps). Importantly, the pattern derived by sweet tooth is complete in the sense that it captures all programs that can possibly be generated by the transformation. However, sweet tooth is currently limited since we only reimplemented abstract versions of a part of the standard library of core Stratego.

Finally, sweet tooth can match the derived patterns against a concrete Java program. If multiple alternatives of a pattern match the same source location, sweet tooth ranks the matches according to the specificity of the pattern. That is, the more concrete syntax-tree nodes or string snippets a pattern contains, the higher the score of this pattern. A match of a pattern that does not contain any unknown subtrees (e.g., System.out.println()) has score 1, whereas a match of a pattern without any concrete syntax-tree node or string snippet (e.g., Alt(?, ?*)) has score 0. This way a maintainer can efficiently detect those source locations that would benefit most from using the DSL. We have successfully applied sweet tooth to locate code applicable to our DSLs for JPQL and field-accessors.

6   Discussion

The choice of the case to study is an important aspect of a case study with respect to generalisability [13]. With a varied selection of implemented DSLs and the Java Pet Store's status as a research object and reference application, we are confident that the results presented here can be generalised to many other existing applications.

The Accessors DSL shows how simple language extensions can address the specific needs of an application. Similar extensions are imaginable for BigDecimal support in banking applications or parallel looping constructs [1]. In our case, conciseness was the most obvious benefit. In general, another important benefit is localising design decisions, which makes them easy to change and reason about.

The XML and JPQL DSLs improve code quality: Domain-specific syntax reduces visual boilerplate and improves readability; domain-specific static analysis helps to avoid errors; domain-specific semantics isolate code patterns and design decisions; domain-specific editor support aids editing and understanding code.

Domain-specific semantics are of particular interest with respect to safety. For example, Java's semantics prevent access to arbitrary program memory by using array indices that exceed an array's length. This language feature makes Java programs immune to one source of exploits that C programs are frequently vulnerable to because a programmer forgot to restrict access themselves. Sugar libraries provide the tools for programmers to enforce similar restrictions in DSLs. For example, the JPQL DSL prevents injection attacks because queries are proper syntactic entities and query parameters are inserted by the sanitising setParameter method instead of string concatenation. Using sweet tooth, maintainers can find all code that not yet uses the securer DSL and thereby enforce security across the entire code base.

A common criticism of domain-specific languages is that they are hard to design and implement [23]. Our case study cannot confirm this. Since we rely on syntactic sugar, design and implementation of simple DSLs is often reduced to recognising a pattern in existing code, extracting a skeleton of static Java code and filling it with the variable parts. Concrete Java syntax [26] makes this particularly easy. Moreover, most transformations will be easy because the domain semantics are most likely implemented in a traditional class library already, like in the JPQL example.

Our case study demonstrates that it is possible to incrementally introduce DSLs into existing Java applications using SugarJ. New DSLs support can be added at any time and code can be adapted to use it at opportune times. We hope that in the future, adding DSLs and reengineering code to use them will be as common-place as more traditional refactorings are today. This calls for research into DSL-specific code smells and means to guide maintainers in making decisions what kinds of problems are best addressed using DSLs.

To this end, we developed sweet tooth, which identifies code that can be refactored to use a DSL. While our tool already is helpful in locating applicability of DSLs, there are two immediate avenues for improving sweet tooth. First, sweet tooth should not only locate code for DSL usage, but also propose a refactored DSL program. Probably, we won't be able to retain completeness for this kind of automatic program transformation, but have to apply heuristics. Second, when testing DSL applicability, sweet tooth currently applies syntactic matching of the pattern. Often, this is insufficient because semantically equivalent programs written in a different style are not matched. To also match alternative representations, we plan to extend sweet tooth so that it applies semantic matching via equational reasoning when trying to match a program against a pattern.

7   Related Work

Ward and Fowler independently coined the term language-oriented programming for a software design that focuses on DSLs [29,14]. In particular, Ward argues that DSLs improve the maintainability of a software system, mainly due to a reduction in code size. However, like any other work on domain-specific languages that we are aware of, Ward only addresses the design of newly created applications, that is, the use of DSLs must be anticipated from the start. In contrast, we demonstrate the incremental introduction of DSLs into existing applications.

Bennet and Rajlich list language abstraction as one important research direction in their roadmap for software maintenance and evolution [3]. They mention legacy applications as a problem and express some concern about whether software reengineering is a feasible solution. They base this concern partly on Sneed's work [20], which quantifies the cost of reengineering software.

Bianchi et. al. propose an incremental process for reengineering software and argue that it avoids the problems of previous non-incremental approaches [4]. However, their main focus is data migration in the context of a legacy COBOL application. It is not clear how to apply their process to introducing DSLs.

In this work, we employed SugarJ [11,10] to implement and apply DSLs for the following reasons. First, we target existing Java applications and SugarJ is based on Java. Incorporating language based abstractions into applications written in Haskell, Ruby, Scheme, Dylan, C++, and others is possible via embedded DSLs [17,16,5]. Unfortunately, Java has very restricted syntactic options, no metaprogramming and a rather unexpressive type system which makes this approach unsuited for our case. Second, SugarJ implements language extensions as libraries. In contrast to extensible compilers [7,19,24] and language workbenches [18,12] the focus on libraries enables easy extension and modular reasoning about source code. And finally, we are familiar with SugarJ, its strengths and weaknesses, and as our case study shows its support for DSL development is sufficient. A detailed comparison can be found in our previous work [9,8].

8   Conclusion and Future Work

We explored how DSLs can be incrementally introduced into legacy applications to improve maintainability: reduce boilerplate, improve readability, increase static safety through domain-specific analyses, and improve navigation and writing through domain-specific editor support. In this paper, we focused on the technical feasibility of incrementally introducing DSLs into an existing code base without requiring a full rewrite. Our solution is based on introducing high-level language abstractions via semantically transparent syntactic sugar that is modularly activated by library imports.

In future work, we want to explore tool support for introducing DSLs into legacy applications. In particular, we want to answer the following questions: Can we guarantee that a DSL can be introduced into an application conflict-free? Based on sweet tooth, can we reliably detect all application sites for a DSL in a code base? Once we detect a potential application site of a DSL, can we provide an automatic refactoring of the legacy code into code that uses the DSL?

Acknowledgements. We would like to thank Paolo G. Giarrusso, Christian Kästner, and the anonymous reviewers for valuable feedback. This work is supported in part by the European Research Council, grant No. 203099.

References

1. Bachrach, J., Playford, K.: The Java syntactic extender (JSE). In: OOPSLA, pp. 31–42. ACM (2001)
2. Batory, D., Johnson, C., MacDonald, B., von Heeder, D.: Achieving extensibility through product-lines and domain-specific languages: A case study. TOSEM 11(2), 191–214 (2002)

3. Bennett, K.H., Rajlich, V.T.: Software maintenance and evolution: A roadmap. In: FOSE, pp. 73–87. ACM (2000)
4. Bianchi, A., Caivano, D., Marengo, V., Visaggio, G.: Iterative reengineering of legacy systems. Transactions on Software Engineering (TSE) 29(3), 225–241 (2003)
5. Brabrand, C., Schwartzbach, M.I.: Growing languages with metamorphic syntax macros. In: PEPM, pp. 31–40. ACM (2002)
6. Dmitriev, S.: Language oriented programming: The next programming paradigm (2004)
7. Ekman, T., Hedin, G.: The JastAdd extensible Java compiler. In: OOPSLA, pp. 1–18. ACM (2007)
8. Erdweg, S.: Extensible Languages for Flexible and Principled Domain Abstraction. PhD thesis, Philipps-Universiät Marburg (2013)
9. Erdweg, S., Giarrusso, P.G., Rendel, T.: Language composition untangled. In: LDTA, pp. 7:1–7:8. ACM (2012)
10. Erdweg, S., Kats, L.C.L., Rendel, T., Kästner, C., Ostermann, K., Visser, E.: Growing a language environment with editor libraries. In: GPCE, pp. 167–176. ACM (2011)
11. Erdweg, S., Rendel, T., Kästner, C., Ostermann, K.: SugarJ: Library-based syntactic language extensibility. In: OOPSLA, pp. 391–406. ACM (2011)
12. Erdweg, S., et al.: The state of the art in language workbenches. In: Erwig, M., Paige, R.F., Van Wyk, E. (eds.) SLE 2013. LNCS, vol. 8225, pp. 197–217. Springer, Heidelberg (2013)
13. Flyvbjerg, B.: Five misunderstandings about case-study research. Qualitative Inquiry, 219–245 (2006)
14. Fowler, M.: Language workbenches: The killer-app for domain specific languages (2005), http://martinfowler.com/articles/languageWorkbench.html
15. Germán, D.M., Davies, J.: Apples vs. oranges?: An exploration of the challenges of comparing the source code of two software systems. In: MSR, pp. 246–249. IEEE (2011)
16. Gil, J., Lenz, K.: Simple and safe SQL queries with C++ templates. Science of Computer Programming 75(7), 573–595 (2010)
17. Hudak, P.: Modular domain specific languages and tools. In: Proceedings of International Conference on Software Reuse (ICSR), pp. 134–142. IEEE (1998)
18. Kats, L.C.L., Visser, E.: The Spoofax language workbench: Rules for declarative specification of languages and IDEs. In: OOPSLA, pp. 444–463. ACM (2010)
19. Nystrom, N., Clarkson, M.R., Myers, A.C.: Polyglot: An extensible compiler framework for java. In: Hedin, G. (ed.) CC 2003. LNCS, vol. 2622, pp. 138–152. Springer, Heidelberg (2003)
20. Sneed, H.M.: Planning the reengineering of legacy systems. IEEE Software 12(1), 24–34 (1995)
21. Steele Jr., G.L.: Growing a language. Higher-Order and Symbolic Computation 12(3), 221–236 (1999)
22. Sun Microsystems. Java Pet Store (2002), http://www.oracle.com/technetwork/java/index-136650.html (accessed November 14, 2012)
23. van Deursen, A., Klint, P.: Little languages: Little maintenance? Software Maintenance 10(2), 75–92 (1998)
24. Van Wyk, E., Krishnan, L., Bodin, D., Schwerdfeger, A.: Attribute grammar-based language extensions for java. In: Ernst, E. (ed.) ECOOP 2007. LNCS, vol. 4609, pp. 575–599. Springer, Heidelberg (2007)

25. Visser, E.: Syntax Definition for Language Prototyping. PhD thesis, University of Amsterdam (1997)
26. Visser, E.: Meta-programming with concrete object syntax. In: Batory, D., Blum, A., Taha, W. (eds.) GPCE 2002. LNCS, vol. 2487, pp. 299–315. Springer, Heidelberg (2002)
27. Visser, E., Benaissa, Z.-E.-A.: A core language for rewriting. Electronic Notes in Theoretical Computer Science 15, 422–441 (1998)
28. Visser, E., Benaissa, Z.-E.-A., Tolmach, A.P.: Building program optimizers with rewriting strategies. In: ICFP, pp. 13–26. ACM (1998)
29. Ward, M.P.: Language-oriented programming. Software – Concepts and Tools 15, 147–161 (1995)

Micropatterns in Grammars

Vadim Zaytsev

Software Analysis & Transformation Team (SWAT),
Centrum Wiskunde & Informatica (CWI), The Netherlands
vadim@grammarware.net

Abstract. Micropatterns and nanopatterns have been previously demonstrated to be useful techniques for object-oriented program comprehension. In this paper, we use a similar approach for identifying structurally similar fragments in grammars in a broad sense (contracts for commitment to structure), in particular parser specifications, metamodels and data models. Grammatical micropatterns bridge the gap between grammar metrics, which are easy to implement but hard to assign meaning to, and language design guidelines, which are inherently meaningful as stemming from current software language engineering practice but considerably harder to formalise.

1 Introduction

Micropatterns are mechanically recognisable pieces of design that reside on a significantly lower level than design patterns, hence being closer to the implementation than to an abstract domain model, while still representing design steps and decisions [14]. They have been proposed in 2005 by Gil and Maman as a method of comparing software systems programmed in the object-oriented paradigm — the original paper concerned Java as the base language for its experiments, but the presence of similar classification methods for considerably different languages like Smalltalk [26] leads us to believe that the approach is applicable to any object-oriented programming language at the least. In this paper, we investigate whether micropatterns can be detected in grammars in a broad sense and become a useful tool for grammarware.

Grammatical micropatterns are similar in many aspects to the OOP micropatterns, in particular in (cf. [14, §4]):

- **Recognisability.** For any micropattern, we can construct an algorithm that recognises if the given grammar matches its condition. Our approach toward this property is straightforward: we implement all micropattern recognisers in Rascal [21] and expose them at the public open source code repository [42]. Unlike design patterns, no two micropatterns share the same structure.
- **Purposefulness.** Even though there are infinitely many possible micropatterns ("name starts with A", "number of terminals is a prime number", "uses nonterminals in alphabetical order", etc), we collect only those which *intent* can be reverse engineered and clearly identified ("name starts with

M. Erwig, R.F. Paige, and E. Van Wyk (Eds.): SLE 2013, LNCS 8225, pp. 117–136, 2013.

uppercase" — because the metalanguage demands it; "no terminals used" — because it defines abstract syntax; etc).

- **Prevalence** is the fraction of nonterminals that satisfy the micropattern condition. It is a property that strengthens the purposefulness, showing whether the condition happens in practice and if so, how often. We tend to ignore micropatterns with zero prevalence or with prevalence greater than 50 %, with a few notable exceptions.
- **Simplicity** is a requirement that stops us from concocting overcomplicated micropatterns like "uses a nonterminal that is not used in the rest of the grammar", even if they are useful. Mostly we pursued two forms of micropattern conditions: ones that can be formulated with a single pattern matching clause, and ones that assert one simple condition over all its children. (When inspecting the implementation, one can notice multiline definitions as well, which are only made so for readability and maintainability purposes, and utilise advanced Rascal techniques like pattern-driven dispatch).
- **Scope.** Each micropattern concerns one nonterminal symbol, and can be automatically identified based on the production rules of that nonterminal symbol. It does not have to bear any information about how this nonterminal is used or what the real intent was behind its design.
- **Empirical evidence.** The micropatterns from our catalogue are validated against a corpus of grammars in a broad sense. Even if the corpus is not curated and not balanced to yield statistically meaningful results, we have a stronger claim of evidential usage of micropatterns in the practice of grammarware engineering than any software language design patterns or guidelines might have (simply because their claims rely on manual harvest).

However, there are some notable differences in our work:

- **Usability of isolated micropatterns.** One of the distinctive feature of micropatterns versus design patterns and implementation patterns pointed out by Gil and Maman in [14, §4.2], was that a single micropattern is not useful on its own, and only the entire catalogue is a worthy instrument. However, as we found out, isolated micropatterns (single ones and small subsets of the catalogue) can also be useful indicators of grammar properties (e.g., the grammar defines an abstract syntax, if all its nonterminals satisfy the AbstractSyntax micropattern), triggers for grammar mutations (e.g., perform deyaccification for all nonterminals with YaccifiedX micropatterns), assertions of technical compatibility, etc.
- **Coverage** is measured as a combined prevalence of a thematic group of micropatterns (it is not equal to the sum of their prevalences, since micropatterns in most groups are not mutually exclusive) and computed separately for each group. For OOP micropatterns, coverage was calculated for the whole catalogue, but per system: we do it the other way around, to emphasize conceptual gaps between groups and to avoid issues with a non-curated corpus. For groups with low coverage we also report on *frequency*, which is prevalence within the group.

- **Grammar mining** is much less popular than software mining and data mining [39], and hence the fact that we derived our catalogue by mining a repository of versatile grammars, is a unique contribution in that sense.

2   Grammar Corpus

Grammar Zoo is a repository that aims at collecting grammars in a broad sense (per [20]) from various sources: abstract and concrete, large and small, typical and peculiar [39]. Technically and historically, it is a part of the larger initiative titled Software Language Processing Suite (SLPS) and available as a publicly accessible repository online since 2008 [42]. Beside the corpus of grammars, the SLPS project also includes experiments and tools relating to the activities of grammar extraction, recovery, documentation, convergence, maintenance, deployment, transformation, mutation, migration, testing, etc. Contrary to prior practice, we will also not include pointers to individual sources per grammar in this paper, plainly due to sheer impossibility of delivering over 500 bibliographic references. An interested reader is referred to the frontend of the Zoo at http://slps.github.io/zoo to inspect any of the grammars or all of them, together with the metadata concerning their authors, original publication dates, extraction and recovery methods and other details properly structured and presented there.

The corpus mainly consists of the following kinds of grammars:

- grammars extracted from parser specifications composed by students
  - for example, 32 TESCOL grammars were used in [9] for grammar testing
- grammars extracted from language documents
  - ISO, ECMA, W3C, OMG, OASIS and other standardisation bodies publish standards [41] that are possible to process with automated notation-parametric grammar recovery methods [37]
- grammars extracted from document schemata
  - for example, XML Schema and RELAX NG definitions of MathML, SVG, DocBook are available and ready to be researched and compared to definitions of the same languages with other technologies like Ecore
- grammars extracted from metamodels
  - the entire Atlantic Metamodel Zoo[1] is imported into Grammar Zoo by reusing their Ecore metamodel variants with our extractor
- grammars extracted from concrete syntax specs
  - for example, the ASF+SDF Meta-Environment and the TXL framework have their own repositories for concrete grammars, which have been extracted and added to the Grammar Zoo
- grammars extracted from DSL grammars in a versioning system (BGF)
  - various DSLs were spawned by the SLPS itself during its development: they are not interesting on their own, but the presence of many versions of the same grammar is a rare treasure; for example, there are 35 versions available of the unified format for language documents from [41].

---

[1] AtlantEcore Zoo: http://www.emn.fr/z-info/atlanmod/index.php/Ecore.

533 grammars present in the Grammar Zoo[2] make it biggest collection of grammars in a broad sense; the grammars are obtained from heterogeneous sources; they are all properly documented, attributed to their creators and annotated with the data available about their extraction process — the combination of these three factors may set the Zoo apart from its competitors [39], yet it does not make it perfect. Even though Grammar Zoo is the largest of its kind, it does not have enough content to claim any kind of balance between different technologies, grammar sizes, quality levels, etc.

We could not emphasize strong enough that empirical investigation is not the primary contribution of this paper. All presented evidence about prevalence of proposed micropatterns serves as a mere demonstration that they indeed occur in practice. Our grammar corpus consists of as many grammars as we could secure, obtained by different means from heterogeneous sources, and we calculate prevalence and coverage as an estimate of ever encountering the same micropatterns in other real life grammars, not as a prediction of the probability of that. At this point, it is not yet feasible to construct a representative versatile corpus of grammars. However, this effort is an ongoing work.

3   Grammatical Micropatterns

The process of obtaining the micropatterns catalogue is identical to the one undertaken by Gil and Maman [14], and we will spare the space on its details. In short, all possible combinations of metaconstructs were considered and tried on a corpus of grammars; those with no matches were either abandoned or kept purely for symmetrical considerations; the intent behind each of them was manually investigated, leading to naming a micropattern properly; and finally the named micropattern was connected to its context by pointing out key publications related to it.

3.1   Metasyntax

It has been shown before [36] that many metalanguages existing for context-free grammars, commonly referred to as BNF dialects or "Extended Backus-Naur Forms"[3], can be specified by a small set of indicators for their metasymbols, which correspond both to the "grammar for grammars" and to human-perceived aspects like "do we quote terminals in this notation?" or "how do we write down multiple production rules for one nonterminal?".

For every feature of the internal representation of a grammar in a broad sense, we define a ContainsX micropattern, where X is that feature:

---

[2] Counted at the day of paper submission: the actual website may contain more.

[3] By "the EBNF", people usually mean the most influential extended variant of BNF, proposed in 1977 by Wirth [34] as a part of his work on Wirth Syntax Notation. However, almost each of the metalanguages used in language documentation ever since, uses its own concrete notation, which sometimes differs even in expressivity from Wirth's proposal — see [36] for more details.

Table 1. Metasyntax micropatterns

Category	Pattern	Matches	Prevalence
Metasyntax	ContainsEpsilon	4,185	10.20%
	ContainsFailure	69	0.17%
	ContainsUniversal	825	2.01%
	ContainsString	1,889	4.60%
	ContainsInteger	343	0.84%
	ContainsOptional	6,554	15.97%
	ContainsPlus	4,586	11.18%
	ContainsStar	3,080	7.51%
	ContainsSepListPlus	55	0.13%
	ContainsSepListStar	142	0.35%
	ContainsDisjunction	2,804	6.83%
	ContainsSelectors	17,328	42.22%
	ContainsLabels	132	0.32%
	ContainsSequence	19,447	47.39%
	AbstractSyntax	29,299	71.39%
	Total coverage	**36,522**	**89.00%**

– ContainsEpsilon for the empty string metaconstruct (ε, "nothing"),
– ContainsFailure for the empty language metaconstruct (φ, "error"),
– ContainsUniversal for the universal metaconstruct (α, "any symbol")[4],
– ContainsString for a built-in string value,
– ContainsInteger for a built-in integer value,
– ContainsOptional for an optionality metasymbol,
– ContainsPlus for the transitive closure,
– ContainsStar for the Kleene star,
– ContainsSepListPlus for a separator list with one or more elements,
– ContainsSepListStar for a separator list with zero or more elements,
– ContainsDisjunction for inner choice metasymbol,
– ContainsSelectors for named subexpressions,
– ContainsLabels for production labels,
– ContainsSequence for sequential composition metaconstruct.

Furthermore, we add one extra micropattern AbstractSyntax for nonterminals which definitions do not contain terminal symbols — mainly because

---

[4] These three metasymbols may seem confusing, but are commonly needed when representing grammatical knowledge from different technological spaces. ε defines a language with a single empty element: $L(\varepsilon) = \{""\}$, so parsing with it would mean successful parsing of an empty string (or a trivial term), while generating a language from it will immediately and successfully terminate. φ defines an empty language: $L(\varphi) = \varnothing$, which models unconditional failure of parsing and impossibility of generation. Formally, $L(\alpha) = \mathcal{T}$, so parsing with α consumes any input.

investigations of abstract data types and abstract syntax vs. concrete syntax [32] form a valuable subdomain of grammarware research. As can be observed on Table 1, the prevalence of AbstractSyntax is quite high, which can be explained by many Ecore metamodels and XML Schema schemata in our corpus.

3.2   Global Position and Structure

Since the very beginning of grammar research, even when grammars were still considered as structural string rewriting systems and not as commitments to structure, there was a need to denote the initial state for rewriting [5, §4.2]. Such an initial state was quickly agreed to be specified with a *starting symbol*, or a *grammar root* — the nonterminal symbol that initiates the generation, or a root of a parse tree. Not being able to overlook this, we say that a nonterminal exercises the Root micropattern, when it is explicitly marked as a root of its grammar. Contrariwise, we define the Leaf micropattern for nonterminals that do not refer to any other nonterminals — they are the leaves of the nonterminal connectivity graph, not of the parse tree.

In some frameworks, the roots are not specified explicitly: either because such metafunctionality is lacking (such as in pure BNF), or because the information was simply lost during engineering or knowledge extraction. For such cases, found quite often in grammar recovery research, we could speak of the Top micropattern, named after "top sorts" from [23, p.19] and "top nonterminals" from [22, §2.2], which are nonterminals defined by the grammar, but never used. A previously existing heuristic technique in semi-automated interactive grammar adaptation, reported rather reliable, is to establish missing connections to all top nonterminals, until only one non-leaf top remains, and assume it to be the true root [22]. Methods such as this would become much easier to explain in terms of micropatterns and relations between them.

In practical grammarware engineering, grammars are commonly allowed to have multiple starting symbols, while most publications about formal languages use a representation with a single root. The reason behind this is simple: one can always imagine adding another nonterminal that becomes a new starting symbol, defined with a choice of all nonterminals that are the "real" starting symbols. Hence, we define a MultiRoot micropattern for catching such definitions explicitly encoded. Surprisingly, it was not very popular: only one match in the whole Grammar Zoo. However, if we were to investigate an XML-based framework that relied heavily on the fact that each element defined by an XSD is allowed to be the root, then such information can be decided to be propagated by the xsd2bgf grammar extractor, which would then lead to all grammars extracted from XML Schema schemata, to have one MultiRoot nonterminal each. The current implementation of the xsd2bgf grammar extractor leaves the roots unspecified, since it is hardly an intent of every XMLware developer to explicitly rely on such diversity.

Complementary to Top, we propose the Bottom micropattern, which is exhibited by a nonterminal that is used in a grammar but never defined — again, we adopt these terminology from [22,23]. Usually in the same context another

Table 2. Global position micropatterns

Category	Pattern	Matches	Prevalence
Global	Root	563	1.37%
	Leaf	9,467	23.07%
	Top	3,245	7.91%
	MultiRoot	1	0.002%
	Bottom	1,311	3.19%
	Total coverage	**12,459**	**30.36%**
Structure	Disallowed	69	0.17%
	Singleton	29,134	70.99%
	Vertical	3,697	9.01%
	Horizontal	6,043	14.73%
	ZigZag	784	1.91%
	Total coverage	**39,727**	**96.81%**

property of a nonterminal is tested, called "fresh" [24, §3.4], for nonterminals that are not present in the grammar in any way, but this property does not convert well into a micropattern for obvious reasons.

For each nonterminal that is not bottom, there are only four possible ways that it can be defined, and so we make four micropatterns from them: Disallowed (defined by an empty language), Singleton (defined with a single production rule), Vertical (defined with multiple production rules) and Horizontal (defined with one production rule that consist of a top level choice with alternatives). We also introduce a separate ZigZag micropattern for definitions that are both horizontal and vertical (multiple production rules, with at least one of them having a top level choice). These five micropatterns together with Bottom are mutually exclusive and together always cover 100 % of any set of nonterminals, and for the Zoo it can be seen on Table 2. The terms "horizontal" and "vertical" are borrowed from the XBGF grammar transformation framework and publications related to it [25, §4.1], other sources also relate to them as "flat" and "non-flat" [24].

As for the global position micropatterns, unsurprisingly, most of nonterminals do not belong to any of these classes, and this group of micropatterns has a meager total coverage of 30.36 % (Table 2). As an example of how Top and Bottom micropatterns encapsulate grammar quality and design intent, we quote Lämmel and Verhoef [23, p.20]:

> In the ideal situation, there are only a few top sorts, preferably one corresponding to the start symbol of the grammar, and the bottom sorts are exactly the sorts that need to be defined lexically.

In the scope of disciplined grammar transformation [25], a ZigZag nonterminal could also be considered a bad style of grammar engineering, but we have no evidence of what dangers it brings along, only an observation of its surprisingly high prevalence.

Table 3. Sugary micropatterns

Category	Pattern	Matches	Prevalence	Frequency
Sugar	FakeOptional	134	0.33%	10.89%
	FakeSepList	624	1.52%	50.69%
	ExprMidLayer	349	0.85%	28.35%
	ExprLowLayer	39	0.10%	3.17%
	YaccifiedPlusLeft	354	0.86%	28.76%
	YaccifiedPlusRight	6	0.01%	0.49%
	YaccifiedStarLeft	0	0.00%	0.00%
	YaccifiedStarRight	0	0.00%	0.00%
	Total coverage	**1,231**	**3.00%**	

3.3   Metasyntactic Sugar

There are several micropatterns that are conceptually similar to those from the previous section, but without the metafunctionality explicitly present in the metalanguage. When a particular metaconstruct is available in the metalanguage, we can check its use, as we have done in subsection 3.1; when it is not a part of the metalanguage, we can still check if any usual substitute for it, is used. For example, the optionality metasymbol is in fact metasyntactic sugar for "this or nothing" — i.e., a choice with one alternative representing the empty language (ε). We call such explicit encodings FakeOptionals (see Table 3), they mostly indeed found occurring in grammars extracted from technical spaces that lack the optionality metasymbol. Similarly, a FakeSepList micropattern explicitly encodes a separator list, and its prevalence is much higher since there are more metalanguages without separator list metasymbols.

For all metalanguages that do not allow to specify expression priorities explicitly, there exists a commonly used implementation pattern:

```
logical-or-expression ::= logical-and-expression
 | logical-or-expression "||" logical-and-expression ;
logical-and-expression ::= inclusive-or-expression
 | logical-and-expression "&&" inclusive-or-expression ;
              ... (12 layers skipped) ...
primary-expression ::= literal | "this"
 | "(" expression ")" | id-expression ;
                    (ISO/IEC 14882:1998(E) C++)
```

Based on multiple occurrences of such an *implementation pattern* in the Grammar Zoo, we have designed the following two *micropatterns*:

- ExprMidLayer: one alternative is a nonterminal, the others are sequences of a nonterminal, a terminal and another nonterminal;
- ExprLowLayer: one alternative is a sequence of a terminal, a nonterminal and another terminal, where the two terminals form a symmetric bracketing pair, the others are solitary terminals or solitary nonterminals.

As one can see, these micropatterns are defined locally and do not enforce any complicated constraints (e.g., concerning the nonterminal between brackets in ExprLowLayer), which could possibly result in false positives, but satisfies our requirements from section 1.

Similarly, we can look for "yaccified" definitions that emulate repetition meta-symbols with recursive patterns. A yaccified definition [18,22] is named after YACC [17], a compiler compiler, the old versions of which required explicitly defined recursive nonterminals. Instead of writing X ::= Y+ ; one would write:

$$X ::= Y ;$$

$$X ::= X Y ;$$

because in LALR parsers like YACC, left recursion was preferred to right recursion (contrary to recursive descent parsers, which are unable to process left recursion directly at all). The use of metalanguage constructs X+ and X* is technology-agnostic, and the compiler compiler can make its own decisions about the particular way of implementation, and will neither crash nor have to perform any transformations behind the scenes. However, as can be seen from Table 3, many existing grammars contain yaccified definitions, and usually the first step in any project that attempts to reuse such grammars for practical purposes, starts with deyaccification [22,25,35, etc].

3.4   Naming

Research on naming conventions has enjoyed a lot of interest in the scopes of program analysis and comprehension [4] and code refactorings that recommend renaming misspelt, synonymous and inaccurate variable names [29]. Naming conventions have not yet been thoroughly investigated in grammarware engineering, but were noted to be useful to consider as a part of metalanguage for notation-parametric grammar recovery [37] and were used as motivation for some automated grammar mutations [38], usually preceding unparsing a grammar in a specific metalanguage. In the scope of grammar recovery, mismatches like digit vs DIGIT or newline vs NewLine were reported as common in recovering grammars with community-created fragments [35].

Let us distinguish four naming conventions to be recognised by micropatterns, namely: CamelCase (LikeThis), MixedCase (almostTheSame), LowerCase (apparentlyso) and UpperCase (OBVIOUSLY). Given that most of current research on naming conventions in software engineering focuses on tokenisation and disabbreviation, we add one more micropattern called MultiWord. A nonterminal conforms to MultiWord, when its name is either written in camelcase or mixed case and has two or more words; or when its name consists of letter subsequences separated by a space, a dash, a slash, a dot or an underscore, — in other words, when its name can be easily tokenised without any dictionary-based heuristics nor heavy machine learning. Something akin to a SingleWord micropattern would have been useful as well, but we failed to obtain a reasonable definition for it: a single mixed case word name is indistinguishable from a single lower case word;

Table 4. Naming micropatterns

Category	Pattern	Matches	Prevalence
Naming	CamelCase	16704	40.70%
	LowerCase	3323	8.10%
	MixedCase	1706	4.16%
	MultiWord	31816	77.53%
	UpperCase	2073	5.05%
	Total coverage	**40,562**	**98.84%**
Naming, lax	CamelCaseLax	18332	44.67%
	LowerCaseLax	17840	43.47%
	MixedCaseLax	1969	4.80%
	MultiWordLax	32290	78.68%
	UpperCaseLax	2412	5.88%
	Total coverage	**41,038**	**100.00%**

both lower case and upper case names may have no word delimiters; a single word camelcase name could in fact also be a multi word capitalised name; etc.

By looking at the top half of Table 4, one quickly realises that the constraints for naming notations could be formulated in a more relaxed way. The nonterminal `Express_metamodel::Core::GeneralARRAYType` from the EXPRESS metamodel is a nice example of an unclassifiable nonterminal name: it combines four capitalised words, one lowercase and one uppercase one, with three different kinds of concatenation (by an underscore, double colons and an empty separator). Arguably, though, its name can be considered CamelCase, with underscore being a "neutral letter" and word boundaries being either empty or "::". Hence, we define a set of five more lax naming convention micropatterns, that together easily cover the whole corpus by using "neutral letters" (underscores and numbers) and being more tolerant with separators.

In particular, one could notice a remarkably high prevalence of MultiWord micropatterns, both strict and lax. These micropatterns have no directly noticeable use right away, but can become a central part of future research on mining and tokenising nonterminal symbol names in grammars.

3.5 Concrete Syntax

We inherit the term Preterminal from the natural language processing field, where it is used for syntactic categories of the words of the language. Preterminals are the immediate parents of the leaves of the parse tree, and usually define keywords of the language, identifier names, etc, without referring to other nonterminals. Prevalence of the Preterminal micropattern is impressively high in our corpus — 7.92 % — despite the fact that more then half of its grammars have been extracted from metamodels and thus contain few or no terminal symbols at all.

This can be explained by many concrete syntax definitions and parser specifications in the corpus as well — in particular, the common practice in ANTLR is to wrap every terminal symbol in a separate nonterminal with an uppercased name, so the prevalence of the Preterminal micropattern in such grammars can climb up to 46.9 % for big languages (Java 5 grammar by Dieter Habelitz) and up to 71.19 % for small ones (TESCOL grammar 10000).

Mining concrete grammars from the corpus led us to discover several steadily occurring patterns of terminal usage (all subcases of the Preterminal micropattern, reported on Table 5):

- Keyword: defined with one production rule, which right hand side is an alphanumeric word:
  ```
  non_end_of_line_character ::= "character" ;
  ```
  (LNCS 4348, Ada 2005)
  ```
   Retry ::= "retry" ;
  ```
  (ISO/IEC 25436:2006(E) Eiffel)
  ```
  this-access ::= "this" ;
  ```
  (Microsoft C# 3.0)
- Keywords: a horizontal or vertical (recall subsection 3.2) definition with all alternatives being keywords:
  ```
  ConstructorModifier ::= "public" ;
  ConstructorModifier ::= "private" ;
  ConstructorModifier ::= "protected" ;
  ```
  (JLS Second Edition, readable Java grammar)
  ```
  exit_qualifier ::= ("__exit" | "exit__" | "exit" | "__exit__") ;
  ```
  (TXL C Basis Grammar 5.2)
- Operator: defined with one production rule, which right hand side is a strictly non-alphanumeric word:
  ```
  formal_discrete_type_definition ::= "(<>)" ;
  ```
  (Magnus Kempe Ada 95)
  ```
  right-shift-assignment ::= ">>=" ;
  ```
  (Microsoft C# 4.0)
  ```
  empty-statement ::= ";" ;
  ```
  (ECMA-334 C# 1.0)
- Operators: a horizontal or vertical definition with all alternatives being operators:
  ```
  relational_operator ::= ("=" | "/=" | "<" | "<=" | ">" | ">=") ;
  ```
  (Lämmel-Verhoef Ada 95)
  ```
  PostfixOp ::= "++" ;
  PostfixOp ::= "--" ;
  ```
  (JLS Third Edition Java, implementable)
  ```
  equalityOperator ::= ("==" | "!=" | "===" | "!==") ;
  ```
  (Google Dart 0.01)

Table 5. Concrete syntax micropatterns

Category	Pattern	Matches	Prevalence	Frequency
Concrete	Preterminal	3249	7.92%	100.00%
	Keyword	906	2.21%	27.89%
	Keywords	1774	4.32%	54.60%
	Operator	1001	2.44%	30.81%
	Operators	1190	2.90%	36.63%
	OperatorsMixed	110	0.27%	3.39%
	Words	40	0.10%	1.23%
	Tokens	34	0.08%	1.05%
	Modifiers	19	0.05%	0.58%
	Range	730	1.78%	22.47%
	NumericLiteral	51	0.12%	1.57%
	LiteralSimple	15	0.04%	0.46%
	LiteralFirstRest	62	0.15%	1.91%
	SimpleStatement	30	0.07%	0.92%
	Total coverage	**3,249**	**7.92%**	

- OperatorsMixed: a horizontal or vertical definition with some alternatives being operators and some being keywords:
  ```
  typeModifier ::= ("opt" | "repeat" | "list" | "attr" | "see" | "not"
     | "push" | "pop" | ":" | "~" | ">" | "<") ;
  ```
  (TXL Basis Grammar for TXL 10.5)
  ```
  op ::= (">" | "<" | "<=" | ">=" | "<>" | "=" | "in" | "is" | "+" | "-"
     | "or" | "xor" | "*" | "/" | "div" | "mod" | "and" | "shl" | "shr"
     | "DIV" | "AND") ;
  ```
  (TXL Basis Grammar for Borland Delphi Object Pascal 1.1)
  ```
  overloadable_unary_operator ::= ("+" | "-" | "!" | "~" | "++" | "--"
     | "true" | "false") ;
  ```
  (Validated TXL Basis Grammar for C# Edition 3)
- Words: a sequential and/or repetitive composition of keywords:
  ```
  simpleDerivationSet ::= "#all" | ("list" | "union" | "restriction")*
  ```
  (RELAX NG schema for XML Schema)
  ```
  mml.lines.datatype ::= ("none" | "solid" | "dashed")+
  ```
  (TESCOL 10001)
- Tokens: a sequential and/or repetitive composition of nontrivial non-keywords:
  ```
  WS ::= (" " | "\t" | "\r" | "\n")+ ;
  ```
  (TESCOL 10100)

- Modifiers: a horizontal or vertical definition with all alternatives being combinations of same keywords:
  ```
  mode ::= ("in"? | ("in" "out") | "out") ;
  ```
  (LNCS 4348, Ada 2005)
  ```
  static_constructor_modifiers ::=
    (("extern"? "static") | ("static" "extern"?)) ;
  ```
  (Validated TXL Basis Grammar for C# 3)

- Range: a choice of trivial terminals:
  ```
  Integer_base_letter ::= ("b" | "c" | "x" | "B" | "C" | "X") ;
  ```
  (ISO/IEC 25436:2006(E) Eiffel)
  ```
  DIGIT ::= ("0" | "1" | "2" | "3" | "4" | "5" | "6" | "7" | "8" | "9") ;
  ```
  (ANTLR Google Dart)

- NumericLiteral: a possibly signed repetition of choice of digits:
  ```
  HEX_DIGIT ::= ("0" | "1" | ... | "9" | "A" | ... | "F" | "a" | ... | "f") ;
  ```
  (Michael Studman Java 5)
  ```
  INT ::= ("+" | "-")? ("0" | (("1" | ... | "9") ("0" | "1" | ... | "9")*)) ;
  ```
  (TESCOL 00011)

- LiteralSimple: a repetition of a range of trivial terminals:
  ```
  [NT-Digits] Digits ::= ("0" | "1" | "2" | "3" | ... | "8" | "9")+ ;
  ```
  (W3C XPath 1.0)

- LiteralFirstRest: a choice of terminals followed by a Kleene star over a choice of terminals:
  ```
  IDENT ::= ("a" | ... | "z" | "A" | ... | "Z" | "_" | "$")
    ("a" | ... | "z" | "A" | ... | "Z" | "_" | "0" | ... | "9" | "$")* ;
  ```
  (Michael Studman Java 5)
  ```
  VARID ::= ("A" | ... | "Z" | "a" | ... | "z")
    ("A" | ... | "Z" | "a" | ... | "z" | "0" | ... | "9" | "_")* ;
  ```
  (TESCOL 10110)

- SimpleStatement: a keyword followed by a semicolon:
  ```
  terminate_alternative ::= "terminate" ";" ;
  null_statement ::= "null" ";" ;
  ```
  (ISO/IEC 8652/1995(E) LNCS 2219 Ada 95)
  ```
  continue-statement ::= "continue" ";" ;
  break-statement ::= "break" ";" ;
  ```
  (ISO/IEC 23270:2003(E) C# 1.0)

3.6   Normal Forms

A lot can be said about normal forms in formal grammar theory, and in the context of micropatterns we can also view normal forms as conditions on nonterminals and their definitions. In particular, we have implemented the following normal forms as micropatterns by reformulating them for unary grammars:

Table 6. Normal form micropatterns

Category	Pattern	Matches	Prevalence
Normal	CNF	5,365	13.07%
	GNF	3,074	7.49%
	ANF	26,269	64.01%
	Total coverage	**28,168**	**68.64%**

Table 7. Folding/unfolding micropatterns

Category	Pattern	Matches	Prevalence	Frequency
Folding	Empty	3,028	7.38%	32.56%
	Failure	69	0.17%	0.74%
	JustOptional	48	0.12%	0.52%
	JustPlus	199	0.48%	2.14%
	JustStar	130	0.32%	1.40%
	JustSepListPlus	28	0.07%	0.30%
	JustSepListStar	32	0.08%	0.34%
	JustChains	1,045	2.55%	11.24%
	JustOneChain	2,065	5.03%	22.20%
	ReflexiveChain	0	0.00%	0.00%
	ChainOrTerminal	145	0.35%	1.56%
	ChainsAndTerminals	290	0.71%	3.12%
	Total coverage	**9,300**	**22.66%**	

- Chomsky Normal Form, CNF [6]: all production rules of the nonterminal have one of three forms: `A ::= B C;` or `A ::= "a";` or `A ::= ` ε.
- Greibach Normal Form, GNF [15]: all production rules of the nonterminal have a form of either `A ::= "a" B C ···;` or `A ::= ` ε.
- Abstract Normal Form, ANF [40]: a nonterminal is either defined with one production rule without terminals, disjunction and labels on the right hand side, or with several chain production rules in the form of `A ::= B;`.

Unsurprisingly, the prevalence of ANF is rather high due to many abstract syntax definitions in the corpus (Table 6).

3.7   Folding/Unfolding

Not all nonterminals are introduced to the grammar because of the impossibility to express the same language differently: many are simply results of folding/unfolding transformations on a minimal grammar, and are meant to improve readability, maintainability or modularity of the language definition. In this group we collected micropatterns for nonterminals that can be removed from the grammar with relative ease (examples are given only for less intuitive micropatterns):

- Empty: a nonterminal is defined as an empty term ε;
- Failure: a nonterminal is explicitly undefined or prohibited with φ;
- JustOptional: a nonterminal defined only with just an optional reference to another nonterminal;
- JustPlus: a one-or-more repetition of a reference to another nonterminal;
- JustStar: a zero-or-more repetition of a reference to another nonterminal;
- JustSepListPlus: a non-empty separator list;
- JustSepListStar: a possibly empty separator list;
- JustChains: a nonterminal defined only with chain production rules (right hand sides are nonterminals);
- JustOneChain: a nonterminal defined only with exactly one chain production rule (right hand side is a nonterminal);
- ReflexiveChain: a nonterminal is circularly defined as itself: `A ::= A;` (usually only happens as an intermediate transformation result);
- ChainOrTerminal: a choice of a nonterminal and a terminal:
```
return-type ::= (type | "void") ;
```
(Microsoft C# 4.0)

- ChainsAndTerminals: a choice where the all alternatives are either isolated nonterminals or isolated terminals:
```
class-type ::= (type-name | "object" | "dynamic" | "string") ;
```
(Microsoft C# 4.0)

```
TypeDeclaration ::= ClassDeclaration ;
TypeDeclaration ::= ";" ;
TypeDeclaration ::= InterfaceDeclaration ;
```
(JLS Second Edition Java, readable)

- AChain: one production rule for the nonterminal is a chain production rule.

Table 7 summarises the prevalence observations of these micropatterns. The ChainsAndTerminals nonterminals mostly tend to have a terminal as the first alternative and nonterminals as the other ones, or vice versa, but we decided to combine such cases into one micropattern due to their extremely low prevalence (under 0.05 %).

3.8 Templates

In previous sections, we have already seen some micropatterns defined as templates like "opening-bracket, nonterminal, closing bracket" (part of ExprLowLayer), "single terminal" (Keyword or Operator), etc. In fact, there are 2673 such templates in total found in the corpus of grammars, and in this section we present the most prevalent ones of them (Table 8):

- Constructor: a named (non-empty production label or a top-level selector) empty term (ε);
- Bracket: a bracket-delimited nonterminal:
```
Explicit_creation_type ::= "{" Type "}" ;
Actual_generics ::= "[" Type_list "]" ;
Parenthesized ::= "(" Expression ")" ;
External_system_file ::= "<" Simple_string ">" ;
```
(ISO/IEC 25436:2006(E) Eiffel)

Table 8. Template micropatterns

Category	Pattern	Matches	Prevalence	Frequency
Template	Constructor	657	1.60%	13.56%
	Bracket	132	0.32%	2.73%
	BracketedFakeSepList	56	0.14%	1.16%
	BracketedFakeSLStar	10	0.02%	0.21%
	BracketedOptional	117	0.29%	2.42%
	BracketedPlus	6	0.01%	0.12%
	BracketedSepListPlus	8	0.02%	0.17%
	BracketedSepListStar	24	0.06%	0.50%
	BracketedStar	15	0.04%	0.31%
	Delimited	81	0.20%	1.67%
	ElementAccess	25	0.06%	0.52%
	PureSequence	2,999	7.31%	61.91%
	DistinguishByTerm	933	2.27%	19.26%
	Total coverage	**4,844**	**11.80%**	

– BracketedFakeSepList: a bracket-delimited explicitly encoded separator list:
```
typeParameters ::= "<" typeParameter ("," typeParameter)* ">" ;
namedFormalParameters ::= "[" defaultFormalParameter
              ("," defaultFormalParameter)* "]" ;
```
(ANTLR Google Dart)
```
template ::= "{{" title ("|" part)* "}}" ;
tplarg ::= "{{{" title ("|" part)* "}}}" ;
```
(EBNF MediaWiki)
– BracketedFakeSLStar: a bracket-delimited possibly empty separator list;
– BracketedOptional: a bracket-delimited optional reference to another nonterminal;
– BracketedPlus: a bracket-delimited one-or-more repetition of a nonterminal;
– BracketedSepListPlus: a bracket-delimited separator list;
– BracketedSepListStar: a bracket-delimited possibly empty separator list;
– BracketedStar: a bracket-delimited zero-or-more repetition of a nonterminal;
– Delimited: a sequence of symbols delimited by non-bracketing terminals:
```
RecordType ::= "RECORD" Fields "END" ;
LoopStmt ::= "LOOP" Stmts "END" ;
```
(SDF Modula 3)
– ElementAccess: a nonterminal followed by a bracketed nonterminal:
```
slice ::= prefix "(" discrete_range ")" ;
```
(LNCS 4348, Ada 2005)
```
libraryDefinition ::= LIBRARY "{" libraryBody "}" ;
```
(ANTLR Google Dart)
```
ArrayDeclarator ::= VariableName "(" ArraySpec ")" ;
StructureConstructor ::= TypeName "(" ExprList ")" ;
```
(TXL Fortran 77/90)

- PureSequence: a definition that uses purely sequential composition;
- DistinguishByTerm: a choice where each alternative starts with a terminal:

```
wildcard_type_bound ::= ("extends" type_specifier)
 | ("super" type_specifier) ;
```
(TXL Java 1.5 Basis Grammar)
```
default_expression_OR_nodefault ::= ("default" expression)
 | "nodefault" ;
```
(TXL Basis Grammar for Borland Delphi Object Pascal 1.1)
```
image-mode-manual-thumb ::= ("thumbnail=" image-name)
 | ("thumb=" image-name) ;
```
(BNF MediaWiki)

4   Discussion and Related Work

An obviously related research topic to micropatterns are design patterns [13], implementation patterns [3] and architectural patterns [11]. In the software language engineering community, there is no widely accepted collection of "DSL design patterns", but there is no shortage on papers and books with guidelines on language design and implementation [31,16,33,1,27,19,12,30, 1965–2013]. Most of these guidelines encapsulate their authors' vision and experience, but are still waiting to be formally organised, algorithmically expressed and verified. We hope that the catalogue of micropatterns is a step toward that goal, even if a small one. In [10], the main focuses of tool support for patterns were identified as application, validation and discovery — of these three, micropatterns mostly contribute to discovery.

Extending software metrics line of thinking to grammars can also be identified as a related domain to grammatical micropatterns. However, there are three main differences between our work and grammar metric suites like gMetrics [7] and SynC [28]. First, grammar metrics are used mostly for measurements, while the main purpose of micropatterns is classification. One can compare grammars based on their metrics, and one can cluster them by size, McCabe complexity and other computed values, so this gap is not unbridgeable, but it is present. The second issue is that grammar metrics work on the level of grammars, while micropatterns in this paper are formulated on the level of nonterminals. The third difference is that some metrics like Varju height are very complicated and require lengthy computations, which clearly contradicts with the simplicity requirement we have formulated in section 1. It remains to be seen whether micropatterns carry a value for grammar metrics in a form of "how many nonterminals in grammar X satisfy the condition of micropattern Y?".

In [8], it is noted that the expressiveness of the software language that is used to define (micro)patterns, severely affects the complexity of their validation and discovery. By using state of the art technology like Rascal [21], we were able to fit the entire system of classifiers and all the experimental code around it, in 760 lines of code, which is about as concise as one could hope.

Being formulated on the level of nonterminals, which is arguably the most fine-grained level of details one could get when working with grammars, puts grammatical micropatterns closer to OOP nanopatterns [2]. However, there is still enough space for grammatical nanopatterns — one could think of them as continuation of the ContainsX micropatterns from subsection 3.1 and operate with patterns like "contains a semicolon terminal", "contains two consecutive terminals", etc.

Grammar mutations are large scale intentional grammar transformations [38, §3.8.1] that involve enforcing a new naming convention over the entire grammar, performing massive folding/unfolding rewritings, removing all terminal symbols in one sweep, etc. Micropatterns are related to them because they can be used as triggers for actual transformation steps, as preconditions and postconditions. For instance, we can say that some grammar mutation works on all nonterminals satisfying the micropattern LowerCase, and as a result they start being Upper-Case. The change itself can be either inferred or programmed, but still with a lot of control and a strict specification around it.

An alternative mining source to a grammar corpus would be a bibliographic corpus: while we reused some existing notions like CNF/GNF and top/bottom for verifying intentionality of a micropattern, one could also systematically explore all nonterminal properties that have been used in prior publications, and can be reformulated as micropatterns: left factoring, various forms of recursion, all kinds of bracketing, etc. The result of such a mining process would conceivably be different from our results, and converging the two could strengthen any claims about the completeness of the actually mined micropattern set or its domain coverage. Replicating the mining experiment on a curated balanced corpus could give insights about which micropatterns are more natural than others, perhaps per technical space of the grammar sources.

Gil and Maman list four aspects that micropatterns can enhance: more efficient design (by reusing the existing domain knowledge), code learning (understanding code through familiarity with common patterns in it), training (rapid introduction to software engineering), automation (enriching generated documentation) [14]. Now that we have identified various micropatterns actually occurring in grammars in a broad sense, we can make the next steps toward these goals by formalising existing practices in software language design. To facilitate that, micropattern detection has been incorporated as one of the components of the **GrammarLab**, a library for grammar analysis and manipulation[5].

5   Conclusion

We have identified **85** algorithmically recognisable, purposeful, notable, simple micropatterns, by analysing **41038** nonterminal symbols of **533** software language definitions. Many of these micropatterns have been previously researched, used or considered in publications in the domain of grammarware engineering. Both the original corpus of grammars and the implementation of micropattern recognisers is publicly exposed through GitHub projects.

---

[5] GrammarLab, http://grammarware.github.io/lab/

References

1. Ammeraal, L.: On the Design of Programming Languages Including MINI ALGOL 68. In: Mühlbacher, J.R. (ed.) GI 1975. LNCS, vol. 34, pp. 500–504. Springer, Heidelberg (1975)
2. Batarseh, F.: Java Nano Patterns: A Set of Reusable Objects. In: Proceedings of the 48th Annual Southeast Regional Conference, SE 2010, pp. 60:1–60:4. ACM (2010)
3. Beck, K.: Smalltalk. Best Practice Patterns. Prentice Hall (1996)
4. Butler, S.: Mining Java Class Identifier Naming Conventions. In: Proceedings of the International Conference on Software Engineering, ICSE 2012, pp. 1641–1643. IEEE Press (2012)
5. Chomsky, N.: Syntactic Structures. Mouton (1957)
6. Chomsky, N.: On Certain Formal Properties of Grammars. Information and Control 2(2), 137–167 (1959)
7. Črepinšek, M., Kosar, T., Mernik, M., Cervelle, J., Forax, R., Roussel, G.: On Automata and Language Based Grammar Metrics. Computer Science and Information Systems 7(2) (2010)
8. van Emde Boas, P.: Resistance is Futile; Formal Linguistic Observations on Design Patterns. Technical Report ILLC-CT-97-02, Institute for Logic, Language and Computation, University of Amsterdam (1997)
9. Fischer, B., Lämmel, R., Zaytsev, V.: Comparison of Context-Free Grammars Based on Parsing Generated Test Data. In: Sloane, A., Aßmann, U. (eds.) SLE 2011. LNCS, vol. 6940, pp. 324–343. Springer, Heidelberg (2012)
10. Florijn, G., Meijers, M., Winsen, P.: Tool Support for Object-Oriented Patterns. In: Akşit, M., Matsuoka, S. (eds.) ECOOP 1997. LNCS, vol. 1241, pp. 472–495. Springer, Heidelberg (1997)
11. Fowler, M.: Patterns of Enterprise Application Architecture. Addison-Wesley Professional (2002)
12. Fowler, M.: Domain Specific Languages. Addison-Wesley Professional (2010)
13. Gamma, E., Helm, R., Johnson, R., Vlissides, J.: Design Patterns: Elements of Reusable Object-Oriented Software. Addison-Wesley (1995)
14. Gil, J., Maman, I.: Micro Patterns in Java Code. In: Proceedings of OOPSLA 2005, pp. 97–116. ACM (2005)
15. Greibach, S.A.: A New Normal-Form Theorem for Context-Free Phrase Structure Grammars. Journal of the ACM 12(1), 42–52 (1965)
16. Hoare, C.A.R.: Hints on Programming Language Design. Technical report, Stanford University, Stanford, CA, USA (1973)
17. Johnson, S.C.: YACC—Yet Another Compiler Compiler. Computer Science Technical Report 32, AT&T Bell Laboratories, Murray Hill, New Jersey (1975)
18. de Jonge, M., Monajemi, R.: Cost-Effective Maintenance Tools for Proprietary Languages. In: Proceedings of ICSM 2001, pp. 240–249. IEEE (2001)
19. Kleppe, A.: Software Language Engineering: Creating Domain-Specific Languages Using Metamodels. Addison-Wesley Professional (2008)
20. Klint, P., Lämmel, R., Verhoef, C.: Toward an Engineering Discipline for Grammarware. ACM Transactions on Software Engineering Methodology (ToSEM) 14(3), 331–380 (2005)
21. Klint, P., van der Storm, T., Vinju, J.: EASY meta-programming with rascal. In: Fernandes, J.M., Lämmel, R., Visser, J., Saraiva, J. (eds.) GTTSE 2009. LNCS, vol. 6491, pp. 222–289. Springer, Heidelberg (2011)

22. Lämmel, R.: Grammar Adaptation. In: Oliveira, J.N., Zave, P. (eds.) FME 2001. LNCS, vol. 2021, pp. 550–570. Springer, Heidelberg (2001)
23. Lämmel, R., Verhoef, C.: Semi-automatic Grammar Recovery. Software—Practice & Experience 31(15), 1395–1438 (2001)
24. Lämmel, R., Wachsmuth, G.: Transformation of SDF Syntax Definitions in the ASF+SDF Meta-Environment. In: Proceedings of LDTA 2001. ENTCS, vol. 44, Elsevier Science (2001)
25. Lämmel, R., Zaytsev, V.: Recovering Grammar Relationships for the Java Language Specification. Software Quality Journal (SQJ) 19(2), 333–378 (2011)
26. Lanza, M., Ducasse, S.: A Categorization of Classes based on the Visualization of their Internal Structure: The Class Blueprint. In: Northrop, L.M., Vlissides, J.M. (eds.) Proceedings of OOPSLA 2001, pp. 300–311. ACM (2001)
27. Mernik, M., Heering, J., Sloane, A.M.: When and How to Develop Domain-Specific Languages. ACM Computing Surveys 37(4), 316–344 (2005)
28. Power, J.F., Malloy, B.A.: A Metrics Suite for Grammar-based Software. Journal of Software Maintenance and Evolution: Research and Practice 16, 405–426 (2004)
29. Thies, A., Roth, C.: Recommending Rename Refactorings. In: Proceedings of the Second International Workshop on Recommendation Systems for Software Engineering, RSSE 2010, pp. 1–5. ACM (2010)
30. Völter, M., Benz, S., Dietrich, C., Engelmann, B., Helander, M., Kats, L.C.L., Visser, E., Wachsmuth, G.: DSL Engineering: Designing, Implementing and Using Domain-Specific Languages (2013), dslbook.org
31. van Wijngaarden, A.: Orthogonal Design and Description of a Formal Language. In: MR, vol. 76. SMC (1965)
32. Wile, D.S.: Abstract Syntax from Concrete Syntax. In: ICSE, pp. 472–480. ACM (1997)
33. Wirth, N.: On the Design of Programming Languages. In: IFIP Congress, pp. 386–393 (1974)
34. Wirth, N.: What Can We Do about the Unnecessary Diversity of Notation for Syntactic Definitions? Communications of the ACM 20(11), 822–823 (1977)
35. Zaytsev, V.: MediaWiki Grammar Recovery. Computing Research Repository (CoRR) 4661, 1–17 (2011)
36. Zaytsev, V.: BNF WAS HERE: What Have We Done About the Unnecessary Diversity of Notation for Syntactic Definitions. In: Ossowski, S., Lecca, P. (eds.) SAC/PL 2012, pp. 1910–1915. ACM (March 2012)
37. Zaytsev, V.: Notation-Parametric Grammar Recovery. In: Sloane, A., Andova, S. (eds.) Post-Proceedings of LDTA 2012, ACM (June 2012)
38. Zaytsev, V.: The Grammar Hammer of 2012. Computing Research Repository (CoRR) 4446, 1–32 (2012)
39. Zaytsev, V.: Grammar Zoo: A Repository of Experimental Grammarware. In: Fifth Special issue on Experimental Software and Toolkits of Science of Computer Programming (SCP EST5) (Currently under review after major revision 2013)
40. Zaytsev, V.: Guided Grammar Convergence. In: Poster Proceedings of the Sixth International Conference on Software Language Engineering (SLE 2013) (2013) (to appear in CEUR)
41. Zaytsev, V., Lämmel, R.: A Unified Format for Language Documents. In: Malloy, B., Staab, S., van den Brand, M. (eds.) SLE 2010. LNCS, vol. 6563, pp. 206–225. Springer, Heidelberg (2011)
42. Zaytsev, V., Lämmel, R., van der Storm, T., Renggli, L., Wachsmuth, G.: Software Language Processing Suite[6] (2008-2013), http://slps.github.io

---

[6] The authors are given according to the list of contributors at http://github.com/grammarware/slps/graphs/contributors.

Safe Specification of Operator Precedence Rules

Ali Afroozeh[1], Mark van den Brand[3], Adrian Johnstone[4], Elizabeth Scott[4],
and Jurgen Vinju[1,2]

[1] Centrum Wiskunde & Informatica, 1098 XG Amsterdam, The Netherlands
[2] INRIA Lille Nord Europe, France
{ali.afroozeh,jurgen.vinju}@cwi.nl
[3] Eindhoven University of Technology, NL-5612 AZ Eindhoven, The Netherlands
m.g.j.v.d.brand@tue.nl
[4] Royal Holloway, University of London, Egham, Surrey, TW20 0EX, UK
{a.johnstone,e.scott}@rhul.ac.uk

Abstract. In this paper we present an approach to specifying operator precedence based on declarative disambiguation constructs and an
implementation mechanism based on grammar rewriting. We identify a
problem with existing generalized context-free parsing and disambiguation technology: generating a correct parser for a language such as OCaml
using declarative precedence specification is not possible without resorting to some manual grammar transformation. Our approach provides a
fully declarative solution to operator precedence specification for context-
free grammars, is independent of any parsing technology, and is safe in
that it guarantees that the language of the resulting grammar will be the
same as the language of the specification grammar. We evaluate our new
approach by specifying the precedence rules from the OCaml reference
manual against the highly ambiguous reference grammar and validate
the output of our generated parser.

1 Introduction

There is an increasing demand for front-ends for programming and domain-
specific languages. We are interested in parser generation technology that can
cover a wide range of programming languages, their dialects and embeddings.
These front-ends are used for example to implement reverse engineering tools,
to build quality assessment tools, to execute research in mining software repositories, or to build (embedded) domain specific languages. In these contexts the
creation of the parser is a necessary and important step, but it is also an overhead
cost that would preferably be mitigated. In such language engineering applications, as opposed to compiler construction, we may expect frequent updates and
maintenance to deal with changes in the grammar.

Expression grammars are an important part of virtually every programming
language. The natural specification of expressions is usually ambiguous. In programming languages books and reference manuals, the semantic definition of
expressions usually includes a table of binary and unary operators accompanied with their priority and associativity relationships. This approach feels very

M. Erwig, R.F. Paige, and E. Van Wyk (Eds.): SLE 2013, LNCS 8225, pp. 137–156, 2013.
© Springer International Publishing Switzerland 2013

natural, probably because this is the way we learn basic arithmetic expressions at school. Virtually all disambiguation techniques for expression grammars are driven by such precedence rules. However, the implementation of such rules varies considerably.

The implementation of operator precedence in grammars may considerably deviate from the initial design the language engineer had in mind. In manual rewriting approaches, grammars are *factored* to remove ambiguities. These approaches are not attractive for us because the resulting grammars are usually large, and hard to read and understand. For example, programming languages such as OCaml, C# and Java have many operators with a considerable number of priority levels and associativity relations. Manually transforming such expression grammars, to encode precedence rules, is a significant undertaking. To make matters worse, we expect changes and evolution of grammars [1]. Every time a new operator is introduced we have to re-think or even re-do this complex and error-prone transformation process. Therefore, we consider declarative approaches in which the parser is generated from the set of precedence rules.

Generalized context-free parsing algorithms provide the opportunity to write any context-free grammar, and allow for language compositions, which helps in modeling embeddings and dialects. This makes generalized context-free parsing a good starting point for our purpose: satisfying the demand for powerful and maintainable front-ends. This is particularly important in the fields of domain-specific languages and reverse engineering, where grammars should be easy to understand, evolvable, and maintainable. Therefore, the focus of this paper is mainly on providing a declarative framework for specification of precedence rules in generalized context-free parsing algorithms, such as Earley [2], GLR [3,4,5,6] and GLL [7].

1.1   From Yacc to SDF

In this section, we discuss two disambiguation techniques that influenced our work the most, and are related to generating parsers from ambiguous grammars using a set of precedence rules. Aho, Johnson, and Ullman [8] (AJU) present an approach in which the LR(1) [9] parsing tables are modified to eliminate shift/reduce conflicts based on the precedence of operator tokens, as specified by the user. The AJU method is not only a disambiguation mechanism, it is also a *nondeterminism reducer*, meaning that it has to resolve all shift/reduce and reduce/reduce conflicts, even when there is no ambiguity, to make the parser deterministic. This implies that the approach cannot predictably deal with expression grammars that are not inherently LR(1), unless the language engineer understands how additional shift/reduce and reduce/reduce actions, used for making the parser deterministic, affect the language. More importantly, the AJU precedence semantics is defined in terms of the deterministic LR parsers: to understand the semantics of the precedence rules, one must understand what an LR(1) conflict is and why it happens. Finally, this method is not directly applicable to non-LR parsers.

The AJU approach is implemented in Yacc[1] and is very popular. For example, the OCaml parser uses `ocamlyacc`[2], which is a variant of Yacc. However, the OCaml grammar used in `ocamlyacc` is heavily factored and is considerably different from the nice, concise reference manual grammar of OCaml.

Although the AJU method is fast and effective when used in the context of arithmetic expressions, because it is bound to LR(1) parsing, it does not fit into our definition of declarative operator precedence techniques. We require that a mechanism for declarative specification of operator precedence rules (1) be *independent* of the underlying parsing technology, so that we can reason about the precedence semantics or use the mechanism in other parsing technologies, (2) be *safe*, meaning that the disambiguation mechanism derived from precedence rules should not change the underlying sentences of the language, and (3) be *complete*, i.e., be able to resolve all the ambiguities resulting from different precedence of operators.

There has been a number of efforts to formalize a parser-independent semantics for operator precedence, and to provide a declarative disambiguation mechanism. The most notable one is SDF[3] in which the semantics of operator precedence is defined as a filter on derivation trees. SDF precedence filters are implemented by removing transitions corresponding to filtered productions from adapted SLR(1) tables [10]. Although we believe that SDF was in the right direction in defining a declarative precedence mechanism, its filters lack the safety and completeness requirements. For example, precedence rules in SDF fail to disambiguate a left-associative binary operator having higher priority than a unary prefix operator. The limitations of SDF are discussed in detail in Section 2.1.

1.2 Contributions and Roadmap

In this paper we present a new semantics for the declarative specification of precedence rules for context-free grammars. The key enablers of our technique are the safety and support for resolving deeply nested precedence conflicts. We also support indirect precedence conflicts when expression grammars are not expressed using a single recursive nonterminal but rather more. The new algorithms proposed in this paper are part of the implementation of the parser generator for Rascal [11]. Using this implementation, we show that our approach is powerful enough to allow declarative specification of operator precedence in OCaml. More importantly, the semantics of our technique is implemented as a grammar transformation, making it independent of the underlying parsing technology. We also guarantee that the parsers we generate produce the exact same parse trees (as if the original grammar was used). The completeness proof —whether our technique resolves all precedence style ambiguities— and the soundness proof of the transformation —whether the transformation exactly implements the semantics— are future work.

---

[1] http://dinosaur.compilertools.net/yacc/

[2] http://caml.inria.fr/pub/docs/manual-ocaml/manual026.html

[3] http://www.syntax-definition.org

The rest of this paper is organized as follows. After this introduction, we give formal definitions which we need in the rest of this paper. Then, we explain the problems with SDF in detail in Section 2.1. After that, the formal semantics of precedence rules and its implementation as a grammar transformation are presented in sections 3 and 4. We present the results of parsing the OCaml test suite in Section 5. Finally, a discussion of related work and a conclusion of this work are given in sections 6 and 7, respectively.

2   Motivation

A grammar is a 4-tuple (N, T, P, S) where N is a set of nonterminals, T a set of terminals, P a set of production rules of the form $A ::= \alpha$ where A, the *head* of the production rule, is a nonterminal and α, the *body* of the production rule, is a string in $(T \cup N)^*$. We shall assume that there are no repeated rules, so we can identify a production rule by writing its head and body. $S \in N$ is the start symbol of the grammar. By convention, in this paper, nonterminals and terminals start with uppercase and lowercase letters, respectively. In addition, symbols, such as $+$ or $*$ are terminals. We use lowercase letters u, v, w to denote non-empty sequences of terminal symbols. A group of production rules that have the same head can be grouped as $A ::= \alpha_1 | \alpha_2 | ... | \alpha_n$ where each $A ::= \alpha_i$ is a production. In this representation, each α_i is called an *alternate* of A.

A derivation step is of the form $\alpha A \beta \Rightarrow \alpha \gamma \beta$ where $\alpha, \beta \in (T \cup N)^*$ and $A ::= \gamma$ is a production rule. In a derivation step a nonterminal A is replaced with the body of its production rule. A derivation of σ from τ is a possibly empty sequence of derivation steps of the form $\tau \Rightarrow \alpha_1 \Rightarrow \alpha_2 \Rightarrow ... \Rightarrow \sigma$, which is also written as $\tau \overset{*}{\Rightarrow} \sigma$. A derivation is left-most if at each step its left most nonterminal is rewritten. A derivation from the start symbol is called a *sentential form* which is a sequence of terminals or nonterminals. A sentential form consisting only of terminal symbols is called a *sentence*.

A sentence is *ambiguous* if it has more than one left-most derivation. *Disambiguation* is a process which eliminates derivations. A disambiguation is said to be *safe* if it does not remove all derivations. Therefore, a safe disambiguation mechanism does not change the underlying language generated by a grammar.

2.1   Limitations of SDF

SDF features three meta notations $>$, *left*, and *right*, which specify the precedence, left and right associativity of operators, respectively [12]. Having $A ::= \gamma > B ::= \alpha^4$ disallows the derivation steps of $B ::= \alpha$ from all B's in γ. $A ::= A\alpha \ \{left\}$ means that the A in $A\alpha$ should not derive $A ::= A\alpha$ itself. Right associativity is the same as the left, but applied on the right-most A. There are three problems with the semantics of SDF[5] disambiguation filters:

---

[4] SDF adheres to algebraic notations and writes $A ::= \gamma$ as $\gamma \to A$. In this paper we use the more common ::= notation.

[5] We describe here SDF version 2 [12] but we simply call it SDF.

- It is *unsafe*: A filter is applied even when there is no ambiguity. For example, having $(E ::= E \wedge E > E ::= -E)$ rejects the string 1 $\wedge$ - 1, even though this string is not ambiguous. This is because, based on the semantics of SDF, $-E$ cannot appear under any of the E's in the body of the rule. SDF also allows the user to specify under which nonterminal the filtering should be carried out. For example, the user can specify that the filtering should only be carried out under the first E in the body of the rule, written as $(E ::= E \wedge E <0>> E ::= -E)$ in SDF. This solves the problem for these two operators, but this explicit selection of the filtered nonterminal is transitively applied to all levels below, even where it should not be applied, producing wrong results.
- It is *incomplete:* The precedence relationship in SDF is defined as a one-level relationship. As a result, it cannot resolve ambiguities in some cases that require deeper than one level searching in the derivation trees. For example, a left-associative binary operator having higher priority than a prefix unary operator remains ambiguous. The problem with one-level filtering is explained in Section 2.2.
- It is *limited* to directly recursive rules. Although SDF has some extensions to filter priority modulo chain rules, general indirect recursion is not supported. Rules such as $E ::= E\,A$, where the right-most nonterminal, A, can eventually produce an E at the right-most position cannot be filtered using SDF priorities.

These limitations are encountered in practice. For example, the `if-then-else` operator in functional programming languages such as OCaml and Haskell acts as a unary operator with lower priority than left-associative binary operators. Indirect recursion also happens, for example, in the reference grammar of OCaml.

2.2 Problem with One-Level Filtering

To illustrate the problem with one-level filtering, we consider the `if-then-else` construct in OCaml, which has lower priority than +. For example, the expression 1 + if x then 2 else 3 + 4 is interpreted as 1 + (if x then 2 else (3 + 4)) rather than (1 + (if x then 2 else 3)) + 4. For notational simplicity, the if...then..else part is replaced with *if* .

$$E ::= E + E$$
$$| \textit{if } E$$
$$| Num$$

Fig. 1 shows the parse trees resulting from parsing the input 1 + if 2 + 3. For a more compact presentation the terminals (1, 2 , 3) are removed.

In SDF, the precedence and associativity rules for disambiguating this case will be:

$$E ::= E + E \; \{left\} \quad\quad\quad\quad\quad \text{(Rule 1)}$$
$$E ::= E + E > E ::= \textit{if } E \quad\quad\quad \text{(Rule 2)}$$

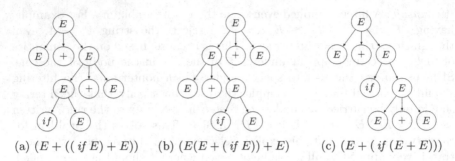

(a) $(E + ((\textit{if } E) + E))$ (b) $(E(E + (\textit{if } E)) + E)$ (c) $(E + (\textit{if } (E + E)))$

Fig. 1. Parse trees from parsing `1 + if 2 + 3`

The disambiguation is not safe in this case: when Rule 2 is applied, $E ::= \textit{if } E$ is removed under both E's, which rejects a sentence such as `1 + if 2 + 3`. We can make it safe by changing Rule 2 into $(E ::= E + E \mathrel{<0>>} E ::= \textit{if } E)$. Now if we examine the effect of the definitions on the shown parse trees in Fig. 1, we can observe that the left-associativity removes the derivation in Fig. 2a. However, none of the definitions affect the remaining two parse trees, and thus the disambiguation fails. The reason that SDF definitions fail to disambiguate this grammar is that patterns of depth greater than two are required. The first E in the body of $E ::= E + E$ can first derive $E ::= E + E$ and then the second E in the body of the newly derived rule derives $E ::= \textit{if } E$. In other words, the following derivation

$$E \Rightarrow E + E \Rightarrow E + E + E \Rightarrow E + \textit{if } E + E$$

remains, which is not rejected by any of the defined patterns, but it is semantically incorrect. The derivation in Fig. 1c is correct and is the only one that should remain after disambiguation.

For this grammar, a two level filtering can solve the problem, but in general, we may need filters of arbitrary depth. For example, consider the following grammar which has an additional expression rule $E ::= E \wedge E$, where $\wedge$ is right associative and has the highest priority.

$$E ::= E \wedge E$$
$$| E + E$$
$$| \textit{if } E$$
$$| Num$$

To illustrate why filters of arbitrary depth may be needed, consider the following derivation:

$$E \Rightarrow E + E \Rightarrow E + E + E \Rightarrow E + E \mathbin{^{\wedge}} E + E \overset{*}{\Rightarrow} E + E \mathbin{^{\wedge}} E \mathbin{^{\wedge}} ... \mathbin{^{\wedge}} E + E$$

As can be seen, after deriving $E + E$, the second E may unboundedly produce $E \wedge E$, leading to derivation trees with wrong precedence levels. Fig. 2 shows

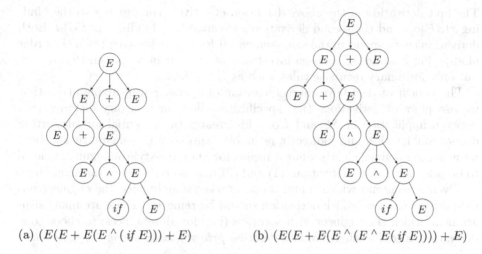

(a) $(E(E + E(E \wedge (if E))) + E)$ (b) $(E(E + E(E \wedge (E \wedge E(if E)))) + E)$

Fig. 2. For some expression grammars filters of arbitrary depth may be required

two of such derivations. For disambiguating such cases, either an infinite number of filters or a mechanism to define filters with variable length is needed. It is not trivial to implement a variable length filter during parsing and it is very likely that the performance of such an implementation will suffer.

We have now established the gap in resolving ambiguities in expression grammars. In the following we propose a general solution that solves the aforementioned limitation, and at the same time improves other quality aspects.

3 Syntax and Semantics for Operator-Style Disambiguation

Expression-style grammar rules display a specific kind of ambiguity, which we call *operator-style* ambiguity. We characterize and define two complementary and safe ambiguity removal schemes for exactly this kind of ambiguity: priority and associativity. Note that this does not imply that our mechanisms completely disambiguate any expression grammar. There may be other ambiguity hidden in the same rules with different causes. This other ambiguity should be left untouched for safety.

3.1 Definitions

Definition 1 (Operator-style ambiguity). *An operator-style-ambiguity exists if for some grammar nonterminal E there exist two leftmost derivations*

$$xE\mu \Rightarrow x\beta E\mu \underset{lm}{\overset{*}{\Rightarrow}} xvE\mu \Rightarrow xvE\alpha\mu \tag{1}$$

$$xE\mu \Rightarrow xE\alpha\mu \Rightarrow x\beta E\alpha\mu \underset{lm}{\overset{*}{\Rightarrow}} xvE\alpha\mu \tag{2}$$

which contain identical sub-derivations $\beta \underset{lm}{\overset{*}{\Rightarrow}} v$.

The first derivation in the above definition effectively corresponds to the binding $x(\beta E)\alpha\mu$ and the second derivation corresponds to binding $x\beta(E\alpha)\mu$. Both derivations correspond to the same sentential form, but between them the order of applying $E\alpha$ and βE as been inverted. Note that it may happen that $\alpha = \beta$, but only for binary recursive rules, such as $E ::= E\gamma E$.

The benefit of the above characterization of operator-style ambiguity is that we use pairs of derivations that specifically allow an arbitrary distance ($\overset{*}{\Rightarrow}$) between application of βE and $E\alpha$. This creates the potential for supporting deeper ambiguities, and indirectly recursive expression grammars. In addition, we now have defined clearly what it means for operator-style ambiguity removal to be safe: never both derivations (1) and (2) may be removed at the same time.

Given a grammar which contains operator-style ambiguity, the engineer has to specify, somehow, which derivation should be removed. There are many situations in which the engineer wishes always (i.e., for all sentences) to choose one derivation over the other. We first describe *priority-based ambiguity removal*.

Definition 2 (Priority-based ambiguity removal via >). *The user specifies a strict partial order $>$ (irreflexive, antisymmetric and transitive) between the alternates of E. For all $\beta E > E\alpha$, derivations which contain derivations of the form (2) are always removed. Vice versa, for all $E\alpha > \beta E$, we choose to remove (1). Note that we do not intend to apply the partial order on other cases of ambiguity, only in the case of the (1) and (2) pair it serves to choose one over the other.*

This definition correlates with the common use of operator priority to specify disambiguation, for example choosing the first derivation gives the β "operator" priority over the α "operator". Since all derivations $\beta\overset{*}{\Rightarrow}v$ are available for both choices, priority disambiguation does not put constraints on other disambiguation choices.

The fact that $>$ is asserted to define a strict partial order is an important detail for satisfying the safety requirement. If there would be both $\alpha > \beta$ and $\beta > \alpha$ for example, then the above definitions would together remove all derivations for both some or all sentences that α and β generate. Similarly $\alpha > \alpha$ is not allowed. The fact that $>$ is allowed to be partial implies that under-specified orderings may leave some operator ambiguity intact. This means it is up to the language engineer to fully declare what the relative precedence of operator is, and also that the priority relation can safely be developed incrementally.

There are, however, common situations in which we do not want to use or cannot enforce a strict partial order as required by $>$. In particular, if an expression-style rule has an alternate with both immediate left and right recursion, $E ::= E\gamma E$, then it is not possible to specify priority with itself, since $>$ must be irreflexive and antisymmetric. More generally, there may be two alternates $E ::= E\gamma E \mid E\delta E$ where γ and δ are required to have a symmetric relation (such as $+$ and $-$ in arithmetic expressions), which also contradicts a strict partial order.

Definition 3 (Symmetric Operator-style Ambiguity). *Instantiating α and β from derivations (1) and (2) above as $\beta = E\delta$ and $\alpha = \gamma E$ both rules are now binary recursive. We can instantiate derivations (1) and (2) above like:*

$$xE\mu \Rightarrow xE\delta E\mu \overset{*}{\underset{lm}{\Rightarrow}} xvE\mu \Rightarrow xvE\gamma E\mu \tag{1'}$$

$$xE\mu \Rightarrow xE\gamma E\mu \Rightarrow xE\delta E\gamma E\mu \overset{*}{\underset{lm}{\Rightarrow}} xvE\gamma E\mu \tag{2'}$$

Also, taking $\beta = E\gamma$ and $\alpha = \delta E$ we can write derivations (1) and (2) above as

$$xE\mu \Rightarrow xE\gamma E\mu \overset{*}{\underset{lm}{\Rightarrow}} xvE\mu \Rightarrow xvE\delta E\mu \tag{1''}$$

$$xE\mu \Rightarrow xE\delta E\mu \Rightarrow xE\gamma E\delta E\mu \overset{*}{\underset{lm}{\Rightarrow}} xvE\delta E\mu \tag{2''}$$

Symmetric operator-style ambiguity is a special case of operator-style ambiguity in which both rules are binary. Often we have $\delta = \gamma$, although this is not necessary. To see why we call the ambiguity symmetric, consider the example where $\gamma = +$ and $\delta = -$, (1') and (2') both derive $y + y - y$ and, (1'') and (2'') both derive $y - y + y$. Then, (1') and (1'') represent $(y + y) - y$ and $(y - y) + y$, respectively.

Definition 4 (Associativity-based ambiguity removal via *left* and *right*). *We define two binary relations "left" and "right" between binary alternates, for which holds that*

$$(left \cap right = \emptyset) \wedge (left \cap \; '>' = \emptyset) \wedge (right \cap \; '>' = \emptyset)$$

In other words, $>$, left and right are mutually exclusive relations.

   When $(\alpha, \beta) \in left$, associativity based ambiguity removal removes the derivations of the form (2'), corresponding to grouping γ and δ to the left, i.e. to choosing $x(w\delta E)\gamma E\mu$ over $w\delta(E\gamma E)\mu$. This correlates with left associativity. Similarly, when $(\alpha, \beta) \in right$, removing derivations with derivations of the form (1') corresponds to right associativity.

The restriction of $>$, *left* and *right* being mutually exclusive is a sufficient restriction for guaranteeing safety since now only one relation is allowed to be active at the same time and each of the relations is safe in itself.

Since $>$, *left* and *right* need to define an order between all alternates of expression languages with dozens of rules, we cannot expect the language engineer to specify each combination manually. This problem is dealt with in our formalism, which is described later, by providing automatic transitive closure for $>$ and a computation akin to Cartesian product for *left* and *right* groups of rules.

In summary, the three relations $>$, *left* and *right* allow a language engineer to remove all operator-style ambiguity of the form in Definition 1, either using an anti-symmetric, irreflexive, transitive relation $>$, or using one of the possibly reflexive, possibly symmetric and possibly non-transitive *left* and *right* relations as long as the three relations exclude each other. Note that in theory all operator-style ambiguity can be removed by simply asserting a full ordering among all recursive alternates using $>$ or by putting all rules in a single *left* or *right* group, but this has no practical value. Instead, complete disambiguation of the operator-style ambiguity in a language definition needs to be considered language-by-language (see Section 5).

3.2   Pattern Notation for Illegal Derivations

As an intermediate step we now introduce a short notation for the derivations (1), (2), (1′) and (2′), called "patterns". Each pattern is specific for a given grammar and combination of two alternate rules. In the next section, we demonstrate how to compute a unified set of patterns from a context-free grammar augmented with $(>, left, right)$ relations, and how to use this set of patterns to compute a grammar transformation that implements the above semantics.

Definition 5 (Operator ambiguity removal pattern). *An operator ambiguity removal pattern (pattern for short) is a 4-tuple of the form (head, parent, i, child), where head is the nonterminal head of the expression grammar for which the precedence rules are defined, parent is an alternate of head, i is the index of a nonterminal in the body of parent, and child is the alternate that should be filtered from the nonterminal at position i of parent. The nonterminal at position i is called the* filtered nonterminal.

In this paper we write a pattern as $(E, \alpha \cdot \beta, \gamma)$ *where E is the head, and* $\alpha \cdot \beta$ *and* γ *are the parent and the child alternates, respectively, and the filtered nonterminal is identified by a dot before it.*

The semantics of patterns are the same as derivations discussed above. For example, the derivations (1) and (2) can be expressed as the patterns $(E, \alpha \cdot E, E\beta)$ and $(E, \cdot E\alpha, E\beta)$, respectively. Note that patterns are not implementation mechanisms. In Section 4 we show a grammar rewriting algorithm to implement patterns.

We now explain informally how to arrive at a set of patterns starting from a context-free grammar augmented with $(>, left, right)$. Table 1 documents the semantics of priority in terms of patterns that are generated for each combination of left, right and binary recursive expression rules. Note that for binary rules sometimes two patterns are generated for the same combination of rules. The semantics of *left* in terms of the patterns is expressed similarly in Table 2. We leave the table for right associativity to the reader.

As can be seen, not all combinations of expression rules generate patterns. Exactly when the combination of rules would *not* be ambiguous and filtering would be unsafe no pattern is generated. This corresponds to the derivations (1), (2), (1′), (2′) using specific combinations of left and right recursive rules. In Section 4 we implement these tables.

3.3   Defining $>$, *left* and *right* in Practice

The following three features, which are taken from the design of SDF [13], are described here for the sake of completeness. They are essential for having concise expression grammars, as mentioned above.

Table 1. The semantics of the $>$ operator in terms of patterns

$>$	$E ::= E\alpha_2 E$	$E ::= E\alpha_2$	$E ::= \alpha_2 E$
$E ::= E\alpha_1 E$	$(E, \bullet E\alpha_1 E, \ E\alpha_2 E)$ $(E, E\alpha_1 \bullet E, \ E\alpha_2 E)$	$(E, E\alpha_1 \bullet E, \ E\alpha_2)$	$(E, \bullet E\alpha_1 E, \ \alpha_2 E)$
$E ::= E\alpha_1$	$(E, \bullet E\alpha_1, \ E\alpha_2 E)$	—	$(E, \bullet E\alpha_1, \ E\alpha_2)$
$E ::= \alpha_1 E$	$(E, \alpha_1 \bullet E, \ E\alpha_2 E)$	$(E, \alpha_1 \bullet E, \ E\alpha_2)$	—

Table 2. The semantics of *left* associativity

left	$E ::= E\alpha_1 E$	$E ::= E\alpha_2 E$
$E ::= E\alpha_1 E$	$(E, E\alpha_1 \bullet E, \ E\alpha_1 E)$	$(E, E\alpha_1 \bullet E, \ E\alpha_2 E)$
$E ::= E\alpha_2 E$	$(E, E\alpha_2 \bullet E, \ E\alpha_1 E)$	$(E, E\alpha_2 \bullet E, \ E\alpha_2 E)$

Firstly, our formalism automatically transitively (but not reflexively) closes the $>$ relation precedence operator. As a result, when the language engineer defines $p_1 > p_2$ and $p_2 > p_3$ we automatically derive $p_1 > p_3$. Furthermore, when they accidentally define $p_1 > p_1$, or both $p_1 > p_2$ and $p_2 > p_1$, either directly, or indirectly via the closure, an error message must be produced. Now we can allow the short-hand $p_1 > p_2 > p_3$ to obtain elegant definitions. Note that the transitive closure step is carried out before generating the actual patterns. The actual patterns are generated from the calculated priority pairs only when is there is an operator-style ambiguity, as defined in Section 3.2 and documented in Table 1.

Secondly, many programming languages have groups of binary operators that have the same precedence level. For example, in $E ::= E + E \mid E - E$ both operators have the same precedence level but should be left associative with respect to each other. We define a left associative group containing a set of rules $(p_1 \mid \ldots \mid p_n)(left)$ to generate a set of associativity declarations:

$$\bigcup_{1 \leq i,j \leq n} p_i \ left \ p_j, \mathbf{when} \ (p_i, p_j) \notin right \wedge (p_i, p_j) \notin \ '>' \ \wedge (p_j, p_i) \notin \ '>'$$

We do similarly for right associative groups. The groups simply compute the Cartesian product, but do not add tuples that would contradict a relation defined elsewhere. Finally, associativity groups may occur in the middle of a priority chain, as in $(p_1 \mid \ldots \mid p_n)(A) > (q_1 \mid \ldots \mid q_n)(B)$. In this case $>$ will be extended by combining each element of the two groups pairwise (and before closure). An additional safety feature (which is novel) is to simply statically check for $>$, *left* and *right* to be non-overlapping, as required.

Finally, some expression languages disallow certain direct nesting while indirect nesting is allowed. For example 1 == 2 == 3 should not be allowed while

$E ::= E\ Arg+$ //function application

	Operator	Associativity
$\mid - E$ //unary minus	function application	–
$\mid E ** E$	unary minus	–
$\mid E + E$	**	right
$\mid E - E$	+, -	left
$\mid$ *if E then E else E*	if-then-else	–
$\mid Id$		

$Arg ::=\ E$
　　　$\mid\ \sim label : E$

Fig. 3. Excerpt from OCaml's grammar with "challenging" operator precedence

$$E ::= E\ Arg+ \qquad\qquad (non-assoc)$$
$$> - E$$
$$> E ** E \qquad\qquad (right)$$
$$>(E + E\mid E - E) \qquad (left)$$
$$> if\ E\ then\ E\ else\ E$$
$$\mid Id$$
$$Arg ::=\ E$$
$$\mid\ \sim label : E$$

Fig. 4. Example definition of challenging operator precedence rules

`true == (2 == 2)` is allowed. Normally we have to introduce a new expression nonterminal just to disallow this direct nesting. So, in order to be able to write concise grammars we add *non−assoc* declarations with the following semantics. If p_1 *non−assoc* p_2, then $(p_1$ *left* $p_2) \wedge (p_1$ *right* $p_2)$. Notice that *non−assoc* declarations are not safe: they intentionally and explicitly remove sentences from the language as generated by the grammar. We extend the associativity group semantics with *non−assoc* as well. Necessarily, any static safety checks on *left* and *right* need to be done before the tuples from *non−assoc* have been added.

To illustrate the syntax of our approach we use the example grammar in Fig. 3 and its priority and associativity properties, which both are taken from the OCaml reference manual[6]. The grammar and the precedence rules can now be written as in Fig. 4. We use ::=, >, *left*, *right* and *non−assoc* meta notation to encode both the syntax and the precedence table in one go.

4   Grammar Rewriting to Exclude Illegal Derivations

In this section we present an algorithm for transforming a grammar accompanied with a set of priority and associativity rules to a grammar that prevents the generation of illegal derivations (see figures 5 and 6).

---

[6] `http://caml.inria.fr/pub/docs/manual-ocaml-4.00/expr.html`

function EXTRACTDEFINITIONS(G)
    $'{>}' \leftarrow '{>}' \cup \{(p_i, q_j) | (p_1 \dots p_i)(A) > (q_1 \dots q_j)(B) \in G\}$ ▷ expand the groups
    $P \leftarrow \{(p_1, p_2) \mid p_1 > p_2 \in G\}+$ ▷ note the transitive closure
    $L \leftarrow \{(p, p) \mid p \text{ left } p \in G\}, L' \leftarrow L$
    $R \leftarrow \{(p, p) \mid p \text{ right } p \in G\}$
    $L \leftarrow L \cup \bigcup_{0 \leq i, j \leq n} \{(p_i, p_j) \mid (p_1 | \dots | p_n)(\text{left}) \in G, (p_i, p_j) \notin R\}$
    $R \leftarrow R \cup \bigcup_{0 \leq i, j \leq n} \{(p_i, p_j) \mid (p_1 | \dots | p_n)(\text{right}) \in G, (p_i, p_j) \notin L'\}$
    return $P \cup L \cup R$
function RIGHTRECURSIVE(G, N)   ▷ LEFTRECURSIVE is elided for brevity
    $R \leftarrow \{N\}$
    while R changes **do** $R \leftarrow R \cup \{X | X ::= \alpha Y \in G, Y \in R\}$
    return R
function PLAIN$(x) = x$ in which all N_i are replaced by N.
function RULES$(G, N) = \{\beta | N ::= \beta \in G\}$
function FRESH$(N) = N_i$ where the integer index i has not been used before.
function GENERATEPATTERNS(G)
    $D \leftarrow$ EXTRACTDEFINITIONS(G)
    $R \leftarrow \{\}$
    for all $(A ::= X\alpha, A ::= \beta Y) \in D$ **do**
        if $X \in$ LEFTRECURSIVE$(G, A) \wedge Y \in$ RIGHTRECURSIVE(G, A) **then**
            $R \leftarrow R \cup \{(A, \bullet X\alpha, \beta Y)\}$
    for all $(A ::= \alpha X, A ::= Y\beta) \in D$ **do**
        if $X \in$ RIGHTRECURSIVE$(G, A) \wedge Y \in$ LEFTRECURSIVE(G, A) **then**
            $R \leftarrow R \cup \{(A, \alpha \bullet X, Y\beta)\}$
    return R

Fig. 5. Translating priority and associativity definitions to safe patterns

1. We translate the definitions to a set of patterns (GENERATEPATTERNS).
2. We apply these patterns to transform the grammar (REWRITEGRAMMAR)

The generation of patterns in Fig. 5 follows exactly the semantics as defined earlier in tables 1 and 2. EXTRACTDEFINITIONS produces a set of binary tuples which represent the associativity and priority declarations in a grammar. This set is an over-approximation of the patterns that will be generated later, since they are not specific for positions in the parents yet and may be ignored entirely if no ambiguity may arise. For a specific nonterminal, RIGHTRECURSIVE and LEFTRECURSIVE compute which other nonterminals contribute to an eventual left/right recursion of that nonterminal. The GENERATEPATTERN function then filters the extracted definitions making sure to introduce a pattern only where left recursion tangles with right recursion and vice versa, i.e., simulating exactly the priority and associativity semantics of Section 3.

Given the set of patterns generated by GENERATEPATTERNS, we can now transform the grammar using the REWRITEGRAMMAR function as shown in Fig. 6. It is important to note that we use indexed nonterminals names, such that when building parse trees, no new names for nonterminals are generated

1: **function** ApplyPattern(G, W, δ, $V ::= \mu'W'\tau'$)
2:     $Y_{alts} = \emptyset$
3:     **for all** $\rho \in$ rules(G, W) **do**
4:         **if** plain$(\rho) \neq$ plain(δ) **then** add ρ to Y_{alts}
5:     **if** $\exists Z \in G :$ (plain$(Z) =$ plain$(W)) \vee$ (rules$(G, Z) = Y_{alts})$ **then**
6:         $Y' \leftarrow Z$
7:     **else**
8:         $Y' \leftarrow$ fresh(W)
9:         **for all** $\beta \in Y_{alts}$ **do** add $Y' ::= \beta$ to G
10:     remove $V ::= \mu'W'\tau'$ from G
11:     add $V ::= \mu'Y'\tau'$ to G
12:     **return** (G, Y')
13: **function** RewriteGrammar$((G, P))$
14:     New $\leftarrow \emptyset$
15:     Slots[ ] $\leftarrow \emptyset$ ▷ an empty map from indexed nonterminal names to dotted rules
16:     **for all** patterns $(Y, \beta \cdot Y\gamma, \delta)$ in P **do**   ▷ Stage 1, reserve nonterminal names
17:         $Y_i \leftarrow$ fresh(Y)
18:         Slots$[Y_i] \leftarrow \beta \cdot Y\gamma$
19:         add Y_i to New
20:         $G_1 \leftarrow G$
21:     **for all** patterns $(Y, \beta \cdot Y\gamma, \delta)$ in P **do**
22:         **if** Slots$[Y_i] = \beta \cdot Y\gamma$ **then**   ▷ Stage 2, update use sites
23:             replace $Y ::= \beta Y\gamma$ in G_1 with $Y ::= \beta Y_i\gamma$
24:     **for all** Y_i in New **do**   ▷ Stage 3, add definitions for new nonterminals
25:         **if** Slots$[Y_i] = \beta \cdot Y\gamma$ **then**
26:             **for all** $Y ::= \alpha$ in G_1 **do**
27:                 **if** $\nexists$ a pattern $(Y, \beta \cdot Y\gamma, \delta) \in P$ **with** plain$(\alpha) = \delta$ **then**
28:                     add $Y_i ::= \alpha$ to G_1
29:     $(G'', G') \leftarrow (G_1, G)$ ▷ Stage 4, look for nested ambiguity
30:     **while** $G' \neq G''$ **do**
31:         $(G', \text{New}') \leftarrow (G'', \text{New})$
32:         **for all** $Y_i \in$ New$'$ **do**
33:             **if** Slots$[Y_i] = \cdot Y\gamma$ **then**
34:                 **for all** grammar rules $Y_i ::= \mu W \in G'$ **do**
35:                     **if** plain$(W) = Y \wedge \exists Z($plain$(Z) = Y$ **then**
36:                         $\wedge W \in$ RightRecursive$(G_1, Z))$ **then**
37:                         **for all** patterns $(Y, \cdot Y\gamma, \delta)$ **do**
38:                             $(G'', U) \leftarrow$ ApplyPattern$(G'', W, \delta, Y_i ::= \mu W)$
39:                             $(\text{Slots}[U], \text{New}) \leftarrow (\text{Slots}[W], \text{New} \cup \{U\})$
40:             **if** Slots$[Y_i] = \beta \cdot Y$ **then**
41:                 **for all** grammar rules $Y_i ::= W\mu$ in G'' **do**
42:                     **if** plain$(W) = Y \wedge \exists Z : ($plain$(Z) = Y$
43:                         $\wedge W \in$ LeftRecursive$(G_1, Z))$ **then**
44:                         **for all** patterns $(Y, \beta \cdot Y, \delta)$ **do**
45:                             $(G'', U) \leftarrow$ ApplyPattern$(G'', W, \delta, Y_i ::= W\mu)$
46:                             $(\text{Slots}[U], NT) \leftarrow (\text{Slots}[W], \text{New} \cup \{U\})$
47:     **return** G''

Fig. 6. Core algorithm that rewrites a grammar, applying patterns to remove alternates from indexed nonterminals (indices can be removed easily). As each rewrite action can only remove some alternates, no new shapes of rules are created by the algorithm (no additional chain rules). This preserves the shape of the parse forest as the language engineer specified in the original grammar.

The algorithm first deterministically generates a set of nonterminals to implement single-level filtering. Lines 14–20 reserve fresh nonterminal names. Lines 21–23 change existing rules to use the new nonterminals at the right positions. Lines 24–28 generate definitions for the new nonterminals by cloning the original while leaving out the filtered alternate. Then, in a fixed point computation (lines 29–46) we treat each level of newly generated nonterminals to a procedure for eliminating deeply nested cases. For left recursive positions (lines 40–46), we make sure that a nonterminal is generated which cannot derive a given postfix operator at arbitrary depth at the right-most position which has lower priority. For right recursive positions we do the opposite (lines 33–39). The APPLYPATTERN helper function does the same as lines 21–46 for the first level, but it includes an explicit check for the existence of generated nonterminals to reuse. This check is necessary for termination as well as efficiency. The fixed point computation will terminate because a new nonterminal is only created in APPLYPATTERN if a nonterminal which defines the same subset of alternates does not already exist. Since every step removes an alternate, eventually —in a worst case scenario— all singleton sets will have been generated and the algorithm terminates.

We can illustrate the algorithm using the following example: Grammar G:

$$E ::= E + E \;\; (\textit{left}) \; > \; iE \mid a;$$

generates patterns P (see Fig. 5): $\{(E, \cdot E + E, iE), (E, E + \cdot E, E + E)\}$. Now the algorithm in Fig. 6 can start. Lines 14–23 create the following grammar rule in G_1, having found two patterns to apply and allocating two fresh nonterminals: $E ::= E_1 + E_2 \mid iE \mid a$

Then, at lines 24–28 we define the two new nonterminals and extend G_1 with their definition:

$$E ::= E_1 + E_2 \mid iE \mid a$$

$$E_1 ::= E_1 + E_2 \mid a$$

$$E_2 ::= iE \mid a$$

Finally we search for nested cases in lines 30–46. The outer loop executes twice. The first time, E_1 results in a new nonterminal E_3 and E_2 does nothing. The second time nothing changes and we terminate with the final grammar:

$$E ::= E_1 + E_2 \mid iE \mid a$$

$$E_1 ::= E_1 + E_3 \mid a$$

$$E_2 ::= iE \mid a$$

$$E_3 ::= a$$

5 Validation Using the OCaml Case

We have conducted an extensive validating experiment. The goal is to show that our approach is indeed more powerful than SDF, and to provide evidence that the algorithm works for complicated, real-world examples.

5.1 Method

For this case study, we selected the OCaml (.ml) files in the test suite directory of the source release of OCaml 4.00.1. OCaml features the kind of ambiguity that SDF filtering semantics cannot solve and our method should be able to solve. The test suite contains numerous examples of different sizes and complexity, testing the language features. We believe the test suite is a good choice for testing our parser on safety and completeness, as the suite rigorously tests the language itself. The suite contains 387 files of which 158 (in the `tool-ocaml` folder) contain only source code comments that document expected output (assembler code) of the compiler. The other 229 files are examples of OCaml code that exercise all features of the language in different combinations to test the compiler.

We performed the experiments in Rascal [11], which is a meta-programming DSL, supporting embedded syntax definitions. The parsing mechanism of Rascal is based on GLL [7].

Our goal is to provide solid evidence of the complete equivalence between the original OCaml parser and the parser generated from our approach. This means that no parse error should be produced by the Rascal parser if no parse error was produced by the original OCaml parser, and the generated parser should produce single parse trees (no ambiguities), and that the structure of the abstract syntax trees should be exactly the same.

To compare parse trees we adapted both the parser from the OCaml compiler and the output of our generated parser to produce exactly the same bracketed forms. The resulting files are then compared with `diff`, ignoring whitespace, to check for equivalence. It should be noted that the ASTs from the OCaml compiler were normalized, for example flat lists were converted to cons list. We performed the same transformation steps on our ASTs.

OCaml programs are basically composed of groups of expressions. The AST produced by the OCaml parser is complex and contains many features. However, because of the expression-like nature of the language, most of the unnecessary information can be removed, resulting in a bracketed form. We modified the default AST printer[7] to produce the bracketed form. For example, the original AST and its bracketed form, resulting from parsing the string 1+2*3 is shown in Fig. 7. The bracketed forms of all the examples we examined are on GitHub[8].

---

[7] The `parsing/printast.ml` file in the OCaml source release.

[8] https://github.com/cwi-swat/ocaml-operator-ambiguity-experiment

```
Ptop_def                                              (
  [                                                     +
    structure_item ([1,0+0]..[1,0+5]) ghost             (
      Pstr_eval                                           1
      expression ([1,0+0]..[1,0+5])                       *
        Pexp_apply                                        (
        expression ([1,0+1]..[1,0+2])                       2
          Pexp_ident "+"                                    3
        [                                                 )
          <label> ""                                    )
            expression ([1,0+0]..[1,0+1])              )
              Pexp_constant Const_int 1
          <label> ""
            expression ([1,0+2]..[1,0+5])
              Pexp_apply
              expression ([1,0+3]..[1,0+4])
                Pexp_ident "*"
              [
                <label> ""
                  expression ([1,0+2]..[1,0+3])
                    Pexp_constant Const_int 2
                <label> ""
                  expression ([1,0+4]..[1,0+5])
                    Pexp_constant Const_int 3
              ] ] ]
```

Fig. 7. The original AST print from the OCaml parser (left) and the stripped version containing only the structure and the labels (right)

For conducting the experiments we wrote a Rascal grammar definition using the notations defined in this paper. The grammar is obtained from the OCaml reference manual[9]. We tried to be as faithful as possible to the grammar in the reference manual, avoiding changes as much as possible.

5.2   Results

The priority and associativity properties, retrieved from the precedence tables in the language manual, resulted in a grammar that uses $>$ and *left, right* and *non−assoc* declarations. These declarations result in 830 ambiguity removal patterns. The rewriting was performed as explained in Section 4.

The rewritten grammar provided us with a very close over-approximation of what the OCaml language designers had in mind. Only a handful of ambiguities, such as the dangling-else ambiguity and identifier conflicts with keywords, remained, which were resolved using other ambiguity resolution features of Rascal. The OCaml grammar written in Rascal is available at: https://github.com/cwi-swat/ocaml-operator-ambiguity-experiment/

We have performed the parsing and comparison process for the given 229 number of files in the case study. 215 files parse correctly and without ambiguity, of which, 182 files (84%) generate ASTs that are identical in both versions. This means that our parser produces the same grouping as the original OCaml parser,

---

[9] http://caml.inria.fr/pub/docs/manual-ocaml-400/language.html

providing evidence for the correctness of our algorithms. For the rest (16%), our manual examination of the `diff` files shows that the differences are minor and are caused by AST de-sugaring and normalization steps in the OCaml compiler, and are not related to the operator precedence.

5.3   Discussion and Threats to Validity

One of the difficulties in this study was how to compare ASTs. The AST from the OCaml parser, in some places, is significantly different from the grammar written in the reference manual. The reason is that the parse trees have been normalized by the front-end for easier processing later in the compiler. For example, flat argument lists are converted to cons lists, presumably to simplify currying and partial function features in OCaml. These changes are not documented in the reference manual. We resolved them by observing the original AST output to deduce the normalization step. We then mimicked these normalization steps as rewrite rules in Rascal before outputting the final bracketed form.

Moreover, OCaml has some language extension and syntax varieties that are not documented in the main language reference document. The use of semicolon was particularly confusing. Semicolon is used in OCaml to separate expressions, defined by the rule $E ::= E ; E$ which is right associative. However, in the inputs we parsed, we observed several occasions in which semicolon can end an expression regardless of being preceded by another expression. We resolved this issue by allowing optional semicolons at the end of expressions.

6   Related Work

Besides the AJU and SDF methods which have been described so far, there are a number of work which present similar ideas. Aasa [14] proposes a framework for the specification of precedences for implementing programming language. To the best of our knowledge, this is the only declarative model that supports deeper patterns. In this work, a parse tree is considered precedence correct based on the weights given to operators in its sub-trees. This work correctly recognizes that, for example, a unary operator can be placed under the right most operand of a binary rule, regardless of their precedence. Our approach in defining precedence semantics is different in that instead of focusing on parse trees, we defined the semantics of precedence as derivations, which is closer to our implementation technique. The main shortcoming of this work is that operators must be unique. They are considered separately from their context, e.g., there cannot be a unary minus and a binary minus at the same time. In addition, there is no discussion of indirect recursions. Similar to us, the disambiguation technique in this work is implemented as a grammar rewriting.

Thorup [15] presents an algorithm for transforming an ambiguous grammar with a set of partial illegal parse trees to a grammar excluding those deriva- tions. On the surface, the approach looks very similar to our technique shown in Section 4, but the inner working is very different. The rewriting technique in this work expects a set of illegal parse trees, and in case the set is unbounded, as in Section 2.2, a set of parse forests with cycles. Then, the algorithm works bottom up, generating all production rules which do not produce any of those illegal parse trees. The resulting grammar of this step should go through another transformation to be simplified. The problem of how to find sufficient illegal parse trees is addressed in another work by the same author [16]. The rewriting presented by Thorup is not directly aiming at providing a declarative disambiguation mechanism, rather it is more an implementation mechanism. It also covers a wider range of rewriting provided that enough illegal parse trees are given, but the overall procedure is complicated. We are not aware of any practical parser generator that uses this technique.

Visser presents "From context-free grammars with priorities to character class grammars" [17], which describes a grammar transformation to give semantics to the SDF2 priority relation similar to our transformation. In a first step, a grammar's nonterminals are replaced by explicit sets of identities (integers) of its alternates. Then, elements are removed from these sets based on the precedence relations. Since every rule is identified, the resulting parse trees do not show the signs of grammar transformation. Character class grammars do not guarantee to preserve the language and do not support indirect recursion, like our semantics do. Although character class grammars are formalized quite differently from our approach that directly manipulates grammars using indexed nonterminals, both methods use grammar transformation to implement the precedence relations.

7   Conclusions

Constructing a parser that correctly implements precedence rules, for a language such as OCaml, using its ambiguous reference manual and the set of precedence rules is not possible without resorting to some manual grammar transformation. In this paper, we defined a parser-independent semantics for operator-style ambiguities that is safe and is able to deal with deeper level and indirect precedence ambiguities. We evaluated our approach using an extensive experiment by comparing the output of the standard OCaml compiler front-end with the output of our own parser, generated from Rascal. The result is promising and shows that our approach is powerful enough to parse OCaml.

For other languages such as Haskell, F#, and Lua, which offer similar expression languages, our approach is expected to be equally beneficial. Although the focus of this paper is mainly on generalized parsing algorithms, we should also emphasize that our approach can be used by any parser generator that supports left recursion.

Acknowledgments. We would like to thank Peter Mosses who has originally identified the problem in OCaml. Also many thanks to Davy Landman and Mark Hills from CWI who assisted us in performing the validation experiments.

References

1. Klint, P., Lämmel, R., Verhoef, C.: Toward an engineering discipline for grammar-ware. ACM Trans. Softw. Eng. Methodol. 14(3), 331–380 (2005)
2. Earley, J.: An efficient context-free parsing algorithm. Commun. ACM 13(2), 94–102 (1970)
3. Tomita, M. (ed.): Generalized LR parsing. Kluwer Academic Publishers (1991)
4. Rekers, J.: Parser Generation for Interactive Environments. PhD thesis, University of Amsterdam, The Netherlands (1992)
5. McPeak, S., Necula, G.C.: Elkhound: A fast, practical GLR parser generator. In: Duesterwald, E. (ed.) CC 2004. LNCS, vol. 2985, pp. 73–88. Springer, Heidelberg (2004)
6. Baxter, I.D., Pidgeon, C., Mehlich, M.: DMS®: Program transformations for practical scalable software evolution. In: Proceedings of the 26th International Conference on Software Engineering, ICSE 2004, pp. 625–634. IEEE Computer Society, Washington, DC (2004)
7. Scott, E., Johnstone, A.: GLL parse-tree generation. Science of Computer Programming (2012) (to appear) ISSN:0167-6423
8. Aho, A.V., Johnson, S.C., Ullman, J.D.: Deterministic parsing of ambiguous grammars. In: Proceedings of the 1st Annual ACM SIGACT-SIGPLAN Symposium on Principles of Programming Languages, POPL 1973, pp. 1–21. ACM (1973)
9. Aho, A.V., Lam, M.S., Sethi, R., Ullman, J.D.: Compilers: Principles, Techniques, and Tools, 2nd edn. Addison-Wesley Longman Publishing Co., Inc., Boston (2006)
10. Visser, E.: Scannerless generalized-LR parsing. Technical Report P9707, Programming Research Group, University of Amsterdam (July 1997)
11. Klint, P., van der Storm, T., Vinju, J.: EASY meta-programming with rascal. In: Fernandes, J.M., Lämmel, R., Visser, J., Saraiva, J. (eds.) Generative and Transformational Techniques in Software Engineering III. LNCS, vol. 6491, pp. 222–289. Springer, Heidelberg (2011), http://www.rascal-mpl.org
12. Klint, P., Visser, E.: Using filters for the disambiguation of context-free grammars. In: Pighizzini, G., San Pietro, P. (eds.) Proc. ASMICS Workshop on Parsing Theory, Milano, Italy, Tech. Rep. 126–1994, pp. 1–20. Dipartimento di Scienze dell'Informazione, Università di Milano (1994)
13. Visser, E.: Syntax Definition for Language Prototyping. PhD thesis, University of Amsterdam (1997)
14. Aasa, A.: Precedences in specifications and implementations of programming languages. Theor. Comput. Sci. 142(1), 3–26 (1995)
15. Thorup, M.: Disambiguating grammars by exclusion of sub-parse trees. Acta Informatica 33(5), 511–522 (1996)
16. Thorup, M.: Controlled grammatic ambiguity. ACM Trans. Program. Lang. Syst. 16(3), 1024–1050 (1994)
17. Visser, E.: From context-free grammars with priorities to character class grammars. In: van Deursen, A., Brune, M., Heering, J. (eds.) Dat Is Dus Heel Interessant, Liber Amicorum Dedicated to Paul Klint, pp. 217–230. CWI (1997)

Detecting Ambiguity in Programming Language Grammars

Naveneetha Vasudevan and Laurence Tratt

Software Development Team, King's College London
http://soft-dev.org/
naveneetha@yahoo.com, laurie@tratt.net

Abstract. Ambiguous Context Free Grammars (CFGs) are problematic for programming languages, as they allow inputs to be parsed in more than one way. In this paper, we introduce a simple non-deterministic search-based approach to ambiguity detection which non-exhaustively explores a grammar in breadth for ambiguity. We also introduce two new techniques for generating random grammars – Boltzmann sampling and grammar mutation – allowing us to test ambiguity detection tools on much larger corpuses than previously possible. Our experiments show that our breadth-based approach to ambiguity detection performs as well as, and generally better, than extant tools.

1 Introduction

Context Free Grammars (CFGs) are widely used for describing formal languages, including Programming Languages (PLs). The full class of CFGs (grammars from now on) includes ambiguous grammars—those which can parse inputs in more than one way. Needless to say, ambiguous grammars are highly undesirable. If an input can be parsed in more than one way, which one of those parses should be taken? We would not enjoy using a compiler if it were to continually ask us to choose which parse we want. Unfortunately, we know that, in general, it is undecidable as to whether a given grammar is ambiguous or not [1]. While there are various parsing approaches which allow a user to manually disambiguate amongst multiple parses, one can not in general know if all possible points of ambiguity have been covered. Perhaps because of this, most tools use parsing algorithms such as LL and LR, which limit themselves to parsing only a subset of unambiguous grammars. This leads to other trade-offs: grammars have to be contorted to fit them within these subsets; and these subsets rule out the ability to compose grammars [2].

As a consequence, there has been a steady stream of work trying to detect ambiguity in arbitrary grammars, in order to bring most of the benefits of the full class of CFGs without the disadvantages. Exhaustive methods such as AMBER [3] systematically generate strings to uncover ambiguity, but for even medium-sized grammars, this quickly leads to infinite state spaces. Approximation techniques, on the other hand, sacrifice accuracy for termination. ACLA [4] transforms a language to an alternative whose accepted inputs are a

M. Erwig, R.F. Paige, and E. Van Wyk (Eds.): SLE 2013, LNCS 8225, pp. 157–176, 2013.
© Springer International Publishing Switzerland 2013

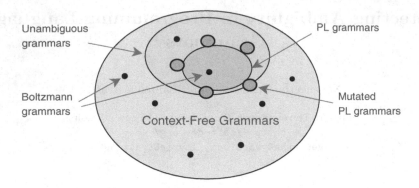

Fig. 1. An intuition about the relation between various classes of CFGs

superset of the original; it never reports false negatives, but may report false positives. Hybrid approaches marry approximation techniques with exhaustive search. Basten's hybrid approach [5] first applies a noncanonical unambiguity test to filter out provably unambiguous portions of a grammar before running AMBER on the result. However, such hybrid approaches still rely on an exhaustive search, although on a smaller state space. Bounded length approaches are in a sense a subset of exhaustive methods: they exhaustively explore a small, fixed part of the search space. CFGAnalyzer [6] uses a SAT solver to explore strings of bounded length. Cheung and Uzgalis' method [7] deterministically expands rules from the start terminal until a fixed bound is reached.

Whereas previous ambiguity detection approaches are deterministic and explore a grammar in 'depth', our hypothesis is that approaches which explore a grammar in 'breadth' have a greater chance of discovering ambiguity. By depth we mean that a subset of the grammar is explored in (possibly exhaustive) detail; by breadth that a large portion of the grammar is explored but not exhaustively so. In other words, we suspect that a scatter-gun approach to detecting ambiguity will be more successful than a focused beam.

To that end, we have created a tool *SinBAD* which houses a number of ambiguity detection approaches. This paper details one of SinBAD's non-deterministic ambiguity detection algorithms which is intended to explore a grammar in breadth rather than depth. The algorithm is extremely simple, with its core explained in less than a page. Despite the simplicity of the algorithm, experimental results show that it performs at least as well as, and generally better than, more complex deterministic approaches. Furthermore, good results are found more quickly than by previous approaches.

Understanding the relation between grammars, and its various subsets is key to understanding the motivation for, and the results of, our work. Figure 1 is our attempt to give an intuition about these relations. Since all the sets involved are infinite, this diagram is necessarily an approximation, but is hopefully helpful. The set of unambiguous grammars is a strict subset of the grammars. Virtually all PL grammars reside within this unambiguous subset. Our underlying hypothesis is that PL grammars often stretch to the very edge of the class of unambiguous grammars. Stated differently, we suspect that PL grammars are often only a small step away from being ambiguous.

This paper also provides new techniques for evaluating the effectiveness of ambiguity detection tools. We believe that evaluating such tools requires much larger input corpuses than previously used: ours contains over 20,000 grammars of various types. In order to generate such a large corpus, we cannot rely on hand-written grammars. We therefore provide two classes of random grammars. The first is generated using Boltzmann sampling, an approach which provides some statistical guarantees about the randomness of the resulting generators. The second class is generated by mutating existing PL grammars. This latter category is particularly interesting as we, like most others working in this field, are particularly interested in the ambiguity of PL-like grammars. There is an inevitable problem with this: most PLs are written for approaches such as LR parsing that accept only unambiguous grammars. Basten hand-modified 20 PL grammars to be ambiguous [8] which we reuse in our suite for comparison purposes. However, one can easily, and inadvertently, create a solution which works well for such a small corpus but little beyond it. By generating a huge number of possibly ambiguous PL-like grammars, we can explore a much wider set of possibilities than is practical by hand.

To summarise, our work has two hypotheses:

H1. Covering a grammar in breadth is more likely to uncover ambiguity than covering it in depth.

H2. PL grammars are only a small step away from being ambiguous.

The contributions of this paper are as follows. First, we show a new search-based approach to ambiguity detection, which is simpler than previous approaches. Second, we provide new means of evaluating the effectiveness of ambiguity tools by providing the ability to produce large quantities of grammars using Boltzmann sampling and grammar mutation. Third, we provide the first large-scale evaluation of such tools. In so doing, we show that our simple search-based approach performs at least as well as, and generally better than, existing tools. The basic idea of our search-based approach was first presented in a workshop paper [9]. This paper extends that with Boltzmann sampled grammars, grammar mutation, and a significantly larger experiment. SinBAD, the grammar generators, the grammar corpus we used, and the results obtained can be downloaded from our experimental suite:

http://figshare.com/articles/cfg_amb_experiment/774614

The structure of this paper is as follows. In Section 3 we describe our search-based approach to ambiguity detection. Sections 4 and 5 describe our algorithms for generating Boltzmann and mutated grammars respectively. In Section 6 we set out the methodology for our experiment, which is split into 3 sub-experiments. In section 10 we consider our hypotheses in the light of our experimental results.

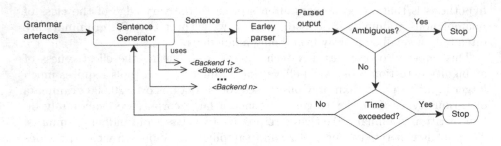

Fig. 2. SinBAD architecture

2 Definitions

Before presenting our algorithms and descriptions, we first introduce some brief definitions (mostly standard) and notations.

A grammar is a tuple $G = \langle N,T,P,S \rangle$ where N is the set of non-terminals, T is the set of terminals, P is the set of production rules over $N \times (N \cup T)^*$ and S is the start non-terminal of the grammar. A production rule $A\!: \alpha$ is denoted as $P[A]$ where $A \in N$, and α is a sequence of strings drawn from $(N \cup T)^*$. N_ϵ denotes set containing non-terminals that have at least one empty alternative. For a rule $P[A]$, $P[A]_{alt}$ denotes a single alternative and $\Sigma P[A]_{alt}$ all its alternatives. We define the size of a grammar as $size(G) = |N|$. We define a sentence of a grammar as a string over T^*. A sentence is ambiguous if it can be parsed in more than one way. A grammar is ambiguous if there exists a sentence which is both accepted and ambiguous. We define 'symbol' to mean either a terminal or a non-terminal.

For a list ℓ, let $\ell[i]$ denote the element at position i, and $\ell[i\!:\!j]$ the items from positions i (inclusive) to j (exclusive). Let $insert(\ell, i, \alpha)$ denote insertion of α into ℓ at position i and $delete(\ell, i)$ denote deletion of element from ℓ from position i. Let $append(\ell, \alpha)$ denote appending element α to list ℓ. For a dictionary $\mathcal{D}$ containing key-value pairs, $\mathcal{D}[x \mapsto a]$ denotes an update to key x with value a, $\mathcal{D}[x]$ denotes a lookup of key x, $\mathcal{D}_{values}$ denotes its list of values. Let $\mathcal{R}(\ell, n)$ denote a list of n items chosen randomly from the list ℓ. Further, let $\mathcal{R}[m..n]$ denote a number chosen randomly between m (inclusive) and n (inclusive).

3 Search-Based Ambiguity Detection

Search-based techniques seek to find 'good enough' solutions for problems that have no feasible algorithmic solution and whose search space is too big to exhaustively scan. Such techniques have been applied to a wide range of problems including software itself (see e.g. [10]). Search-based techniques are either random or guided by a fitness function.

In order to apply search-based techniques to ambiguity detection, we created *SinBAD*, a simple tool with pluggable backends. Figure 2 shows SinBAD's architecture. Given a grammar and a lexer, the *Sentence Generator* component generates random sentences using a given *backend*. A backend, in essence, is an algorithm that governs how sentences are generated. For instance, a backend can use a unique scoring mechanism to favour an alternative when expanding a non-terminal, or one that can generate sentences of bounded length. The generated sentence is then fed to a parser to check for ambiguity (we use ACCENT [11], a fast Earley parser for this). The search stops when an ambiguity is found or when a time limit is exceeded. In this paper we consider the most successful SinBAD backend we have created so far: *dynamic1*[1].

3.1   The *dynamic1* Backend

Given a grammar, the *dynamic1* backend shown in Algorithm 1 non-deterministically creates a valid sentence which can then be used to test for ambiguity. In essence, the algorithm continually picks random alternatives to follow for sentence generation, recursing into the grammar. However, doing this naively leads to frequent non-termination [9]. Therefore, the backend is parameterised by a user-configurable integer D[2]. Once the algorithm has recursed beyond depth D, it favours alternatives which immediately terminate (i.e. rules that contain no non-terminals). When this is not possible – some rule's alternatives all contain non-terminals – the favouritism then chooses whichever rules have been least visited. In this way, the generator tends not only to terminate in reasonable time, but also to explore a grammar's rules semi-uniformly.

The function START is initialised with a user-defined grammar G and threshold depth D. The current depth d is set to zero. We initiate sentence generation by deriving the start symbol S of the grammar. We keep a note of when we have entered a rule and when we have exited. To derive a non-terminal, we randomly select one of its alternatives (line 11). When the depth of the recursion exceeds a certain threshold depth, we start favouring alternatives (lines 8 and 9).

The FAVOUR-ALTERNATIVE function is called when the algorithm wishes to try and terminate. Given a rule, the function generates a score for each alternative and the one with the lowest score is selected. In the event of a tie, one of the lowest scoring alternatives is arbitrarily selected. Terminals are scored as 0. Non-terminals are scored as a ratio of the number of derivations that haven't been fully derived yet to the total number of derivations (line 30).

dynamic1's simplicity means that our experimental corpus has uncovered a handful of cases (1.4% of grammars in the corpus) where it doesn't terminate. This is due, in an unintended irony, to the one deterministic part of *dynamic1*: the favouring of alternatives. When FAVOUR-ALTERNATIVE is called, it scores rules, selects those with the equal lowest score, and then non-deterministically picks amongst them. If one alternative always has the lowest score, then it will be picked every time. Consider the rules P: Q and Q: P | R S. If, at a given point of time, the scores for the first and second alternatives

---

[1] For a discussion of some other backends, see [9].

[2] Setting D to ∞ provides equivalent behaviour to the naive non-terminating approach.

Algorithm 1. The *dynamic1* algorithm

1: **function** START(G, D)
2:     $Sen \leftarrow \varnothing$
3:     GENERATE($P[S]$, G, Sen, $d = 0$, D)
4:     **return** Sen
5: **end function**

6: **function** GENERATE($P[A]$, G, Sen, d, D)
7:     $P[A].entered \leftarrow P[A].entered + 1$
8:     **if** $d \geq D$ **then**
9:         $P[A]_{alt} \leftarrow$ FAVOUR-ALTERNATIVE($P[A]$, G)
10:     **else**
11:         $P[A]_{alt} \leftarrow \mathcal{R}(\Sigma P[A]_{alt}, 1)$
12:     **end if**
13:     **for** $Sym \in P[A]_{alt}$ **do**
14:         **if** $Sym \in N$ **then**
15:             $Sen \leftarrow Sen +$ GENERATE($P[Sym]$, G, Sen, $d + 1$, D)
16:         **else**
17:             $Sen \leftarrow Sen + Sym$
18:         **end if**
19:     **end for**
20:     $P[A].exited \leftarrow P[A].exited + 1$
21:     $d \leftarrow d - 1$
22: **end function**

23: **function** FAVOUR-ALTERNATIVE($P[A], G$)
24:     $scores \leftarrow \{ \}$
25:     $scores \leftarrow \{scores[alt \mapsto 0] \mid alt \in \Sigma P[A]_{alt}\}$
26:     **for** $P[A]_{alt} \in \Sigma P[A]_{alt}$ **do**
27:         **for** $Sym \in P[A]_{alt}$ **do**
28:             **if** $Sym \in N$ **then**
29:                 **if** $P[Sym].entered > 0$ **then**
30:                     $score_{alt} \leftarrow score_{alt} + (1 - (P[Sym].exited / P[Sym].entered))$
31:                 **end if**
32:             **end if**
33:         **end for**
34:         $scores \leftarrow scores[P[A]_{alt} \mapsto score_{alt}]$
35:     **end for**
36:     $alts_{min} \leftarrow \{alt \in \Sigma P[A]_{alt} \mid scores[alt] = min(scores_{values})\}$
37:     **return** $\mathcal{R}(alts_{min}, 1)$
38: **end function**

---

of rule Q are <1 and >1 respectively, then the alternative favouring will always select the first alternative, as it has the lowest score. We briefly outline a possible solution for this in Section 12.

```
Cfg = Cfg Rule ... Rule
Rule = SingleAlt Alt | RuleAlts1 Rule Alt
Alt = EmptyAltSyms | SingleAltSyms1 Symbol | AltSyms1 Alt Symbol
Symbol = NonTerm NonTerm | Term Term
NonTerm = NonTerm1 | NonTerm2 | ... | NonTermN
Term = Term1 | Term2 | ... | TermN
```

Fig. 3. Tree specification for generating grammars

4   Boltzmann Sampled Grammars

Boltzmann sampling is a framework for random generation of combinatorial structures (see [12] for further details). The basic idea is to give the sampler a class specification of a combinatorial structure and a value to control the size of the generated objects. For a given class C, and size n, the sampler provides approximate-size uniform random generation—objects are generated with approximate size $n\pm\epsilon$, where ϵ is a fixed tolerance, but objects of the same size occur with equal probability. This allows the sampler to generate large objects in linear time. In this section we provide the first Boltzmann sampler for grammars.

4.1   Class Specification

A Boltzmann sampler class specification is a grammar containing a set of productions. A production is of the form: A: $\langle \mathrm{rhs} \rangle$, where A is the name of the class being defined and $\langle \mathrm{rhs} \rangle$ is a set of definitions. A definition is of the form $DefX$ Y, where $DefX$ denotes a constructor and Y is either a reference to a definition (if a definition Y exists) or a literal otherwise.

Since, as far as we are aware, this is the first time that Boltzmann sampling has been used to generate grammars, we were forced to create a class specification ourselves. Determining a good class specification is arguably the hardest part of Boltzmann sampling, and is complicated by the fact that grammars do not have a single, obvious specification. Furthermore, since grammars are unbounded in size, we necessarily have to restrict the size of the those generated to make using them practical. This immediately leads us to a difficult question: what style of grammars do we want? In reality, we are most interested in grammars which somewhat resemble PL grammars. Generating grammars with 2 rules containing 100 alternatives each may tell us something about grammars in general – though getting enough coverage to say something useful may be much harder – but little about programming languages. We have therefore crafted our use of Boltzmann sampling to lead to grammars which roughly resemble real PLs. In order to do this, we are forced to apply post-filters to restrict the grammars generated to those we are most interested in, as we shall soon see.

Our class specification is shown in Figure 3. Using [13] as a guiding principle, our specification is designed to give us control over three things: the number of empty alternatives, the number of alternatives per rule, and the number of symbols per alternative. `Cfg` denotes a context-free grammar, `Rule` a production rule, `Alt` a production alternative, and `Symbol` denotes either a non-terminal (a `NonTerm`) or a terminal (a `Term`) symbol. A CFG consists of 1 or more production rules (hence the references to multiple Rule definitions). `Rule` has two outcomes: it can either be called recursively to build a list of alternatives; or just build a list with single alternative. `Alt` has three choices: it can either be called recursively to build a sequence of symbols; or just build a sequence with one symbol (middle choice); or an empty string (`EmptyAltSyms`). The specification enforces equal numbers of `NonTerms` and `Terms` in a grammar, the 1:1 ratio seeming to us a reasonable heuristic based on our observations of real grammars.

While we do not claim that our specification is perfect, it is the result of considerable experimentation and the resulting grammars are close to those we might expect to see for PLs. Minor variations to the specification can lead to significantly differing "styles" of grammars being generated. For instance: replacing `SingleAlt Alt` by `EmptyAlt` would cause a much higher percentage of empty alternatives to be generated.

4.2   Precision

A Boltzmann sampler is parameterised by two values that control the size of the generated objects: singular precision and value precision. To get an efficient sampler, these two values need to be set as low as possible [12]. However, the lower these values are, the greater the likelihood of large objects being generated. This is a problem for us, as "large" means rules would have more alternatives and symbols per alternative than we desire. The challenge, then, is to find values that generate large numbers of relevant grammars in reasonable time. We settled on values of $1.0e^{-7}$ and $1.0\text{-}e^{-4}$ for the singular and value precisions respectively.

4.3   Grammar Generation and Filtering

Our Boltzmann class specification gets us in the rough neighbourhood of PL grammars, but some obvious differences remain. We also struggled to generate grammars of all sizes that we wished for.

The sampler struggled to generate grammars when we restricted the number of symbols per alternative to 5, so we relaxed this criterion. Approximately 10–15% of alternatives from each grammar generated by the sampler have more than 5 symbols per alternative.

Similarly, the sampler tends to generate a much larger number of empty alternatives than are typical of PL grammars. Using Basten's PL grammar corpus as an example, the proportion of empty alternatives varied between 4% (Java) to 12% (Pascal). We therefore wrote a filter to remove all grammars that had a proportion of empty alternatives above 5%. Such filters are needed if one wishes to generate PL-like grammars.

Because the sampler is unaware of the precise semantics of grammars, it can and does produce grammars which are non-sensical or trivially ambiguous. We filter out all grammars which contain non-terminating cycles of the form A :

B and B: A as they consume no input and generate the empty language. We also filter out grammars which contain alternatives with the same sequence of symbols (e.g. A: X | X | ...) which are trivially ambiguous.

We wanted to generate grammars of size ranging from 10 to 50 inclusive. However, the sampler was unable to generate any grammars for sizes 16, 20, 25, 26, 29, 32, 40, 42, and 49. This can be solved by making the precision greater than 0.005, but this causes other issues (see Section 4.2), so we did not do so.

5   Mutated Grammars

Random grammar generators have one major problem from our perspective: even if they produce grammars in the general style of those used by PLs, it can be reasonably argued that they are never close enough. Of course, exactly what *is* close enough is impossible to pinpoint: it seems unlikely that any metric, or set of metrics, can reliably classify PL vs. non-PL grammars. Instead, we have little choice but to fall back on the intuitive notion that "we know one when we see one." This means that past work has struggled to understand how ambiguity affects PL-like grammars: we simply can't get hold of enough of them to perform adequate studies. The best attempt of which we are aware is the work of Basten, who took 20 unambiguous PL grammars and manually altered them to introduce ambiguity [14]. Manually altering grammars is tedious, hard to scale, and always open to the possibilities of unintentional human bias.

We have therefore devised a simple way of generating arbitrary numbers of 'PL-like' grammars with possible ambiguity. Our approach to grammar mutation bears no relation to grammar evolution or grammar recovery. Instead, our basic tactic is inspired by Basten's manual modifications: we take in a real (unambiguous) grammar for a PL and perform a single random alteration to a single rule. Although there are numerous possible mutations, we restrict ourselves to the following four, each of which is applied to a single rule:

Add empty alternative. This is only possible if a rule does not already have an empty alternative.

Mutate symbol. Randomly select a symbol from an alternative and change it. A non-terminal can be replaced by a terminal and vice versa.

Add symbol. Randomly pick an alternative and add a symbol at a random place within it.

Delete symbol. Randomly delete a symbol from an alternative. Only non-empty alternatives are considered.

Our mutated grammars are therefore identical to a real PL grammar, with only a single change. This is the best way that we can imagine of solving the "we know it when we see it" problem. As we will see later, these simple mutations introduce a surprising number of ambiguities. The full algorithm is presented in Appendix A.

6   Experiment Methodology

The objective of our experiment is to understand how well search-based approaches perform in detecting ambiguities. Since ambiguity is inherently undecidable, it is impossible to evaluate such a tool in an absolute sense. Instead, we evaluated our tool against three others: ACLA, AMBER, and AmbiDexter [14]. Each tool takes a different approach: ACLA uses an approximation technique; AMBER uses an exhaustive search; AmbiDexter uses a hybrid approach; and SinBAD uses a random search-based approach.

All the tools except ACLA have run-time options which adjust the way they operate and thus affect which ambiguities they find. We believe the fairest comparison is between the tools at their best and that we need to use the "best" run-time option values possible. However, discovering what the best options are by trying all possibilities on our full set of grammars is prohibitively expensive. Instead, we first run a "mini" experiment on a small set of grammars to determine good tool options. We do not claim that the option values discovered necessarily allow each tool to operate at its maximum potential; rather, we believe that they allow the tool to operate close enough to its maximum potential to make a meaningful comparison.

Using the run-time options determined by the mini experiment, we then run the "main" experiment on a larger set of grammars (about 7 times bigger) with each tool. Finally, we check that the proportion of grammars discovered as ambiguous scales up, by running a "validation" experiment using only *dynamic1* on a larger set of grammars again (about 5 times bigger than the main experiment).

Since grammars can specify infinite languages, grammar ambiguity tools can run forever. We are therefore also interested in how long it takes each tool to give quality results. For the mini and main experiments, we therefore run each tool for 10, 30, 60, and 120 seconds, enforcing the limit with the timeout tool. For AMBER the parser generation time is not included in the limit, whereas for SinBAD it is (as we were unable to break the two apart). Since this time is rather small (0.4s), we believe it does not unduly colour the results.

We evaluated the various tools on three different sets of grammars: Boltzmann sampled, altered PL grammars, and mutated grammars. Boltzmann sampled grammars were described in Section 4. Basten's altered PL grammars are taken from [5], where Pascal, SQL, Java, and C grammars were manually modified to produce 5 ambiguous variations of each. The mutated grammars were described in Section 5. Table 1 shows the size of the grammar sets used in each experiment. For the Boltzmann sampled grammars, each size (10-50) is represented equally (i.e. for the main experiment, 50 grammars of each size are used). Similarly, for the mutated grammars, each mutation category (add empty alternative, mutate symbol, add symbol, and delete symbol) is equally represented (e.g. for the main experiment, 500 grammars from each category are used). Note that we are not worried about differences in the ambiguous fragments identified: we care only whether a tool uncovers ambiguity in a grammar or not.

All experiments were performed on a cluster of identical Intel i7-2600 CPU 3.4GHz machines with 8GiB memory. For the mini experiment, where perfect

Table 1. The number of grammars used in the various experiments

	Mini	Main	Validation
Boltzmann	384	1600	9600
Altered PL	20	20	20
Mutated	160	2000	11200
Total	564	3620	20820

Table 2. Options tried in the mini experiment

Tool	Option	Values
AMBER	Search by length	5, 10, 15, 20, 25, 50, 100
	Search by example	10^{10}, 10^{20}, 10^{30}
	Ellipsis	Yes / No
AmbiDexter	From 0 to N	5, 10, 15, 20, 25, 50, 100
	From N to ∞	0
	Filter	None, LR0, SLR1, LALR1, LR1
dynamic1	Depth	5, 6, 7, ..., 30

precision was not necessary, we used 8 cores (4 real and 4 hyperthreading) per machine. For the main and validation experiments, where precision is important, we disabled hyperthreading and restricted ourselves to utilising 3 cores per machine. We used `parallel`[3] to parallelise our experiment. The experiments took around 3400 core-hours in total, broken down into: 600 hours for the mini experiment; 2000 for the main experiment; and 800 for the validation experiment.

Our experimental setup is fully repeatable and is available through our downloadable experimental suite.

7 Mini Experiment

In the mini experiment, we wish to uncover what reasonable values for various options are. ACLA has no options, so does not to be considered further. The options and their values tried for the other tools are outlined in Table 2.

AMBER can search either by length (sentences up to a fixed length) or by example (search limited by number of sentences with no restriction on sentence length). The 'ellipsis' option causes non-terminals to be treated as tokens, which increases the chances of finding long ambiguous fragments. We found that in most cases, turning on the 'ellipsis' option led to better results: 22 with it set vs. 18 without. Only for the 'add empty alternative' variant of mutated grammars did the ellipsis option perform worse.

---

[3] http://www.gnu.org/software/parallel

Table 3. Best performing options for each tool

Grammar set	ACLA	AMBER[a]	AmbiDexter[b]	*dynamic1*[c]
Boltzmann	n/a	ell+N=10^{10}	ik+unf	D=11
Altered PL	n/a	ell+len=10	k=15+LR0	D=9
Mutated	n/a	len=15	k=15+SLR1	D=17

[a] ell, len, N ≜ AMBER options *ellipsis*, *length* and *examples* respectively.
[b] ik, k, unf ≜ AmbiDexter options incremental length, maximum length of sentences to check, unfiltered version of a grammar respectively.
[c] D ≜ Threshold depth for *dynamic1*.

AmbiDexter has two modes of sentence generation: searching for sentences up to length N, or searching for sentences from a starting length N to ∞. AmbiDexter also supports filters that can identify and remove provably unambiguous subsets of a grammar. These filters are of varying power: LR0 (low) to LR1 (high). The more powerful a filter is, the greater the portion of a grammar it can filter out, but the longer it takes to do so. We evaluated the tool with both unfiltered and filtered versions of a grammar. Generating a filtered version of a grammar is included in the time limit.

SinBAD's *dynamic1* backend requires a depth option D to determine when it should attempt to unwind recursion. We evaluated D for values from 5 to 30. For lower values of D, *dynamic1* starts favouring alternatives much earlier, and therefore sentences are short and quick to generate. For higher values of D, *dynamic1* generates longer sentences. In the cases where *dynamic1*'s sentence generator did not terminate, we re-ran it (in such cases, the normal time limit still applied, preventing infinite re-runs).

The values we chose for the mini experiment were based on our experience of using the tools in question, and our need to choose a reasonable subset of options in order to have a tractable experiment. To check that the values we chose were not biased against the tools, we performed a brief sanity check on each of the 'best' values found, checking several of its near neighbours. Only with AMBER was there a measurable difference (when searching by example). Using a value of 10^{10} with the 'search by example' option, 238 Boltzmann sampled grammars were found to be ambiguous; with a value of 10^8, 240 were found to be ambiguous. For the mutated grammars, 10^{10} found 6 ambiguities whereas 10^7 found 7 ambiguities. In both cases, the differences are sufficiently small to make us comfortable with sticking with the original values.

Table 3 lists the best performing options for each tool. All the data involved are available from our downloadable experimental suite.

8   Main Experiment

The main experiment is the largest cross ambiguity detection tool experiment to date. All the data involved are available from our downloadable experimental suite.

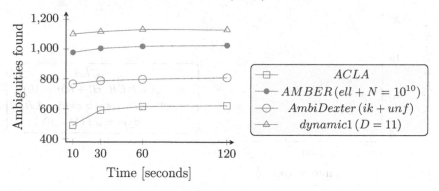

Fig. 4. Number of ambiguities found for Boltzmann sampled grammars

Figures 4, 5, and 6 show the results of our experiments for each grammar set, for each time limit. In analysing some of the results from the main experiment, we had to perform additional experiments. In most cases, we used grammars from the main experiment. In only one case, for collecting data for sentence and ambiguous fragment length, have we used grammars from the mini experiment.

Our results from the main experiment indicated that three of our grammar sets were highly ambiguous: Boltzmann sampled (70%), the 'add empty alternative' mutated grammars (60%), and 'delete symbol' mutated grammars (45%). Manual observation of ambiguous grammars led to two observations:

Cyclic ambiguity. Rules that contain cycles of the form (A: A | ...) or (A: B | ...; B: A | ...) contribute to cyclic ambiguity [15]. We manually calculated the percentage of cyclically ambiguous grammars to be: 22% (Boltzmann sampled), 0% (Altered PL), and 0.009% (Mutated). This appears to be by far the most common type of ambiguity we encounter.

Multiple ambiguity. A grammar has multiple ambiguity if it has more than one ambiguous subset. 36% of Boltzmann grammars contained 2.5 ambiguities per grammar. For mutated grammars the figures are: 37% and 2.8 for 'add empty alternative'; 13% and 3 for 'mutate symbol'; 4% and 2.7 for 'add symbol'; and 23% and 2.6 for 'delete symbol'.

In the rest of this section, we explore what the results mean for each tool (in alphabetical order).

8.1 ACLA

Given a grammar, ACLA will report it to be ambiguous, unambiguous, or possibly ambiguous (that is, it is unsure if the grammar is ambiguous). ACLA's approach to ambiguity detection is based on two linguistic properties: vertical and horizontal ambiguity. Vertical ambiguity means that during the parsing of

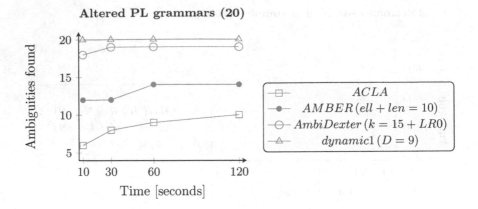

Fig. 5. Number of ambiguities found for altered PL grammars

Table 4. Maximum sentence ('Sen') and ambiguous fragment ('Amb') length detected by each tool using the options from Table 3. Note: we were unable to determine the sentence length for ACLA.

	ACLA		AMBER		AmbiDexter		*dynamic1*	
	Sen	Amb	Sen	Amb	Sen	Amb	Sen	Amb
Boltzmann	-	15	58	14	27	21	1554664	2671
Altered PL	-	11	10	9	15	15	281	88
Mutated	-	15	15	6	15	15	4392	502

a string, there is a choice between the alternatives of a non-terminal. Horizontal ambiguity means that, when parsing a string according to a production alternative, there is a choice in how the string can be split.

For Boltzmann and mutated grammars, ACLA reported only one or two grammars to be unambiguous. On average across the grammar sets, ACLA was unsure whether 50–60% of the grammars were ambiguous or not. ACLA did not detect 12% of cyclically ambiguous grammars as being ambiguous. ACLA detects ambiguity in a grammar by iterating through each non-terminal, and checking its language for vertically or horizontally ambiguous strings. Although it is not clear what sort of string length it searches for, the length of ambiguous fragments that it detects, on average, ranges between 10 and 15 (see Table 4). In most cases, where the ambiguous subset is deeply nested, ACLA is unsure if the grammar is ambiguous. For most grammar sets, ACLA reaches a point of diminishing returns at 120s. Only in the case of mutated grammars, did our results (see Figure 6) seem to indicate that given additional time, ACLA might uncover further ambiguities. Running ACLA for an extended time limit of 240s only uncovered in 4 additional ambiguities being found.

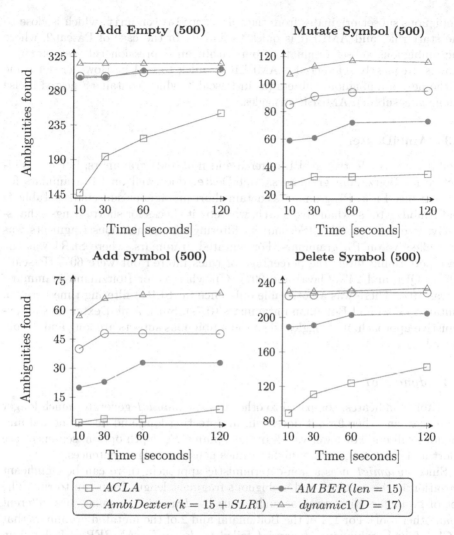

Fig. 6. Number of ambiguities found for mutated grammars

8.2   AMBER

AMBER performs extremely well on the Boltzmann grammars, but less well on manually altered or mutated grammars. AMBER uses an exhaustive approach to ambiguity detection, whereby it systematically enumerates strings for a given grammar, and checks for ambiguity. There are two possible reasons why AMBER does well on Boltzmann grammars. First, these grammars contain multiple ambiguities, and a relatively high percentage of cyclically ambiguous grammars. AMBER was quick to detect these ambiguities. Second, the ambiguous subsets found are easily reachable, in the sense that they are referenced from very near the start of the grammar. For instance, in the case of Java.1, where the ambiguous subset originates from the rule `compilation_unit`, which is close to the start rule, and AMBER is quick to find it. In the case of Pascal.2, where the ambiguous subset originates from within an expression rule set (`term`) – that is, frequently referenced – AMBER is quick to find it. However, for some of the nested ambiguous subsets (as in Pascal.3, which contains a nested if-else ambiguous subset), AMBER struggles.

8.3   AmbiDexter

AmbiDexter is effective for PL (altered and mutated) grammars, but is less effective for Boltzmann grammars. AmbiDexter does well on PL grammars for two reasons. First, PL grammars contain short ambiguous subsets (see Table 4) and AmbiDexter's exhaustive search, whereby it checks for short strings exhaustively, is quick to find it. Second, its filtering of unambiguous fragments was very effective on PL grammars. For mutated grammars, where SLR1 was the best performing filter, the percentage of rules filtered out were 60% (Pascal), 90% (SQL), and 24% (Java) and 20% (C), whereas for Boltzmann grammars, it was 19%. There was a noticeable difference in (SLR1) filtering time between mutated (1.3s) and Boltzmann grammars (0.7s). Since AmbiDexter uses an exhaustive approach, it struggles when the ambiguous subsets are long and deeply nested.

8.4   *dynamic1*

As Table 4 indicates, compared to other tools, *dynamic1* generates much longer sentences, and therefore, it does well, in detecting long and deeply nested ambiguous subsets. For lower values of the *dynamic1*'s depth option, sentences are short and quick to generate; higher values generate longer sentences.

Since *dynamic1* uses a non-deterministic approach, there can be significant variation in the sentence and ambiguous fragment length from run to run. The set of grammars discovered as ambiguous by *dynamic1* is sometimes different than other tools. For 111 of the Boltzmann and 2 of the mutated grammars that ACLA found ambiguous, *dynamic1* failed to do so; for AMBER, 4 Boltzmann and 2 mutated PL grammars; for AmbiDexter, 2 Boltzmann and 8 mutated grammars. Some of the grammars amongst these sets are common, but by no means all.

Of the 111 Boltzmann grammars for which ACLA detected ambiguity and *dynamic1* failed to detect any, 110 of them contained ambiguous subsets that were unreachable from the start rule. For instance, a grammar with rules `root: 'p'` and `A: 'q' | 'q'` contains an ambiguous subset that is unreachable from the start rule. Since ACLA's approach to ambiguity detection is by searching for ambiguous strings for each non-terminal, it can detect ambiguities that are unreachable from the start rule. We did not anticipate our Boltzmann sampler generating such non-sensical grammars, and recommend that future experiments filter them out. The remaining one grammar for ACLA, and the grammars for AMBER and AmbiDexter, contained common subsets, totalling 4 Boltzmann grammars. For

2 of them, *dynamic1* did not terminate, exited and re-ran (roughly 500 times for one of the grammars). For the remaining two grammars, one of them contained a short but deeply nested ambiguous subset, whereas for the other the ambiguous fragment was long and, for D=11 (the best performing option for Boltzmann grammar), *dynamic1* didn't generate sufficiently long sentences to uncover ambiguity.

For the mutated grammar set, *dynamic1* didn't detect ambiguity for a total of 9 grammars for which the other tools detected ambiguity. For 4 of these grammars, the ambiguous subsets were short but deeply nested. For 2 of these grammars, the ambiguous fragments were long, and D=17 (the best performing option for mutated grammars) did not generate sufficiently long sentences to uncover ambiguity. The remaining 3 grammars were cyclically ambiguous, and *dynamic1*'s sentence generator did not terminate for them.

9 Validation Experiment

In order to ensure that the results of Figures 4, 5, 6 scale to larger sets of grammars, we used *dynamic1* to perform a validation experiment on a much larger set of grammars (see Table 1). The number of ambiguities found for 120 seconds were 70% (Boltzmann) and 63%, 21%, 13%, and 45% (for mutated types: add empty alternative, mutate symbol, add symbol and delete symbol respectively). The proportion of ambiguities found in our validation experiment is close to the number of ambiguities found in the main experiment (see Figures 4 and 6). All the data involved are available from our experimental downloadable suite.

10 Validating the Hypotheses

In Section 1, we stated two hypotheses which informed our work. In this section, we revisit the hypotheses in the light of our results.

Hypothesis H1 postulates that "covering a grammar in breadth is more likely to uncover ambiguity than covering it in depth." *dynamic1*'s non-deterministic approach tends to naturally generate sentences which cover much larger portions of a grammar than previous approaches. It is therefore more successful at uncovering ambiguity against our grammar corpus than other tools. Although non-determinism clearly plays its part, we believe that *dynamic1*'s coverage is key and strongly validates hypothesis H1.

Hypothesis H2 postulates that "PL grammars are only a small step away from being ambiguous." The mutated grammars are our attempt to explore this hypothesis and as the validation experiment shows, just over a third of mutations to real PL grammars result in *dynamic1* detecting ambiguity. This proportion is a lower-bound: it is possible that there is further ambiguity in the mutated grammars that *dynamic1* (and, indeed, any other tool) does not discover. We consider this validation of hypothesis H2.

11   Threats to Validity

The most obvious threat to the validity of our results are the grammars used.

In a previous experiment [9] we used a hand-written generator to create random grammars. In this paper we created a Boltzmann sampler to reduce the chances of bias in our hand-written generator. Interestingly, this made relatively little difference to the number of ambiguous grammars we found. However, it is impractical to generate completely arbitrary grammars, since they have no size limit. Our Boltzmann specification is therefore geared towards generating grammars which are "somewhat PL like". It is possible that it still produces overly biased grammars, particularly as we are forced to use filters to remove some grammars we consider irrelevant or unrepresentative. Our current Boltzmann sampler can create grammars which have subsets of rules which are not reachable from the start rule; ironically, these grammars penalise *dynamic1* relative to other ambiguity tools such as ACLA. However, we believe that, overall, it is more trustworthy than any previous random grammar generator.

The mutated grammars are also a potential threat to validity as we might have chosen unrepresentative grammars as a base. Since they come from an external source, we have some level of confidence in them.

The final threat to validity is our use of a mini experiment to determine a reasonable set of run-time options for the various tools used. It is possible that the grammars used in the mini experiment were unrepresentative of those used in the main experiment, though our measurements suggest this is unlikely. The percentage of ambiguous Boltzmann grammars were 67% (mini) and 70% (main). The percentage of ambiguous mutated grammars (add empty alternative, mutate symbol, add symbol, delete symbol) were mini (60%, 30%, 10%, and 42%) and main (63%, 22%, 13%, and 46%).

12   Conclusions

In this paper, we introduced the concept of a search-based approach to CFG ambiguity detection with the SinBAD tool and its *dynamic1* backend. Using the largest grammar corpus to date, we showed that *dynamic1* can detect a larger number of ambiguities than previous approaches. The key to its success is its use of non-determinism, which has several surprising consequences. It frees us from having to design many complex heuristics. *dynamic1*'s only heuristic relates to the need to terminate the sentence generator. In turn, this allows *dynamic1* to explore a much larger portion of a grammar than by previous approaches and it increases the chances of detecting ambiguous fragments nested deep within a grammar. In essence, our results suggest that covering the breadth of a grammar's state space is more important than covering it in depth.

dynamic1's chief weakness is that its single deterministic point causes it not to terminate on some grammars. We suspect that a probabilistic approach which gives a lower chance to frequently derived alternatives – in other words, which makes it less likely, but not impossible, that they are picked – will make non-termination less likely whilst preserving *dynamic1*'s general approach.

We also introduced two new ways of generating large grammar corpuses: Boltzmann sampling and grammar mutation. The grammars created using Boltzmann sampling were highly ambiguous and thus not entirely representative of PL grammars. The mutated grammars, on the other hand, are representative of PL grammars although how ambiguous they are depends on the mutation. Our results indicate that certain mutations tend to cause grammars to be highly ambiguous whereas others less so. Our experience suggest that for uses that require exploring wide class of grammars, one should use Boltzmann sampling whereas, uses that require exploring PL grammars, one should use grammar mutation.

Acknowledgements. We are extremely grateful to Alexis Darrasse (LIP6) for his advice in creating a Boltzmann sampler specification. We thank the Department of Informatics at King's College for giving extended access to computing facilities. Edd Barrett and Carl Friedrich Bolz gave insightful comments on drafts of this paper.

References

1. Cantor, D.G.: On the ambiguity problem of backus systems. Journal of the ACM 9(4), 477–479 (1962)
2. Tratt, L.: Parsing: The solved problem that isn't. Hacker Monthly, 37–42 (June 2011)
3. Schröer, F.W.: Amber, an ambiguity checker for context-free grammars. Technical report (2001), http://accent.compilertools.net/Amber.html
4. Brabrand, C., Giegerich, R., Møller, A.: Analyzing ambiguity of context-free grammars. Science of Computer Programming 75(3), 176–191 (2010)
5. Basten, H.J.S., Vinju, J.J.: Faster ambiguity detection by grammar filtering. In: Proc. LDTA, pp. 5:1–5:9 (2010)
6. Axelsson, R., Heljanko, K., Lange, M.: Analyzing context-free grammars using an incremental SAT solver. In: Aceto, L., Damgård, I., Goldberg, L.A., Halldórsson, M.M., Ingólfsdóttir, A., Walukiewicz, I. (eds.) ICALP 2008, Part II. LNCS, vol. 5126, pp. 410–422. Springer, Heidelberg (2008)
7. Cheung, B.S.N., Uzgalis, R.C.: Ambiguity in context-free grammars. In: Proc. SAC, pp. 272–276. ACM (1995)
8. Basten, H.J.S.: Ambiguity detection methods for context-free grammars. Master's thesis, Universiteit van Amsterdam (August 2007)
9. Vasudevan, N., Tratt, L.: Search-based ambiguity detection in context-free grammars. In: Proc. ICCSW, pp. 142–148 (September 2012)
10. Harman, M.: The current state and future of search based software engineering. In: FOSE, pp. 342–357 (2007)
11. Schröer, F.W.: Accent, a compiler compiler for the entire class of context-free grammars. Technical report (2000), http://accent.compilertools.net/Accent.html
12. Canou, B., Darrasse, A.: Fast and sound random generation for automated testing and benchmarking in objective caml. In: Proc. Workshop on ML, pp. 61–70 (2009)
13. Mougenot, A., Darrasse, A., Blanc, X., Soria, M.: Uniform random generation of huge metamodel instances. In: Paige, R.F., Hartman, A., Rensink, A. (eds.) ECMDA-FA 2009. LNCS, vol. 5562, pp. 130–145. Springer, Heidelberg (2009)
14. Basten, H.J.S., van der Storm, T.: Ambidexter: Practical ambiguity detection. In: Proc. SCAM 2010, pp. 101–102 (2010)
15. Tomita, M.: An efficient context-free parsing algorithm for natural languages. In: Proc. IJCAI, pp. 756–764 (1985)

A   Mutated Grammar Generation Algorithm

Algorithm 2 shows how we generate a mutated version of a grammar. $\mu_{type} \in$ $\{empty, mutate, add, delete\}$ indicates the type of mutation to be performed for a given grammar. The function MUTATE-GRAMMAR first creates a deep copy of the grammar. For the 'add empty alternative' mutation, we first identify non-terminals which do not already have an empty alternative (line 4), before randomly selecting one, and adding an empty alternative. For mutations of type 'add symbol' we randomly select a non-terminal, before randomly selecting one of its alternatives. From the selected alternative, we randomly pick a position and insert a randomly selected symbol from V (line 12). For mutation s of type 'mutate symbol' and 'delete symbol', we randomly select a non-terminal, before randomly selecting one of its non empty alternatives. To mutate a symbol, we randomly pick a position from the selected alternative and replace it with a randomly selected symbol from V (line 18). To delete a symbol, we randomly pick a position from the selected alternative, and delete it (line 20).

Algorithm 2. An algorithm to generate a mutated version of a grammar

---

1: **function** MUTATE-GRAMMAR(G, μ_{type})
2:    $G_c \leftarrow copy(G)$ ▷ $Gc = \langle N_c, T_c, P_c, S_c \rangle$
3:    **if** $\mu_{type} = empty$ **then**
4:        $N_\psi \leftarrow \{A \in N_c \mid A \notin N_\epsilon \}$
5:        $A \leftarrow \mathcal{R}(N_\psi, 1)$
6:        $\Sigma P[A]_{alt} \leftarrow append(\Sigma P[A]_{alt}, [\,])$
7:    **else**
8:        $A \leftarrow \mathcal{R}(N_c, 1)$
9:        **if** $\mu_{type} = \{add\}$ **then**
10:            $alt \leftarrow \mathcal{R}(\Sigma P[A]_{alt}, 1)$
11:            $k \leftarrow \mathcal{R}[0, |alt|)$
12:            $alt \leftarrow insert(alt, k, \mathcal{R}(V, 1))$
13:        **else if** $\mu_{type} \in \{mutate, delete\}$ **then**
14:            $alts \leftarrow \{alt \in \Sigma P[A]_{alt} \mid |alt| > 0 \}$
15:            $alt \leftarrow \mathcal{R}(alts, 1)$
16:            $k \leftarrow \mathcal{R}[0, |alt|\text{-}1)$
17:            **if** $\mu_{type} = \{mutate\}$ **then**
18:                $alt[k] \leftarrow \mathcal{R}(V, 1)$
19:            **else**
20:                $alt \leftarrow delete(alt, k)$
21:            **end if**
22:        **end if**
23:    **end if**
24:    **return** G_c
25: **end function**

A Pretty Good Formatting Pipeline

Anya Helene Bagge and Tero Hasu

Bergen Language Design Laboratory
Dept. of Informatics, University of Bergen, Norway

Abstract. Proper formatting makes the structure of a program apparent and aids program comprehension. The need to format code arises in
code generation and transformation, as well as in normal reading and
editing situations. Commonly used pretty-printing tools in transformation frameworks provide an easy way to produce indented code that is
fairly readable for humans, without reaching the level of purpose-built
reformatting tools, such as those built into IDEs. This paper presents a
library of pluggable components, built to support style-based formatting
and reformatting of code, and to enable further experimentation with
code formatting.

1 Introduction

Pretty-printing and code formatting are fundamental in the software language
engineering toolbox. There are two main aspects to pretty-printing: creating
textual output from an internal representation, and ensuring that the textual
representation is visually pleasing and/or structurally clear. The ideal code formatting results in text that conveys the semantics as clearly as possible within
the constraints of the medium.

In this paper, we will focus mainly on the formatting aspect, rather than on
producing text output from an internal representation. Code formatting must
take into account the syntactic and maybe also the semantic structure of the
code in order to maximise the readability of the output. For example, the treat-
ment of spacing around a minus symbol depends on whether it occurs as a binary
operator (typically spaced on both sides), a unary operator (typically with no
space after), or in some other context. For this reason, the input to the formatting must either contain the necessary syntactic and semantic information, or it
must be reconstructed prior to formatting (via lexical, syntactic and/or semantic
analysis).

We may consider several formatting concerns:

- *Horizontal spacing.* Good placement of spaces can make the details easier
  to grasp. For example, an expression such as a+x * y may easily confuse a
  casual reader as to the operator precedence, compared to a + x*y or even
  the neutrally spaced a + x * y (assuming normal operator priorities).
- *Indentation* has long been considered important to visual recognition of
  scope and nesting structures in program text [12]. This insight goes back
  at least to the 1960s [11].

M. Erwig, R.F. Paige, and E. Van Wyk (Eds.): SLE 2013, LNCS 8225, pp. 177–196, 2013.

- *Line breaking* may be necessary to fit the program to the screen or output medium. Line breaking must trade off efficient use of the human field of vision against program comprehension concerns such as keeping related things together and less related things further apart.
- Other processing, such as colourising or highlighting, attaching additional information such as hover text for HTML output and so on.

This paper describes our *pretty good formatter* (PGF) and associated experimental formatting components. PGF uses a pipeline of connected components to format or reformat code, where the various concerns of producing pretty code are separated into different *processors*; one for inserting horizontal space, one for breaking lines, one for adding colour and so on. PGF is designed to be useful for code generation, reformatting, or just reindenting code – depending on which components are plugged into the pipeline. PGF provides basic building blocks for making processing components, and the included components are designed to be reusable for different languages, with appropriate customisation.

The pipeline architecture itself is reusable for other purposes, and offers support for processing data concurrently in a pipeline, one data item at a time. Each processing component has access to a stream of input and a stream of output, and may specify a desired level of look-ahead and output history, in order to process based on a sliding window of information.

PGF is implemented as a reusable Java library, with experiments and prototypes in the Rascal meta-programming language [10] and the Scheme variant Racket [4]. The paper presents a mixture of the library proper, and the associated experiments. All source code and related content is online.[1]

The contributions of this paper include:

- *Pipeline processing*: a pipelined framework for building flexible code formatters and rule-based token processors (Section 2);
- *Line breaking*: a new heuristic line-breaking algorithm, and a reformulation of two other algorithms to fit our architecture (Section 3).
- *Pipeline plumbing*: a stream-based plugin architecture for connecting components in a pipeline, and a technique for grouping tokens and building pipelines dynamically (Section 4)

After presenting the contributions, the paper continues with a discussion and related work (Section 5), and conclusion (Section 6).

2 The Formatting Pipeline

Our formatter is built from a pipeline of *token processors*. Each processor receives a stream of tokens, processes them one by one, and feeds them to the next processor. The pipeline is illustrated in Fig. 1, which shows an input tree, an output text and two different pipeline arrangements, one doing line breaking and another one doing colourising and indentation. More details about the pipeline infrastructure is provided in Section 4.

---

[1] http://nuthatchery.org/pgf/

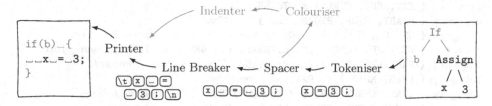

Fig. 1. A PGF pipeline. Starting with a program tree (rightmost), we translate it to a stream of tokens, then insert spaces, do indentation and line breaking, before producing program text (leftmost). The alternative path (light blue), adds colour and does indentation without line breaking. The token stream is shown below each step. In this example, each token is only one character wide; this is not generally the case.

2.1   Tokens and Categories

Tokens are either *data tokens* or *control tokens*. Each data token represents an atomic piece of source code to be output, while the control tokens (if used) may convey information about nesting, indentation levels, etc.

Each data token contains a string of characters, and is associated with a *category*, and possibly other metadata. The categories are user-definable, but we have selected a set of default categories (see Fig. 2), in order to aid reusability of components.

In this paper, we write data tokens enclosed in quotes, optionally followed by a colon and the category; for example, $"if"$:KEYWORD, $" "$:WS, $"("$:LPAR. Control tokens are marked by a hash character followed by the category and possibly a list of parameters, e.g., #BEGIN(expr). The PGF library itself uses slightly different conventions, depending on the implementation language.

Each token has only one specified category, but each category may be a subcategory of zero or more supercategories, with A <: B indicating that A is a subcategory of B – implying that any token categorised as A can also be categorised as B:

$$\frac{t : A \qquad A <: B}{t : B}$$

We will use A <: B also for the case where A is connected to B through one or more intermediate steps. Note that, in this case, there may be multiple paths through the supercategory chain, since each category can have multiple supercategories.

The use of categories is crucial for achieving reusability and language independence of processors. For example, languages that mostly follow the same spacing rules can reuse the same processor as long as the language-specific tokens are mapped to the same, general categories – possibly with a few additional language-specific rules.

When customising a processor for a particular language, it may be useful to have a one-to-one correspondence between token text and category, for instance, in the case of keywords. So, we may have $"if"$:IF and $"else"$:ELSE, with

```
category { TXT, SPC, CTRL } <: TOKEN;
category { START, STOP, BEGIN, END } <: CTRL;
category { WS, NL, COM } <: SPC; // horizontal, vertical space; comments
category { KEYWORD, PUNCT, ID, LITERAL, OP, GRP } <: TXT; // non—space
category { PAR, BRC, BRT } <: GROUPING; // parens, braces, brackets
category { LPAR, RPAR } <: PAR; // parentheses
category { LPAR, LBRC, LBRT } <: LGROUPING; // left grouping tokens
category { COMMA, SEMI, COLON, DOT } <: PUNCT; // punctuation
```

Fig. 2. A selection of the default token categories. In the notation, `category` defines one or more new categories (left-hand side), listing any supercategories to the right of the <: sign.

{IF, ELSE} <:KEYWORD, and a rule stating that we should never break the line between IF and ELSE.

Token processors make their decisions primarily based on token categories, and not by inspecting token data. The flexible category hierarchy allows several aspects to be encoded. For example, with a default categorisation of "(" as LPAR, a left parenthesis token will belong to both its own category, as well as PAR (parentheses in general), LGRP (left grouping tokens), GRP (groupings in general), TXT (printable, non-space tokens), TOKEN (any token), and decisions may be made on the basis of any of these.

2.2   The Tokeniser

The first processor in a pipeline is the *tokeniser*, which turns the input (whatever that might be) into a stream of tokens. We envisage three kinds of input:

- a parse tree, containing both structural and lexical information, or
- an abstract syntax tree, containing mostly structural information (maybe including semantic information), or
- a token sequence from a lexer, containing mostly lexical information.

With an abstract syntax tree, the lexical information must be reconstructed, for example using a pretty-print table generated from the grammar, or by a hand-written tokeniser which traverses the AST and outputs appropriate tokens for each AST node.

Lexer output might be more or less directly usable, possibly with mapping of the lexer's token categories to the formatter's. As we've only been using scannerless parsers, we have not explored this option further.

With a parse tree as input, all necessary information for printing and formatting should be available, and we can use a generic parse tree tokeniser to obtain the token stream. We have written such tokenisers that accepts parse trees in the UPTR and AsFix2 formats.[2]

---

[2] UPTR is the *Universal Parse Tree Representation*; it is used by Rascal, and is fairly similar to its predecessor, AsFix2, which is used by SDF2 and the SGLR and JSGLR parsers.

Generic Parse Tree Tokeniser. The parse tree tokeniser (available in UPTR and AsFix2 versions) traverses a parse tree, and produces data tokens for leaf node; i.e., lexical (corresponding to identifies, numbers and such), literal (corresponding to keywords and punctuation) or layout (corresponding to white space and comments) nodes. The layout nodes are split into horizontal space (WS), newlines (NL) and comments (COM), and literals and lexicals are categorised according to a customisable scheme:

- the text of each token is checked against a category mapping table (one for lexicals and one for literals) either by exact string matching or regular expression matching;
- the parse tree node is checked for a category annotation (such annotations can be added automatically by a parser); and/or
- all tokens of the same syntactic sort can be mapped to the same category.

Remaining non-space tokens are categorised as the default TXT.

Additionally, control tokens may be emitted for some non-leaf nodes in the parse tree – for example, indentation may require #BEGIN/#END control tokens around lists of statements and other parts of the code that should be indented.

Mapping tables for literals, lexicals and sorts are all configurable, allowing the tokeniser to be customised to a particular language, and having it output tokens categorised according to a common scheme.

As an example, consider the following Java code input:

```
if(b) { x = 3; }
```

After parsing it using an SDF2 grammar[3], the AsFix2 tokeniser yields the following token stream:

`"if":IF  "(":LPAR  "b":ID  ")":RPAR  " ":WS  "{":LBRC #BEGIN  " ":WS  "x":ID  " ":WS  "=":EQ  " ":WS  "3":NUM  ";":SEMI  " ":WS #END  "}":RBRC`

A further refinement would be to tokenise comments, so they can be reformatted as well.

2.3 Token Processors

A token processor accepts a stream of input tokens, and produces a stream of output tokens. Each processor has a **process** method which performs one step of the processor. The pipeline framework will ensure that **process** is called whenever there is available input to process.

The processor connects to the overall pipeline through a *pipe connector* which provides buffering (if needed), a history of recently outputted tokens (if needed) and may also provide transparent handling of control tokens for processors that are only interested in data tokens.

We are free to implement a process in any way, as long as it satisfies the general interface, but for convenience and performance, we provide a rule-based framework for specifying processors. This should be suitable for most simple

---

[3] JavaFront – http://strategoxt.org/Stratego/JavaFront

cases; more advanced processors can be programmed in a general purpose language. Section 2.4 and Section 2.5 give examples of token processors for adjusting spacing and breaking lines, respectively. Full versions of the processors and additional processors (including a general indenter) can be found in the online materials.

Rule-Based Token Processors. A rule-base processor makes decisions based on a set of prioritised rules. Each rule consists of a condition and an action. In our Java library, conditions and actions are built using static methods returning condition and action objects. Two kinds of conditions are currently supported:

- `at(CAT...)` true if the next incoming token(s) match `CAT...` ("looking at")
- `after(CAT...)` true if the last emitted token(s) match `CAT...`

For example, the condition `after(A, B).at(C, D)` matches if the next tokens match category C and D, and the last emitted token was a B preceded by an A.[4] A token $t:C_t$ matches a category C iff $C_t = C$ or $C_t <: C$.

An action may be arbitrary Java code, or selected from a simple library of actions:

- `insert("txt", CAT)` – insert a token before the current token
- `move` – move the current token from input to output
- `seq(a1, a2, ...)` – execute actions in sequence
- `drop` – delete the current token without producing output

Rules are added to the processor using the `addRule` method. For example, the following processing rule deletes all spaces:

```
addRule(at(SPC), drop);
```

We'll see more examples in Section 2.4.

Rule processing is implemented using decision tables, where a pair of categories are looked up, resulting in an action to be executed. We currently only support matching with two categories – either a `after(A).at(B)` pair, or a two token look-ahead, `at(A, B)`. If only one category is given in a rule, the other is assumed to be `TOKEN`, the supercategory of all categories.

Rule Priorities. It will often be the case that there is more than one matching rule in a given situation. The general rule for resolving such ambiguities is that the more specific rule should apply. In this context, "more specific" means, for a rule with two categories:

- Assuming we are looking at a token with categories C, D, and we have two rules r_1 and r_2 with conditions involving C_1, D_1 and C_2, D_2 respectively, with $C <: C_1$, $C <: C_2$, $D <: D_1$, and $D <: D_2$;

---

[4] It is useful to think of the tokens as flowing in from the right (or, equivalently, that the token processor moves left-to-right over the token stream).

- rule r_1 is more specific than rule r_2 if $dist(C, C_1) + dist(D, D_2) < dist(C, C_2) + dist(D, D_2)$,
- where $dist(A, B)$ is the number of steps in the shortest supercategory chain $A <: \ldots <: B$ from A to B.

In addition to this priority rule we may also state that one set of rules should always have priority over another set of rules. When building a rule processor, this can be accomplished with the `addPriorityLevel` method.

Potential conflicts can be determined when the decision table is built, and a suitable warning will be provided to the programmer.

2.4   Token Processor: Spacer

The duty of the *spacer* is to process a stream of tokens, and insert spaces as appropriate. This is used to control horizontal spacing in a document.

Spacing can increase readability, even though many languages do not treat spaces as significant. A naive pretty-printing may insert spaces between all tokens, just to be on the safe side (e.g., preventing identifiers from running into each other). A more refined approach is to insert spaces according to style rules.

Spacing is readily implemented with a rule-based processor. Since many spacing rules are similar across languages (e.g., "`(x, y)`" is preferable to "`( x ,y)`"), we expect to be able to reuse much of the spacing code for multiple languages.

For a Java or a similar language, some sensible spacing rules might be:

- No spaces on the inner side of parentheses
- Always (or never) space between an `if` and the parenthesis
- Always space after a comma, never before
- No space before semicolon
- Always space around a binary operator
- Always spaces between any other tokens

We may implement these rules using the code in Fig. 3. The rule set removes all spaces from the input (highest priority level), and – unless otherwise specified – adds a new space between all text tokens (lowest priority level).

If we apply the rules to the following Java code:

```
if(b) {x=3;}else{x=4;}
if(b) x = f ( 1,2,3);
```

we get the following result, with some spaces inserted and some removed:

```
if (b) { x = 3; } else { x = 4; }
if (b) x = f(1, 2, 3);
```

A user-friendly configuration frontend could present customisation choices to the user, and then select appropriate rules to implement them. Note that it is also possible to specify certain rules to be followed (e.g., no space before comma, always after), while not otherwise changing the input.

```
addRule(at(WS), drop);  // delete all incoming spaces

addPriorityLevel();  // rules above have highest priority

addRule(after(LPAR), nop);  // no space after left parenthesis
addRule(at(PAR), nop);  // no spaces before parentheses
addRule(after(IF).at(LPAR), space);  // but always between 'if' and '('

addRule(at(PUNCT), nop);  // no space before comma, semicolon, etc.

addRule(after(TXT).at(BINOP), space);  // space around binary operators (this
addRule(after(BINOP).at(TXT), space);  // actually follows from the general rule)

addPriorityLevel();  // rules below have lowest priority

addRule(after(TXT).at(TXT), space);  // general rule
```

Fig. 3. A selection of sample spacing rules. The full spacing code for Java is available online. The command *space* inserts a space before the token we're looking **at**; *drop* deletes the token, and *nop* keeps the token (used for overriding a more general rule).

2.5   Token Processor: Line Breaker

The *line breaker* is responsible for turning a token stream into something that is ready for printing or converting into a string. This means reducing all formatting related stream content into nothing but text and line breaks. If line breaking is done, any indentation must be done together with it, since indentation has an impact on line width (though it is certainly possible to do only indentation in a pipeline, without line breaking).

Line breaking is easily the most challenging part of code formatting, involving trade-offs between horizontal and vertical space usage, code clarity and aesthetics. Also, earlier breaking decisions can impact later ones, in terms of how much space is available on a line – making the 'wrong' choice can make it impossible to achieve a pleasing result later.

We have experimented with three different line breakers. One is experimental, and based on assigning a 'breakability' value to each space (based, e.g. on how deeply nested an expression is); the higher its value, the more breakable it is, and the more likely it is that we break the line at that point, particularly as we get closer to the end of the line (Section 3.2). Another one is a refinement of an algorithm by Wadler [18]; some extensions have been added, and adjustments have been made to accept stream-based input in order to fit the pipeline (Section 3.3). The third one is a recent algorithm by Kiselyov et al. [9], with a novel implementation technique, reliant on stream-based processing (Section 3.4).

The experimental algorithm is implemented in Rascal only, and is not yet optimised for performance. The Wadler algorithm is implemented in both Rascal and Racket (with Racket offering decent performance). The Kiselyov algorithm is implemented in Racket only, with a present shortcoming denying us the algorithm's theoretically pleasing performance characteristics. We have no clear favourite among these line breakers, but with our library of pluggable components we aim to avoid "lock-in" to any particular choice – and also to allow comparison of the different algorithms.

3 Line Breaking

3.1 Nesting and Indentation

Proper indentation relies on information about the current nesting level of the code. Additionally, one of our algorithms (Section 3.2) relies on nesting for making line-breaking decisions.

As we are working on a stream of data rather than a tree where nesting is explicit, we rely on control tokens to tell us about changes in the nesting level. The current nesting level can be tracked using a stack.

In addition to the usual increasing and decreasing of indentation levels, our nesting primitives supports absolute (specified column), relative (to the current column), and string-based indentation, as well as non-indenting nesting. Absolute indentation is useful for printing #ifdef and other CPP directives starting from the first column, or Lisp ;;; comments. Relative indentation support makes it easier to align related text appearing over multiple lines. String-based indentation is necessary for pretty-printing "line comments" (e.g., comments starting with // in C++), if they are to be allowed to be broken over multiple lines.

The available indentation controls are:

- LvInc(n) – increase level by n (negative OK)
- LvStr(s) – append indentation string s
- LvAbs(n) – set new indentation level to n
- LvRel(n) – set level relative to current output cursor column

For example, a list of statements in a block may be surrounded by #BEGIN(LvInc(1)) ... #END, causing the statements to be indented one level more that the surrounding context. Relative indentation is useful inside parentheses. For example, the control tokens in the following stream would cause the line breaker to store the current column c, and indent the following line to $c + 0$ if the line is broken inside the parentheses:

... "(":LPAR #BEGIN(LvRel(0)) ... #END ")":RPAR ...

A plain #BEGIN ... #END is ignored by the indentation code, but may be used for other purposes, such as the algorithm in Section 3.2.

Our indentation control tokens are similar to Chitil's [2], who provides Open-Nest and CloseNest. The difference is that OpenNest takes a function rather than an interpreted level value. This solution is more flexible than ours in that any function computing a new indentation level in terms of the current indentation level and "cursor" column is allowed. However, the function signature only permits integers, and hence the equivalent of LvStr is inexpressible.

3.2   A New Line-Breaking Algorithm

This line breaking algorithm tries to balance simplicity with the desire to keep related code on the same line. It is based on assigning breakability factors to spaces in the document (we'll assume that we always break lines at a space; if necessary, an empty space may be used as a break-point). The algorithm assumes that control tokens are inserted into the stream to indicate nesting, and the breakability is chosen based on this; the deeper the nesting, the less breakable a point is. Additionally, breakability can be set directly on space tokens, for "always break" and "never break". In our experiments, we've used nesting for each level of declarations, statements and expressions in our parse tree.

The Algorithm

- We keep track of
  - the desired line width (W),
  - the current breakability level (B) – a number between 0 and 1,
  - a stack of indentation levels (I),
  - and the current horizontal position, as a fraction of the line (P).
- Furthermore we have
  - A queue of processed tokens that have not yet been output
  - The last space that seemed like a good place to break (S)
  - The desirability of breaking at the last space (D) – computed based on P and B (based on experimentation, $P * B^2$ seems to be a good starting point). Initially zero, higher is better.
- For each incoming token, we do:
  1. • *if text*: append to queue
     • *if explicit line break*: flush queue, break line, indent, reset variables
     • *if nesting start*: decrease breakability by some factor (e.g., nestFactor=0.75)
     • *if nesting end*: increase breakability again
     • *if space*: we must decide whether this is a better place to break than our previous candidate. We compute the desirability of breaking at the current point, if it is higher or equal to D, we:
       (a) flush the queue
       (b) store this space as the best break point
       (c) store the new value of D
       Otherwise, the space is added to the queue.
  2. If the current position + queue length is larger than W, we:
     (a) break line, indent, reset variables
     (b) flush queue, reset best break point to empty, D=0.0

The algorithm never examines a token more than once, and has linear time complexity. In terms of memory, it needs a queue buffer proportional to the desired line width. Note that we only make the final decision on where to break when we reach the end of the line. Some tuning is necessary in order to find the best way to calculate how "desirable" a particular potential break is.

In the small example below, the algorithm has been applied to a code fragment with nested expressions, with line width 15. Compared to naive breaking nearest the end of line (right), our algorithm (left) tries to keep the deeper nested expressions on the same line; in this case, at the cost of using an extra line.

```
  x = a * b                    x = a * b + c
2 + c / d                    2 / d + (c / d
  + (c / d * f)                * f) + c / d;
4 + c / d;
```

3.3   Adaptation of Wadler's Pretty-Printing Algorithm

Our next line breaker is based on a pretty-printing algorithm described in a paper by Wadler [18]. We discuss the key concepts and characteristics of the original algorithm, and present our stream-adapted version and its extensions.

Wadler's Pretty-Printing Algorithm. The original implementation [18] of the algorithm is Haskell based. The input given to the algorithm is specified as a *document*, which can be composed using provided operations. The most important operations include: `nil` (empty document), `text`, `line` (line break), `<>` (concatenation), `nest` (indented block), and `group`. The `group` constructor may produce a document whose layout involves line-breaking decisions, as the layout may differ depending on page width w.

The Haskell-based algorithm operates on primitive document types, which are: `NIL`, `:<>` (concatenation), `NEST`, `TEXT`, `LINE`, and `:<|>`. All except `:<|>` have a direct counterpart in the list of operations given above. The `:<|>` primitive signifies a *union* (or choice) of two possible sets of layouts, and any line-breaking sensitivity within documents (including those produced by `group`) must ultimately be expressible in terms of unions. The semantics of a union is that the left choice is taken if and only if it (fully, or up to any `LINE` break) fits on the line (i.e., the line width will not exceed w characters).

Use of the union primitive easily results in huge documents due to combinatorial explosion. For performance it is crucial for implementations of Wadler's algorithm to: (i) never inspect more than w characters per choice, and to (ii) not build (parts of) documents that are not inspected. Together these two measures achieve the property of *boundedness* [18] (of a pretty-printing algorithm), which Wadler defines as not looking at more than the next w characters in making line-breaking decisions. Measure (ii) is implementable by means of *lazy evaluation*, which one gets "for free" in Haskell as it is the default semantics. Laziness leads to a kind of co-routine computation [2], and it is also possible to encode sufficient laziness in strict languages [19].

Our Adaptation of the Algorithm. Our layout algorithm is the same as Wadler's in the sense that the same primitive document types are supported. They may appear somewhat different, however, due to our requirement for a stream-based interface; `NIL`, for example, is simply represented as the empty stream, whereas any two consecutive tokens in a stream can be thought to have been composed by :<>. Another difference to the original algorithm is that we chose to extend the NEST primitive to support the indentation controls of Section 3.1, for additional flexibility. The extension adds expressive power without taking anything away or affecting the general performance characteristics of the original algorithm.

We have implementations in both the Racket and Rascal languages. These bear little resemblance to the original Haskell-based implementations, both due to Haskell's different evaluation semantics (lazy vs strict) and the different "document model" (objects vs streams).

Complexity Bounding Measures. In the original implementation Haskell's need-driven evaluation automatically takes care of the bounding measures required for good performance. Rascal and Racket are both strict languages, and we had to implement both of the measures explicitly.

To account for measure (i) we implemented the actual layout algorithm in a strict manner, making state and modifications to it explicit. All state is stored in structures, and no recursion is used by the algorithm proper. This makes the evaluation order and control flow clear, and no information enabling early pruning of fruitless search paths is "hiding" somewhere up the call stack. Decisions about whether or not to backtrack are made as soon the right margin is crossed when examining a choice (of a union). Backtracking is implemented by switching to an older, stored state, which is possible as state updates are purely functional.

Measure (ii) is more externally visible as documents are provided as input, and operations for constructing documents, whether lazily or otherwise, must be made available to the user. In many cases the required laziness can be hidden by accepting reasonably-sized (and complete) "instructions" for building documents as arguments to operations, and then performing the construction lazily within said operations as appropriate. The on-demand construction in a stream setting is enabled by defining a lazy (functional) stream type. Many of our document construction operations return such lazy streams, conforming to the "even" style of laziness [19].

While we do expose our Union primitive and the lazy stream API to allow for full document building flexibility, a variety of typical layouts can be achieved using the higher-level operations that we provide. These operations include flatten, group, and fill, as documented by Wadler [18]: flatten replaces each line break (and its associated indentation) by a single space; group adds a flattened form of a document as the preferred choice; and fill takes a list of documents and creates a fill layout for them, so that whenever there are two or more documents left, the first two are laid out flattened and a single space between them if they fit on the line, and otherwise the first document is laid out unflattened and followed by a line break.

3.4   Kiselyov et al's Pretty-Printing Algorithm

We have also made a Racket port of the linear-time, backtracking-free, bounded-latency pretty-printing algorithm by Kiselyov et al [9]. The algorithm is faster than Wadler's, and operates on a token stream, after any initial tokenisation. The set of supported formatting operations is like Oppen's [14]. The algorithm is particularly interesting for us as it suggests a potentially convenient way to organise a pipeline with interleaved operation of token processors, similar to our own formatting pipeline.

The Kiselyov algorithm itself has an internal token pipeline making use of a `yield` construct similar to what one finds in Ruby and many other languages [7]. Kiselyov's implementation of `yield` however does not require first-class delimited continuations (such as created by Racket's `call-with-continuation-prompt`), but rather is based on much lighter-weight *simple generators*. Their idea is to bind each token processor's `yield` target in the dynamic environment as a function. Our implementation of `yield` uses Racket's built-in support for dynamic binding (i.e., "parameterization"), which is semantically equivalent to the original Haskell implementation's use of the `Reader` (or "environment") monad.

Our initial impressions of using the simple generator style of co-routines for building pipelines are positive. One can just write "regular" Racket functions that may invoke `yield` to emit tokens, and the bindings can be established only once composing the pipeline. Processors requiring state may simply retain it in their closure.

The one problem with our current implementation is that one of its auxiliary data structures does not have all of the required stringent algorithmic properties. We are currently using an implementation of Okasaki's *banker's deque* [13], which does not enable concatenation and iteration with the required properties. The pipeline itself requires no explicit data structure, thanks to the `yield`-based approach of immediately passing tokens from one processor to another, without any pipe data structure in between.

4   Plumbing

4.1   Java Pipeline Design

We have so far described the details of token processors and formatting components, we'll now go into the details of the pipeline itself and how components are coupled together – the plumbing.

Our generic pipeline framework for Java is built on three concepts:

- *processors* that manipulate a stream of objects;
- *pipe components* that control the processors, and are connected together in a pipeline; and
- *pipe connectors* that connect processors to pipe components, and provide buffering and various utility services.

The framework is designed to support (optional) concurrency with each processor running in its own thread. The framework takes care of transporting the information through the pipeline, without the processor implementer having to worry about locking or concurrency issues (unless the processor accesses non-local information). Streams may be of any kind of object – in our PGF formatting framework the objects are tokens.

Pipe components supports a `connect` method for connecting the output to another component, `put` for sending an object into the component, `end` for signalling the end of a stream, and `restart` for resetting any internal state and preparing for a new stream of data. In a concurrent setting, the pipe component will take care of managing a processing thread.

Each pipe component connects to its processor through a pipe connector. The connector can provide input and output buffering, and can also maintain histories of the last seen or last output data items. The buffering is useful to provide look-ahead for the processor, and also to reduce the amount of locking in a concurrent setting. Multiple connectors may be layered to provide filtering or translation of the data stream (for example, processing control tokens).

Each processor has a `process` method, which is called by the pipe component whenever there is input available through the pipe connector. The processor may inspect or get objects from the input buffer, and also send objects to the output. The processor can state the amount of look-ahead and output history needed, and also how the start and end of the stream should be signalled.

Activity is driven by putting objects into the pipeline; `put` calls to the first component will propagate calls through the entire pipeline; the output from one processor triggering a `put` to the next component which triggers the next processor, and so on.

4.2   Grouping and Dynamic Processors in Racket

The pretty printer adaptation in Section 3.3 is designed for pipelining, in the sense of contributing to a result as input becomes available. For example, the formatting of a nested range of tokens can proceed before the end marker of the range has been seen. The nesting construct is easy to handle in a stream setting as any tokens within a nested range may be processed unconditionally. This is unfortunately not the case with *union* primitive.

As mentioned in the subsection on complexity bounding measures, it is imperative for performance not to inspect (or even build) all the content of "large" unions. Hence such content should not appear within the stream in a "flat" form, as then it would be necessary to scan through any union contents just to get past them. We are forced to "unnaturally" express a union as a token containing the left and right choices as embedded streams. These nested streams can then be inspected to the appropriate extent.

Alternative and lazy constructions may not be natural within a token *sequence*, but often such constructions are just the low-level expression of what really is a concrete sequence with some associated semantics. For instance, consider the `group` function, defined in Racket as shown below, involving the `Union` primitive and a lazy `flatten` operation. In the (commented out) example `group` expression, we essentially just have the word sequence of "a" followed by "b", with the semantics that the words should be laid out horizontally if they fit on a line, and vertically otherwise.

```
;; E.g. (group (tseq "a" br "b"))
(define (group ts) ;; tseq → tseq
  (Union (flatten ts) ts))
```

tseq is our token sequence datatype in Racket: `empty-tseq` is an empty sequence, `tseq` is a constructor, and `tseq-put` appends a token, with functional update.

As can be seen from the listing, implementing `group` as a function in terms of other operations is trivial when the full token stream `ts` to be grouped is available. We want to retain this ease of implementation, but would still like to allow `group`s to be emitted incrementally, token by token, as is fitting for a stream setting. Chitil, in his pretty printer [2], enables this specifically for `group` by supporting `Open` and `Close` tokens for delimiting the contents of a `group`. To a similar and more general effect we want to be able to "encode" the argument value for `group` as a sub-sequence of tokens, and then have the result of invoking `group` with that argument used as input for the actual layout algorithm.

To allow for such encoding, we introduce a *grouping* mechanism, which dynamically inserts a processor into the pipeline, along with a substream of tokens to be processed. While this kind of preprocessing happens to be particularly essential for Wadler's algorithm (unlike e.g. for Kiselyov's and our own), we have implemented the grouping processor in a fairly general way, and might find useful applications for it elsewhere within our token pipeline.

In a general sense the grouping facility makes it possible for "foreign language" (e.g., arguments to a function) to appear within an input stream, provided that it is known where the "foreign expression" begins and ends, and that a translator (to "native" language) is provided – for example, doing special formatting of comments. The former condition is met with opening and closing control tokens indicating the foreign range. The latter condition is met in an open-ended way by specifying a translator in the opening `Begin` token. A translator must conform to the `Grouping` abstraction, which includes functions for managing state for the delimited token range.

Below we define XML-inspired `group/` and `/group` delimiters, and use `tseq-put` to cache arguments for the `group` function. We then have `group` called with its entire cached argument upon seeing an `End` token. In this example the result is a single `Union` token, and hence there is no possibility of returning result tokens incrementally. The `Union` token may be lazily constructed, however. Here the specified `#:end` operation produces the full result (as a stream), which indeed is lazily constructed. The `#:put` operation is expected to receive and incorporate both new input as well as the results of any contained, nested groupings.

```
(define group-grouping ;; Grouping
  (make-grouping 'group
    #:new (thunk empty-tseq) ;; create fresh state
    #:put tseq-put ;; incorporate token into state
```

```
#:end group))  ;; finalise by calling 'group' with state
```

```
;; E.g. (tseq group/ "a" br "b" /group)
(define group/ (Begin group-grouping))
(define /group (End group-grouping))
```

A grouping implemented in such a manner (i.e., call a function to get the result) may cause prohibitive space consumption for some applications, as depending on grouping semantics one may have to first buffer the entire input and then the entire result, and these can generally be of arbitrary length. However, depending on the grouping it may be possible to reduce space consumption by: (i) having "argument" tokens incorporated into a (small) result as they are read, without having to buffer them (cf. a hash function); and/or (ii) returning the result as a (small) lazy stream which will compute the full result sequence one token at a time (cf. a generator).

The `group` function gives us (ii), but (i) appears impossible, and we are still left with worst-case linear space consumption for our grouping implementation. We presently have no solution to avoid such overhead for all groupings, and to begin to achieve that we suspect that our grouping mechanism would have to be made less generic, more closely integrated with the algorithm proper, or both. As shown by Chitil and Swierstra [2,17], achieving theoretically pleasing layout performance can be challenging and intricate.

The grouping support mechanism is implemented by maintaining grouping state within token sequences to ensure correct ordering as tokens flow in and out of grouping processing. Multiple groupings may nest, and groupings may output groupings; there is no guarantee of termination. No token reaches the layout algorithm proper before any grouping processing concerning it is complete; the algorithm proper is unaware of groupings.

5   Discussion

5.1   Plumbing Considerations

The concept of organising a code formatter as a pipeline is appealing. It offers four benefits, as far as we can tell:

- a clear separation of concerns,
- flexibility in that components can be plugged together to achieve different effects (e.g., indent only; spacing + indentation; line breaking + indentation),
- ease of prototyping and experimentation, since multiple interchangeable versions of one component can be tried,
- a possibility for fairly simple concurrent processing.

There are different ways to achieve pipelining. Our Java library uses a series of interconnected objects to achieve fairly straight-forward pipelining in Java. The technique of Kiselyov et al [9] uses the `yield` language construct to achieve "native" pipelining in languages that support it, without having to manage the pipeline as a data structure. The grouping construct of Section 4.2 is designed for use in a surrounding pipeline, but also provides a way to dynamically build a more complex pipeline based on the control tokens in the incoming token stream.

Our Java version has advantages in the relative ease of doing buffered look-ahead and concurrency; a `yield`-based pipeline offers relative simplicity for languages that have it or where it can be added. Overall, we feel the choice comes down to the preferred (or required) implementation language.

5.2   Performance

Although performance may be of some importance in an interactive setting, it is of less concern than the quality of output, as long as "decent" performance is offered. In our experiments with our Java implementation of PGF, the most time consuming part of formatting is the tokenisation of parse tree – but even this is dominated by the time spend on parsing. Formatting a 2 MiB file of Java source takes around 6s (excluding parsing) on our workstations, which is a bit slower than Eclipse's Java formatter, but not much.

5.3   Quality and Reusability of Processors

We had an expectation that the various processing components that make up the formatting pipeline should be fairly easy to adapt to different languages, provided that the tokenisation has been customised for the particular languages. Our results so far are promising; generic spacing, indentation and line-breaking processors do a fair (but by no means perfect) job of formatting Java and Magnolia code. Producing high quality output requires careful tuning, and will of course also have to take into account styling preferences. Examples of output can be found in the online materials.

More work is needed on composing and combining rule sets of rule-based processors; extending a generic processor with rules for a particular language has a tendency to result in rule conflicts or unexpected behaviour.

5.4   Related Work

Oppen's pretty printer [14] is also stream oriented. Unlike Wadler's, it exploits streams to allow two communicating sequential processes to coordinate their work. This results in performance characteristics of time $\mathcal{O}(n)$ and space $\mathcal{O}(w)$, with input length n and page width w. In comparison, the worst case time complexity of Wadler's algorithm is $\mathcal{O}(nw)$ [2], i.e. superlinear if w is considered variable.

While Oppen's solution is unbeaten in performance, it is also monolithic. The constructs of his layout language only exist as part of a whole, without a meaningful description in isolation [5]. The variety of parameters for Oppen's *blank* tokens add expressiveness to the language. For example, *consistent* and *inconsistent* blanks loosely correspond to `group` and `fill`, respectively. The *variable offset* of blanks has the same motivation as the `LvRel` parameter we introduced in Section 3.1.

Hughes' pretty printer [5] is based on algebraic design, and served as a major influence for Wadler's. The `Union` operator, for instance, has its origins in Hughes' algebra, and indeed in the set theoretical ∪ operator. Hughes' layout operator set is expressive, able to express some layouts that Wadler's cannot [18], but also such that a bounded implementation is impossible [18].

Chitil [2] managed to devise a purely functional pretty printer with Oppen-level efficiency. In it he also opts to represent documents as token sequences rather than trees, due to sequences appearing more amenable to efficient processing.[5] Chitil maintains context information in explicit data structures, and notes that this is important for achieving high efficiency. Our implementation of Wadler's algorithm shares these two design choices, though for reasons of architecture and clarity.

Swierstra's and Chitil's joint work on a pretty printer [17] resulted in two linear-time implementations that are simpler and clearer than Chitil's earlier work. They provide the insight that such solutions can be achieved by utilising two mutually recursive processes running asynchronously, but that such solutions are hard to express in purely algebraic style. Wadler's algorithm was derived based on algebraic techniques.

Kiselyov et al. found a still simpler and clearer way to implement a linear-time, bounded-latency solution to the pretty printing problem [9]. Their algorithm, discussed in Section 3.4, is similar to Swierstra and Chitil's second solution in that instead of relying on Haskell's lazy evaluation to interleave processing, a co-routine style approach is used; Swierstra and Chitil's approach is more heavyweight in that it involves building and storing "continuation" functions. Kiselyov et al. point out a sometimes overlooked [16] corner case in the processing of `groups`, offering normalisation of document trees as the solution. We believe such normalisation cannot be done efficiently on token streams, meaning that bounded look-ahead is lost unless we can ensure that earlier token processors only produce normalised output.

The Box [1,3,8] formatting model is based on composing two-dimensional boxes of code. This produces good quality output, but the complexity of the algorithm is high, leading to poor performance on large documents (often dominating the other processing steps in a source-to-source transformation). Additionally, some forms of indentation are difficult to express.

Jackson et.al. [6] provide an efficient, stable peephole pretty-printing algorithm, suitable for use in an interactive editor. The peephole property means that it is capable of pretty-printing just a part of a program, corresponding to an editor view. The running time of the pretty-printer is thus independent of the full length of the program—only the size of the editor's view (or peephole) matters. The algorithm is *stable*, in that it gives the same result as if the entire program was pretty-printed, avoiding reformatting artefacts as the user

---

[5] Swierstra has shown that a tree representation does not preclude Oppen-level efficiency [16].

scrolls the editor view. The stable peephole is achieved by identifying *anchors* in the program; places where the indentation level is the same, no matter which choices are made by the formatter. The line-breaking algorithm itself is a variant of Wadler's [18].

Our new line breaker has (we believe) fewer choices than the Wadler algorithm, so it should be easier to identify anchors, and provide stable peephole functionality. However, peepholing may not work so well with a pluggable architecture. We need to explore this more.

Reiss [15] has shown that given samples of existing source code in the desired style, machine learning can be used to deduce formatting rules for the style. This approach should also apply to deducing rule tables for our spacer engine, for example.

6 Conclusion

PGF is a general framework for code formatting, based on a flexible pipeline of formatting components. We aim to use the framework as a basis for further experimentation into customisable, language-independent formatting components. The flexibility of offered by pluggable components seems useful for conducting such experiments. We provide both a rule system for implementing components, and support for using general purpose languages.

We have built components for spacing, indentation and three variants of line breaking, as well as tokenisers accepting parse trees in UTPR and AsFix2 format. Although we are implementing PGF as a Java library, we also perform experiments and prototyping in Rascal and Racket. This has allowed us to rapidly try out various techniques, including three different line breaking algorithms.

The general pipelining framework should be reusable for other purposes than just code formatting – it is built to be independent of the type of data processed. We have applied the PGF formatter to the Java and Magnolia languages, so far with promising results, though further tuning is needed to produce high quality output, and to determine the level of code reuse possible when implementing formatters for multiple languages.

Online materials are available at http://nuthatchery.org/sle13/

Acknowledgements. Thanks to Eivind Jahren, who has helped us understand unfamiliar Haskell concepts. This research has been funded by the Research Council of Norway.

References

1. van den Brand, M.G.J., Visser, E.: Generation of formatters for context-free languages. ACM Transactions on Software Engineering and Methodology 5(1), 1–41 (1996)

2. Chitil, O.: Pretty printing with lazy dequeues. ACM Trans. Program. Lang. Syst. 27, 163–184 (2005)
3. Coutaz, J.: A layout abstraction for user-system interface. SIGCHI Bull. 16(3), 18–24 (1985), http://doi.acm.org/10.1145/1044201.1044202
4. Flatt, M.: PLT: Reference: Racket. Tech. Rep. PLT-TR-2010-1, PLT Inc (2010), http://racket-lang.org/tr1/
5. Hughes, J.: The design of a pretty-printing library. In: Jeuring, J., Meijer, E. (eds.) AFP 1995. LNCS, vol. 925, pp. 53–96. Springer, Heidelberg (1995)
6. Jackson, S., Devanbu, P., Ma, K.L.: Stable, flexible, peephole pretty-printing. Science of Computer Programming 72(1-2), 40–51 (2008)
7. James, R.P., Sabry, A.: Yield: Mainstream delimited continuations. In: First International Workshop on the Theory and Practice of Delimited Continuations, TPDC 2011 (May 2011)
8. de Jonge, M.: A pretty-printer for every occasion. In: Ferguson, I., Gray, J., Scott, L. (eds.) Proceedings of the 2nd International Symposium on Constructing Software Engineering Tools (CoSET 2000), University of Wollongong, Australia, pp. 68–77 (June 2000)
9. Kiselyov, O., Peyton-Jones, S., Sabry, A.: Lazy v. Yield: Incremental, linear pretty-printing. In: Jhala, R., Igarashi, A. (eds.) APLAS 2012. LNCS, vol. 7705, pp. 190–206. Springer, Heidelberg (2012)
10. Klint, P., van der Storm, T., Vinju, J.: Rascal: A domain specific language for source code analysis and manipulation. In: SCAM 2009: Proceedings of the 2009 Ninth IEEE International Working Conference on Source Code Analysis and Manipulation, pp. 168–177. IEEE Computer Society, Washington, DC (2009)
11. McKeeman, W.M.: Algorithm 268: Algol 60 reference language editor. Commun. ACM 8(11), 667–668 (1965)
12. Miara, R.J., Musselman, J.A., Navarro, J.A., Shneiderman, B.: Program indentation and comprehensibility. Commun. ACM 26(11), 861–867 (1983)
13. Okasaki, C.: Purely Functional Data Structures. Cambridge University Press (1999)
14. Oppen, D.C.: Prettyprinting. ACM Trans. Program. Lang. Syst. 2, 465–483 (1980)
15. Reiss, S.P.: Automatic code stylizing. In: 22nd IEEE/ACM International Conference on Automated Software Engineering (ASE), Atlanta, Georgia, pp. 74–83 (November 2007)
16. Swierstra, S.D.: Linear, online, functional pretty printing (corrected and extended version). Tech. Rep. UU-CS-2004-025a, Department of Information and Computing Sciences, Utrecht University (2004)
17. Swierstra, S.D., Chitil, O.: Linear, bounded, functional pretty-printing. Journal of Functional Programming 19(1), 1–16 (2009)
18. Wadler, P.: A prettier printer. In: Gibbons, J., de Moor, O. (eds.) The Fun of Programming. Cornerstones of Computing. Palgrave Macmillan (June 2005)
19. Wadler, P., Taha, W., Macqueen, D.: How to add laziness to a strict language without even being odd. In: Workshop on Standard ML, Baltimore, Maryland (1998)

The State of the Art in Language Workbenches
Conclusions from the Language Workbench Challenge

Sebastian Erdweg[1], Tijs van der Storm[2,3], Markus Völter[4], Meinte Boersma[5],
Remi Bosman[6], William R. Cook[7], Albert Gerritsen[6], Angelo Hulshout[8],
Steven Kelly[9], Alex Loh[7], Gabriël D.P. Konat[10], Pedro J. Molina[11], Martin Palatnik[6],
Risto Pohjonen[9], Eugen Schindler[6], Klemens Schindler[6], Riccardo Solmi[12],
Vlad A. Vergu[10], Eelco Visser[10], Kevin van der Vlist[13],
Guido H. Wachsmuth[10], and Jimi van der Woning[13]

[1] TU Darmstadt, Germany
[2] CWI, Amsterdam, The Netherlands
[3] INRIA Lille Nord Europe, Lille, France
[4] voelter.de, Stuttgart, Germany
[5] DSL Consultancy, Leiden, The Netherlands
[6] Sioux, Eindhoven, The Netherlands
[7] University of Texas, Austin, US
[8] Delphino Consultancy, Best, The Netherlands
[9] MetaCase, Jyväskylä, Finland
[10] TU Delft, The Netherlands
[11] Icinetic, Sevilla, Spain
[12] Independent, Bologna, Italy
[13] Universiteit van Amsterdam

Abstract. Language workbenches are tools that provide high-level mechanisms
for the implementation of (domain-specific) languages. Language workbenches
are an active area of research that also receives many contributions from industry.
To compare and discuss existing language workbenches, the annual Language
Workbench Challenge was launched in 2011. Each year, participants are chal-
lenged to realize a given domain-specific language with their workbenches as a
basis for discussion and comparison. In this paper, we describe the state of the art
of language workbenches as observed in the previous editions of the Language
Workbench Challenge. In particular, we capture the design space of language
workbenches in a feature model and show where in this design space the participants of the 2013 Language Workbench Challenge reside. We compare these
workbenches based on a DSL for questionnaires that was realized in all workbenches.

1 Introduction

Language workbenches, a term popularized by Martin Fowler in 2005 [19], are tools
that support the efficient definition, reuse and composition of languages and their IDEs.
Language workbenches make the development of new languages affordable and, therefore, support a new quality of *language engineering*, where sets of syntactically and
semantically integrated languages can be built with comparably little effort. This can

M. Erwig, R.F. Paige, and E. Van Wyk (Eds.): SLE 2013, LNCS 8225, pp. 197–217, 2013.
© Springer International Publishing Switzerland 2013

lead to multi-paradigm and language-oriented programming environments [8, 61] that can address important software engineering challenges.

Almost as long as programmers have built languages, they have also built tools to make language development easier and language use more productive. The earliest language workbench probably was SEM [52]; other early ones include MetaPlex [7], Metaview [51], QuickSpec [43], and MetaEdit [48]. Graphical workbenches that are still being developed today include MetaEdit+ [28], DOME [24], and GME [38]. On the other hand, language workbenches that supported textual notations include Centaur [5], the Synthesizer generator [46], the ASF+SDF Meta-Environment [30], Gem-Mex/Montages [2], LRC [36], and Lisa [42]. These systems were originally based on tools for the formal specification of general purpose programming languages [20]. Nonetheless, many of them have been successfully used to build practical domain-specific languages (DSLs) as well [41]. Textual workbenches like JastAdd [49], Rascal [32, 33], Spoofax [27], and Xtext [17] can be seen as successors of these systems, leveraging advances in editor technology of mainstream IDEs. At the same time, projectional language workbenches like MPS [57] and Intentional [47] are reviving and refining the old idea of structure editors [9], opening up the possibility of mixing arbitrary notations.

Throughout their development, language workbenches and domain-specific languages have been used in industry. Examples include:

- Eurofighter Typhoon [1], with IPSYS's HOOD toolset (later ToolBuilder).
- Nokia's feature phones [44], with MetaEdit+.
- RISLA, a DSL for interest-rate products [3], with ASF+SDF.
- Polar's heart rate monitors and sports watches [26], with MetaEdit+.
- WebDSL [56] and Mobl [22] for building Web applications and mobile applications respectively, with Spoofax.
- File format DSL for digital forensics tool construction [53], with Rascal.
- mbeddr [58, 59] a C-based language for embedded software development, including extensions such as units of measure, components, requirements tracing, and variability, based on MPS.

Language workbenches are currently enjoying significant growth in number and diversity, driven by both academia and industry. Existing language workbenches are so different in design, supported features, and used terminology that it is hard for users and developers to understand the underlying principles and design alternatives. To this end, a systematic overview is helpful.

The goal of the Language Workbench Challenge (LWC) is to promote understanding and knowledge exchange on language workbenches: Each year a language engineering challenge is posed and the submissions (often but not exclusively by tool developers) implement the challenge; documentation is required as well, so others can understand the implementation. All contributors then meet to discuss the submitted solutions. By tackling a common challenge, the approaches followed by different workbenches become transparent, and understanding about design decisions, capabilities, and limitations increases. In this paper, we channel the lessons learnt from the previous iterations of the LWC and document this knowledge for the scientific community at large. In particular, we make the following contributions:

- We describe the history of the LWC.
- We establish a feature model that captures the design space of language workbenches as observed in the previous LWCs.
- We present and discuss the 10 language workbenches participating in LWC'13 by classifying them according to our feature model.
- We present empirical data on 10 implementations of the LWC'13 assignment (a questionnaire DSL).
- Based on our investigation, we document the state of the art of language workbenches.

2 Background

The idea of the LWC was born during discussions at the 2010 edition of the Code Generation conference. Since then, LWC has been held three times, each year with a different language to implement as assignment. Below we briefly review the assignments of 2011, 2012, and 2013. Then we describe the methodology we followed in this paper.

2.1 The Challenges of LWC

The LWC'11 assignment[1] consisted of a simple language for defining entities and relations. At the basic level, this involved defining syntax for entities, simple constraint checking (e.g., name uniqueness), and code generation to a general-purpose language. At the more advanced level, the challenge included support for namespaces, a language for defining entity instances, the translation of entity programs to relational database models, and integration with manually written code in some general-purpose language. To demonstrate language modularity and composition, the advanced part of the assignment should be realized without modifying the solution of the basic assignment.

In the LWC'12 assignment[2], two languages had to be implemented. The first language captured piping and instrumentation models which can be used, for instance, to describe heating systems. The elements of this language included pumps, valves, and boilers. The second language consisted of a state machine-like controller language that could be used to describe the dynamic behavior of piping and instrumentation models. Developers were supposed to combine the two languages to enable the simulation of piping and instrumentation systems.

The LWC'13 assignment[3] consisted of a DSL for questionnaires, which should be rendered as an interactive GUI that reacts to user input to present additional questions. The questionnaire definition should be validated, for instance, to detect unresolved names and type errors. In addition to basic editor support, participants should modularly develop a styling DSL that can be used to configure the rendering of a questionnaire. We describe the details of the LWC'13 assignment in Section 5.

---

[1] http://www.languageworkbenches.net/index.php?title=LWC_2011
[2] http://www.languageworkbenches.net/index.php?title=LWC_2012
[3] http://www.languageworkbenches.net/index.php?title=LWC_2013

2.2   Research Methodology

The main goal of this paper is to document the state of the art of language workbenches in a structured and informative way. We assemble the relevant information based on our experience and involvement in the LWC from 2011 to 2013. Nevertheless, for this paper we focused on the most recent challenge of 2013. We invited all participants of LWC'13 to contribute to the domain analysis and to the language workbench comparison as described below.

Domain Analysis. The first part of our methodology addresses the goal of accurately describing the domain of language workbenches. We have asked all participants of LWC'13 to provide a detailed list of features supported by their language workbench. The first three authors then started to "mine" a feature model [25] to capture the relevant aspects of the language-workbench domain. Since non-functional features have not been in scope of any previous LWC, we solely focused on the functional properties of language workbenches. The extracted feature model was then presented to all participants for feedback. The refined feature model presented in Section 3 provides a way to categorize language workbenches according to which features they support.

Empirical Data. In addition to a general overview of language workbenches, we investigated empirical data on the solutions submitted to the LWC'13. We constructed a feature model for the features of the questionnaire DSL and asked the participants to indicate which features they realized in their solution. We present a description of the assignment and the feature model in Section 5.

To get an impression about how different language workbenches achieve various (subsets of) features of the questionnaire DSL, we also asked all participants to answer the following three questions:

- *What is the size of your solution?* The suggested metric for the answer was SLOC (Source Lines of Code)[4].
- *What are the static, compile-time dependencies?* This captures the various libraries, frameworks, and platforms that are needed to run the compiler and IDE of the questionnaire DSL.
- *What are the dynamic, runtime dependencies?* This addresses the additional software components that are needed to run the generated questionnaires GUIs.

We present the answers to these questions and discuss the language workbenches in view of these results in Section 6 and Section 7 respectively.

Generality of the Survey. Not all existing language workbenches were represented at LWC'13. Language workbenches that contributed to earlier challenges, but not to LWC'13, include commercial ones, such as the Intentional workbench [47], OOMega[5], and Obeo Designer[6], as well as academic systems such as Atom3 [37], Cedalion [39], and EMFText [21]. As we show in Section 4, the language workbenches covered in our study are very diverse regarding the features they support. To our knowledge, the

---

[4] SLOC does not count comments or empty lines. Note that SLOC only works for textual languages; we come back to this problem in Section 6.

[5] http://www.oomega.net/

[6] http://www.obeodesigner.com/

features of aforementioned language workbenches are covered by our feature model. Hence, even though not all language workbenches are part of this survey, we consider the *domain* of language workbenches sufficiently covered.

3   A Feature Model for Language Workbenches

Language workbenches exist in many different flavors, but they are united by their common goal to facilitate the development of (domain-specific) languages. Based on input provided by the participants of LWC'13, we derived the feature model shown in Fig. 1. It outlines the most important features of language workbenches. We use standard feature-diagram notation and interpretation [4]: The root node (*Language workbench* in Fig. 1) is always selected. A mandatory feature (filled circle) has to be selected if its parent is selected. An optional feature (empty circle) does not have to be selected even if its parent is selected. In a list of *Or* children (filled edge connector), at least one feature has to be selected if the parent is selected.

We separate language workbench features into six subcategories. A language workbench *must* support notation, semantics, and an editor for the defined languages and its models. It *may* support validation of models, testing and debugging of models and the language definition, as well as composition of different aspects of multiple defined languages. In the remainder of this section, we explain the feature model in more detail.

Every language workbench must support the mandatory feature *notation*, which determines how programs or models are presented to users. The notation can be a mix of textual, graphical, and tabular notations, where textual notation may optionally support symbols such as integrals or fraction bars embedded in regular text.

A language workbench must support the definition of language *semantics*. We distinguish translational semantics, which compiles a model into a program expressed in another language, and interpretative semantics, which directly executes a model without prior translation. For translational semantics we distinguish between model-to-text translations, which are based on concatenating strings, and model-to-model translations, which are based on mapping abstract model representations such as trees or graphs. To simplify the handling of abstract model representations, some language workbenches support concrete syntax for source and target languages in transformation rules.

Editor support is a central pillar of language workbenches [19] and we consider user-defined editor support mandatory for language workbenches. The two predominant editing modes are free-form editing, where the user freely edits the persisted model (typically the source code), and projectional editing, where the user edits a projection of the persisted model in a standard, fixed layout. In addition to a plain editor, most language workbenches provide a selection of syntactic and semantic editor services. Syntactic editor services include:

– Customizable visual *highlighting* in models, such as language-specific syntax coloring for textual languages or language-specific node shapes for graphical languages.
– Navigation support via an *outline* view.
– *Folding* to hide part of a model.
– Code assist through *syntactic completion* templates that suggest code, graph, or tabular fragments to the user.

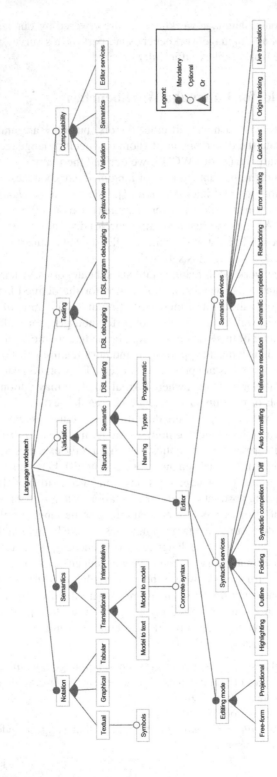

Fig. 1. Feature model for language workbenches. With few exceptions, all features in the feature model apply to the languages that can be defined with a language workbench, and not to the definition mechanism of the language workbench itself.

- Comparison of programs via a *diff*-like tool (the basis for version control).
- *Auto formatting*, restructuring, aligning, or layouting of a model's presentation.

Semantic editor services include:

- *Reference resolution* to link different concepts of the defined language such as declarations and usages of variables.
- Code assist through *semantic completion* that incorporates semantic information such as reference resolution or typing into the completion proposal.
- Semantics-preserving *refactorings* of programs or models, ranging from simple renaming to language-specific restructuring.
- In case an error is detected in the model, an *error marker* highlights the involved model element and presents the error message to the user.
- *Quick fixes* may propose ways of fixing such an error. When the user selects any of the proposed fixes, the faulty model is automatically repaired.
- When transforming models, keeping track of a model's *origin* enables linking elements of the transformation result back to the original input model. This is particularly useful for locating the origin of a static or dynamic error in generated code. It is also useful in debugging.
- To better understand the behavior of a model, it can be useful to have a view of the code that a model compiles to. Language workbenches that feature *live translation* can display the model and the generated code side-by-side and update the generated code whenever the original model changes.

In addition to the above services, the language editor provided by most language workbenches can display information about the result of language-specific *validations*. We distinguish validations that are merely structural, such as containment or multiplicity requirements between different concepts, and validations that are more semantic, such as name or type analysis. Language workbenches may facilitate the definition of user-defined type systems or name binding rules. However, many language workbenches do not provide a declarative validation mechanisms and instead allow the definition of validation rules programmatically in a general-purpose programming language.

Another important aspect of building languages is *testing* of the language definition. Testing a language definition may be supported by unit-testing the different language aspects: the syntax (parser or projections), semantics (translation or interpretation), editor (completion, reference resolution, refactoring, etc.), and validation (structure or types). Some language workbenches support debugging. We distinguish between support for debugging the language definition (validation or semantics), and support for constructing debuggers for the defined language. The latter allows, for instance, the definition of domain-specific views to display variable bindings, or specific functionality for setting breakpoints.

Finally, *composability* of language definitions is a key requirement for supporting language-oriented programming [8, 61] where software developers use multiple languages to address different aspects of a software system. Language workbenches may support *incremental extension* (syntactic integration of one language into another) and *language unification* (independent languages can be unified into a single language) [12]. This composition should be achieved for all aspects of a language: syntax, validation, semantics, and editor services.

In summary, our feature model captures most of the design space for language work-benches. In creating this feature model, we ignored *how* the various features can be supported by a language workbench. This is the focus of the subsequent section.

4 Language Workbenches

In this section, we introduce the language workbenches that participated at LWC'13 and show which features of our feature model they support.

4.1 Introduction of the Tools

Ensō (since 2010, http://www.enso-lang.org) is a greenfield project to enable a soft-ware development paradigm based on interpretation and integration of executable spec-ification languages. Ensō has its roots in an enterprise application engine developed at Allegis starting in 1998, which included integrated but modular interpreters for seman-tic data modeling, policy-based security, web user interfaces, and workflows. Between 2003 and 2010 numerous prototypes were produced that sought to refine the vision and establish an academic foundation for the project. The current version (started in 2010) is implemented in Ruby. Rather than integrate with an existing IDE, Ensō seeks to even-tually create its own IDE. The goal of the project is to explore new approaches to the model-based software development paradigm.

Más (since 2011, http://www.mas-wb.com) is a web-based workbench for the creation of domain-specific languages and models. Más uses projectional editing to provide con-venient styling of models and an intuitive editor experience for "non-dev" users, and makes language definition as simple as possible. Language semantics is defined through "activations", consisting, for instance, of declarative code generation templates. Más aims at lowering the entry barrier for language creation far enough to allow adoption and scaling of the model-driven approach across disciplines and industries.

MetaEdit+ (since 1995, http://www.metacase.com) is a mature, platform-independent, graphical language workbench for domain-specific modeling [28]. MetaEdit+ aims to be the easiest domain-modeling tool to learn and to use, removing accidental complexity to allow users to concentrate on creating productive languages and good models. MetaEdit+ is commercially successful, used by customers in both industry and academia. Empirical research has consistently shown that MetaEdit+ increases productivity of developers by a factor of 5–10 compared to programming [26, 29, 44].

MPS (since 2003, http://www.jetbrains.com/mps/) is an open-source language work-bench developed by JetBrains. Its most distinguishing feature is a projectional editor that supports integrated textual, symbolic, and tabular notations, as well as wide-ranging sup-port for composition and extension of languages and editors. MPS realizes the language-oriented programming paradigm introduced by Sergey Dmitriev [8] and has evolved into a mature and well-documented tool. It is used by JetBrains internally to develop various web-based tools such as the Youtrack bugtracker. It has also been used to develop var-ious systems outside of JetBrains, the biggest one probably being the mbeddr tool for embedded software development [58].

Onion (since 2012) is a language workbench and base infrastructure implemented in .NET for assisting in the creation of DSLs. Onion has evolved from Essential (2008), a textual language workbench with a focus on model interpretation and code generation. The main goals of the Onion design is to provide the tools to speed up DSL creation for different notations (text, graphical, projectional) and provide scalability for big models via partitioning and merging capabilities. Onion emphasizes speed of parsing and code generation, enabling real-time synchronization of models and generated code.

Rascal (since 2009, `http://www.rascal-mpl.org`) is an extensible metaprogramming language and IDE for source code analysis and transformation [23, 32, 33, 54]. Rascal combines and unifies features found in other tools for source code manipulation and language workbenches. Rascal provides a simple, programmatic interface to extend the Eclipse IDE with custom IDE support for new languages. Rascal is currently used as a research vehicle for analyzing existing software and the implementation of DSLs. It provides the implementation platform for a real-life DSL in the domain of digital forensics [53]. The tool is accompanied with interactive online documentation and is regularly released as a self-contained Eclipse plugin.

Spoofax (since 2007, `http://www.spoofax.org`) is an Eclipse-based language workbench for efficient development of textual domain-specific languages with full IDE support [27]. In Spoofax, languages are specified in declarative meta-DSLs for syntax (SDF3 [60]), name binding (NaBL [34]), editor services, and transformations (Stratego [6]). From these specifications, Spoofax generates and dynamically loads an Eclipse-based IDE which allows languages to be developed and used inside the same Eclipse instance. Spoofax is used to implement its own meta-DSLs. Spoofax has been used to develop WebDSL [56] and Mobl [22], and is being used by Oracle for internal projects.

SugarJ (since 2010, `http://www.sugarj.org`) is a Java-based extensible programming language that allows programmers to extend the base language with custom language features [11,14]. A SugarJ extension is defined with declarative meta-DSLs (SDF, Stratego, and a type-system DSL [40]) as part of the user program and can be activated in the scope of a module through regular import statements. SugarJ also comes with a Spoofax-based IDE [13] that can be customized via library import on a file-by-file basis. A language extension can use arbitrary context-free and layout-sensitive syntax [15] that does not have to align with the syntax or semantics of the base language Java. Therefore, SugarJ is well-suited for the implementation of DSLs that combine the benefits of internal and external DSLs. Variants of SugarJ support other base languages: JavaScript, Prolog, and Haskell [16].

Whole Platform (since 2005, `http://whole.sourceforge.net`) is a mature projectional language workbench supporting language-oriented programming [50]. It is mostly used to engineer software product lines in the financial domain due to its ability to define and manage both data formats and pipelines of model transformations over big data. The Whole Platform aims to minimize the explicit metamodeling efforts, so that users can concentrate on modeling. The Whole Platform aims to reduce the use of monolithic languages and leverages grammar-based data formats for integrating with legacy systems.

Xtext (since 2006, http://www.eclipse.org/Xtext/) is a mature open-source framework for development of programming languages and DSLs. It is designed based on proven compiler construction patterns and ships with many commonly used language features, such as a workspace indexer and a reusable expression language [10]. Its flexible architecture allows developers to start by reusing well-established and commonly understood default semantics for many language aspects, but Xtext scales up to full programming language implementations, where every single aspect can be customized in straightforward ways by means of dependency injection. Companies like Google, IBM, BMW and many others have built external and internal products based on Xtext.

4.2 Language Workbench Features

We position the language workbenches above in the design space captured by our feature model as displayed in Table 1. In the remainder of this subsection, we reflect on some of the findings.

Notation and Editing Mode. Most language workbenches provide support for textual notations. Only MetaEdit+ is strictly non-textual. Más, MetaEdit+, MPS, and the Whole Platform provide support for tabular notations. Más, MPS and Onion employ projectional editing, which simplifies the integration of multiple notation styles. Currently, only Ensō combines textual and graphical notations by providing support for custom projections into diagram editors. All other language workbenches only support textual notation, edited in a free-form text editor. MetaEdit+, MPS, and the Whole Platform also support mathematical symbols, such as integral symbols or fractions.

Semantics. Except for Ensō, all language workbenches follow a generative approach, most of them featuring both model-to-text and model-to-model transformations, and many additionally supporting interpretation of models. In contrast, Ensō eschews generation of code and is solely based on interpreters, following the working hypothesis that interpreters compose better than generators.

Validation. Some language workbenches lack dedicated support for type checking and/or constraints. These concerns are either dealt with programmatically, or assumed to be addressed by the use of semantically rich meta models. MPS, SugarJ [40], and Xtext provide declarative languages for the definition of type systems. Spoofax has a declarative language for describing name binding rules [34].

Testing. MPS, Spoofax, and Xtext feature dedicated sublanguages for testing aspects of a DSL implementations, such as parsing, name binding, and type checking. Rascal partially supports testing for DSLs through a generic unit testing and randomized testing framework. Five language workbenches provide debuggable specification languages. Four language workbenches support the debugging of DSL programs. For example, Xtext automatically supports debugging for programs that build on Xbase and compile to Java. MPS has a debugger API that can be used to build language-specific debuggers. It also defines a DSL for easily defining how debugging of language extension works. Both Xtext and MPS rely on origin tracking of data created during generation. In the Whole Platform both metalanguage and defined language can be debugged using the same infrastructure which has support for conditional breakpoints and variable views.

Table 1. Language Workbench Features (● = full support, ◐ = partial/limited support)

		Ensō	Más	MetaEdit+	MPS	Onion	Rascal	Spoofax	SugarJ	Whole	Xtext
Notation	Textual	●	●		●	●	●	●	●	●	●
	Graphical	●	◐	●			◐			●	
	Tabular			●	●	●				●	
	Symbols				●	●				●	
Semantics	Model2Text		●	●	●	●	●	●	●	●	●
	Model2Model			●	●	●	●	●	●	●	●
	Concrete syntax			●	●	●	●	●	●		
	Interpretative	●		●	●		◐	●		●	●
Validation	Structural	●	●	●	●	●	●	●	●	●	●
	Naming	◐	●	●	●	●		●		●	◐
	Types				●				●		●
	Programmatic	●			●	●	●	●	●		●
Testing	DSL testing				●		◐	●		●	●
	DSL debugging	●		●	●			●		●	●
	DSL prog. debugging	●			●					●	●
Composability	Syntax/views	●			●	●	●	●	●	●	◐
	Validation				●	●	●	●	●	●	●
	Semantics	●			●	●	●	●	●		●
	Editor services				●	●	●	●	●		●
Editing mode	Free-form	●			●	●	●	●	●		●
	Projectional		●		●	●				●	
Syntactic services	Highlighting		◐	●	●	●	●	●	●	●	●
	Outline			●	●	●	●	●	●	●	●
	Folding		●	●	●	●	●	●	●	●	●
	Syntactic completion			●	●	●		●	●	●	●
	Diff	●			●	●	●	●	●	●	●
	Auto formatting	●	●	●	●	●	●	●		●	●
Semantic services	Reference resolution	●	●	●	●	●	●	●			●
	Semantic completion	●	●	●	●	●	●	●		●	●
	Refactoring	◐		●	●			●	●	●	
	Error marking	●	●	●	●	●	●	●	●	●	●
	Quick fixes				●						●
	Origin tracking	●		●	●		●	●	●		●
	Live translation			●			●	◐	●	●	●

Composability. Composability allows languages to be built by composing separate, reusable building blocks. Ensō, Rascal, Spoofax, and SugarJ obtain syntactic composability through the use of generalized parsing technology, which is required because only the full class of context-free grammars is closed under union. The composability of Xtext grammars is limited, since it is built on top of ANTLR's LL(*) algorithm [45]. Syntactic composition in Onion is based on composing PEG [18] grammars. The language workbenches MPS and MetaEdit+, which do not use parsing at all, allow arbitrary notations to be combined.

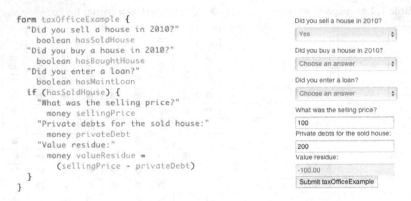

Fig. 2. An example of a textual QL model (left) and its default rendering (right)

The composability of validation and semantics in Rascal, Spoofax, and SugarJ is based on the principle of composing sets of rewrite rules. In Ensō, composition of semantics is achieved by using the object-oriented principles of inheritance and delegation in interpreter code. In MPS, different language aspects use different means of composition. For example, the type system relies on declarative typing rules which can be simply composed. On the other hand, the composition of transformations relies on the pair-wise specification of relative priorities between transformation rules.

Editor. The free-form textual language workbenches that are built on Eclipse (Rascal, Spoofax, SugarJ, Xtext) all provide roughly the same set of IDE features: syntax coloring, outlining, folding, reference resolution, and semantic completion. Spoofax, SugarJ, and Xtext have support for syntactic completion. Rascal, Spoofax, and Xtext allow the definition of custom formatters to automatically layout DSL programs. Projectional editors such as MPS, Whole Platform or Más always format a program as part of the projection rules, so this feature is implicit. Textual free-form language workbenches get the Diff feature for free by reusing existing version-control systems. MPS comes with a dedicated three-way diff/merge facility that works at the level of the projected syntax. MetaEdit+ provides a dedicated differencing mechanism so that modelers can inspect recent changes; for version-control a shared repository is used.

5   LWC 2013 Assignment: A DSL for Questionnaires

We use the assignment of LWC'13 for comparing the language workbenches introduced in the previous section. In the present section, we briefly introduce the assignment and its challenges, which was to develop a Questionnaire Language (QL)[7]. A questionnaire

---

[7] Original assignment text: http://www.languageworkbenches.net/images/5/53/Ql.pdf. The questionnaire language was selected based on the expectation that it could be completed "after-hours" and that it would not be biased towards one particular style of language workbenches (e.g., graphical or textual). We have had no feedback indicating that the assignment was infeasible or unsuitable.

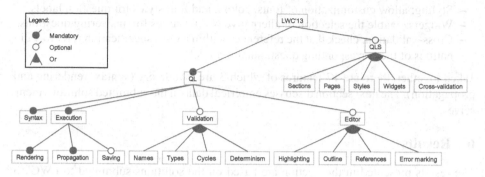

Fig. 3. Feature model of the QL assignment

consists of a sequence of questions and derived values. A question may be conditionally visible based on the values of earlier questions. A questionnaire is presented to a user by rendering it as a GUI, as exemplified in Fig. 2. In addition to these mandatory features, we asked participants to realize a number of optional features. All features are shown in the feature model of Fig. 3. Specifically, we asked for a QL language and IDE implementation supporting the following features:

- Syntax: provide concrete and abstract syntax for QL models.
- Rendering: compile to code that executes a questionnaire GUI (or interpret directly).
- Propagation: generate code that ensures that computed questions update their value as soon as any of their (transitive) dependencies changes.
- Saving: generate code that allows questionnaire users to persist the values entered into the questionnaire.
- Names: ensure that no undefined names are used in expressions.
- Types: check that conditions and expressions are well-typed.
- Cycles: detect cyclic dependencies through conditions and expressions.
- Determinism: check that no two versions of equally-named questions are visible simultaneously (requires SAT solving or model checking).
- Highlighting: provide customized visual clues to distinguish language constructs.
- Outline: provide a hierarchical view or projection of QL models.
- References: support go-to-definition for variables used in conditions and expressions.
- Error marking: visually mark offending source-model elements in case of errors.

We also asked participants to develop a second language called QLS for declaring the style and layout of QL questionnaires. QL has the requirement that it should be possible to apply a QLS specification to an existing questionnaire without anticipation in the definition of the questionnaire itself. Specifically, we asked for the following features:

- Sectioning: allow questions to be (re)arranged in sections and subsections.
- Pagination: allow questions to be distributed over multiple pages.

- Styling: allow customization of fonts, colors, and font styles for question labels.
- Widgets: enable the selection of alternative widget styles for answering questions.
- Cross-validation: check that the references within a QLS specification refer to valid entities of the corresponding questionnaire model.

Taken together, there are 17 features of which 3 are mandatory (syntax, rendering and propagation). The next section discusses empirical data on the submitted solutions themselves.

6   Results

The results presented in this section are based on the solutions submitted to LWC'13 (links to the sources of these solutions are listed in Table 2). In Table 3 show for each language workbench which features the corresponding QL/QLS implementation supports. The feature-based categorization of the solutions provides a qualitative frame of reference for interpreting the size and dependency results given in Table 4. To indicate the completeness of a solution, we computed feature coverage as shown in the bottom row of Table 3. The coverage is computed by counting the number of supported features ($\bullet = 1$, $\ominus = 0.5$), and then dividing by the total number of features (17).

Table 4 summarizes the results on the size of each QL/QLS solution. As a size metric, we use the number of source lines of code (SLOC), excluding empty lines and comments. Because in some language workbenches non-textual notations are used to realize (parts of) the solution, SLOC does not tell the whole story. In these cases, we also count and report the number of model elements (NME). Model elements include any kind of structural entity that is used to define aspects of a language. For example, in MetaEdit+, modeling elements include graphs, objects, relationships, roles, and properties.

For the textual language workbenches Ensō, Onion, Rascal, Spoofax, SugarJ, and Xtext, SLOC were measured using the script cloc.pl[8] or by manual count. For Más, MetaEdit+, and the Whole Platform we counted the number of model elements and measured the size additional code artifacts. Since MPS is purely projectional but still provides a textual presentation of languages, we use an approximate SLOC count: We counted modeling elements and computed SLOC of an equivalent Java program by multiplying the number of model elements with different factors for different types of modeling elements [59]. In addition we report the number of SLOC/NME per feature. The number is obtained by dividing the total SLOC/NME by the number of supported features. Finally, the table also shows the compile-time and runtime dependencies of each solution to appreciate the complexity of deploying the resulting QL/QLS IDE and the generated questionnaire applications.

It is important to realize it is not our intention to present the quantitative results of Table 4 as an absolute measure of implementation effort or complexity (as is, e.g., done in [35]). They cannot be used to rank language workbenches. Factors that prevent such ranking include:

- The SLOC count is incomplete in systems where non-textual languages are used, such as in Más, MetaEdit+, MPS and Whole Platform. The NME count only partially makes up for this.

---

[8] http://cloc.sourceforge.net

Table 2. Published sources of the QL solutions

Lang. Workbench	Links to the corresponding QL solutions
Ensō	`https://github.com/enso-lang/enso/tree/master/demos/Questionaire`
Más	`http://www.mas-wb.com/secure/concrete/language?id=120001&securityToken=` `restricted_public_token` `http://www.mas-wb.com/languages/inspector?id=120001`
MetaEdit+	`http://www.metacase.com/support/50/repository/LWC2013.zip`
MPS	`http://code.google.com/p/mps-lwc13`
Onion	`https://bitbucket.org/icinetic/lwc2013-icinetic`
Rascal	`https://github.com/cwi-swat/QL-R-kemi`
Spoofax	`https://github.com/metaborg/lwc2013`
SugarJ	`https://github.com/seba--/sugarj/tree/questionnaire/case-studies/` `questionnaire-language`
Whole Platform	`https://github.com/wholeplatform/whole-examples/tree/master/org.whole.` `crossexamples.lwc13`
Xtext	`http://code.google.com/a/eclipselabs.org/p/lwc13-xtext/`

- A single number of SLOC is presented, but in each language workbench (a multiplicity of) different programming, modeling, and specification languages are used.
- The architecture and design may be substantially different across QL/QLS solutions. For instance, chosing a client-server Web architecture over a desktop GUI design may or may not affect SLOC.
- Different QL/QLS features may require varying amounts of effort, which may not be reflected in SLOC. Furthermore, the degree as to how much effort is needed for a particular feature may vary per language workbench. The coarse granularity of the QL feature model may obscure this even more. For instance, the feature model does not distinguish between the number of questionnaire data types that are supported.
- Even though, intuitively, more features would imply more effort, this relation is almost certainly not linear, since more features increase the risk of feature interaction. The SLOC/feature metric ignores this aspect.
- The SLOC count may be influenced by the developer's familiarity with the language workbench. For instance, some of the solutions have been developed by the language workbench implementors themselves (e.g., Más, SugarJ), whereas others are built by first-time (e.g., MPS) or second-time (e.g., Rascal) users of a language workbench. We did not record the time spent on a particular solution.
- Even if all risks above could be mitigated, our data set is to small to derive any statistically significant conclusions. Moreover, in the low end of the SLOC data set there are very few data points, and in the upper region of the data set there is high variability.

In summary, we are aware that the presented numbers are a gross simplification of reality. Nevertheless, juxtaposing the size, size per feature, and dependencies helps to spot outliers and can enable interesting observations. Furthermore, this can guide future investigations by workbench users or implementors. In the next section, we present our findings based on the results above.

Table 3. Implemented QL and QLS features per language workbench (● = "fully implemented", ◔ = "partially implemented")

		Ensō	Más	MetaEdit+	MPS	Onion	Rascal	Spoofax	SugarJ	Whole	Xtext
Execution	Syntax	●	●	●	●	●	●	●	●	●	●
	Rendering	●	●	●	●	●	●	●	●	●	●
	Propagation	●	●	●	●	●	●	●	●	●	●
	Saving	●		●	●	●	●	●		●	●
Validation	Names		●	●	●	●	●	●	●	●	●
	Types		◔	●	●	●	●	●	●		●
	Cycles						●	●			●
	Determinism							◔	●		
IDE	Coloring		●	●	●	●	●	●	●	●	●
	Outline			●	◔	●	●	●	●	●	●
	References		●	●	●		●	●	●	●	●
	Marking			●	●	◔	●	●	●	●	●
QLS	Sectioning			●		●	●	●		●	●
	Pagination			●			●	●			●
	Styling			●	◔	●	●	●		●	●
	Widgets			●	●	●	●	●		●	●
	Validation			●	●	●	●	●		●	●
Feature coverage (in percent)		24	44	88	74	82	88	97	59	65	94

Table 4. Size metrics and dependency information on the QL/QLS solutions

	SLOC / NME	SLOC/NME per feature	Compile-time dependencies	Runtime dependencies
Ensō	83 / –	21 / –	Ensō, NodeJS or Ruby 1.9	Ensō, NodeJS, browser with JavaScript, jQuery
Más	413 / 56	55 / 9	Más, browser with JavaScript	browser with JavaScript, jQuery
MetaEdit+	1177 / 68	78 / 5	MetaEdit+	browser with JavaScript
MPS	1324 / –	106 / –	MPS, JDK, Sacha Lisson's Richtext Plugins	JRE
Onion	1876 / –	134 / –	Onion, .NET 4.5, StringTemplate	browser with JavaScript
Rascal	2408 / –	161 / –	Rascal, Eclipse, JDK, IMP	PHP server, browser with JavaScript, jQuery and validator
Spoofax	1420 / –	86 / –	Spoofax, Eclipse, JDK, IMP, WebDSL	WebDSL runtime, SQL database, browser with JavaScript
SugarJ	703 / –	70 / –	SugarJ, JDK, Eclipse, Spoofax	JRE
Whole	645 / 313	59 / 28	Whole Platform, Eclipse, JDK	JRE, SWT, Whole LDK
Xtext	1040 / –	65 / –	Xtext, Eclipse, ANTLR, Xtend	JRE, JSF 2.1, JEE container

7 Observations

Completeness. All solutions fulfilled the basic requirements of rendering and executing QL models. Furthermore, 9 out of 10 solutions provide IDE support for the QL language. Additionally, 7 of those solutions also provide confusing IDE support for the optional QLS language. All of the solutions achieve these results with fewer than 2 500 SLOC; for the language workbenches based on non-textual notations, the raw SLOC count is below 1 200. For comparison, a simple QL implementation in Java, consisting of a (generated) parser, type checker and interpreter, rougly requires around 3 100 SLOC, *excluding* IDE support and QLS features[9]. This shows that state of the art language workbenches indeed provide advanced support for language engineering, and confirms earlier research providing evidence that the use of DSL tools leads to language implementations which are easier to maintain [31].

Diversity. Reflecting upon Tables 1 and 4 we can observe a striking diversity among the tools, even though they perform more or less equally well in terms of the assignment. In our study, half of the workbenches are developed in an academic context (Ensō, Rascal, Spoofax, SugarJ, and the Whole Platform) and the other half in industry (Más, MetaEdit+, MPS, Onion, and Xtext). Feature coverage and SLOC per feature show no bias to either side. Similarly, the age of the language workbenches varies from 18 years (MetaEdit+) to 1 year (Onion). Yet, again there seems to be no bias towards a particular age category. It is to be expected that the maturity, stability, and scalability of industrial and academic tools differ; however, this has not been focus of our study. Indeed, scalability will likely be one of the focuses of the next LWC, from which we hopefully gain further insight into the field of language workbenches.

Another interesting distinction is whether a language workbench provides a single, generic metalanguage or a combination of smaller metalanguages. For instance, Rascal provides a unified language with domain-specific features (grammars, traversal, relational calculus, etc.) to facilitate the construction of languages. Similarly, apart from metamodels in Más and grammars and metamodels in Onion, these two language workbenches interface with general purpose languages for the heavy lifting (Xtend in Más, C# in Onion). Both MPS and Xtext provide escapes to Java should the need arise.

On the other hand, Spoofax provides a multiplicity of declarative languages dedicated to certain aspects of a language implementation (e.g., SDF3 for parsing and pretty printing, Stratego for transformation, NaBL for name binding, etc.). Along the same lines, MPS and SugarJ provide support for building such sub-languages on top of an open, extensible base language. In this way, SugarJ integrates SDF, Stratego and a language for type systems into the base language. MPS uses specialized languages for type system rules, transformation rules and data flow specification, among others.

Finally, considering editor model and notation style, there seems to be no predominant language-workbench style: textual, projectional and graphical notations are well represented and have been found equally able to realize the QL/QLS assignment. It is interesting to note however, that such boundaries are blurring. MPS already supports tabular, symbolic, and textual notations. Both MPS and Spoofax are currently working towards integrating graphical notations (see e.g., [55]). In the Onion language workbench, textual parsing is combined with projectional editing. Finally, Ensō apriori does

---

[9] This number is based on computing the median SLOC of hand-written, non-test Java code and ANTLR, Rats! or JACC grammar definitions over 48 QL implementations, constructed by students of the Software Construction course in the Master Software Engineering, University of Amsterdam, 2013. See:
https://github.com/software-engineering-amsterdam/sea-of-ql

not commit to one particular style and supports both textual and graphical editing. Thus there seems to be a convergence towards language workbenches where multiple, heterogeneous notations or editing modes may co-exist within one language, similar to the original vision of intentional programming [47].

Language Reuse and Composition. An important goal of language-oriented programming [61] is the ability to combine different languages describing different aspects of software systems. The results on the QL/QLS assignment reveal first achievements in this direction. First of all, as indicated above, a number of language workbenches approach language-oriented programming at the meta level: language definitions in MPS, Spoofax, and SugarJ are combinations of different metalanguages. Second, some of the language workbenches achieve high feature coverage using relatively low SLOC numbers. Notably, the low SLOC/feature number of Ensō, MPS, Spoofax, SugarJ and Xtext can be explained by reusing existing languages or language fragments. The Ensō, MPS, SugarJ, and Xtext solutions reuse a language for expressions, thus getting aspects like syntax, type checking, compilation or evaluation for free. The Spoofax solution targets the WebDSL platform, thus reusing execution logic at runtime. In contrast, the Rascal solution includes full implementations of both syntax and semantics of expressions and the execution logic of questionnaires.

Another observation in line with language-oriented programming is the fact that all language workbenches considered in this paper are themselves compile-time dependencies for the QL/QLS IDE. This suggests that the goal of state-of-the-art language workbenches is not so much to facilitate the construction of independent compilers and IDEs, but to provide an extensible environment where those compilers and IDEs can live in. In Ensō, MetaEdit+, MPS, SugarJ, and the Whole Platform, new languages are really extensions of or additions to the language workbench itself. MPS, Ensō and SugarJ go sofar as to even facilitate extension of the metalanguages. Furthermore, with the exception of Xtext, all language workbenches allow new languages or language extensions to be activated dynamically within the same instance of the IDE.

8   Concluding Remarks

To document the state of the art of language workbenches, we established a feature model that captures the design space of language workbenches. We positioned existing language workbenches in this design space by identifying the features they support. As our study reveals, all features of our feature model are realized by some language workbench, but no language workbench realizes all features. To investigate the 10 language workbenches of our study in more detail, we collected empirical data on feature coverage, size, and required dependencies of implementations of a language for questionnaires with styling (QL/QLS) in each language workbench. Based on the results, our observations can be summarized as follows:

- Language workbenches provide adequate abstractions for implementing a language like QL. The results show a marked advantage over manual implementation.
- The language workbench space is very diverse: different sets of supported features, age ranging from 1 to 18 years, single metalanguage or multiple metalanguages,

industry or research, etc. Based on our results it is impossible to conclude that any particular category performs better than others.

Finally, we have observed trends towards:

- Integrating different notation styles (textual, graphical, tabular, symbolic) and editing modes (free-form and projectional).
- Reuse and composition of languages, leading to language-oriented programming both at the object level and meta level.
- Viewing language workbenches as an extensible environments, instead of a tools to create other tools.

References

1. Alderson, A.: Experience of bi-lateral technology transfer projects. In: Diffusion, Transfer and Implementation of Information Technology (1997)
2. Anlauff, M., Kutter, P.W., Pierantonio, A.: Tool support for language design and prototyping with montages. In: Jähnichen, S. (ed.) CC 1999. LNCS, vol. 1575, pp. 296–300. Springer, Heidelberg (1999)
3. Arnold, B.R.T., Van Deursen, A., Res, M.: An algebraic specification of a language for describing financial products. In: Formal Methods Application in Software Engineering, pp. 6–13. IEEE (1995)
4. Batory, D.: Feature models, grammars, and propositional formulas. In: Obbink, H., Pohl, K. (eds.) SPLC 2005. LNCS, vol. 3714, pp. 7–20. Springer, Heidelberg (2005)
5. Borras, P., Clement, D., Despeyroux, T., Incerpi, J., Kahn, G., Lang, B., Pascual, V.: Centaur: the system. SIGPLAN Not. 24(2), 14–24 (1988)
6. Bravenboer, M., Kalleberg, K.T., Vermaas, R., Visser, E.: Stratego/XT 0.17. A language and toolset for program transformation. Sci. Comput. Program. 72(1-2), 52–70 (2008)
7. Chen, M., Nunamaker, J.: Metaplex: An integrated environment for organization and information system development. In: ICIS, pp. 141–151. ACM (1989)
8. Dmitriev, S.: Language oriented programming: The next programming paradigm. JetBrains on Board 1(2) (2004)
9. Donzeau-Gouge, V., Huet, G., Kahn, G., Lang, B.: Programming environments based on structured editors: The MENTOR experience. Technical Report 26, INRIA (1980)
10. Efftinge, S., Eysholdt, M., Köhnlein, J., Zarnekow, S., von Massow, R., Hasselbring, W., Hanus, M.: Xbase: Implementing domain-specific languages for Java. In: GPCE, pp. 112–121 (2012)
11. Erdweg, S.: Extensible Languages for Flexible and Principled Domain Abstraction. PhD thesis, Philipps-Universität Marburg (2013)
12. Erdweg, S., Giarrusso, P.G., Rendel, T.: Language composition untangled. In: LDTA, pp. 7:1–7:8. ACM (2012)
13. Erdweg, S., Kats, L.C.L., Rendel, T., Kästner, C., Ostermann, K., Visser, E.: Growing a language environment with editor libraries. In: GPCE, pp. 167–176. ACM (2011)
14. Erdweg, S., Rendel, T., Kästner, C., Ostermann, K.: SugarJ: Library-based syntactic language extensibility. In: OOPSLA, pp. 391–406. ACM (2011)
15. Erdweg, S., Rendel, T., Kästner, C., Ostermann, K.: Layout-sensitive generalized parsing. In: Czarnecki, K., Hedin, G. (eds.) SLE 2012. LNCS, vol. 7745, pp. 244–263. Springer, Heidelberg (2013)
16. Erdweg, S., Rieger, F., Rendel, T., Ostermann, K.: Layout-sensitive language extensibility with SugarHaskell. In: Haskell Symposium, pp. 149–160. ACM (2012)

17. Eysholdt, M., Behrens, H.: Xtext: Implement your language faster than the quick and dirty way. In: SPLASH Companion, pp. 307–309. ACM (2010)
18. Ford, B.: Parsing expression grammars: A recognition-based syntactic foundation. In: POPL, pp. 111–122. ACM (2004)
19. Fowler, M.: Language workbenches: The killer-app for domain specific languages? (2005), http://martinfowler.com/articles/languageWorkbench.html
20. Heering, J., Klint, P.: Semantics of programming languages: a tool-oriented approach. SIG-PLAN Not. 35(3), 39–48 (2000)
21. Heidenreich, F., Johannes, J., Karol, S., Seifert, M., Wende, C.: Derivation and refinement of textual syntax for models. In: Paige, R.F., Hartman, A., Rensink, A. (eds.) ECMDA-FA 2009. LNCS, vol. 5562, pp. 114–129. Springer, Heidelberg (2009)
22. Hemel, Z., Visser, E.: Declaratively programming the mobile web with Mobl. In: OOPSLA, pp. 695–712. ACM (2011)
23. Hills, M., Klint, P., Vinju, J.J.: Meta-language support for type-safe access to external resources. In: Czarnecki, K., Hedin, G. (eds.) SLE 2012. LNCS, vol. 7745, pp. 372–391. Springer, Heidelberg (2013)
24. Honeywell Technology Center. Dome guide (1999)
25. Kang, K.C., Cohen, S.G., Hess, J.A., Novak, W.E., Peterson, A.S.: Feature-oriented domain analysis (FODA) feasibility study. Technical report, CMU Software Engineering Institute (1990)
26. Kärnä, J., Tolvanen, J.-P., Kelly, S.: Evaluating the use of domain-specific modeling in practice. In: DSM (2009)
27. Kats, L.C.L., Visser, E.: The Spoofax language workbench: Rules for declarative specification of languages and IDEs. In: OOPSLA, pp. 444–463. ACM (2010)
28. Kelly, S., Lyytinen, K., Rossi, M.: MetaEdit+: A fully configurable multi-user and multi-tool CASE and CAME environment. In: Constantopoulos, P., Vassiliou, Y., Mylopoulos, J. (eds.) CAiSE 1996. LNCS, vol. 1080, pp. 1–21. Springer, Heidelberg (1996)
29. Kelly, S., Tolvanen, J.-P.: Domain-Specific Modeling: Enabling Full Code Generation. Wiley-IEEE Computer Society Press (2008)
30. Klint, P.: A meta-environment for generating programming environments. TOSEM 2(2), 176–201 (1993)
31. Klint, P., van der Storm, T., Vinju, J.: On the impact of DSL tools on the maintainability of language implementations. In: LDTA. ACM (2010)
32. Klint, P., van der Storm, T., Vinju, J.: EASY meta-programming with rascal. In: Fernandes, J.M., Lämmel, R., Visser, J., Saraiva, J. (eds.) GTTSE III. LNCS, vol. 6491, pp. 222–289. Springer, Heidelberg (2011)
33. Klint, P., van der Storm, T., Vinju, J.J.: RASCAL: A domain specific language for source code analysis and manipulation. In: SCAM, pp. 168–177. IEEE (2009)
34. Konat, G., Kats, L., Wachsmuth, G., Visser, E.: Declarative name binding and scope rules. In: Czarnecki, K., Hedin, G. (eds.) SLE 2012. LNCS, vol. 7745, pp. 311–331. Springer, Heidelberg (2013)
35. Kosar, T., López, P.E.M., Barrientos, P.A., Mernik, M.: A preliminary study on various implementation approaches of domain-specific language. Inf. Softw. Technol. 50(5), 390–405 (2008)
36. Kuiper, M.F., Saraiva, J.: Lrc – a generator for incremental language-oriented tools. In: Koskimies, K. (ed.) CC 1998. LNCS, vol. 1383, pp. 298–301. Springer, Heidelberg (1998)
37. de Lara, J., Vangheluwe, H.: AToM^3: A tool for multi-formalism and meta-modelling. In: Kutsche, R.-D., Weber, H. (eds.) FASE 2002. LNCS, vol. 2306, pp. 174–188. Springer, Heidelberg (2002)
38. Ledeczi, A., Maroti, M., Bakay, A., Karsai, G., Garrett, J., Thomason, C., Nordstrom, G., Sprinkle, J., Volgyesi, P.: The generic modeling environment. In: Intelligent Signal Processing (2001)

39. Lorenz, D.H., Rosenan, B.: Cedalion: A language for language oriented programming. In: OOPSLA, pp. 733–752. ACM (2011)
40. Lorenzen, F., Erdweg, S.: Modular and automated type-soundness verification for language extensions. In: ICFP (to appear, 2013)
41. Mernik, M., Heering, J., Sloane, A.M.: When and how to develop domain-specific languages. ACM Comput. Surv. 37(4), 316–344 (2005)
42. Mernik, M., Lenič, M., Avdicauševic, E., Zumer, V.: LISA: An interactive environment for programming language development. In: Nigel Horspool, R. (ed.) CC 2002. LNCS, vol. 2304, pp. 1–4. Springer, Heidelberg (2002)
43. Meta Systems Ltd. Quickspec reference guide (1989)
44. MetaCase. MetaEdit+ revolutionized the way Nokia develops mobile phone software (2007), http://www.metacase.com/cases/nokia.html (June 5th, 2013)
45. Parr, T., Quong, R.W.: ANTLR: A predicated-LL(k) parser generator. Software Practice and Experience 25(7), 789–810 (1995)
46. Reps, T., Teitelbaum, T.: The synthesizer generator. SIGPLAN Not. 19(5), 42–48 (1984)
47. Simonyi, C., Christerson, M., Clifford, S.: Intentional software. In: OOPSLA, pp. 451–464. ACM (2006)
48. Smolander, K., Lyytinen, K., Tahvanainen, V.-P., Marttiin, P.: MetaEdit—a flexible graphical environment for methodology modelling. In: Andersen, R., Solvberg, A., Bubenko Jr., J.A. (eds.) CAiSE 1991. LNCS, vol. 498, pp. 168–193. Springer, Heidelberg (1991)
49. Söderberg, E., Hedin, G.: Building semantic editors using JastAdd: tool demonstration. In: LDTA, p. 11 (2011)
50. Solmi, R.: Whole platform. PhD thesis, University of Bologna (2005)
51. Sorenson, P.G., Tremblay, J.-P., McAllister, A.J.: The Metaview system for many specification environments. IEEE Software 5(2), 30–38 (1988)
52. Teichroew, D., Macasovic, P., Hershey III, E., Yamato, Y.: Application of the entity-relationship approach to information processing systems modeling (1980)
53. van den Bos, J., van der Storm, T.: Bringing domain-specific languages to digital forensics. In: ICSE SEIP, pp. 671–680. ACM (2011)
54. van der Storm, T.: The Rascal Language Workbench. CWI Technical Report SEN-1111, CWI (2011)
55. van Rest, O., Wachsmuth, G., Steel, J., Süss, J.G., Visser, E.: Robust real-time synchronization between textual and graphical editors. In: ICMT (2013)
56. Visser, E.: WebDSL: A case study in domain-specific language engineering. In: Lämmel, R., Visser, J., Saraiva, J. (eds.) GTTSE II. LNCS, vol. 5235, pp. 291–373. Springer, Heidelberg (2008)
57. Voelter, M., Pech, V.: Language modularity with the MPS language workbench. In: ICSE, pp. 1449–1450. IEEE (2012)
58. Voelter, M., Ratiu, D., Kolb, B., Schaetz, B.: mbeddr: Instantiating a language workbench in the embedded software domain. Journal of Automated Software Engineering (2013)
59. Voelter, M., Ratiu, D., Schaetz, B., Kolb, B.: mbeddr: an extensible C-based programming language and IDE for embedded systems. In: SPLASH Wavefront, pp. 121–140. ACM (2012)
60. Vollebregt, T., Kats, L.C.L., Visser, E.: Declarative specification of template-based textual editors. In: LDTA (2012)
61. Ward, M.P.: Language-oriented programming. Software – Concepts and Tools 15, 147–161 (1995)

A Model-Driven Approach
to Enhance Tool Interoperability Using
the Theory of Models of Computation

Papa Issa Diallo, Joël Champeau, and Loïc Lagadec

Lab-STICC, ENSTA Bretagne, UEB - 2, Rue F. Verny 29806 Brest cedex 9, France
{papa_issa.diallo,joel.champeau,loic.lagadec}@ensta-bretagne.fr

Abstract. In the context of embedded systems design, the growing heterogeneity of systems leads to increasingly complex and unreliable tool chains. The Model-Driven Engineering (MDE) community has been making considerable efforts to abstract tool languages in meta-models, and to offer model transformation mechanisms for model exchanges. However, the interoperability problems are recurring and still not consistently addressed. For instance, when it comes to executable model exchanges, it is very difficult to ensure the preservation of the models behavior from one tool to another. This is mainly due to a lack of understanding of the Models of Computation (MoC) and execution semantics behind the models within different environments. In this paper, we introduce a methodology and a framework to: make explicit the execution semantics of models (based on the theory of MoC); provide semantics enrichment mechanisms to ensure the preservation of the execution semantics of models between tools. Our case study is an integration between a UML specification tool and an industrial Intensive Data Flow processing tool. This contribution helps to highlight execution semantics concerns within the tool integration context.

Keywords: Model-Driven Engineering, Model of Computation, Tool Interoperability.

1 Introduction

Embedded systems design expectations have greatly evolved in the last few decades. Accordingly, the number of engineering domains and tools involved during the development phases have considerably increased.

In this context, tool interoperability became a major topic for tool integration and several solutions have been proposed to tackle the arising issues. Among other contributions, A. Wasserman et al. [1] or I. Thomas et al. [2] have contributed to establish an important basis for the resolution of tool interoperability. Their contribution helped to classify tool integration in four main integration concerns (*presentation*, *process*, *control* and *data*) that have been included in several tool integration methodologies.

M. Erwig, R.F. Paige, and E. Van Wyk (Eds.): SLE 2013, LNCS 8225, pp. 218–237, 2013.

More recently, Model-Driven Engineering (MDE) has proposed promising so-lutions by promoting the use of models and meta-models for the interchange between tools [3] [4]. Not only does MDE allow the definition of meta-models that focus on the intrinsic properties of an engineering domain (e.g., signal-processing, control systems), it also offers solutions for the automation of tool exchanges during the design phases. For instance, model transformation tools allow automatic model-to-model transformations and code generation. This en-ables tool integration to take advantage of the several standardized languages to describe meta-models [5] and to transform models [6].

1.1 Problematic and Contribution

In the embedded systems community, the reuse of exchanged models between tools is difficult despite numerous contributions of MDE [7]. The known ap-proaches for tool interoperability have struggled to be accepted, mainly because they failed to provide solutions for consistent data interoperability within a do-main where models are highly parallel and heterogeneous in nature.

For instance, to perform design and analysis during the development process, the *execution semantics* of the exchanged models is a major factor to preserve the models behavior. In particular, if those environments have potentially different runtimes based on different execution semantics (e.g., IBM Rational Rhapsody Modeler [8] with Discrete Events [9] semantics, or Gaspard2 [10] with Array-OL [11] semantics).

Execution semantics describes the evolution of a model and/or its behavior over time. In the context of embedded systems design, execution semantics is based on a theory of computation called Model of Computation (MoC). The MoC defines the execution rules underlying execution semantics; every rule represents how a machine will execute a program. The most popular MoC includes Communicating Sequential Processes [12] and Synchronous Data Flow [13] models.

The execution semantics of models has been addressed in the MDE community through the work of J.M. Jézéquel *et al.* [14] and D. Di Ruscio *et al.* [15]. In these works, execution semantics is discussed to give executability to models. However, they do not clearly relate execution semantics to the MoC theory. Moreover, in the literature there is a lack of contributions addressing their use as key elements for consistent tool interoperability. Usually, the execution semantics is not visible to the designers i.e., it is implicitly defined in the execution engine or within the transformation rules. This results in a low reuse of models, and their faulty interpretation. The identified issues can be summarized as follows:

- the exchanges between tools are limited to structural alignments. In this case, one is more interested in the interpretation of the static semantics;
- the modeling languages rarely explain the way in which the parallelism is controlled by tools. In fact, this cannot be expressed without taking into ac-count the execution semantics of the models. How such semantics is handled during model exchanges remains an open question. Especially when the lack of execution semantics causes poor quality and consistency of the analysis activities;

- the current approaches for execution semantics definition do not explicitly identify the underlying MoC of the tools. Consequently, it is difficult to formally reason about the links between several execution semantics of different tools;

To address these issues, we provide a methodology for the explicit identification of execution semantics and support for the specification of the *parallelism control* at the meta-model level using MoC theory. This contributes to highlight the importance of MoC definitions for the exchange of semantically enriched models. The paper presents the following contributions:

- A methodology to disambiguate the semantics of models from a MoC viewpoint. This methodology is based on the work of D. Harel *et al.* [16] and A. Sangiovanni-Vincentelli *et al.* [17]. Its purpose is to use MoC theory to characterize the interoperability between tools and languages;
- A framework to define semantic enrichments and semantic adaptations for models from different tools. The framework is illustrated through a novel design flow [1] integrating the Unified Modeling Language (UML) IBM Rhapsody Modeler [8] and the Spear Development Environment (Spear DE) [18] industrial tool that performs *design space exploration*[2] activities. The illustration includes the capture of the Array-OL [11] MoC semantics with Cometa (properties and execution control mechanisms);
- Finally, an experiment based on the intensive data processing model (section 4.2). In this experiment, thanks to the abstracted execution semantics, we were able to simulate the Array-OL MoC within Rhapsody which does not implement such semantics natively.

1.2   Outline

The rest of the paper is structured as follows: Section 2 presents background information; Section 3 presents the methodology for MoC identification within tool chains; Section 4 presents the semantics enrichment definitions, in particular using the Cometa framework and our experimentation on a *Chirp*[3] model; Section 5 presents related work; finally Section 6 concludes our work.

2   Background on Syntactic and Semantic Interoperability

The challenges regarding the tool interoperability have been addressed in several communities (Information Systems, Web Semantics, Embedded systems, etc.).

---

[1] The research leading to these results has received funding from the ARTEMIS Joint Undertaking under grant agreement n° 100203 (see Article II.9. of the JU Grant Agreement).
[2] Design Space Exploration is an activity during the development process aiming to provide the design possibilities before any implementation.
[3] The Chirp model defines a pseudo-periodic signal that is filtered and processed by several sub-modules (see Section 4.2).

For instance, in the context of embedded systems, Pimentel *et al.* [19] discuss the need for a Common Design Flow Infrastructure (CDFI) framework to build and adapt design flows offering reliable tool interoperability. Each tool within the framework must formally specify its input requirements, its semantics to fit in the framework. More importantly, interoperability must ensure semantics consistency for accurate analysis activities of embedded systems.

Elsewhere, for modeling and simulation purposes, A. Tolk *et al.* [20] define a conceptual model of interoperability called Levels of Conceptual Interoperability Model (LCIM) describing different levels of interoperability for systems and tools. Their contribution highlights two major challenges for the analysis of systems towards different tools: the syntactic interoperability and the semantic interoperability (Figure 1/ Level 2, 3, 4).

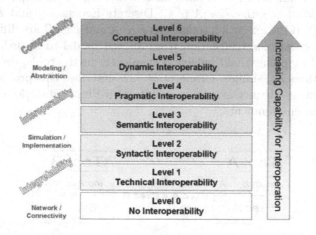

Fig. 1. Levels of Conceptual Interoperability Model [21]

The syntactic interoperability (Level 2) is reached when several tools are able to exchange data using a common format, such concern is currently quite well addressed. In our context, meta-models are used for syntactic interoperability. The data are described as models conforming to meta-models, which in turn conform to the standards such as the Meta-Object Facility (MOF) [5]. Consequently, the communicating tools must define their corresponding meta-models of data for exchanges.

Besides, semantics preservation (static and dynamic) is a major challenge for tools interoperability and both should be addressed with lot of care in design flows.

A. Tolk *et al.* defines the semantic interoperability as reaching a compromise on the unambiguous meaning of models to be exchanged (level 3), regardless of their representation. Similarly, D. Harel *et al.* [16] define a language as: a syntax (abstract or concrete, see Figure 2) whose meaning is specified by its semantic domain. The relation to semantic domains is described by semantic mapping rules from the syntax to the domain where the different elements of syntax

Fig. 2. Semantic Mapping of Language to Semantic Domain

make sense. However, this description only tackles the syntax interpretation issue (static semantics). Because models should preserve their behavior towards different tools, having a formal description of the dynamic semantics of models is also mandatory. The example of Figure 3 highlights this shortcoming.

The A and B simulation tools have their model execution respectively driven by the execution semantics *ExecA* (e.g., Discrete Events [9]) and *ExecB* (e.g., Array-OL [11]). If the execution semantics *ExecA* and *ExecB* are different, there is no guarantee that the translation from an *mA* model to an *mB* model (after syntactical mappings) will behave equivalently in the tools, even when the model's structures are similar. Crane *et al.* [22] describes this problem with experiments showing distinct execution results of a Finite State Machine (FSM) within different environments.

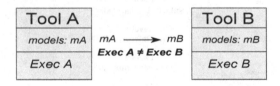

Fig. 3. Simple example of execution semantics issue for Tool Interoperability

In [23], B. Combemale *et al.* argue that the description of a language must also consider the formal description of the evolution of model elements; such formal description is provided by MoC rules.

The MoC provide a framework for formal description of the different rules that apply to execution of the models. By making explicit the MoC information, not only are we able to identify the exchanges of models that will ensure preservation of the execution semantics, but also we will be able to define (when necessary) adaptations between execution semantics to preserve the overall behavior of models through different tools.

In this paper, we argue the ability to do such identifications and adaptations mainly because the execution semantics relationships are strongly related to the MoC relationships. Consequently, we can use the classification of MoCs to establish links between execution semantics. For instance, A. Sangiovanni-Vincentelli *et al.* [17] define the following classification (Figure 4), which reflects the level of compatibility between a set of MoCs.

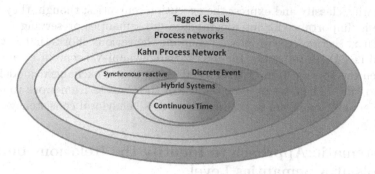

Fig. 4. MoC Classification according to A. Sangiovanni-Vincentelli *et al.*

The classification uses set theory to define relationships (union, intersection, difference) between MoCs starting from the less flexible (more constrained e.g., Continuous Time [24]), to the more flexible (less constrained e.g., Tagged Signals [25]). In our work, we use the above classification to specify consistency of tool chains with regards to their formal execution semantics (MoC).

Afterwards, our idea is to use the framework Cometa to capture the execution semantics adaptations for the models using the MoC theory. Cometa [26] reproduces scheduling mechanisms of concurrent entities based on the theory of MoC to control the parallelism. It defines schedulers and communication protocols that implement the synchronization of the system's components. For specific MoC properties capture, the meta-model abstracts four concerns previously defined by A. Jantsch [27].

- *The Data concern* defines *DataTypes*. The *DataTypes* are used to create elements representing the kind of data manipulated in a given semantic domain e.g., booleans, integers, or complex structured types.
- *The Communication concern* highlights the description of the communication. This concern is based on the definition of ports and connectors. According to the MoC, specific properties are added to these communication elements.
- *The Time concern* abstracts concepts to capture time definition for timed systems. The Concepts such as *TimeBase, Instant* or *Clock* in the meta-model are based on the time model of Modeling and Analysis of Real-time and Embedded systems (MARTE) profile [28].
- *The Behavioral concern* is used to describe the operational semantics of parallel entities. The behaviors of the schedulers and communication protocols are described with event-based Finite State Machine (FSM). A FSM is a theoretical and formal model which allows to switch easily from an abstract representation of behavior to its implementation (e.g., C, Java) [8].

At this stage, we have depicted the importance of explicitly and formally expressing the execution semantics of models in the context of tool interoperability. In addition, we as well have presented several approaches in the literature that aim to clarify, classify and express the execution semantics; though, they do not reference its importance for interoperability and semantics preserving.

In the next sections, we propose to combine the various efforts that have been presented i.e., D. Harel *et al.* [16] and A. Sangiovanni-Vincentelli *et al.* [17] to strengthen the specification of the formal semantics of exchanged models with regards to MoC. Then, we propose the use of the Cometa framework to provide semantic adaptation layers to ensure the models behavioral consistency.

3   Systematic Approach to Identify the Relations between Tools at a Semantics Level

3.1   Principles and Techniques

In this section, we describe the characterization of the tools semantics interoperability using the semantic domains and the underlying execution semantics of the tools.

The semantic domain as defined by D. Harel *et al.* [16] is reused in a formal context with the MoC theory. Therefore, we define a new term *MoC-Based Semantic Domain* as the MoC domain on which the syntax of a given language has its execution formally defined. Consequently, the produced models become executable and follow the execution rules induced by the MoC. Before any further argumentation, we introduce some definitions.

Within a design flow, each interconnected tool uses a language L_{Tool} to describe models. From the language syntax, one defines semantic mappings M to well-defined semantic domains. More particularly, mappings can be directed to so-called *MoC-Based semantic domains* $MBSD_{MoC}$ to specify the models execution rules. The mapping relation is denoted by $M : L_{Tool} \rightarrow MBSD_{MoC}$.

The relations between the $MBSD_{MoC}$ allows exhibiting feasible model exchanges that emphasize semantics and behavior preservation. These relations are provided by the classification of MoC as defined in [17]. The classification is based on a description of the properties underlying each MoC and their degree of expressiveness. According to A. Jantsch [27], the main axes to characterize MoC properties are time, communication, behavior and data. Therefore, a $MBSD_{MoC}$ is defined by the tuple $\langle D_{MoC}, B_{MoC}, C_{MoC}, T_{MoC} \rangle$ where: D_{MoC} characterizes the data types specific to the MoC domain; B_{MoC} represents the underlying behaviors induced by the MoC rules; C_{MoC} represents how the communication is expressed in the MoC; T_{MoC} represents the way in which the time is expressed.

When $MBSD_{MoC}$ are compliant, it is possible to define a transformation T on the subset of compliant properties (tuples) to provide their translation. For instance, a transformation can be $T : D_{MoC1} \rightarrow D_{MoC2}$. Based on this, we can study the relationship between languages and the $MBSD_{MoC}$. In Figure 5, we depict the four main scenarios of relations.

In the first scenario, the language's syntaxes are mapped to the same semantic domain; e.g., L_1 and L_2 have their mapping to the same $MBSD_{SR}$. Here, even if

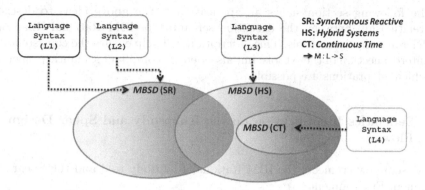

Fig. 5. Language and MoC-Based semantic domains

the syntactic representations are different, there is a clear and common definition of the MoC domain elements where each syntactic element of L_1 and L_2 is mapped. The explicit definition of semantic mappings according to the four axes should allow the description of the relationship between the syntactic elements of languages.

In the second scenario, languages are mapped to different $MBSD_{MoC}$ that are disjoint; e.g., L_1 and L_4 have their respective mapping to $MBSD_{SR}$ and $MBSD_{CT}$, plus $MBSD_{SR} \cap MBSD_{CT} = \emptyset$. Consequently, the set of properties used to characterize $MBSD_{SR}$ and $MBSD_{CT}$ are disjoint (e.g., $D_{SR} \cap D_{CT} = \emptyset$). Therefore, the exchanges of data between tools from these domains cannot be achieved consistently because their underlying MoCs are not compliant.

In the third scenario, the languages are mapped to different semantic domains. However, the semantic domains are not completely disjoint (the semantic domains intersection is not empty); e.g., L_1 and L_3 have their respective mapping to $MBSD_{SR}$ and $MBSD_{HS}$. $MBSD_{SR} \cap MBSD_{HS} \neq \emptyset$, which means they have a subset of common properties. Here, at least one of the intersection between the tuples describing $MBSD_{SR}$ and $MBSD_{HS}$ is not empty. Hence, there exists a subset of properties exchangeable between these domains. As a result, a transformation T (e.g., $T : C_{SR} \rightarrow C_{HS}$) can be defined for the tuples that have compliant elements. However, having no control over the rest of the MoC properties for each tool is error-prone. Consequently, it is still difficult to guarantee consistent model interpretation towards different tools.

In the fourth scenario, the languages are mapped to different semantic domains and the semantic domains are fully compliant (e.g., inclusion relation on the property sets); In this case, the properties of a source $MBSD_{MoC1}$ can all be transformed to equivalent $MBSD_{MoC2}$ properties on a target domain, while keeping the fundamental rules of the source MoC domain. For instance, $MBSD_{CT}$ and $MBSD_{HS}$ are fully compliant and the semantics expressed by CT [24] is expressible from HS semantics [29]. In this context, we can define a semantic transformation on each of the tuples to complement or transform a CT model into a HS model conforming to the constraints defined in CT.

The following section shows an application of the above ideas to describe the relationship between the execution semantics of IBM Rational Rhapsody Modeler and the Spear tools. This description will help ensure the consistency of the interconnection of these tools; but also identify compliant semantic properties for which adaptations are possible.

3.2 Semantics Identification on the Rhapsody and Spear Design Flow

The design flow connects the IBM Rational Rhapsody tool and the Spear Development Environment.

Rhapsody [8] is a proprietary tool that provides a system development environment (mostly embedded systems) based on the use of UML language and profiles. Rhapsody incorporates several activities of software development cycle (requirements specification, high-level system specification, code generation, simulation and testing, etc.). Regarding the specification of systems, the tool integrates UML component models to specify communicating concurrent entities. In such models, the components are interconnected via ports and connectors (see the conceptual model on the left in Figure 6), these elements are classes that may have a behavior (*UML Statechart*) and attributes (*UML Attributes*). Besides, the communication is provided by events (signals) exchanges e.g., *callEvent, receptionEvent*.

DE semantics: The simulation tool provides a runtime based on discrete events (DE) semantics. Thus, the exchanges between the system components are considered as sequences of event requests temporarily stored in storage elements (queue, FIFO, LIFO, etc). The system model defines execution end conditions (e.g., stop Event, variable defining the number of allowed executions, etc). While the execution stop condition is not reached, the scheduling behavior constantly observes the storage elements to process events to the target components, and updates the static values which may affect the execution stop condition.

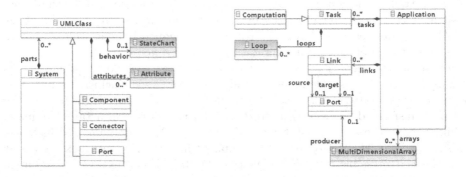

Fig. 6. Conceptual description of Rhapsody and Spear syntax elements

Spear [18] is a tool for parallelization of intensive processing tasks on multidimensional data arrays and implements the Array-OL specification. At the application level, Spear has components communicating via ports and connectors (on the right in Figure 6). The Components (*Computation*) have a vector defining the number of executions (*Loops*); arrays are described at the application level by their shape and elementary operations (*ET* - Elementary Transform). The *Multidimensional* data define references to ports that produce them. Above this description, an implementation of a scheduling mechanism allows components to run following the Array-OL semantics.

Array-OL semantics: Array-OL is a specification for intensive data flow processing. The idea is to parallelize tasks that extract and process multidimensional arrays of data. The specification gathers two main definitions to exploit and process the data:

- *Task Parallelism* is done by defining a dependency graph where every node is a component of type *compound.*
- *Data Parallelism* is the definition of a *repetition* component which has a *repetitionSpace*. A *repetitionSpace* defines how many times a component is executed. These components extract, process and build multidimensional arrays of predefined sizes (*Shape*'s).

The extraction mechanisms and pattern building properties are provided by the definition of a *"Tiler"* connected to the ports or connectors. The Tiler consists of a vector "Origin" (to determine the starting position for the extraction or the point to start building a pattern in the output array), a fitting matrix to determine the spacing between the selected elements in the Array, and a paving matrix to change the origin at each repetition of the component.

Array-OL scheduling depends on the topology of the application (directed acyclic graphs) which gives the dependency relationships between the system components. The scheduling depends also on the expression of data-parallelism where, the number of times each component must be executed to produce or consume an array is given.

Figure 7 shows the positioning of the semantics domains for the Rhapsody and Spear design flow. We define the semantic mappings of the UML (L_uml) and Spear (L_spear) languages to their respective $MBSD_{DE}$ and $MBSD_{ArrayOL}$ domains.

The Array-OL and DE semantics have distinct levels of flexibility and expressiveness for semantics. One of the very basic conditions for the use of DE semantics is that communication between components is performed using lists (queues) of events and a scheduler to transmit events to the communicating components. From this point of view, Array-OL is more constrained in terms of properties. If we consider the previously defined tuples, we can identify the following relations between the semantics:

- $D_{ArrayOL} \bigcap D_{DE} \neq \emptyset$. Array-OL defines multidimensional arrays of data. The arrays are read and written concurrently by the system components. Such data structures do not exist natively in Rhapsody. However, the UML

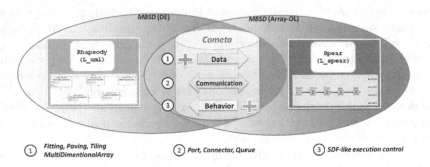

Fig. 7. Rhapsody-Spear design flow and the semantics positioning

language concepts (e.g., class diagrams) model structures similar to multi-dimensional arrays. Here, a formal description of the array's characteristics (sizes, number of vectors) must be provided. From this description, we can define a transformation between Array-OL data models to UML.

– $B_{ArrayOL} \cap B_{DE} \neq \emptyset$. The Array-OL specification defines rules for scheduling concurrent entities. The scheduling requirements combine: managing dependency relations between entities, taking into account the relations between the multi-dimensional arrays, and finally taking into account the vectors that define the number of executions allowed for each component. Any algorithm or execution control mechanism that meets the requirements is capable of simulating the components with respect to the semantics.

Algorithms solving these constraints have already been studied for the SDF MoC [30]. The resulting solution is based on the resolution of linear Diophantine equations [31] that take into account different production and consumption rates. Such components execution control is describable in DE as a program or using more abstract description mechanisms such as event-based FSM. We present in section 4.1 mechanisms for the execution control based on FSM.

– $C_{ArrayOL} \cap C_{DE} \neq \emptyset$. For communication, the same resources are used in both specifications. Indeed, the components communicate through ports and connectors and data are stored in storage entities accessible for the components or the scheduler. However, in DE, the components exchange events. Therefore, the stored elements in the queues are events. This representation is different with the direct storage of data with Array-OL. The formal description of events allows adding parameters on events and parameters can represent values or data. Therefore, it is possible to define a transformation which is an encapsulation of arrays into events.

– The temporal aspect is not described in the Array-OL specification. For the sake of simplicity, we do not consider time description in this experiment.

Considering the above information, the semantic domains are not disjoint at least for Data, Communication, and Behavior viewpoints as shown in Figure 7. This suggests that it is possible to define the appropriate adaptations to move models from one tool to the other while keeping the execution semantics of the source tool.

The transformation ① must take into account the addition of the properties related to data manipulation (enrichment). These properties correspond with the capture of multidimensional data structures, information related to the allowed array sizes on each port (*Shape*) and the vectors defining how patterns of data are selected in the arrays. Section 4.1 shows the capture of this information in Cometa. Further, we enrich the models that are candidates for translation with the capture of execution control mechanisms to guarantee the preserving of the rules imposed by the Array-OL execution semantics from Spear to Rhapsody. This work corresponds to the translation ③ and is detailed in Section 4.1.

The explicit definition of $MBSD_{MoC}$ and their relations (mapping) enhance the reasoning on tool interoperability definition. It ensures less focus on the technical support for interoperability and offers the opportunity to make decisions on the consistency and feasibility of certain tool connexions. These mappings help to assess compliance between tools, as well as to find the possible semantic adaptations based on the relationships between MoC.

4   Semantics Enrichments and Adaptations Using Cometa

In our design flow, we want to alternate Design Space Exploration and Simulation activities with Spear and Rhapsody, respectively. The translation of a Spear model in Rhapsody will not make sense if Rhapsody is not able to interpret the model while preserving the execution semantics from Spear (Array-OL). Therefore, the proper mechanisms (adaptations) to represent the semantics of Array-OL in the context of the DE semantics have to be defined.

4.1   Adding Semantics Properties for the Design Flow

Adding New Properties from Rhapsody to Spear. In this section, we present the usage of Cometa to abstract the data properties ($D_{ArrayOL}$) of the $MBSD_{ArrayOL}$ domain. As shown in Figure 8 (Structure Concern), in Cometa the description of the structural part is done by using *BasicComponent* and *CompositeComponent*. *BasicComponent* owns communication ports, a behavior and parameters that can be used to capture the repetitionSpace. The behavior is defined to capture the execution semantics and is explained in the next sub-section. The abstracted concepts (metaclasses) in the Data concern are used to capture the specific data properties of the specification: The concept *Matrix* is used to capture the vectors that extract the patterns of data (*Matrix MetaClass* → (*Tiler, Fitting, Paving*)); The concept *Vector* is used to capture the accepted data sizes on each port (*Vector MetaClass* → (*Shape, Origin*)); and the concept *Parameter* for the capture of the repetition space (*Parameter MetaClass* → (*repetitionSpace*)).

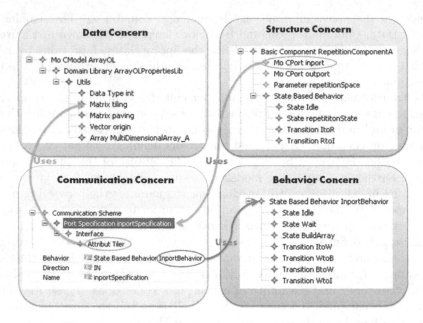

Fig. 8. Array-OL semantic domain capture in a Cometa Model and relations between concerns

Adding Execution Control from Spear to Rhapsody. In Cometa, the execution control and scheduling mechanisms for Array-OL consists in the description of three state machines for control and communication of (*BasicComponent* and *MoCPort* (Input/Output)). The tiling mechanism is placed on I/O ports. The two state machines presented in Figure 9 describe the behavior of components and ports (*input* ports) to process data (Behavior Concern).

BasicComponent behavior has 2 states (cf. Figure 9 (B)): *Idle* and *repetition-State*. In the *Idle* state, the component waits for the *MoCPort* to notify the arrival of an array. On the reception of a notification, *BasicComponent* requests data extraction as many times as the product of the defined values in its *repetitionSpace*. At each repetition, the component waits for *MoCPort* to extract the data before sending another extraction request.

The *MoCPort* behavior has three states (cf. Figure 9 (A)): *Idle*, *Wait* and *BuildArray*. In the *Idle* state, the port waits for data arrival. On reception of data array, it notifies the *BasicComponent* and waits for a response (*Wait* state). After the data extraction request is received from the *BasicComponent*, the port uses the *Tiler* matrix defined to extract array samples from the input array. These FSM descriptions are generic and can be reused in several environments. In the same way, a generic FSM is defined to build the array on output ports.

The example of Figure 9 represents an abstract description of the interaction mechanisms between components that integrate the finite state machines.

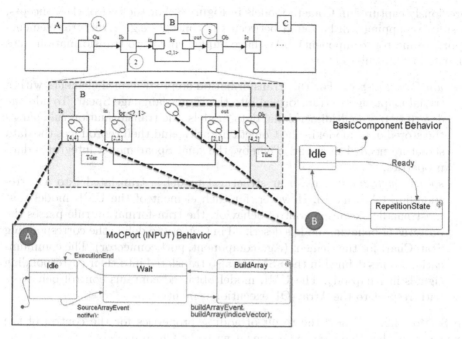

Fig. 9. Example of 3 inter-connected components with Array-OL semantics

A, B and C are composite components, and *br* is a repetition component. In Phase ① the scheduler enables the execution of component A, which produces an array of a predifined size on its port *Oa*. The array and its size are defined using the MetaClass *Array* of Cometa. The data is received by the port and sent to *br* → *Ib* in the subcomponent *br*. In phase ②, the port *br* → *in* has a generic behavior and mechanism of extracting patterns (*Tiler*). Once the Array is received, it notifies the state machine of the *br* component that data is available. The *BasicComponent* after receiving the notification will run 2 times (2x1) every execution, it will send to *br* → *in* request for the construction of sub-array and produce a sub-array output on *br* → *out*. In phase ③, the sub-array output is received by the port *Ob* which also has a generic behavior and Tiler mechanism. At each receiving of a sub-array, using the Tiler, *Ob* places the elements of the sub-arrays on a defined position in the output array. Once all repetitions of *br* are reached, an output array is built and sent to *Ic* from *Ob*. *Ic* on receipt of this Array, will make other processings.

Mappings and Transformations. For the transformation rules, there are two questions to answer: What are the required elements for Spear to run correctly the Array-OL semantics that UML cannot provide natively? What are the elements that Rhapsody needs to execute the Array-OL semantics and Spear does not provide? For the first question the missing elements are the Loops parameters and multidimensional data types. For the second question, the missing elements are the behaviors for the control of the execution. This information was previously captured in Cometa models in Figure 8. For the rest of the concepts, a simple mapping can be found between the concepts e.g., structural elements (port, connector, component) [4]. We have implemented two transformation rules that follow the rules below:

- *umlCometa2spear*: For this transformation step, structural elements with a trivial mapping are transformed into the target language Spear. To add the description of multidimensional data models, the transformation rule parses the stored data model in the Cometa libraries, and then reproduces the data structure needed in Spear. Thereby, the final Spear model integrates data properties.
- *spearCometa2uml*: The spear structural model is translated into a corresponding UML model. However, for each element of the UML model that must handle execution control behavior, the transformation rule parses the patterns of behavior models described in Cometa to define the corresponding StateChart for the element (e.g., component, port connector). The communication events defined in the FSM are also translated into their corresponding signals in Rhapsody. The UML model obtained contains control behaviors with respect to the Array-OL execution semantics.

In Section 4.2, we show the result of adding properties for the control of the execution in the Rhapsody environment with the Chirp model.

4.2   Use Case: The Chirp Model

The Chirp model is a signal processing sub-system. All the modules process intensively multidimensional arrays of data. The experiment presented in this section corresponds with the simulation of the Chirp model in the Rhapsody specification and simulation environment. The transformation *spearCometa2uml* was used for the structural transformation of the Chirp Spear model to its corresponding UML Rhapsody model. For the control of the execution, the model integrates the execution control FSM that was captured with Cometa and presented in Section 4.1.

The system consists of five modules (cf. Figure 10 (1)): *Gen_Chirp* produces a multidimensional array containing information of a radar signal, the *Comp_Imp* module performs pulse compression on the data received; *Filt_Dop* performs doppler filter on the data produced from *Comp_Imp*; finally, *reduce* and *Module* process the data produced by *Filt_Dop* to retrieve the relevant data signal without any loss of information. The modules can be launched in parallel. However, to avoid loss of information, the sizes of the array they can produce or receive rule their scheduling. The above Cometa models are reused entirely for the specification (cf. Figure 10 (2)) and simulation of the Chirp model in IBM Rational Rhapsody environment. The Execution of the Chirp model in the UML environment provides traces as shown in Figure 10 (3). At each repetition of the BasicComponent A (*Gen_Chirp*) an array is built (extracted) and transmitted

---

[4] We showed excerpts of concepts in Section 3, Figure 6.

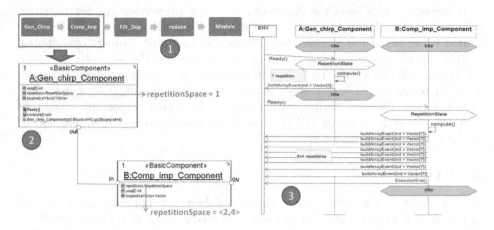

Fig. 10. (1) Excerpt of the Chirp Model (UML) enriched with Cometa properties and FSMs; 2) Excerpt of the execution of Gen_Chirp and Comp_Imp with Array-OL Semantics in Rhapsody.

to the next component BasicComponent B (*Comp_Imp*) for processing. The *repetitionSpace* of A is 1, which means that A executes once. The *repetitionSpace* of B is 2x4 which implies that it executes 2x4 times.

The experiment shows that it is possible to keep the underlying behavioral logic of Array-OL from Spear to UML Rhapsody, because we have provided the necessary semantic adaptation for controlling the execution in an environment where the execution semantics is not Array-OL but is based on DE.

4.3   Conclusion and Benefits

Figure 11 presents a subset of activities (first column) that highlights the gain from Cometa for tool interoperability. In the second column, Rhapsody provides support for UML specification and discrete events simulation activities.

Activities/ Tools	IBM Rhapsody UML Modeler	Rhapsody / Cometa MoC	Spear DE
UML Specification	Yes	Yes	No
Discrete Events (DE) Simulation	Yes	Yes	No
Array-OL Simulation	No	Yes [Cometa DE-FSM Capture]	Yes
Design Space Exploration	No	No	Yes

Fig. 11. Semantics as articulation to connect Design and Implementation Tools

However, at this level the Array-OL semantic properties are not natively present in the UML environment, and the way Array-OL models should be executed is not defined. Therefore, they cannot be simulated. Cometa contributes in this specific concern, using the relationship between the semantic domains Array-OL, DE and FSMs. Thus, in column 3 the specification model is enriched and can be simulated with respect to Array-OL. As a result, design space exploration activities are available with Spear, given that important semantics properties have been integrated into the UML model; Array-OL simulation is also available within Rhapsody.

5 Related Work

In this paper, our interest goes to the use of MoCs to improve the semantics of the models exchanged between tools in the context of tool interoperability. Historically, communities around MoCs and those around tool interoperability have evolved separately. Indeed, their efforts have never been combined, despite they both agree on the difficulty to preserve the behavioral semantics of models between tools. Our contribution is precisely at this level. Nevertheless in this section, we will present some of the contributions of both communities to innovate MoC concerns or tool interoperability.

For instance, the Ptolemy [32] tool provides an environment to define models of communicating systems based on hierarchical components. They have the two main concepts that are the actors and directors. An actor can be seen as a component that communicates with other components through MoC rules well-defined by the Director which describes the communication. However, the way MoCs are implemented is unique and the tool is not dedicated for model exchanges between tools. Similarly, in ModHel'X [33], the author defines the concept of hierarchical blocks and interface point for communication and a system based on snapshot (triggering updates of data passing among components) to simulate the system. However, this approach presents the same shortcomings as in Ptolemy.

Elsewhere, tackling tool interoperability, the work of [34] addresses the semantic interoperability by defining model transformations based on the mapping between concepts of meta-models. This approach also advocates the use of point-to-point transformation with a "bridge" metamodel to define the mapping between concepts of language tools. Unfortunately, the approach is not dedicated to the identification of semantic domains and semantic enrichment of models to ensure their proper execution. Our approach is complementary as it can automatically define the mapping and transformation between a given source metamodel, our semantic domain metamodel and the target metamodel.

In [35] the authors define an interesting approach to the definition of a mapping metamodel to make semantic equivalence between source concepts and output concepts of metamodel elements. Thanks to this metamodel, they derive a "semantic translator" that implements the model transformation. Nevertheless, the approach is not generic because for each semantic mapping a new DSL defining the mapping might be necessary to define the mapping.

6   Conclusion

The tools integration domain has several shortcomings that motivated many ongoing research activities. Despite considerable efforts to provide solutions, semantic interoperability remains an open issue mainly due to the multiplicity of the design tools. In the MDE context, there is no new approach addressing this issue. On the opposite, we propose a different and complementary way to look at semantic interoperability. We advertise a method of abstracting semantic domains underlying tools in the co-design domain. The Cometa approach allows grouping languages according to their MoC-based semantic domains. We also contribute to the execution semantic aspects of models to ensure equivalent behavior of models in different environments.

This contribution offers great perspectives for solving the problem of behavior preservation for models exchanges by integrating the tools formal execution semantics definitions. In particular, it provides a solid foundation that will makes it easier to include the activities of formal verification and validation for tool chains.

References

1. Wasserman, A.I.: Tool integration in software engineering environments. In: Long, F. (ed.) Software Engineering Environments. LNCS, vol. 467, pp. 137–149. Springer, Heidelberg (1990)
2. Thomas, I., Nejmeh, B.A.: Definitions of tool integration for environments. IEEE Softw. 9(2), 29–35 (1992)
3. Brunelière, H., Cabot, J., Clasen, C., Jouault, F., Bézivin, J.: Towards model driven tool interoperability: Bridging eclipse and microsoft modeling tools. In: Kühne, T., Selic, B., Gervais, M.-P., Terrier, F. (eds.) ECMFA 2010. LNCS, vol. 6138, pp. 32–47. Springer, Heidelberg (2010)
4. Blanc, X., Gervais, M.-P., Sriplakich, P.: Model bus: Towards the interoperability of modelling tools. In: Aßmann, U., Akşit, M., Rensink, A. (eds.) MDAFA 2003. LNCS, vol. 3599, pp. 17–32. Springer, Heidelberg (2005)
5. Object Management Group: Meta object facility (MOF) 2.0 core specification. Technical Report formal/06-01-01, Object Management Group, OMG Available Specification (2001)
6. Object Management Group: Meta Object Facility (MOF) 2.0 Query/View/ Transformation Specification, QVT (2008)
7. The ModelCVS Project, http://www.modelcvs.org/publications/conference.html
8. IBM Telelogic: Rational Rhapsody UML modeler., http://www.telelogic.com/products/rhapsody/index.cfm
9. Muliadi, L.: Discrete event modeling in Ptolemy II. Master's report, Dept. of EECS, University of California, Berkeley, CA (1999)
10. Labbani, O., Dekeyser, J.-L., Boulet, P., Rutten, É.: Introducing Control in the Gaspard2 Data-Parallel Metamodel: Synchronous Approach. In: International Workshop MARTES: Modeling and Analysis of Real-Time and Embedded Systems, Montego Bay, Jamaica (October 2005)

11. Boulet, P.: Array-OL Revisited, Multidimensional Intensive Signal Processing Specification. Rapport de recherche RR-6113, INRIA (2007)
12. Hoare, C.A.R.: Communicating sequential processes. Prentice Hall International (1985)
13. Lee, E.A., Messerschmitt, D.G.: Synchronous data flow. In: Proceedings of the IEEE, vol. 75(9), pp. 1235–1245. IEEE Computer Society (1987)
14. Jézéquel, J.-M., Barais, O., Fleurey, F.: Model driven language engineering with kermeta. In: Fernandes, J.M., Lämmel, R., Visser, J., Saraiva, J. (eds.) GTTSE 2009. LNCS, vol. 6491, pp. 201–221. Springer, Heidelberg (2011)
15. Di Ruscio, D., Jouault, F., Kurtev, I., Bézivin, J., Pierantonio, A.: Extending AMMA for Supporting Dynamic Semantics Specifications of DSLs. RR 06.02 RR 06.02
16. Harel, D., Rumpe, B.: Meaningful modeling: What's the semantics of "semantics"? Computer 37(10), 64–72 (2004)
17. Sangiovanni-Vincentelli, A.L., Shukla, S.K., Sztipanovits, J., Yang, G., Mathaikutty, D.: Metamodeling: An emerging representation paradigm for system-level design. IEEE Design & Test of Computers 26(3), 54–69 (2009)
18. Lenormand, E., Edelin, G.: An Industrial Perspective: A pragmatic High end Signal processing Design Environment at Thales (2003)
19. Pimentel, A.D., Stefanov, T., Nikolov, H., Thompson, M., Polstra, S., Deprettere, E.F.: Tool integration and interoperability challenges of a system-level design flow: A case study. In: Bereković, M., Dimopoulos, N., Wong, S. (eds.) SAMOS 2008. LNCS, vol. 5114, pp. 167–176. Springer, Heidelberg (2008)
20. Tolk, D. A., Muguira, J.A.: The levels of conceptual interoperability model. In: 2003 Fall Simulation Interoperability Workshop (2003)
21. Wang, W., Tolk, A., Wang, W.: The levels of conceptual interoperability model: applying systems engineering principles to M&S. In: Proceedings of the 2009 Spring Simulation Multiconference, SpringSim 2009, pp. 168:1–168:9. Society for Computer Simulation International, San Diego (2009)
22. Crane, M.L., Dingel, J.: UML vs. classical vs. rhapsody statecharts: not all models are created equal. Software and Systems Modeling 6(4), 415–435 (2007)
23. Combemale, B., Hardebolle, C., Jacquet, C., Boulanger, F., Baudry, B.: Bridging the Chasm between Executable Metamodeling and Models of Computation. In: Czarnecki, K., Hedin, G. (eds.) SLE 2012. LNCS, vol. 7745, pp. 184–203. Springer, Heidelberg (2013)
24. Liu, J.: Continuous time and mixed-signal simulation in Ptolemy II. Technical Report UCB/ERL M98/74, Dept. of EECS, University of California, Berkeley, CA (1998)
25. Lee, E.A., Sangiovanni-Vincentelli, A.: A framework for comparing models of computation. IEEE Transactions on Computer-Aided Design of Integrated Circuits and Systems 17, 1217–1229 (1998)
26. Diallo, P.I., Champeau, J., Leilde, V.: An approach for describing concurrency and communication of heterogeneous systems. In: Proceedings of the Third Workshop on Behavioural Modelling, BM-FA 2011, pp. 56–63. ACM, New York (2011)
27. Jantsch, A.: Modeling Embedded Systems and SoCs - Concurrency and Time in Models of Computation. Systems on Silicon. Morgan Kaufmann Publishers (June 2003)
28. Object Management Group: UML profile for MARTE, beta 1. Technical Report ptc/07-08-04, Object Management Group (2007)
29. Liu, J., Liu, X., Lee, E.A.: Modeling distributed hybrid systems in Ptolemy ii. In: Proceedings of the American Control Conference, pp. 4984–4985 (2001)

30. Lee, E.A., Messerschmitt, D.G.: Synchronous data flow. Proceedings of the IEEE 75, 1235–1245 (1987)
31. Clausen, M., Fortenbacher, A.: Efficient solution of linear diophantine equations. J. Symb. Comput. 8(1-2), 201–216 (1989)
32. Buck, J., Ha, S., Lee, E.A., Messerschmitt, D.G.: Ptolemy: a framework for simulating and prototyping heterogeneous systems. IEEE 10, 527–543 (2002)
33. Boulanger, F., Hardebolle, C.: Simulation of Multi-Formalism Models with Modhel'X. In: ICST 2008: Proceedings of the 2008 International Conference on Software Testing, Verification, and Validation, pp. 318–327. IEEE Computer Society, Washington, DC (2008)
34. Kappel, G., Wimmer, M., Retschitzegger, W., Schwinger, W.: Leveraging model-based tool integration by conceptual modeling techniques. In: Kaschek, R., Delcambre, L. (eds.) The Evolution of Conceptual Modeling. LNCS, vol. 6520, pp. 254–284. Springer, Heidelberg (2011)
35. Karsai, G., Lang, A., Neema, S.: Design patterns for open tool integration. Software and Systems Modeling 4(2), 157–170 (2005)

Whiley: A Platform for Research in Software Verification

David J. Pearce and Lindsay Groves

Victoria University of Wellington
Wellington, New Zealand
{djp,lindsay}@ecs.vuw.ac.nz

Abstract. An ongoing challenge for computer science is the development of a tool which automatically verifies programs meet their specifications, and are free from runtime errors such as divide-by-zero, array out-of-bounds and null dereferences. Several impressive systems have been developed to this end, such as ESC/Java and Spec#, which build on existing programming languages (e.g. Java, C#). However, there remains a need for an open research platform in this area. We have developed the Whiley programming language, and its accompanying verifying compiler, as an open platform for research. Whiley has been designed from the ground up to simplify the verification process. In this paper, we introduce the Whiley language and it accompanying verifying compiler tool.

1 Introduction

Prof. Sir Tony Hoare (ACM Turing Award Winner, FRS) proposed the creation of a *verifying compiler* as a grand challenge for computer science [1]. A verifying compiler *"uses automated mathematical and logical reasoning to check the correctness of the programs that it compiles."* There have been numerous attempts to construct a verifying compiler system, although none has yet made it into the mainstream. Early examples include that of King [2], Deutsch [3], the Gypsy Verification Environment [4] and the Stanford Pascal Verifier [5]. More recently, the Extended Static Checker for Modula-3 [6] which became the Extended Static Checker for Java (ESC/Java) — a widely acclaimed and influential work [7]. Building on this success was JML and its associated tooling which provided a standard notation for specifying functions in Java [8]. Finally, Microsoft developed the Spec# system which is built on top of C# [9].

Both ESC/Java and Spec# build on existing object-oriented languages (i.e. Java and C#) but, as a result, suffer numerous limitations. The problem is that such languages were not designed for use with verifying compilers. Ireland, in his survey on the history of verifying compilers, noted the following [10]:

> *"The choice of programming language(s) targeted by the verifying compiler will have a significant effect on the chances of success."*

Likewise, a report on future directions in verifying compilers, put together by several researchers in this area, makes a similar comment [11]:

> *"Programming language design can reduce the cost of specification and verification by keeping the language simple, by automating more of the work, and by eliminating common errors."*

M. Erwig, R.F. Paige, and E. Van Wyk (Eds.): SLE 2013, LNCS 8225, pp. 238–248, 2013.
© Springer International Publishing Switzerland 2013

This paper introduces Whiley, a programming language designed from scratch in conjunction with a verifying compiler. The intention of this is to provide an open framework for research in automated software verification. The initial goal is to automatically eliminate common errors, such as *null dereferences*, *array-out-of-bounds*, *divide-by-zero* and more. In the future, the intention is to consider more complex issues, such as termination, proof-carrying code and user-supplied proofs. Finally, several works have already been published which focus primarily on Whiley's type system [12–14].

The Tool. The main tool underlying Whiley is the verifying compiler. This is been in development for over three years, and has become a large (and relatively mature) code base. Numerous student projects have been conducted already based on this compiler, and the hope is to use it for teaching next year. The compiler is released under an open source license (BSD), can be downloaded from `http://whiley.org` and forked at `http://github.com/DavePearce/Whiley/`. Some interesting statistics are available from `http://www.ohloh.net/p/whiley` and a fun demonstration on writing loop invariants is available here: `http://www.youtube.com/watch?v=WwnxHugabrw`. Finally, a prototype Eclipse plugin is available and can be installed via the update site: `http://whiley.org/eclipse`.

2   Language Core

We begin by exploring the Whiley language and highlight some of the choices made in its design. For now, we stick to the basic issues of syntax, semantics and typing and, in the following section, we will focus more specifically on using Whiley for verification. Perhaps one of our most important goals was to make the system as accessible as possible. To that end, the language was designed to superficially resemble modern imperative languages (e.g. Python), and this decision has significantly affected our choices.

Overview. Languages like Java and C# permit arbitrary side-effects within methods and statements. This presents a challenge when such methods may be used within specifications. Systems like JML and Spec# require that methods used in specifications are *pure* (i.e. side-effect free). An important challenge here is the process of checking that a function is indeed pure. A significant body of research exists on checking functional purity in object-oriented languages (e.g. [15, 16]). Much of this relies on interprocedural analysis, which is too costly for a verifying compiler. To address this, Whiley is a hybrid object-oriented and functional language which divides into *a functional core* and an *imperative outer layer*. Everything in the functional core can be modularly checked as being side-effect free. To make this possible, Whiley incorporates first-class sets, lists and maps which are *values* (rather than mutable objects) and, hence, allow call-by-value semantics (more on this later).

Flow Typing. An unusual feature of Whiley is the use of a *flow typing system* (see e.g. [17, 18, 13, 14]). This gives Whiley the look-and-feel of a dynamically typed language (e.g. Python). Furthermore, automatic variable retyping through conditionals is supported using the **is** operator (similar to `instanceof` in Java) as follows:

```
define Circle as {int x, int y, int radius}
define Rect as {int x, int y, int width, int height}
define Shape as Circle | Rect

real area(Shape s):
    if s is Circle:
        return PI * s.radius * s.radius
    else:
        return s.width * s.height
```

A Shape is either a Rect or a Circle (which are both record types). The type test "s is Circle" determines whether s is a Circle or not. Unlike Java, Whiley automatically retypes s to have type Circle (resp. Rect) on the true (resp. false) branches of the if statement. There is no need to explicitly cast variable s to the appropriate Shape before accessing its fields.

Union Types. Another unusual feature of Whiley is the use of *union types* (see e.g. [19, 20]), which complement the flow type system. Consider the following example:

```
null|int indexOf(string str, char c):
    ...

[string] split(string str, char c):
    idx = indexOf(str,c)
    // idx has type null|int
    if idx is int:
        // idx now has type int
        below = str[0..idx]
        above = str[idx..]
        return [below,above]
    else:
        // idx now has type null
        return [str]
```

Here, indexOf() returns the first index of a character in the string, or **null** if there is none. The type **null** | **int** is a union type, meaning it is either an **int** *or* **null**. The system seamlessly ensures **null** is never dereferenced because the type **null** | **int** cannot be treated as an **int**. Instead, one must first check it *is* an **int** using e.g. "idx **is int**".

Recursive Data Types. Whiley provides recursive types which are similar to the abstract data types found in functional languages (e.g. Haskell, ML, etc). For example:

```
define LinkedList as null | {int data, LinkedList next}

int length(LinkedList l):
    if l is null:
        return 0 // l now has type null
    else:
        return 1 + length(l.next) // l now has type {int data, LinkedList next}
```

Here, we again see how flow typing gives an elegant solution. More specifically, on the false branch of the type test "1 **is null**", variable 1 is automatically retyped to {**int** data, LinkedList next} — thus ensuring the subsequent dereference of 1.next is safe. No casts are required as would be needed for a conventional imperative language (e.g. Java). Finally, like all compound structures, the semantics of Whiley dictates that recursive data types are passed by value (or, at least, appear to be from the programmer's perspective).

Value Semantics. The prevalence of pointers — or references — in modern programming languages (e.g. Java, C++, C#) has been a major hindrance in the development of verifying compilers. Indeed, Mycroft recently argued that (unrestricted) pointers should be "considered harmful" in the same way that Dijkstra considered goto harmful [21]. To address this, all compound structures in Whiley (e.g. lists, sets, and records) have *value semantics*. This means they are passed and returned by-value (as in Pascal, MATLAB or most functional languages). But, unlike functional languages (and like Pascal), values of compound types can be updated in place. Whilst this latter point may seem unimportant, it serves a critical purpose: to give Whiley the appearance of a modern *imperative* language when, in fact, the functional core of Whiley is pure. This goes towards our goal of making the language as accessible as possible.

Value semantics implies that updates to a variable only affect that variable, and that information can only flow out of a function through its return value. Consider:

```
int f([int] xs):
    ys = xs
    xs[0] = 1
    ...
```

The semantics of Whiley dictate that, having assigned xs to ys as above, the subsequent update to xs does not affect ys. Arguments are also passed by value, hence xs is updated inside f() and this does not affect f's caller. That is, xs is not a *reference* to a list of **int**; rather, it *is* a list of **int**s and assignments to it do not affect state visible outside of f().

Unbound Arithmetic. Modern languages typically provide fixed-width numeric types, such as 32bit two's compliment integers, or 64-bit IEEE 754 floating point numbers. Such data types are notoriously difficult for an automated theorem prover to reason about [22]. Systems like ESC/Java and Spec# assume (unsoundly) that numeric types do not overflow or suffer from rounding. To address this, Whiley employs *unbounded integers* and *rationals* in place of their fixed-width alternatives and, hence, does not suffer the limitations of soundness discussed above.

Performance. Many of our choices (e.g. value semantics and unbound arithmetic) have a potentially detrimental effect on performance. Whilst this is a trade-off we accept, there are existing techniques which can help. For example, using reference counting to minimise unnecessary cloning of compound structures (see e.g. [23]); and, integer range analysis (see e.g. [24]) to place variables into native data types where possible.

3 Verification

The key goal of the Whiley project is to develop an open framework for research in automated software verification. As such, we now explore verification in Whiley.

Example 1 — Constrained Types. The following Whiley code defines a function accepting a positive integer and returning a non-negative integer (i.e. natural number):

```
int f(int x) requires x > 0, ensures $ >= 0 && $ != x:
    return x-1
```

Here, the function `f()` includes a **requires** and **ensures** clause which correspond (respectively) to its *pre-condition* and *post-condition*. In this context, $ represents the return value, and must be used in the **ensures** clause. The Whiley compiler statically verifies that this function meets its specification.

The above illustrates a function specification given through explicit pre- and post-conditions. However, we may also employ *constrained types* to simplify it as follows:

```
define nat as int where $ >= 0
define pos as int where $ > 0

nat f(pos x) ensures $ != x:
    return x-1
```

Here, the **define** statement includes a **where** clause constraining the permissible values for the type ($ represents the variable whose type this will be). Thus, `nat` defines the type of non-negative integers (i.e. the natural numbers). Likewise, `pos` gives the type of positive integers and is implicitly a subtype of `nat` (since the constraint on `pos` implies that of `nat`). We consider that good use of constrained types is critical to ensuring that function specifications remain as readable as possible.

The notion of type in Whiley is more fluid than found in typical languages. In particular, if two types T_1 and T_2 have the same *underlying* type, then T_1 is a subtype of T_2 iff the constraint on T_1 implies that of T_2. Consider the following:

```
define anat as int where $ >= 0
define bnat as int where 2*$ >= $

bnat f(anat x):
    return x
```

In this case, we have two alternate (and completely equivalent) definitions for a natural number (we can see that `bnat` is equivalent to `anat` by subtracting $ from both sides). The Whiley compiler is able to reason that these types are equivalent and statically verifies that this function is correct.

Example 2 — Implicit Retyping. Variables in Whiley are described by their underlying type and those constraints which are shown to hold. As the automated theorem prover learns more about a variable, it automatically takes this into consideration when checking constraints are satisfied. For example:

```
define nat as int where $ >= 0

nat abs(int x):
    if x >= 0:
        return x
    else:
        return -x
```

The Whiley compiler statically verifies that this function always returns a non-negative integer. This relies on the compiler to reason correctly about the implicit constraints implied by the conditional. A similar, but slightly more complex example is that for computing the maximum of two integers:

```
int max(int x, int y) ensures $ >= x && $ >= y
                          && ($==x || $==y):
    if x > y:
        return x
    else:
        return y
```

Again, the Whiley compiler statically verifies this function meets its specification. Here, the body of the function is almost completely determined by the specification — however, in general, this not the case.

Example 3 — Bounds Checking. An interesting example which tests the automated theorem prover more thoroughly is the following:

```
null|int indexOf(string str, char c):
    for i in 0..|str|:
        if str[i] == c:
            return i
    return null
```

In this case, the access str[i] must be shown as within the bounds of the list str. The Whiley compiler statically verifies this is true and, hence, that indexOf() cannot cause an out-of-bounds error.

Example 4 — Loop Invariants. Another example illustrates the use of *loop invariants* in Whiley:

```
define natlist as [int] where all { x in $ | x >= 0 }

int sum(natlist list) ensures $>=0:
    r = 0
    for v in list where r >= 0:
        r = r + v
    return r
```

Here, bounded quantifiers are used to define a list of natural numbers which is accepted by the sum() function. Equivalently, we could have used [nat] (with nat defined as before) — and these two alternative definitions of the same concept are, in a strong sense, identical.

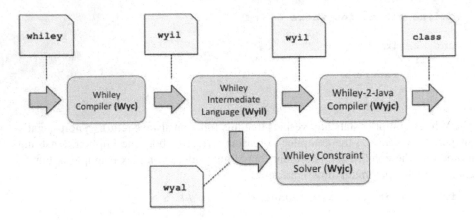

Fig. 1. Illustrating the compilation and verification pipeline

A key constraint is that summing a list of natural numbers yields a natural number (recall arithmetic is unbounded and does not overflow in Whiley). The Whiley compiler statically verifies that sum() does indeed meet this specification. The loop invariant is necessary to help the compiler generate a sufficiently powerful verification condition to prove the function meets the post condition. In the future, we hope to automatically synthesize simple loop invariants such as this.

4   Compiler Architecture

The Whiley verifying compiler is structured as a number of distinct modules. This has proved invaluable for keeping a clear separation of concerns between the major components, and for testing and debugging — since many modules can be tested in isolation from others. The main modules of the verifying compiler are:

- **Whiley Build System (WyBS).** Responsible for information flow throughout the compiler, managing source and binary roots, and determining compilation orders.
- **Whiley Compiler (WyC).** Responsible for parsing and type checking whiley source files, and compiling them into binary wyil files.
- **Whiley Intermediate Language (WyIL).** A register-based intermediate language similar to Java bytecode along with an accompanying binary file format.
- **Whiley-2-Java Compiler (WyJC).** A back-end which converts wyil files into JVM class files.
- **Whiley-2-C Compiler (WyCC).** An experimental back-end which converts wyil files into C source files.
- **Whiley Constraint Solver (WyCS).** An automated theorem prover responsible for accepting input files in a variant of first-order logic called the *Whiley Assertion Language (WyAL)* and verifying they are correct.

Figure 1 provides an overview of the flow of information within the compiler. Here we see that whiley source files are converted into (binary) wyil files; in turn, these are converted into binary `class` files (for execution) and `wyal` source files (for verification). The latter is, in turn, converted into the more concise binary `wycs` form. Note that, in the general course of events, not all of these files are physically produced. For example, when compiling a `whiley` source file into a `class` file, no other files are written to disk (unless specifically requested).

From Figure 1, we see that a strong emphasis has been placed on the use of different file formats. Whilst this may seem overly complex, it helps the testing and debugging process significantly. For example, consider diagnosing a bug presenting as a `whiley` source file that incorrectly verifies. There are numerous places within the compiler which could be causing the problem. For example, it could be a problem with the translation of the `whiley` source to the `wyil` file. Likewise, it could be a problem with the *verification condition generator* which generates `wyal` files from `wyil` files. In debugging this, one can generate each of these files and inspect them individually to identify the misbehaving module; furthermore, one can modify any of these files and push them back into the pipeline to see the effect. Likewise, each module can be tested in isolation of others by providing tests written in its given input format.

Another advantage of the modularisation in the verifying compiler, is that it enables interesting possibilities for reuse. For example, other researchers could build a front-end for a different language and compile down to our intermediate language — thereby gaining the ability to verify their programs for free. Likewise, other researchers developing their own verifying compiler with a different intermediate representation might still generate verification conditions in the `wyal` format and reuse our theorem prover. Similarly, we can e.g. replace the WyCS theorem prover with another (e.g. Z3 [25] or Simplify [26]) by writing a wrapper which converts files in the `wyal` format into the appropriate input language of the external tool[1].

4.1 Intermediate Language

The *Whiley Intermediate Language (WyIL)* is a register-based intermediate language which resembles Java Bytecode. The following illustrates a Whiley function (left) and the corresponding WyIL code (right):

```
int abs(int x) ensures $ >= 0:        int abs(int):
    if x >= 0:                        ensures:
        return x                          const %3 = 0 : int
    else:                                 assertge %0,%3 "..." : int
        return -x                     body:
                                          const %2 = 0 : int
                                          iflt %0,%2 goto label0 : int
                                          return %0 : int
                                      .label0
                                          neg %5 = %0 : int
                                          return %5 : int
```

As can be seen from above, every WyIL bytecode is associated with a type. Furthermore, registers are prefixed with % (e.g. %3); the `const` bytecode loads a constant

---

[1] And, indeed, a student project run this year has been investigating doing exactly this.

value into a register; the `iflt` bytecode branches to a label if its first operand is less than its second; the `neg` bytecode negates its operand and assigns to a given register; finally, the `return` bytecode returns its operand.

4.2 Assertion Language

The *Whiley Assertion Language* is a dialect of first-order logic with various additional theories (e.g. for arithmetic, sets, lists, etc). A given `wyil` file will generate a single `wyal` file that may contain numerous assertions. The following illustrates the two assertions generated from our example above (written side-by-side to conserve space):

```
assert "...":                   assert "...":
    forall(int r0):                 forall(int r0):
        if:                             if:
            r0 >= 0                         r0 < 0
        then:                           then:
            r0 >= 0                         -r0 >= 0
```

Here, the left assertion corresponds to the execution path through the true branch of the **if** statement in the original Whiley function; likewise, the right assertion corresponds to the path through the false branch. Finally, each **assert** statement is given a message to report if it is found to be invalid (note, these are elided above for brevity).

4.3 Build System

The *Whiley Build System (WyBS)* controls the overall flow of information within the compiler. Every build operates over a *project* which contains one or more *source roots*, and one or more corresponding *binary roots*. A source root gives the root location of a Whiley package (e.g. a file system directory). A binary root indicates where binary files should be located (e.g. a file system directory, a `jar` file, etc). Observe that some binary files (e.g. `wyil`) are written during compilation, but may also be read (e.g. from the standard library). A key design feature is that roots may be *virtual* — meaning they are not written physically to disk. A command-line option can then determine whether or not a given root should be virtual (i.e. whether or not a given set of files need to be physically generated). A further advantage of this approach is that it aids integration with other tools (e.g. `ant`, `eclipse`, etc). For example, `eclipse` maintains its own filesystem representation and, hence, integrating our compiler requires integrating with this. In fact, this was straightforward: we simply created a range of `root` classes which interface with `eclipse` and replace those used by the stand-alone compiler.

5   Conclusion

In this paper, we have presented the Whiley language and its accompanying verifying compiler tool. Our goal is to provide an open framework for research in automated software verification, and work continues on this front.

Acknowledgements. This work is supported by the Marsden Fund, administered by the Royal Society of New Zealand.

References

1. Hoare, T.: The verifying compiler: A grand challenge for computing research. Journal of the ACM 50(1), 63–69 (2003)
2. King, S.: A Program Verifier. PhD thesis, Carnegie-Mellon University (1969)
3. Peter Deutsch, L.: An interactive program verifier. Ph.d. (1973)
4. Good, D.I.: Mechanical proofs about computer programs. In: Mathematical Logic and Programming Languages, pp. 55–75 (1985)
5. Luckham, D.C., German, S.M., von Henke, F.W., Karp, R.A., Milne, P.W., Oppen, D.C., Polak, W., Scherlis, W.L.: Stanford pascal verifier user manual. Technical Report CS-TR-79-731, Stanford University, Department of Computer Science (1979)
6. Detlefs, D.L., Leino, K.R.M., Nelson, G., Saxe, J.B.: Extended static checking. SRC Research Report 159, Compaq Systems Research Center (1998)
7. Flanagan, C., Leino, K.R.M., Lillibridge, M., Nelson, G., Saxe, J.B., Stata, R.: Extended static checking for Java. In: Proc. PLDI, pp. 234–245 (2002)
8. Leavens, G.T., Cheon, Y., Clifton, C., Ruby, C., Cok, D.R.: How the design of JML accommodates both runtime assertion checking and formal verification. Science of Computer Programming 55(1-3), 185–208 (2005)
9. Barnett, M., Leino, K.R.M., Schulte, W.: The spec# programming system: An overview. Technical report, Microsoft Research (2004)
10. Ireland, A.: A Practical Perspective on the Verifying Compiler Proposal. In: Proceedings of the Grand Challenges in Computing Research Conference (2004)
11. Leavens, G.T., Abrial, J., Batory, D., Butler, M., Coglio, A., Fisler, K., Hehner, E., Jones, C., Miller, D., Peyton-Jones, S., Sitaraman, M., Smith, D.R., Stump, A.: Roadmap for enhanced languages and methods to aid verification. In: Proc. of GPCE, pp. 221–235 (2006)
12. Pearce, D., Noble, J.: Implementing a language with flow-sensitive and structural typing on the JVM. Electronic Notes in Computer Science 279(1), 47–59 (2011)
13. Pearce, D.J.: Sound and complete flow typing with unions, intersections and negations. In: Giacobazzi, R., Berdine, J., Mastroeni, I. (eds.) VMCAI 2013. LNCS, vol. 7737, pp. 335–354. Springer, Heidelberg (2013)
14. Pearce, D.J.: A calculus for constraint-based flow typing. In: Proc. FTFJP, page Article 7 (2013)
15. Rountev, A.: Precise identification of side-effect-free methods in Java. In: Proc. ICSM, pp. 82–91. IEEE Computer Society Press (2004)
16. Sălcianu, A., Rinard, M.: Purity and side effect analysis for Java programs. In: Cousot, R. (ed.) VMCAI 2005. LNCS, vol. 3385, pp. 199–215. Springer, Heidelberg (2005)
17. Tobin-Hochstadt, S., Felleisen, M.: Logical types for untyped languages. In: Proc. ICFP, pp. 117–128 (2010)
18. Guha, A., Saftoiu, C., Krishnamurthi, S.: Typing local control and state using flow analysis. In: Barthe, G. (ed.) ESOP 2011. LNCS, vol. 6602, pp. 256–275. Springer, Heidelberg (2011)
19. Barbanera, F., Caglini, M.D.-C.: Intersection and union types. In: Ito, T., Meyer, A.R. (eds.) TACS 1991. LNCS, vol. 526, pp. 651–674. Springer, Heidelberg (1991)
20. Igarashi, A., Nagira, H.: Union types for object-oriented programming. Journal of Object Technology 6(2) (2007)
21. Mycroft, A.: Programming language design and analysis motivated by hardware evolution. In: Riis Nielson, H., Filé, G. (eds.) SAS 2007. LNCS, vol. 4634, pp. 18–33. Springer, Heidelberg (2007)

22. Bryant, R.E., Kroening, D., Ouaknine, J., Seshia, S.A., Strichman, O., Brady, B.A.: Deciding bit-vector arithmetic with abstraction. In: Grumberg, O., Huth, M. (eds.) TACAS 2007. LNCS, vol. 4424, pp. 358–372. Springer, Heidelberg (2007)
23. Lameed, N., Hendren, L.: Staged static techniques to efficiently implement array copy semantics in a MATLAB JIT compiler. In: Knoop, J. (ed.) CC 2011. LNCS, vol. 6601, pp. 22–41. Springer, Heidelberg (2011)
24. Nielson, F., Nielson, H.R., Hankin, C.L.: Principles of Program Analysis. Springer (1999)
25. de Moura, L., Bjørner, N.S.: Z3: An efficient SMT solver. In: Ramakrishnan, C.R., Rehof, J. (eds.) TACAS 2008. LNCS, vol. 4963, pp. 337–340. Springer, Heidelberg (2008)
26. Detlefs, Nelson, Saxe: Simplify: A theorem prover for program checking. JACM 52 (2005)

Method and Tool Support for Classifying Software Languages with **Wikipedia**

Ralf Lämmel, Dominik Mosen, and Andrei Varanovich

University of Koblenz-Landau, Software Languages Team

Abstract. Wikipedia provides useful input for efforts on mining taxonomies or ontologies in specific domains. In particular, Wikipedia's categories serve classification. In this paper, we describe a method and a corresponding tool, WikiTax, for exploring Wikipedia's category graph with the objective of supporting the development of a classification of software languages. The category graph is extracted level by level. The extracted graph is visualized in a tree-like manner. Category attributes (i.e., metrics) such as depth are visualized. Irrelevant edges and nodes may be excluded. These exclusions are documented while using a manageable and well-defined set of 'exclusion types' as comments.

1 Introduction

Ever since 2008, the calls for papers for the *Software Language Engineering* (SLE) conference[1] have contained slightly different, more implicit or more explicit definitions of the term 'software language'. Other community material contains yet other definition attempts; see, for example, the IEEE TSE special section on SLE in 2009 [8]. At SLEBOK 2012 (i.e., an SLE 2012 satellite event dedicated to the the SL(E) body of knowledge), the attendees were also getting into the issue of what exactly a software language is.

A *classification* of software languages is a useful (if not necessary) pillar of a definition of 'software language'. Such classification is the topic of the present paper. One branch of software languages appears to be well understood. That is, *programming languages* are obviously *software languages* and they may be classified in terms of criteria and concepts as organized, for example, in textbooks on programming languages, programming paradigms, and programming language theory such as [13,16]. There is also scholarly (dated) work on the classification of programming languages [1,6]. Actually quite a few sets of criteria or concepts exist for programming languages; there is no obvious contender; there is no comprehensive classification. Several classes of languages (other than programming languages) have been classified in scholarly work, e.g., model transformation languages [5], business rule modeling languages [17], visual languages [3,4,11], and architecture description languages [12]. The ultimate taxonomy of software languages should subsume and integrate existing, fragmented classifications in a

---

[1] http://planet-sl.org/

M. Erwig, R.F. Paige, and E. Van Wyk (Eds.): SLE 2013, LNCS 8225, pp. 249–259, 2013.

transparent manner. The *101companies* project[2] hosts efforts targeted at such a taxonomy, but the results are of limited use and quality so far.

In this paper, we try to inform the apparent classification challenge for software languages by means of exploring Wikipedia. Obviously, Wikipedia contains substantial amounts of taxonomy-like (if not ontology-like) information—also for software languages (without though embracing the actual term, at the time of writing). For instance, there are hierarchically organized categories such as *Computer languages*, *Programming languages*, and *Programming language classification* that seem to apply; yet other categories may be relevant. Accordingly, we describe a method and a corresponding tool, WikiTax, for exploring Wikipedia's category graph. Exploration is supported in a manner such that a domain expert can reduce the category graph so that a classification emerges. The overall approach is not specific to software languages, but we apply it to software languages throughout the paper.

Contribution. We do not claim to have converged on a good candidate taxonomy for software languages. Rather we contribute procedural, tool-supported elements of a method towards development of the ultimate taxonomy. The resulting tool, WikiTax, is a rather simple graph exploration tool, which however includes a few domain-specific features not available in more generic functionality for searching and exploring Wikipedia's category graph.

Road-map. §2 describes the overall exploration approach and sketches corresponding tool support as implemented by WikiTax. §3 explores Wikipedia categories related to software languages. §4 concludes the paper. The source code of WikiTax, a comprehensive manual, and all data covered in this paper are available online.[3]

2 Exploring Wikipedia with WikiTax

Wikipedia's Category Graph. Wikipedia uses several means of organizing its information: plain links giving rise to an article graph, designated article lists, portals meant to introduce users to key topics, info-boxes for semantic ('typed') data, and categories giving rise to a category graph for the classification of articles. When it comes to taxonomy mining, the category graph is particularly relevant; the graph is accessible, for example, through the MediaWiki API, which is the access path chosen by WikiTax.

Graph Extraction. Initially, WikiTax is pointed to a root category (level 0) for extraction. Iteratively, subcategories and pages (in fact, page titles) can be extracted level by level or exhaustively. Exhaustive extraction may take minutes to hours depending on the root category. The Wikipedia category graph contains many surprising edges, which would easily imply inclusion of large, arguably irrelevant subgraphs. Thus, extraction is controllable.

---

[2] http://101companies.org/
[3] https://github.com/dmosen/wiki-analysis

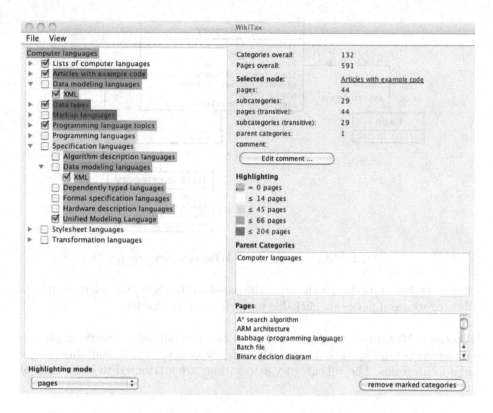

Fig. 1. Exploration of level 1 and 2 subcategories of *Computer languages*

Graph Reduction. WikiTax supports reduction of the graph—both during (level-by-level) extraction and post extraction. Reduction boils down to the exclusion of nodes, i.e., categories. (In fact, we may also remove individual edges, given that a category may have multiple parent categories.) A category would be removed, if domain knowledge suggests that the category at hand does not serve the intended kind of classification, e.g., classification of software languages in our case. When exclusion is performed during extraction, then the excluded nodes (edges) are ignored during subsequent extraction steps. When exclusion is performed post extraction, then nodes (edges) are only blacklisted, without actually reducing the graph. In this manner, exclusion decisions can be revisited.

WikiTax's Visualization. Figure 1 shows the WikiTax exploration view after the extraction of levels 1 and 2 starting from the category *Computer languages*. Some edges are marked for exclusion. (Exclusion would be confirmed with the 'removal' button.) The marked categories are to be excluded because domain knowledge suggests that these categories do not serve language classification in a conceptual manner. Highlighting is applied to the categories according to the metric of immediate member pages. In the figure, the category *Articles with example code* is

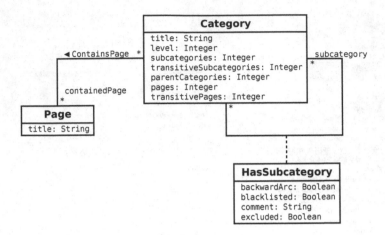

Fig. 2. Metamodel of the WikiTax category graph

selected so that extra data is shown in the panel on the right, e.g., member pages. All categories and pages are clickable to navigate to Wikipedia.

WikiTax's Metamodel. WikiTax operates on an enhanced category graph; see the metamodel in Figure 2. Thus, each category associates with contained pages and subcategories. The subcategory associations are attributed to keep track of metadata as follows:

backwardArc Marker for cyclic edges in the category graph.
blacklisted Marker for categories blacklisted past extraction.
excluded Marker for categories excluded during reduction.
comment Label ('reason for exclusion') to be associated with the edge.

Categories are associated with measures as follows:

level The level 0, 1, 2, ... of the category in the graph with the root at level 0.
subcategories The number of immediate subcategories.
transitiveSubcategories The number of all subcategories.
pages The number of immediately contained pages.
transitivePages The number of all pages in this category.

The implementation of WikiTax uses the Java-based JGraLab library[4] for the representation of (annotated) graphs with JSON as an export format.

Exclusion Types. A methodologically important aspect of graph reduction is that reasons for category exclusion are not just simply documented by a comment, but a manageable, well-defined set of exclusion types is to be developed over time. For instance, the category *Unified Modeling Language* could be said to be of an exclusion type 'Singleton classifier' to mean that this category, by

---

[4] https://github.com/jgralab

design, is primarily concerned with a single language, i.e., UML in this case; the other members or subcategories of the category are concerned with UML concepts, tools, and other related artifacts. §3 lists several more exclusion types. The aggregation and use of exclusion types captures domain knowledge and insight into Wikipedia's category graph in a transparent manner.

3   Explorative Study

In this study, we examine some Wikipedia categories with two objectives: a) to retrieve some candidate classifiers of an emerging taxonomy of software languages; b) to get some experience with Wikipedia's approach to classification and related issues of style and consistency.[5]

Designation of a Root. Wikipedia's classification hierarchies are complex and thus, it is not straightforward to determine a root for exploration unambiguously. However, we have established by an ad-hoc search that the category *Computer languages* may be a suitable root: its intended coverage may be similar to what the SL(E) community has in mind for the notion of software languages.

Figure 1 showed all the immediate (i.e., level 1) subcategories of the category *Computer languages*. Several of these immediate subcategories are excluded because they are not directly concerned with the *classification* of languages: *Lists of computer languages*, *Articles with example code*, *Data types*, and *Programming language topics*. One of the remaining immediate subcategories is the category *Programming languages*. We found another major classifier for programming languages, namely *Programming language classification*, which is reachable through the excluded category *Programming language topics*.

Level-by-level Extraction. We decided to extract another level to obtain a graph of manageable size. Again, we excluded several categories, if they did not meet our objective of language classification. As a result, we obtained the categories shown in Figure 3. This is a pretty manageable set of language classifiers. It happens that they all end on "... languages" except for two subcategories of *Markup languages* which end on "... formats". In contrast, most of the excluded categories (see below) do not end on "... languages" . We take this to provide a hint at the different classification styles of Wikipedia.

Exclusion Types. In order to obtain the reduced result of Figure 3, we had to exclude 29 categories. This may seem like a small number, but it is clear that yet more categories must be excluded once deeper levels are explored. We used these 29 exclusions to develop a small set of exclusion types for the study; see Figure 4 for the list of excluded categories with the associated exclusion type:

Alternative classifier. The category classifies software languages in a manner that is not related to software concepts. For instance, the category

---

[5] All Wikipedia data for this study and this paper was retrieved 7-18 June 2013.

Category	Subcategories
Data modeling languages	–
Markup languages	*Declarative markup languages, GIS file formats,* *Knowledge representation languages,* *Lightweight markup languages,* *Mathematical markup languages,* *Musical markup languages, Page description markup languages,* *Playlist markup languages, User interface markup languages,* *Vector graphics markup languages,* *Web syndication formats, XML markup languages*
Programming languages	*.NET programming languages,* *Agent-based programming languages,* *Agent-oriented programming languages,* *Concatenative programming languages,* *Concurrent programming languages,* *Data-structured programming languages,* *Declarative programming languages,* *Dependently typed languages,* *Domain-specific programming languages,* *Dynamic programming languages,* *Extensible syntax programming languages,* *Formula manipulation languages, Function-level languages,* *Functional languages, High Integrity Programming Language,* *High-level programming languages,* *ICL programming languages,* *Intensional programming languages,* *Low-level programming languages,* *Multi-paradigm programming languages,* *Nondeterministic programming languages,* *Object-based programming languages,* *Pattern matching programming languages,* *Procedural programming languages,* *Process termination functions,* *Prototype-based programming languages,* *Reactive programming languages,* *Secure programming languages,* *Set theoretic programming languages,* *Statically typed programming languages,* *Synchronous programming languages,* *Term-rewriting programming languages,* *Text-oriented programming languages,* *Tree programming languages, Visual programming languages,* *XML-based programming languages*
Specification languages	*Algorithm description languages,* *Dependently typed languages, Formal specification languages,* *Hardware description languages*
Stylesheet languages	–
Transformation languages	*Macro programming languages*

Fig. 3. Reduced subcategory lists for subcategories of *Computer languages*

Category	Exclusion type
Academic programming languages	Alternative classifier
Articles with example code	Deviating classifier
Cascading Style Sheets	Singleton classifier
Data types	Deviating classifier
Discontinued programming languages	Alternative classifier
DocBook	Singleton classifier
Esoteric programming languages	Alternative classifier
Experimental programming languages	Alternative classifier
HTML	Singleton classifier
JSON	Singleton classifier
Lists of computer languages	List classifier
Lists of programming languages	List classifier
Markup language comparisons	Deviating classifier
Markup language stubs	Maintenance classifier
Non-English-based programming languages	Alternative classifier
Programming language families	Deviating classifier
Programming language standards	Deviating classifier
Programming language topics	Deviating classifier
Programming languages by creation date	Alternative classifier
Programming languages conferences	Deviating classifier
Software by programming language	Deviating classifier
SyncML	Singleton classifier
TeX	Singleton classifier
Text Encoding Initiative	Singleton classifier
Troff	Singleton classifier
Uncategorized programming languages	Maintenance classifier
Unified Modeling Language	Singleton classifier
Wikipedia categories named after programming languages	Deviating classifier
XML	Singleton classifier

Fig. 4. Exclusion types for levels 1 and 2 of *Computer languages*; this list is produced by the WikiTax tool based on metadata (comments) entered by us interactively

Academic programming languages describes itself as being concerned with languages that are "influential in computer science and programming language theory".

Deviating classifier. The category does not actually classify software languages. It rather classifies something else. For instance, category *Articles with example code* describes itself as being concerned with "articles which include reference implementations of algorithms".

Singleton classifier. The category is effectively concerned with a single software language for which it serves as a container of related entities such as technologies or standards. For instance, category *Cascading Style Sheets* contains pages on all kinds of topics related to the CSS language.

List classifier. The category collects lists or categories of lists (rather than plain categories) of software languages. For instance, category *Lists of computer languages* has *Lists of programming languages* as a subcategory, which in turn contains pages for some lists of languages, such as the *List of BASIC dialects*.

Maintenance classifier. The category is used by the Wikipedia authors to capture some information related to the maintenance of pages or categories. For instance, the category *Uncategorized programming languages* describes itself as serving categories or pages "which need to be classified under more specific categories". Also: "This category may be empty occasionally or even most of the time."

An Observation Regarding Wikipedia Style. The resulting classification of Figure 3 with the remaining level-1 and level-2 subcategories is of a manageable size. We may review the classification and observe some of its characteristics in this manner. During the study, we realized, for example, an asymmetry between 'query' versus 'transformation'. That is, there is a category *Transformation languages* at level 1, but there is apparently no category for 'query languages', not even at level 2. Let us inspect the page for *SQL*, which is an obvious query language. It turns out that *SQL* is a member of various categories including a category *Query languages* which in turn is a subcategory of various categories including the category *Domain-specific programming languages* which occurred in Figure 3. Let us compare this classification scheme with the one of *XSLT*, which is an obvious transformation language: it is a member of the categories *Transformation languages*, *Declarative programming languages*, *Functional languages*, *Markup languages*, *XML-based programming languages*, and yet other categories that may count as 'alternative classifiers'. However, *XSLT* (unlike *SQL*) is not a member of the category *Domain-specific programming languages*.

WikiTax is helpful in making such observations regarding consistency (or lack thereof) of classification on Wikipedia.

Programming Languages: All Levels According to Figure 3, the subcategory of *Computer languages* with by far the most subcategories is *Programming languages*. Thus, we embarked on a more comprehensive exploration of category *Programming languages*:

Initially, we extracted 423 categories over 8 levels with 7515 pages. The automatic extraction took several minutes. We performed exclusion in two steps. First, we (re-) excluded those direct subcategories that already appeared in Figure 4. After such initial pruning, 288 categories with 6671 pages remained. We completed reduction at all levels of the category graph. This process required about 2 hours of manual work to determine what categories to remove and for what reason. This effort is intrinsically manual; it requires domain knowledge and involves consultation of the relevant and additional Wikipedia pages. Ultimately, 79 categories over 4 levels with 1560 pages remained. Figure 5 visualizes the reduced taxonomy for two different metrics supported by WikiTax.

On the left, the metric for the *number of transitive member pages* is applied for visualization. No category is grayed out, which means that there is no category without members. Most of the categories are shown in a plain font, which means that they all carry members, but less than 25 % of the total members in the category *Programming languages* (which has 1560 member pages). There is actually one heavyweight: category *Domain-specific programming languages* carries 976 members, which is more than 50 % of all members; this status is expressed by highlighting the category.

Pages

Categories

Programming languages

- ☐ ICL programming languages
- ☐ Agent-based programming languages
- ☐ Agent-oriented programming languages
- ☐ Concatenative programming languages
- ☐ Concurrent programming languages
- ▶ ☐ Data-structured programming languages
- ▶ ☐ Declarative programming languages
- ☐ Dependently typed languages
- ▶ ☐ **Domain-specific programming languages**
- ▶ ☐ Dynamic programming languages
- ☐ Extensible syntax programming languages
- ☐ Formula manipulation languages
- ☐ Function-level languages
- ☐ Functional languages
- ☐ High Integrity Programming Language
- ☐ High-level programming languages
- ☐ Intensional programming languages
- ☐ Low-level programming languages
- ▶ ☐ Multi-paradigm programming languages
- ☐ .NET programming languages
- ☐ Nondeterministic programming languages
- ▶ ☐ Object-based programming languages
- ☐ Pattern matching programming languages
- ▶ ☐ Procedural programming languages
- ☐ Process termination functions
- ☐ Prototype-based programming languages
- ☐ Reactive programming languages
- ☐ Secure programming languages
- ☐ Set theoretic programming languages
- ☐ Statically typed programming languages
- ☐ Synchronous programming languages
- ☐ Term-rewriting programming languages
- ☐ Text-oriented programming languages
- ☐ Tree programming languages
- ☐ Visual programming languages
- ☐ XML-based programming languages

Programming languages

- ☐ ICL programming languages
- ☐ Agent-based programming languages
- ☐ Agent-oriented programming languages
- ☐ Concatenative programming languages
- ☐ Concurrent programming languages
- ▶ ☐ Data-structured programming languages
- ▶ ☐ Declarative programming languages
- ☐ Dependently typed languages
- ▶ ☐ Domain-specific programming languages
- ▶ ☐ Dynamic programming languages
- ☐ Extensible syntax programming languages
- ☐ Formula manipulation languages
- ☐ Function-level languages
- ☐ Functional languages
- ☐ High Integrity Programming Language
- ☐ High-level programming languages
- ☐ Intensional programming languages
- ☐ Low-level programming languages
- ▶ ☐ Multi-paradigm programming languages
- ☐ .NET programming languages
- ☐ Nondeterministic programming languages
- ▶ ☐ Object-based programming languages
- ☐ Pattern matching programming languages
- ▶ ☐ Procedural programming languages
- ☐ Process termination functions
- ☐ Prototype-based programming languages
- ☐ Reactive programming languages
- ☐ Secure programming languages
- ☐ Set theoretic programming languages
- ☐ Statically typed programming languages
- ☐ Synchronous programming languages
- ☐ Term-rewriting programming languages
- ☐ Text-oriented programming languages
- ☐ Tree programming languages
- ☐ Visual programming languages
- ☐ XML-based programming languages

Fig. 5. Metrics-based views on *Programming languages* graph

On the right, the metric for the number of transitive subcategories is applied for visualization. Most subcategories of *Programming languages* do not have any subcategories; thus, they are grayed out. 7 out of 36 level-1 categories carry subcategories. 6 out of these 7 categories carry only very few subcategories (less than 5). Category *Domain-specific programming languages* carries 18 subcategories, which is more than 25 % of all subcategories; this status is expressed by highlighting the category.

4   Conclusion

Any domain with large data to explore ('large' in terms of what the user needs to understand) may benefit from interactive exploration possibly with editing or annotation; see tools for ontologies [2], graphs [9], semantic data [7], software bugs [10], API usage [15]. In this paper, we described an approach to the exploration of Wikipedia's category graph so that candidate taxonomies can be extracted from the graph. We were specifically interested in understanding Wikipedia's classification of software languages. To this end, we developed a domain-specific exploration tool, WikiTax, which supports level-by-level graph extraction, metrics-based graph visualization as well as transparent and revisable graph reduction. Such designated exploration support is missing in more generic tools for searching or exploring the category graph.

The described method of graph reduction is deliberately interactive and relies on domain knowledge for transparent exclusion decisions, as opposed to any means of automated ontology extraction / generation [18,19]. (Without such validation, there is little hope that the resulting taxonomy would be readily meaningful.) An important conceptual contribution is our proposal to document exclusion decisions with (comments for) exclusion types, thereby making reduction more systematic and transparent. This interactive approach can be contrasted with related work on taxonomy or ontology mining, where categories are classified and additional relationships are inferred automatically, e.g., by analyzing the structure of compound category names [14].

We contend that the described approach provides the initial core of a method for actually developing a taxonomy for software languages (and possibly other taxonomies) on the grounds of Wikipedia. Collaborative work and further improved tool support are needed to actually arrive at a comprehensive taxonomy. We imagine that we need powerful refactoring operations on the category graph to facilitate taxonomy extraction and enforcement of consistent style. The exploration of the category graph could also be supported by additional forms of visualization, e.g., for understanding the overlap of categories. Also, we need to generally better understand (perhaps based on an automated analysis) the different classifier styles used by Wikipedia.

References

1. Babenko, L.P., Rogach, V.D., Yushchenko, E.L.: Comparison and classification of programming languages. Cybernetics 11, 271–278 (1975)
2. Baskaya, F., Kekäläinen, J., Järvelin, K.: A tool for ontology-editing and ontology-based information exploration. In: Proc. of ESAIR 2010, pp. 29–30. ACM (2010)
3. Bottoni, P., Grau, A.: A suite of metamodels as a basis for a classification of visual languages. In: Proc. of VL/HCC 2004, pp. 83–90. IEEE Computer Society (2004)
4. Burnett, M.M., Baker, M.J.: A classification system for visual programming languages. J. Vis. Lang. Comput. 5(3), 287–300 (1994)
5. Czarnecki, K., Helsen, S.: Feature-based survey of model transformation approaches. IBM Systems Journal 45(3), 621–646 (2006)
6. Doyle, J.R., Stretch, D.D.: The classification of programming languages by usage. International Journal of Man-Machine Studies 26(3), 343–360 (1987)
7. Dumas, B., Broché, T., Hoste, L., Signer, B.: ViDaX: an interactive semantic data visualisation and exploration tool. In: Proc. of AVI 2012, pp. 757–760. ACM (2012)

8. Favre, J.-M., Gasevic, D., Lämmel, R., Winter, A.: Guest editors' introduction to the special section on software language engineering. IEEE Trans. Software Eng. 35(6), 737–741 (2009)
9. Haun, S., Nürnberger, A., Kötter, T., Thiel, K., Berthold, M.R.: CET: A tool for creative exploration of graphs. In: Balcázar, J.L., Bonchi, F., Gionis, A., Sebag, M. (eds.) ECML PKDD 2010, Part III. LNCS, vol. 6323, pp. 587–590. Springer, Heidelberg (2010)
10. Hora, A., Anquetil, N., Ducasse, S., Bhatti, M.U., Couto, C., Valente, M.T., Martins, J.: Bug Maps: A tool for the visual exploration and analysis of bugs. In: Proc. of CSMR 2012, pp. 523–526. IEEE (2012)
11. Marriott, K., Meyer, B.: On the classification of visual languages by grammar hierarchies. J. Vis. Lang. Comput. 8(4), 375–402 (1997)
12. Medvidovic, N., Taylor, R.N.: A classification and comparison framework for software architecture description languages. IEEE Trans. Software Eng. 26(1), 70–93 (2000)
13. Mosses, P.D.: Action Semantics. Cambridge University Press (1992)
14. Nastase, V., Strube, M.: Decoding Wikipedia categories for knowledge acquisition. In: Proc. of AAAI 2008, pp. 1219–1224. AAAI Press (2008)
15. Roover, C.D., Lämmel, R., Pek, E.: Multi-dimensional exploration of API usage. In: Proc. of ICPC 2013, 10 pages. IEEE (to appear, 2013)
16. Sebesta, R.W.: Concepts of Programming Languages, 10th edn. Addison-Wesley (2012)
17. Skalna, I., Gawel, B.: Model driven architecture and classification of business rules modelling languages. In: Proc. of FedCSIS 2012, pp. 949–952 (2012)
18. Suchanek, F.M., Kasneci, G., Weikum, G.: YAGO: A large ontology from Wikipedia and WordNet. J. Web Sem. 6(3), 203–217 (2008)
19. Wu, F., Weld, D.S.: Automatically refining the Wikipedia infobox ontology. In: Proc. of WWW 2008, pp. 635–644. ACM (2008)

A Language Independent Task Engine
for Incremental Name and Type Analysis

Guido H. Wachsmuth[1,2], Gabriël D.P. Konat[1], Vlad A. Vergu[1],
Danny M. Groenewegen[1], and Eelco Visser[1]

[1] Delft University of Technology, The Netherlands
{g.h.wachsmuth,v.a.vergu,d.m.groenewegen}@tudelft.nl,
{gkonat,visser}@acm.org
[2] Oracle Labs, Redwood City, CA, USA

Abstract. IDEs depend on incremental name and type analysis for responsive feedback for large projects. In this paper, we present a language-independent approach for incremental name and type analysis. Analysis consists of two phases. The first phase analyzes lexical scopes and binding instances and creates deferred analysis tasks. A task captures a single name resolution or type analysis step. Tasks might depend on other tasks and are evaluated in the second phase. Incrementality is supported on file and task level. When a file changes, only this file is recollected and only those tasks are reevaluated, which are affected by the changes in the collected data. The analysis does neither re-parse nor re-traverse unchanged files, even if they are affected by changes in other files. We implemented the approach as part of the Spoofax Language Workbench and evaluated it for the WebDSL web programming language.

1 Introduction

Integrated development environments (IDEs) provide a wide variety of language-specific editor services such as syntax highlighting, error marking, code navigation, content completion, and outline views in real-time, while a program is edited. These services require syntactic and semantic analyses of the edited program. Thereby, timely availability of analysis results is essential for IDE responsiveness. Whole-program analyses do not scale because the size of the program determines the performance of such analyses.

Incremental analysis reuses previous analysis results of unchanged program parts and reanalyses only parts affected by changes. The granularity of the incremental analysis directly impacts the performance of the analysis. A more fine-grained incremental analysis is able to reanalyze smaller units of change, but requires a more complex change and dependency analysis. At program level, any change requires reanalysis of the entire program, which might consider the results of the previous analysis. At file level, a file change requires reanalysis of the entire file and all dependent files. At program element level, changes to an element within a file require reanalysis of that element and dependent elements, but typically not of entire files. Incremental analyses are typically implemented

M. Erwig, R.F. Paige, and E. Van Wyk (Eds.): SLE 2013, LNCS 8225, pp. 260–280, 2013.

manually. Thereby, change detection and dependency tracking are cross-cutting the implementation of the actual analysis. This raises complexity of the implementation and negatively affects maintenance, reusability, and modularity.

In this paper, we focus on incremental name and type analysis. We present a language-independent approach which consists of two phases. The first phase analyzes lexical scopes, collects information about binding instances, and creates deferred *analysis tasks* in a top-down traversal. An analysis task captures a single name resolution or type analysis step. Tasks might depend on other tasks and are evaluated in the second phase. Incrementality is supported on file level by the collection phase and on task level by the evaluation phase. When a file changes, only this file is recollected and only those tasks are reevaluated, which are affected by the changes in the collected data. As a consequence, the analysis does neither re-parse nor re-traverse unchanged files, even if they are affected by changes in other files. Only the affected analysis tasks are reevaluated.

Our approach enables language engineers to abstract over incrementality. When applied directly, language engineers need to parametrize the collection phase, where they have full freedom to create and combine low-level analysis tasks. Thereby, they can focus solely on the name binding and typing rules of their language while the generic evaluation phase provides the incrementality. The approach can also form the basis for more high-level meta-languages for specifying the static semantics of programming languages. We use the task engine to implement incremental name analysis for name binding and scope rules expressed in NaBL, Spoofax' declarative name binding language [16].

We have implemented the approach as part of the Spoofax language workbench [14] and evaluated it for WebDSL, a domain-specific language for the implementation of dynamic web applications [7], designed specifically to enable static analysis and cross-aspect consistency checking in mind [11]. We used real change-sets from the histories of two WebDSL applications to drive experiments for the evaluation of the correctness, performance and scalability of the obtained incremental static analysis. Experiment input data and the obtained results are publicly available.

We proceed as follows. In the next section, we introduce the basics of name and type analysis and introduce the running example of the paper. In Sects. 3 and 4, we discuss the two analysis phases of our approach, collection and evaluation. In Sect. 5, we discuss the implementation and its integration into the Spoofax language workbench. In Sect. 6, we discuss the evaluation of our approach. Sects. 7 and 8 are for related work and conclusions.

2   Name and Type Analysis

In this section, we discuss name and type analysis in the context of the running example of the paper, a multi-file C# program shown in Fig. 1.

Name Analysis. In textual programming languages, an *identifier* is a name given to program elements such as variables, methods, classes, and packages. The

```
class A {                class B {                class C:A {
  B b; int m;              int i; float f;          int n() {
  float m() {              int m() {                  return m(); }}
    return 1 + b.f; }}       return 0; }}
```

Fig. 1. C# class declarations in separate files with cross-file references. The underlined expression causes a type error.

```
class A {                class B {                namespace N {
  B b; int m;              int i; float f;          class C:B {
  int m(B b) {             int m() {                  int n() {
    return 1 + b.i; }}       return 1; }}               return m(); }}}
```

Fig. 2. C# class declarations after editing. Changes w.r.t. Fig. 1 are highlighted.

same identifier can have multiple *instances* in different places in a program. Name analysis establishes relations between a *binding instance* that *defines* a name and a *bound instance* that *uses* that name [17]. Name analysis is typically defined programmatically through a name resolution algorithm that connects *binding prospects* to binding instances. When a prospect is successfully connected, it becomes a bound instance. Otherwise, it is a *free instance*.

The C# class declarations in Fig. 1 contain several references, some of which cross file boundaries. The declared type of field b in class A refers to class B in a separate file. Also, the return expression of method m in class A accesses field f in class B. The parent of class C refers to class A in a separate file and the return expression of method n in class C is a call to method m in class A.

Languages typically distinguish several *namespaces*, i.e. different kinds of names, such that an occurrence of a name in one namespace is not related to an occurrence of that same name in another. In the example, class A contains a field and a homonym method m, but C# distinguishes field and method names.

Scopes restrict the visibility of binding instances. They can be nested and name analysis typically looks for binding instances from inner to outer scopes. In the example, b is resolved by first looking for a variable b in method A.m, before looking for a field b in class A. A *named scope* is the context for a binding instance, and scopes other binding instances. In the example, class A is a named scope. It is the context for a class name and a scope for method and field names.

An *alias* introduces a new binding instance for an already existing one. An *import* introduces binding instances from one scope into another one. In the example, class C imports fields and methods from its parent class A.

Type Analysis. In statically typed programming languages, a *type* classifies program elements such as expressions according to the kind of values they compute [20]. Fig. 1 declares method C.n of type **int**, meaning that this method is expected to compute signed 32-bit integer values. Type analysis assigns types to program elements. Types are typically calculated compositionally, with the type of a program element depending only on the types of its sub-elements [20].

Type checking compares expected with actual types of program elements. A *type error* occurs if actual and expected type are incompatible. Type errors reveal at compile-time certain kinds of program misbehavior at run-time. In the example, the return expression in method C.n causes a type error. The expression is of type **float**, since the called method m returns values of this type. But the declaration of C.n states that it evaluates to values of type **int**.

Incremental Analysis. When a program changes, it needs to be reanalyzed. Different kinds of changes influence name and type analysis. First, adding a binding instance may introduce bindings for free instances, or rebind bound instances. Removing a binding instance influences all its bound instances, which are either rebound to other binding instances or become free instances. Changing a binding instance combines the effects of removing and adding. Second, adding a binding prospect requires resolution, while removing it makes a binding obsolete. Changing a binding prospect requires re-binding, resulting either in a new binding or a free instance. Third, addition, removal, or change of scopes or imports influence bound instances in the affected scopes, which might be rebound to different binding instances or become free instances. Similarly, they influence bound instances which are bound to binding instances in the affected scopes. Finally, addition of a typed element requires type analysis, while removing it makes a type calculation obsolete. Changing a typed element requires reanalysis.

Furthermore, changes propagate along dependencies. When bound instances are rebound to different binding instances or become free instances, this influences bindings in the context of these bound instances, the type of these instances, the type of enclosing program elements, and bindings in the context of such types. Consider Fig. 2 for an example. It shows edited versions of the C# class declarations from Fig. 1. We assume the following editing sequence:

1. The return type of method A.m is changed from **float** to **int**. This affects the type of the return expression of method C.n and solves the type error, but raises a new type error in the return expression of A.m.
2. The return expression of method A.m is changed to b.i. This requires resolution of i and affects the type of the expression, solving the type error.
3. Parameter B b is added to method A.m. This might affect the resolution and by this the type of b and i in the return expression, the type of the return expression, the resolution of m in method C.n, and the type of its return expression. Actually, only the resolution of b and m and the type of the return expression in C.n are affected. The latter resolution fails, causing a resolution error and leaving the return expression untyped.
4. The parent of class C is changed from A to B. This affects the resolution of m in method C.n and the type of its return expression. It fixes the resolution error and the return expression becomes typed again.
5. Class C is enclosed in a new namespace N. This might affect the resolution of parent class D, the resolution of m in N.C.n, and the type of the return expression in N.C.n. Actually, it does not affect any of those.
6. The return expression of method m in class B is changed. This might affect the type of this expression, but actually it does not.

We discuss incremental analysis in the next sections. We start with the collection phase in Sect. 3, and continue with the evaluation phase in Sect. 4.

3   Semantic Index

We collect name binding information for all units in a project into a *semantic index*, a central data structure that is persisted across invocations of the analysis and across editing sessions. For the purpose of this paper, we model this data structure as binary relations over keys and values. As keys, we use URIs, which identify bindings uniquely across a project. As values, we use either URIs or terms. We use $\mathcal{U}$ and $\mathcal{T}$ to denote the set of all URIs and terms, respectively.

URIs. We assign a URI to each binding instance, bound instance, and free instance. A bound instance shares the URI with its corresponding binding instance. A URI consists of a language name, a list of scope segments, the namespace of the instance, its name, and an optional unique qualifier. This qualifier helps to distinguish unique binding instances by numbering them consecutively. A segment for a named scope consists of the namespace, the name, and the qualifier of the scoping binding instance. Anonymous scopes are represented by a segment anon(u), where u is a unique string to distinguish different scopes. For example, C#://*Class*.A.1/*Method*.m.1 identifies method m in class A in the C# program in Fig. 1. The qualifier 1 distinguishes the method. Possible homonym methods in the same class would get subsequent qualifiers.

Index Entries. The index stores binding instances ($B \subseteq \mathcal{U} \times \mathcal{U}$), aliases ($A \subseteq \mathcal{U} \times \mathcal{U}$), transitive and non-transitive imports for each namespace ns ($TI_{ns} \subseteq \mathcal{U} \times \mathcal{U}$ and $NI_{ns} \subseteq \mathcal{U} \times \mathcal{U}$), and types of binding instances ($P_{type} \subseteq \mathcal{U} \times \mathcal{T}$). For a binding instance with URI u, B contains an entry (u', u), where u' is retrieved from u by omitting the unique qualifier. u' is useful to resolve binding prospects, as we will show later. An alias consists of the new name, that is a binding instance, and the old name, that is a binding prospect. For each alias, A contains an entry (a, u), where a is the URI of the binding instance and u is the URI of the binding prospect. For a transitive wildcard import from a scope with URI u into a scope with URI u', TI_{ns} contains an entry (u', u). Similarly, NI_{ns} contains entries for non-transitive imports. Finally, for a binding instance of URI u and of type t, P_{type} contains an entry (u, t). P can also store other properties of binding instances, but we focus on types for this paper.

Example. Fig. 3 shows the index for the running example. It contains entries in B for binding instances of classes A, B, and C, fields A.b, A.m, B.i, and B.f, and methods A.m, B.m, and C.n. Corresponding entries for P_{type} contain the types of all fields and methods in the program. Since the running example does not define any aliases, A does not contain any entries. It also contains corresponding entries for NI_{Field}, TI_{Field}, NI_{Method}, and TI_{Method}. These entries model inheritance by a combination of a non-transitive and a transitive import. C first inherits the fields and methods from A (non-transitive import). Second, C inherits the fields and methods which are inherited by A (transitive import).

Relation	Key	Value
B	C#:/*Class*.A	C#:/*Class*.A.1
	C#:/*Class*.A.1/*Field*.b	C#:/*Class*.A.1/*Field*.b.1
	C#:/*Class*.A.1/*Field*.m	C#:/*Class*.A.1/*Field*.m.1
	C#:/*Class*.A.1/*Method*.m	C#:/*Class*.A.1/*Method*.m.1
	C#:/*Class*.B	C#:/*Class*.B.1
	C#:/*Class*.B.1/*Field*.i	C#:/*Class*.B.1/*Field*.i.1
	C#:/*Class*.B.1/*Field*.f	C#:/*Class*.B.1/*Field*.i.1
	C#:/*Class*.B.1/*Method*.m	C#:/*Class*.B.1/*Method*.m.1
	C#:/*Class*.C	C#:/*Class*.C.1
	C#:/*Class*.C.1/*Method*.n	C#:/*Class*.C.1/*Method*.n.1
NI_{Field}, TI_{Field}	C#:/*Class*.C.1	Task:/31
NI_{Method}, TI_{Method}	C#:/*Class*.C.1	Task:/31
P_{type}	C#:/*Class*.A.1/*Field*.b.1	Task:/6
	C#:/*Class*.A.1/*Field*.m.1	int
	C#:/*Class*.A.1/*Method*.m.1	([], float)
	C#:/*Class*.B.1/*Field*.i.1	int
	C#:/*Class*.B.1/*Field*.f.1	float)
	C#:/*Class*.B.1/*Method*.m.1	([], int)
	C#:/*Class*.C.1/*Method*.n.1	([], int)

Change	Key	Value
$\Delta^1_{P_{type}}$	C#:/*Class*.A.1/*Method*.m.1	([], float)
	C#:/*Class*.A.1/*Method*.m.1	([], int)
Δ^3_{B}	C#:/*Class*.A.1/*Method*.m.1/*Var*.b	C#:/*Class*.A.1/*Method*.m.1/*Var*.b.1
$\Delta^3_{P_{type}}$	C#:/*Class*.A.1/*Method*.m.1/*Var*.b.1	Task:/6
	C#:/*Class*.A.1/*Method*.m.1	([], int)
	C#:/*Class*.A.1/*Method*.m.1	([Task:/6], int)
$\Delta^4_{I_{Field}}$	C#:/*Class*.C.1	Task:/31
	C#:/*Class*.C.1	Task:/6
$\Delta^4_{I_{Method}}$	C#:/*Class*.C.1	Task:/31
	C#:/*Class*.C.1	Task:/6
Δ^5_{B}	C#:/Ns.N	C#:/Ns.N.1
	C#:/*Class*.C	C#:/*Class*.C.1
	C#:/Ns.N.1/*Class*.C	C#:/Ns.N.1/*Class*.C.1
	C#:/*Class*.C.1/*Method*.n	C#:/*Class*.C.1/*Method*.n.1
	C#:/Ns.N.1/*Class*.C.1/*Method*.n	C#:/Ns.N.1/*Class*.C.1/*Method*.n.1
$\Delta^5_{I_{Field}}$	C#:/*Class*.C.1	Task:/6
	C#:/Ns.N.1/*Class*.C.1	Task:/54
$\Delta^5_{I_{Method}}$	C#:/*Class*.C.1	Task:/6
	C#:/Ns.N.1/*Class*.C.1	Task:/54
$\Delta^5_{P_{type}}$	C#:/*Class*.C.1/*Method*.n.1	([], int)
	C#:/Ns.N.1/*Class*.C.1/*Method*.n.1	([], int)

Fig. 3. Initial semantic index for the C# program in Fig. 1 (top) and changes for the C# program from Fig. 2 (bottom)

Initial Collection. We collect index entries in a generic top-down traversal, which needs to be instantiated with language-specific name binding and scope rules. During the traversal, a dictionary S is maintained to keep track of the current scope for each namespace. At each node, we perform the following actions:

1. If the node is the context of a binding instance of name n in namespace ns, we create a new unique qualifier q, construct URIs $u' = S(ns)/ns.n$ and $u = u'.q$, and add (u', u) to B. If the instance is of type t, we add (u, t) to P_{type}. If the node is a scope for a namespace ns', we update $S(ns)$ to u.
2. If the current node is an anonymous scope for a namespace ns, we extend $S(ns)$ with an additional anonymous segment.
3. If the current node defines an alias, transitive, or non-transitive wildcard import, we add corresponding pairs of URIs to A, TI_{ns}, or NI_{ns}.

Collection does not consider binding prospects which need to be resolved. Furthermore, entries in TI_{ns}, NI_{ns}, and P_{type} might still require project-wide name resolution and type analysis. Instead of performing this analysis during the collection, we defer the remaining analysis tasks to a second phase of analysis and store unique placeholder URIs in the index. For example, the type of field A.b contains a class name B, which needs to be resolved. The index in Fig. 3 does not contain an actual type, but a reference to a deferred resolution task. Also, the index entries for wildcard imports refers to a deferred task, since the name of the base class of class C needs to be resolved first.

The semantic index is a project-wide data structure, but collection can be split over separate partitions. A *partition* is typically a file, but can also be a smaller unit. The only constraint we impose on partitions is that they need to be in global scope. This ensures that index collection is independent of other partitions. Collection for a partition p will provide us with a partial index consisting of B_p, A_p, $TI_{p,ns}$, $NI_{p,ns}$, and $P_{p,type}$. The overall index can be formed by combining all partial indices of a project.

Incremental Collection. When a partition is edited, reanalysis is triggered. But only the partial index of the changed partition needs to be recollected, while partial indices of other partitions remain valid. Partial recollection will result in an updated relation B'_p. Given the original B_p, we define a change set $\Delta_B = (B'_p \setminus B_p) \cup (B_p \setminus B'_p)$ of entries added to or removed from B. In the same way, we can define Δ_A, and $\Delta_{P_{type}}$. For imports, the situation is slightly different, since we need to consider changes in transitive import chains. We keep a change set $\Delta_{I_{ns}}$ for a derived relation $I_{ns} = TI^*_{ns} \circ NI_{ns}$, where TI^* is the reflexive transitive closure of TI and I is the composition of this closure with NI.

Example. Fig. 3 shows non-empty change sets for the running example. Thereby, superscripts indicate editing steps. In step 1, changing the return type of method A.m causes a change in P_{type}. In step 3, adding a parameter to the same method causes changes to B and P_{type}. In step 4, changing the parent of class C causes changes in I_{Field} and I_{Method}. In step 5, enclosing class C in a namespace affects all index entries for the class and its contained elements. The next section discusses how change-sets trigger reevaluation of deferred analysis tasks.

4   Deferred Analysis Tasks

In the previous section, we discussed the collection of index entries. This collection is efficient, since it requires only a single top-down traversal. When a partition changes, recollection is even more efficient, since it can be restricted to the changed partition, while the collected entries from other partitions remain valid. This is achieved by deferring name resolution and type analysis tasks, which might require information from other partitions or from other tasks.

Tasks are collected together with index entries and evaluated afterwards in a second analysis phase. For evaluation, no traversal is needed. Instead, inter-task dependencies determine an evaluation order. When a partition changes, only the tasks for this partition are recollected in the first phase. Change sets determine which tasks need to re-evaluated, including affected tasks from other partitions.

Instructions. Each *task* consists of a special URI, which is used as a placeholder in the semantic index, its dependencies to other tasks, and an instruction. Fig. 4 lists the instructions which can be used in tasks. Their semantics is given with respect to the semantic index, a type cast relation $C \subseteq \mathcal{T} \times \mathcal{T}$, where $(t, t') \in C$ iff type t can be cast to type t', and a partial function $\delta_C : \mathcal{T} \times \mathcal{T} \to \mathbb{N}$ for the distance between types. We write $R[S]$ to denote the image of a set S under a

Instruction	Semantics
resolve uri	$B[\text{uri}]$
resolve alias uri	$A[\text{uri}]$
resolve import ns **into** uri	$I_{\text{ns}}[\text{uri}]$
lookup type of uri	$P_{type}[\text{uri}]$
check type t **in** T	$\{t\} \cap \text{T}$
cast type t **to** T	$C[t] \cap \text{T}$
assign type t	$\{t\}$
s1 + s2	$R[\text{s1}, \text{s2}]$
s1 <+ s2	$\begin{cases} R[\text{s1}], \text{if} \neq \emptyset \\ R[\text{s2}], \text{otherwise} \end{cases}$
filter s1 + s2 **by type** T	$\{u \in R[\text{s1}, \text{s2}] \mid P_{type} \circ C[u] \cap \text{T} \neq \emptyset\}$
filter s1 <+ s2 **by type** T	$\begin{cases} \{u \in R[\text{s1}] \mid (P_{type} \circ C)[u] \cap \text{T} \neq \emptyset\}, \text{if} \neq \emptyset \\ \{u \in R[\text{s2}] \mid P_{type} \circ C[u] \cap \text{T} \neq \emptyset\}, \text{otherwise} \end{cases}$
disambiguate s1 + s2 **by type** T	$\{u \in R[\text{s1}, \text{s2}] \mid \forall u' \in R[\text{s1}, \text{s2}] : \delta_C(u', \text{T}) \geq \delta_C(u, \text{T})\}$
disambiguate s1 <+ s2 **by type** T	$\begin{cases} \{u \in R[\text{s1}] \mid \forall u' \in R[\text{s1}, \text{s2}] : \delta_C(u', \text{T}) \geq \delta_C(u, \text{T})\}, \text{if} \neq \emptyset \\ \{u \in R[\text{s2}] \mid \forall u' \in R[\text{s1}, \text{s2}] : \delta_C(u', \text{T}) \geq \delta_C(u, \text{T})\}, \text{ow.} \end{cases}$

Fig. 4. Syntax and semantics of name and type analysis instructions. uri denotes a URI, ns a namespace, t a type, T a set of types, and s1, s2 subtask IDs.

relation R and omit set braces for finite sets, that is, we write $R[e]$ instead of $R[\{e\}]$. We provide three name resolution instructions for looking up binding instances from B (**resolve**), named imports from A (**resolve alias**), and wildcard imports from the derived relation I_{ns} (**resolve import**), and four type analysis instructions for type look-up from P_{type} (**lookup**), for checks with respect to expected types (**check**), for casts to an expected type according to C (**cast**), and for assigning types to program elements (**assign**).

Example. Fig. 5 shows tasks and their solutions for the running example. Tasks 1 to 6 try to resolve class name B. Task 1 looks for B directly in the global scope. It finds an entry in B and *succeeds*. Task 2 looks for aliases, which task 3 tries to resolve next. Instead of a concrete URI, the task 3 has a reference to task 2. Since task 2 *fails* to find any named imports, task 3 also fails. Task 5 tries to resolve B inside imported scopes, which are yielded by task 4. Both tasks fail. Task 6 combines resolution results based on local classes, aliases, and imported classes. We will discuss such combinators in the next example.

Tasks 7 to 25 are involved in type checking the return expression of A.m() in Fig. 1. Task 7 assigns type **int** to the integer constant. Tasks 8 to 18 are an example for the interaction between name and type analysis. The first six tasks try to resolve b either as a local variable, a field in the current class, or an inherited field. Next, task 14 looks up the type of the resolved field A.b, before the remaining tasks resolve field f with respect to that type B. Task 19 looks up the type of the referred field. The remaining tasks analyse the binary expression: Tasks 20 and 21 check if the subexpressions are numeric or string types. Tasks 22 and 23 try to coerce the left to the right type and vice versa. Both tasks are combined by task 24. Finally, task 25 checks if the type of the return expression can be coerced to the declared return type of the method.

Combinators. Fig. 4 also shows six instructions to combine the results of subtasks. The semantics of these combinators are expressed in terms of a relation R, where $(t, r) \in R$ iff r is a result of task t. Notably, tasks can have multiple results. We will revisit R later, when we discuss task evaluation.

The simplest combinators are a non-deterministic choice + and a deterministic pendant <+. The result of the non-deterministic choice is the union of the results of its subtasks. while the result of the deterministic choice is the result of its first non-failing subtask. Furthermore, we provide combinators **filter** and **disambiguate**. Both can be used in a non-deterministic or deterministic fashion to combine the result sets of resolution tasks with respect to expected types. **filter** keeps only compliant results. **disambiguate** keeps only results which fit best with respect to the expected types. The non-deterministic variant keeps all of them, while the deterministic variant chooses the first subtask which contributes to the best fitting results.

Example. In Fig. 5, task 6 combines resolution results based on local classes, aliased classes, and imported classes. The non-deterministic choice ensures that no result is preferred over another. Similarly, task 24 combines the results of alternative coercion tasks. In tasks 12 and 13, deterministic choices ensure that local fields win over inherited fields and variables win over fields, respectively.

ID Instruction	Results
1 **resolve** C#:/*Class*.B	C#:/*Class*.B.1
2 **resolve alias** C#:/*Class*.B	
3 **resolve** Task:/2	
4 **resolve import** *Class* **into** C#:/	
5 **resolve** Task:/4/*Class*.B	
6 Task:/1 + Task:/3 + Task:/5	C#:/*Class*.B.1
7 **assign type** int	int
8 **resolve** C#:/*Class*.A.1/*Method*.m.1/*Var*.b	
9 **resolve** C#:/*Class*.A.1/*Field*.b	C#:/*Class*.A.1/*Field*.b.1
10 **resolve import** *Field* **into** C#:/*Class*.A.1	
11 **resolve** Task:/10/*Field*.b	
12 Task:/9 <+ Task:/11	C#:/*Class*.A.1/*Field*.b.1
13 Task:/8 <+ Task:/12	C#:/*Class*.A.1/*Field*.b.1
14 **lookup type of** Task:/13	C#:/*Class*.B.1
15 **resolve** Task:/14/*Field*.f	C#:/*Class*.B.1/*Field*.f.1
16 **resolve import** *Field* **into** Task:/14	
17 **resolve** Task:/16/*Field*.f	
18 Task:/15 <+ Task:/17	C#:/*Class*.B.1/*Field*.f.1
19 **lookup type of** Task:/18	float
20 **check type** Task:/7 **in** {int, long, float, double, String}	int
21 **check type** Task:/19 **in** {int, long, float, double, String}	float
22 **cast type** Task:/21 **to** Task:/20	
23 **cast type** Task:/20 **to** Task:/21	float
24 Task:/22 + Task:/23	float
25 **cast type** Task:/24 **to** float	float
26 **cast type** Task:/20 **to** int	int
27 **resolve** C#:/*Class*.A	C#:/*Class*.A.1
28 **resolve alias** C#:/*Class*.A	
29 **resolve** Task:/28	
30 **resolve** Task:/4/*Class*.A	
31 Task:/27 + Task:/29 + Task:/30	C#:/*Class*.A.1
32 **resolve** C#:/*Class*.C.1/*Method*.m	
33 **resolve import** *Method* **into** C#:/*Class*.C.1	C#:/*Class*.A.1
34 **resolve** Task:/33/*Method*.m	C#:/*Class*.A.1/*Method*.m.1
35 **assign type** []	[]
36 **disambiguate** Task:/32 <+ Task:/34 **by type** Task:/35	C#:/*Class*.A.1/*Method*.m.1
37 **lookup type of** Task:/36	([], float)
38 **cast type** Task:/37 **to** int	

Fig. 5. Tasks and their solutions for the C# program in Fig. 1

Method call resolution in the presence of overloaded methods is a well-known example for interaction between name and type analysis. Actual and formal argument types need to be considered by the resolution, since they need to comply. Furthermore, relations between these types indicate which declaration is more applicable. As an example, consider tasks 32 to 36 in Fig. 5. They resolve method call m() in the return expression of C.n() from Fig. 1. Task 32 tries to resolve it locally, while tasks 33 and 34 consider inherited methods. Task 35 assigns an empty list as the type of the actual parameters of the call. Task 36 selects only these methods which fits this type best, preferring local over inherited methods. Finally, the last two tasks check the return expression of C.n. Task 37 looks up the type of A.m. Task 38 tries to casts this to the declared return type, but fails.

Initial Evaluation. During the generic traversal in the collection phase, we do not only collect semantic index entries but also instructions of tasks $(T \subseteq \mathcal{U} \times \mathcal{I})$ and inter-task dependencies $(D \subseteq \mathcal{U} \times \mathcal{U})$. Language-specific collection rules are needed to control the collection of name resolution and type analysis tasks. D imposes an evaluation order for tasks. First, we can evaluate independent tasks. Next, we can evaluate tasks which only depend on already evaluated tasks. This will evaluate all tasks except those with cyclic dependencies, which we consider erroneous. As mentioned earlier, we capture task results in a relation $R \subseteq \mathcal{U} \times (\mathcal{U} \cup T)$.

The instruction of each task is evaluated according to the semantics given in Fig. 4. However, this only works, if we replace placeholders of dependent subtasks with their results. When a subtask has multiple results, we evaluate the dependent task for each of these results. Consider task 14 from Fig. 5 as an example. It can only be evaluated after replacing the placeholder Task:/13 with a result of the corresponding task. Since this task has a single result C#:/Class.A.1/Field.b.1, we actually need to evaluate the instruction **lookup type** C#:/Class.A.1/Field.b.1, yielding C#://Class.B.1 as its only result.

Incremental Evaluation. When a partition is edited, the partial index and tasks for this partition will be recollected, resulting in an updated relation T'_p. We need to evaluate new tasks, which did not exist in another partition before. We collect the URIs of these tasks in a change set: $\Delta_{T_p} = \mathrm{dom}(T'_p \setminus T_p)$. Furthermore, a changed semantic index might affect the results of the tasks from all partitions, requiring the reevaluation of those tasks. The various change sets determine which tasks need to be reevaluated:

$(u', u) \in \Delta_B$: tasks which evaluated an instruction **resolve** u'.
$(a, u) \in \Delta_A$: tasks which evaluated an instruction **resolve alias** a.
$(u', u) \in \Delta_I$: tasks which evaluated an instruction **resolve import** u'.
$(u, t) \in \Delta_{P_{type}}$: tasks which evaluated an instruction **lookup type of** u and
   filter or **disambiguate** tasks with a subtask s with $u \in R[s]$.

We maintain the URIs of these tasks in another change set Δ_T. The URIs of tasks which require evaluation is given by the set $\Delta_{T_p} \cup D^*[\Delta_T]$.

Example. In step 1 of the running example, task 25 becomes obsolete, since the return expression needs to be checked with respect to a new type, which is done by a new task 39, shown in Fig. 6. Furthermore, the disambiguation in task 36 depends on an element in $\Delta^1_{P_{type}}$, which is to be reevaluated. Transitive dependencies trigger also the reevaluation of tasks 37 and 38. Since task 38 succeeds now, it does no longer indicate a type error in C.n. But the new task 39 fails, indicating a new type error in A.m. In step 2, tasks 15, 17 to 19, 21 to 24, and 39 become obsolete, since another field needs to be resolved. The semantic index was not changed, and only the corresponding new tasks 40 to 48 need to be evaluated. In step 3, the additional variable parameter causes changes in the semantic index. Δ^3_B requires the reevaluation of task 8 and its dependent tasks 14, 16, and 40 to 48. Furthermore, $\Delta^3_{P_{type}}$ requires the reevaluation of task 36 and its dependent tasks 37 and 38. Similarly, $\Delta^4_{I_{Field}}$ requires the reevaluation of task 33 and its dependent tasks 34 and 36 to 38. Finally, the new enclosing namespace introduced in step 5 makes tasks 32 to 34 and 36 to 38 obsolete and introduces new tasks 49 to 61, which take the new namespace into account.

ID	Instruction	Results
39	**cast type** Task:/24 **to** int	
40	**resolve** Task:/14/*Field*.i	C#:/*Class*.B.1/*Field*.i.1
41	**resolve** Task:/16/*Field*.i	
42	Task:/40 <+ Task:/41	C#:/*Class*.B.1/*Field*.i.1
43	**lookup type of** Task:/42	int
44	**check type** Task:/43 **in** {int, long, float, double, String}	int
45	**cast type** Task:/44 **to** Task:/20	int
46	**cast type** Task:/20 **to** Task:/44	int
47	Task:/45 + Task:/46	int
48	**cast type** Task:/47 **to** int	int
49	**resolve** C#:/Ns.N.1/*Class*.B	
50	**resolve alias** C#:/Ns.N.1/*Class*.B	
51	**resolve** Task:/50	
52	**resolve import** *Class* **into** C#:/Ns.N.1	
53	**resolve** Task:/52/*Class*.B	
54	Task:/49 + Task:/51 + Task:/53	
55	Task:/31 + Task:/54	C#/*Class*.B.1
56	**resolve** C#:/Ns.N.1/*Class*.C.1/*Method*.m	
57	**resolve import** *Method* **into** C#:/Ns.N.1/*Class*.C.1	C#:/*Class*.B.1
58	**resolve** Task:/57/*Method*.m	C#:/*Class*.B.1/*Method*.m.1
59	**disambiguate** Task:/56 + Task:/58 **by type** Task:/35	C#:/*Class*.B.1/*Method*.m.1
60	**lookup type of** Task:/59	([], int)
61	**cast type** Task:/60 **to** int	int

Fig. 6. New tasks and their solutions for the C# program in Fig. 2

5   Implementation

We have implemented the approach as three components of the Spoofax language workbench [14]. The first component is a Java implementation of the semantic index. It maintains a multimap storing relations B, A, I, and P, a set keeping partition names, and another multimap from partitions to their index entries. During collection, it calculates change sets on the fly, maintaining two multisets for newly added and removed elements.

The second component is a task engine implemented in Java. It maintains a map from task IDs to their instructions and bidirectional multimaps between task IDs and their partitions, between task IDs and index entries they depend on, and for task dependencies. Just as the semantic index, the task engine exposes a collection API and calculates change sets on the fly, maintaining a set of added and a set of removed tasks. Additionally, it exposes an API for task evaluation. During evaluation, it maintains a queue of scheduled tasks and a bidirectional multimap of task dependencies which are discovered dynamically. Results and messages of tasks are kept in maps. Both components use hash-based data structures which can be persisted to file. They support Java representations of terms as values and expose their APIs to Stratego [2], Spoofax' term rewriting language for analysis, transformation, and code generation.

```
Class(NonPartial(), c, _, _): defines Class c scopes Field, Method
Field(_, f)                   : defines Field f
Method(_, m, _, _)            : defines Method m scopes Var

Base(c):
  imports Field, imported Field, Method, imported Method from Class c

ClassType(c)   : refers to Class c
FieldAcc(e, f) : refers to Field f in Class c where e has type c
VarRef(x)      : refers to Var x otherwise refers to Field x
ThisCall(m, p*): refers to best Method m of type t* where p* has type t*
```

```
overlays
  NUMERIC() = [Int(), Long(), Float(), Double()]
  STRING()  = ClassType(PackRef("System"), "String")

type-of(|ctx):
  Add(e1, e2) → <choose(|ctx)> [ty1', ty2']
  where
    ty1  := <type-check(|ctx)> (e1, [STRING() | NUMERIC()])
  ; ty2  := <type-check(|ctx)> (e2, [STRING() | NUMERIC()])
  ; ty1' := <type-match(|ctx, Coerce())> (ty1, ty2)
  ; ty2' := <type-match(|ctx, Coerce())> (ty2, ty1)
```

Fig. 7. Declarative name binding and scope rules for C# in NaBL (top) and manually written Stratego rule for typing additions and string concatenations in C# (bottom)

The third component implements index and task collection as a generic traversal in Stratego. At each tree node, the traversal applies language-specific rewrite rules for name and type analysis. These rules can either be generated from name binding and scope rules defined in NaBL, or manually written in Stratego. For example, Fig. 7 shows an extract of NaBL rules as well as a manually written Stratego rule for C#. The latter involves callbacks to the collection component, which creates the corresponding tasks in the task engine. type-check creates a **check** task, type-match creates a **cast** task, and choose creates a non-deterministic choice. The rule looks very similar to an ordinary typing rule in Stratego, but instead of calculating types, it calculates tasks, which are evaluated later. The API hides the internals of our approach from the language engineer, who can specify an incremental static analysis in NaBL and Stratego in the same way as a regular static analysis.

6   Evaluation

We evaluate the *correctness, performance*, and *scalability* of our approach with an implementation for name and type analysis of WebDSL programs. Correctness is interesting since we only analyze affected program elements. We expect incremental analysis to yield the same result as a full analysis. Performance and scalability are crucial since they are the main purpose of incremental analysis. We want to assess whether performance is acceptable for practical use in IDEs and how the approach scales for large projects. Specifically, we evaluate the following research questions: *RQ1*) Does incremental name and type analysis of WebDSL applications yield the same results as full analysis? *RQ2*) What is the performance gain of incremental name and type analysis of WebDSL applications compared to full analysis? *RQ3*) How does the size of a WebDSL application influence the performance of incremental name and type analysis? *RQ4*) Is incremental name and type analysis suitable for a WebDSL IDE?

Research Method. In a controlled setting, we quantitatively compare the results and performance of incremental and full analysis of different versions of WebDSL applications. We have reimplemented name and type analysis for WebDSL, using NaBL to specify name binding and scope rules and Stratego to specify type analysis. We apply the same algorithm to perform full and incremental analyses to the source code histories of two WebDSL applications. We run a fullanalysis on all files in a revision, and and incremental analysis only on changed files with respect to the result of a full analysis of the previous revision.

Subjects. WebDSL is a domain-specific language for the implementation of dynamic web applications [7]. It was designed from the ground up with static analysis and cross-aspect consistency checking in mind [11]. This focus makes it is an ideal candidate to evaluate its static analysis. WebDSL provides many language constructs on which constraints have to be checked. It also embodies a complex expression language that is representative of expressions in general purpose languages such as Java and C#. It has been used for several applications in production, including the issue tracker Yellowgrass[1], which is a subject of this evaluation, the digital library Researchr, and the online education platform WebLab. When developing such larger applications, the usability of the WebDSL IDE sometimes suffered from the lack of incremental analyses. We focus on two open source WebDSL applications, Blog, a web application for wikis and blogs, and Yellowgrass, a tag-based issue tracker. In their latest revisions, their code bases consist of approximately 7 and 9 KLOC.

Data collection. We perform measurements by repeating the following for every revision of each application. We run an incremental and a full analysis. During each of the analyses we record execution timings. After each analysis we preserve the data from the semantic index and the task engine which we analyse afterwards. Each analysis is sequentially executed on command line in a separate invocation of the Java Virtual Machine (JVM) and garbage collection is invoked before each analysis. After starting the virtual machine, we run three analyses and discard results allowing for the warmup period of the JVM's JIT compiler. All executions are carried out on the same machine with 2.7 Ghz Intel Core i-7, 16 GB of memory, and Oracle Java Hotspot VM version 1.6.0 45 in server JIT mode. We fix the JVM's heap size at 4 GB to decrease the noise caused by garbage collection. We set the maximum stack size at 16 MB.

Analysis procedure. For *RQ1*, we evaluate the structural equality of data from the semantic index and the task engine produced by full and incremental analysis. For *RQ2*, we determine absolute execution times of full and incremental analysis and the relative speed up. We calculate the relative performance gain between analyses separately for each revision. We report geometric mean and distribution of absolute and relative performance of all revisions. For *RQ3*, we determine the number of lines and the number of changed lines of a revision. We relate the incremental analysis time to these numbers. For *RQ4*, we filter revisions which changed only a single file. On these revisions, we determine the execution time of incremental analysis.

Results and Interpretation. We published the collected data and all analysis results in a public repository[2], including instructions on reproducing our experiments. Since both applications yield similar results, we discuss only Yellowgrass data here. Data for Blog can be found in the repository. For the future, we plan to collect data on more WebDSL applications and on more programming languages. Our implementation and the subjects are also open source.

RQ1) For all revisions of both applications, incremental and full analysis produce structurally equal data in semantic index and task engine. This is the expected outcome and supports the equivalence of both analyses.

RQ2) Fig. 8 show the absolute execution times of full and incremental analyses of all revisions. Full analysis takes between 4.74 and 13.31 seconds. Incremental analysis takes between 0.37 and 4.97 seconds. The mean analysis times are 9.75 seconds and 0.96 seconds, with standard deviations of 2.29 and 0.61

---

[1] http://yellowgrass.org

[2] https://bitbucket.org/slde/opendata-experiments

seconds, respectively. Incremental analysis takes between 3.06% and 43.75% of the time of a full analysis. The mean ratio between incremental and full analysis is 10.56%. Thus, incremental analysis gives huge performance gains.

RQ3) Fig. 9 shows incremental analysis times per revision, ordered by LOC and changed LOC, respectively. The size of a project does not seem to influence incremental analysis time (correlation coefficient −0.18), but the size of the change does. This is the expected outcome, but more experiments will be needed.

RQ4) There were 137 revisions which affected only a single file. Incremental analysis takes between 0.37 and 1.12 seconds. There is only one revision where incremental analysis takes longer than one second. The mean incremental analysis time is 0.56 seconds. All analysis times would be acceptable response times in an interactive IDE setting, where analysis is performed in the background without blocking the user interface. Single responses which take slightly more than one second would still be acceptable, if regular responses are fast. Furthermore,

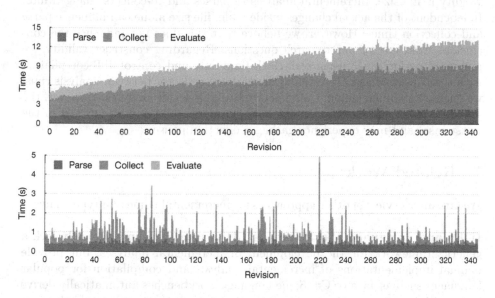

Fig. 8. Analysis time for full (top) and incremental (bottom) analyses

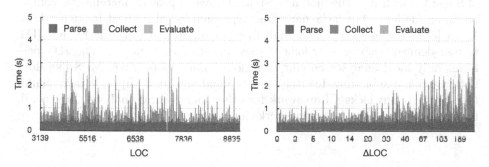

Fig. 9. Incremental analysis time ordered by LOC (left) and ΔLOC (right)

changes between two revisions are more coarse grained and should require more re-evaluation than changes in an editing scenario.

Threats to Validity. An important threat to external validity is that we analyzed only WebDSL applications and only two of them. We are convinced that WebDSL's name and type analysis is representative for other languages, but our evaluation cannot generalize beyond WebDSL and its sublanguages. Furthermore, other WebDSL applications, particularly those of different size, might show different characteristics. Additional threats are the large distance between revisions and the correctness of revisions. In real-time editing scenarios, distances might be much smaller and revisions might switch between correct and erroneous states. We believe that smaller distances would only be in the benefit of incremental analysis. Erroneous revisions should not affect parse and collection times but evaluation times, which tend to be small. A threat to internal validity is file size. Incremental analysis re-parses and re-collects changed files. Independent of the actual changes inside a file, file size alone can influence parse and collection times. However, we believe that this does not influence the conclusions from any of our research questions. Regarding construct validity, we measured performance using wall-clock time only and control JIT compilation with a warm-up phase. By running the garbage collector between analysis runs, we ensured a similar amount of memory available to all analyses. However, the semantic index and the task engine store large amounts of data (13 MB in the worst case) and may experience garbage collection pauses.

7   Related Work

We give an overview of other approaches for incremental name and type analysis.

IDEs and Language Workbenches. IDEs such as Eclipse typically lack a generic framework for the development of incremental analyses, but provide manual implementations of incremental analysis and compilation for popular languages such as Java or C#. Some language workbenches automatically derive incremental analyses. In SugarJ [5], extensions inherit the incremental behaviour of SugarJ, which uses the module system of Java to provide incremental compilation on file-level, but lacks name and type analysis of its host language Java. Xtext [6] leverages incremental analysis and compilation from the Eclipse JDT to user-defined languages, as long as they map to Java concepts. The JDT performs only local analyses on edit and global analyses on save. MPS [30] does not require name binding due to its projectional nature. It supports incremental type analysis but lacks a framework for other incremental analyses. In general, language workbenches lack frameworks for developing incremental analyses.

Attribute Grammars. Attribute grammars [15] provide a formal way of specifying the semantics of a context-free language, including name and type analysis. One of the first incremental attribute evaluators is proposed in [3]. It only evaluates changed attributes and propagates evaluation to affected attributes. A similar incremental evaluation algorithm is shown in [31,32] for ordered attributed grammars [13]. In [22,24,23,12], extensions to propagation are shown that stop propagation if an attribute value is unchanged from its previous attribution.

Similar to attribute grammars, our approach exploits static dependencies, caching, and change propagation. Similar to ordered attribute grammars, we assume an evaluation order of tasks. Though tasks can be cyclic, we just do not evaluate them. While attributes are (re-)evaluated in visits to the tree, our collection separates tasks from the tree and they are (re-)evaluated independent of the tree. As a consequence, we do not require incremental parsing techniques and are not restricted to editing modes. For name analysis, attribute grammars typically pass environments throughout the tree. Incremental name analysis suffers from this as a single change in the environment requires a full re-evaluation of the aggregated environment and all dependent attributes. In our approach, we have a predefined notion of an environment, the semantic index, which is globally maintained. It enables fine-grained dependency tracking for name and type analysis tasks solely based on changing entries, not on changing environments.

Reference Attribute Grammars. A popular extension to attribute grammars is the addition of reference attributes. These simplify the specification of algorithms that require non-local information, including name resolution. Door Attribute Grammars [8,9] extend attribute grammars with reference attributes and door objects which facilitate analysis of object-oriented languages. A similar but more general extension is shown in [21]. Reference Attributed Grammars [10] are a generalization of door attribute grammars where the door objects are removed. In [26], an incremental evaluator for reference attributed grammars is shown which is used by the JastAdd [4] meta-compilation system. JastAdd also adds parametrized attributes which allow attributes to be parametrized, forming a mapping. The approach is compared to traditional attribute grammars in [27] and shows that the use of reference attribute grammars reduces the number of affected attributes for name and type analysis significantly.

Our approach has two mechanisms similar to reference attributes. First, we can refer to binding instances by URIs and can look up their properties in the semantic index. Second, properties and tasks can refer to arbitrary other tasks. Reference attribute grammars discover dependencies during evaluation. We detect inter-task dependencies after collection. This already helps in establishing an ordering for evaluation. Only dependencies from properties to tasks are discovered during evaluation. Similar to ordinary attribute grammars, reference attribute grammars also do not provide a solution for aggregate attributes.

Some attribute grammar formalisms take a functional approach to evaluation. In [19] attributes are evaluated using visit-functions with memoization. A more general extension to attribute grammars is the higher order attribute grammar [28,25] for which an incremental evaluator is presented in [29]. Similar to this approach, our approach employs a global cache and uses hash consing to efficiently share tasks and to make look-ups into the cache extremely fast. Tasks can also be seen as functions, but the evaluation strategy differs. Visit-functions are still applied on subtrees while tasks are completely separated from the tree.

Other Approaches. Pregmatic [1] is an incremental program environment generator that uses extended affix grammars for specification. It uses an incremental propagation algorithm similar to the one used by attribute grammar approaches which were discussed earlier. Instead of separating parsing and semantic analysis, all evaluation is done during parse-time which differs significantly from our parse, collect and evaluate approach. Incremental Rewriting [18] describes efficient algorithms for incrementally rewriting programs based on algebraic specifications. An algorithm for incrementally evaluating functions on aggregated values is also shown. The approach does not support non-local dependencies, making specification of name binding less intuitive as it requires copying of information.

8   Conclusion

We have proposed an approach for incremental name and type analysis in two phases, collection and deferred evaluation of analysis tasks. The collection is instantiated with language-specific name binding and type rules and incremental on file level. Unchanged files are neither re-parsed nor re-traversed. The evaluation phase is incremental on task level. When a file changes, all tasks that are affected by this change are reevaluated. This might include dependent tasks from other files.

Tasks execute low-level instructions for name resolution and type analysis, and can form a basis for the definition of declarative meta-languages at a higher level of abstraction. For example, we map declarative name binding and scope rules expressed in NaBL to an instantiation of the presented approach. We implemented the approach as part of the Spoofax language workbench. It frees language engineers from the burden of manually implementing incremental analysis. We applied the implementation to WebDSL and empirical evaluation has shown this analysis to be responsive to changes in analyzed programs and suitable to the interactive requirements of an IDE setting.

Acknowledgements. This research was supported by NWO/EW Free Competition Project 612.001.114 (Deep Integration of Domain-Specific Languages) and by a research grant from Oracle Labs. We would like to thank Lennart Kats for his contribution to the start of NaBL and to Spoofax' incremental analysis project. We would also like to thank Karl Kalleberg for valuable discussions on the interpretation of name binding and scoping rules.

References

1. van den Brand, M.G.J.: PREGMATIC - a generator for incremental programming environments. Ph.D. thesis, University Nijmegen (1992)
2. Bravenboer, M., Kalleberg, K.T., Vermaas, R., Visser, E.: Stratego/XT 0.17. A language and toolset for program transformation. SCP 72(1-2), 52–70 (2008)
3. Demers, A.J., Reps, T.W., Teitelbaum, T.: Incremental evaluation for attribute grammars with application to syntax-directed editors. In: POPL, pp. 105–116 (1981)
4. Ekman, T., Hedin, G.: The jastadd system - modular extensible compiler construction. SCP 69(1-3), 14–26 (2007)
5. Erdweg, S., Rendel, T., Kástner, C., Ostermann, K.: Sugarj: Library-based syntactic language extensibility. In: OOPSLA, pp. 391–406 (2011)
6. Eysholdt, M., Behrens, H.: Xtext: implement your language faster than the quick and dirty way. In: OOPSLA, pp. 307–309 (2010)
7. Groenewegen, D.M., Hemel, Z., Kats, L.C.L., Visser, E.: WebDSL: a domain-specific language for dynamic web applications. In: OOPSLA, pp. 779–780 (2008)
8. Hedin, G.: Incremental static-semantic analysis for object-oriented languages using door attribute grammars. In: SAGA, pp. 374–379 (1991)
9. Hedin, G.: Incremental Semantic Analysis. Ph.D. thesis (1992)
10. Hedin, G.: Reference attributed grammars. Informatica SI 24(3) (2000)
11. Hemel, Z., Groenewegen, D.M., Kats, L.C.L., Visser, E.: Static consistency checking of web applications with WebDSL. JSC 46(2), 150–182 (2011)
12. Johnson, G.F., Fischer, C.N.: A meta-language and system for nonlocal incremental attribute evaluation in language-based editors. In: POPL, pp. 141–151 (1985)
13. Kastens, U.: Ordered attributed grammars. ACTA 13, 229–256 (1980)
14. Kats, L.C.L., Visser, E.: The Spoofax language workbench: rules for declarative specification of languages and IDEs. In: OOPSLA, pp. 444–463 (2010)
15. Knuth, D.E.: Semantics of context-free languages. MST 2(2), 127–145 (1968)
16. Konat, G., Kats, L., Wachsmuth, G., Visser, E.: Declarative name binding and scope rules. In: Czarnecki, K., Hedin, G. (eds.) SLE 2012. LNCS, vol. 7745, pp. 311–331. Springer, Heidelberg (2013)
17. Krishnamurthi, S.: Programming Languages: Application and Interpretation (2007)
18. Meulen, E.A.V.D.: Incremental Rewriting. Ph.D. thesis, University of Amsterdam (1994)
19. Pennings, M.C.: Generating incremental attribute evaluators. Ph.D. thesis, Computer Science, Utrecht University (November 1994)
20. Pierce, B.C.: Types and Programming Languages. MIT Press, Cambridge (2002)
21. Poetzsch-Heffter, A.: Programming language specification and prototyping using the max system. In: PLIPL, pp. 137–150 (1993)
22. Reps, T.W.: Optimal-time incremental semantic analysis for syntax-directed editors. In: POPL, pp. 169–176 (1982)
23. Reps, T.W.: Generating language-based environments. Massachusetts Institute of Technology, Cambridge (1984)
24. Reps, T.W., Teitelbaum, T., Demers, A.J.: Incremental context-dependent analysis for language-based editors. TOPLAS 5(3), 449–477 (1983)
25. Swierstra, S.D., Vogt, H.: Higher order attribute grammars. In: SAGA. pp. 256–296 (1991)

26. Söderberg, E.: Contributions to the Construction of Extensible Semantic Editors. Ph.D. thesis (2012)
27. Söderberg, E., Hedin, G.: A comparative study of incremental attribute grammar solutions to name resolution (2012)
28. Vogt, H., Swierstra, S.D., Kuiper, M.F.: Higher-order attribute grammars. In: PLDI, pp. 131–145 (1989)
29. Vogt, H., Swierstra, S.D., Kuiper, M.F.: Efficient incremental evaluation of higher order attribute grammars. In: PLIPL, pp. 231–242 (1991)
30. Völter, M., Solomatov, K.: Language modularization and composition with projectional language workbenches illustrated with MPS. In: SLE (2010)
31. Yeh, D.: On incremental evaluation of ordered attribute grammars. BIT 23(3), 308–320 (1983)
32. Yeh, D., Kastens, U.: Improvements of an incremental evaluation algorithm for ordered attribute grammars. SIGPLAN 23(12), 45–50 (1988)

A Generic Framework for Symbolic Execution

Andrei Arusoaie[1], Dorel Lucanu[1], and Vlad Rusu[2]

[1] Faculty of Computer Science, Alexandru Ioan Cuza University, Iaşi, Romania
andrei.arusoaie@gmail.com, dlucanu@info.uaic.ro
[2] Inria Lille Nord Europe, France
vlad.rusu@inria.fr

Abstract. We propose a language-independent symbolic execution framework for languages endowed with a formal operational semantics based on term rewriting. Starting from a given definition of a language, a new language definition is automatically generated, which has the same syntax as the original one but whose semantics extends data domains with symbolic values and adapts semantical rules to deal with these values. Then, the symbolic execution of concrete programs is the execution of programs with the new symbolic semantics, on symbolic input data. We prove that the symbolic execution thus defined has the properties naturally expected from it. A prototype implementation of our approach was developed in the $\mathbb{K}$ Framework. We demonstrate the genericity of our tool by instantiating it on several languages, and show how it can be used for the symbolic execution and model checking of several programs.

1 Introduction

Symbolic execution is a well-known program analysis technique introduced in 1976 by James C. King [12]. Since then, it has proved its usefulness for testing, verifying, and debugging programs. Symbolic execution consists in executing programs with symbolic inputs, instead of concrete ones, and it involves the processing of expressions involving symbolic values [19]. The main advantage of symbolic execution is that it allows reasoning about multiple concrete executions of a program, and its main disadvantage is the state-space explosion determined by decision statements and loops. Recently, the technique has found renewed interest in the formal-methods community due to new algorithmic developments and progress in decision procedures. Current applications of symbolic execution are diverse and include automated test input generation [13], [27], invariant detection [18], model checking [11], and proving program correctness [26,7]. We believe there is a need for a formal and generic approach to symbolic execution, on top of which language-independent program analysis tools can be developed.

The *state* of a symbolic program execution typically contains the next statement to be executed, symbolic values of program variables, and the *path condition*, which constrains past and present values of the variables (i.e., constraints on the symbolic values are accumulated on the path taken by the execution for reaching the current instruction). The states, and the transitions between them induced by the program instructions generate a *symbolic execution tree*. When

M. Erwig, R.F. Paige, and E. Van Wyk (Eds.): SLE 2013, LNCS 8225, pp. 281–301, 2013.

the control flow of a program is determined by symbolic values (e.g., the next instruction to be executed is a conditional statement, whose Boolean condition depends on symbolic values) then there is a branching in the tree. The path condition can then be used to distinguish between different branches.

Our Contribution. The main contribution of the paper is a formal, language-independent theory and tool for symbolic execution, based on a language's operational semantics defined by term-rewriting[1]. To our best knowledge, our framework is the only one supporting automatic derivation of the symbolic semantics of languages from their concrete semantics. On the theoretical side, we introduce a transformation between languages such that the symbolic execution in the source language is defined as the concrete execution in the transformed language. We prove that the symbolic execution thus defined has the following properties, which ensure that it is related to concrete program execution in a natural way:

Coverage: to every concrete execution there corresponds a feasible symbolic one;

Precision: to every feasible symbolic execution there corresponds a concrete one;

where two executions are said to be corresponding if they take the same path, and a symbolic execution is feasible if the path conditions along it are satisfiable.

On the practical side, we present a prototype implementation of our approach in $\mathbb{K}$ [20], a framework dedicated to defining formal operational semantics of languages. Developing our tool within the $\mathbb{K}$ framework enables us to benefit from the many existing language definitions written in $\mathbb{K}$. We briefly describe our implementation as a language-engineering tool, and demonstrate its genericity by instantiating it on several nontrivial languages defined in $\mathbb{K}$. We emphasize that the tool uses the $\mathbb{K}$ language-definitions as they are, without requiring modifications, and automatically harnesses them for symbolic execution. The examples illustrate program execution as well as Linear Temporal Logic model checking and bounded model checking using our tool.

We note that the proposed approach deals with symbolic data, not with symbolic code. Hence, it is restricted to languages in which data and code are distinct entities that cannot be mixed. This excludes, for example, higher-order functional languages in which code can be passed as data between functions.

Related Work. There is a substantial number of tools performing symbolic execution available in the literature. However, most of them have been developed for specific programming languages and are based on informal semantics. Here we mention some of them that are strongly related to our approach.

Java PathFinder [28] is a complex symbolic execution tool which uses a model checker to explore different symbolic execution paths. The approach is applied to Java programs and it can handle recursive input data structures, arrays, preconditions, and multithreading. Java PathFinder can access several Satisfiability Modulo Theories (SMT) solvers and the user can also choose between

---

[1] Most existing operational semantics styles (small-step, big-step, reduction with evaluation contexts, ...) have been shown to be representable in this way in [25].

multiple decision procedures. We have instantiated our generic approach to a formal definition of Java defined in the $\mathbb{K}$ framework, and have performed symbolic execution on several programs. This shows that our tool can tackle real languages.

Another approach consists in combining concrete and symbolic execution, also known as *concolic* execution. First, some concrete values given as input determine an execution path. When the program encounters a decision point, the paths not taken by concrete execution are explored symbolically. This type of analysis has been implemented by several tools: DART [9], CUTE [23], EXE [4], PEX [5]. We note that our approach allows mixed concrete/symbolic execution; it can be the basis for language-independent implementations of concolic execution.

Symbolic execution has initially been used in automated test generation [12]. It can also be used for proving program correctness. There are several tools (e.g. Smallfoot [3]) which use symbolic execution together with separation logic to prove Hoare triples. There are also approaches that attempt to automatically detect invariants in programs([18], [22]). Another useful application of symbolic execution is the static detection of runtime errors. The main idea is to perform symbolic execution on a program until a state is reached where an error occurs, e.g., null-pointer dereference or division by zero. We show that the implementation prototype we developed is also suitable for such static code analyses.

Another body of related work is symbolic execution in term-rewriting systems. The technique called *narrowing*, initially used for solving equation systems in abstract datatypes, has been extended for solving reachability problems in term-rewriting systems and has sucessfully been applied to the analysis of security protocols [17]. Such analyses rely on powerful unification-modulo-theories algorithms [8], which work well for security protocols since there are unification algorithms modulo the theories involved there (exclusive-or, ...). This is not always the case for programming languages with arbitrarily complex datatypes.

Regarding performances, our generic and formal tool is, quite understandably, not in the same league as existing pragmatic tools, which are dedicated to specific languages (e.g. Java PathFinder for Java, PEX for C#, KLEE for LLVM) and are focused on specific applications of symbolic execution. Our purpose is to automatically generate, from a formal definition of any language, a symbolic semantics capable of symbolically executing programs in that language, and to provide users with means for building their applications on top of our tool. For instance, in order to generate tests for programs, the only thing that has to be added to our framework is to request models of path conditions using, e.g., SMT solvers. Formal verification of programs based on deductive methods and predicate abstractions are also currently being built on top of our tool.

Structure of the Paper. Section 2 introduces our running example (the simple imperative language IMP) and its definition in $\mathbb{K}$. Section 3 introduces a framework for language definitions, making our approach generic in both the language-definition framework and the language being defined; $\mathbb{K}$ and IMP are just instances for the former and latter, respectively. Section 4 shows how the definition of a language $\mathcal{L}$ can be automatically transformed into the definition

$Id ::=$ domain of identifiers

$Int ::=$ domain of integer numbers (including operations)

$Bool ::=$ domain of boolean constants (including operations)

$AExp :: = Int \quad\quad | \; AExp \; / \; AExp$ [strict]

$\quad\quad | \; Id \quad\quad\quad | \; AExp * AExp$ [strict]

$\quad\quad | \; (AExp) \;\; | \; AExp + AExp$ [strict]

$BExp :: = Bool$

$\quad\quad | \; (BExp) \quad\quad\quad\quad | \; AExp \; \texttt{<=} \; AExp$ [strict]

$\quad\quad | \; \texttt{not} \; BExp$ [strict] $\;\; | \; BExp \; \texttt{and} \; BExp$ [strict(1)]

$Stmt :: = \texttt{skip} \; | \; \{ \; Stmt \; \} \; | \; Stmt \; ; \; Stmt \; | \; Id := AExp$

$\quad\quad | \; \texttt{while} \; BExp \; \texttt{do} \; Stmt$

$\quad\quad | \; \texttt{if} \; BExp \; \texttt{then} \; Stmt \; \texttt{else} \; Stmt$ [strict(1)]

$Code ::= Id \; | \; Int \; | \; Bool \; | \; AExp \; | \; BExp \; | \; Stmt \; | \; Code \curvearrowright Code$

Fig. 1. $\mathbb{K}$ Syntax of IMP

of a language $\mathcal{L}^s$ by extending the data of $\mathcal{L}$ with symbolic values, and by providing the semantical rules of $\mathcal{L}$ with means to process those values. Section 5 deals with the symbolic semantics and with its relation to the concrete semantics, establishing the coverage and precision results stated in this introduction. Section 6 describes an implementation of our approach in the $\mathbb{K}$ framework and show how it is automatically instantiated to nontrivial languages defined in $\mathbb{K}$. An Appendix (for the reviewers only, not to be included in the final version) contains more detailed descriptions of the examples and of the tool.

2 A Simple Imperative Language and Its Definition in $\mathbb{K}$

Our running example is IMP, a simple imperative language intensively used in research papers. The syntax of IMP is described in Figure 1 and is mostly self-explainatory since it uses a BNF notation. The statements of the language are either assignments, *if* statements, *while* loops, *skip* (i.e., the empty statement), or blocks of statements. The attribute *strict* in some production rules means the arguments of the annotated expression/statement are evaluated before the expression/statement itself. If *strict* is followed by a list of natural numbers then it only concerns the arguments whose positions are present in the list.

The operational semantics of IMP is given as a set of (possibly conditional) rewrite rules. The terms to which rules are applied are called *configurations*. Configurations typically contain the

$Cfg ::= \langle\langle Code \rangle_\texttt{k} \langle Map_{Id,Int} \rangle_\texttt{env} \rangle_\texttt{cfg}$

Fig. 2. $\mathbb{K}$ Configuration of IMP

program to be executed, together with any additional information required for program execution. The structure of a configuration depends on the language being defined; for IMP, it consists only of the program code to be executed and an environment mapping variables to values.

Configurations are written in $\mathbb{K}$ as nested structures of *cells*: for IMP this consists of a top cell **cfg**, having a subcell k containing the code and a subcell

$$\langle\langle I_1 + I_2 \cdots\rangle_k \cdots\rangle_{cfg} \Rightarrow \langle\langle I_1 +_{Int} I_2 \cdots\rangle_k \cdots\rangle_{cfg}$$

$$\langle\langle I_1 * I_2 \cdots\rangle_k \cdots\rangle_{cfg} \Rightarrow \langle\langle I_1 *_{Int} I_2 \cdots\rangle_k \cdots\rangle_{cfg}$$

$$\langle\langle I_1 / I_2 \cdots\rangle_k \cdots\rangle_{cfg} \wedge I_2 \neq_{Int} 0 \Rightarrow \langle\langle I_1 /_{Int} I_2 \cdots\rangle_k \cdots\rangle_{cfg}$$

$$\langle\langle I_1 \mathrel{<=} I_2 \cdots\rangle_k \cdots\rangle_{cfg} \Rightarrow \langle\langle I_1 \leq_{Int} I_2 \cdots\rangle_k \cdots\rangle_{cfg}$$

$$\langle\langle true \text{ and } B \cdots\rangle_k \cdots\rangle_{cfg} \Rightarrow \langle\langle B \cdots\rangle_k \cdots\rangle_{cfg}$$

$$\langle\langle false \text{ and } B \cdots\rangle_k \cdots\rangle_{cfg} \Rightarrow \langle\langle false \cdots\rangle_k \cdots\rangle_{cfg}$$

$$\langle\langle \text{not } B \cdots\rangle_k \cdots\rangle_{cfg} \Rightarrow \langle\langle \neg B \cdots\rangle_k \cdots\rangle_{cfg}$$

$$\langle\langle \text{skip} \cdots\rangle_k \cdots\rangle_{cfg} \Rightarrow \langle\langle \cdots\rangle_k \cdots\rangle_{cfg}$$

$$\langle\langle S_1; S_2 \cdots\rangle_k \cdots\rangle_{cfg} \Rightarrow \langle\langle S_1 \curvearrowright S_2 \cdots\rangle_k \cdots\rangle_{cfg}$$

$$\langle\langle \{ S \} \cdots\rangle_k \cdots\rangle_{cfg} \Rightarrow \langle\langle S \cdots\rangle_k \cdots\rangle_{cfg}$$

$$\langle\langle \text{if } true \text{ then } S_1 \text{ else } S_2 \cdots\rangle_k \cdots\rangle_{cfg} \Rightarrow \langle\langle S_1\rangle_k \cdots\rangle_{cfg}$$

$$\langle\langle \text{if } false \text{ then } S_1 \text{ else } S_2\rangle_k \cdots\rangle_{cfg} \Rightarrow \langle\langle S_2\rangle_k \cdots\rangle_{cfg}$$

$$\langle\langle \text{while } B \text{ do } S \cdots\rangle_k \cdots\rangle_{cfg} \Rightarrow$$
$$\langle\langle \text{if } B \text{ then}\{ S \text{ ;while } B \text{ do } S \}\text{else skip} \cdots\rangle_k \cdots\rangle_{cfg}$$

$$\langle\langle X \cdots\rangle_k \langle M\rangle_{env}\rangle_{cfg} \Rightarrow \langle\langle lookup(X, M) \cdots\rangle_k \langle M\rangle_{env}\rangle_{cfg}$$

$$\langle\langle X := I \cdots\rangle_k \langle M\rangle_{env}\rangle_{cfg} \Rightarrow \langle\langle \cdots\rangle_k \langle update(X, M, I)\rangle_{env}\rangle_{cfg}$$

Fig. 3. $\mathbb{K}$ Semantics of IMP

env containing the environment (cf. Figure 2). The code inside the k cell is represented as a list of computation tasks $C_1 \curvearrowright C_2 \curvearrowright \ldots$ to be executed in the given order. Computation tasks are typically statements and expressions. The environment in the env cell is a set of bindings of identifiers to values, e.g., $a \mapsto 3, b \mapsto 1$.

The semantics of IMP is shown in Figure 3. Each rewrite rule from the semantics specifies how the configuration evolves when the first computation task from the k cell is executed. Dots in a cell mean that the rest of the cell remains unchanged. Most syntactical constructions require only one semantical rule. The exceptions are the conjunction operation and the if statement, which have Boolean arguments and require two rules each (one rule per Boolean value).

In addition to the rules shown in Figure 3 the semantics of IMP includes additional rules induced by the *strict* attribute. We show only the case of the if statement, which is strict in the first argument. The evaluation of this argument is achieved by executing the following rules:

$$\langle\langle \text{if } BE \text{ then } S_1 \text{ else } S_2 \curvearrowright C\rangle_k \cdots\rangle_{cfg} \Rightarrow \langle\langle BE \curvearrowright \text{if } \square \text{ then } S_1 \text{ else } S_2 \curvearrowright C\rangle_k \cdots\rangle_{cfg}$$

$$\langle\langle B \curvearrowright \text{if } \square \text{ then } S_1 \text{ else } S_2 \curvearrowright C\rangle_k \cdots\rangle_{cfg} \Rightarrow \langle\langle \text{if } B \text{ then } S_1 \text{ else } S_2 \curvearrowright C\rangle_k \cdots\rangle_{cfg}$$

Here, BE ranges over $BExp \setminus \{false, true\}$, B ranges over the Boolean values $\{false, true\}$, and $\square$ is a special variable, destined to receive the value of BE once it is computed, typically, by the other rules in the semantics.

3 The Ingredients of a Language Definition

In this section we identify the ingredients of language definitions in an algebraic and term-rewriting setting. The concepts are explained on the $\mathbb{K}$ definition of IMP. We assume the reader is familiar with the basics of algebraic specification and rewriting. A language $\mathcal{L}$ can be defined as a triple $(\Sigma, \mathcal{T}, \mathcal{S})$, consisting of:

1. A many-sorted algebraic signature Σ, which includes at least a sort Cfg for *configurations* and a sort $Bool$ for *constraint formulas*. For the sake of presentation, we assume in this paper that the constraint formulas are Boolean terms built with a subsignature $\Sigma^{\mathsf{Bool}} \subseteq \Sigma$ including the boolean constants and operations. Σ may also include other subsignatures for other data sorts, depending on the language $\mathcal{L}$ (e.g., integers, identifiers, lists, maps, . . .). Let Σ^{Data} denote the subsignature of Σ consisting of all *data* sorts and their operations. We assume that the sort Cfg and the syntax of $\mathcal{L}$ are not data, i.e., they are defined in $\Sigma \setminus \Sigma^{\mathsf{Data}}$. Let T_Σ denote the Σ-algebra of ground terms and $T_{\Sigma,s}$ denote the set of ground terms of sort s. Given a sort-wise infinite set of variables Var, let $T_\Sigma(Var)$ denote the free Σ-algebra of terms with variables, $T_{\Sigma,s}(Var)$ denote the set of terms of sort s with variables, and $var(t)$ denote the set of variables occurring in the term t.

2. A Σ^{Data}-model $\mathcal{D}$, which interprets the data sorts and operations. We assume that the model $\mathcal{D}$ is *reachable*, i.e., for all $d \in \mathcal{D}$ there exists a term $t \in T_{\Sigma^{\mathsf{Data}}}$ such that $d = \mathcal{D}_t$. Let $\mathcal{T} \triangleq \mathcal{T}(\mathcal{D})$ denote the free Σ-model generated by $\mathcal{D}$, i.e., $\mathcal{T}$ interprets the non-data sorts as ground terms over the signature

$$(\Sigma \setminus \Sigma^{\mathsf{Data}}) \cup \bigcup_{d \in Data} \mathcal{D}_d \tag{1}$$

where $\mathcal{D}_d$ denotes the carrier set of the sort d in the algebra $\mathcal{D}$, and the elements of $\mathcal{D}_d$ are added to the signature $\Sigma \setminus \Sigma^{\mathsf{Data}}$ as constants of sort d. The satisfaction relation $\rho \models b$ between valuations ρ and constraint formulas $b \in T_{\Sigma,Bool}(Var)$ is defined by $\rho \models b$ iff $\rho(b) = \mathcal{D}_{true}$. For simplicity, we often write in the sequel $true, false, 0, 1 \ldots$ instead of $\mathcal{D}_{true}, \mathcal{D}_{false}, \mathcal{D}_0, \mathcal{D}_1, \ldots$

3. A set $\mathcal{S}$ of rewrite rules. Each rule is a pair of the form $l \wedge b \Rightarrow r$, where $l, r \in T_{\Sigma,Cfg}(Var)$ are the rule's *left-hand-side* and the *right-hand-side*, respectively, and $b \in T_{\Sigma,Bool}(Var)$ is the *condition*. The formal definitions for rules and for the transition system defined by them are given below.

We explain these concepts on IMP. Nonterminals in the syntax $(Id, Int, Bool, \ldots)$ are sorts in Σ. Each production from the syntax defines an operation in Σ; e.g, the production $AExp ::= AExp + AExp$ defines the operation $\_+\_ : AExp \times AExp \to AExp$. These operations define the constructors of the result sort. For the sort Cfg, the only constructor is $\langle\langle \_ \rangle_\mathsf{k} \langle \_ \rangle_\mathsf{env}\rangle_\mathsf{cfg} : Code \times Map_{Id,Int} \to Cfg$. The expression $\langle\langle X := I \curvearrowright C \rangle_\mathsf{k}\langle X \mapsto 0 \; Env\rangle_\mathsf{env}\rangle_\mathsf{cfg}$ is a term of $T_{Cfg}(Var)$, where X is a variable of sort Id, I is a variable of sort Int, C is a variable of sort $Code$ (the rest of the computation), and Env is a variable of sort $Map_{Id,Int}$ (the rest of the environment). The data algebra $\mathcal{D}$ interprets Int as the set of integers, the operations like $+_{Int}$ (cf. Figure 3) as the corresponding usual operation on integers, $Bool$ as the set of Boolean values $\{false, true\}$, the operation like $\wedge$ as the usual Boolean operations, the sort $Map_{Id,Int}$ as the set of maps $X \mapsto I$, where X ranges over identifiers Id and I over the integers. The value of an identifier X is an environment M is $lookup(X, M)$, and the environment M, updated by binding an identifier X to a value I, is $update(X, M, I)$. Here, $lookup()$ and $update()$ are operations in a signature $\Sigma^{\mathsf{Map}} \subseteq \Sigma^{\mathsf{Data}}$ of maps. The other sorts, $AExp$, $BExp$, $Stmt$, and $Code$, are interpreted in the algebra $\mathcal{T}$ as ground terms over a modification of the form (1) of the signature Σ, in which data subterms are replaced by their interpretations in $\mathcal{D}$. For instance, the term if 1 $>_{Int}$ 0 then skip else skip is interpreted as if $\mathcal{D}_{true}$ then skip else skip. We now formally introduce the notions required for defining semantical rules.

Definition 1 (Pattern [21]). *A pattern is an expression of the form $\pi \wedge b$, where $\pi \in T_{\Sigma,Cfg}(Var)$ is a basic pattern and $b \in T_{\Sigma,Bool}(Var)$. If $\gamma \in T_{Cfg}$ and $\rho : Var \to \mathcal{T}$ we write $(\gamma, \rho) \models \pi \wedge b$ for $\gamma = \rho(\pi)$ and $\rho \models b$.*

A basic pattern π defines a set of (concrete) configurations, and the condition b gives additional constraints these configurations must satisfy.

Remark 1. The above definition is a particular case of a definition in [21]. There, a pattern is a first-order logic formula with configuration terms as sub-formulas. In this paper we keep the conjunction notation from first-order logic but separate basic patterns from constraints. Note that first-order formulas can be encoded as terms of sort *Bool*, where the quantifiers become constructors. The satisfaction relation $\models$ is then defined, for such terms, like the usual FOL satisfaction.

We identify basic patterns π with patterns $\pi \wedge true$. Sample patterns are $\langle\langle I_1 + I_2 \curvearrowright C\rangle_{\mathsf{k}}\langle Env\rangle_{\mathsf{env}}\rangle_{\mathsf{cfg}}$ and $\langle\langle I_1 / I_2 \curvearrowright C\rangle_{\mathsf{k}}\langle Env\rangle_{\mathsf{env}}\rangle_{\mathsf{cfg}} \wedge I_2 \neq_{Int} 0$.

Definition 2 (Rule, Transition System). *A rule is a pair of patterns of the form $l \wedge b \Rightarrow r$ (note that r is in fact the pattern $r \wedge true$). Any set S of rules defines a labelled transition system $(\mathcal{T}_{Cfg}, \Rightarrow_S)$ such that $\gamma \overset{\alpha}{\Longrightarrow}_S \gamma'$ iff there exist $\alpha \triangleq (l \wedge b \Rightarrow r) \in S$ and $\rho : Var \to \mathcal{T}$ such that $(\gamma, \rho) \models l \wedge b$ and $(\gamma', \rho) \models r$.*

4   Symbolic Semantics by Language Transformation

In this section we show how a new definition $(\Sigma^s, \mathcal{T}^s, S^s)$ of a language $\mathcal{L}^s$ is automatically generated from a given a definition $(\Sigma, \mathcal{T}, S)$ of a language $\mathcal{L}$. The new language $\mathcal{L}^s$ has the same syntax as $\mathcal{L}$, but its semantics extends $\mathcal{L}$'s data domains with symbolic values and adapts the semantical rules of $\mathcal{L}$ to deal with the new values. Then, the symbolic execution of $\mathcal{L}$ programs is the concrete execution of the corresponding $\mathcal{L}^s$ programs on symbolic input data, i.e., the application of the rewrite rules in the semantics of $\mathcal{L}^s$. Building the definition of $\mathcal{L}^s$ amounts to:

1. extending the signature Σ to a symbolic signature Σ^s;
2. extending the Σ-algebra $\mathcal{T}$ to a Σ^s-algebra $\mathcal{T}^s$;
3. turning the concrete rules S into symbolic rules S^s.

We then obtain the symbolic transition system $(\mathcal{T}^s_{Cfg^s}, \Rightarrow^{\mathcal{T}^s}_{S^s})$ by using Definitions 1,2 for $\mathcal{L}^s$, just like the transition system $(\mathcal{T}_{Cfg}, \Rightarrow^{\mathcal{T}}_S)$ was defined for $\mathcal{L}$. Section 5 deals with the relations between the two transition systems.

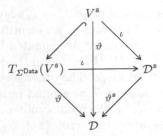

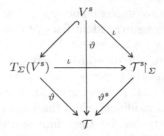

Fig. 4. Diagram Characterising Data Symbolic Domain $\mathcal{D}^s$

Fig. 5. Lifting Diagram in Fig. 4 to from Data Domain $\mathcal{D}$ to $\mathcal{T}^s|_\Sigma$

4.1   Extending the Signature Σ to a Symbolic Signature Σ^s

The signature Σ^s extends Σ with a sort Cfg^s and a constructor $\langle \_, \_ \rangle : Cfg \times Bool \to Cfg^s$, which builds symbolic configurations as pairs of configurations over symbolic data and Booleans term denoting path conditions.

Example 1. For the IMP example we enrich the configuration with a new cell:

$$Cfg^s ::= \langle\langle Code \rangle_k \langle Map_{Id,Int} \rangle_{env} \langle Bool \rangle_{cnd} \rangle_{cfg}$$

where the new cell cnd includes a formula meant to express the path condition.

4.2   Extending the Model $\mathcal{T}$ to a Symbolic Model $\mathcal{T}^s$

We first deal with the *symbolic domain* $\mathcal{D}^s$, a Σ^{Data}-algebra with the following properties:

1. The Σ^{Data}-algebra $\mathcal{D}$ is a sub-algebra of $\mathcal{D}^s$.
2. We assume an infinite, sort-wise set of *symbolic values* V^s of the data sorts, disjoint from Var and from symbols in Σ, and assume that there is an injection $\iota : V^s \to \mathcal{D}^s$ such that for any valuation $\vartheta : V^s \to \mathcal{D}$ there exists a unique algebra morphism $\vartheta^s : \mathcal{D}^s \to \mathcal{D}$ such that the diagram in Figure 4 commutes. The diagram essentially says that the interpretation of terms like $a^s +_{Int} b^s$ via ϑ is the same as that given by the composition of ι with ϑ^s.
3. The satisfaction relation $\models$ is extended to constraint formulas $\phi^s \in \mathcal{D}^s_{Bool}$ and valuations $\vartheta : V^s \to \mathcal{D}$ such that $\vartheta \models \phi^s$ iff $\vartheta^s(\phi^s) = \mathcal{D}_{true}$.

For instance, $\mathcal{D}^s$ can be the algebra of ground terms over the signature $\Sigma^{Data}(V^s \cup \mathcal{D})$, or the quotient of this algebra modulo the congruence defined by some set of equations (which can be used in practice as simplification rules).

We leave some freedom in choosing the symbolic domain, to allow the use of decision procedures or other efficient means for handling symbolic artefacts.

By the definition of $\mathcal{T} = \mathcal{T}(\mathcal{D})$, there is a unique Σ-morphism $\mathcal{T} \to \mathcal{T}(\mathcal{D}^s)$. We note that the extended definition $(\Sigma, \mathcal{S}, \mathcal{T}(\mathcal{D}^s))$ is not suitable for symbolic executions because the symbolic values in V^s are constrained by the computations and decisions taken up to that point. This is why we extended the signature to Σ^s, in which the path condition becomes a component of the configuration.

Next, we naturally define the model $\mathcal{T}^s$ as being the free Σ^s-model generated by $\mathcal{D}^s$. Since there is an inclusion signature morphism $\Sigma \hookrightarrow \Sigma^s$, $\mathcal{T}^s$ can also be seen as a Σ-model $\mathcal{T}^s\!\upharpoonright_\Sigma$, where only the interpretations of the symbols from Σ are considered. This allows us to lift up the diagram in Figure 4 at the level of the model $\mathcal{T}^s\!\upharpoonright_\Sigma$ and in particular to define $\vartheta^s : \mathcal{T}^s\!\upharpoonright_\Sigma \to \mathcal{T}$ as the unique function from $\mathcal{T}^s\!\upharpoonright_\Sigma$ to $\mathcal{T}$ that makes the diagram in Figure 5 commute. Furthermore, Σ and Σ^s have the same data sub-signature and $\mathcal{D}$ is a sub-algebra of $\mathcal{D}^s$, hence there is a unique Σ-morphism $\mathcal{T} \to \mathcal{T}^s\!\upharpoonright_\Sigma$. All these properties of the model $\mathcal{T}^s$ show that it is a suitable model for both concrete and symbolic executions.

However, the semantical rules $\mathcal{S}$ still have to be transformed into rules on symbolic configurations including path conditions. Moreover, we must ensure that the transition system defined by the new rules has the properties of coverage and precision with respect to the transition system defined by $(\Sigma, \mathcal{S}, \mathcal{T})$. This requires some transformations of the rules $\mathcal{S}$, to be presented later in the paper.

The following lemma is crucial for obtaining symbolic executions via matching.

Lemma 1 (Semantic Unification is Reduced to Matching). *Let us consider $l \in T_\Sigma(Var)$, $\rho : Var \to \mathcal{T}$, $\pi^s \in \mathcal{T}^s\!\upharpoonright_\Sigma$, $\vartheta : V^s \to \mathcal{T}$ such that l is linear, any data sub term of l is a variable, and $\rho(l) = \vartheta^s(\pi^s)$ (i.e., l and π^s are semantically unifiable in $\mathcal{T}$). Then there is a (symbolic) valuation $\sigma : Var \to \mathcal{T}^s\!\upharpoonright_\Sigma$ such that $\sigma(l) = \pi^s$ and $\vartheta^s(\sigma(x)) = \rho(x)$ for each $x \in Var$.*

Proof. We first prove the slightly weaker property $(\Diamond)$: there exists a valuation $\sigma : var(l) \to \mathcal{T}^s\!\upharpoonright_\Sigma$ such that $\sigma(l) = \pi^s$ and $\vartheta^s(\sigma(x)) = \rho(x)$ for each $x \in var(l)$.

To prove $(\Diamond)$ we proceed by structural induction on l. If l is a variable x, then we take $\sigma(x) = \pi^s$ and the conclusion of the lemma is obviously satisfied. We assume now that $l = f(l_1, \ldots, l_n)$, $n \geq 0$. The result sort of f is a non-data sort by the hypotheses, hence $\mathcal{T}_f(a_1, \ldots, a_n) = f(a_1, \ldots, a_n)$ and $\mathcal{T}_f^s(b_1, \ldots, b_n) = f(b_1, \ldots, b_n)$ by the definition of $\mathcal{T}$ and $\mathcal{T}^s$, respectively. Consequently, $\rho(l) = f(\rho(l_1), \ldots, \rho(l_n))$, $\pi^s = f(\pi_1^s, \ldots, \pi_n^s)$, $\vartheta^s(\pi^s) = f(\vartheta^s(\pi_1^s), \ldots, \vartheta^s(\pi_n^s))$, and $\rho(l_i) = \rho^s(\pi_i^s)$, $i = 1, \ldots, n$, for certain $\pi_1^s, \ldots, \pi_n^s \in \mathcal{T}^s\!\upharpoonright_\Sigma$. Recall that for each sort s in Σ, $(\mathcal{T}^s\!\upharpoonright_\Sigma)_s = \mathcal{T}_s^s$. Each term l_i preserves the properties of l, hence there is σ_i satisfying the conclusion of lemma for l_i and π_i^s, i.e. $\sigma_i(l_i) = \pi_i^s$ and $\rho(x) = \vartheta^s(\sigma_i(x))$ for each $x \in var(l_i)$. Since l is linear, $var(l) = var(l_1) \uplus \ldots \uplus var(l_n)$. It follows we may define $\sigma : var(l) \to \mathcal{T}^s\!\upharpoonright_\Sigma$ such that $\sigma(x) = \sigma_i(x)$ iff $x \in var(l_i)$. We have $\sigma(l) = f(\sigma(l_1), \ldots, \sigma(l_n)) = f(\sigma_1(l_1), \ldots, \sigma_n(l_n)) = f(\pi_1^s, \ldots, \pi_n^s) = \pi^s$. The property $\rho(x) = \vartheta^s(\sigma(x))$ for each $x \in var(l)$ is inherited from σ_i.

The prove the lemma, we need to extend the valuation σ to Var such that $\vartheta^s(\sigma(x)) = \rho(x)$ for all $x \in Var$, using the reachability of the data domain $\mathcal{D}$:

- first, we prove that the function $\vartheta^s : \mathcal{T}\!\upharpoonright_\Sigma \to \mathcal{T}$ is surjective. For this, consider any $\tau \in \mathcal{T}$, thus, $\tau \triangleq C[\tau_1, \ldots \tau_n]$ with $\tau_1, \ldots, \tau_n \in \mathcal{D}$ and C a Σ-context, since $\mathcal{T}$ is the free Σ-model generated by $\mathcal{D}$. Since $\mathcal{D}$ is reachable, $\tau_i = \mathcal{D}_{t_i}$ for some $t_i \in T_{\Sigma^{\mathrm{Data}}}$, $i = 1, \ldots, n$. Then, we have $\vartheta^s(\iota(C[t_1, \ldots t_n])) = \vartheta(C[t_1, \ldots t_n])$ per the diagram in Figure 5, and since $C[t_1, \ldots t_n] \in T_\Sigma$ we have $\vartheta(C[t_1, \ldots t_n]) = \mathcal{T}_{C[t_1, \ldots t_n]} = \mathcal{T}_t = \tau$ (as $\vartheta : T_\Sigma(V^s) \to \mathcal{T}$ maps ground terms in $T_\Sigma(\emptyset)$ to their interpretation in $\mathcal{T}$). Thus, for an arbitrary $\tau \in \mathcal{T}$ we found $\mu \triangleq \iota(C[t_1, \ldots t_n])$ satisfying $\vartheta(\mu) = \tau$, i.e., $\vartheta^s : \mathcal{T}\!\upharpoonright_\Sigma \to \mathcal{T}$ is surjective.
- thus, for each $x \in Var \setminus var(l)$, we choose $\sigma(x)$ s.t. $\vartheta^s(\sigma(x)) = \rho(x)$. $\qquad\square$

Definition 3 (Satisfaction Relation for Configurations). *A concrete configuration* $\gamma \in \mathcal{T}_{Cfg}$ *satisfies a symbolic configuration* $\langle \pi^s, \phi^s \rangle \in \mathcal{T}^s_{Cfg^s}$, *written* $\gamma \models \langle \pi^s, \phi^s \rangle$, *if there exists* $\vartheta : V^s \to \mathcal{D}$ *such that* $\gamma = \vartheta^s(\pi^s)$ *and* $\vartheta^s(\phi^s) = true$.

Example 2. Assume b^s is a symbolic value of sort *Bool*. The configuration
$$\gamma \triangleq \langle\langle \text{if } true \text{ then skip else skip}\rangle_k \langle . \rangle_{\text{env}}\rangle_{\text{cfg}}$$
satisfies the symbolic configuration
$$\langle \pi^s, \phi^s \rangle \triangleq \langle\langle \text{if } b^s \text{ then skip else skip}\rangle_k \langle . \rangle_{\text{env}} \langle b^s \rangle_{\text{cnd}}\rangle_{\text{cfg}}$$
thanks to any valuation ϑ that maps b^s to *true*.

4.3   Turning the Concrete Rules $\mathcal{S}$ into Symbolic Rules $\mathcal{S}^s$

We show how to automatically build the symbolic-semantics rules $\mathcal{S}^s$ from the concrete semantics-rules $\mathcal{S}$, by applying the three steps described below.

1. Linearising Rules A rule is (left) linear if any variable occurs at most once in its left-hand side. A nonlinear rule can always be turned into an equivalent linear one, by renaming the variables occurring several times and adding equalities between the renamed variables and the original ones to the rule's condition. For example, the last rule from the original IMP semantics (Fig. 3) could have been written as a nonlinear rule:
$$\langle\langle X \cdots \rangle_k \langle X \mapsto I \cdots \rangle_{\text{env}} \cdots \rangle_{\text{cfg}} \qquad \Rightarrow \langle\langle I \cdots \rangle_k \langle X \mapsto I \cdots \rangle_{\text{env}} \cdots \rangle_{\text{cfg}}$$
To linearise it we just add a new variable, say X', and a condition, $X' = X$:
$$\langle\langle X \cdots \rangle_k \langle X' \mapsto I \cdots \rangle_{\text{env}} \cdots \rangle_{\text{cfg}} \wedge X = X' \Rightarrow \langle\langle I \cdots \rangle_k \langle X \mapsto I \cdots \rangle_{\text{env}} \cdots \rangle_{\text{cfg}}$$

2. Replacing Data Subterms by Variables Let $Dpos(l)$ be the set of positions ω[2] of the term l such that l_ω is a maximal subterm of a data sort. The next step of our rule transformation consists in replacing all the maximal data subterms of l by fresh variables. The purpose of this step is to make rules match any configuration, including the symbolic ones.

Thus, we transform each rule $l \wedge b \Rightarrow r$ into the rule
$$l[l_\omega/X_\omega]_{\omega \in Dpos(l)} \wedge (b \wedge \bigwedge_{\omega \in Dpos(l)}(X_\omega = l_\omega)) \Rightarrow r,$$
where each X_ω is a new variable of the same sort as l_ω.

Example 3. Consider the following rule for *if* from the IMP semantics:
$$\langle\langle \text{if } true \text{ then } S_1 \text{ else } S_2 \cdots \rangle_k \cdots \rangle_{\text{cfg}} \Rightarrow \langle\langle S_1 \cdots \rangle_k \cdots \rangle_{\text{cfg}}$$

We replace the constant *true* with a Boolean variable B, and add the condition $B = true$:
$$\langle\langle \text{if } B \text{ then } S_1 \text{ else } S_2 \cdots \rangle_k \cdots \rangle_{\text{cfg}} \wedge B = true \Rightarrow \langle\langle S_1 \cdots \rangle_k \cdots \rangle_{\text{cfg}}$$

3. Adding Formulas to Configurations and Rules The last transformation step consists in transforming each rule $l \wedge b \Rightarrow r$ in $\mathcal{S}$ obtained after the previous steps, into the following one:
$$\langle l, \psi \rangle \Rightarrow \langle r, \psi \wedge b \rangle \tag{2}$$

---

[2] For the notion of position in a term and other rewriting-related notions, see, e.g., [2].

where $\psi \in Var$ is a fresh variable of sort *Bool* (i.e. it does not occur in the rules $\mathcal{S}$) and $\langle \_, \_ \rangle$ is the pairing operation in Σ^s. This means that when a symbolic transition is performed on a symbolic configuration the current path condition is enriched with the rule's condition.

Example 4. The last rule for if from the (already transformed) IMP semantics is further transformed into the following rule in $\mathcal{S}^s$:

$$\langle\langle \text{if } B \text{ then } S_1 \text{ else } S_2 \cdots\rangle_k \langle\psi\rangle_{\text{cnd}} \cdots\rangle_{\text{cfg}} \Rightarrow \langle\langle S_1 \cdots\rangle_k \langle\psi \wedge (B = true)\rangle_{\text{cnd}} \cdots\rangle_{\text{cfg}}$$

4.4 Defining the Symbolic Transition System

The triple $(\Sigma^s, \mathcal{T}^s, \mathcal{D}^s)$ defines a language $\mathcal{L}^s$. Then, the transition system $(\mathcal{T}^s_{Cfg^s}, \Rightarrow_{\mathcal{S}^s})$ can be defined using Definitions 1 and 2 applied to $\mathcal{L}^s$. For this, we note that both sides of the rules of the form (2) are terms in $T_{\Sigma^s, Cfg^s}(Var)$, thus, according to Definition 1 applied to $\mathcal{L}^s$, they are (basic) patterns of $\mathcal{L}^s$, and then Definition 2 for $\mathcal{L}^s$ gives us the transition system $(\mathcal{T}^s_{Cfg^s}, \Rightarrow_{\mathcal{S}^s})$.

5 Relating the Concrete and Symbolic Semantics of $\mathcal{L}$

We now relate the concrete and symbolic semantics of $\mathcal{L}$, i.e., the transition systems $(\mathcal{T}_{Cfg}, \Rightarrow_{\mathcal{S}}^{\mathcal{T}})$ and $(\mathcal{T}^s_{Cfg^s}, \Rightarrow_{\mathcal{S}^s}^{\mathcal{T}^s})$. We prove certain simulation relations between them and obtain the coverage and precision properties as corollaries.

The next lemma shows that the symbolic transition system forward-simulates the concrete transition system. We denote by $\alpha^s \in \mathcal{S}^s$ the rule obtained by transforming $\alpha \in \mathcal{S}$ (Section 4.3).

Lemma 2. $(\mathcal{T}^s_{Cfg^s}, \Rightarrow_{\mathcal{S}^s})$ *forward simulates* $(\mathcal{T}_{Cfg}, \Rightarrow_{\mathcal{S}})$: *for all configurations* γ, *symbolic configurations* $\langle \pi^s, \phi^s \rangle$ *and rules* $\alpha \in \mathcal{S}$, *if* $\gamma \models \langle \pi^s, \phi^s \rangle$ *and* $\gamma \xRightarrow{\alpha}_{\mathcal{S}} \gamma'$ *then there exists* $\langle \pi'^s, \phi'^s \rangle$ *such that* $\langle \pi^s, \phi^s \rangle \xRightarrow{\alpha^s}_{\mathcal{S}^s} \langle \pi'^s, \phi'^s \rangle$ *and* $\gamma' \models \langle \pi'^s, \phi'^s \rangle$.

Proof. From $\gamma \xRightarrow{\alpha}_{\mathcal{S}} \gamma'$ we obtain $\alpha \triangleq (l \wedge b \Rightarrow r) \in \mathcal{S}$ and $\rho : Var \to \mathcal{T}$ such that $\gamma = \rho(l)$, $\rho \models b$, and $\gamma' = \rho(r)$. Recall that $\alpha^s \triangleq (\langle l, \psi \rangle \Rightarrow \langle r, \psi \wedge b \rangle)$.

From $\gamma \models \langle \pi^s, \phi^s \rangle$ we obtain $\vartheta : V^s \to \mathcal{D}$ such that $\gamma = \vartheta(\pi^s)$ and $\vartheta \models \phi^s$.

Using Lemma 1 we obtain the valuation σ such that $\sigma(l) = \pi^s$ and $\rho(x) = \vartheta(\sigma(x))$ for each $x \in Var$.

We define $\pi'^s \triangleq \sigma(r)$ and $\phi'^s \triangleq \sigma(b) \wedge \phi^s$. Consider the valuation $\sigma[\psi \mapsto \phi^s]$, which behaves like σ on $Var \setminus \{\psi\}$ and maps ψ to ϕ^s.

We prove $\langle \pi^s, \phi^s \rangle \xRightarrow{\alpha^s}_{\mathcal{S}^s} \langle \pi'^s, \phi'^s \rangle$ using the valuation $\sigma[\psi \mapsto \phi^s]$.

- First, $(\sigma[\psi \mapsto \phi^s])(\langle l, \psi \rangle) = \langle \sigma(l), \phi^s \rangle = \langle \pi^s, \phi^s \rangle$, since ψ does not occur in the rule, thus, the left-hand side $\langle l, \psi \rangle$ of the rule α^s matches $\langle \pi^s, \phi^s \rangle$. Second, $\langle \pi'^s, \phi'^s \rangle = \langle \sigma(r), \sigma(b) \wedge \phi^s \rangle = \langle (\sigma[\psi \mapsto \phi^s])(r), (\sigma[\psi \mapsto \phi^s])(\psi \wedge b) \rangle = (\sigma[\psi \mapsto \phi^s])(\langle r, \psi \wedge b \rangle)$. Thus, α^s rewrites $\langle \pi^s, \phi^s \rangle$ to $\langle \pi'^s, \phi'^s \rangle$.

This proves $\langle \pi^s, \phi^s \rangle \xRightarrow{\alpha^s}_{\mathcal{S}^s} \langle \pi'^s, \phi'^s \rangle$. There remains to prove $\gamma' \models \langle \pi'^s, \phi'^s \rangle$.

For this we use the same valuation $\vartheta : V^{s} \to \mathcal{D}$ as above. We have $\vartheta(\pi'^{s}) = \vartheta(\sigma(r))$, which, using Lemma 1, is $\rho(r)$, and the latter equals γ', cf. beginning of the proof. Thus, $\gamma' = \vartheta(\pi'^{s})$.

On the other hand, $\vartheta(\phi'^{s}) = \vartheta(\sigma(b) \wedge \phi^{s}) = \vartheta(\sigma(b)) \wedge \vartheta(\phi^{s}) = \rho(b) \wedge \vartheta(\phi^{s})$. We have:

- $\rho(b) = true$ because we have $\rho \models b$ from the beginning of the proof;
- $\vartheta(\phi^{s}) = true$ because $\vartheta \models \phi^{s}$, also from the beginning of the proof;

which implies $\rho(b) \wedge \vartheta(\phi^{s}) = true$, thus, $\vartheta(\phi'^{s}) = true$, which together with $\gamma' = \vartheta(\pi'^{s})$ proved above implies $\gamma' \models \langle \pi'^{s}, \phi'^{s} \rangle$, which completes the proof. $\square$

For $\beta \triangleq \beta_1 \cdots \beta_n \in \mathcal{S}^*$ we write $\gamma_0 \stackrel{\beta}{\Longrightarrow}_S \gamma_n$ for $\gamma_i \stackrel{\beta_{i+1}}{\Longrightarrow}_S \gamma_{i+1}$ for all $i = 0, \ldots, n-1$, and use a similar notation for sequences of transitions in the symbolic transition system, where we denote β^{s} the sequence $\beta_1^{s} \cdots \beta_n^{s} \in \mathcal{S}^{s,*}$.

We can now state the coverage theorem as a corollary to the above lemma:

Theorem 1 (Coverage). *If $\gamma \stackrel{\beta}{\Longrightarrow}_S \gamma'$ and $\gamma \models \langle \pi^{s}, \phi^{s} \rangle$ then there is a symbolic configuration $\langle \pi'^{s}, \phi'^{s} \rangle$ such that $\gamma' \models \langle \pi'^{s}, \phi'^{s} \rangle$ and $\langle \pi^{s}, \phi^{s} \rangle \stackrel{\beta^{s}}{\Longrightarrow}_{S^s} \langle \pi'^{s}, \phi'^{s} \rangle$*

The coverage theorem says that if a sequence β of rewrite rules can be executed starting in some initial configuration, the corresponding sequence of symbolic rules can be fired as well. That is, if a program can execute a certain control-flow path concretely, then it can also execute that path symbolically.

We would like, naturally, to prove the converse result (precision) based on a simulation result similar to Lemma 2: *for all configurations γ and symbolic configuration $\langle \pi^{s}, \phi^{s} \rangle$, if $\gamma \models \langle \pi^{s}, \phi^{s} \rangle$ and $\langle \pi^{s}, \phi^{s} \rangle \stackrel{\alpha^{s}}{\Longrightarrow}_{S^s} \langle \pi'^{s}, \phi'^{s} \rangle$ then there is a configuration γ' such that $\gamma \stackrel{\alpha}{\Longrightarrow}_S^{\mathcal{T}} \gamma'$ and $\gamma' \models \langle \pi'^{s}, \phi'^{s} \rangle$.* But this is obviously false, since it would imply that ϕ'^{s} is satisfiable, which is not true in general.

Thus, we need another way of proving the precision result. The next lemma says that the concrete semantics backwards-simulates the symbolic one:

Lemma 3. *$(\mathcal{T}_{Cfg}, \Rightarrow_S)$ backward simulates $(\mathcal{T}_{Cfg^s}^{s}, \Rightarrow_{S^s})$: for all configurations γ' and all symbolic configurations $\langle \pi^{s}, \phi^{s} \rangle$ and $\langle \pi'^{s}, \phi'^{s} \rangle$, if $\langle \pi^{s}, \phi^{s} \rangle \stackrel{\alpha^{s}}{\Longrightarrow}_{S^s} \langle \pi'^{s}, \phi'^{s} \rangle$ and $\gamma' \models \langle \pi'^{s}, \phi'^{s} \rangle$ then there exists $\gamma \in \mathcal{T}_{Cfg}$ such that $\gamma \models \langle \pi^{s}, \phi^{s} \rangle$ and $\gamma \stackrel{\alpha}{\Longrightarrow}_S \gamma'$.*

Proof. The transition $\langle \pi^{s}, \phi^{s} \rangle \stackrel{\alpha^{s}}{\Longrightarrow}_{S^s} \langle \pi'^{s}, \phi'^{s} \rangle$ is obtained by applying a symbolic rule $\alpha^{s} \triangleq (\langle l, \psi \rangle \Rightarrow \langle r, \psi \wedge b \rangle) \in \mathcal{S}^{s}$, with some valuation that has the form $(\sigma[\psi \mapsto \phi^{s}]) : Var \to \mathcal{T}^{s}|_{\Sigma}$. Thus, $\sigma(l) = \pi^{s}$, $\pi'^{s} = \sigma(r)$, and $\phi'^{s} = \phi^{s} \wedge \sigma(b)$.

From $\gamma' \models \langle \pi'^{s}, \phi'^{s} \rangle$ we obtain $\vartheta : V^{s} \to \mathcal{T}$ such that $\gamma' = \vartheta^{s}(\pi'^{s}) = \vartheta^{s}(\sigma(r)) = (\vartheta^{s} \circ \sigma)(r)$ and $true = \vartheta^{s}(\phi'^{s}) = \vartheta^{s}(\phi^{s}) \wedge (\vartheta^{s} \circ \sigma)(b)$, thus, $\vartheta^{s}(\phi^{s}) = true$ and $(\vartheta^{s} \circ \sigma)(b) = true$.

Consider also $\rho : Var \to \mathcal{T} \triangleq \vartheta^{s} \circ \sigma$, and let $\gamma \triangleq \rho(l)$. We have:

- on the one hand, $\gamma = \rho(l) = (\vartheta^{s} \circ \sigma)(l) = \vartheta^{s}(\sigma(l)) = \vartheta^{s}(\pi^{s})$, i.e., $\gamma = \vartheta^{s}(\pi^{s})$;

– on the other hand, $\vartheta^s(\phi^s) = true$ was obtained above;

which proves $\gamma \models \langle \pi^s, \phi^s \rangle$. There remains to prove $\gamma \overset{\alpha}{\Longrightarrow}_S \gamma'$. To prove this we consider the rule $\alpha = (l \wedge r \Rightarrow b) \in S$ whose symbolic version is α^s from the beginning of the proof, and the valuation $\rho = \vartheta^s \circ \sigma$ from above. We have:

– $\gamma = \rho(l)$ by definition of γ;
– $\rho(b) = true$, which is just $(\vartheta^s \circ \sigma)(b) = true$ that we obtained above;
– $\gamma' = \rho(r)$, since we obtained above $\gamma' = (\vartheta^s \circ \sigma)(r)$.

This proves $\gamma \overset{\alpha}{\Longrightarrow}_S \gamma'$ and completes the proof.   □

A consequence of this lemma is the *precision* theorem; it says that if a sequence β^s of symbolic rules can be executed starting in some initial symbolic configuration and reaches a satisfiable final symbolic configuration (thus, implicitly, all intermediary path conditions are satisifiable, since the final path condition is logically stronger than all the intermediary ones) then the corresponding sequence of concrete rules can be fired as well.

Theorem 2 (Precision). *If* $\langle \pi^s, \phi^s \rangle \overset{\beta^s}{\Longrightarrow}_{S^s} \langle \pi'^s, \phi'^s \rangle$ *and* $\gamma' \models \langle \pi'^s, \phi'^s \rangle$ *then there exists a configuration* γ *such that* $\gamma \models \langle \pi^s, \phi^s \rangle$ *and* $\gamma \overset{\beta}{\Longrightarrow}_S \gamma'$.

6   Implementation

In this section we present a prototype tool implementing our symbolic execution approach. In Section 6.1 we briefly present our tool and its integration within the $\mathbb{K}$ framework. In Section 6.2 we illustrate the most significant features of the tool by the means of use cases involving nontrivial languages and programs.

6.1   Symbolic Execution within the $\mathbb{K}$ Framework

Our tool is part of $\mathbb{K}$ [20,24], a semantic framework for defining operational semantics of programming languages. In $\mathbb{K}$ the definition of a language, say, $\mathcal{L}$, is compiled into a rewrite theory. Then, the $\mathbb{K}$ runner executes programs in $\mathcal{L}$ by applying the resulting rewrite rules to configurations containing programs.

Our tool follows the same process. The main difference is that our new $\mathbb{K}$ compiler includes the transformations presented in Section 4.3. The effect is that the compiled rewrite theory defines the symbolic semantics of $\mathcal{L}$ instead of its concrete semantics. We note that the symbolic semantics can execute programs with concrete inputs as well. In this case it behaves like the concrete semantics.

The current version of the tool provides symbolic support for some of the most standard $\mathbb{K}$ data types: Booleans, integers, strings, as well as arrays whose size, index, and content can be symbolic. The symbolic semantics is in general nondeterministic: when presented with symbolic inputs, a program can take several paths. Therefore the $\mathbb{K}$ runner can be called with several options: it can execute one nondeterministically chosen path, or all possible paths, up to a given depth; it can also be run in a step-by-step manner. During the execution, the path conditions (which are computed by the symbolic semantics) are checked for satisfiability using the axioms of the symbolic data domains as simplification rules and, possibly, calls to the Z3 SMT solver[6]. For efficiency reasons the SMT solver is called only if the rules add non-trivial formula to path conditions, which cannot be simplified to *true* or *false* by the axioms of the symbolic domains. Users can also fine-tune the amount of calls to the solver in order to achieve a balance between the precision and the execution time of their symbolic execution. There is also an option for displaying the transformed 𝕂 definitions.

The current version of the tool has some limitations, which we are planning to deal with in the future: only data constants, not full data subterms, are replaced with variables, the tool is connected to only one prover (Z3), and it provides only a limited support for building applications based on symbolic execution.

6.2   Use Cases

We show three use cases for our tool: the first one illustrates the execution and LTL model checking for IMP programs extended with I/O instructions, the second one demonstrates the use of symbolic arrays in the SIMPLE language – an extension of IMP with functions, arrays, threads and several other features, and the third one shows symbolic execution in an object-oriented language called KOOL [10]. The SIMPLE and KOOL languages have existed almost as long as the 𝕂 framework and have intensively been used for teaching programming language concepts. Our tool is applied on the current definitions of SIMPLE and KOOL.

IMP with I/O Operations. We first enrich the IMP language (Figure 1) with **read** and **print** operations. This enables the execution of IMP programs with symbolic input data. We then compile the resulting definition by calling the 𝕂 compiler with an option telling it to generate the symbolic semantics of the language by applying the transformations described in Section 4.3.

```
int n, s;
n = read();
s = 0;
while (n > 0) {
    s = s + n;
    n = n - 1;
}
print("Sum = ", s, "\n");
```

```
int k, a, x;
a = read();
x = a;
while (x > 1) {
    x = x / 2;
    k = k + 1;
    L : {}
}
```

Fig. 6. sum.imp   **Fig. 7.** log.imp

Programs such as sum.imp shown in Figure 6 can now be run with the 𝕂 runner in the following ways:

1. with symbolic or with concrete inputs;
2. on one arbitrary execution path, or on all paths up to a given bound;
3. in a step-wise manner, or by letting the program completely execute a given number of paths.

For example, by running `sum.imp` with a symbolic input n (here and thereafter we use mathematical font for symbolic values) and requiring at most five completed executions, the $\mathbb{K}$ runner outputs the five resulting, final configurations, one of which is shown below, in a syntax slightly simplified for readability:

```
<k> . </k>
<path-condition> n > 0 ∧ (n − 1 > 0) ∧ ¬((n − 1) − 1 > 0) </path-condition>
  <state>
    n |-> (n − 1) − 1
    s |-> n + (n − 1)
  </state>
```

The program is finished since the `k` cell has no code left to execute. The path condition actually means $n = 2$, and in this case the sum `s` equals $n+(n-1) = 2+1$, as shown by the `state` cell. The other four final configurations, not shown here, compute the sums of numbers up to 1, 3, 4, and 5, respectively. Users can run the program in a step-wise manner in order to see intermediary configurations in additional to final ones. During this process they can interact with the runner, e.g., by choosing one execution branch of the program among several, feeding the program with inputs, or letting the program run on an arbitrarily chosen path until its completion.

LTL Model Checking. The $\mathbb{K}$ runner includes a hook to the Maude LTL (Linear Temporal Logic) model checker [16]. Thus, one can model check LTL formulas on programs having a finite state space (or by restricting the verification to a finite subset of the state space). This requires an (automatic) extension of the syntax and semantics of a language for including labels that are used as atomic propositions in the LTL formulas. Predicates on the program's variables can be used as propositions in the formulas as well, using the approach outlined in [15].

Consider for instance the program `log.imp` in Figure 7, which computes the integer binary logarithm of an integer read from the input. We prove that whenever the loop visits the label L, the inequalities $x * 2^k \leq a < (x + 1) * 2^k$ hold. The invariant was guessed using several step-wise executions. We let `a` be a symbolic value and restrict it in the interval (0..10) to obtain a finite state space. We prove that the above property, denoted by `logInv(a,x,k)` holds whenever the label L is visited and `a` is in the given interval, using the following command (again, slightly edited for better readability):

```
$ krun log.imp -cPC="a >Int 0 ∧Bool a <Int 10" -cIN="a"
           -ltlmc "□Ltl (L →Ltl logInv(a, x, k))"
```

The $\mathbb{K}$ runner executes the command by calling the Maude LTL model-checker for the LTL formula $\square_{Ltl} (\text{L} \rightarrow_{Ltl} \text{logInv}(a, x, k))$ and the initial configuration having the program `log.imp` in the computation cell k, the symbolic value a in the input cell in, and the constraint $a >_{Int} 0 \wedge_{Bool} a <_{Int} 10$ in the path condition. The result returned by the tool is that the above LTL formula holds.

SIMPLE, Symbolic Arrays, and Bounded Model Checking. We illustrate symbolic arrays in the SIMPLE language and shows how the $\mathbb{K}$ runner can directly

```
void init(int[] a, int x, int j){        void main() {
    int i = 0, n = sizeOf(a);                int n = read();
    a[j] = x;                                int j = read();
    while (a[i] != x && i < n) {              int x = read();
        a[i] = 2 * i;                        int a[n], i = 0;
        i = i + 1;                           while (i < n) {
    }                                            a[i] = read();
    if (i > j) {                                 i = i + 1;
        print("error");                      }
    }                                        init(a, x, j);
}                                        }
```

Fig. 8. SIMPLE program: `init-arrays`

be used for performing bounded model checking. In the program in Figure 8, the `init` method assigns the value `x` to the array `a` at an index `j`, then fills the array with ascending even numbers until it encounters x in the array; it prints *error* if the index `i` went beyond `j` in that process. The array and the indexes `i`, `j` are parameters to the function, passed to it by the `main` function which reads them from the input. In [1] it has been shown, using model-checking and abstractions on arrays, that this program never prints *error*.

We obtain the same result by running the program with symbolic inputs and using the $\mathbb{K}$ runner as a bounded model checker:

```
$ krun init-arrays.simple -cPC="n >Int 0" -search -cIN="n j x a1 a2 a3"
                          -pattern="<T> <out> error </out> B:Bag </T>"
Search results:
No search results
```

The initial path condition is $n >_{Int} 0$. The symbolic inputs for `n,j,x` are entered as $n \ j \ x$, and the array elements $a1 \ a2 \ a3$ are also symbolic. The `-pattern` option specifies a pattern to be searched in the final configuration: the text *error* should be in the configuration's output buffer. The above command thus performs a bounded model-checking with symbolic inputs (the bound is implicitly set by the number of array elements given as inputs - 3). It does not return any solution, meaning that that the program will never print *error*.

The result was obtained using symbolic execution without any additional tools or techniques. We note that array sizes are symbolic as well, a feature that, to our best knowledge, is not present in other symbolic execution frameworks.

KOOL: Testing Virtual Method Calls on Lists. Our last example (Figure 9) is a program in the KOOL object-oriented language. It implements lists and ordered lists of integers using arrays. We use symbolic execution to check the well-known virtual method call mechanism of object-oriented languages: the same method call, applied to two objects of different classes, may have different outcomes.

The `List` class implements (plain) lists. It has methods for creating, copying, and testing the equality of lists, as well as for inserting and deleting elements in a list. Figure 9 shows only a part of them. The class `OrderedList` inherits from `List`. It redefines the `insert` method in order to ensure that the sequences of

```
class List {                         class OrderedList extends List {
  int a[10];                           ...
  int size, capacity;                  void insert(int x){
  ...                                    if (size < capacity) {
                                           int i = 0, k;
  void insert (int x) {                    while(i < size && a[i] <= x) {
    if (size < capacity) {                   i = i + 1;
      a[size] = x;  ++size;                 }
    }                                      ++size; k = size - 1;
  }                                        while(k > i) {
                                             a[k] = a[k-1]; k = k - 1;
  void delete(int x) {                     }
    int i = 0;                             a[i] = x;
    while(i < size-1 && a[i] != x) {     }
      i = i + 1;                        }
    }                                 }
    if (a[i] == x) {                  class Main {
      while (i < size - 1) {            void Main() {
        a[i] = a[i+1];                     List l1 = new List();
        i = i + 1;                         ... // read elements of l1 and x
      }                                    List l2 = l1.copy();
      size = size - 1;                     l1.insert(x); l1.delete(x);
    }                                      if (l2.eqTo(l1) == false) {
  }                                          print("error\n");
}                                          }
  ...                                    }
}                                      }
```

Fig. 9. lists.kool: implementation of lists in KOOL

elements in lists are sorted in increasing order. The Main class creates a list l1, initializes l1 and an integer variable x with input values, copies l1 to a list l2 and then inserts and deletes x in l1. Finally it compares l1 to l2 element by element, and prints *error* if it finds them different. We use symbolic execution to show that the above sequence of method calls results in different outcomes, depending on whether l1 is a List or an OrderedList. We first try the case where l1 is a List, by issuing the following command to the $\mathbb{K}$ runner:

```
$ krun  lists.kool   -search -cIN="e1 e2 x"
                     -pattern="<T> <out> error </out> B:Bag </T>"
 Solution 1, State 50:
<path-condition>
    e1 = x ∧Bool ¬Bool (e1 = e2)
</path-condition>
 ...
```

The command initializes l1 with two symbolic values (e_1, e_2) and sets x to the symbolic value x. It searches for configurations that contain *error* in the output. The tool finds one solution, with $e_1 = x$ and $e_1 \neq e_2$ in the path condition. Since insert of List appends x at the end of the list and deletes the first instance of x from it, l1 consists of (e_2, x) when the two lists are compared, in contrast to l2, which consists of (e_1, e_2). The path condition implies that the lists are different.

The same command on the same program but where l1 is an OrderedList finds no solution. This is because insert in OrderedList inserts an element in a unique place (up to the positions of the elements equal to it) in an ordered list, and `delete` removes either the inserted element or one with the same value. Hence, inserting and then deleting an element leaves an ordered list unchanged.

Thus, virtual method call mechanism worked correctly in the tested scenarios. An advantage of using our symbolic execution tool is that the condition on the inputs that differentiated the two scenarios was discovered by the tool. This feature can be exploited in other applications such as test-case generation.

6.3   The Implementation of the Tool

Our tool was developed as an extension of the $\mathbb{K}$ compiler. A part of the connection to the Z3 SMT solver was done in $\mathbb{K}$ itself, and the rest of the code is written in Java. The $\mathbb{K}$ compiler (`kompile`) is organized as a list of transformations applied to the abstract syntax tree of a $\mathbb{K}$ definition. Our compiler inserts additional transformations (formally described in Section 4.3). These transformations are inserted when the $\mathbb{K}$ compiler is called with the `-symbolic` option.

The compiler adds syntax declarations for each sort, which allows users to use symbolic values written as, e.g., `#symSort(x)` in their programs. The tool also generates predicates used to distinguish between concrete and symbolic values.

For handling the path condition, a new configuration cell, `<path-condition>` is automatically added to the configuration. The transformations of rules discussed in Subsection 4.3 are also implemented as transformers applied to rules. There is a transformer for linearizing rules, which collects all the variables that appear more than once in the left hand side of a rule, generates new variables for each one, and adds an equality in the side condition. There is also a transformer that replaces data subterms with variables, following the same algorithm as the previous one, and a transformer that adds rule's conditions in the symbolic configuration's path conditions. In practice, building the path condition blindly may lead to exploration of program paths which are not feasible. For this reason, the transformer that collects the path condition also adds, as a side condition to rewrite rules, a call to the SMT solver of the form `checkSat`$(\phi) \neq$ `"unsat"`, where the `checkSat` function calls the SMT solver over the current path condition ϕ. When the path condition is found unsatisfiable the current path is not explored any longer. A problem that arises here is that, in $\mathbb{K}$, the condition of rules may also contain internally generated predicates needed only for matching. Those predicates should not be part of the path condition, therefore they had to be filtered out from rule's conditions before the latter are added to path conditions.

Not all the rules from a $\mathbb{K}$ definition must be transformed. This is the case, e.g., of the rules computing functions or predicates. We have created a transformer that detects such rules and marks them with a tag. The tag can also be used by the user, in order to prevent the transformation of other rules if needed. Finally, in order to allow passing symbolic inputs to programs we generated a variable `$IN`, initialized at runtime by `krun` with the value of the option `-cIN`.

7   Conclusion and Future Work

We have presented a formal and generic framework for the symbolic execution of programs in languages having operational semantics defined by term-rewriting. Starting from the formal definition of a language $\mathcal{L}$, the symbolic version $\mathcal{L}^s$ of the language is automatically constructed, by extending the datatypes used in $\mathcal{L}$ with symbolic values, and by modifying the semantical rules of $\mathcal{L}$ in order to make them process symbolic values appropriately. The symbolic semantics of $\mathcal{L}$ is then the (usual) semantics of $\mathcal{L}^s$, and symbolic execution of programs in $\mathcal{L}$ is the (usual) execution of the corresponding programs in $\mathcal{L}^s$, which is the application of the rewrite rules of the semantics of $\mathcal{L}^s$ to programs. Our symbolic execution has the natural properties of *coverage*, meaning that to each concrete execution there is a feasible symbolic one on the same path of instructions, and *precision*, meaning that each feasible symbolic execution has a concrete execution on the same path. These results were obtained by carefully constructing definitions about the essentials of programming languages, in an algebraic and term-rewriting setting. We have implemented a prototype tool in the $\mathbb{K}$ framework and have illustrated it by instantiating it to several languages defined in $\mathbb{K}$.

Future Work. We are planning to use symbolic execution as the basic mechanism for the deductive systems for program logics also developed in the $\mathbb{K}$ framework (such as reachability logic [21] and our own circular equivalence logic [14]). More generally, our symbolic execution can be used for program testing, debugging, and verification, following the ideas presented in related work, but with the added value of being language independent and grounded in formal operational semantics. In order to achieve that, we have to develop a rich domain of symbolic values, able to handle e.g., heaps, stacks, and other common data types.

Acknowledgements. The results presented in this paper would not have been possible without the valuable support from the $\mathbb{K}$ tool development team (http://k-framework.org). We would like to thank the reviewers for their helpful comments. The work presented here was supported in part by Contract 161/15.06.2010, SMIS-CSNR 602-12516 (DAK).

References

1. Armando, A., Benerecetti, M., Mantovani, J.: Model checking linear programs with arrays. In: Proceedings of the Workshop on Software Model Checking, vol. 144-3, pp. 79–94 (2006)
2. Baader, F., Nipkow, T.: Term rewriting and all that. Cambridge University Press, New York (1998)
3. Berdine, J., Calcagno, C., O'Hearn, P.W.: Symbolic execution with separation logic. In: Yi, K. (ed.) APLAS 2005. LNCS, vol. 3780, pp. 52–68. Springer, Heidelberg (2005)

4. Cadar, C., Ganesh, V., Pawlowski, P.M., Dill, D.L., Engler, D.R.: EXE: automatically generating inputs of death. In: Juels, A., Wright, R.N., di Vimercati, S.D.C. (eds.) ACM Conference on Computer and Communications Security, pp. 322–335. ACM (2006)

5. de Halleux, J., Tillmann, N.: Parameterized unit testing with pex. In: Beckert, B., Hähnle, R. (eds.) TAP 2008. LNCS, vol. 4966, pp. 171–181. Springer, Heidelberg (2008)

6. de Moura, L., Bjørner, N.: Z3: An efficient SMT solver. In: Ramakrishnan, C.R., Rehof, J. (eds.) TACAS 2008. LNCS, vol. 4963, pp. 337–340. Springer, Heidelberg (2008)

7. Dillon, L.K.: Verifying general safety properties of Ada tasking programs. IEEE Trans. Softw. Eng. 16(1), 51–63 (1990)

8. Escobar, S., Meseguer, J., Sasse, R.: Variant narrowing and equational unification. Electr. Notes Theor. Comput. Sci. 238(3), 103–119 (2009)

9. Godefroid, P., Klarlund, N., Sen, K.: DART: directed automated random testing. In: PLDI, pp. 213–223. ACM (2005)

10. Hills, M., Roşu, G.: KOOL: An application of rewriting logic to language prototyping and analysis. In: Baader, F. (ed.) RTA 2007. LNCS, vol. 4533, pp. 246–256. Springer, Heidelberg (2007)

11. Khurshid, S., Păsăreanu, C.S., Visser, W.: Generalized symbolic execution for model checking and testing. In: Garavel, H., Hatcliff, J. (eds.) TACAS 2003. LNCS, vol. 2619, pp. 553–568. Springer, Heidelberg (2003)

12. King, J.C.: Symbolic execution and program testing. Commun. ACM 19(7), 385–394 (1976)

13. Li, G., Ghosh, I., Rajan, S.P.: KLOVER: A symbolic execution and automatic test generation tool for C++ programs. In: Gopalakrishnan, G., Qadeer, S. (eds.) CAV 2011. LNCS, vol. 6806, pp. 609–615. Springer, Heidelberg (2011)

14. Lucanu, D., Rusu, V.: Program equivalence by circular reasoning. In: Johnsen, E.B., Petre, L. (eds.) IFM 2013. LNCS, vol. 7940, pp. 362–377. Springer, Heidelberg (2013)

15. Lucanu, D., Şerbănuţă, T.F., Roşu, G.: K Framework Distilled. In: Durán, F. (ed.) WRLA 2012. LNCS, vol. 7571, pp. 31–53. Springer, Heidelberg (2012)

16. Meseguer, J.: Rewriting logic and Maude: Concepts and applications. In L. Bachmair, editor, RTA. In: Bachmair, L. (ed.) RTA 2000. LNCS, vol. 1833, pp. 1–26. Springer, Heidelberg (2000)

17. Meseguer, J., Thati, P.: Symbolic reachability analysis using narrowing and its application to verification of cryptographic protocols. Higher-Order and Symbolic Computation 20(1-2), 123–160 (2007)

18. Păsăreanu, C.S., Visser, W.: Verification of Java Programs Using Symbolic Execution and Invariant Generation. In: Graf, S., Mounier, L. (eds.) SPIN 2004. LNCS, vol. 2989, pp. 164–181. Springer, Heidelberg (2004)

19. Păsăreanu, C.S., Visser, W.: A survey of new trends in symbolic execution for software testing and analysis. STTT 11(4), 339–353 (2009)

20. Roşu, G., Şerbănuţă, T.F.: An overview of the K semantic framework. Journal of Logic and Algebraic Programming 79(6), 397–434 (2010)

21. Roşu, G., Ştefănescu, A.: Checking reachability using matching logic. In: Leavens, G.T., Dwyer, M.B. (eds.) OOPSLA, pp. 555–574. ACM (2012)

22. Schmitt, P.H., Weiß, B.: Inferring invariants by symbolic execution. In: Proceedings of 4th International Verification Workshop, VERIFY 2007 (2007)

23. Sen, K., Marinov, D., Agha, G.: CUTE: a concolic unit testing engine for C. In: Proceedings of the 10th European Software Engineering Conference Held Jointly with 13th ACM SIGSOFT International Symposium on Foundations of Software Engineering, ESEC/FSE-13, pp. 263–272. ACM (2005)
24. Serbanuta, T.F., Arusoaie, A., Lazar, D., Ellison, C., Lucanu, D., Rosu, G.: The K primer (version 2.5). In: Hills, M. (ed.) K 2011. Electronic Notes in Theoretical Computer Science (2011) (to appear)
25. Şerbănuţă, T.-F., Roşu, G., Meseguer, J.: A rewriting logic approach to operational semantics. Inf. Comput. 207(2), 305–340 (2009)
26. Siegel, S.F., Mironova, A., Avrunin, G.S., Clarke, L.A.: Using model checking with symbolic execution to verify parallel numerical programs. In: ISSTA, pp. 157–168. ACM (2006)
27. Staats, M., Păsăreanu, C.S.: Parallel symbolic execution for structural test generation. In: Tonella, P., Orso, A. (eds.) ISSTA, pp. 183–194. ACM (2010)
28. Visser, W., Păsăreanu, C.S., Khurshid, S.: Test input generation with Java PathFinder. In: Avrunin, G.S., Rothermel, G. (eds.) ISSTA, pp. 97–107. ACM (2004)

Circular Higher-Order Reference Attribute Grammars

Emma Söderberg and Görel Hedin

Department of Computer Science, Lund University, Sweden
{emma.soderberg,gorel.hedin}@cs.lth.se

Abstract. Reference attribute grammars (RAGs) provide a practical declarative means to implement programming language compilers and other tools. RAGs have previously been extended to support both circular attributes and context-dependent declarative rewrites of the abstract syntax tree. In this previous work, dependencies between circular attributes and rewrites are not considered. In this paper, we investigate how these extensions can interact, and still be well defined. We introduce a generalized evaluation algorithm that can handle grammars where circular attributes and rewrites are interdependent. To this end, we introduce circular higher-order attributes, and show how RAG rewrites are a special form of such attributes.

1 Introduction

Reference attribute grammars (RAGs) [14] provide a practical declarative means to implement programming language compilers and other tools. Examples include a full Java compiler [11], as well as extensions to aspect-oriented, context-oriented and feature-oriented programming languages [3,2,1]. RAGs are an extension of Knuth's attribute grammars (AGs) [18], and support attributes with references to remote abstract syntax tree (AST) nodes as values. Over the years, AGs and RAGs have been subject to a multitude of extensions. For instance, RAGs have previously been extended to support circular attributes [13,15,20], and attribute-dependent rewrites [9], performing in-place transformations in the AST. In this previous work, dependencies between circular attributes and rewrites are not considered.

In this paper, we investigate how circular attributes and rewrites can interact, and still be well defined. We consider the similarities of rewritten values and higher-order attributes [26], from here on referred to as *non-terminal attributes* (NTAs). We introduce a generalized evaluation algorithm that can handle grammars with interdependent circular attributes and rewrites. To this end, we introduce circular higher-order attributes, and show how RAG rewrites are a special form of such attributes. The contributions of this paper are as follows:

- A definition of circular NTAs, together with an evaluation algorithm.
- A mapping from circular NTAs to rewrites.
- An evaluation of the presented algorithm on a typical rewrite problem.

The rest of this paper is structured as follows: Section 2 walks through the preliminaries of this paper, Section 3 gives a motivating example, Section 4 presents circular NTAs, Section 5 presents a mapping to rewrites, Section 6 evaluates the presented mechanism, Section 7 discusses related work, and finally Section 8 concludes the paper.

M. Erwig, R.F. Paige, and E. Van Wyk (Eds.): SLE 2013, LNCS 8225, pp. 302–321, 2013.

2 Preliminaries

To illustrate examples, and to present solutions, we use the syntax and evaluation code supported and provided by the JastAdd system [12].

2.1 Attribute Grammars

Attribute grammars (AGs) were introduced by Knuth [18] and provide a means to compute context-sensitive information for context-free grammars. The information is defined by attributes associated with non-terminals, and equations associated with productions. In JastAdd, the non-terminals and productions are viewed as types and subtypes, and attributes and equations belong to such node types, that is, they are *hosted* by node types. Abstract syntax trees (ASTs) consist of nodes instantiated from node types, and each node hosts instances of the attributes hosted by its node type.

An equation defines an attribute (on the left-hand side), using an expression (on the right-hand side) that may use attributes in the hosting node, or its children. This expression is called the *semantic function* of the attribute. Attributes are either *synthesized* or *inherited*. A synthesized attribute hosted by a node of type n, has a value defined by an equation also hosted by n, while an inherited attribute has a value defined by an equation hosted by the *parent* of n.

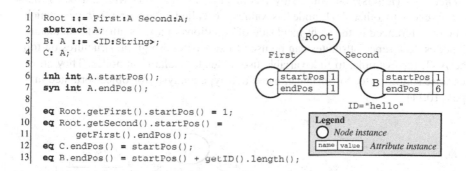

```
1| Root ::= First:A Second:A;
2| abstract A;
3| B: A ::= <ID:String>;
4| C: A;
5|
6| inh int A.startPos();
7| syn int A.endPos();
8|
9| eq Root.getFirst().startPos() = 1;
10| eq Root.getSecond().startPos() =
11|     getFirst().endPos();
12| eq C.endPos() = startPos();
13| eq B.endPos() = startPos() + getID().length();
```

Fig. 1. AG example A simple attribute grammar and an example of an attributed AST

Figure 1 shows a simple example of a JastAdd attribute grammar, and an AST following this grammar. The grammar defines a `Root` node type with two children of the abstract type `A`. This type `A` has two subtypes `B` and `C`, where `B` has a token `ID` of type `String`. A token is seen as an *intrinsic* attribute, i.e., an attribute whose value is defined during the AST construction, rather than by an equation. The attribution defines an inherited attribute `startPos` and a synthesized attribute `endPos` for `A` nodes, along with equations defining the values of the attributes.

An equation has the form `H.getC().i()` = *exp* for an inherited attribute, or `H.s()` = *exp* for a synthesized attribute. Here, `H` is the host type, `getC()` is an accessor to a child of `H`, `i()` is an inherited attribute of `C()`, and `s()` is a synthesized attribute of H. A right-hand side expression *exp* executes in the context of H. For example, on line 10, an equation hosted by Root defines its second A's startPos to be equal to its first A's endPos. The AST, with attribute instances and their values, is illustrated to the right in the figure.

A simple and powerful way to compute the value of an attribute instance a_0 is to locate its defining equation and evaluate its right-hand side expression, recursively evaluating any attribute instances $a_1...a_n$ used when evaluating the expression [17]. The attribute a_0 is said to *depend* on $a_1...a_n$. Note that these dependencies are dynamic: the dependencies themselves may depend on the values of attributes. For example, in an equation $a = b\,?\,c : d$, an instance of a will depend on b and on *either c or d*, depending on the value of b.

This dynamic evaluation technique is called *demand evaluation*, since only those attributes whose values are demanded are actually evaluated. The attribute values can be cached after evaluation, so that a second demand for an attribute value will return the value immediately, rather than evaluating the equation again. Despite being so simple, this technique is very powerful, and is used in JastAdd. It can handle many extensions to Knuth's attribute grammars, including reference attributes and nonterminal attributes, and it can be extended to support circular attributes and rewrites.

2.2   Reference Attributes

Reference AGs (RAGs), introduced by Hedin [14], extend AGs with attributes that have references to other AST nodes as values, so called *reference attributes*, which may be de-referenced in the right-hand side of equations to access attributes in distant AST nodes. Reference attributes can be used to super-impose graph structures on top of the AST, for example, to link variable use nodes to declaration nodes. They allow for concise solutions to, for instance, name and type analysis for object-oriented languages [10,11].

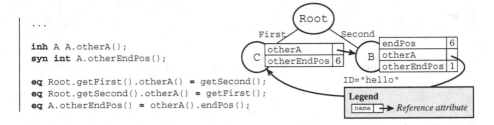

Fig. 2. RAG example Extends the grammar from Figure 1 with two attributes, of which one is a reference attribute (otherA). For conciseness, most attributes from Figure 1 are omitted.

Figure 2 shows a simple example of a system with reference attributes, where the grammar of Figure 1 has been extended with an inherited reference attribute otherA and a synthesized attribute otherEndPos. The latter attribute is defined by dereferencing otherA and accessing that node's endPos attribute. Note that the reference attributes super-impose a cyclic structure on top of the AST, but that the attribute *dependencies* are not cyclic. The demand-driven evaluation algorithm works without any problems.

2.3 Non-terminal Attributes

Higher-order AGs, introduced by Vogt, Swierstra and Kuiper [26], extend AGs with *non-terminal attributes* (NTAs), i.e., attributes for which the semantic function computes a fresh sub-AST, rooted by a given non-terminal. These sub-ASTs may themselves have attributes, hence the term higher-order. This extension makes it possible to let the attribution decide parts of the AST structure, which otherwise would be decided entirely during construction. NTAs can, for example, be used to de-sugar language constructs by constructing an alternative representation of a part of the AST. Like any attribute, an NTA is hosted by a node type of the grammar and each node of that type will host its own instance of the NTA.

Unlike other attributes, the value of an NTA is in itself attributable, and inherited attributes are evaluated in the context of the node hosting the NTA. That is, the hosting node becomes the parent of the NTA, and must provide equations defining the inherited attributes of the NTA. In JastAdd, an equation defining the inherited attribute of a child automatically applies to all nodes in the child sub-AST, so called *broadcasting* [12]. Thus, often there is already a suitable equation further up in the AST, and if not, the host can provide an appropriate equation, overriding any broadcasting equation higher up in the AST. Figure 3 shows an example. The demand-driven recursive evaluation algorithm works directly for NTAs.

2.4 Circular Attributes

Circular attributes are attributes that depend (transitively) on themselves. They are useful for describing many problems, for example, dataflow. Circular attributes are well-defined as the least fixed-point solution to their equations, if their semantic functions are monotonic and yield values over a lattice of bounded height [16,13]. Farrow describes how an evaluator can compute a fixed-point by successive approximation of attribute

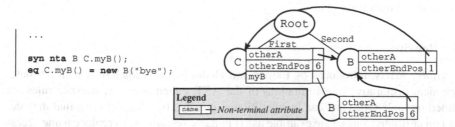

Fig. 3. Non-terminal attributes The grammar from Figure 2 is extended with an NTA computing a new B node under C. The NTA value gets the same inherited values as C. This behavior could be modified by adding more equations to C.

values [13], as shown in Figure 4. The algorithm solves the equation $X = F(X)$ by starting from the *bottom value* ($\bot$) and then iterating until a fixed-point is reached. That is, $X = \bot \cup F(\bot) \cup F(F(\bot)) \cup \ldots F^l(\bot) \ldots$ until $F^l(\bot) = F^{l+1}(\bot)$, where $\cup$ is monotonic on the domain and co-domain of F.

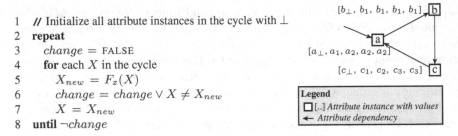

```
1   // Initialize all attribute instances in the cycle with ⊥
2   repeat
3       change = FALSE
4       for each X in the cycle
5           X_new = F_x(X)
6           change = change ∨ X ≠ X_new
7           X = X_new
8   until ¬change
```

Fig. 4. Fixed-point evaluation of attribute instances in a cycle. Example of cycle shown to the right. Starting at $\bot$, attribute instance values are updated each iteration until there is no change.

To support circular attributes in RAGs, the recursive demand-driven evaluation is extended to do fixed-point iteration, as described by Magnusson and Hedin [20] and shown in Figure 5. When the value of a circular attribute instance is demanded, there are three different cases: Case 1 covers the case when the attribute instance is called from "outside", i.e., from an attribute not involved in any cyclic evaluation. This part of the algorithm contains the loop that drives the fixed-point iteration. Cases 2 and 3 cover cases when a circular attribute is called from "inside", i.e., when a circular evaluation is already ongoing. Case 2 computes the next value in the iteration for the attribute. Case 3 covers the case when the computation of the next value is already ongoing, in which case the function immediately returns the current value. A global flag, IN_CIRCLE, keeps track of if any cyclic evaluation is ongoing. Figure 6 illustrates the evaluation stack for the example used in Figure 5.

As a simple example, Figure 7 shows a circular attribute in JastAdd that computes whether any `endPos` of nodes, connected through the `otherA` references, are over 5. The attribute is boolean, and the values can be viewed as arranged in a simple lattice with *false* at the bottom and *true* at the top, and the semantic function uses the monotonic *or* operator ($||$).

2.5   Rewrites

Rewritable RAGs, introduced by Ekman and Hedin [9], extends RAGs with attribute-dependent declarative transformations of the AST, called *rewrites*. Rewrite rules are defined on node types and can be conditional, guarded by `when` clauses that may depend on attribute values. One example use is in name resolution, to replace name access nodes by more specific nodes depending on context, for example, field accesses or local variable accesses [10]. A node is in a consistent state, with respect to rewrites, when it has no applicable rewrite rules. An evaluator thus needs to automatically apply rewrite

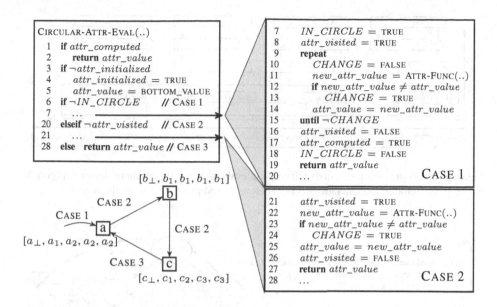

Fig. 5. Recursive fixed-point evaluation Listing of the algorithm divided into three cases, exemplified for the dependency graph from Figure 4. ATTR-FUNC refers to the actual semantic function of the attribute.

rules, intertwined with attribute evaluation, until no applicable rewrites remain. Figure 8 shows an example, where a new subtype D is defined that extends the type A. A rewrite rule for the type B declares that it should be replaced by a D node in case the value of its endPos attribute is larger than 4.

Like RAG attributes, rewrites are evaluated on demand, and with the use of a recursive evaluation strategy. When a node is accessed for the first time (through the getter in its parent), the rewrite rules for the node are applied repeatedly until there are no more applicable rewrites, i.e., the node is in its final state. Thus, the client accessing the child never sees the initial or any intermediate states, but only the final state of the node. The root node itself is not allowed to have any rewrite rules. Initially, the root of the AST is final, and as the AST is traversed, this final region is expanded from parent to child. For instance, after building the initial AST in Figure 8, suppose we access first the root node, and then its second child. The second child will then be rewritten, and a reference to the final D node is returned.

The evaluation of rewrites, shown as the child access method ASTNODE.GETCHILD in Figure 9[1], starts with a check of the current state of the child to be accessed. If the child is NULL, if it is already in the final state, or if it has no rewrite rules, its current value is returned immediately without any further evaluation. Alternatively, the rewrite evaluation continues. Beyond the initial part, the ASTNODE.GETCHILD method handles two cases: CASE 1 covers the case when the node is accessed for the first time, in which case a loop is entered which drives the evaluation of the rewrite. CASE 2 covers

---

[1] ASTNODE is a supertype of all node types.

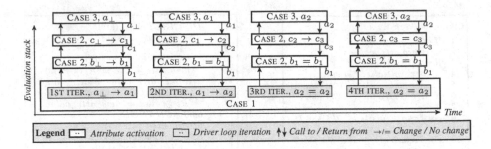

Fig. 6. **Evaluation stack** for recursive fixed-point evaluation and the example shown in Figure 5. CASE 1 goes through three iterations (ITER) before a fixed point is found in the fourth.

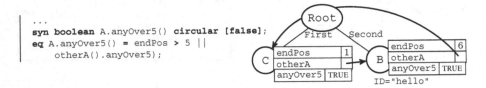

```
...
syn boolean A.anyOver5() circular [false];
eq A.anyOver5() = endPos > 5 ||
   otherA().anyOver5();
```

Fig. 7. **Circular attribute example** Extending the grammar from Figure 2 with a circular attribute anyOver5 with `false` as bottom value

the case when the node is already in the process of being rewritten, but accessed again, in which case the current value is returned.

CASE 1 contains a driver loop, similar to the first case for circular attributes in Figure 5. A difference is that each rewritten node is driven by its own driver loop, which is kept track of using the boolean field INCIRCLE in the node. Another difference is that the change check is not done by comparing values, but instead using a boolean flag that is set in the beginning of each iteration (CHANGE), and reset (to NOCHANGE) by the REWRITETO method, in case no when clause applies. These flags are pushed on a stack (STACK), so that nested rewrites of different nodes each have their own flag.

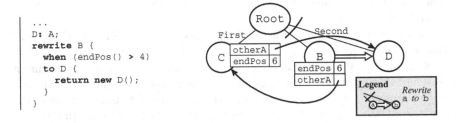

```
...
D: A;
rewrite B {
  when (endPos() > 4)
  to D {
    return new D();
  }
}
```

Fig. 8. **Rewrite example** Extends the grammar in Figure 2 with a node type D and a rewrite rule, replacing a B node with a D node, depending on the value of endPos (shown to the right)

Because rewrites change the AST, attribute instance values may not be cached (memoized) if they depend on nodes which have not yet become final. This requires additional bookkeeping not shown in Figure 9.

ASTNODE.GETCHILD(*index*)

```
1   node = this.GETCHILDNOTRANSFORM(index)
2   if node = NULL ∨ node.ISFINAL()
3     return node
4   if ¬node.MAYHAVEREWRITE()
5     node.SETFINAL(parent.ISFINAL())
6     return node
7   if ¬node.INCIRCLE() // CASE 1
8     repeat
9       STACK.PUSH(CHANGE)
10      node.SETINCIRCLE(TRUE)
11      new_node = node.REWRITETO()
12      if new_node ≠ node
13        this.SETCHILD(index, new_node)
14        node = new_node
15      node.SETINCIRCLE(FALSE)
16      state = STACK.POP()
17    until state ≠ CHANGE
18    if state = NOCHANGE ∧ this.ISFINAL()
19      node.SETFINAL(TRUE)
20    return node
21  else
22    return node    // CASE 2
```

ASTNODE.REWRITETO

```
1   STACK.POP()
2   STACK.PUSH(NOCHANGE)
3   return this
```

ASTNODE.MAYHAVEREWRITE

```
1   return FALSE
```

NODE.REWRITETO

```
1   // when clauses in lexical order
2   return super.REWRITETO()
```

NODE.MAYHAVEREWRITE

```
1   return TRUE
```

Fig. 9. Rewrite evaluation The pseudo code for the initial part, together with the two evaluation cases, is listed to the left, and node-specific code for controlling the change check and triggering of rewrite evaluation, is listed to the right

3 Motivating Example

In the previous section, we walked through the evaluation of attribute grammars with focus on two extensions: circular attributes and rewrites. The evaluation mechanisms of these extensions are similar; both use a loop to drive the evaluation until there is no change, both base their evaluation on some initial value, and both mechanisms may create intermediate values on their way to a final value. That is, if a circular attribute is called, entering CASE 2 or CASE 3, a potentially intermediate value is returned, and the same goes for rewrites, entering CASE 2. The presented evaluation mechanisms handle circular attributes and rewrites in isolation from each other, i.e., assuming there are no interdependencies between them.

As an example of such an interdependency, consider the grammar specified in Figure 10. It includes one rewrite, one circular attribute and one inherited attribute (for convenience). The rewrite needs the value of the circular attribute to evaluate its when clause, and the circular attribute, for the sake of the example, uses the A child of Root to compute its value. Effectively, there are dependencies between the circular attribute and the rewrite, and vice versa, as shown in the figure. The values in the figure are the expected final values, that is, we expect the circular attribute to receive the value 2, and we expect the child to receive the value C.

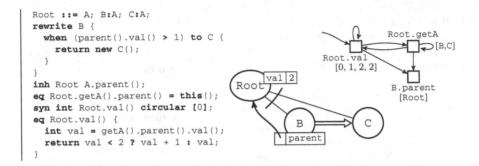

```
Root ::= A; B:A; C:A;
rewrite B {
  when (parent().val() > 1) to C {
    return new C();
  }
}
inh Root A.parent();
eq Root.getA().parent() = this();
syn int Root.val() circular [0];
eq Root.val() {
  int val = getA().parent().val();
  return val < 2 ? val + 1 : val;
}
```

Fig. 10. Interdependent rewrite and circular attribute Example of a simple RAG system with one rewrite and one circular attribute, depending on each other. The rewrite is shown in the AST, and the attribute graph shows expected values and dependencies. The val equation uses a block, which may have local state but no external side-effects, and getA corresponds to a child access via ASTNode.getChild.

In just using the algorithms from Section 2, the interdependencies are not accounted for, and the final value of the child becomes B rather than C, i.e., the rewrite terminates too soon. Figure 11 illustrates the evaluation stack for the example, showing how the initial call to the circular attribute enters circular CASE 1, and how the first child access enters rewrite CASE 1. In both of these cases, a loop is started to drive the evaluation. The first iteration of the rewrite driver loop results in a call to the circular attribute, and this call becomes the second call to the circular attribute. At this point, the circular attribute is already driving its own evaluation (CASE 1), hence it enters CASE 3 and returns its current value. This current value is the bottom value of the circular attribute (0), and with this value the when clause of the rewrite becomes false. With only false when clauses, NOCHANGE is pushed on to the rewrite stack (STACK), causing the rewrite evaluation to terminate.

Interdependencies, like the above, can either be disallowed or handled. Using the global evaluation state (IN_CIRCLE, STACK) presented in Section 2, a runtime exception can be thrown if a circular attribute instance uses a rewrite, or vice versa. Alternatively, interdependencies can be handled, either by adding bookkeeping to each algorithm to account for the other, or by generalizing the algorithms. The current JastAdd implementation uses an extended version of the REWRITE algorithm to allow for more caching during evaluation. This extension results in handling of interdependencies like in the

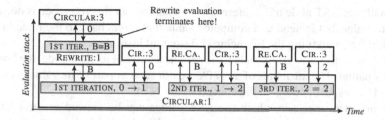

Fig. 11. Evaluation stack of interdependent rewrite and circular attribute specified in Figure 10. Without handling of interdependencies, the rewrite terminates prematurely, because of unawareness of changes to the circular attribute, and returns a cached rewritten value (RE.CA. = REWRITE CACHED). Legend is described in Figure 6, and colon is used to indicate case number for calls. Abbreviations: ITER. = ITERATION, CIR. = CIRCULAR

above example, but requires additional bookkeeping, making the algorithm more complex. In this paper, we instead present a generalization, based on a unification of the two mechanisms. We do this by introducing the notion of *circular NTAs* (Section 4), of which rewrites can be seen as a special form (Section 5). This unification allows us to account for interdependencies without special bookkeeping, using a simpler algorithm with fewer conceptual entities. It also allows us to cache more attribute values during rewrites (i.e., during the evaluation of circular NTAs), resulting in better performance.

4   Circular Non-terminal Attributes

In this section, we introduce circular NTAs, and show how these can be used to compute the attribute values described in Section 3.

4.1   AST values

As for ordinary circular attributes, we require circular NTAs to take their values from a lattice of bounded height, that the semantic function is monotonic, and that a bottom value is provided as the starting point of the fixed-point iteration. Consider the following circular NTA:

```
syn nta ReturnType HostType.attribute() circular [BottomNode] = SemanticFunction();
```

Here, `SemanticFunction` has the `HostType` node as its implicit argument, and via this node, other attributes can be accessed. The `SemanticFunction` should be side-effect free, and return a fresh subtree rooted by a node of type `ReturnType`. An NTA value is seen as an unattributed subtree, defined as follows:

Definition 1. *An AST value v is either* `null`, *or an AST node, where an AST node is a tuple <*`Type`, `Tokens`, `Children`*>, where* `Type` *is an AST node type,* `Tokens` *is a list of zero or more tokens, and* `Children` *is a list of zero or more AST values. Two AST values are equal if they are both* `null`, *or if their types, tokens and children are equal.*

Additionally, an AST node has a reference to its parent, but this reference is not seen as part of the value, but instead as a computed value that refers back to the node of which it is a child, i.e., satisfying the following child-parent invariant:

$n.child(i).parent() == n$. As an NTA is seen as a child of its host node, the host node will be its parent. The attributes of an NTA are not seen as part of its value, as they are computed values, depending on the context of the NTA.

There are many ways in which the AST values can be viewed as on a lattice of bounded height. One simple way is to consider all values with the same Type to be incomparable, and to order the types. But it is also possible to consider AST values with the same Type as comparable, and to place an ordering on the tokens and children.

4.2 Evaluation

To evaluate circular NTAs we alter the demand-driven fixed-point evaluation algorithm from Figure 5, to account for AST values. The result, listed in Figure 12, maintains the three evaluation cases from Figure 5 (CASE 1, CASE 2, and CASE 3), but with a different change check (ISEQUAL) and assignment of values. The change check corresponds to a call to a boolean function ISEQUAL, complying with Definition 1. The assignment of values must account for the possible null value of AST values, and establish the child-parent invariant of the new AST value. For cases when there are several attributes in a cycle, ordinary or NTA, these will be driven to a common fixed point.

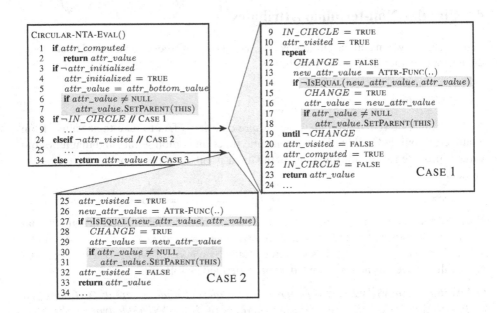

Fig. 12. Circular NTA evaluation ATTR-FUNC contains the actual attribute function. Lines differing from Figure 5 are marked.

Given that the AST values of NTAs are attributable, circular NTAs may be nested and dependent on each other. A case where an outer circular NTA depends on an inner circular NTA, and vice versa, may arise. In such a case, there may be several possible orderings of iteration steps, for example, they may be interleaved, or one of them may take a step as soon as possible. Due to the fixed-point properties, the result will be the same, regardles of iteration order.

During the evaluation of a circular NTA, it may happen that an ordinary attribute is evaluated that uses the NTA, in which case an intermediate value of the NTA may be returned by CASE 1 or CASE 2. In this case, the value of that attribute should not be cached, because it depends on a non-final value. To prevent caching in this situation, a check is added to the evaluation of ordinary non-circular attributes, setting an extra flag that is reset by the CASE 1 and CASE 2 code.

4.3 Revisiting Our Example

Revisiting the example from Section 3, we now compute the same values by using a circular NTA instead of a rewrite, as seen in Figure 13. The evaluation of the `val` attribute is illustrated in Figure 14.

```
Root ::= A;                        syn nta A Root.child()
B : A;                                 circular [getA().fullCopy()];
C : A;                             eq Root.child() = child().rewriteTo();

inh Root A.parent();               syn A A.rewriteTo() = this;
Root.child().parent() = this();    eq B.rewriteTo() {
                                     if (parent().val() > 1) {
                                       return new C();
syn int Root.val() circular [0];     }
eq Root.val() {                      return super.rewriteTo();
  int val = child().parent().val(); }
  return val < 2 ? val + 1 : val;
}
```

Fig. 13. Interdependent example revisited Alternative grammar where the rewrite is replaced by a circular NTA. The same values as in Figure 10 are computed.

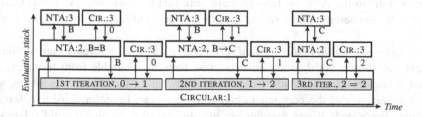

Fig. 14. Evaluation stack for revisited example An illustration of the evaluation of the `val` attribute in Figure 13. Legend described in Figure 6. Abbreviations: ITER. = ITERATION, CIR. = CIRCULAR

The important difference from the rewrite solution is the unification of the evaluation cycles. The circular NTA and the circular attribute are evaluated in the same cycle, and are aware of each others' changes. Thus, the evaluation produces consistent values. In comparing the rewrite and the NTA solution (Figure 10 and Figure 13), we see that the rewrite solution transforms the children directly, while the NTA solution defines an extra attribute (`child`). In the next section, we will see how rewrites in general can be mapped to circular NTAs, allowing rewrites and circular attributes to be mixed freely.

5   Rewrites as Circular Non-terminal Attributes

In the previous section we replaced a rewrite with a circular NTA, in effect making a child a computed entity, just like an attribute. We will now have a closer look at what happens if we compute *all* children, and based on this idea, we will present a mapping of rewrites to circular NTAs.

5.1   Considering Children as Attributes

An attribute grammar is in essence a complex function from an *initial* AST, typically constructed by a parser, to the attributes of nodes in that AST. What we are now considering is to instead view the attribute grammar as defining an attribution of an AST that is *computed* from the initial AST, using attributes. This makes sense if we consider the computed AST to initially be the same as the initial AST, which by a fixed-point computation gradually turns into the final computed AST. This way, both the computed AST and the attributes of the computed AST is a function of the initial AST. Note that the initial AST remains unchanged during the evaluation – it is only the attribution that changes, including the computed AST, until it has reached its final state, where all equations are satisfied. To consider a computed AST raises questions about the parent-child relation, and how to represent the initial and the computed AST:

The parent-child relation. The parent-child relation has a special role in an AG system, since parents have the obligation to provide equations defining the inherited attributes of their children. For our demand-driven evaluator, each node has a parent reference, satisfying the parent-child invariant, which is used by the evaluator when computing inherited attributes. In moving the AG to define an attribution over the computed AST, rather than the initial AST, we have to make sure that the computed AST is actually a tree, and that the parent-child invariant holds for both the initial and the computed AST.

Representation of initial and computed AST The initial child references are similar to reference attributes, but they are *intrinsic*, i.e., they are available from the start, and are not defined by equations, just like tokens. They can in fact be seen as tokens with reference values, and the computed child references can be defined using reference attributes. For a node where rewrites are not desired, the computed child references can simply be defined as copies of the initial child references, by using synthesized attributes. For a node where rewrites are desired, a circular NTA can be defined in its parent, and the computed child reference can be defined to refer to this NTA. In both cases, a tree structure for the computed AST is guaranteed, and parent references can be automatically added by the evaluator, whenever the computed child reference is updated by the fixed-point computation.

Although equations that refer to children will access the computed children, it is still possible to explicitly access the initial child references. This is useful, for example, to define the bottom values for computed children that are defined by circular NTAs.

5.2   Mapping Rewrites to Circular Non-terminal Attributes

As will be demonstrated in this section, rewrites can be translated to circular NTAs. We will take the solution presented in the earlier example in Figure 13 as a starting point, and extend it to a parameterized attribute `child(int)`, to handle all children of a node. However, in order to make the mapping efficient, we will take the following two properties into account: First, a rewrite is consistent when all when clauses are false, and therefore, no value comparison is needed to decide that the rewrite has terminated. Second, not all nodes have rewrites. These properties should be taken into account to avoid expensive value comparisons and unnecessary creation of NTAs.

Design A

```
syn nta ASTNode ASTNode.child(int i)
  circular [getChild(i).fullCopy()]{
  return child(i).rewriteTo();
}
syn ASTNode ASTNode.rewriteTo();
eq ASTNode.rewriteTo() = this;
eq Node.rewriteTo() {
  // list of when clause
  return super.rewriteTo();
}
```

Design B

```
public ASTNode ASTNode.child(int i) {
  if (getChild(i).mayHaveRewrite())
    return rewriteChild(i);
  return getChild(i);
}
syn boolean ASTNode.mayHaveRewrite();
eq ASTNode.mayHaveRewrite() = false;
eq Node.mayHaveRewrite() = true;
syn nta ASTNode ASTNode.rewriteChild(int i)
  circular [getChild(i).fullCopy()] {
  return rewriteChild(i).rewriteTo();
}
```

Design C

ASTNODE.REWRITETO	CASE 1/CASE 2
	...
STACK.POP()	STACK.PUSH(NTA_CHANGE)
STACK.PUSH(NTA_NO_CHANGE)	new_value = ATTR-FUNC(..)
return THIS	state = STACK.POP()
	if state ≠ NTA_NO_CHANGE
	CHANGE = TRUE
	...

Fig. 15. Mapping Design A extends the solution in Figure 13 to a parameterized circular NTA covering all children. Design B limits the construction of NTAs to children with statically declared rewrites using `mayHaveRewrite`. Design C reuses the stack of change flags from Figure 9 to avoid value comparisons for rewrites mapped to circular NTAs.

Figure 15 lists code for three mappings; designs A, B, and C. Starting with design A, we extend the `child` attribute from Figure 13 to handle an index parameter. Other than that, the solution is the same; the initial child is copied and an attribute `rewriteTo` maps to when clauses. With the above optimizations in mind, this solution is inefficient in that there is a circular NTA for every child, despite the fact that we know statically that nodes of certain types do not have any rewrites.

To address this problem, design B represents the computed children by an ordinary function child(int) that calls a circular NTA rewriteChild(int), but only in case the node may have rewrites. Because of the demand-driven evaluation, the circular NTAs will be created only when they are actually needed. For nodes that do not have any rewrites, getChild(i) is returned, i.e., the node from the initial AST. The rewrite check is implemented by a synthesized attribute mayHaveRewrites, similar to the namesake in Figure 9. This attribute is simple to generate from the grammar: it is defined as *false* for the most general node type ASTNode, and then an overriding equation that defines it as *true* is added for subclasses with rewrites.

With prevention of copies, the remaining efficiency concern in design B is the change check, which still compares values. Given that we generate the mapping from a rewrite specification, we know if a circular NTA is a replacement for a rewrite, and we can use this knowledge to prevent value comparisons: if no rewrite is applicable, the next value will be the same as the current one, so no value check is necessary. Design C in Figure 15 shows how the implementation of rewriteTo uses a stack of CHANGE/NO_CHANGE flags, in the same way as the rewrite evaluation in Figure 9.

5.3 Mapping Circular NTAs to Rewrites

In the reverse direction, circular NTAs may be mapped to rewrites. That is, the comparison of AST values performed in the evaluation of circular NTAs can be moved into the when clause of a rewrite, as follows:

```
rewrite Node {
  when (!this.IS_EQUAL(nextValue())) to Node2 {
    return nextValue();
  }
}
```

This when clause would become false when there is no change, that is, when there is a fixed-point, and this would be in accordance with the rewrite rules. Still, to support interdependencies with circular attributes, the underlying rewrite evaluation would have to be carried out in the same cycle as circular attributes, as discussed in Section 3.

6   Evaluation

We will now compare the new algorithm for rewrites, CIRCULAR-NTA, as listed in design C in Figure 12, with the current algorithm used in the JastAdd system, REWRITE-OPT, i.e., the one listed in Figure 9 extended with bookkeeping for caching. We also compare to REWRITE-INIT, which is a variant of REWRITE-OPT that additionally saves initial AST values. This variant is used to support incremental evaluation for RAGs with rewrites, as described in [23]. The evaluation code in this section is available at [8].

For the comparison, we use the scaled-down language DemoJavaNames, that demonstrates name resolution for Java, where contextually ambiguous dot-expressions like a.b.c are resolved to package, type, and expression names using rewrites [10]. The

```
Prog ::= CompUnit*;
CompUnit ::= .. ClassDecl*;                    rewrite AmbiguousName {
ClassDecl ::= .. BodyDecl*;                      when(..) to Name new ExpressionName(..);
abstract BodyDecl;                               when(..) to Name new TypeName(..);
FieldDecl:BodyDecl::= Name .. Expr;              when(..) to Name new PackageName(..);
MemberClassDecl:BodyDecl ::=ClassDecl;         }
abstract Expr;                                 rewrite PackageOrTypeName {
abstract Name:Expr::=<name:String>;              when(..) to Name new TypeName(..);
Dot:Name ::= Left:Name Right:Name;               when(..) to Name new PackageName(..);
ExpressionName:Name;                           }
PackageName:Name;
TypeName:Name;
ParseName:Name;
PackageOrTypeName : Name;
AmbiguousName : Name;
rewrite ParseName {
when(..) to Name new PackageName(..);
when(..) to Name new TypeName(..);
when(..) to Name new ExpressionName(..);
when(..) to Name new PackageOrTypeName(..);
when(..) to Name new AmbiguousName(..);
}
```

Fig. 16. DemoJavaNames An excerpt from the DemoJavaNames RAG. The rewrite value lattice is shown bottom right. Names are abbreviated for conciseness.

rewrites directly encode the rules in the Java language specification for reclassification of parsed names, using intermediate classifications like `AmbiguousName` and `PackageOrTypeName`. Figure 16 shows an excerpt from the DemoJavaNames RAG, together with a lattice over rewrite AST values. Each when clause corresponds to an arrow in the lattice.

The example programs in Figure 17 each contains at least one assignment with a dot-expression on the right-hand side. To test the impact of nested dot-expressions, the examples are expanded to different sizes, where the examples shown have size 1, and an example of size K has $K + 1$ dots in the dot-expression (second dot-expression for Program II). To obtain programs that are sufficiently large to measure performance accurately, we have scaled up the program code in two different ways. In Program I, the class is replicated 1000 times (mangling the names to avoid name conflicts), $N = 1000$. In Program II, the class is replicated 10 times, $N = 10$, 10 inner classes are added inside each outer class, $M = 10$, and finally, the inner assignment is replicated 100 times. The result is that Program I has 1000 assignments and Program II has 10 000 assignments.

Given a set of Programs I and II, for different values of K, we do a full traversal of each program using all three algorithms, to trigger all rewrites, or circular NTA computations. We count the number of computations using an instrumented version of each algorithm, and we measure performance on a non-instrumented version. To measure performance we use the multi-iteration approach described in [4], and measure on a Lenovo X230 with OpenJDK 1.7.0/Linux Mint.

Figure 18 shows the results for values of K between 1 and 10. In the left side diagrams, we see that the CIRCULAR-NTA algorithm reduces the number of attribute computations compared to REWRITE-OPT and REWRITE-INIT, which both have the same number of computations. This remarkable decrease is due to the opportunity to cache

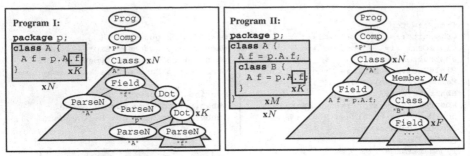

Fig. 17. Expandable evaluation programs Program I is described to the left, and Program II is described to the right. Each program is based on a small program which is expanded (xN,xM,xK,xF), as indicated with boxes in the left-side code samples. The corresponding initial ASTs, and expansions, are shown to the right for each program. The inner field in Program II is expanded xK, as described for Program I.

attributes during the rewrites in the CIRCULAR-NTA algorithm. As the same attribute instance may be evaluated several times, early caching of attributes can make a big difference in the number of attribute computations that need to be done.

The middle diagrams show the number of node copies made for each algorithm. REWRITE-OPT makes no copies, while CIRCULAR-NTA and REWRITE-INIT both make copies in order to keep the initial AST unmodified. The REWRITE-INIT algorithm makes a copy during initialization before CASE 1. This is the same for CIRCULAR-NTA, and non-surprisingly they end up making the same number of copies.

The right-side diagrams show the execution times for the algorithms. As we can see, the CIRCULAR-NTA is faster than REWRITE-INIT for all K, for both Program I and II, and that the gap grows for larger values of K. The REWRITE-OPT algorithm is slightly faster for low values of K, for Program I, although with overlapping confidence intervals, but for larger values of K, CIRCULAR-NTA is faster, and with an increasing amount. For Program II, CIRCULAR-NTA is faster than REWRITE-OPT for all K.

7   Related Work

Knuth's original attribute grammar definition assumes non-circular attributes, and provides an algorithm for determining statically if attribute grammars are cyclic or not [18]. However, for attribute grammars with remote attribute access, like in RAGs, determining circularity statically is an undecidable problem [5]. In JastAdd, it is assumed that the user explicitly declares circular attributes as circular. If an attribute is not declared as circular, but in fact turns out to be circularly defined for a given AST, this can be detected dynamically [20].

RAG rewrites have similarities to tree transformation systems like Stratego [25], ASF+SDF [24], and TXL [6]. These systems typically rely on user-defined rewrite application strategies. RAG rewrites, in contrast, can depend on arbitrary attribute values, that may themselves depend on rewrites, and the rewriting order is implicit, and driven by the dependencies.

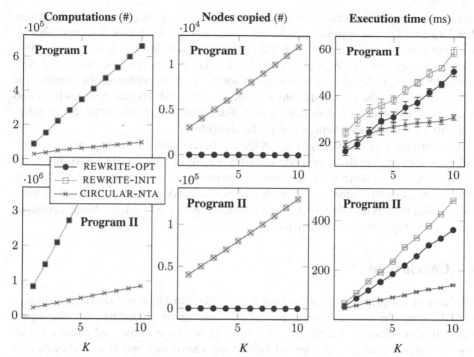

Fig. 18. Results The rows show results for Program I (top row) and Program II (bottom row). For each row, the left-side diagram shows number of attribute instance computations, the middle diagram shows the number of node copies made, and the right-side diagram shows the execution time, with an included confidence interval of 95%. The titles give the labels for the y axes.

An alternative approach to supporting transformations for attribute grammars is *forwarding* [27]. Here, the transformed AST is constructed as an NTA, and synthesized and inherited attributes can be automatically forwarded to the NTA, giving the effect of a transformation. If the transformation includes several steps, all intermediate steps will be kept when using forwarding, whereas with rewrites, the nodes are replaced. A major difference between rewrites and forwarding is the open syntax provided by rewrites, allowing conditional rewrite steps to be added in separate modules.

Martins, Fernandes and Saraiva suggest the use of *functional zippers* to provide a functional embedding of attribute grammars in Haskell, including support for reference attributes, higher-order attributes, and circular higher-order attributes [21]. They give an example of implementing a circular higher-order attribute using fixed-point iteration. Similar to our mapping of rewrites to circular NTAs, they terminate the iteration based on changes, rather than value equality. In contrast to our work, they use a manually encoded fixed-point iteration, rather than a general algorithm. Furthermore, they do not address rewrites or cases where several attribute instances are mutually dependent, and they do not give any performance results.

In editor applications, the initial AST can be modified as a response to edits done interactively by the user, causing attributes to become inconsistent. For demand-driven evaluators, consistency can be restored simply by flushing all cached attribute values. For large ASTs, this approach might not scale, and an alternative is to apply an incremental evaluator that reuses unaffected attribute values. Incremental evaluators have been presented both for AGs [7,22] and for RAGs [23]. In any case, the initial AST needs to be kept. To use the REWRITE/REWRITE-OPT algorithm in this setting, the evaluator needs to be modified to store the initial AST nodes before rewrites [23], corresponding to the algorithm REWRITE-INIT. For the new algorithm (CIRCULAR-NTA), the initial AST nodes are kept as part of the algorithm.

Concerning termination, a circular NTA can be compared to constructing one new NTA for each step in the fixed-point iteration. Krishnan and Van Wyk have suggested an approach to conservatively determine termination for such multi-level NTAs [19]. It is based on ordering the nonterminals (the node types), so that each new NTA has a lower order than its host. We used a similar technique for the DemoJavaNames example, where node types were ordered in a lattice.

8   Conclusions

We have investigated the interplay between circular attributes and rewrites, and introduced a generalized evaluation algorithm that can handle grammars with interdependent circular attributes and rewrites. To this end, we have introduced circular NTAs, and shown how rewrites are a special form of such attributes, and how their evaluation can be optimized. As a performance evaluation, we have compared the new and old algorithms on a typical rewrite problem. The results suggest that the new algorithm, while being more general, has similar performance for simple programs, and that the performance is substantially improved for more complex programs. Further experiments on full scale grammars and programs are needed to confirm these results.

The presented mapping of rewrites to circular NTAs provides a compelling simplification of the meta-compilation system that can handle more general grammars with fewer evaluation mechanisms, and with similar or improved performance.

Acknowledgements. We would like to thank Niklas Fors and Jesper Öqvist for valuable feedback. This research was partially funded by the Swedish Research Council (Vetenskapsrådet) under grant 621-2012-4727.

References

1. Apel, S., Kolesnikov, S., Liebig, J., et al.: Access control in feature-oriented programming. Sci. Comp. Prog. 77(3), 174–187 (2012)
2. Appeltauer, M., Hirschfeld, R., Masuhara, H., Haupt, M., Kawauchi, K.: Event-specific software composition in context-oriented programming. In: Baudry, B., Wohlstadter, E. (eds.) SC 2010. LNCS, vol. 6144, pp. 50–65. Springer, Heidelberg (2010)
3. Avgustinov, P., Ekman, T., Tibble, J.: Modularity first: a case for mixing AOP and attribute grammars. In: AOSD, pp. 25–35. ACM (2008)
4. Blackburn, S.M., McKinley, K.S., Garner, R., et al.: Wake up and smell the coffee: evaluation methodology for the 21st century. CACM 51(8), 83–89 (2008)
5. Tang Boyland, J.: Remote attribute grammars. J. ACM 52(4), 627–687 (2005)

6. Cordy, J.R.: The TXL source transformation language. Sci. Comp. Prog. 61(3), 190–210 (2006)
7. Demers, A.J., Reps, T.W., Teitelbaum, T.: Incremental evaluation for attribute grammars with application to syntax-directed editors. In: White, J., Lipton, R.J., Goldberg, P.C. (eds.) POPL, pp. 105–116. ACM Press (1981)
8. Söderberg, E.: Paper examples (2013), http://fileadmin.cs.lth.se/sde/publications/papers/2013-Soderberg-SLE-CircularNTA
9. Ekman, T., Hedin, G.: Rewritable reference attributed grammars. In: Odersky, M. (ed.) ECOOP 2004. LNCS, vol. 3086, pp. 147–171. Springer, Heidelberg (2004)
10. Ekman, T., Hedin, G.: Modular name analysis for Java using JastAdd. In: Lämmel, R., Saraiva, J., Visser, J. (eds.) GTTSE 2005. LNCS, vol. 4143, pp. 422–436. Springer, Heidelberg (2006)
11. Ekman, T., Hedin, G.: The Jastadd Extensible Java Compiler. In: OOPSLA, pp. 1–18. ACM (2007)
12. Ekman, T., Hedin, G.: The JastAdd system - modular extensible compiler construction. Sci. Comp. Prog. 69(1-3), 14–26 (2007)
13. Farrow, R.: Automatic generation of fixed-point-finding evaluators for circular, but well-defined, attribute grammars. In: SIGPLAN 1986: Proceedings of the 1986 SIGPLAN Symposium on Compiler Construction, pp. 85–98. ACM, New York (1986)
14. Hedin, G.: Reference Attributed Grammars. Informatica (Slovenia) 24(3), 301–317 (2000)
15. Jones, L.G.: Efficient evaluation of circular attribute grammars. ACM TOPLAS 12(3), 429–462 (1990)
16. Jones, L.G., Simon, J.: Hierarchical vlsi design systems based on attribute grammars. In: POPL, pp. 58–69. ACM (1986)
17. Jourdan, M.: An optimal-time recursive evaluator for attribute grammars. In: Paul, M., Robinet, B. (eds.) Programming 1984. LNCS, vol. 167, pp. 167–178. Springer, Heidelberg (1984)
18. Knuth, D.E.: Semantics of Context-free Languages. Mathematical Systems Theory 2(2), 127–145 (1968); Correction: Mathematical Systems Theory 5(1), 95–96 (1971)
19. Krishnan, L., Van Wyk, E.: Termination analysis for higher-order attribute grammars. In: Czarnecki, K., Hedin, G. (eds.) SLE 2012. LNCS, vol. 7745, pp. 44–63. Springer, Heidelberg (2013)
20. Magnusson, E., Hedin, G.: Circular reference attributed grammars - their evaluation and applications. Sci. Comp. Program. 68(1), 21–37 (2007)
21. Martins, P., Fernandes, J.P., Saraiva, J.: Zipper-based attribute grammars and their extensions. In: Du Bois, A. (ed.) SBLP 2013. LNCS, vol. 8129, pp. 135–149. Springer, Heidelberg (2013)
22. Reps, T.W.: Optimal-time incremental semantic analysis for syntax-directed editors. In: DeMillo, R.A. (ed.) POPL, pp. 169–176. ACM Press (1982)
23. Söderberg, E., Hedin, G.: Incremental Evaluation of Reference Attribute Grammars using Dynamic Dependency Tracking. Technical Report 98, Lund University, LU-CS-TR:2012-249, ISSN 1404-1200 (April 2012)
24. den van Brand, M.G.J., et al.: The ASF+SDF meta-environment: A component-based language development environment. In: Wilhelm, R. (ed.) CC 2001. LNCS, vol. 2027, pp. 365–370. Springer, Heidelberg (2001)
25. Visser, E.: Stratego: A language for program transformation based on rewriting strategies system description of stratego 0.5. In: Middeldorp, A. (ed.) RTA 2001. LNCS, vol. 2051, pp. 357–361. Springer, Heidelberg (2001)
26. Vogt, H., Swierstra, S.D., Kuiper, M.F.: Higher order attribute grammars. In: PLDI, pp. 131–145 (1989)
27. Van Wyk, E., de Moor, O., Backhouse, K., Kwiatkowski, P.: Forwarding in attribute grammars for modular language design. In: Nigel Horspool, R. (ed.) CC 2002. LNCS, vol. 2304, pp. 128–142. Springer, Heidelberg (2002)

Mapping-Aware Megamodeling: Design Patterns and Laws*

Zinovy Diskin[1,2], Sahar Kokaly[1], and Tom Maibaum[1]

[1] NECSIS, McMaster University, Canada
{diskinz,kokalys,maibaum}@mcmaster.ca
[2] University of Waterloo, Canada
zdiskin@gsd.uwaterloo.ca

Abstract. Megamodeling is the activity of specifying systems of models and mappings, their properties, and operations over them. The latter functionality is the most important for applications, and megamodels are often used as an abstract workflow language for model processing. To be independent of a particular modeling language, typical megamodels reduce relationships between models to unstructured edges encoding nothing but a labeled pair of models, thus creating a significant gap between megamodels and code implementing them. To bridge the gap, we propose *mapping-aware* megamodels, which treat edges as model mappings: structured sets of links (pairs of model elements) rather than pairs of models. The workflow can then be represented as an algebraic term built from elementary operations with models and model mappings.

1 Introduction

Model driven software engineering (MDE) puts models at the heart of software development, and makes it heavily dependent on the provision of intelligent model management (MMt) frameworks and tools. A common approach to implementing MMt tasks is to present models as collections of objects, and to program model operations in terms of operations applied to these objects; we can call this *object-at-a-time programming (ObjATP)*. Since models may contain thousands of interrelated objects, ObjATP can be laborious and error-prone. In a sense, it is similar to the infamous *record-at-a-time programming (RecATP)* in data processing, and has similar problems of "micro-management".

Replacing RecATP by *relation-ATP* ("macro-management") has raised data processing technology to a qualitatively new level in semantic transparency and programmer productivity. Similarly, one can expect that *model-ATP*, in which an engineer can think of MMt routines in terms of operations over models as integral entities, could significantly facilitate development of MMt applications. Lately, this program has been pursued by the database community [3], and is being gradually developed by the MDE community under the umbrella of *megamodeling* [4].

---

* This work was done as part of the NECSIS project, funded by Automotive Partnership Canada and NSERC.

M. Erwig, R.F. Paige, and E. Van Wyk (Eds.): SLE 2013, LNCS 8225, pp. 322–343, 2013.

Megamodeling is the activity of specifying systems of models and mappings, their properties, and operations over them. The latter functionality is the most important for applications, and megamodels are often used as an abstract work-flow language for model processing. A simple megamodel is presented in Fig. 1(a). Names A_i, A, B refer to models, and edges refer to different types of intermodel relationships: arc o denotes an overlap between models A_1 and A_2, arrows e_i are model embeddings, and arrow t specifies model B as the result of transformation t applied to model A. Label [merge] specifies A as the merge of A_1, A_2 modulo overlap o. For example, one may think of A_1 and A_2 as a class and a sequence diagram, A as an UML model merging them, and B as Java code generated from A. In practical applications, this megamodel would also contain other models A_i and their overlaps in the direction A_1, A_2: think of other class, sequence, stat-echart and other types of diagrams. A typical megamodel would also contain models preceding and succeeding those A_i via transformation/refinement chains along the direction AB.

With a suitable implementation of a megamodeling language, the megamodel in Fig. 1(a) could be understood dynamically as a simple workflow described by a pseudo-script in Fig. 1(b). While the megamodel Fig. 1(a) helps to understand what the script does, it provides little help for the script implementation. Indeed, there is a rich structure, and important structural dependencies, not explicated by the meg-amodel. We will show in the paper that edges of a typical metamodel like that in Fig. 1 are actually structured sets of links between the models—we will say *model mappings*, and even a single model is a mapping from its data graph to its type graph. MMt operations are thus operations over

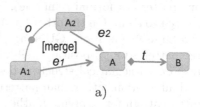

a)

```
import models A1, A2
import overlap O=O(A1, A2)
merge (A1,A2) into A by O
import transformation t
apply t to A result B
```

b)

Fig. 1. Workflow megamodel

models and model mappings: they take a configuration of models and map-pings as their input, and return a configuration of models and mappings as their output with the added constraint that certain structural dependencies between mappings must be respected. In contrast, in typical megamodeling languages [24,19], edges are considered as binary relationships (labeled pairs of models): overlap(A1,A2), embedsIn(Ai,A), isTransformOf(A,B), and conformsTo(A,M) for a model A and a metamodel M. Rich semantics of mappings and operations over them is hidden in names and not anyhow made explicit. This semantics will then be implicit in code but not specified, which leads to well known problems in testing and maintenance. Moreover, unclear semantics hinders tool acceptance by the user (cf. [34]).

In databases, SQL replaced RecATP by RelATP and achieved great success. Megamodeling strives to repeat this experience by replacing ObjATP by ModATP, but is not yet successful. An important cause of this failure is that a crucial ingredient of the megamodeling landscape—model mappings—is missing from the picture. At least, so far mappings are not properly placed into the general megamodeling framework, and are not first-class citizens there.

Our goal is to demonstrate the primary role that model mappings can (and must) play in megamodeling. We propose a new type of megamodel, the *mapping-aware (MA-)megamodel*, which is built from two elementary blocks: graphs and graph mappings. Models and complex intermodel relationships are composed from these blocks, and the workflow appears as an algebraic term built from elementary operations over them. We show how classical megamodeling constructs (conformance, overlap, consistency, and transformation) can be composed from graphs, graph mappings, and operations over them. Then, *edges-are-relationships* megamodels appear as formally specified abstractions of our MA-megamodels. Moreover, by combining the same blocks we can build new useful constructs, e.g., bidirectional transformations and heterogeneous merge. In this way, we are building a library of structural design patterns for megamodel engineering. We give our patterns a formal semantics, and identity several basic mathematical laws related to them. On the other hand, our notation for specifying MA-megamodels can be usable in tools, GUIs, and "back of the envelope" designs. Importantly, the patterns we propose are well-known and tested in category theory in the context of mathematical structure design. What we do is thus more pattern reuse and adaptation rather than pattern discovery, which, we believe, is itself a good meta-pattern for applying mathematics to engineering disciplines.

Our plan is as follows. In Sections 2 and 3, we introduce MA-megamodels via a series of simple examples, specify our library of elementary building blocks, and demonstrate how to combine them into a complex workflow. Section 2 is devoted to basic intermodel relations, and Section 3 is about basic operations over models and mappings crucial for model transformations. In Section 3.4 we will finish our tour of megamodeling blocks and unfold the megamodel in Fig. 1 into an ma-megamodel In Section 4 we discuss how to adapt the framework for more general situations and show that richer mappings can be packaged into the simple syntax developed in Sections 2 and 3. Related work is discussed in Section 5, and Section 6 concludes.

2   Models, Mappings and Model Overlap

2.1   Elementary Blocks: Models

Fig. 2(a) presents a simple object model A describing John, Mary and their happy relations. Normally, OIDs would be anonymous, and names would be attributes, but to simplify presentation, we use names as OIDs.

Objects and their attributes are typed by elements of the class diagram M (the metamodel for model A). The metamodel consists of a class Person and two unidirectional associations (we will say *maps*), 'loves' and 'helps', with multiplicities: every person loves at most one person, and helps from 1 to 3 persons. The arrow denotes an implication constraint: if x loves y, then x helps y. To be

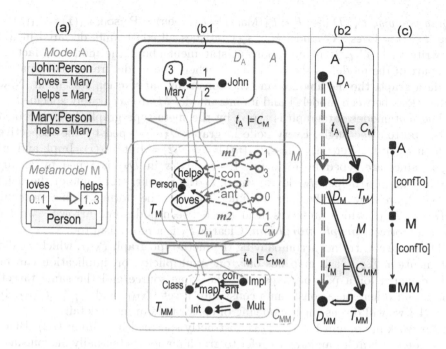

Fig. 2. A sample model and its formalization via graphs and graph mappings

a legal instance of the metamodel, an object diagram typed over M must satisfy the constraints; e.g., model A satisfies them.

A typical megamodeling abstraction of (a) is shown in (c). The diagram specifies a relationship $(A, M) \in$ conformsTo (a *link*) between models. The problem with this specification is an essential gap between the real model and its abstract description. The compact syntax of UML diagrams hides a multitude of structural connections not shown in (c). We plan to zoom into models in column (a), reveal their structure and relations, and build an ma-megamodel less abstract than (c), but still independent of the specifics of the concrete case in (a).

We first accurately formalize the metamodel. The latter consists of three types (UML says classifiers): one class and two maps, which form the *type graph* T_M in column Fig. 2(b1) framed by a roundtangle. The three constraints are not types but are important elements of the metamodel: they are represented by blank nodes (red with a color display) connected to the types they constrain by dashed (red) arrows: nodes $m1$, $m2$ denote multiplicities, and node i is implication. Constraints form the *constraint graph*, C_M, dashed-framed in Fig. 2(b1). The intersection graph $T_M \cap C_M$ consists of types that are in the scope of at least one constraint (i.e., all types for the case). Types and constraints together form the data graph $D_M = T_M \cup C_M$ of the metamodel (the outer roundtangle).

Model A is given by its data graph D_A (the upper roundtangle in Fig. 2b1), whose elements are *typed* as shown by curved (orange) links in Fig. 2(b1) (two node typing links are skipped to avoid clutter). These links together make a

typing mapping $t_A \colon D_A \to T_M \colon t_A(\mathsf{Mary}) = t_A(\mathsf{John}) = \mathsf{Person}$, $t_A(1) = t_A(3) =$
help, $t_A(2) = \mathsf{loves}$. As model (D_A, t_A) satisfies all constraints declared in M,
we write $t_A \models C_M$. It is an important statement about the model; in fact, it
is a part of the model as shown in Fig. 2, where the model frame encompasses
its data graph, the metamodel, and the constraint satisfaction statement. Now
connections between model A and its metamodel M are accurately specified.

The metamodel datagraph is typed by the meta-type graph T_{MM} specified
in the bottom rectangle. Every node in graph D_M is typed by the respective
node in $T_{MM} \colon t_M(\mathsf{Person}) = \mathsf{Class}$, $t_M(m1) = t_M(m2) = \mathsf{Mult}$, $t_M(i) = \mathsf{Impl}$, and integer values are typed by node Int. Every arrow in D_M is typed by an ar-
row in $T_{MM} \colon t_M(\mathsf{helps}) = t_M(\mathsf{loves}) = \mathsf{map}$, $t_M(\mathsf{:ant}) = \mathsf{ant}$, etc. Some of the pairs
$[x, t_M(x)]$ are shown in the figure by links. Together they form a typing mapping
$t \colon D_M \to T_{MM}$, which preserves incidence between nodes and arrows – we say
t_M is a (correct) *graph morphism*. Clearly, t_A is a morphism too.

There are constraints accompanying the meta-type graph T_{MM}, which we did
not mention. E.g., each map has only one multiplicity, or, implication can be
only declared for a pair of maps with the same source and the same target.
These and other meta-constraints constitute a set C_{MM}, and $t_M \models C_{MM}$. In
Sect. 4.3 we will discuss metamodeling of constraints in more detail.

Our work in column Fig. 2(b1) is abstractly specified in column (b2). Black
circles denote graphs, and arrows refer to graph mappings (actually morphisms):
vertical ones provide typing, and horizontal ones are inclusions of type graphs
into data graphs. Dashed (blue with color display) mappings are compositions of
typing mappings with inclusions (we will motivate this visualization in Section
3). A dashed arrow comprises the same set of links as the solid arrow from the
same source, but has a different target; by the abuse of notation, we will denote
both mappings by the same symbol.

With one more abstraction step, we can denote all data embodied into models
by roundtangle black nodes, and conformance relationships between models by
bullet-tail arrows as shown in Fig. 2(c). The meaning of such relationships is
hidden in the label [confTo] (and described in column (b2)), but what is exactly
specified is two links labeled by a relationship type. Here and below we denote
links by thin arrows with bullet-tails. In contrast, mappings between structures,
which themselves are sets of links, are denoted by thick double-body arrows.

Thus, a metamodel is a pair of interrelated graphs, $M = (T, C)$. It is assigned
with two classes of instances. Those that are legally typed but perhaps do not
satisfy the constraints will be called *premodels*; the class of all premodels is
$\mathsf{Inst}^\circ(M) \stackrel{\text{def}}{=} \{A = (D_A, t_A) \mid t_A \colon D_A \to T \text{ is a correct graph mapping}\}$, Those
that are legally typed *and* satisfy all constraints are called *models*; they make
a class $\mathsf{Inst}^\bullet(M) = \{A \mid t_A \models C_M\} \subset \mathsf{Inst}^\circ(M)$. This distinction is important in
formalization of a multimodel's consistency via merge (discussed later).

Pattern 1. A model is a total *typing* mapping from model's *data* graph to
model's *metadata* graph, which comprises a type graph and a constraint graph.
The Laws. Typing must be a correct graph morphism, and all constraints declared in the metamodel are to be satisfied.

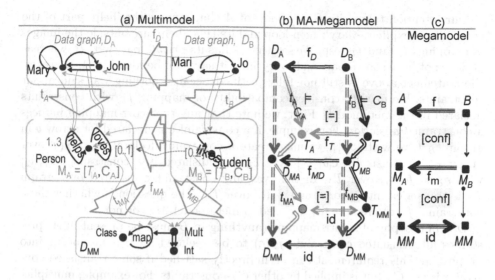

Fig. 3. Model mapping

2.2 Elementary Blocks: Model Mappings

The idea behind a mapping from model B to model A is that everything described by B must be present in A. Consider an example. Model A in Fig. 3(a) presents the next step of our story: now Mary and John love each other. Model B (created, perhaps, by a different team) is a view of A in which the help-side of the story is ignored (recall that names here are OIDs and hence are different in B). To explicate B as a view of A, we map each B's element to a respective A's element as shown in Fig. 3(a) by curved (orange with a color display) *correspondence* links (we will say *corr-links*). Together, these links form a totally defined graph morphism $f_D: D_A \leftarrow D_B$. However, these links do not respect typing and map Students to Persons, and 'like'-links to 'love-links. To make correspondence type-safe, we need to match the respective types and map B's types to A's types as shown by two links making mapping $f_T: T_A \leftarrow T_B$ (inside bigger mapping $f_M: M_A \leftarrow M_B$ in Fig. 3(a) with M referring to metadata. In a heterogeneous environment, each model X refers to its own metamodel M_X, and we write T_X for T_{M_X}.) [1] Thus, our corr-mapping $f: A \leftarrow B$ consists of two parts: data mapping $f_D: D_A \leftarrow D_B$ and metadata mapping $f_T: T_A \leftarrow T_B$, which are both graph morphism that together with vertical typing morphisms form the back-face square diagram in Fig. 3(b). Type-safety is *commutativity* requirement for this diagram: $b.f_D.t_A = b.t_B.f_T$ for any element b of datagraph D_B.

---

[1] If Mari, Student etc. were values of attribute name rather than OIDs, we could simply exclude them from the domain of the mapping, as we would exclude other auxiliary (wrt. modeling as such) attributes, e.g., timestamps. On the other hand, if we do want to pay attention to names, then we have a conflict between the models, and their correspondence must be specified by a span of mappings, rather than by a mapping, as will be explained in Sect. 2.3.

Our intention to specify B as a view of A that ignores the 'help'-part of the story is now explicit: Mary's help-loop and its type 'help' are outside the images of mappings f_D and f_T resp. We say that A has its *private* part wrt. B, whereas B does not have such a part and everything it says can be found in A. However, the statement above is still not fully justified because nothing was said about constraints. We need to consider compatibility of mapping f_T with constraints declared in the metamodels. First, we note that any type corr-mapping induces a constraint *translation*. For example, if a constraint c is declared for arrow b in graph T_B (we write c$[b]$), we may create a constraint declaration c$[f_T(b)]$ over graph T_A. A constraint c$[b_1, b_2]$ over T_B is translated into constraint c$[a_1, a_2]$ with $a_i = f_T(b_i)$ over T_A. In this way any constraint c declared over graph T_B is translated into a constraint $f_T(\mathsf{c})$ over T_A. The question is whether these constraints $f_T(\mathsf{c})$ are actually declared in metamodel M_A, or not.

Our philosophy of a corr-mapping (anything in B must be present in A) prescribes all translated constraints $f_T(\mathsf{c})$ to be declared in M_A, i.e., occur into graph C_A. This requirement can be indirectly satisfied if some translated constraint is not C_A but is implied by other C_A-constraints. For example, multiplicity 0..2 for link help in T_B is translated into mult. 0..2 for link 'love'=f_T('help') in T_A, which is implied by mult. 0..1 declared in M_A (indeed, "not more than one" implies "not more than two"). Hence, we may informally map mult. 0..2 for 'like' into mult. 0..1 for 'love' as shown in Fig. 3(a). For complex constraints, to check $C_A \models f_T(\mathsf{c})$, we check consistency of theory $C_A \cup \{\mathsf{not} f_T(\mathsf{c})\}$ with a model checker. This gives us a bigger mapping $f_M \colon M_A \leftarrow M_B$. Clearly, this mapping must commute with two (meta)typing mappings t_{M_A}, t_{M_B} as shown in the lower part of Fig. 3(a)—metatype-safety condition. Note that we need to revise the philosophy underlying the notion of corr mapping $f \colon A \leftarrow B$. Now it reads: everything in B must be present, *perhaps indirectly*, in A. In Sect. 4.3, we will consider yet another indirection in model mappings, when data elements from the source model are mapped to queries against the target model.

To treat constraint correspondence formally, we introduce graph $C_A^{\models} \supset C_A$ encompassing all constraints implied by C_A, and if all translated constraints are indeed declared in $C_A^{\models}$, we have mapping $f_C \colon C_A^{\models} \leftarrow C_B$. Then we also have mapping $(f_T \cup f_C) \colon (T_A \cup C_A^{\models}) \leftarrow (t_B \cup C_B)$ or $f_M \colon M_A^{\models} \leftarrow M_B$ as shown in Fig. 3(b) (where superindex $\models$ near M_A is skipped).

Fig. 3(b) abstracts our work with example in terms of graphs and their morphisms. As both models share the same meta-metamodel, the meta-metadata mapping f_{MM} is identity; for different MM_A and MM_B, it would be some nontrivial corr-mapping. All arrows in the diagram denote graph morphisms. For mappings f_M and f_{MM}, it implies compatibility with constraints. For vertical (typing) mappings, constraint satisfaction is a special requirement (discussed later in Sect. 4.1). Diagram Fig. 3(c) is an abstraction of diagram (b): horizontal arrows encode the respective commutative diagrams (hence, the triple-body of the arrows); vertical arrows are conformance relationships as in Fig. 2.

Pattern 2. *A model mapping is a pair of total correspondence mappings between the respective data and metadata parts of the models. Together with the respective typing mappings, they form a square of mappings.*

The Laws. To ensure type-safety, the model mapping square is required to be commutative. Moreover, translations of constraints declared for the source of a mapping are to be implied by the constraints in the target: the target is to be at least as constrained, perhaps more constrained, than the source.

2.3 Model Overlap and Consistency

2.3.1 Simple Overlaps

Models A and B in Fig. 4 present two views of the same domain. The views overlap as Mary and John in model A and Mari and Jo in model B correspond (refer to the same real world objects), and the 'love' and 'like' links between them do too.

However, we cannot specify this overlap by a totally defined mapping from one model to another because each of them has its own private information: attribute 'age' in A and attribute 'gpa' in B. In addition, corr-links constitute an important part of the megamodel, and we may want to annotate them with auxiliary metadata (e.g., timestamp, authorship). Both issues (totality and annotation) can be managed by *reifying* the correspondence links with a new model O(verlap) as shown in the figure. Elements of O could be thought of as pairs of elements $(a, b) \in A \times B$, and total mappings, $f: A \leftarrow O$ and $g: O \to B$, as projections identifying the corresponding parts of the components.

A pair of mappings with a common source is called a (binary) *span*, model O is its *head*, projection mappings f, g are *legs*, and their targets A, B are *feet* of the span. There are also m-ary spans with m legs and feet.

Below we will refer to Mary/Mari and John/Jo as to M and J resp. Note that model O satisfies neither constraints C_A nor C_B. Indeed, as model A misses an important fact that M loves herself while model B misses that she likes J, neither of these two

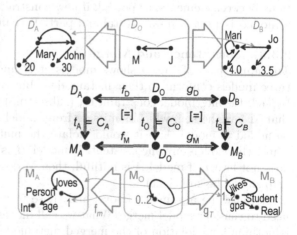

Fig. 4. Overlapping models

links occurs in the overlap model O. Hence, we need to relax multiplicity in the metamodel M_O to a $(0,.1)$ value. This is a general rule: the head of the overlap span is always less constrained than its feet.

2.3.2   Complex Overlap via Constraints

In the example above, the overlap model M_O declares only a set of "equations" (John=Jo=J, Mary=Mari=M, etc.) specifying a correspondence between models A and B. However, models can interact in a more complex way. An example is shown in Fig. 5, in which maps in the models ('loves' and 'helps', resp.) are different, but are logically related by a constraint c_{hl}: "if X helps Y, then X loves Y". This constraint is declared in the new metamodel M_O and denoted there by a double-body (red) arrow between the maps. Note that constraint c_{hl} is an essentially new piece of data, it belongs to neither M_A nor M_B and cannot be declared in either of them. Respectively, projection mappings are partially defined (note links that go into projection arrows and vanish there). We call such spans *partial*, and overlaps *complex*. Finally, we show in [8] that specifying overlap of n-models may need several m-ary (total and partial) spans ($2 \leq m \leq n$).

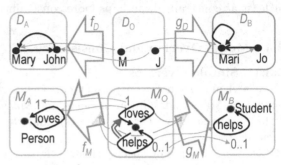

Fig. 5. Overlap via constraints

Pattern 3 (Model Overlap). Overlap of two models is a span of model mappings. The latter are either total, if overlapping amounts to correspondence equations between elements, or partial, if new constraints are introduced. Overlap of n-models is a set of m-ary (total and partial) spans with $2 \leq m \leq n$.

2.3.3   Consistency and Merge

The upper part of Fig. 5 shows models A, B and their overlap model O. All three models conform to their metamodels, but together they are inconsistent. Indeed, the intermodel constraint c_{lh} (subsetting) together with model B imply that M loves herself, which is missing from model A. Moreover, this fact cannot be added to model A as it would violate the multiplicity 1 in the metamodel. Thus, the models are inconsistent: if model B is faithful (to reality), then M does not love J; if model A is faithful, then M does not help herself (indeed, J's help should be sufficient).

To make the arguments above, and those in Section 2.3.1, more precise, we need to consider model merge. What we call inconsistency of a system of models is nothing but violation of the merged metamodel's constraints by the merged model (all computed modulo their overlap). Examples and details can be found in [33] for the homogeneous case, and in [8] for the heterogeneous case.

Pattern 3 Completed: The Laws. The merge of a system of models modulo their overlap span is a correct premodel. However, it can violate inter-model constraints. This is what we call *inconsistency*.

3   Model Transformations

There are two fundamental operations over models: computing a view of a given source, and generating a source from a given view. The roles played by the view models in these scenarios are entirely different: the view is *descriptive* for the former, and *prescriptive* for the latter (cf. analytical vs. synthetic views in [28]). We consider these operations in Sections 3.1 and 3.2 resp. In Section 3.3 we show that complex model transformations can be seen as combinations of the two operations, and in Section 3.4 we consider a complex workflow scenario described in Fig. 1.

To differentiate between given (*basic*) objects, and those computed with an operation (*derived*), we will use the following formatting (different from the static figures above). Basic models and mappings are shaded, and their nodes and links are solid. Derived models and mappings are blank, and their nodes and links are blank and dashed (and additionally blue with a color display).

To simplify diagrams, having two metamodels M, N and a mapping $v \colon M \leftarrow N$, we will skip graph inclusions $T_M \hookrightarrow D_M$, $T_N \hookrightarrow D_N$, and only keep metadata mapping $v \colon D_M \leftarrow D_N$. Also, to ease presentation, we will use the same names Mary , John for both interrelated models.

3.1   Descriptive Views

We return to the case described in Fig. 3, but now consider it in a different context (see Fig. 6). We have two metamodels, M and N with datagraphs $D_M = (T_M, C_M)$ and $D_N = (T_N, C_N)$, and a mapping $v \colon D_M \leftarrow D_N$ that describes N as a view of M. We want to consider this mapping as a *view definition* in the technical sense, i.e., as a declarative specification that can be executed for any instance of M, e.g., model A shown in the figure. The result should be an instance of N, model $V = \mathsf{get}_v(A)$ (read "get the view v of A"). In contrast to Fig. 3 where model B and mapping f are given, model V and traceability mapping $trace_V$ are to be computed, as a database view would be.

The computing procedure works as follows. We take an element $n \in D_N$, find all elements a in D_A whose type is $v(n)$ and copy them to V with type n. In detail, if $t_A(a) = v(n)$, we create a copy $a^* \in D_V$ and set $t_V(a^*) = n$ (the figure shows how it works). Thus, all elements in graph D_A, whose types belong to the image $v(T_N)$, are copied into graph D_V and respectively retyped. It is easy to see that the graph structure (incidence of nodes and arrows) is preserved as soon as both mappings, v and t_A, are structure preserving. This is formally proven in category theory, where the operation just described is called a *pull-back*, PB in short (we also say that arrow t_A is *pulled-back along* arrow v) [17]. We have thus specified a function $\mathsf{get}_v \colon \mathsf{Inst}^\circ(M) \to \mathsf{Inst}^\circ(N)$. (Note that as all constraints in D_M are beyond the image $t_A(D_A)$, only the v_T-part of v works here.)

Note that pulling back also produces a traceability mapping $trace_V \colon D_A \leftarrow D_V$ such that the entire square diagram commutes. This means that the pair $(v, trace_V)$ is a (pre)model mapping $\overline{v_A} \colon A \leftarrow V$.

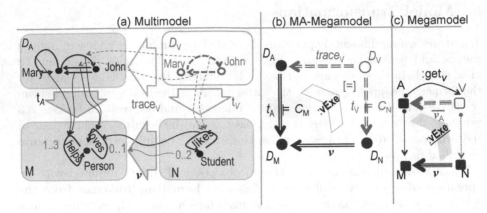

Fig. 6. Operation of view computation

Does view $\mathsf{get}_v(A)$ satisfy the constraints C_N declared in metamodel N? Suppose $c[x] \in C_N$ is a multiplicity constraint for arrow $x \in T_N$, which is translated into a constraint $v(c) = c[v(x)]$ for arrow $v(x) \in T_M$. If $A \models v(c)$, then $\mathsf{get}_v(A) \models c$ as view computation amounts to copying and retyping of the corresponding part of D_A. But, a legal M-instance $A \models C_M$, and so if $C_M \models v(c)$ (the case in our example), then $\mathsf{get}_v(A) \models c$ as well. In other words, if the view definition mapping is compatible with the constraints, then pulling-back a legal model A produces a legal view model $V = \mathsf{get}_v(A)$, and we have a total function $\mathsf{get}_v \colon \mathsf{Inst}^\bullet(M) \to \mathsf{Inst}^\bullet(N)$. This gives a semantics for metamodel morphisms, which we discussed in Sect. 2.1.2 purely syntactically.

In Fig. 6(b), our considerations are presented in an abstract way as the diagram operation of *view execution* (note the chevron labeled :vExe): it takes two solid (black) arrows as its input, and produces two dashed (blue) arrows as its output. The colon in the chevron's label says that we specify an *application instance* of the operation: for another source A' and another view definition v', we would have another instance of vExe and another computed view $V' = \mathsf{get}_{v'}(A')$. Note also that constraint satisfaction pre-conditions for vExe are shaded (with red) while derived post-conditions are not shaded (and blue). Also, not shown in the diagram, but important, is the following fact: if mapping v is injective (a precondition that we normally assume by default), then mapping $trace_V$ is injective too (because pullbacks preserve injectivity [17]).Finally, Fig. 6(c) presents an even more abstract setting: models are encapsulated as nodes, and model mappings (= commutative squares of graph mappings) as arrows, from which metamodels and their mappings can be projected out. As before, vertical arrows are just links. The shaded chevron denotes an operation abstracted from the blank chevron in Fig. 6(b): the latter works with graphs, whereas the former works with models and metamodels. Note that the direction of the operation is diagonally-opposite to the direction of the view definition mapping; for the function $\mathsf{get}_v \colon \mathsf{Inst}^\bullet(M) \to \mathsf{Inst}^\bullet(N)$, this opposition is somewhat striking: the directions of get_v and v are opposite. Our fine-tuned work with constraints is also embodied in the diagram: if v is a metamodel morphism and A a (legal) model, then V is also a model, and $\overline{v_A}$ is a legal model mapping.

The view $V = \mathsf{get}_v(A)$ possesses a remarkable property: it is a maximal model amongst models that can be mapped to A over v, e.g., model B in Fig. 3 is mapped to model V in an evident (and uniquely determined!) way. Some reflection on how the pullback works shows that it is a general property: for any model B and mapping $f\colon A \leftarrow B$ such that $f_T = v$ (think of node B placed to the north-east of node V), there is a unique mapping $!_f\colon D_V \leftarrow D_B$ such that both triangles commute: $!_f; t_V = t_B$ and $!_f; trace_V = f_D$. In other words, any mapping $f\colon A \leftarrow B$ factors through $\mathsf{get}_v(A)$ and we have $f = !_f; \overline{v_A}$.

Pattern 4 (Descriptive Views). A view definition is a metamodel mapping $v\colon M \leftarrow N$. Its execution goes in the opposite direction: it maps pre-instances of the target metamodel to pre-instances of the source metamodel, and is specified by a function $\mathsf{get}_v\colon \mathsf{Inst}^\circ(M) \to \mathsf{Inst}^\circ(N)$.

The Laws. (a) Legal instances are mapped to legal instances as soon as the view definition mapping is compatible with constraints declared in the metamodels: $C_M \models v(C_N)$. Then get_v is a total function $\mathsf{Inst}^\bullet(M) \to \mathsf{Inst}^\bullet(N)$. (b) For any view definition v and model A, the view $\mathsf{get}_v(A)$ is maximal amongst models mappable to A over v.

3.2   Prescriptive Views

In the example above, model A was given and model $V = \mathsf{get}_v(A)$ served a purely descriptive function: to present a view of model A, in which 'helps' relations are ignored, and other elements are retyped. In other words, the source A was primary while the view V was secondary. A typical MDE example is when a model is reverse engineered from code (the challenge of this task is to find a proper view definition mapping).

Now consider the opposite situation of code generation: the view model V is given and primary, while the source (code) A is to be built. For example, suppose that Mary wants to achieve (implement) the situation in which John helps her as specified by the "platform-independent" model V (see Fig. 7 (a)). For this goal, she is going to use the "platform" of personal relations (specified by metamodel M), which satisfies the implementation law "If X loves Y, then X helps Y". This law is specified by a view definition mapping $v\colon M \leftarrow N$ shown in the figure: If "X loves Y" in some instance A of M, then "X helps Y" in the view $\mathsf{get}_v(A)$ according to the algorithm of view execution specified above. Thus, Mary should build a model A over M such that $V = \mathsf{get}_v(A)$. Of course, Mary would be interested in building a minimal A satisfying the requirement, and it is enough to place in A two objects, John and Mary, and a 'John-loves-Mary' link between them. This link would implement the 'John-helps-Mary' link as shown by mapping $trace_A$ in Fig. 7 (ignore the second link in graph D_A and objects inside the outer square $D_V N M D_A$ for a while). Thus, A can be considered as a (platform-dependent) model generated by V over implementation definition v, and we write $A = \mathsf{gen}_v(V)$.

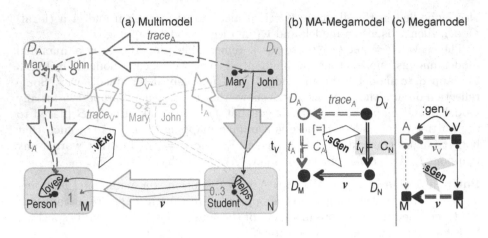

Fig. 7. Operation of source generation

This would be the end of the story except for the multiplicity constraint in M requiring every person to love somebody. To satisfy this constraint, Mary must add to model A either a link from herself to John, or a self-loop (or both, but this would violate both the multiplicity 1 and minimality of A). Figure 7 shows the case in which Mary chooses 'Mary-loves-John'. (In the model synchronization jargon, such a choice is defined by a *(synchronization) policy*.) However, now an extra help-link appears in the view $V^* = \mathsf{get}_v(A)$ (note the chevron :vExe, which "computes" view V^*), so that Mary needs to help John, which is not assumed by the original view V. Thus, the platform of personal relations with its constraint is not suitable for implementing given view V exactly; $V^* \neq V$. Nonetheless, implementation works in a weaker sense: view V^* properly includes V via embedding $!_{trace_A} : V^* \leftarrow V$ ensured by V^*'s maximality (if $trace_A$ is injective, then $!_{trace_A}$ is injective too [17]). We will refer to this inclusion as the GenGet law, as it specifies a common case: to implement all the necessary requirements, we may need to implement something extra. This extra thing should appear in our computation only once: if we implement V^* and build $A^* = \mathsf{gen}_v(V^*)$, then a reasonable implementation must ensure $A^* = A$ since all implementation details are already reflected in V^*. Conversely, given a source A and its view $V = \mathsf{get}_v(A)$, we should have $V = \mathsf{get}_v(\mathsf{gen}_v(V))$ so that the source and the view are synchronized after, at most, two synchronization steps. We call these conditions the GenGetGen and the GetGenGet laws (see [12]).

Column (b) in the figure presents our considerations in an abstract way as a diagram operation of *source generation* (note the :sGen-chevron in the middle): it takes two solid (black) mappings and produces two dashed (blue) ones. Column (c) is analogous to column (c) in Fig. 6, but works in the opposite direction from the view to the source.

Pattern 5 (Prescriptive Views). Implementation of an instance of metamodel N within a platform specified by M is an operation opposite to view execution, and unfolds over a view definition mapping $v: M \leftarrow N$. Constraints in M may prevent the existence of a unique minimal implementation; then a policy is required to choose one implementation amongst all possiblilities.

The Laws. Implementation is specified by a function $\mathsf{gen}_v: \mathsf{Inst}^\bullet(M) \leftarrow \mathsf{Inst}^\bullet(N)$ satisfying GenGet, GenGetGen, and GetGenGet laws.

3.3 Model Transformations

Abstractly, a model transformation is a function $\mathsf{t}: \mathsf{Inst}^\bullet(M) \to \mathsf{Inst}^\bullet(N)$ sending instances of metamodel M to instances of metamodel N. However, this widely used setting is far too abstract. The key point missed from the abstract definition above is that if a model $A \in \mathsf{Inst}^\bullet(M)$ is transformed into a model $B = \mathsf{t}(A) \in \mathsf{Inst}^\bullet(N)$, then a majority of B's elements should be traceable back to A's elements responsible for their generation (while other B elements could only be generated to conform to the metamodel's constraints). Thus, a (partial) traceability mapping $r_{AB}: A \Leftarrow B$ between models is a crucial part of model transformation. In addition, such a traceability mapping must be compatible with typing, that is, we should also have a mapping between metamodels $r: M \Leftarrow N$ so that we have something like a commutative diagram formed by these two mappings and two typing mappings. Moreover, as we have seen in Sections 3.1-2, mappings between metamodels can be executed.

We thus come to the idea of trying to consider mapping r as a declarative definition of t, and computation of $\mathsf{t}(A)$ as the execution of r for the instance $A \in \mathsf{Inst}^\bullet(M)$, in analogy with how we considered view execution and source generation. However, in general, neither of the metamodels could be considered a view of the other. There may be *private* types in M not relevant for the transformation, and, dually, there are private types in N. Thus, a more practically applicable case is when a transformation t is based on a common "shared view" metamodel S_t in-between M and N (Fig. 8) with view definition mappings v_t and w_t. related. A span $r_t = (v_t, w_t)$ of view definitions can be executed for an arbitrary model $A \in \mathsf{Inst}^\bullet(M)$ as shown in the top row of Fig. 8. We first compute the intermediate view $V = \mathsf{get}_{v_t}(A)$ by treating v_t descriptively. Then we generate model B from this view by treating w_t prescriptively. The same span can be executed in

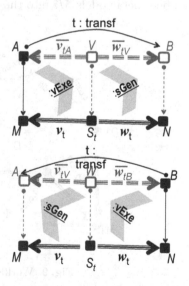

Fig. 8. Assembling model transformations

the opposite direction as shown in the lower row: at first, mapping w_t is executed descriptively, then v_t is executed prescriptively. If both mappings are compatible with constraints, both transformations map legal instances to legal instances. Note also that traceability mappings between models are also spans. Thus, with suitable technological support, the span can be executed in either direction providing bidirectional transformation. This facility is especially effective if both models can be updated, and the changes are to be propagated to the other side in an incremental mode. This scenario is discussed in the TR.

Pattern 6. *A model transformation definition is a span of metamodel mappings, which can be executed in both directions. A full set of laws is an open question. Two basic laws , identity propagation and weak invertibility, are specified in [9].*

3.4   Workflow Example Revisited

In this section we represent the megamodel from Fig. 1 as a composition of several operations over models and mappings introduced above. To make the scenario in Fig. 1 certain, we will make several additional assumptions.

We begin with two given heterogenous models $t_i: Di \to Mi$, $i = 1, 2$ with a known overlap span $(M0, v1, v2)$ (Fig. 9) between their metamodels. Here and below we will refer to models by their data graph names (the upper plane in Fig. 9), all typing mappings are vertical (or inclined) and unnamed. Merge is realized by invoking the colimit operation over graphs: invocation 1:colimit takes span $(M0, v1, v2)$ as its input, and returns cospan $(M, v1^*, v2^*)$ as shown in the lower face of the cube in Fig. 9 (M is the merged metamodel and mappings vi^* embed metamodels Mi into the merge).

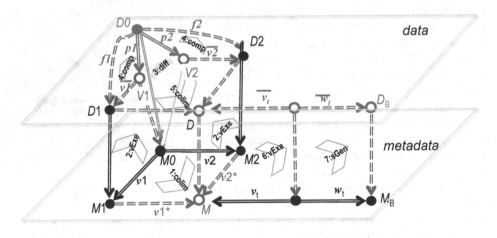

Fig. 9. Worlflow megamodel Fig. 1 revisited

Now we need to merge data graphs. As the latter can contain thousands of user-defined elements, discovering their overlap span requires a model matching/differencing tool. However, the latter normally work with homogeneous models. Retyping Di to the merge metamodel would result in differencing two big models, which is not necessary if we proceed in a more intelligent way. To wit, first, we execute mappings $v1$, $v2$ treated as view definitions (note two chevrons

2:vEXe working in the left and the back faces of the cube), and obtain projections (views) Vi of models Di with traceability mappings $\overline{vi}: Vi \to Di$. These views can be essentially smaller (less information) than the original models, and we can effectively run a model differencing tool that returns an overlap span $(D0, p1, p2)$ in the data plane. We encode this procedure as a "quasi-operation" diff (note greenish chevron 3:diff) that takes two models and returns a span between them so that the two triangle diagrams commute. Diff is not a truly algebraic operation as a) its results need correction by the user, and b) normally diff uses complex heuristics, and its input actually includes several contextually-dependent parameters in addition to the two models. That is why we color the output of diff green rather than blue. Formal (i.e., algebraically), the elements $D0, p1, p2$ form a part of the input for the entire workflow and should be black.

The next step is to invoke mapping composition and produce mappings fi (note two chevrons 4:comp in the upper plain). Now we have a span of data graphs $(D0, f1, f2)$ correctly typed over a span of metadata graphs $(M0, v1, v2)$. Next we can invoke 5:colimit (the upper face of the cube) for span $(D0, f1, f2)$, which returns span $(D, f1^*, f2^*)$ correctly typed over span $(M, v1^*, v2^*)$ (because, in fact, we apply colimit to a span of (vertical) graph morphisms $ti: Di \to Mi$ $(i = 0, 1, 2)$, which always exists). However, the resulting typing mapping $t: D \to M$ does not necessarily satisfy constraints in M, in which case we say that the models are inconsistent. A detailed discussion and examples can be found in [8]. Thus, if models are consistent, they can be merged into a correct model $t: D \to M$. Finally, we specify model transformation t as a span of view definitions (v_t, w_t), which is executed as explained in Sect.3.3 (note chevrons 6:vExe and 7:sGen).

The entire diagram in Fig. 9 encodes an algebraic term, i.e., a composed operation, over graphs and graph mappings: black and green elements are input variables, chevrons are operation names, and blue elements are the output (see [11] for a formal definition of such diagram operations and their composition). Numbers before the operation names impose execution order: equally numbered operations cna be executed in paralell, and a greater number points out that the input for the operation needs the output of the preceding operation. We have a worlkflow of MMt operations, which realizes a complex MMt scenario.

4   Beyond Simple Examples

We will argue that the way we specified our simple examples (typing, corr-linking, and their composition) can be extended far beyond them. We need to answer three main questions. 1) Does the machinery work for graphs more complex than those considered in the examples? 2) Can any constraint declaration be specified via typed graphs? 3) Do our simple notions of model correspondence and view capture complex practically interesting intermodeling cases? We will address these questions consecutively in Sections 4.1-3.

4.1 Beyond Simple Graphs

Operations of mapping composition, pullback, merge/colimit can be performed
with any graphs (see, e.g., [17]). As for source generation, it is non-trivial for our
simple examples, and is even more complicated for complex graphs: the choice
of a reasonable policy to make the source unique is always an issue. There are
no universal solutions, but existence of many code generating, and other similar
transformations shows that in certain practical situations a reasonable solution
can be found.

4.2 Beyond Simple Constraints

Any constraint declaration has its scope: a configuration of a metamodel's elements, whose instantiation is constrained by requiring it to have a specified
property P. Hence, to add a constraint to metamodel M, we begin with a predicate P with a specified *arity* graph $art(P)$, and then substitute M's elements
(maps) for $art(P)$'s elements (arrows). For example, the arity of the implication
of Sect. 2.1 is some fixed graph with two arrows between the same nodes. This
constraint amounts to a formula $\mathsf{Impl}(m1, m2)$ with $m1, m2$ two maps in the
metamodel, which can be specified by a "graph" $m1\leftarrow(\mathsf{Impl})\rightarrow m2$ with links
from the constraint node to the maps it constrains (see Fig. 2). Maps $m1, m2$
must have the same source and the same target as prescribed by Impl's arity.
Similarly, the arity of commutativity predicate Comm is some fixed triangle-
graph (with two consecutive arrows $N_1\rightarrow N_2\rightarrow N_3$ and the third arrow $N_1\rightarrow N_3$).
The commutativity constraint is then described by a formula $\mathsf{Comm}(m1, m2, m3)$
with mi being three maps forming a triangle as required. It can be specified by
a star "graph" with node Comm in the center and three links from the center to
nodes mi representing three maps.

The mechanism above can be made precise
with ordinary graphs (rather than "graphs")
as specified by meta-metamodel MM in
Fig. 10, where we consider three constraints:
Impl, Comm, and Mult(iplicity). For a predicate P, metaclass P will be instantiated
by P-declarations as described above: arrows
$P\rightarrow$Map correspond to arrows in $art(P)$ (we

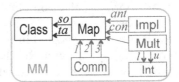

Fig. 10. Meta-metamodel for constraints

assume that arity graphs do not have isolated nodes) and are instantiated by
M-arrows from the constraint node to maps to be constrained; in fact, maps
are substituted for $art(P)$ arrows. To ensure a correct substitution, the metamodel must be endowed with equational meta-constraints: x.$ant.so$ = x.$con.so$,
x.$ant.ta$ = x.$con.ta$ for any Impl declaration x, and x.1.ta = x.2.so, x.1.so =
x.3.so, x.3.ta = x.2.ta for any Comm declaration x. Any MM-instance is a correct
metamodel, and conversely, e.g., the metamodel in Fig. 2 is. As MM is a graph
with equational constraints, the class of all its instances is a category with many
good properties (a presheaf topos in the categorical jargon); in particular, it has
all limits and colimits, and so is closed under pullback and merge operations.

A detailed discussion can be found in [26], which originated the metamodeling idea above.

4.3   Beyond Simple Correspondence Mappings: Queries

All corr-mappings considered so far consisted of links relating directly the given model elements. Such linking works only for a part of practically interesting cases. Often, an element in a model, say, B, is to be linked to a *derived* element in another model, A, which is not present in A but can be computed with a query against A.

Consider our example of view execution in Fig. 6, where mapping v says that Students are Persons. Suppose now that only *young* Persons with age less than 30 can be Students, and inter-Student relation 'likes' is the same as 'love' between young Persons. This new situation is specified by a mapping v in Fig. 11. The target of the mapping is metamodel M^+ obtained by augmenting M (the inner roundtangle) with several elements specifying a query definition; we call such elements *derived*. We first specify the sub-

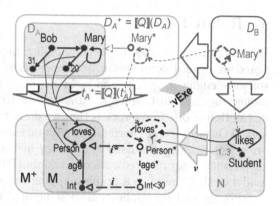

Fig. 11. View computation with queries

set of integers less than 30 (note inclusion arrow i). Then a simple query Q "Select those objects P in class Person, for which (a) P.age < 30 and (b) P.loves.age< 30" is represented by class Person* for the query results and its inclusion i^* into Person, attribute age^* into the domain of integers less than 30, and reference $loves^*$. Algebraically, metamodel M^+ can be considered as a term freely generated by applying a diagrammatic operation Q to graph M, and we write $M^+ = Q(M)$ (it can be made precise within diagram algebra described in [11]). A query language also provides an execution mechanism for query definitions: for any model A typed over graph T_M, query Q can be executed and produce an augmented model $A^+ = [\![\,Q\,]\!](A)$ typed over $M^+ = Q(M)$ (Fig. 11).

We call view definition mappings involving queries *q-mappings*. A q-mapping is executed in two steps. First, the query is executed as explained above. Then the query results are retyped according to mapping v as it was explained in Sect. 3.1. Composition of two steps results in the same diagram operation pattern that we used for ordinary views Fig. 6(b,c) — querying is hidden inside. Moreover, in paper [7] we show that q-mappings (and their execution) can be composed and have other properties making their encapsulation consistent: one can manipulate q-mappings as if they were ordinary mappings.

In more detail, in [7] we show that a query language can be modeled by a monad, and q-mappings are so called *Kleisli mappings* of this monad. Kleisli mappings can be composed and form a category. Since ordinary (typing) mappings can be pulled back over a Kleisli mapping (producing a Kleisli mapping for traceability), our dynamic patterns and laws defined in Section 3 hold also for view definitions based on complex queries. Also, as Kleisli categories are closed under colimits, our model overlap patterns and laws hold for cases when one or several legs of the overlap span are Kleisli mappings, i.e., involve queries. We conclude that our patterns work for complex mappings involving queries.

A formal framework integrating constraints and queries is described in [6]. It is based on the notion of *fibration* [2], which is, basically, CT's way of saying "view execution", as specified in Fig. 6 (c).

5   Related Work

Categorical approaches to megamodeling broadly understood have been proposed in several domains: in databases [1,10], in ontology engineering [27], in software engineering [23], and in MDE [5]. They all can be traced back to the pioneering ideas of Goguen & Burstall's institution theory [21]. A fundamental distinction of our framework is that we do not encode a model as a conventional logical theory given by formulas, and a metamodel as an institution of such theories. For us, a model itself is a theory in the sense of categorical logic, i.e., a graph with diagram predicate constraints (DP-graph in short), and a semantic model of that theory is a graph mapping satisfying the constraints.

DP-logic and its application to structural modeling were initially developed by Diskin et al in the *functorial semantics* setting [15,14]. In this setting, a model is a DP-graph G, and its instance is a graph morphisms $[\![..]\!] : G \to \mathsf{SetMap}$ into some predefined universe of sets and mappings, which satisfies the predicate constraints declared in G. The dual but equivalent semantics, in which an instance is a typing mapping $t_A : G \leftarrow D_A$ as described in Section 2, was proposed in [10], and accurately formalized in [16]. DP-graphs with this semantics were applied to several MDE problems in [13,31,30]. Specifying constraints by typed graphs as we did in this paper is new. Also, DP-framework of Rutle *et al* does not have a query mechanism and, correspondingly, q-mappings (Kleisli morphisms), which are a crucial ingredient of our view of megamodeling. Q-mappings in the universe of logical theories were used in [23,25]; their use for megamodeling as such was proposed in [10,11] and formalized in [7].

Attributed typed graphs as a mathematical framework are well-elaborated [17], and applied to MDE by the graph-transformation community, e.g., for view integration in [18] and for model transformation in [22]. However, they only consider simple constraints whereas the DP-graph framework allows us to treat all constraints in a uniform way. Specification of model tranformations (MTs) with DP-graphs is developed in [32]. They specify an MT by a *cospan* of DP-graph embeddings, whose execution is defined by a set of graph transformation. Our pattern in Section 3 is different: an MT is specified by a *span* of q-mappings between DP-graphs, whose execution is defined by query execution; as the latter is not specialized, any query engine can be plugged-in. Other relevant surveys of related work can be found in in [11,8].

6 Conclusion

We have proposed a megamodeling framework based on graphs and graph mappings, and operations over them. Using these elementary blocks, we reconstructed classical megamodeling constructs: conformance, overlap, consistency, and transformation relationships, in a mathematically correct way, and revealed how they are built in terms of a small number of basic operations. We have also shown that new constructs can be built by combining the same blocks, e.g., bidirectional transformations. In this way, we provided a library of structural design patterns for megamodel engineering, and outlined a mathematical framework in which these patterns can be provided with formal semantics. Though the full details are not presented in the paper, they can be filled in using standard concepts of category theory along the lines of [6,7].

Our structural patterns are fairly abstract structural blocks applicable to a wide class of MMt situations and scenarios. Applying them in a concrete domain as real design patterns, as the latter are understood in OO design [20], needs instantiation and adaptation. In fact, each of the patterns is a separate research topic that needs a separate paper for a reasonable presentation, but in the present paper we have intensionally focused on breadth rather than depth. We aimed to show that major megamodeling constructs can be made precise and accurately specified in a uniform way within a framework provided by category theory. We believe that a categorical unification is crucial for proper composition of separate MMt blocks into a single workflow (simply because any categorical framework is inherently compositional).

Going forward, we intend to elaborate these ideas both theoretically and practically: there is further theory to develop, respective engineering practices to create, and evaluation studies to do. Particularly, we are going to explore the engineering applications of MA-megamodeling within the NECSIS research network — a collaborative project between academia, the automotive industry (General Motors Canada) and IBM Canada, [29] which focuses on MDE-based design of embedded systems.

References

1. Alagić, S., Bernstein, P.A.: A model theory for generic schema management. In: Ghelli, G., Grahne, G. (eds.) DBPL 2001. LNCS, vol. 2397, pp. 228–246. Springer, Heidelberg (2002)
2. Barr, M., Wells, C.: Category theory for computing science. Prentice Hall (1995)
3. Bernstein, P., Melnik, S.: Model management 2.0: manipulating richer mappings. In: SIGMOD Conference, pp. 1–12 (2007)
4. Bézivin, J., Jouault, F., Rosenthal, P., Valduriez, P.: Modeling in the large and modeling in the small. In: Aßmann, U., Akcsit, M., Rensink, A. (eds.) MDAFA 2003. LNCS, vol. 3599, pp. 33–46. Springer, Heidelberg (2005)
5. Boronat, A., Knapp, A., Meseguer, J., Wirsing, M.: What is a multi-modeling language? In: Corradini, A., Montanari, U. (eds.) WADT 2008. LNCS, vol. 5486, pp. 71–87. Springer, Heidelberg (2009)

6. Diskin, Z.: Towards generic formal semantics for consistency of heterogeneous multimodels. Tech. Rep. GSDLAB 2011-02-01, University of Waterloo (2011)
7. Diskin, Z., Maibaum, T., Czarnecki, K.: Intermodeling, queries, and kleisli categories. In: de Lara, J., Zisman, A. (eds.) FASE 2012. LNCS, vol. 7212, pp. 163–177. Springer, Heidelberg (2012)
8. Diskin, Z., Xiong, Y., Czarnecki, K.: Specifying overlaps of heterogeneous models for global consistency checking. In: Dingel, J., Solberg, A. (eds.) MODELS 2010. LNCS, vol. 6627, pp. 165–179. Springer, Heidelberg (2011)
9. Diskin, Z., Xiong, Y., Czarnecki, K., Ehrig, H., Hermann, F., Orejas, F.: From state- to delta-based bidirectional model transformations: The symmetric case. In: Whittle, et al. [35], pp. 304–318
10. Diskin, Z.: Mathematics of generic specifications for model management. In: Rivero, L.C., Doorn, J.H., Ferraggine, V.E. (eds.) Encyclopedia of Database Technologies and Applications, pp. 351–366. Idea Group (2005)
11. Diskin, Z.: Model synchronization: Mappings, tiles, and categories. In: Fernandes, J.M., Lämmel, R., Visser, J., Saraiva, J. (eds.) GTTSE 2009. LNCS, vol. 6491, pp. 92–165. Springer, Heidelberg (2011)
12. Diskin, Z.: Lax lenses. Tech. Rep. GSDLab-TR 2013-03-01, University of Waterloo (2013)
13. Diskin, Z., Easterbrook, S.M., Dingel, J.: Engineering associations: From models to code and back through semantics. In: Paige, R.F., Meyer, B. (eds.) TOOLS (46). LNCS, vol. 11, pp. 336–355. Springer, Heidelberg (1974)
14. Diskin, Z., Kadish, B.: Variable set semantics for keyed generalized sketches: formal semantics for object identity and abstract syntax for conceptual modeling. Data Knowl. Eng. 47(1), 1–59 (2003)
15. Diskin, Z., Kadish, B., Piessens, F., Johnson, M.: Universal arrow foundations for visual modeling. In: Anderson, M., Cheng, P., Haarslev, V. (eds.) Diagrams 2000. LNCS (LNAI), vol. 1889, pp. 345–360. Springer, Heidelberg (2000)
16. Diskin, Z., Wolter, U.: A diagrammatic logic for object-oriented visual modeling. Electr. Notes Theor. Comput. Sci. 203(6), 19–41 (2008)
17. Ehrig, H., Ehrig, K., Prange, U., Taenzer, G.: Fundamentals of Algebraic Graph Transformation (2006)
18. Ehrig, H., Heckel, R., Taentzer, G., Engels, G.: A combined reference model- and view-based approach to system specification. Int. Journal of Software and Knowledge Engeneering 7, 457–477 (1997)
19. Favre, J.-M., NGuyen, T.: Towards a megamodel to model software evolution through transformations. In: SETRA Workshop. Elsevier ENCTS (2004)
20. Gamma, E., Helm, R.: Johnson, R., Vlissides, J.: Design Patterns: Elements of Reusable Object-Oriented Software. Addison-Wesley Professional (1994)
21. Goguen, J.A., Burstall, R.M.: Institutions: Abstract model theory for specification and programming. Journal of ACM 39(1), 95–146 (1992)
22. Hermann, F., Ehrig, H., Orejas, F., Czarnecki, K., Diskin, Z., Xiong, Y.: Correctness of model synchronization based on triple graph grammars. In: Whittle et al. [35], pp. 668–682
23. Jüllig, R., Srinivas, Y.V., Liu, J.: Specware: An advanced evironment for the formal development of complex software systems. In: Nivat, M., Wirsing, M. (eds.) AMAST 1996. LNCS, vol. 1101, pp. 551–554. Springer, Heidelberg (1996)
24. Kling, W., Jouault, F., Wagelaar, D., Brambilla, M., Cabot, J.: MoScript: A DSL for querying and manipulating model repositories. In: Sloane, A., Aßmann, U. (eds.) SLE 2011. LNCS, vol. 6940, pp. 180–200. Springer, Heidelberg (2012)

25. Maibaum, T.S.E.: Conservative extensions, interpretations between theories and all that! In: Bidoit, M., Dauchet, M. (eds.) CAAP 1997, FASE 1997, and TAPSOFT 1997. LNCS, vol. 1214, pp. 40–66. Springer, Heidelberg (1997)
26. Makkai, M.: Generalized sketches as a framework for completeness theorems. Journal of Pure and Applied Algebra 115, 49–79, 179–212, 214–274 (1997)
27. Mossakowski, T., Tarlecki, A.: Heterogeneous logical environments for distributed specifications. In: Corradini, A., Montanari, U. (eds.) WADT 2008. LNCS, vol. 5486, pp. 266–289. Springer, Heidelberg (2009)
28. Muller, P.-A., Fondement, F., Baudry, B., Combemale, B.: Modeling modeling modeling. SoSym 11(3), 347–359 (2012)
29. NECSIS: Network for the Engineering of Complex Software-Intensive Systems for Automotive Systems (2011), https://www.necsis.ca/
30. Rossini, A., de Lara, J., Guerra, E., Rutle, A., Lamo, Y.: A graph transformation-based semantics for deep metamodelling. In: Schürr, A., Varró, D., Varró, G. (eds.) AGTIVE 2011. LNCS, vol. 7233, pp. 19–34. Springer, Heidelberg (2012)
31. Rutle, A., Rossini, A., Lamo, Y., Wolter, U.: A diagrammatic formalisation of MOF-based modelling languages. In: Oriol, M., Meyer, B. (eds.) TOOLS EUROPE 2009. LNBIP, vol. 33, pp. 37–56. Springer, Heidelberg (2009)
32. Rutle, A., Rossini, A., Lamo, Y., Wolter, U.: A formalisation of constraint-aware model transformations. In: Rosenblum, D.S., Taentzer, G. (eds.) FASE 2010. LNCS, vol. 6013, pp. 13–28. Springer, Heidelberg (2010)
33. Sabetzadeh, M., Nejati, S., Liaskos, S., Easterbrook, S.M., Chechik, M.: Consistency checking of conceptual models via model merging. In: RE. pp. 221–230 (2007)
34. Stevens, P.: Bidirectional model transformations in qvt: semantic issues and open questions. Software and System Modeling 9(1), 7–20 (2010)
35. Whittle, J., Clark, T., Kühne, T. (eds.): MODELS 2011. LNCS, vol. 6981. Springer, Heidelberg (2011)

Partial Instances via Subclassing

Kacper Bąk[1], Zinovy Diskin[1], Michał Antkiewicz[1], Krzysztof Czarnecki[1],
and Andrzej Wąsowski[2]

[1] GSD Lab, University of Waterloo, Canada
{kbak,zdiskin,mantkiew,kczarnec}@gsd.uwaterloo.ca
[2] IT University of Copenhagen, Denmark
wasowski@itu.dk

Abstract. The traditional notion of instantiation in Object-Oriented Modeling (OOM) requires objects to be complete, i.e., be fully certain about their existence and attributes. This paper explores the notion of *partial instantiation* of class diagrams, which allows the modeler to omit some details of objects depending on modeler's intention. Partial instantiation allows modelers to express optional existence of some objects and slots (links) as well as uncertainty of values in some slots. We show that partial instantiation is useful and natural in domain modeling and requirements engineering. It is equally useful in architecture modeling with uncertainty (for design exploration) and with variability (for modeling software product lines).

Partial object diagrams can be (partially) completed by resolving (some of) optional objects and replacing (some of) unknown values with actual ones. Under the Closed World Assumption (CWA), completion reduces uncertainty of already existing objects, or deletes them if their existence is optional. Under the Open World Assumption (OWA), completion may additionally introduce new elements, perhaps uncertain. The paper presents a simple theory of partial instantiation and completion under the CWA. It shows that partial object diagrams can be modeled by subclassing and multiplicity constraints. As a result, class diagrams can implement partial instances with the well-known notions of subtyping and inheritance.

1 Introduction

Instances play a major role in modeling. They represent real-world objects for which models provide abstractions. In Object-Oriented Modeling (OOM), an instance of a class diagram is an *object diagram*, i.e., a collection of objects and links instantiating, respectively, classes and associations. For a link $l: o \to v$, we will also say that object o owns *slot* l that holds value v.

Traditionally, objects are complete. Their types are known, and all slots have well-defined values. Such a notion of an instance, however, is restrictive when modeling involves uncertainty, variability, or simply underspecification. This is because classic (we will also say complete) instantiation requires that all slots are assigned values simultaneously. We discuss the notion of a *partial instance*

M. Erwig, R.F. Paige, and E. Van Wyk (Eds.): SLE 2013, LNCS 8225, pp. 344–364, 2013.
© Springer International Publishing Switzerland 2013

that enriches the traditional instantiation. It allows object diagrams to have partiality, by which we assume that (a) existence of some objects and slots can be optional, and (b) there are slots with unknown values. By resolving optionality and replacing unknown values with actual ones, a partial object diagram becomes *complete*. There are many different completions of the same partial instance, and so the latter implicitly represents a set of instances. In this sense, a partial instance works like a class; in the paper we will make this observation precise.

Partial instances represent partial knowledge. They leave out knowledge that is unavailable at a given time, either due to uncertainty, variability, or under-specification. In uncertainty, the modeler captures several options but is unsure which one is the correct one (which one is correct is the missing knowledge). In variability, the modeler captures several options, each of which are correct and should be supported (the missing knowledge is the set of choices for a particular application). In underspecification, the modeler leaves out information that is irrelevant with respect to the modelers viewpoint. Thus, they differ in the intention. Partial instances, under various names, occur in:

- *Models with uncertainty.* Uncertainty captures possible choices that the modeler is unsure about ("don't know" semantics). An example would be a mobile device with hands-free input; this could be head gestures or voice input; the designer is uncertain about the choice, but the final solution will pick on them. Partial instances of meta-models can represent uncertainty in models. They can treat uncertainty in requirements [4,10] and in architectural models [11].
- *Models with variability.* Several choices are possible, each for a different product configuration (e.g., for a different customer). Partial instances of meta-models represent variability in models [6]. They are used to represent requirements models for product lines (including the product line scope), product line architectures [3], and product line tests. The variabilities in tests can be configured when the application is configured.
- *Models with underspecification.* Modelers focus on certain system aspects and can leave other aspects, which are outside their scope, underspecified ("don't care" semantics). Partial instances allow us to express partial specification of test cases as in Test-Driven Development (TDD) [13,17].
- *Variability models* (e.g., feature models [14]). Instances of variability models represent system configurations; their partial instances represent partial configurations and support staged configuration [5,3]. Variability models are related to models with variability, but they do not consider further instantiations of the configurations (linguistically), because they are not meta-models.
- *Data with uncertainty.* Partial instances of data schemas represent uncertainty in application data. They are useful in databases [12], exchanging web data [2], and model finding [21].

The above applications of partial instances are difficult (if at all possible) to manage with complete instances. Partial instances allow one to delay design decisions and to construct instances incrementally. The missing parts of partial instances can be completed either by the modeler, or automatically by tools.

Despite the important applications, the traditional notion of instantiation in OOM offers limited support for partial instances. For example, UML object diagrams cannot express optionality of objects. One can use, however, UML class diagrams "as is" to encode partial instances. Our contribution makes this encoding precise and general. We show that partial object diagrams can be encoded by subclassing and strengthening multiplicity constraints. One of the implications is that **OOM languages with no direct support for partial instances can support them via class-based modeling.**

The paper is organized as follows. Section 2 demonstrates the usefulness of partial instances in requirements elicitation. It introduces completion under the Closed World Assumption (CWA) and Open World Assumption (OWA). Section 3 shows the intuition behind encoding partial object diagrams as class diagrams. Section 4 presents a simple theory of partial instantiation and completion under the CWA. Section 5 discusses related work and Section 6 concludes.

2   Requirements Elicitation with Partial Instances: An Example

Example-Driven Modeling (EDM) [4] systematically uses examples for eliciting, modeling, verifying, and validating complex business knowledge. During requirements elicitation a Subject Matter Expert (SME) transfers their knowledge to a Business Analyst (BA) who then explicates it as documents, models, and code. This section motivates the necessity of partial instances for eliciting and validating requirements, and in OOM in general. First, we consider partial instances under the CWA, where completion of partial instances means reduction of uncertainty, variability, or underspecification. Later, we discuss partial instances under the OWA, in which new objects and slots (perhaps, optional) can be added.

2.1   Completion under the Closed World Assumption

Alice is an SME and her organization needs a system for booking meeting rooms. She hires Charlie, a BA, to build such a system. Charlie's task is to implement room booking functionality. He is concerned with the timing aspect of scheduling meetings. Requirements elicitation is a complex task and, in practice, can only be done iteratively. The first session between Alice and Charlie goes as follows:

ALICE: We need to keep track of bookings to ensure that rooms and people are not double-booked. Recently, for example, Sue, the head of research, had scheduled two meetings at the same day at 10am.

CHARLIE: How did that happen?

ALICE: First, she organized a meeting at 10am. The other meeting was organized by Sam also at 10am. Sue somehow understood that Sam wanted to attend her meeting and confirmed her attendance of Sam's meeting. It wasn't the first time that miscommunication happened.

CHARLIE: I see. So how does Sue deal with conflicting meetings?

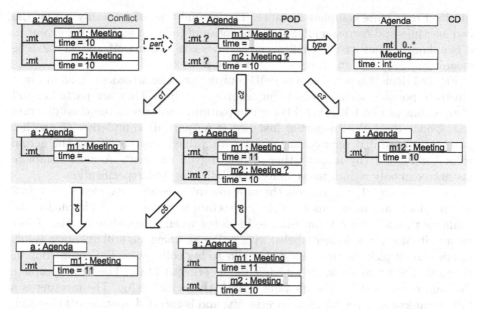

Fig. 1. Several cases of completion of partial object diagrams. Changes between object diagrams are highlighted in yellow.

ALICE: In several ways. First, she may cancel one of the meetings. Alternatively, she confirms only one of the meetings while keeping the other one unconfirmed. She can also confirm the two meetings but they cannot overlap. Sometimes she combines the two meetings into one if the topics are similar. Each employee should have a daily agenda of meetings. Based on that they should be able to confirm or decline each meeting.

CHARLIE: That's quite complex. I think I understand...

[CHARLIE writes down the possible ways of scheduling meetings (Fig. 1).]

Figure 1 Conflict models the situation where Sue has two meetings scheduled at 10am. The object diagram shows her agenda with the meetings m1 and m2. It conforms to the class diagram in Fig. 1 CD, where time of the meeting is mandatory. The object diagram violates an important constraint that one person cannot have several meetings scheduled at the same time. To manage conflict resolution, Charlie creates a template for inserting information about the two meetings, in fact, a partial instance POD as shown in Fig. 1. The dashed arrow *part* indicates this activity. The initial partial instance must be as uncertain as possible. However, Sue cannot manage time of Sam's meeting, hence, this attribute cannot be uncertain. By completing the partial instance incrementally, Charlie can arrive at a non-conflicting schedule. The partial instance conforms to the class diagram in Fig. 1 CD.

The partial instance POD has two types of partiality. First, the time of meeting m1 is unknown (has value _). As an organizer, Sue may pick the time later. The meaning of _ is that the concrete value exists but is unknown and it may be specified by a more complete instance. The second type of partiality is that the two meetings and corresponding slots are optional (labeled with ?). For example, it is unknown whether Sue confirms or declines the meeting m1 and/or m2. The meaning of ? is that an element may or may not exist.

Figure 1 depicts several cases of POD completion. The arrows $c1 \ldots c6$ in Fig. 1 illustrate possible ways of scheduling meetings by Sue. They are partial or full completions of Fig. 1 POD. All these completions conform to the class diagram CD. Under the CWA, a partial instance is a (partial) completion of another partial instance if it removes some unknown value _ (by specifying the actual value) or label ? (by instantiating or deleting an element). A more complete instance can only reduce uncertainty, variability, or underspecification.

COMPLETION $c1$. Sue cancels the meeting m2. Elements labeled with ? (m2 and its slot) have no instances in the more complete diagram. Additionally, she confirms the meeting m1, but may decide later when to schedule it. The object m1 and its slot are no longer labeled with ?. The slot time has still unknown value, as Sue cannot pick the time unless she talks to her colleagues. The completion $c4$ shows that Sue may decide to schedule the meeting at 11am. The more complete diagram replaces the unknown value _ with the actual value. The meeting is a fully complete instance without uncertainty, and is encoded as an object diagram.

COMPLETION $c2$. Sue confirms the meeting m1 and schedules it at 11am. In the partial object diagram, the label ? is removed from m1 and its slot. The value of time is specified as 11. Sue keeps the meeting m2 unconfirmed (still labeled as ?). The diagram can be further completed in two ways. First, Sue can cancel the meeting m2 as in the completion $c5$. Alternatively, as in the completion $c6$, she can confirm the meeting m2; its time does not overlap with m1. There may be several completion chains (e.g., $c1.c4$ and $c2.c5$) leading to the same result.

COMPLETION $c3$. Sue decides to merge her meeting with Sam's one because the topics are similar. Formally, two objects are combined into one named m12 (we will also say that objects are glued together).

2.2 Completion under the Open World Assumption

Charlie works with his partner, Bob, to build the room booking system. The two BAs are interested in different aspects of the system. Charlie's task is to take care of scheduling; Bob needs to keep track of the available equipment. The session between Alice and Bob goes as follows:

ALICE: Each meeting is organized by a chair who is responsible for book-ing the room. Chair also notifies other participants about the meeting. Rooms have different equipment, and obviously, different numbers.

BOB: Let's understand a concrete meeting. Could you please give me an example of room booking? What equipment is used?

ALICE: Sure. For example, Sue organizes meetings for her research group. They use an electronic whiteboard, as it simplifies sharing notes online. [BOB writes down the example (see Fig. 2 Bob I).]

BOB: Perfect. Do all rooms have an electronic whiteboard?

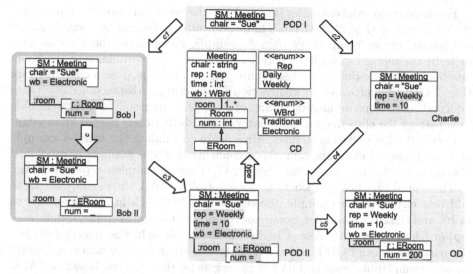

Fig. 2. Abstraction and partial completion of examples. Changes between object diagrams are highlighted in yellow. Note that Bob II refines the type of room r.

ALICE: No. All rooms have a traditional whiteboard, but only some rooms offer the electronic one.

[BOB completes the example (see Fig. 2 Bob II).]

In the next session Alice talks to Charlie again:

ALICE: As you may know, each meeting is organized by a chair.
BOB: Right, such as Sue. Alice, how often are the meetings scheduled? Can you give me a concrete example?
ALICE: For example, Sue organizes weekly meetings at 10am. They discuss progress done on research projects.

[CHARLIE writes down the example (see Fig. 2 Charlie).]

After the two sessions Bob and Charlie meet to consolidate their knowledge of different aspects of the system. Their goal is to come up with a consistent picture. Bob learned about rooms and equipment, whereas Charlie learned that meetings may repeat. Figure 2 shows the elicited examples and that the process of adding details can be modeled as instance completion.

Bob's first example (Fig. 2 Bob I) specifies that there is a meeting SM organized by Sue and that the meeting requires an **Electronic** whiteboard. He also specifies that the meeting takes place in some room r, but he does not know the room number **num**. After clarifying some details, Bob learned that only certain rooms provide the electronic equipment that Sue needs. He completes the previous example by refining the type of r to an assumed subtype **ERoom** (Fig. 2 Bob II). Charlie's example (Fig. 2 Charlie) shows that he learned that Sue schedules meetings at 10am and they repeat weekly.

Based on the partial examples Bob and Charlie create an example that merges their knowledge (Fig. 2 POD II). The partial object diagram is a combination of Charlie's example and Bob's refined example. Fortunately, there are no conflicts in the merged example. There is, however, still one unknown: the room number num where Sue meets her group. The two BAs propose a class diagram (Fig. 2 CD) that provides an abstraction for meetings. Abstractions generalize information to improve understanding of a set of examples. The BAs were able to construct the class diagram only after consolidating their partial knowledge.

Bob and Charlie decide to meet Alice again to validate the merged example and the proposed class diagram. Alice confirms that the example is valid. She also says that Sue uses room 200. Figure 2 OD shows a complete object diagram.

The completion in Fig. 2 works under the OWA. OWA allows completions to add new elements. For example, the completion POD II adds new elements to Bob's and Charlie's examples. Some slots do no exist in the example of Bob (e.g., rep) or Charlie (e.g., wb). Also, Charlie's initial example had no uncertainty, but the partial instance POD II has uncertainty: the room number num is unknown. Clearly, completion based on OWA is more general than the one based on CWA.

Partial instances naturally express stakeholder's partial view of the world. When BAs focus on different aspects of the system, they construct partial examples. Modeling with partial instances has an important advantage over modeling with always complete instances. It explicates what is known and unknown given current knowledge. Our example showed that completion of partial examples may work under the CWA or the OWA. The former is useful for conflict resolution and exploring a set of configurations. The latter is adequate for requirements elicitation by various parties. OWA-completions subsume CWA-ones.

3   Modeling Partial Examples with Subclassing

This section shows that instantiation (partial and complete) of a class diagram can be encoded as extending the latter via subclassing. The main idea is that objects of class C are encoded as singleton subtypes of C; then links instantiating C's associations are naturally encoded as associations either inherited from C to the subclasses, or redefined in the subclasses.

3.1   Extension under the CWA

Figure 1 showed possible ways of resolving a conflict between two overlapping meetings. Let us now model all the solutions with subclassing as shown in Fig. 3. It parallels the structure of the previous figure. Instead of typing and completion, the diagrams are related by subclassing (arrows with hollow heads placed between class name and its superclass) and extension (hollow arrows between diagrams). Extension is a relation expressing that a more complete diagram includes the less complete one.

Figure 3 CD+ encodes Fig. 1 POD as a class diagram. The class diagram CD+ includes classes from Fig. 3 CD (the same as in Fig. 1 CD), but makes them abstract, and introduces subclasses. The class A is a singleton subclass of

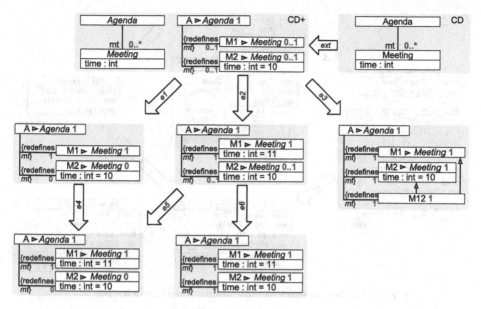

Fig. 3. Several cases of extension of class diagrams (compare with Fig. 1)

Agenda. Its class multiplicity is 1 (following class name and superclass), meaning that there is exactly one instance of this class. The two optional meetings are modeled by subclasses M1 and M2 with multiplicities 0..1. The two references from A to the meetings are also optional. As A is a subclass of *Agenda*, the two references redefine mt, i.e., they restrict the targets of mt to the two subclasses of *Meeting*. Both subclasses inherit the attribute time from *Meeting*. The class M1 says nothing about time and keeps its value unknown. The class M2 redefines the attribute time by specifying its value to be 10.

The extensions $e1 \ldots e6$ parallel the completions $c1 \ldots c6$ from Fig. 1. Informally, extension means that each element of the less complete diagram can be mapped to an element of the more complete one. Under the CWA the extensions reduce uncertainty. Class diagrams can do that by: introducing singleton subclasses, restricting multiplicities of classes/references/attributes, and redefining targets of references and values of attributes. All the extensions should include the class diagram from Fig. 3 CD, but with classes made abstract (similarly to CD+). We omit these classes to ease reading.

The extension $e1$ models a situation when Sue confirms one of the meetings and cancels the other one. The multiplicity of M1 (and its slot) is redefined as 1. The multiplicity of M2 (and its slot) is redefined a 0. The diagram shows M2 to make it explicit that its multiplicity is 0. Removal of M2 from the diagram would have the same meaning. Furthermore, the value of time in M1 is kept unknown. The extension $e2$ can be understood analogically. The extension $e3$ describes a situation where Sue combines two meetings. It introduces a class M12 that merges information from classes M1 and M2 by subclassing them. Additionally,

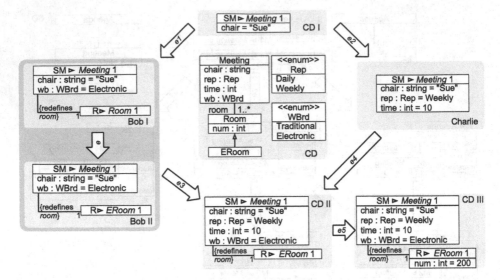

Fig. 4. Partial examples as subclassing (compare with Fig. 2)

it refines class and slots multiplicities to be 1. In the case of diamond inheritance, the properties from the common base are not duplicated. Thus M12 redefines the merge of the redefinitions of mt from M1 and M2.

3.2   Extension under the OWA

Bob & Charlie elicited examples of booking a meeting in Fig. 2. Figure 4 encodes the diagram with subclassing and extension. The class model in Fig. 4 CD is exactly the same as in Fig. 2. Other models are created as previously: objects are encoded as singletons, slots are encoded as redefined references/attributes, and each model includes classes from Fig. 4 CD but makes them abstract (omitted to avoid repetition). The mapping completion is replaced by extension.

Working under the OWA is natural when using subclassing and extension. For example, regardless of the definition of class Meeting, Charlie's class SM can easily add new attributes. They may have defined or undefined values. All the arrows $e1 \ldots e6$ could, in principle, be replaced by subclassing. The subclasses would need to be renamed to avoid name clashes.

3.3   Encoding Partial Instances as Class Diagrams

We denote the encoding of partial object diagrams as class diagrams by a function *cdenc*. It takes a partial instance and encodes it as a class diagram that extends the class diagram that the partial instance conforms to. Figure 5 shows the previously defined class diagram from Fig. 1 CD and the partial instance from Fig. 1 POD that conforms to it. It also shows the completion *c6* of POD. All derived elements are shown as dashed and blue. The result of function *cdenc*

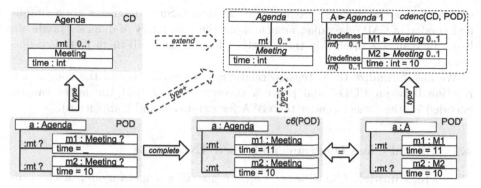

Fig. 5. Example of partial instantiation via subclassing

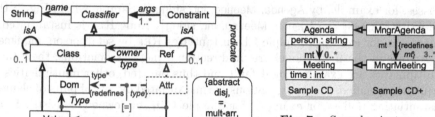

Fig. 6. Meta-model of formal class diagrams

Fig. 7. Sample instance: class diagram Sample CD and Sample CD+

is shown in the upper right corner of Fig. 5. The function *cdenc* takes POD, and extends CD with singleton classes (that encode objects) and references/attributes (that encode slots). It respects the labels ? by placing multiplicities in the class diagram. If an attribute has undefined value, then it is skipped in the resulting class diagram, because it is inherited from one of the superclasses.

The derived class diagram (*cdenc*(CD, POD) in Fig. 5) has two important properties. First, it is an extension of CD that POD partially instantiates. Hence, the partial instance POD can be typed over the derived class diagram by *type+*. Second, all the completions of POD that are instances of CD must be isomorphic with instances of the derived class diagram. In the example, the completion *c6*(POD) is isomorphic with POD', i.e., an instance of *cdenc*(CD, POD). The partial object diagrams are not exactly the same due to different typing. The partial object diagram *c6*(POD) is typed over CD, whereas POD' is typed over *cdenc*(CD, POD). We formally show that the typing of *c6*(POD) over *cdenc*(CD, POD) and the typing of POD' over CD can be derived under the CWA.

4 Partial Instantiation as Subclassing

This section formalizes class diagrams (CDs) and partial object diagrams (PODs) used in Sections 2 and 3 by building their meta-models. Meta-models are themselves *formal class diagrams*, i.e., graphs (collections of nodes and arrows) endowed with constraints (predicate declarations). Such diagrams are a simplified version of UML class diagrams, and use the machinery of diagram predicate logic [9,8,20]. We often skip the adjective 'formal' and call them just class diagrams.

We also formalize the extension relations between CDs, and the completion relation between PODs, and prove a theorem stating that the latter can be encoded by the former (under the CWA for extension and completion).

4.1   Formal Class Diagrams and Their Extensions

The Meta-model: Classifiers. Figure 6 specifies a meta-model of class diagrams. It is a graph whose nodes are meta-classes to be interpreted by sets; elements of those sets *instantiate* meta-classes. Node CLASS is instantiated by classes, for example, by Agenda, Meeting, int, string in Sample CD in Fig. 7; then we write $[\![\text{CLASS}]\!] = \{$Agenda, Meeting, int, string$\}$. Node REF is instantiated by references, for example, Sample CD instantiates REF by set $\{$person, mt, time$\}$.

Arrows in the meta-model are unidirectional meta-associations; their target multiplicities are exactly 1 by default and thus omitted; other multiplicities are explicitly specified. Meta-associations are instantiated by sets of pairs of elements instantiating nodes; for example, for Sample CD, set $[\![\text{owner}]\!]$ consists of pairs (person, Agenda), (mt, Agenda), (time, Meeting). The default multiplicity 1 makes such sets of pairs single-valued totally-defined mappings (or functions). Thus, for Sample CD, sets $[\![\text{owner}]\!]$ and $[\![\text{type}]\!]$ are functions from set $[\![\text{REF}]\!]$ to set $[\![\text{CLASS}]\!]$.

Subclassing relation between classes is modeled by the meta-association *isA*. If this meta-association is instantiated — e.g., in the Sample CD+ , set $[\![isA]\!]$ has two elements (pairs of classes): (mngrAgenda, Agenda) and (mngrMeeting, Meeting) — it means that mngrAgenda is a subclass of Agenda, and mngrMeeting is a subclass of Meeting. Following UML, we denote subclassing by arrows with triangle arrow head. Semantics of *isA* is subsetting: $[\![\text{mngrAgenda}]\!] \subset [\![\text{Agenda}]\!]$, and $[\![\text{mngrMeeting}]\!] \subset [\![\text{Meeting}]\!]$. We will also often interpret subsetting by inclusion mappings and write, e.g., $[\![isA]\!]$: $[\![\text{MngrAgenda}]\!] \hookrightarrow [\![\text{Agenda}]\!]$.

The keyword *redefines* means inclusion $[\![mt^*]\!] \subset [\![mt]\!]$ of the corresponding set of pairs. In such a case, UML says mt^* *subsets* mt, and thus defines a meta-association loop *isA* for references too.

The *isA* (subsetting) mechanism is used in the meta-model itself (Fig. 6), where triangle-head arrows are used for declaring meta-*isA* for meta-classes. The upper such arrow says that CLASS and REF are classifiers, and another such arrow from DOM to CLASS says that some of meta-classes are domains. For example, in Sample CD, $[\![\text{DOM}]\!]=\{$string, int$\} \subset [\![\text{CLASS}]\!]$ is the set of primitive domains used in the class diagram. Node ATTR denotes the result of the query *"Select all references whose type is a domain"*; for Sample CD, $[\![\text{ATTR}]\!]=\{$person, time$\}$. We will say that it is a *derived* node (its frame is dashed and blue). The query also produces derived arrow *type**, which subsets (redefines) *type*.

As an attribute can be initialized with a concrete value (to be final in our context), the meta-model has a partially-defined meta-association *val*. Its target VAL is instantiated by values of the primitive domains and by singleton classes that represent these values, $[\![\text{VAL}]\!] = [\![\text{int}]\!] \cup [\![\text{string}]\!] \cup \{\{i\} : i \in [\![\text{int}]\!]\} \cup \{\{s\} :$ $s \in [\![\text{string}]\!]\}$, and function $[\![\textit{Type}]\!]$ provides their type: if $x \in [\![\text{VAL}]\!]$ is in $[\![\text{int}]\!]$, then $[\![\textit{Type}]\!](x)=$int. We require that for any object diagram instantiating the meta-model, and for any its attribute $a \in [\![\text{ATTR}]\!]$, if a is initialized with a value, then the value has to be of the same type as the attribute, i.e., $a.[\![\textit{val}]\!].[\![\textit{Type}]\!] = a.[\![\textit{type*}]\!]$. We encode this constraint by labeling the three arrows with commutativity predicate [=].

Metamodel II: Constraints. Constraints are an important part of formal class diagrams. Specification of constraints begins with a *signature Sign of predicate symbols (or labels)*, each one is supplied with its *arity*, i.e., a configuration (graph) of nodes and arrows for which the predicate can be declared. In our examples, the signature is $Sign = $ mult-node $\sqcup$ mult-arr $\sqcup$ {abstract, disj, =}. Set mult-node=int×int* consists of pairs of integers (including * for int*), which can be declared for classes, i.e., the arity of each predicate in mult-node is some fixed single-node graph. Set mult-arr=int×int* consists of pairs of integers (including *), which can be declared for associations, i.e., the arity of each predicate in mult-arr is some fixed single-arrow graph. The arity of predicate abstract is also a singleton node graph. If a class is abstract, it can only be instantiated via its subclasses. In other words, there are no elements whose typing mapping points to the abstract class, but must point to one of the subclasses. UML's notation for declaring a class abstract is to display its name in *italic*.

The arity of predicate disj is the family of all graphs consisting of a finite set of arrows with a common target. For example, we may declare disj for two arrows MngrAgenda $\rightarrow$ Agenda and SecretaryAgenda $\rightarrow$ Agenda. In any legal instance of this class diagram, sets $[\![\text{MngrAgdenda}]\!]$ and $[\![\text{SecretaryAgenda}]\!]$ are disjoint. To ease notation, we assume that any set of subclasses that *do not have a common subclass* is declared disjoint by default.

Predicate = (commutativity) can be declared for any arrow diagram, in which there are two paths between the same source and target, like in the lower part of Fig. 6. The declaration ensures that for any element instantiating the source class, the two instantiated paths lead to the same element instantiating the target class. Note that having commutativity actually allows us to define subsetting (redefinition) of associations. For example, in Fig. 7 Sample CD+, declaring mt^* *redefines* mt means commutativity: for any object diagram instantiating the diagram, and any object $a \in [\![\text{MngrAgenda}]\!]$, we have $a.[\![mt^*]\!].[\![isA]\!] = a.[\![isA]\!].[\![mt]\!]$.

A *constraint declaration* or just a *constraint* is an expression $P(e_1, ..., e_n)$ with P a predicate symbol (label) from the signature $Sign$, and $e_1...e_n$ a list of its arguments conforming to P's arity graph. For example, for commutativity label, the argument list consists of two sublists giving two paths. In diagrams, expression $P(e_1, ..., e_n)$ is declared by placing label P close to the members of the argument list so that it should be clear what the elements e_i are. Such placing can be easily done for node and arrow multiplicities. By default, all classes have multiplicity 0..*, and different default policies can be set for arrow multiplicities.

Extension Relation. We first give a formal definition and then explain its meaning with special cases. Let CD be a consistent class diagram, i.e., $\text{INST}(CD) \neq \varnothing$. (Note that an empty instance is legal if allowed by the constraints.) We say that a class diagram CD' *extends* CD (write $CD \leq CD'$), if

1. CD graph is a subgraph of CD' graph, particularly, they may coincide.
2. if a class A' belongs to $CD' - CD$, then
   (a) there exists a family of CD classes $\text{sup}(A') = (A_0, A_1, ..., A_n)$ with A_0 being the parent of $A_1..A_n$, which are all ($i = 0..n$) declared abstract in CD' and such that A' is a child of all $A_1..A_n$ (and hence of A_0 too). The case n=0, hence, $\text{sup}(A') = (A_0)$, is not excluded.
   (b) if B' is another class (not equal to A') in $CD' - CD$ with $\text{sup}(B') = (B_0, B_1, ..., B_m)$ and $B_0 = A_0$, then A' and B' are declared disjoint.
   (c) if a reference r' is owned by class A' in $CD' - CD$, then there is some A_i in the family $\text{sup}(A')$ such that r' is either inherited from A_i or redefines some of its references r. In the latter case, if $type(r) = B$ and $type(r') = B'$, then B occurs into $\text{sup}(B')$.
3. all constraints in CD go into CD'. New constraints introduced in CD' are consistent with constraints in CD so that CD' is also consistent.

Thus, $CD \leq CD'$ means that there is an embedding mapping $e : CD \to CD'$ satisfying the conditions above. There are several special cases of extension.

1. *Strengthening constraints.* CD is one class A with multiplicity 0..n and some attributes. CD' is composed of classes A and A', such that A is abstract and A' is a subclass of A, and the multiplicity of A' is $0 \leq m' \ldots n' \leq n$ with attributes inherited and/or redefined. Then because A is abstract in CD', CD' actually amounts to class A' with all its attributes inherited/redefined from A, that is, A' is A but with stronger multiplicity. For example, Fig. 3 shows that extension *e1* makes M1 a singleton.
2. *Deletion.* If in the first case the multiplicity is strengthened to be 0..0 for A', then the class A in CD will be effectively deleted. For example, Fig. 3 shows that extension *e1* deletes M2.
3. *Gluing.* CD consists of class A with two subclasses, A_1 and A_2, with multiplicities $m_1..n_1$ and $m_2..n_2$ respectively. CD' has in addition class A'$_{12}$ subclassing both A_1 and A_2, which are declared abstract in CD', and its multiplicity is m'..n'. Because all (grand) parents of A'$_{12}$ are abstract in CD', the latter, in fact, amounts to class A'$_{12}$ with attributes inherited from A_1 and A_2. Thus, A_1 and A_2 have glued in CD' into A'$_{12}$. For example, Fig. 3 shows that extension *e3* introduces M12 that subclasses M1 and M2. To prohibit extensions with gluing, it is enough to specialize the general definition by setting $n = 0$, i.e., $\text{sup}(A') = (A_0)$: a class in the extension has exactly one superclass.

For a class diagram CD, we write $\text{EXT}(CD)$ for the set of all its extensions.

4.2   Partial Instances and Their Completion

Instantiation of Class Diagrams by Object Diagrams. A class diagram is a pair $CD = (G_{CD}, C_{CD})$ with G_{CD} a graph with some additional structure

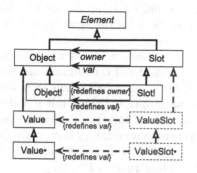

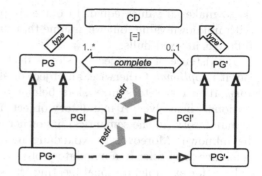

Fig. 8. Meta-model of partial object diagrams

Fig. 9. Rules of instance completion

specified in the previous section, and C_{CD} a set of constraints declared over the graph. An *object diagram* OD over CD is a graph G_{OD} equipped with a typing mapping $type_{OD} : G_{OD} \rightarrow G_{CD}$. Nodes in graph G_{OD} represent objects and values; arrows are links between them. As in UML, we also call links *slots*: for a link $time$: M1 $\rightarrow$ 10, we say that object M1 owns slot $time$ that holds value 10, and for a link $room$: M1 $\rightarrow$ R, we say that slot $room$ holds a reference to object R. The typing mapping is a correct graph morphism compatible with partition into classes and domains. For example, if a node in G_{OD} is typed by int, then it must be an integer value.

We call an OD correctly typed over a CD's *preinstance*, and write $\text{PINST}(CD)$ for the set of CD's preinstances.

Inverting the typing mapping maps nodes of graph G_{CD} into sets, and arrows into mappings. For example, if C is a class in G_{CD}, then $type_{OD}^{-1}(\mathsf{C})$ is the set of objects typed by C. In Sect. 4.1 we denoted such sets by $[\![\mathsf{C}]\!]$. Similarly, if $r : \mathsf{C} \rightarrow \mathsf{C}'$ is a reference arrow in G_{OD}, then $type_{OD}^{-1}(r)$ is the set of links (i.e., pairs of objects) typed by r. In Sect. 4.1, we denoted such sets by $[\![r]\!]$, and noted that such a set defines a mapping $[\![r]\!] : [\![\mathsf{C}]\!] \rightarrow [\![\mathsf{C}']\!]$. Hence, we can check whether multiplicities and other constraints declared in CD are satisfied.

We say that an OD over CD is its *correct (or legal) instance* if all constraints are satisfied. Let $\text{INST}(CD)$ denote the set of all legal CD's instances. Clearly, $\text{INST}(CD) \subset \text{PINST}(CD)$.

Instantiation of Class Diagrams by Partial Object Diagrams. A *partial object diagram* is an object diagram, where some values in slots may be unknown, and some objects and slots may not exist (our examples marked such by label ?). To deal with unknown values, we add to every primitive domain a countable set of null values $\{\_1, \_2, \ldots\}$ called *indexed nulls*. (In the database literature, they are called labeled nulls.) For a given domain, say, int, we need many nulls (not just one), because different attributes of type integer may have (potentially different) unknown values. Making attributes certain means replacing nulls by actual (non-null) integer values, but having only one null value would force us to make all values equal. In our examples, we placed symbol _ into a slot with unknown value, but we assume that different slots (of the same type) hold different indexed nulls.

If existence of an object or slot is declared uncertain, we label it by ? and say it is *optional*. Otherwise, an object or slot is considered certain and *mandatory*. If in concrete syntax slots belong to an optional object, then they are optional themselves. A mandatory object may have optional slots, but if a slot is mandatory (in the semantics), its owner is mandatory too (but the value may be unknown). Moreover, to avoid dangling references, a mandatory slot holding a reference must refer to a mandatory object. We admit optional slots with known values (for example, optional meeting M2 with certain time in Fig. 1).

The Metamodel. Metamodel in Fig. 8 makes the discussion precise. The upper part (ELEMENT, OBJECT, SLOT) says that a partial object diagram is a graph. Meta-classes OBJECT! and SLOT! represent mandatory objects and slots; mandatory elements form a correct subgraph of the partial object diagram graph.

Metaclass VALUE represent values of primitive domains (e.g., integers and strings) together with the indexed nulls. For simplicity, values are assumed to be special objects (class VALUE is a subclass of OBJECT). Class VALUE$^\bullet$ represents actual values of primitive domains (nulls excluded). Derived class VALUESLOT is for slots holding values rather than references, and VALUESLOT$^\bullet$ is subclass of slots holding actual known values.

To be precise, instances of the meta-model in Fig. 8 are *partial graphs* rather than partial object diagrams: the latter are endowed with typing mapping into some class diagram. The meta-model states that a partial graph is a triple $PG = (G, G!, G^\bullet)$ with G a graph, $G!$ its subgraph of *mandatory* elements, and $G^\bullet$ a subgraph of slots with *known values*.

Given a class diagram CD, a *partial object diagram* over it, POD, is a partial graph $PG_{POD} = (G_{POD}, G!_{POD}, G^\bullet_{POD})$ with a totally defined typing mapping (graph morphism) $type_{POD} : G_{POD} \to G_{CD}$, which maps proper objects to classes and values to value domains. The pair $(G_{POD}, type_{POD})$ is denoted by $|POD|$; it is the POD with all ?-labels removed.

Given a CD, we say that a POD is a *(partial) preinstance* if $type_{POD}$ is a correct graph morphism (thus, the set $\text{PINST}(CD)$ also includes well-typed graphs with unknown values). We call a preinstance POD an *(partial) instance* if $G_{POD} = G^\bullet_{POD}$ (i.e., all values are known) and all constraints are satisfied, i.e., $|POD| \in \text{INST}(CD)$. We denote the set of (partial) preinstances by $\text{PPINST}(CD)$ and of (partial) instances by $\text{PINST}(CD)$.

Partial Object Diagram Completion. Let $PG = (G, G!, G^\bullet)$ be a partial graph. Its *(partial) completion* comprises another partial graph $PG' = (G', G'!, G'^\bullet)$ and a partially defined graph mapping $c : G \to G'$, which is compatible with the extra partial graph structure. To wit: both restrictions of mapping c to the two subgraphs, $c! : G! \to G'$ and $c^\bullet : G^\bullet \to G'$, are actually inclusion mappings into the respective subgraphs of G', i.e., mapping c provides

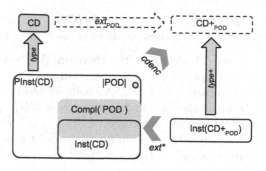

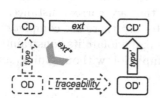

Fig. 10. Projection of preinstances

Fig. 11. Instances of CD^+ are instances of CD and completions of POD

two inclusions $c! : G! \rightarrow G'!$ and $c^\bullet : G^\bullet \rightarrow G^\bullet$ as shown in Fig. 9 (and so $G!$ $\subset G'!$ and $G^\bullet \subset G^\bullet$). Completion of partial object diagrams, i.e., typed partial graphs, requires, in addition, commutativity with typing mappings as shown in the upper part of the figure.

Let us see how this definition works. Given a CD, we say that a partial object diagram POD' is more complete than partial object diagram POD, if some unknown values _ in POD are replaced by actual values, and some of labels ? are removed by either removal of labels ? from objects/slots, or removal of objects/slots labeled by ?. The former removal means that an ?-element in POD certainly exists in POD', the latter removal means that a ?-element certainly does not exist in POD'. The multiplicities on the *complete* arrow in Fig. 9 are important. The multiplicity $0..1$ means that an element of POD may have only one completion in POD'. The multiplicity $1..^*$ means that a completion completes at least one element, i.e., it can reduce uncertainty by gluing elements (if the multiplicity was 1, gluing would be prohibited). Generally, we have a partially defined mapping $c : POD \rightarrow POD'$ commuting with typing of POD and POD'. We call this mapping *complete* (see Fig. 9), and write $c : POD \leq POD'$.

We write $\text{COMPL}(POD) = \{|POD'| \in \text{PINST}(CD) : POD \leq POD'\}$ for the set of all completions of POD.

4.3 Partial Object Diagrams via Class Diagrams

We first note that an extension $ext : CD \rightarrow CD'$ of diagram CD gives rise to a function $ext^* : \text{PINST}(CD') \rightarrow \text{PINST}(CD)$ that projects preinstances of CD' to preinstances of CD (see Fig. 10). Let OD' be a preinstance of CD', e' is its element, and $t' = type'(e)$ is its type in CD'. If $t' = ext(t)$ for some type $t \in CD$, then ext^* copies e into OD and gives it the type t. If $t' \in (CD' \setminus CD)$, then e is not copied into OD. In this way, by traversing all elements in OD', we build a CD's preinstance OD and traceability mappings from OD to OD'.

Theorem. *For any class diagram CD and its partial preinstance POD there is a class diagram CD^+_{POD} and an extension $ext_{POD} : CD \rightarrow CD^+_{POD}$ such that the mapping*

$$ext^* : \text{INST}(CD^+_{POD}) \to \text{INST}(CD) \cap \text{COMPL}(POD)$$

is a bijection. Moreover, if $POD \neq POD'$, then $CD^+_{POD} \neq CD^+_{POD'}$.

Figure 11 visualizes the theorem. Any correct instance of the class diagram CD^+_{POD}, projected onto preinstances of CD, is a correct instance of CD and is a completion of POD. All completions of POD, that are correct instances of CD, must also be correct instances of CD^+_{POD}. Note that there are completions of POD that are not correct instances of CD (they may violate its constraints).

We prove the theorem for the simpler case of completion without gluing, and correspondingly CD^+_{POD} without multiple inheritance.

Proof. The proof consists of two parts. In Part 1, we specify a function *cdenc*, which for a given pair (CD, POD), as above, produces CD^+_{POD} and an extension mapping $ext_{POD} : CD \to CD^+_{POD}$. In Part 2, we prove that ext^* is a bijection.

Part 1. (Below we will skip the index POD near CD^+ and ext)

Function *cdenc* encodes any partial object diagram POD as a class diagram CD^+, such that CD^+ is an extension of CD ($CD \leq CD^+$). For a given class diagram CD, any partial object diagram POD, such that $|POD| \in \text{PINST}(CD)$, the function $cdenc(CD, POD)$ constructs $CD^+ \in \text{EXT}(CD)$ as follows.

1. Copy all elements of CD to CD^+.
2. Label all classes of CD^+ that belong to CD as [abstract].
3. For each $o \in \text{OBJECT}$ belonging to POD, create a singleton class $c \in \text{CLASS}$ belonging to CD^+. The class subclasses o's class, i.e., $isA(c) = type(o)$. If $o \in \text{OBJECT!}$ then the multiplicity of c is $1..1$, otherwise it is $0..1$.
4. For each $s \in \text{SLOT}$ where $owner(s) = o$ and $val(s) = v$, such that $v \neq \_$, create a reference $r \in \text{REF}$ belonging to CD^+. Let us assume that the objects o and v are mapped to classes c and d, respectively, in CD^+. The reference r is defined so that $owner(r) = c$. Additionally, the reference redefines its type from CD, i.e., $isA(r) = type(s)$. If $s \in \text{VALUESLOT}$, then $type(r) = Type(type(v))$ and $val(r) = d$, otherwise $type(r) = d$. In the former case, the type of r is one of the primitive domains. If $s \in \text{SLOT!} \cup \text{VALUESLOT}^\bullet$ then the multiplicity of r is $1..1$, otherwise it is $0..1$.

Part 2. For the function *cdenc*, as defined above, the mapping ext^* defined at the very beginning of Sect. 4.3 is a bijection.

2.1) *Given a correct instance I in* $\text{INST}(CD) \cap \text{COMPL}(POD)$, *there is* I^+ *in* $\text{INST}(CD^+)$ *such that* $ext^*(I^+) = I$.

The partial graph of POD can be typed over CD^+, because of encoding by *cdenc*. Each element e_{POD} of POD can be typed over CD^+ by $type_{POD} : GP_{POD} \to CD^+$. If I completes POD, then for each element e belonging to I, we have $e = complete(e_{POD})$. The instance I^+ can be constructed by having the same partial graph as I and typing each e of I over CD^+ by $type^+(e) = type_{POD}(e_{POD})$. The instance I^+ is correct, as CD^+ preserves the constraints of CD and POD.

Furthermore, $ext^*(I^+) = I$ holds. The instance $ext^*(I^+)$ is a correct instance of CD, because extension is compatible with constraints. That is, we also have a function $ext^* : \text{INST}(CD^+) \to \text{INST}(CD)$ (denoted again by ext^*). That way each correct instance of CD^+ can be projected onto a correct instance of CD.

2.2) *Given a correct instance* $I^+ \in \text{INST}(CD^+)$*, the projection* $ext^*(I)^+$ *is in* $\text{INST}(CD) \cap \text{COMPL}(POD)$.

As shown previously, any correct instance I^+ of CD^+ can be projected onto a correct instance of CD, i.e., $ext^*(I^+) \in \text{INST}(CD)$.

Furthermore, I^+ also belongs to $\text{COMPL}(POD)$. It is because, POD can be typed over CD^+. Each element belonging to I^+ has exactly one type t^+ such that exactly one element of POD is mapped to t (it is established by $cdenc$). This correspondence establishes completion between elements of I^+ and $|POD|$, and from that follows that $ext^*(I^+) \in \text{COMPL}(POD)$.

As it is seen from the proof, the constructions b_1 and b_2 are mutually inverse. The last statement of the theorem is also evident by construction.   □

We conjecture that the theorem remains true for the general case of POD completions with gluing, but an accurate proof is our future work.

5   Related Work

Partial instances, under the name of incomplete information, is a classical topic in databases, from a seminal (and still influential) paper [12] to lattice-theoretic models [15] to semistructured data [2]. However, this work is based on the *value-oriented* relational data model; optionality of objects and slots is not considered.

UML object diagrams [19] offer partial support for partial instances. Slots may have unknown values, called nulls, that correspond to our _. Objects and slots, however, cannot be labeled as optional. Our work provides syntax for both partialities and supplies it with formal semantics. UML class diagrams, on the other hand, can support partial instances "as is" via subclassing of classes, attributes, and associations. Our work makes this encoding precise; it assumes, however, that the typing mapping from object diagrams to class diagrams is total. UML object diagrams allow partial typing for objects, i.e., objects may have missing classifier. Partial typing is also supported by subclassing, as new attributes and associations can be introduced in subclasses (as in Fig. 4) but the presented theory needs to be extended to cover that case (extension for OWA).

MOF [18] is a standardized meta-modeling language. Similarly to UML object diagrams, properties may have unknown values. They are specified as a question mark ? (we use _ for the same purpose). MOF does not consider the second type of partiality, i.e., optional existence of elements (that we label as ?).

Partial instances of meta-models occur in the context of uncertainty, variability, or underspecification. Partial models [10] express uncertainty about a concrete model variant. Model templates [6] express variability and model multiple variants simultaneously. Both works use annotations (similar to our labels ?) to indicate optional elements. The annotations go beyond the semantics of assumed base languages. The subclassing approach may encode labeled models at the level of meta-models to make them compatible with the base languages [3].

Modal Object Diagrams (MODs) [16] extend UML object diagrams with positive/negative and example/invariant modalities. Our work focuses on positive examples; the conflicting example in Sect. 2 would be a negative example in

MODs. MODs have two further extensions: partial and parametrized object diagrams. The former are related to our labels ? and extension relation. The latter are related to unknown values _. We provide concrete syntax and semantics for both. MODs were encoded in Alloy as partial instances via existentially quantified formulas, whereas we encode them generically via singletons. Existentially quantified formulas do not reflect explicitly the structure of diagrams.

Alloy [7] is a structural modeling language based on sets and relations. Kodkod [21] is its relational model finder. Although Kodkod has direct support for partial instances, Alloy does not expose it in the concrete syntax. One way of encoding partial instances is through singletons. We make this encoding precise. Alloy has no first-class support for redefinition of references. It can be done via constraints. AlloyPI [17] extends Alloy with special syntax for partial instances; i.e., types and partial instances have distinct notations. There are tradeoffs between separate notations and a unified notation for partial instances. The latter allows keeping the language small, and there is no need to extend tools to deal with new syntax; however, users may prefer an explicit notation for instances in some situations; the tradeoffs should be investigated further in user studies.

Clafer [3] is a meta-modeling language with first-class support for variability modeling. In contrast to mainstream OOM languages, Clafer allows for arbitrary property nesting (classes/attributes/associations) in the containment hierarchy. It encodes partial instances via singletons, as described in this paper. Similarly to Alloy, a reasoner generates completions that, again, can be encoded as singletons.

Also, architectural languages, such as AADL [11] and AUTOSAR [1], support subclassing of classes and associations. They are used to define partial architectures and refine subcomponents.

While several previous works listed above encode partial instances as singletons (natively in Clafer; singleton idiom in Alloy; in AADL and in AUTOSAR, the components are nested and they have cardinalities—AUTOSAR calls them prototypes), we are not aware of a formalization of this idea. The presented theory makes the concept of partial instances via subclassing and its relation to explicit partial instances precise, improving the understanding of both approaches to language design and their tradeoffs.

We see several advantages of this encoding: 1) any OOM language without native support for partial instances can support them at the class level; 2) the encoding can be relatively easily implemented on top of existing languages solely by syntactical means, i.e., the semantics of underlying language is kept unchanged; 3) encoding (partial) instances as class diagrams allows the modeler to specify constraints in the context of each such instance – in contrast, objects in object diagrams cannot contain constraints; and 4) a user of such a language has fewer concepts to learn. On the other hand, we also see two main drawbacks of this syntactical unification. A general disadvantage is that fundamental OOM concepts (instances and types) are not directly visible in the syntax, which may lead to confusion. Second, the class diagrams that encode partial instances are, arguably, bulky and convoluted. In the presented encoding, we abused class modeling by specifying "degenerated" class diagrams composed of singleton classes. It is unlikely that practitioners would work directly with such diagrams.

A dedicated UML profile could address this problem. Clafer avoids this problem by a suitable syntax design.

6   Conclusion and Future Work

Partial instances enable modeling with uncertainty, variability, and underspecification. We showed their use in requirements elicitation and validation. The first example involved uncertainty; the second underspecification. We considered partial instances and their completion under the CWA and the OWA. Despite many applications, support for partial instances in OOM languages is limited.

Our work contributes to the design of modeling notations. It showed that under the CWA partial instances can be encoded as class diagrams by strengthening multiplicity constraints, redefinition, and subclassing. In other words, partial instantiation and subclassing/redefinition are formally equivalent for modeling partialities within the presented scope. One of the implications is that any OOM language can support partial instances as long as it offers the notion of subclassing for classes and properties (associations and attributes). Our work makes this encoding generic and precise; the presented concepts may be widely applicable.

The formal part of our work focused on completion and extension under the CWA. It omitted the case of completion with gluing instances. The latter case and formalization under the OWA remain future work. Another line of future work is to formally consider instantiation and subtyping to understand if, and to what degree, the two relationships can be unified.

References

1. AUTOSAR Partnership: Release 4.1, http://www.autosar.org/ (online; accessed August 2013)
2. Barceló, P., Libkin, L., Poggi, A., Sirangelo, C.: XML with incomplete information: models, properties, and query answering. In: PODS (2009)
3. Bąk, K., Czarnecki, K., Wąsowski, A.: Feature and meta-models in Clafer: Mixed, specialized, and coupled. In: Malloy, B., Staab, S., van den Brand, M. (eds.) SLE 2010. LNCS, vol. 6563, pp. 102–122. Springer, Heidelberg (2011)
4. Bąk, K., Zayan, D., Czarnecki, K., Antkiewicz, M., Diskin, Z., Wąsowski, A., Rayside, D.: Example-Driven Modeling. Model = Abstractions + Examples. In: ICSE (2013)
5. Czarnecki, K., Helsen, S., Eisenecker, U.: Staged configuration through specialization and multilevel configuration of feature models. SPIP 10(2) (2005)
6. Czarnecki, K., Pietroszek, K.: Verifying feature-based model templates against well-formedness ocl constraints. In: GPCE (2006)
7. Daniel, J.: Software Abstractions: Logic, Language, and Analysis. The MIT Press (2006)
8. Diskin, Z., Kadish, B.: Variable set semantics for keyed generalized sketches: Formal semantics for object identity and abstract syntax for conceptual modeling. DKE 47 (2003)
9. Diskin, Z., Kadish, B., Piessens, F., Johnson, M.: Universal arrow foundations for visual modeling. In: Anderson, M., Cheng, P., Haarslev, V. (eds.) Diagrams 2000. LNCS (LNAI), vol. 1889, pp. 345–360. Springer, Heidelberg (2000)

10. Famelis, M., Salay, R., Chechik, M.: Partial models: Towards modeling and reasoning with uncertainty. In: ICSE (2012)
11. Feiler, P.H., Gluch, D.P.: Model-Based Engineering with AADL: An Introduction to the SAE Architecture Analysis & Design Language. Addison-Wesley Professional (2012)
12. Imieliński, T., Lipski, W.: Incomplete information in relational databases. JACM 31(4) (1984)
13. Janzen, D., Saiedian, H.: Test-driven development concepts, taxonomy, and future direction. Computer 38(9) (2005)
14. Kang, K.C., Cohen, S.G., Hess, J.A., Nowak, W.E., Peterson, A.S.: Feature-oriented domain analysis (FODA) feasibility study. Tech. Rep. CMU/SEI-90-TR-21, CMU (1990)
15. Libkin, L.: Approximation in databases. In: Vardi, M.Y., Gottlob, G. (eds.) ICDT 1995. LNCS, vol. 893, pp. 411–424. Springer, Heidelberg (1995)
16. Maoz, S., Ringert, J.O., Rumpe, B.: Modal Object Diagrams. In: Mezini, M. (ed.) ECOOP 2011. LNCS, vol. 6813, pp. 281–305. Springer, Heidelberg (2011)
17. Montaghami, V., Rayside, D.: Extending Alloy with Partial Instances. In: Derrick, J., Fitzgerald, J., Gnesi, S., Khurshid, S., Leuschel, M., Reeves, S., Riccobene, E. (eds.) ABZ 2012. LNCS, vol. 7316, pp. 122–135. Springer, Heidelberg (2012)
18. OMG: Meta Object Facility (MOF) Core Specification (2011)
19. OMG: OMG Unified Modeling Language (2011)
20. Rutle, A., Rossini, A., Lamo, Y., Wolter, U.: A diagrammatic formalisation of MOF-based modelling languages. In: Oriol, M., Meyer, B. (eds.) TOOLS EUROPE 2009. LNBIP, vol. 33, pp. 37–56. Springer, Heidelberg (2009)
21. Torlak, E., Jackson, D.: Kodkod: A relational model finder. In: Grumberg, O., Huth, M. (eds.) TACAS 2007. LNCS, vol. 4424, pp. 632–647. Springer, Heidelberg (2007)

Reifying Concurrency for Executable Metamodeling*

Benoît Combemale[1], Julien De Antoni[2], Matias Vara Larsen[2], Frédéric Mallet[2],
Olivier Barais[1], Benoit Baudry[1], and Robert B. France[3]

[1] University of Rennes 1, IRISA, Inria
[2] Univ. Nice Sophia Antipolis, CNRS, I3S, Inria
[3] Colorado State University

Abstract. Current metamodeling techniques can be used to specify the syntax
and semantics of domain specific modeling languages (DSMLs). Still, there is
little support for explicitly specifying concurrency semantics of DSMLs. Often,
such semantics are provided by the implicit concurrency model of the execution environment supported by the language workbench used to implement the
DSMLs. The lack of an explicit concurrency model has several drawbacks: it
prevents from developing a complete understanding of the DSML's behavioral semantics, as well as effective concurrency-aware analysis techniques, and explicit
models of semantic variants. This work reifies concurrency as a metamodeling
facility, leveraging formalization work from the concurrency theory and models
of computation (MoC) community. The essential contribution of this paper is a
language workbench for binding domain-specific concepts and models of computation through an explicit event structure at the metamodel level. We present a
case study that serves to demonstrate the utility of the novel metamodeling facilities and clarify the scope of the approach.

1 Introduction

In a context where software-intensive systems must handle an increasing number of
issues in diverse domains, for example, issues related to providing functional features
and qualitative guarantees, and to supporting heterogeneous hardware platforms, the
use of domain-specific modeling languages (DSMLs) can result in increased productivity while providing effective support for separating concerns. DSMLs can make it
easier for stakeholders from different domains (*e.g.*, experts in fault tolerance, security,
communication) to participate in the design of a system, by providing linguistic concepts tailored to their specific needs. However, for a DSML to be an effective system
design tool, it must be defined as precisely as possible and supported by sound analysis
tools [1].

The specification, design and tooling of DSMLs leverage the rich state of the
art in language theory. Several metamodeling environments support the specification
of the syntax and the (static and dynamic) semantics of a DSML. These two elements of a DSML specify the domain-specific concepts, as well as the meanings of
domain-specific actions that manipulate these concepts. Examples of metamodeling

---

* This work is partially supported by the ANR INS Project GEMOC (ANR-12-INSE-0011), and
the CNRS PICS Project MBSAR.

M. Erwig, R.F. Paige, and E. Van Wyk (Eds.): SLE 2013, LNCS 8225, pp. 365–384, 2013.
© Springer International Publishing Switzerland 2013

environments include Microsoft's DSL tools[1], Eclipse Modeling Framework (EMF) [2], Generic Modeling Environment (GME) [3], and MetaEdit+ [4]. A significant limitation of current metamodeling environments is the lack of support for explicitly modeling concurrency semantics. Concurrency semantics is currently defined implicitly in DSMLs that support concurrent execution in their models. It is typically embedded in the underlying execution environment supported by the language workbench used to implement the DSMLs (*e.g.*, if the language runs on top of a Java Virtual Machine, the semantics of Java threads defines concurrent behavior).

The lack of an explicit concurrency model has several drawbacks. It not only hinders a comprehensive understanding of the behavioral semantics, it also prevents developing effective concurrency-aware analysis techniques. For instance, knowing that a data-flow model (*e.g.*, an activity diagram) follows Kahn process networks semantics ensures *de facto* properties like latency-insensitive functional determinism but imposes communications through unbounded FIFOs. Restricting the data-flow model to the Synchronous Data Flows semantics allows the computation of finite bounds on the communication buffer sizes. Furthermore, having an implicit concurrency model also prevents the distinction of semantic variants in a model. For example, the fUML specification identifies several semantic variation points. As stated in the fUML specification, some semantic areas "are not explicitly constrained by the execution model: The semantics of time, the semantics of concurrency, and the semantics of inter-object communications mechanism" [2]. The lack of an explicit model of concurrency, including time and communication, prevents one from understanding the impact of these variation points on the execution of a conforming model.

In previous work, we developed an approach that bridges the gap between models of computation and DSMLs [3]. In this paper we use that work as the base for reifying concurrency as a metamodeling facility. We leverage formalization work on concurrency and time from concurrency theory, specifically, theoretical work on tagged structures [4] and on heterogeneous composition of models of computation [5,6]. The primary contribution of this paper is an approach supported by a language workbench for binding domain specific concepts and models of computation through an explicit event structure at the metamodel level. We illustrate these novel metamodeling facilities by designing a DSML specifying concurrent and timed finite state machines. We highlight the benefits and the flexibility of the approach by making a semantic variation on the concurrency specification of the DSML. We also provide pointers to other examples to show that our approach applies to different MoCs and DSMLs.

The paper is organized as follows. Section 2 uses background on language and concurrency theories to identify the key ingredients of a concurrency-aware executable DSML, and to reify them as the association of four language units. Section 3 describes the language workbench built to implement the proposal, and the associated environment for concurrent model execution. Section 4 demonstrates and discusses the DSML implementation and execution environment obtained thanks to our language

---

workbench. The approach is illustrated throughout the paper with the design, implementation and use of timed finite state machines. A comparison to related work and a
conclusion follow.

2 Ingredients of a Concurrency-Aware Executable DSML

2.1 Background Knowledge

Current metamodeling environments support defining a modeling language through the
specification of the concrete and the abstract syntaxes as well as the mapping from the
syntactic domain to the semantic domain. Over the last 50 years, the language theory
community has studied the mapping between the syntactic domain and the semantic
domain extensively. This has led to three primary ways of defining semantics: *operational semantics*, where a virtual machine uses guard(s) on the execution state to drive
the evolution of the models expressed in the language [7,8,9,10]; *axiomatic semantics*,
where predicates on the execution state allow reasoning about the models expressed in
the language and its correct evolution [11,12,13]; and *translational semantics* [14] that
defines an exogenous transformation from the syntactic domain to an existing language
(either an existing computer language or a mathematical denotation, *i.e.,* a denotational
semantics [15]). A drawback of such approaches is that none of them supports the specification of concurrency in a manner that would allow systematic reasoning (chapter
14 of [13]). Even if these approaches could support the definition of concurrency, the
concurrency model would be scattered through the semantic specification, making it
difficult to understand and analyze the properties related to concurrency (*e.g.*, deadlock
freeness, determinism).

In most language implementations, the concurrency semantics is implicitly embedded in the underlying execution environment used to execute the conforming models.
For instance, some executable models supporting concurrent execution rely on the Java
concurrent model. On one hand, the concurrency of the model depends on the Java
concurrency and on the other hand it does not guarantee similar execution/analysis on
platforms with different parallelism possibilities (*e.g.*, single core vs. many cores, processor arrays).

Work on formal and explicit models of concurrency has been the focus of some research programs since the fifties. Early work in this area resulted in three well-known
contemporary approaches: CCS [16], CSP [17] and Petri Nets [18]. Unlike the approaches from language theory, these solutions focus on concurrency, synchronizations
and the, possibly timed, causalities between actions. In these approaches, the focus is
on concurrency and, thus, the actions are opaque and abstract away details on data
manipulations and sequential control aspects of the system. Such models have proven
useful for reasoning about concurrent behavior, but they are not tailored to support the
description of a *domain-specific* modeling language dedicated to a domain expert. After many years, work on models of concurrency has consolidated, from an analytical
point of view, into two different approaches, namely, event structures [19] and tagged
structures [4]. In these approaches the non-relevant parts of a model are abstracted away
into *events* (also named signal) and the focus is on how such events are related to each
other through causality, timed or synchronization relationships. Both event structures

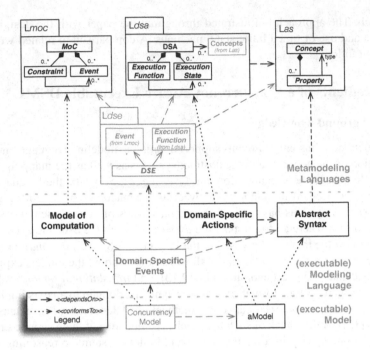

Fig. 1. Modular Design of a Concurrency-Aware Executable Modeling Language

and tagged structures have been used to formally specify or compare concurrency models underlying system models expressed in modeling languages. These concurrency models and can be viewed as the concurrent specification of a specific system model. However, such approaches are not related to the computational part of a model and have not been used to specify the concurrency semantics of a language.

2.2 Language Units Identification

Taking a step back from these seminal approaches, we explicitly identify the common language units that constitute the design and implementation of an executable concurrency-aware modeling language (see middle level of Fig. 1). Each language unit is independent of the way it is implemented, and directly benefits from language and concurrency theories described above.

Language Unit #1. The first language unit is the description of the language *abstract syntax* (see Fig. 1). Older approaches build the semantics of the language on top of the concrete syntax but the benefits of using the abstract syntax as a foundation for language reasoning (first introduced in [20]) have been well understood since the 1960s. In the MDE community, the abstract syntax is a first class part of a language definition. The abstract syntax specifies the syntactic domain and is used to anchor the semantics. It is however important to avoid blurring the syntactic domain with language elements that represent the execution state of the model.

Definition 1. *The Abstract Syntax (*AS*) specifies the concepts of the language and their relationships. An instance of the* AS *is a model.*

Consequently, a meta-language for modeling AS (*Las* in Fig. 1) must provide facilities to define the language concepts (*Concept*) and the relationships between them (*Property*).

Language Unit #2. The second language unit, called *Domain Specific Actions* (see Fig. 1), adds new properties that represent the *execution state* of a model and a set of *execution functions* that operate on these properties during the execution of a model.

The execution state can be represented, for example, by the *current state* in a Finite State Machine (FSM). It can also be specified independently of the abstract syntax, as in, for example, the incidence matrix that encodes the state of a Petri net. Such information is needed to specify the state of a model during its execution but is not needed to specify the model's static structure. It is consequently part of the semantic domain.

The DSA is also composed of *execution functions* that specify how the execution state sequentially evolves during the model execution. For instance, when a transition is fired in a FSM, the current state is updated. This is one of the roles of the execution functions. They also specify how the concepts of a language behave. For instance if the language contains a *Plus* concept, then an execution function must specify how the *Plus* instances actually behave during the model execution.

Definition 2. *The Domain Specific Actions (*DSA*) represent both the execution state and the execution functions of a DSML. An instance of the* DSA *represent the state of a specific model during the execution and the functions to manipulate such a state.*

No hypothesis is made on how to specify the DSA (*Ldsa* in Fig. 1). However, the specification of the DSA depend on the AS since it describes a part of its semantic domain. The execution state would be defined with structural properties representing the semantic domain, in the same way *Las* supports the definition of the syntactic domain. The execution functions can be specified in very concrete terms (*e.g.*, operational semantics that uses an action language to specify rewriting rules), or in more abstract terms (*e.g.*, denotational semantics that provides functions specifying the execution functions). The latter approach only denotes mathematical properties about the result, and does not specify any details on how to implement the resulting functions. This is even more abstract in an axiomatic semantics, where pre/post conditions on the execution state of the system are specified and all the functions that respect such conditions are considered as correct execution functions.

Note that the global ordering of the execution functions is not specified in the DSA since it can be concurrent (and timed). This is the role of the third language unit.

Language Unit #3. Concurrency theory has proposed many approaches, but roughly speaking a concurrency model is a way to specify how different events are causally and temporally related during an execution (in our case, the execution of a model conforming to a DSML). These ideas have been used in the notion of Model of Computation (MOC) [6,21,5]. All definitions of MOCs share the fact that a MOC acts as a director for some pieces of code. The MOC is then acting as an explicit concurrency pattern, which provides MOC-dependent analysis properties. The third language unit is then called *Model of Computation* (see Fig. 1) and explicitly specifies the concurrency.

Definition 3. *The Model of Computation (*MOC*) represents the concurrency aspects in a language, including the synchronizations and the, possibly timed, causality relationships between the execution functions. An instance of a* MOC *is defined for a specific model, conforming to the DSML. It is the part of the* concurrency model *that specifies the possible partial orderings between the events instantiated with regards to the model.*

A meta-language for modeling MOC (*Lmoc* in Fig. 1) would allow the definition of events and the specification of causal relationships (and synchronizations) such as scheduling, temporal constraints, and communications. The events can be discrete (*i.e.,* a discrete event is a possibly infinite sequence of occurrences), or dense (*i.e.,* a dense event is an infinite set of occurrences and there are an infinity of occurrences between any two event occurrences in the set). *Lmoc* must be independent of a specific AS or DSA.

2.3   Reifying Language Units Coordination

In our approach, all language units previously presented are specified separately (see middle level of Fig. 1). This separation benefits modularity, reuse and the identification of the concurrency related analyses supported by the language. The modeling units must then be consistently coordinate to provide an executable modeling language with reified concurrency. This coordination has to keep the language units separated while providing a natural articulation between them.

The AS and the DSA are kept separated to support several implementations of the DSA for a single AS (to deal with semantic variation points, or with semantics for different purposes, *e.g.*, interpreter or compiler). There exists a mapping between the DSA and the AS, however the DSA is dedicated to a specific AS (see dependency between AS and DSA in Fig. 1), and both AS and DSA are dedicated to the DSML under design. Consequently, we did not reify this mapping. The mapping is more conveniently described directly in the DSA.

The definition of the DSML behavioral semantics then consists in specifying the coordination of a given MOC with the DSA. This coordination must keep the MOC and DSA independent to enable the (re)use of a MOC on different AS/DSA or changing the MOCs on a single AS/DSA. Hence, the coordination specification can be put neither directly in the MOC nor in the DSA. For this reason, we reify the binding as a proper language unit that bridges the gap between the MOC and the DSA. This is done through the notion of *Domain Specific Event*, a novel metamodeling facility that we propose to reify.

Language Unit #4. The *Domain Specific Events* (DSE, see Fig. 1) specify the coordination between the events from the MOC and the execution function calls from the DSA. The DSE depend on both the MOC and the DSA. This coordination contains four parts:

DSE → DSA   The DSE specify events that are associated with one or more execution functions. When such an event occurs, it results in the call of the associated execution functions. The meta language for modeling DSE (*Ldse* on Fig. 1) has to make some choices about how much associated functions can be associated with an event (*e.g.*, single one, any) and if several functions are associated with a single event, it must specify how these calls must be done (*e.g.*, in sequence, in parallel).

MOC → DSE   The MOC events can be specified at a abstraction level different than the execution functions from the DSA. For this reason, the DSE specify how the defined events are obtained from the ones constrained by the MOC. This specification can be, for example, the filtering of occurrences from an event or the detection of an occurrence pattern from various events. It can also be the observation of some dense events from the MOC. In this case the DSE are used to specify the relevant observations on the dense event from the MOC and, in such a way, they specify the events that can be observed by looking at the execution of the conforming models. Such an adaptation between the low level events from the MOC and the ones in the DSE can be arbitrarily complex (ranging from a simple mapping to a complex event processing). However, when *Ldse* allows adaptations more complex than a simple mapping, one must ensure that the adaptation is not breaking any concurrency-related assumptions from the MOC.

DSA → DSE   The MOC and the DSE represent the specification, at the language level of the concurrency model (dedicated to a specific model conforming to the DSML). This concurrency model specifies the acceptable partial orderings of both the events constrained by the MOC and the ones from the DSE. During a specific execution, the call to some execution functions can restrict such partial orderings. For instance, if the DSML specifies a conditional concept (*e.g.*, *if-then-else*), a MOC usually specifies that going through the *then* branch or through the *else* branch depends on the evaluation of the condition (*i.e.,* the condition evaluation causes either the *then* or the *else* branch, exclusively). Both paths are specified in the concurrency model as acceptable but the actual path taken during an execution depends on the result of the call to an execution function. The specification of the feedback from the execution function calls to the execution engine of the concurrency model must be specified in the DSE.

MOC ← DSE → AS   Finally , the DSE must specify how the MOC is applied on a specific model that conforms to the DSML (*i.e.,* how to create the concurrency model according to the MOC constraints and the AS concepts). Depending on the language used for the MOC modeling, this specification can be of a different nature, however it requires the capacity to query the AS to retrieve the parameters needed for the creation of the concurrency model. For instance, in a FSM the DSE can specify that a specific constraint must be instantiated for all the *Transition* instances in the model. Also, it can retrieve the actual parameter of the constraint by querying the AS. Once again, depending on the possibility offered by *Ldse*, one must ensure the preservation of the MOC assumptions (*e.g.*, by using proven compilers or a language supporting clear and simple composition of constraints from the MOC).

Definition 4. *The Domain Specific Events (DSE) represent a coordination between the* MOC *and the* DSA *to establish the concurrency-aware semantic domain. It is composed of a set of domain specific events, a mapping between these events and the execution functions from the* DSA, *a possibly complex mapping between the events constrained by the* MOC *and the domain specific events; the specification of the impact of the execution* *function results in the execution of the concurrency model and finally the specification of the* MOC *application on a specific model that conforms to the DSML.*

As highlighted by the previous description, the coordination between the MOC and the DSA (*i.e.*, the DSE) is a key point to enable concurrency-aware semantic domain. However, this coordination is often implicit or hard coded. We believe that its reification enables effective use of a language that includes concurrency and computational aspects. In this section, we have identified the key ingredients for designing a concurrency-aware executable DSML that leads to the architectural pattern proposed in Figure 1. Consequently, we consider in this paper the following definition for a concurrency-aware executable DSML:

Definition 5. *A concurrency-aware executable DSML is a domain-specific modeling language whose conforming models are executable according to an explicit concurrency model. Its definition includes at least the abstract syntax and the behavioral semantics (including the DSA, the MOC and the DSE to coordinate them). In the context of this paper, a concurrency-aware executable DSML (xDSML) is defined as a tuple* $\langle AS, DSA, MOC, DSE \rangle$.

3   A Language Workbench to Design and Implement Concurrency-Aware Executable DSMLs

The reification of concurrency for executable metamodeling has been presented in its general form and several implementations of it can be realized. In this section we present the actual implementation of our language workbench that was used to validate the proposition. We have tried to take the most adequate language/technology for each language unit so that the model expressed in the resulting language can actually be executed. Our implementation solution is illustrated by the definition of a concurrent Timed Finite State Machine (TFSM) language; a language where different state machines augmented with timed transitions can be concurrently executed. Here timed transitions possibly refer to different (independent) clocks.

This section is organized according to the implementation choices presented in Figure 3. It starts with the description of the AS, then the DSA, followed by the MOC and to finish, the DSE reification is specified.

3.1   Abstract Syntax Design

In model-driven engineering, the abstract syntax is usually expressed in an object-oriented manner. For example the *de facto* standard meta-language EMOF (Essential Meta Object Facility) [22] specified by the Object Management Group (OMG) can be used. EMOF provides the following language constructs for specifying an abstract syntax: package, class, property, multiple inheritance (specialization) and different kinds of associations among classes. The semantics of these core object-oriented constructs is close to a standard object model (*e.g.*, Java, C#, Eiffel).

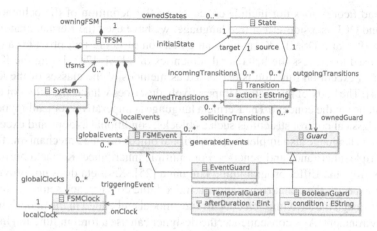

Fig. 2. Abstract Syntax of TFSM (using Ecore)

In practice, we have chosen Ecore to design abstract syntax, a meta-language part of the *Eclipse Modeling Framework* (EMF) [23] and aligned with EMOF. This choice is motivated by the wide acceptance of Ecore and its correspondence to the MOF standard. Additionally, EMF is well tooled and many other tools are based on it (*e.g.*, XText, OCL, GMF, Obeo Designer), so that a language developed in our workbench can benefit from such tools. Note that any meta-language aligned with EMOF can be used in our approach.

Briefly, the AS of TFSM starts with a *System* composed of a set of *TFSMs*, a set of global *FSMEvents* and a set of global *FSMClocks* (see Fig. 2). Each TFSM is composed of *States* among which an initial state is identified. Each state can be the source of outgoing guarded *Transitions*. A guard can be specified by the reception of a *FSMEvent* (*EventGuard*), by a duration relative to the entry time in the incoming state of the transition (*TemporalGuard*) or by a boolean condition (*BooleanGuard*). The duration of a temporal guard is measured on an explicit reference clock. An action is associated with a transition and is represented in the abstract syntax as a *String*. The condition of the boolean guard is also specified as a *String*. These strings represent model level code defined by the designer (*i.e.*, written using an opaque action language). In our experiments such model level code is written in the Groovy language[5]. Groovy was chosen for its capacity to be dynamically invoked. However any other action language could be used. Finally, a transition can also generate a set of event occurrences when fired.

Note that in the abstract syntax, we refrain from adding concepts about the execution state or functions. These concepts are specified in the DSA.

3.2 Domain Specific Actions Design

The domain-specific actions (DSA) enriches the abstract syntax with data representing the execution state and with functions representing the execution functions. Since

---

[5] http://groovy.codehaus.org/

EMOF (and Ecore) does not include concepts for the definition of the behavioral semantics and OCL is a side-effect free language, we have used the Kermeta language to define the DSA of a DSML. Kermeta is an extension of Ecore that provides an action language used to express the behavioral semantics of a DSL [24]. Using the Kermeta language, an execution function is expressed as methods of the classes of the abstract syntax [24]. The body of the method imperatively describes what is the effect of executing an instance of the concept. The Kermeta language is imperative, statically typed, and includes classical control structures such as blocks, conditionals, loops and exceptions. The Kermeta language also implements traditional object-oriented mechanisms for handling multiple inheritance and generics. For multiple inheritance, Kermeta borrows the semantics from the Eiffel programming language [25]. Kermeta does not provide any solution to specify the concurrency model. Indeed, the concurrency semantic model is provided through the Java implicit concurrency model embedded in the underlying execution environment. As a consequence, the designer can use a foreign function interface mechanism to call the Java Thread API but there is no specific support to describe the concurrency model explicitly.

In the approach and the language workbench proposed, the AS and the DSA are conceptually and physically (at the file level) defined in two different modules. The aspect keyword enables DSML engineers to bind the AS and the DSA together. It allows DSML engineers to reopen a previously created class in the abstract syntax to add some new pieces of information such as new methods (execution functions) or new properties (execution state representing the semantic domain). It is inspired by open-classes (aka. static introduction) [26].

In the case of TFSM (cf. Listing 1.1), we have added the *currentState* as an attribute of $TFSM$. We have also added *numberOfTicks* as an integer attribute of $FSMClock$. All the instances of $TFSM$ in a system possess a current state. Also, all instances of $FSMclock$ have an integer representing their actual time. The execution state of the system is then a set of current states and a set of Integers. The choice of what should be added as attribute depends on the information we want to capture in the execution state of the models. Such information can usually be specified in various ways. For instance, we could have specified the execution state by a set of sensitive transitions instead of a set of current states. Kermeta aspects are also used to specify operations on metaclasses. They provide an operational specification of the execution functions as described in the DSA language unit. The advantage is then the executability of such operations. In TFSM, we have added six operations:

- *init()* on $TSFM$: Operation *init()* is used to initialize the execution state of the $TFSM$ (*i.e.,* the current state in our case, lines 5 to 8).
- *fire()* on $Transition$: Operation *fire()* is in charge of changing the current state from the source state to the target state of the transition. It is also in charge of executing the groovy code specified in the action attribute (lines 12 to 18).
- *init()* on $FSMClock$: Operation *init()* is used to initialize the *numberOfTicks* (not shown in the listing).
- *ticks()* on $FSMClock$: Operation *ticks()* is used to increment the *numberOfTicks* of $FSMClock$ (line 24 to 27).

Listing 1.1. Part of the Kermeta aspects specifying the DSA

```
1   aspect class TFSM
2   {
3     //Attribute used at runtime to store the current state
4     attribute currenteState : tfsm::State
5     operation init() : String is do
6       currentState := self.initialState
7       result:= "call␣to␣init()␣:␣" + name
8     end
9   }
10  aspect class Transition
11  {
12    operation fire() : String is do
13      var groovyExpression : String init self.action
14      var res1 : kermeta::standard::Object init extern org::
15        kermeta::extra::groovyembedded::GroovyEmbeder.runOnScript(
             groovyExpression)
16      self.source.owningFSM.currentState := self.target
17      result := "fire:␣" + name + "␣->␣" +self.action
18    end
19  }
20  aspect class FSMClock
21  {
22    //Attribute used at runtime to store the number of tick
23    attribute numberOfTicks : Integer
24    operation ticks() : void is do
25      numberOfTicks := numberOfTicks + 1
26      result := "ticks:␣" + name
27    end
28  }
```

Note that while the DSAs are described by Kermeta aspects over the concepts of the AS, none of them specifies the execution workflow (like a *main()* operation). The schedule of the different operation calls is made by the concurrency model according to the MOC used in the DSML.

3.3   Model of Computation Design

The MOC defines the concurrency, the synchronizations and the possibly timed causality relationships in a DSML. The meta-language used for the specification of the MOC must be able to specify constraints on events independently of the AS and the DSA on which it is applied. We have chosen the Clock Constraint Specification Language (CCSL) [27] for specifying the MOC (at the DSML level), as well as to represent its instances as concurrency models (at the model level). In CCSL, a concurrency model is a set of constraints whose definitions and formal parameters are given in libraries. We use the library mechanism to specify MOC specific constraints. These constraints specify the correct evolution of the events given as formal parameters of the constraints. More precisely it is a reusable set of constraints considered as consistent with regards to a specific MOC; it defines the possibly timed synchronizations and causality relationships between some events and has already been shown to be a good candidate for the specification of the concurrent and temporal aspects of a language [27]. It is not possible to specify any computational aspects in CCSL so that it fits with the separation of the concurrent and temporal aspects in the MOC from the computational aspects in the DSA.

We have defined new constraints dedicated to the TFSM MOC in a specific library. For instance we have defined *TemporalTransition* and *EventTransition* constraints whose declarations are presented in Listing 1.2[6]. Each declaration exposes a set of formal parameters, which are needed to specify the constraint between the events (named *clocks* in CCSL). For instance, for the temporal transition relationship, four events are important, the event that starts the "timer", the event used to measure the time, the event that disables the transition (*i.e.*, makes it non fireable until the next timer starts), and the clock that actually fires the transition. Additionally, the integer representing the delay after which the transition should be fired is also a parameter. Such parameters represent the information that should be provided by a DSML so as the MOC can be used. Such declarations do not make any assumptions about AS and DSA. These constraints define the acceptable concurrency and the possibly timed synchronizations and causalities at the language level. A change in the library affects the execution of all models expressed in a language that uses the MOC (*i.e.*, the constraints).

Listing 1.2. Excerpt of a MoC library used for TFSM (using CCSL)

```
1  RelationDeclaration TemporalTransition(TemporalTransition_MakeFireable:clock,
       TemporalTransition_RefClock:clock, TemporalTransition_Reset:clock,
       TemporalTransition_delay:int, TemporalTransition_Fire:clock)
2  RelationDeclaration EventTransition(EventTransition_MakeFireable:clock,
       EventTransition_Trigger:clock, EventTransition_Reset:clock,
       EventTransition_Fire:clock)
```

3.4 Domain Specific Event Design

The DSE put MOC and DSA together to constitute the behavioral semantics of the DSML. They contain the events relevant to the DSML perspective and how they are linked to the execution functions of the DSA; and on the other hand they specify queries on the AS to specify the actual parameters that have to be used by the concurrency model on a specific model. To do so, a specific meta-language named ECL (standing for *Event Constraint Language* [28]) is developed as an extension of OCL [29] with events. The ECL file specifies the constraints used in the concurrency model for a specific model, by specifying the link between the MOC, the DSA and the AS of a DSML. ECL benefits from the OCL query language and its possibility to augment an abstract syntax with additional attributes (without any side effects). Using ECL it is then possible to define new DSE in the context of a specific concept of the AS. DSE also specify, if needed, the execution function that must be called when specific events occur. For instance, in the TFSM example which is partially represented in Listing 1.3, we have defined three domain specific events in the context of *FSMEvent*, *FSMClock* and *Transition* (lines 5–10 in Listing 1.3). The events defined in the context of *FSMClocks* and *Transition*, respectively call when they occur the execution function *ticks*() defined in the context of *FSMClock* and the execution function *fire*() defined in the context of *Transition*.

The ECL file imports a MOC library (line 2 in Listing 1.3). It is used to define some invariants that specify in which context and with which parameter(s) a constraint from the MOC is used. The specification of the actual parameters are specified by querying the AS. To specify the mapping between MOC and DSA, it is also possible to create

---

[6] The definitions are not given for the sake of clarity.

intermediate events by using expressions over existing DSE. For instance, lines 13 to 23 represents the invariant that specifies that for each transition of the AS whose guard is of type *TemporalGuard*, if the source state of this transition has more than one other outgoing transition (line 16), then there is a constraint of type *TemporalTransition* in the concurrency model (line 21). The parameters of the constraints can be queried on the AS like in the line 17 or 22 and 23. It can also be specified by an expression over existing domain specific events like specified in line 18 to 20, which specify a new event defined by the *Union* of all the fire events from other outgoing transitions from the same source state. It is used here to specify when the event transition must be disabled (see the formal parameters line 8 in Listing 1.2). These queries define how the structure of the AS is used to retrieve the actual parameters. For instance, the actual duration of the temporal transition is defined by the *afterDuration* attribute defined in the AS (line 17).

Listing 1.3. Excerpt of the Domain-Specific Events of TFSM (using ECL)

```
1    import 'http://fr.inria.aoste.gemoc.example.tfsm'
2    ECLImport "TFSMMoC.ccslLib"
3    package tfsm
4    // DSE definition, and mapping of the DSE to the DSA (i.e., Kermeta method)
5      context FSMEvent
6        def: occurs : Event()
7      context FSMClock
8        def: ticks : Event(self.ticks())
9      context Transition
10       def: fire : Event(self.fire())
11   // Mapping of the DSE to the MOC
12     context Transition
13       inv fireWhenTemporalGuardHoldsVariousTransition:
14         (self.ownedGuard.oclIsKindOf(TemporalGuard)
15         and self.source.outgoingTransitions->
16           select(t|t <> self)->size() > 0) implies
17             let guardDelay : Integer = self.ownedGuard.oclAsType(
                   TemporalGuard).afterDuration in
18             let otherFireFromTheSameState: Event =
19               Expression Union (self.source.outgoingTransitions->
20                     select(t|t <> self).fire) in
21           Relation TemporalTransition(self.source.entering,
22                     self.ownedGuard.oclAsType(
                           TemporalGuard).onClock.ticks,
23                     otherFireFromTheSameState, guardDelay,
                           self.fire )
24   // Using a MoC constraint specifying a rendez-vous semantics
25     context FSMEvent
26       inv occursWhenSolicitate:
27         (self.sollicitingTransitions->size() >0) implies
28         let AllTriggeringOccurrences : Event = Expression
29         Union(self.sollicitingTransitions.fire) in
30         Relation FSMEventRendezVous(AllTriggeringOccurrences, self.occurs)
```

Listing 1.3 shows another invariant, which defines the *FSMEventRendezVous* constraint on the MOC. This constraint is changed in section 4 to highlight the impact of a MOC variation. From such a specification, it is possible to generate a CCSL specification that represents the concurrency model for any model that conforms to the AS; *i.e.*, a model that contains the actual constraints and their parameters according to a specific model. ECL restricts the requirements expressed in section 2. For instance, it is not possible yet to specify how the result of an execution function call influences the execution path taken by the execution engine at runtime. Such information is for now defined in the configuration of the execution engine. Information about the execution engine is given in the next subsection.

3.5 Execution Engine

Each unit of a DSML is described in our language workbench using technologies built on top of the Eclipse Modeling Framework (EMF). To summarize, we describe the AS with the meta-language Ecore part of EMF (*1* in Fig. 3). Then we describe the DSA (both execution state and functions) with Kermeta [24] (*2* in Fig. 3). We mainly use Kermeta for its weaving capability on the abstract syntax. DSA are specified using aspects on metaclasses that enable the addition of execution state attributes and execution functions. Then, we specify the MOC by constraints definition as a CCSL library (*3* in Fig. 3). Finally we define DSE and link them with the execution functions by using ECL (*4* in Fig. 3). ECL is also used to specify, at the language level, the constraints used in a concurrency model for a specific model.

In the workbench, EMF generates an API for the AS that can load and save models conforming to the DSML. Kermeta methods and properties are compiled as a set of Scala traits that are woven within this model API [30]. As a result, Kermeta provides an extended version of the Java API, encapsulated in a jar file, on which it is possible to call the execution functions weaved within the AS (*5* in Fig. 3). Then, for a specific model conforming to the DSML, the ECL file can be used to automatically create a concurrency model in CCSL (*6* in Fig. 3). The concurrency model is directly linked to the model elements. This model represents all the partial ordering of events considered as correct with regards to the MoC. In our workbench, it is interpreted by a tool named TIMESQUARE [31] to provide one partial ordering between the domain specific events in the model (*7* in Fig. 3). To call the execution functions defined in the DSA, TIMESQUARE has been extended in our language workbench with a new back-end able to use the jar files to execute the model (*8* in Fig. 3). In the proposed language workbench, EMF serves as a common technical foundation. Kermeta provides an API fully compatible with EMF that eases the integration within the language workbench.

As a result, this language workbench provides a set of Java libraries allowing to call execution functions on a model. The call to the execution functions is driven by TIMESQUARE. The (possibly simultaneous) ordering of the calls to the execution functions represents the concurrent-aware execution of the model. We illustrate in the next section the use of the TFSM language on five concurrent TFSMs, which model road traffic lights and their controller.

4   Demonstration and Discussion: Using TFSM on Concurrent Road Traffic Lights

To go further in our approach, we present an example of five concurrent TFSMs built using the executable language proposed in the previous sections and the tools mentioned above. Our case study is a simple modeling of crossroad traffic lights. In our example, the traffic lights regulate the traffic on a main road and a secondary road. The traffic lights are synchronized differently during the day or the night. During the day, the two

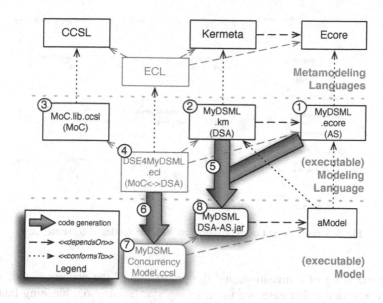

Fig. 3. Architecture of the language workbench and the associated execution engine for concurrent model execution

traffic lights on the main road are red during two minutes and then switch to green. They remain green until a controller sends the *switch* event that makes the two main traffic lights become red again. The two other traffic lights have exactly the same behavior but are green when the main traffic lights are red and red when the main traffic lights are green. The controller has two states Day and Night that change depending on the reading of a sensor answering whether it is night or day. During the day it sends a switch event every 4th minute and during the night every 6th minute. In Figure 4, the controller TFSM (named *Control*) and one of the main road traffic lighs (named *Semaphore0*) are shown. The abstract syntax has been tooled with Obeo designer to obtain a graphical concrete syntax.

By using this example we want to highlight the impact of a simple change in a MOC applied on the same AS/DSA. The MOC variation consists in the synchronization

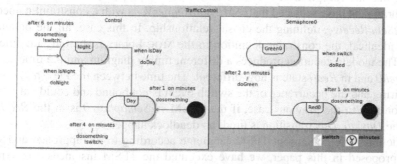

Fig. 4. Partial traffic light model

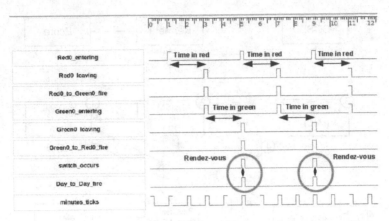

Fig. 5. Timing output of the simulation with the rendez-vous semantics

between the firing of a transition, and the production of the occurrences of its *generatedEvents*. In the first case, we use a strong synchronization, meaning that if one transition is fired and generates an event occurrence, all the transitions waiting for this event are simultaneously fired (The transitions with an event guard on this event). For that purpose, we use a constraint named *FSMEventRendezVous* in the MOC library (see the lines 27 to 32 of the Listing 1.3). Once the concurrency model has been generated for the model of Figure 4, we can execute the concurrency model in TIMESQUARE. The model execution produced a timing diagram representing the occurrences of the event according to the time (Figure 5). On this picture we can see that the firings of the transition named *Day_to_Day* from the traffic light controller are simultaneous with the occurrences of the switch event, themselves simultaneous with the firings of the *Green0_to_Red0* transition. In this case, the time spent in the *Red0* state and the time in the *Green0* state is the same: 2 minutes. This mechanism is a strong synchronization so that if the TFSM of *Semaphore0* (Figure 4) is in the *Red0* state when the *Day_to_Day* transition is fired, a deadlock happens.

In a second case, we have changed this strong synchronization with a causal relationship, meaning that if one transition is fired and generates an event occurrence, all the transitions waiting for this event must be fired in a later step (it abstracts the sending and the reception of a FSMEvent). For this purpose, we have modified the MOC library and have replaced the *FSMEventRendezVous* with a constraint named *FSMEventSendReceive*, defining the causal relationship. In this case, all the parameters remain identical, the constraint definition in the MOC library is the only modification made. The model execution produces a different timing diagram and the time spent in the *Green0* and in *Red0* state is now different. The time between the *Day_to_Day* transition firing and the occurrence of the switch event is not bound and could vary. In this case, contrary to the previous case, if the TFSM of *Semaphore0* is in the *Red0* state when the *Day_to_Day* transition is fired, no deadlock happens.

By defining the concurrent TFSM language according to the approach and workbench proposed in this paper, we have executed the TFSM instances concurrently. By changing a single constraint in the MOC library, we get a different behavior of

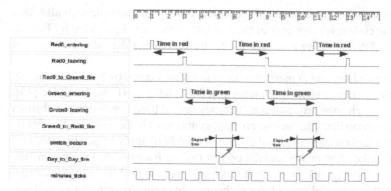

Fig. 6. Timing output of the simulation with the send-receive semantics

the system, highlighting the importance to make explicit and to reify the MOC and DSE. The presentation of the whole example with video of its compilation and execution (including diagram animation) can be found on the companion web page: http://gemoc.org/sle13. This web page also introduces two other usages of the language workbench. The first one shows the definition of the Actor Computing Model using the workbench. It allows the simulation of the behavior of a set of Actors. The second one illustrates an example of the Logo language[7] with two turtles sharing the same playground.

5 Related Work

Much work has been done on the design and implementation of both DSML and models of computation. In this paper, we propose a conceptual and technical framework to take benefits from both underlying theory. This section presents related work in the field of language design and implementation, and then in the field of models of computation.

The problem of the modular design of languages has been explored by several authors (*e.g.*, [32,33]). For example, JastAdd [33] combines traditional use of higher order attribute grammars with object-orientation and simple aspect-orientation (static introductions) to get a better modularity mechanism. With a similar support for object-orientation and static introductions, Kermeta and its aspect paradigm can be seen as an analogue of JastAdd in the DSML world. The major drawback of such approach is that none of them provides a native support for concurrency.

A language workbench is a software package for designing software languages [34]. For instance, it may encompass parser generators, specialized editors, DSLs for expressing the semantics and others. Early language workbenches include Centaur [35], ASF+SDF [36], and TXL [37]. Among more recent proposals, we can cite Generic Model Environment (GME) [38], Metacase's MetaEdit+ [39], Microsoft's DSL Tools [40], Krahn et al's Monticore [41], Kats and Visser's Spoofax [42], Jetbrain's MPS [43]. The important difference of our approach is that we explicitly reify the concurrency concern in the design of an executable language, providing a dedicated tooling

---

[7] http://en.wikipedia.org/wiki/Logo_(programming_language)

for its implementation and reuse. Our approach is also 100% compatible with all EMF-based tools (at the code level, not only at the abstract syntax level provided by Ecore), hence designing a DSL with our approach easily allows reusing the rich ecosystem of Eclipse/EMF.

Models of computation, and in particular the concurrency concern, have been mainly tooled in three different workbench: Ptolemy [6], ModHel'X [44] and ForSyDe [45]. Each of them have their own pros and cons but they are all based on a specific abstract syntax and API. On one hand the unique abstract syntax avoids their use in the context of specific DSMLs and on the other hand the use of an API to apply a specific MOC creates a gap between the MOC theory and the corresponding framework. In our approach we use the notion of DSE to link a MOC to the DSA of a specific DSML and we use CCSL to specify the MOC in a formal way, closer to theory like event structures or tagged signals. A similar approach has been used in BIP [46], where a specific algebra is used to describe the interactions through connectors between behaviors expressed in timed automata. From the properties of the connectors, it is possible to predict global properties of the models. This approach is interesting in its analysis capacity but is tailored to the composition of timed automata. Finally another approach based on CCSL has been used in [47] to describe two MOC and the interactions between heterogeneous models of computation. This approach improved ModHel'X workbench but is still dedicated to apply a MOC to a specific abstract syntax. However, it gives good hint for the use of the approach proposed in this paper for the composition of heterogeneous executable modeling languages.

6   Conclusion and Perspectives

This work proposes an approach that reifies the key concerns to design and implement a concurrency-aware executable DSML (AS, DSA, MOC and DSE). The approach is supported by a language workbench based on EMF, including a meta-language dedicated to each concern to design concurrency-aware executable DSMLs in a modular way. Then, the implementation of a DSML automatically results in a dedicated environment for concurrent execution of the conforming models. The explicit modeling of concurrency as first-class concern paves the way to a full understanding and configuration ability of the behavioral semantics. Additionally, the modular design enables the reuse of existing MoCs that come with specific analysis capabilities and tool support. We illustrate our approach and language workbench on the design, the implementation and the use of variants, of concurrent and timed finite state machine. A complementary video is available on the companion webpage, as well as other DSML families implemented according to our approach: http://gemoc.org/sle13.

In future works, we plan to focus more on the DSA and DSE relationships. Up to now, the events are driving the execution of actions, but only a crude feedback is allowed from the actions. The understanding of what kind of feedback is expected needs to be further explored. Finally, the explicit definition of concurrency in the behavioral semantics of DSML opens many perspectives. In particular, we are exploring the way to support heterogeneous execution models (*e.g.*, synchronization and composition of interpreter or compiler). The goal here is to make explicit the composition of heterogeneous DSMLs by using the information provided by the reified language units.

References

1. Combemale, B., Crégut, X., Pantel, M.: A Design Pattern to Build Executable DSMLs and associated V&V tools. In: APSEC. IEEE (December 2012)
2. Object Management Group, Inc.: Semantics of a Foundational Subset for Executable UML Models (fUML), v1.0 (2011)
3. Combemale, B., Hardebolle, C., Jacquet, C., Boulanger, F., Baudry, B.: Bridging the Chasm between Executable Metamodeling and Models of Computation. In: Czarnecki, K., Hedin, G. (eds.) SLE 2012. LNCS, vol. 7745, pp. 184–203. Springer, Heidelberg (2013)
4. Lee, E.A., Sangiovanni-Vincentelli, A.L.: A framework for comparing models of computation. IEEE Trans. on CAD of Integrated Circuits and Systems 17(12), 1217–1229 (1998)
5. Jantsch, A.: Modeling Embedded Systems and SoCs. Morgan Kaufmann Publishers Inc. (2004)
6. Eker, J., Janneck, J.W., Lee, E.A., Liu, J., Liu, X., Ludvig, J., Neuendorffer, S., Sachs, S., Xiong, Y.: Taming heterogeneity – the Ptolemy approach. Proc. of the IEEE 91(1) (2003)
7. Plotkin, G.D.: A structural approach to operational semantics (1981)
8. Karsai, G., Agrawal, A., Shi, F., Sprinkle, J.: On the use of graph transformations for the formal specification of model interpreters. Journal of Universal Computer Science 9 (2003)
9. Bendraou, R., Jezéquél, J.-M., Fleurey, F.: Combining aspect and model-driven engineering approaches for software process modeling and execution. In: Wang, Q., Garousi, V., Madachy, R., Pfahl, D. (eds.) ICSP 2009. LNCS, vol. 5543, pp. 148–160. Springer, Heidelberg (2009)
10. Knuth, D.E.: Semantics of context-free languages. Theory of Computing Systems 2(2), 127–145 (1968)
11. Hoare, C.A.R.: An axiomatic basis for computer programming. Communications of the ACM 12(10), 576–580 (1969)
12. Gries, D.: The science of programming, vol. 198. Springer (1981)
13. Winskel, G.: The formal semantics of programming languages: an introduction. MIT press (1993)
14. Fredlund, L.A., Jonsson, B., Parrow, J.: An implementation of a translational semantics for an imperative language. In: Baeten, J.C.M., Klop, J.W. (eds.) CONCUR 1990. LNCS, vol. 458, pp. 246–262. Springer, Heidelberg (1990)
15. Scott, D.S., Strachey, C.: Toward a mathematical semantics for computer languages. Oxford University Computing Laboratory, Programming Research Group (1971)
16. Milner, R.: A calculus of communicating systems. Springer (1982)
17. Hoare, C.A.R.: Communicating sequential processes. Communications of the ACM 21(8), 666–677 (1978)
18. Petri, C.A.: Introduction to general net theory. In: Advanced Course: Net Theory and Applications, pp. 1–19 (1975)
19. Winskel, G.: Event structures. In: Brauer, W., Reisig, W., Rozenberg, G. (eds.) Petri Nets: Applications and Relationships to Other Models of Concurrency. LNCS, vol. 255, pp. 325–392. Springer, Heidelberg (1987)
20. McCarthy, J.: Towards a mathematical science of computation. Information Processing 62, 21–28 (1962)
21. Boulanger, F., Hardebolle, C.: Simulation of Multi-Formalism Models with ModHel'X. In: ICST, pp. 318–327. IEEE (2008)
22. Object Management Group, Inc.: Meta Object Facility (MOF) 2.0 Core (2006)
23. Steinberg, D., Budinsky, F., Paternostro, M., Merks, E.: EMF: Eclipse Modeling Framework, 2nd edn. Addison-Wesley (2008)
24. Muller, P.-A., Fleurey, F., Jézéquel, J.-M.: Weaving Executability into Object-Oriented Meta-Languages. In: Briand, L.C., Williams, C. (eds.) MoDELS 2005. LNCS, vol. 3713, pp. 264–278. Springer, Heidelberg (2005)

25. Meyer, B.: Eiffel: The language. Prentice-Hall, Inc. (1992)
26. Clifton, C., Leavens, G.T.: Multijava: Modular open classes and symmetric multiple dispatch for java. In: OOPSLA, pp. 130–145 (2000)
27. Mallet, F., DeAntoni, J., André, C., de Simone, R.: The Clock Constraint Specification Language for building timed causality models. Innovations in Systems and Software Engineering 6, 99–106 (2010)
28. Deantoni, J., Mallet, F.: ECL: The Event Constraint Language, an Extension of OCL with Events. Research report RR-8031, INRIA (July 2012)
29. Object Management Group, Inc.: UML Object Constraint Language (OCL) 2.0 (2003)
30. Jézéquel, J.M., Combemale, B., Barais, O., Monperrus, M., Fouquet, F.: Mashup of metalanguages and its implementation in the kermeta language workbench. In: SoSyM (2013)
31. DeAntoni, J., Mallet, F.: TimeSquare: Treat Your Models with Logical Time. In: Furia, C.A., Nanz, S. (eds.) TOOLS 2012. LNCS, vol. 7304, pp. 34–41. Springer, Heidelberg (2012)
32. Van Wyk, E., de Moor, O., Backhouse, K., Kwiatkowski, P.: Forwarding in attribute grammars for modular language design. In: Nigel Horspool, R. (ed.) CC 2002. LNCS, vol. 2304, pp. 128–142. Springer, Heidelberg (2002)
33. Ekman, T., Hedin, G.: The JastAdd system – modular extensible compiler construction. Sci. Comput. Program, 14–26 (2007)
34. Volter, M.: From Programming to Modeling-and Back Again. IEEE Software 28(6) (2011)
35. Borras, P., Clement, D., Despeyroux, T., Incerpi, J., Kahn, G., Lang, B., Pascual, V.: Centaur: the system. In: 3rd ACM Software Engineering Symposium on Practical Software Development Environments, pp. 14–24. ACM (1988)
36. Klint, P.: A meta-environment for generating programming environments. ACM TOSEM 2(2), 176–201 (1993)
37. Cordy, J.R., Halpern, C.D., Promislow, E.: TXL: a rapid prototyping system for programming language dialects. In: Conf. Int Computer Languages, pp. 280–285 (1988)
38. Sztipanovits, J., Karsai, G.: Model-Integrated Computing. IEEE Computer 30(4) (1997)
39. Tolvanen, J., Rossi, M.: MetaEdit+: defining and using domain-specific modeling languages and code generators. In: Companion of the 18th Annual ACM SIGPLAN Conference OOPSLA, 92–93. ACM (2003)
40. Cook, S., Jones, G., Kent, S., Wills, A.: Domain-Specific Development with Visual Studio DSL Tools. Addison-Wesley Professional (2007)
41. Krahn, H., Rumpe, B., Volkel, S.: MontiCore: Modular Development of Textual Domain Specific Languages. In: Paige, R.F., Meyer, B. (eds.) TOOLS EUROPE 2008. LNBIP, vol. 11, pp. 297–315. Springer, Heidelberg (2008)
42. Kats, L.C., Visser, E.: The spoofax language workbench: rules for declarative specification of languages and IDEs. In: OOPSLA, pp. 444–463. ACM (2010)
43. Voelter, M.: Language and IDE Modularization and Composition with MPS. In: Lämmel, R., Saraiva, J., Visser, J. (eds.) GTTSE 2011. LNCS, vol. 7680, pp. 383–430. Springer, Heidelberg (2013)
44. Hardebolle, C., Boulanger, F.: Multi-Formalism Modelling and Model Execution. International Journal of Computers and their Applications 31(3), 193–203 (2009)
45. Sander, I., Jantsch, A.: System Modeling and Transformational Design Refinement in ForSyDe. IEEE Transactions on Computer-Aided Design of Integrated Circuits and Systems 23(1), 17–32 (2004)
46. Basu, A., Bozga, M., Sifakis, J.: Modeling heterogeneous real-time systems in BIP. In: 4th IEEE SEFM, pp. 3–12 (September 2006)
47. Boulanger, F., Dogui, A., Hardebolle, C., Jacquet, C., Marcadet, D., Prodan, I.: Semantic Adaptation Using CCSL Clock Constraints. In: Kienzle, J. (ed.) MODELS 2011 Workshops. LNCS, vol. 7167, pp. 104–118. Springer, Heidelberg (2012)

Author Index